Environmental Crime

ASPEN SELECT SERIES

Environmental Crime:
Pollution and Wildlife Enforcement

Jared C. Bennett
Adjunct Professor of Law
S.J. Quinney College of Law
University of Utah

Wolters Kluwer

Printed in the United States of America.

1 2 3 4 5 6 7 8 9 0

ISBN: 978-1-5438-1383-8

Library of Congress Cataloging-in-Publication Data

Names: Bennett, Jared C., author.
Title: Environmental crime : pollution and wildlife enforcement / Jared C. Bennett, Adjunct Professor of Law, S.J. Quinney College of Law, University of Utah.
Description: New York : Wolters Kluwer, [2019] | Series: Aspen Select Series | Includes index.
Identifiers: LCCN 2019014995 | ISBN 9781543813838
Subjects: LCSH: Offenses against the environment--Law and legislation--United States. | Pollution--Law and legislation--United States--Criminal provisions. | Wildlife conservation--Law and legislation--United States--Criminal provisions. | Hazardous wastes--Law and legislation--United States--Criminal provisions. | Liability for environmental damages--United States. | Criminal intent--United States. | LCGFT: Casebooks (Law)
Classification: LCC KF3775 .B393 2019 | DDC 345.73/0245--dc23
LC record available at https://lccn.loc.gov/2019014995

SUSTAINABLE FORESTRY INITIATIVE

Certified Chain of Custody
Promoting Sustainable Forestry

www.sfiprogram.org
SFI-01347

About Wolters Kluwer Legal & Regulatory U.S.

Wolters Kluwer Legal & Regulatory U.S. delivers expert content and solutions in the areas of law, corporate compliance, health compliance, reimbursement, and legal education. Its practical solutions help customers successfully navigate the demands of a changing environment to drive their daily activities, enhance decision quality and inspire confident outcomes.

Serving customers worldwide, its legal and regulatory portfolio includes products under the Aspen Publishers, CCH Incorporated, Kluwer Law International, ftwilliam.com and MediRegs names. They are regarded as exceptional and trusted resources for general legal and practice-specific knowledge, compliance and risk management, dynamic workflow solutions, and expert commentary.

Summary of Contents

Contents

Preface

In September 2005, I had the privilege of joining the United States Attorney's Office as an Assistant United States Attorney chiefly handling civil environmental cases in the District of Utah. On a bright spring day in 2006, the United States Attorney entered my office and said, "You have an environmental background. I'd like you to handle our office's environmental crimes cases."

Stunned by this unexpected turn of events, I sputtered, "O . . . O.K., but I have never handled a criminal case in my life."

"No problem," the United States Attorney replied. "Go find a drug or bank robbery prosecutor and learn how to do it. You'll be fine."

That was it. From that point, I started learning federal criminal procedure and practice in addition to working with the previously unknown criminal provisions of the environmental statutes that I had known well on the civil side. Over the past 13 years, my practice and teaching of environmental law generally and environmental crime specifically has been punctuated with success and mistakes (probably more of the latter than the former), which have provided me with a unique perspective as to both the theory and practice of environmental crimes.

Given this history, I have structured this book to be sensitive to the fact that there may be students who take an environmental crimes course without any previous environmental law background. Additionally, there may be those who, like me, had no real background in federal criminal law but are drawn to environmental prosecutions. To accommodate these various experience and exposure levels, this book's chapters cover the basics in federal criminal procedure and practice and the environmental law background necessary to understand how environmental criminal enforcement functions.

For example, Chapter 1 introduces the players in environmental crimes enforcement and ends with a discussion regarding the concerns about prosecutorial discretion. Congress was reluctant for many years to impose serious criminal penalties on environmental violations, but congressional patience eventually ran out. But when Congress imposed those serious consequences, Congress left to prosecutors the decision as to what should be a civil enforcement matter and what should be a criminal prosecution. Chapter 1 ends with the debate over whether the discretion granted to prosecutors over environmental crime is too much.

Recognizing the concern about prosecutorial discretion, Chapter 2 discusses the purported restraints on investigatory and prosecutorial discretion that environmental law enforcement agencies and the Department of Justice have placed upon themselves to determine whether an environmental enforcement matter is civil or criminal in nature.

Additionally, Chapter 2 introduces students to the roll and functions of the federal grand jury and asks students whether it serves as a check on prosecutorial discretion or merely rubber stamps the indictment that the government seeks.

In addition to internal policy and, possibly, the grand jury to limit prosecutorial discretion, Chapter 3 introduces the range of mens rea concepts upon which the environmental crimes discussed in this book are predicated. This chapter discusses the requirements for proving a willful, knowing, and negligent mens rea in addition to certain strict liability environmental crimes. This chapter also teaches students that simply because one statute uses the same word as another statute to supply mens rea, the word may not have the same meaning between the two statutes. This allows for engaging class discussion about what "knowing," for example, really requires the government to prove.

Chapter 4 then introduces students to the theories of individual and corporate liability that prosecutors must consider before deciding against whom to impose charges and that attorneys representing putative defendants must consider to try and prevent charges from being sought in the first place. Students will see that although most of the liability theories discussed are available in most other criminal matters, one (i.e., the responsible corporate officer doctrine) is uniquely relevant to some environmental criminal matters.

After arming students with the common language of federal criminal basics in Chapters 2-4, Chapter 5 begins with substantive environmental law concepts relating to the Clean Water Act and its most often-used criminal provisions. With an understanding of the Clean Water Act's basics, students will learn about what is required to prosecute unlawful discharges into waters of the United States, publicly owned treatment works and other sewer systems, and wetlands. Additionally, students will learn about the knowing endangerment provisions that Congress enacted, which carry significant prison time. Finally, Chapter 5 discusses the importance of self-reporting in our regulatory regime and the criminal penalties that Congress imposed to ensure that those who have an obligation to self-report do so truthfully.

Chapter 6 briefly discusses potential criminal charges under the lengthy and complex Clean Air Act. Due to its complexity, however, Chapter 6 observes that many potential criminal actions do not materialize. For example, students learn that mens rea under the Clean Air Act changes depending upon the office a putative defendant holds in an organization. Given these comlexities, Clean Air Act prosecutions have mostly been about enforcing hazardous air pollutant regulations and, more recently, compliance with permits issued under the various permitting regimes in the Act.

Chapter 7 marks the last chapter on pollution-related crimes by discussing violations associated with hazardous waste, hazardous substances, and the unlawful use of pesticides. Chapter 7 also observes that although Congress has enacted felony provisions in nearly all pollution-related statutes, the federal pesticide statute (i.e., FIFRA) is one where Congress has been content with misdemeanor prosecutions despite some terrible tragedies that people have experienced by those who do not apply pesticides responsibly.

Chapter 8 pivots away from pollution-related crimes by focusing on another significant area of environmental criminal action: wildlife regulation. Even students with prior exposure to environmental law will likely be introduced for the first time to the Lacey Act—the United States' oldest wildlife trafficking statute—and may be surprised to learn that the Endangered Species Act carries relatively weak criminal penalties, especially when Department of Justice policy limits prosecutors in ways that courts have not. In addition to discussing criminal provisions on migratory birds and bald and golden eagles, the chapter finishes with a brief discussion of some of the newest additions to the environmental crime arsenal: federal animal fighting and anti-crush video statutes.

Finally, Chapter 9 helps students understand some long-standing, conventional criminal statutes that can be brought in conjunction with or in lieu of some of the more complex environmental charges discussed in Chapters 5-8. With a bend toward environmental enforcement, students will learn about mail and wire fraud, false statements, obstruction of justice, and smuggling.

Although this book contains sufficient material to teach a three-credit class, my experience teaching environmental crimes has been limited to a two-credit class. If such is the case for you, then covering every topic will be difficult. Nevertheless, even if time requires you to cut some topics, the chapters in this book will provide your class with engaging material that will give them a well-rounded perspective about environmental enforcement generally and environmental crimes specifically.

In addition to teaching the nuts and bolts of environmental enforcement, I hope that this book helps students appreciate that environmental crimes are unique compared to most criminal statutes because of how young they are relative to many of the other criminal statutes in the federal code. Indeed, the felony provisions of the Clean Water Act, Clean Air Act, and Resource Conservation and Recovery Act have not yet attained middle-age for a person, to say nothing of the long lifespan of the nation's criminal statutes. Given the youth of environmental criminal statutes, practitioners and students alike will encounter many questions that courts or Congress have yet to answer. These questions provide excellent opportunities to engage students in class as they contemplate how they would argue the issue before a judge or a jury if they are called upon to litigate the matter. Additionally, these unanswered questions help educate those students who do not want to litigate and are more interested in orienting clients away from trouble by helping clients think through whether they want to take an action that may be used to answer a previously unanswered question through criminal litigation.

Although this book represents my best efforts to capture years of environmental crimes experience in the courtroom and the classroom, it does not represent the views of any government agency and will undoubtedly include some errors. Whether those errors are in content, perception, opinion, or punctuation, any errors in this work are mine and mine alone. But overcoming and learning from our errors is the greatest part of life and is exactly why law has been and always will be a "practice."

Jared C. Bennett
April 2019

Acknowledgments

I express my sincere gratitude to the environmental pioneers: the late Raymond W. Mushal, from the Department of Justice's Environmental Crimes Section; and professors *nonpareil* Robert Adler and Robert Keiter of the S.J. Quinney College of Law, University of Utah.

As I express gratitude to the pioneers, I also express my hope in the future thanks to Alex, Andrew, Aubrey, Anika, Austin, and Alayna. Finally, my deepest gratitude goes to Pamela who holds the world together.

I also gratefully acknowledge the following sources, which granted permission to reprint excerpts from the works listed below:

Jared C. Bennett, The Soothsayer, Julius Caesar, and Modern-Day Ides: Why You Should Prosecute FIFRA Cases, 59 Dep't of Justice J. of Fed. L. & Practice, July 2011, at 84, 86-90. Copyright © 2011 by Dep't of Justice. Reprinted by permission. All rights reserved.

Preet Bharara, Corporations Cry Uncle and Their Employees Cry Foul: Rethinking Prosecutorial Pressure on Corporate Defendants, 44 Am. Crim. L. Rev. 53 (2007). Copyright © 2007 by Preet Bharara. Reprinted by permission. All rights reserved.

Kathleen F. Brickey, Environmental Crime at the Crossroads: The Intersection of Environmental and Criminal Law Theory, 71 Tul. L. Rev. 487 (1997). Reprinted with the permission of the Tulane Law Review Association, which holds the copyright.

Kathleen F. Brickey, Environmental Crime: Law, Policy, Prosecution, 13-17 (Wolters Kluwer 2008). Copyright © 2008 by CCH. Reprinted by permission. All rights reserved.

John C. Coffee, Jr., Does "Unlawful" Mean "Criminal"?: Reflections on the Disappearing Tort/Crime Distinction in American Law, 71 B.U. L. Rev. 193 (1991). Copyright © 1991 by Boston University Law Review and John C. Coffee, Jr. Reprinted by permission. All rights reserved.

Michael J. McClary, Jessica B. Goldstein, FIFRA at 40: The Need for Felonies For Pesticide Crimes, 47 Envtl. L. Rptr. News & Analysis 10767 (Sept. 2017). Copyright © 2017 by Michael McClary, Jessica Goldstein, and Environmental Law Reporter. Reprinted by permission. All rights reserved.

Environmental Crime:
Pollution and Wildlife Enforcement

CHAPTER 1

WHY ENVIRONMENTAL CRIME?

A. REAL LIFE EXAMPLES

During the early morning hours of February 13, 1981, the city of Louisville, Kentucky was rocked by a series of explosions that decimated roads, shredded the subterranean utility pipes, turned streets into craters, injured drivers, and shook homes throughout the city. Although the photos from this cataclysmic event appear to originate from the set of *The Avengers*, the fact is that this real-life destruction erupted from a source beneath the city that no one thought about. For months leading up to the explosion, a volatile organic compound called hexane was introduced into the sewer system at the local Ralston-Purina plant. As the hexane trickled into the sewer, the resulting vapors from the hexane built up in the pipes and effectively made an enormous pipe bomb, which detonated from a fateful spark near a railroad bridge. Although two miles of Louisville sewer had exploded, miraculously, no one was killed.[1] However, the damage to the city, private property, and lives was catastrophic.

The Louisville sewer explosion came a mere three years after what some have considered "one of the most appalling environmental tragedies in United States history."[2] In the early twentieth century, Love Canal, New York was intended to be an idyllic neighborhood. However, the utopian vision of the original landowner never materialized because a neighborhood was never built upon the intended site until decades after the original owner parted with the property. Prior to development, the land for the would-be utopian neighborhood passed through the corporate hands of Hooker Chemical, which used the property to bury tons of toxic, hazardous waste. Hooker Chemical then sold the property, which was developed. In 1978, the homeowners in that neighborhood realized that the land on which they had built their homes was toxic and that far too many in the area were dying of cancer. Instead of an idyllic neighborhood in which families could realize home

---

[1] For more on this incident, read Matthew Claxton, *The Day Purina Blew Up Louisville*, Vancouver Courier, Feb. 18, 2014, http://www.vancourier.com/opinion/columnists/the-day-purina-blew-up-louisville-1.858693; Winston Williams, *Louisville's Cleanup Begins in Wake of Sewer Explosion*, N.Y. Times, Feb. 18, 1981, at A12, https://www.nytimes.com/1981/02/18/us/louisville-s-cleanup-begins-in-wake-of-sewer-explosion.html.

[2] Eckardt C. Beck, *The Love Canal Tragedy*, EPA Journal, January 1979, https://archive.epa.gov/epa/aboutepa/love-canal-tragedy.html.

ownership and the American dream, Hooker Chemical turned Love Canal into a toxic nightmare.

In addition to having widespread impacts, environmental violations have profound individual effects. For example, in 2009, Nathan and Brenda Toone hired Bugman Pest and Lawn, Inc. to remedy a rodent problem that the Toones had in their yard. Despite clear requirements on the rodenticide label as to the maximum amount and the distance from an inhabited structure that the rodenticide could be applied, the licensed exterminator applied too much far too close to the Toones' home. As moisture from the soil came into contact with the pesticide, it turned into phosphine gas, which seeped into the Toones' house. Sadly, the greatest concentration of phosphine gas found its way into the upstairs bedroom of Rebecca and Rachel Toone, ages 4 years and 15 months respectively. As the little girls slept, they breathed in deadly poison, which took both of their lives and forever affected their surviving family and friends.[3]

In addition to these societal and individual impacts, human interaction with the environment has taken its toll on both flora and fauna. For example, in 1939, the Acting Secretary of the United States Department of Agriculture wrote the following to Congress:

> It is apparent to this Department from its long observations with respect to the wildlife of this country that there are those in any community in which an eagle may appear who are immediately seized with a determination to kill it for no other reason than that it is an eagle and a bird of large proportions. It is equally apparent that if the destruction of the eagle and its eggs continues as in the past this bird will wholly disappear from much the larger part of its former range and eventually will become extinct.[4]

In addition to the bald eagle being hunted, this apex predator was also being killed through contact with human developments like high-voltage power lines, insecticides, rodenticides, other poisons, and automobiles, among other things. All of these impacts on the bald eagle led Congress in 1940 to declare that the bald eagle was "threatened with extinction."[5]

B. THE LEGAL RESPONSE TO THESE EXAMPLES

Having read these real-life examples, place yourself in the role of a policymaker whose constituency is clamoring for tough laws to address the problems that these four above-referenced events created. In fact, more than two-

---

[3] EPA Criminal Case File: Rebecca and Rachel Toone (Nov. 19, 2012), https://www.youtube.com/watch?v=XzAmkfRGFgc&feature=youtu.be.

[4] H.R. Rep. No. 2104, 76th Cong., 3d Sess. 1 (1940). For an excellent summary of the Bald and Golden Eagle Protection Act, 16 U.S.C. § 668, see Rebecca F. Wisch, *Detailed Discussion of the Bald and Golden Eagle Protection Act*, Animal Law Legal and Historical Center (July 7, 2018), https://www.animallaw.info/article/detailed-discussion-bald-and-golden-eagle-protection-act.

[5] June 8, 1940, c. 278, § 1, 54 Stat. 250.

thirds of your constituents favor incarceration for deliberate violations of environmental laws and consider environmental crime as seventh in importance, according to a survey on public attitudes toward crime.[6]

Although many want tough criminal laws to address environmental violations, others remind you that producing the goods on which society relies requires companies to use dangerous chemicals, and, sometimes, those dangerous substances will produce hazardous wastes. They also remind you that regulating otherwise lawful, albeit dangerous, activities can be very complex and that holding someone criminally liable for misunderstanding complex regulations is fundamentally unfair. Others remind you of how many people have died throughout history from the diseases carried by rodents and insects, and point out that although chemicals like rodenticides and pesticides are dangerous, they kill far fewer people than the diseases spread by the chemicals' intended targets. Criminal sanctions, they argue, are too much and are unnecessary because of existing robust administrative and civil enforcement mechanisms against negligent companies and pesticide applicators. Still others argue that hunting has been an activity in which humankind has engaged since its existence, and many people do not hunt animals like the bald eagle for sport but for religious purposes. Consequently, they argue, if criminal sanctions are to be considered at all, they must be narrow.

These complex arguments are over-simplistically stated here, but they illustrate the difficulty of inserting a criminal enforcement mechanism into environmental regulation and help explain why significant criminal penalties have been so slow to join the federal environmental regulatory regime. Although federal environmental regulation of both pollution and wildlife has been on the books since the nineteenth century, the laws were piecemeal and authorized very minor criminal penalties, if any. Even when Congress enacted significant, comprehensive anti-pollution statutes in the 1970s (e.g., Clean Air Act, Clean Water Act, the Resource Conversation and Recovery Act (RCRA), among others), none of these included felony criminal provisions for even deliberate violations. Instead, these laws relied on administrative, civil, and misdemeanor criminal penalties. Unfortunately, these penalties and those in significant wildlife statutes did not sufficiently deter illegal conduct to society's or to Congress's satisfaction.

Accordingly, to increase deterrence, Congress started off the 1980s by enacting significant felony provisions for both pollution and wildlife statutes. For example, in 1980, Congress amended RCRA to include felony criminal sanctions including up to five years in prison for knowingly storing or disposing of a hazardous waste without a permit and up to 15 years for knowingly endangering human life. Similarly, in 1981, Congress introduced felony provisions into the nation's then 81-year old wildlife trafficking statute (i.e., the Lacey Act) that included maximum prison terms between one and five years. Congress's get-tough

---

[6] U.S. Dept of Justice Bureau of Justice Statistics, The National Survey of Crime Severity, vii-viii (1985); Robert Deeb, *Environmental Criminal Liability*, 2 S.C. Envtl. L.J. 159, 160-61 (1993); F. Hentry Habicht, II, *The Federal Perspective on Environmental Criminal Enforcement: How to Remain on the Civil Side*, 17 Envtl. L. Rep. (Envtl. L. Inst.) 10,478, 10,484 & n.64 (1987); Susan Hedman, *Expressive Functions in Environmental Law*, 59 Geo. Wash. L. Rev. 889, 889 & n.1 (1991).

approach on environmental crime continued into the 1990s with the amendments to the Clean Air Act, which included higher fines and prison sentences for violators.

C. INTRODUCING THE CRIMINAL ENFORCERS OF ENVIRONMENTAL LAW

When Congress enacted its comprehensive anti-pollution laws in the 1970s, it created the United States Environmental Protection Agency (EPA). In 1982, after Congress enacted felony provisions in some of its anti-pollution statutes, it created the EPA Criminal Investigation Division (EPA-CID). EPA-CID special agents investigate violations of the anti-pollution statutes that EPA administers, in addition to other federal criminal laws. However, Congress did not give EPA the ability to pursue criminal violations by itself. Instead, Congress requires EPA to work through the United States Department of Justice (DOJ)—which includes the United States Attorney's Offices—to bring criminal charges against violators. Although EPA-CID does not need permission from the DOJ to investigate alleged criminal violations of the EPA's statutes, EPA-CID must work through the DOJ if the investigation requires a grand jury subpoena or an investigatory measure that necessitates judicial approval (e.g., search warrant, vehicle tracker, etc.). If EPA-CID determines through its investigation that criminal charges are warranted, then EPA-CID will refer the case to the DOJ. If the DOJ determines that prosecution is warranted, it, not the EPA, will present the matter to the federal grand jury for indictment. If the grand jury indicts, then the DOJ will litigate the case until its resolution. Although the DOJ litigates the case, EPA-CID still plays an enormous role because EPA-CID gathered the evidence on which the DOJ will rely during the prosecution.

For cases involving fish and wildlife, the criminal investigations are most often carried out by the United States Fish and Wildlife Service (USFWS) within the United States Department of the Interior for all species except oceanic fish. Criminal investigations pertaining to oceanic fish species are conducted by National Oceanic and Atmospheric Administration Fisheries, Office of Law Enforcement (NOAA), which is within the United States Department of Commerce. Similar to the relationship between EPA-CID and the DOJ, law enforcement officers from both USFWS and NOAA investigate criminal violations of wildlife and other laws without needing approval from the DOJ. However, USFWS and NOAA special agents must work through the DOJ to obtain judicial approval for certain investigatory measures and to obtain grand jury subpoenas. If USFWS or NOAA decides that it has enough evidence to pursue a criminal case against a violator, then the agencies will refer the case to the DOJ, which will decide whether to seek a grand jury indictment. If the grand jury issues an indictment, then the DOJ handles all litigation thereafter while relying heavily on the agents from USFWS or NOAA during the pendency of the case.[7]

---

[7] For criminal violations involving plant species, the United States Department of Agriculture is typically the investigating law enforcement agency.

D. THE DEBATE OVER CRIMINAL ENVIRONMENTAL ENFORCEMENT

Although environmental criminal enforcement is a legal reality—with its own police force and prosecutors—one must understand the intellectual underpinnings for and the counterarguments against environmental crime in order to be an effective advocate for a government entity, a defendant, or a victim involved in an environmental crimes case. Consequently, the remainder of this chapter will address these concepts by discussing: (1) how the nature of environmental law makes criminal enforcement challenging, (2) how core criminal law concepts are incorporated into environmental crimes, and (3) the relationship between civil and criminal enforcement.

1. The Nature of Environmental Law

Kathleen F. Brickey, Environmental Crime at the Crossroads: The Intersection of Environmental and Criminal Law Theory
71 Tul. L. Rev. 487 (1997)

A. Aspirational Qualities

Environmental law is "aspirational" or "inspirational" in the sense that it seeks to bring about radical change in human behavior to minimize environmental degradation and hazards to public health. It invokes technology-forcing mandates that are often unrealistic or flatly unobtainable—typically under scientifically or administratively infeasible deadlines.

The earliest notable example of aspirational environmental legislation, the Clean Air Act of 1970, directed states to achieve national ambient air-quality standards commensurate with the protection of public health and welfare within three years. That mandate was issued notwithstanding that these standards could only be achieved by radical changes not only in the pollution-control technology and industrial processes of tens of thousands of major stationary sources of air pollution, but in automobile emission-control technology as well. . . .

No less ambitious in its sweep, the Clean Water Act of 1972 adopted the goal of eliminating all discharges of pollutants into the nation's waters by 1985, an objective we are nowhere close to attaining more than a decade after the compliance date expired. Nor have we met the (somewhat) more modest goal that all of the nation's waters be fishable and swimmable by 1983, a date that preceded extensive contamination of the New Jersey shoreline with medical wastes and the accidental release of more than ten million gallons of oil into Alaska's Prince William Sound. . . .

To be sure, some commentators credit much of the success of the nation's environmental-enforcement program to the aspirational qualities of environmental law, while others regard this phenomenon as "unrealistic and even irrational." But, apart from the merits of this mode of environmental policymaking, one might well postulate that environmental law's aspirational qualities make criminal enforcement less appropriate.

B. Evolutionary Nature

Environmental law is in a constant state of flux. Continual change in environmental regulation is all but inevitable. Setting environmental standards requires making "scientifically informed value judgments" based on evolving and often tentative scientific principles.

Environmental policymaking also reflects the volatile forces of public opinion and political conflict over a hierarchy of competing values and interests. Stated simply, environmental policymaking occurs in a rough-and-tumble world [i]n contrast with the stability normally associated with traditional criminal law. . . .

The evolutionary nature of environmental law creates uncertainty about what the law is or is likely to be, including what conduct will be considered criminal. The unpredictability of the governing legal standards thus may implicate questions of fairness in the context of criminal enforcement. . . .

C. High Degree of Complexity

No one would argue with the premise that environmental law is highly complex. It is fraught with highly technical scientific, engineering, and economic jargon that, even to one schooled in the intricacies of environmental science and economics, can be truly mind-boggling.

Apart from the special expertise needed to penetrate the technical facets of environmental law, the draftsmanship in the statutes and regulations is notoriously flawed. The Clean Water Act has been variously described as a "poorly drafted and astonishingly imprecise statute" that is "difficult to understand, construe and apply" and (needless to say) "devoid of plain meaning." Hazardous waste regulations are so complex that they "defy the comprehension of any one person." . . . And so it goes down the line.

In addition to these barriers to understanding environmental law, much of the law itself is obscure. . . . And as environmental regulations consume literally thousands of pages in the Code of Federal Regulations, "the quantity of minutely detailed language . . . begs description." To complicate this overlay of complexity, much of environmental law is hidden in detailed preambles that are not published in the Code of Federal Regulations with the regulations they explain. . . .

As is true of its evolutionary nature then, the complexity of environmental law contributes to uncertainty about what conduct will be deemed to be in compliance, and raises concerns among environmental scholars about the appropriateness of criminal enforcement in the midst of such uncertainty.

- Are environmental law's qualities more aspirational in nature than millennia-old crimes like homicide, theft, or assault?
- Is environmental law more evolutionary than the laws regarding homicide, theft, or assault?
- Does determining compliance with environmental law involve more complexity than the law prohibiting those aforementioned crimes?
- If so, then is it really appropriate to criminalize environmental violations?
- Do you think Congress adequately took the differences between environmental law and traditional crimes into account before creating environmental criminal violations?

2. Core Criminal Concepts

Traditionally, criminal law theory focuses on the concepts of harm, culpability, and deterrence. In addition to these traditional concepts, modern corporate criminal law also considers the concept of equalizing the economic playing field so that violators do not have an economic advantage over those who seek to comply with the law. Each of these concepts are briefly discussed below.

Kathleen F. Brickey, Environmental Crime: Law, Policy, Prosecution
13-17 (Wolters Kluwer 2008)

A. Harm

Harm is a central value in the criminal law. It is "the fulcrum between criminal conduct . . . and the punitive sanction." Yet despite the centrality of harm in criminal law theory, conduct that falls short of causing actual harm may constitute a punishable crime. That is particularly true of conduct that creates an unjustifiable risk of harm, and this principle is embedded in the law of inchoate crimes like attempt and conspiracy. It is also embedded in specialized criminal statutes such as the laws punish[ing] reckless endangerment, which has close parallels in the Clean Water Act, the Clean Air Act, and the Resource Conservation and Recovery Act.

Even when harm or a serious risk of harm is not an explicit element of a crime, if the actor's conduct actually causes a tangible harm, the presence (and, perhaps, extent) of the harm may be relevant in determining the seriousness of the violation or the applicable range of punishment. Simply put, one of the principle purposes of the criminal law is prevention of unjustifiable harm, however proximate the actor is to actually causing it.

ILLUSTRATION A: An environmental engineer who works for a chemical manufacturer decides to discharge treated chemical waste into a nearby river. The engineer knows it is illegal to discharge the waste without a permit, but he does not apply for one because he doesn't want to bother with the paperwork. Since the waste has been pretreated and there is only a miniscule amount of chemicals in the wastewater, the discharges do not affect water quality and pose no risk of harm to human health or the environment. Had the engineer applied for a permit to discharge the wastewater as required by law, the permit would have been issued and the discharges would be legal.

Here, there is no tangible environmental harm, yet the engineer could be criminally charged for discharging wastewater into the river [without a permit]. Why would his conduct be punishable if, but for the lack of a permit, the discharges would otherwise be legal? Where is the harm in this scenario? [Is failure to follow the required process, by itself, worthy of criminal sanctions?]

ILLUSTRATION B: The owner of a small business illegally dumps hazardous industrial sludge in a gravel pit over a long period of time. The pit is located on property near a small town whose residents rely on town wells for their drinking water. Scientists agree that the sludge could eventually contaminate the wells but disagree on how long it would take the contaminants to traverse the distance between the pit and the wells. Scientists are also uncertain about what health risks the town residents would be exposed to if they drank the water after small amounts of contaminants entered the wells.

In Illustration B, there is a strong possibility that the town's drinking water supply would be contaminated, but no time line for how long it would take before that occurred. And, as in Illustration A, there is as yet no tangible harm to human health or the environment and no certainty that it will occur.

If prosecutors in Illustration B were required to wait until actual harm occurred before they could charge the business owner for the illegal dumping, there could be serious complications. It might take years for the contaminants to reach the wells, for example, and by that time the statute of limitations for the act of dumping might well have expired, making the prosecution time-barred.

Or suppose the owner of a different business located a few miles on the other side of the town wells illegally buried the same or similar hazardous contaminants on the premises. Assuming that the wells eventually became contaminated and that it took a period of years, establishing a causal link between the offending company and the harm done could be an extremely difficult and complex task. And the more time that elapses between the prohibited act and an investigation and trial, the more likely it is that witnesses will be gone and other crucial evidence will be stale.

ILLUSTRATION C: A chemical manufacturer illegally releases flammable waste into a city sewer system, causing a series of underground explosions in the sewer. The explosions injure four people, cause millions of dollars of damage, and require the evacuation of an entire neighborhood. Because much of the sewer was damaged or destroyed, the city had to divert untreated sewage into a river that was the source of drinking water for communities located downstream.

Illustration C poses a case in which there is clearly significant harm. But as in Illustration B, the discharge of flammable waste into the sewer would be been illegal regardless of whether it caused explosions or polluted the river. In what sense is the actual harm caused relevant in a prosecution for the illegal discharge?

B. Culpability

Responsibility for causing harm is not, standing alone, a sufficient predicate for imposing criminal liability. Instead, the criminal law requires a measure of blameworthiness, and blameworthiness depends in large measure on the actor's state of mind. One who undertakes a socially undesirable course of action with the prescribed state of mind—which could run the gamut from willfulness to negligence—is deemed morally blameworthy for exposing another person to an unreasonable risk of serious harm. Once who lacks the required state of mind is not.

ILLUSTRATION D: Assume the facts in Illustration C with the following variation. The employee responsible for the release of flammable waste intended to discharge rinse water, a harmless substance that the manufacturer could legally introduce into the sewer. The employee mistakenly turned the wrong valve, accidentally discharging flammable waste instead.

Is the employee's conduct blameworthy? If the required mental state is intent or knowledge, then the employee likely would not be criminally responsible since the release was accidental. If the statute requires negligence, then the question of blameworthiness would turn on whether he should have known the valve he turned was the wrong one.

C. Deterrence

The decision to criminalize or criminally enforce legal norms invokes the moral force of the law in its most powerful form—the power to punish. The power of the state to impose punishment for blameworthy conduct provides, at least in theory, strong incentives for those in the regulated community to comply with the law.

For individuals, the prospect of jail time and the stigma of criminal conviction will deter wrongdoing if the expected punishment outweighs the anticipated gains. For organizations, the punishment must be sufficiently severe that it cannot reasonably be considered another cost of doing business. That is especially true in the context of government regulation, where the costs of compliance can easily exceed an ordinary criminal fine. Stated differently, only when the maximum authorized fine is greater than the cost of compliance can the threat of a fine realistically serve as a deterrent to noncompliance.

ILLUSTRATION E: The manager of an industrial plant knows that fluorides and fluoride particulates emitted from the plant have harmed the neighborhood property every year for at least 15 years. The contamination was largely preventable through installation of proper fluoride controls, which would reduce the quantity of fluoride particulates released into the air by at least 90 percent. When asked by the neighboring property owner why he had not used more effective controls, the manager replied: "It is cheaper to pay claims than it is to control fluorides."[8]

Even if the claims paid to neighboring businesses were commensurate to the harm, they were clearly not large or bothersome enough to deter the manager from continuing to pollute the surrounding air. A credible threat of criminal prosecution accompanied by potentially large fines and remediation costs would have been more likely to command the manager's attention. [After all, the thought of a corporate manager spending time in federal prison and having a federal felony on his/her record for the rest of his/her life is a strong way to make the costs of compliance seem much cheaper.]

D. Equalize the Economic Playing Field[9]

Related to deterrence is the concept of using criminal prosecution to equalize the industrial playing field. In other words, criminal sanctions seek to remove the economic advantage that scofflaws will have over industries that spend the money to comply with environmental regulations

ILLUSTRATION F: Assume that two furniture restoration and refinishing companies are in competition with each other in City Z. Both companies use the same chemical compound to strip the varnish off furniture that each receives from customers before starting the refinishing process. Once this chemical compound has been used several times, it ceases to be effective and must be replaced by a new bucket of the compound. Because of the toxic nature of this chemical compound, the law considers it to be hazardous waste. Properly disposing of each bucket of hazardous waste at [a] permitted disposal facility costs $300. However,

---

[8] *Reynolds Metals Co. v. Lampert*, 324 F.2d 465, 466 (9th Cir. 1963).
[9] Section D is the author's addition to Professor Brickey's work in sections A-C.

disposing of the chemical compound down the sewer or onto the land somewhere else is free. Suppose that Company A chooses to pay the $300 to properly dispose of the spent chemical compound, but Company B chooses to dump it on the dirt behind its building. Because Company A is paying to comply with the law, it must charge its customers more to restore their furniture. Company B, on the other hand, is able to attract more business because it is able to perform the same furniture restoration services as Company A more cheaply by not having to comply with environmental law.

By not following the law, Company B has a marked competitive advantage over Company A. If Company B maintains its economic advantage over Company A, then Company A will be faced with the dilemma of either going out of business or joining Company B in disobeying the law and putting land, water, and society at risk. If the managers at Company B have a legitimate risk of spending time in a United States Bureau of Prisons facility, enduring a term of supervised release thereafter, and paying fines and any restitution that may be imposed, then Company B may decide that the costs of maintaining its economic advantage are far too high. Therefore, Company B will likely begin to lawfully dispose of its hazardous waste, which levels the economic playing field between competing businesses.

3. The Relationship Between Criminal and Civil Environmental Enforcement

John C. Coffee, Jr., Does "Unlawful" Mean "Criminal"?: Reflections on the Disappearing Tort/Crime Distinction in American Law
71 B.U. L. Rev. 193 (1991)

American criminal law scholarship has always placed the issue of mens rea at center stage. Its greatest achievement—the Model Penal Code—creates a presumption that mens rea applies to every material element in the crime, unless the statute clearly indicates otherwise. In *Morissette v. United States*, the Supreme Court seemed to give such a presumption a quasi-constitutional gloss:

> The contention that an injury can amount to a crime only when inflicted by intention is no provincial or transient notion. It is as universal and persistent in mature systems of law as belief in freedom of the human will and a consequent ability and duty of the normal individual to choose between good and evil. A relation between some mental element and punishment for a harmful act is almost as instinctive as the child's familiar exculpatory 'But I didn't mean to'. . . .

More recently, in *Liparota v. United States*, the Court reaffirmed this presumption, at least with respect to those elements in the crime that establish moral blameworthiness. Simultaneously, however, *Liparota* acknowledged that an exception to this generalization existed for "public welfare offenses." Reviewing its prior decisions on mens rea, the Court explained that in those cases in which it had upheld the omission of a mental element, the statute "rendered criminal a type of conduct that a reasonable person should know is subject to stringent public regulation and may seriously threaten the community's health or safety."

This language frames a central question: what is the scope of this exception for public welfare offenses? Lower courts have read the *Liparota* exception as limited to cases in which the risks created by the defendants' conduct "may be presumed to be regulated because of their inherent danger." As an example, the *Liparota* Court cited *United States v. Freed*, a case in which the Court upheld a conviction for illegal possession of unregistered hand grenades, notwithstanding the defendant's claim (and the trial court's failure to instruct the jury) that he could be convicted only if he had knowledge that the hand grenades were unregistered. Both *Liparota* and *Freed* thus involved defendants who claimed lack of knowledge of the applicable regulations; but Liparota won, and Freed lost. Seemingly, the obvious public safety factor present in *Freed* was not present in *Liparota*, which involved only the unauthorized use of food stamps and not a deadly weapon.

If public safety is the deciding test, the possibility arises that many environmental statutes, which commonly require permits before various conduct (e.g., the disposal of waste, the filling-in of wetlands, etc.) may be engaged in, will fall on the strict liability side of the line. Here, the circuit courts of appeal have recently divided. In *United States v. Hoflin*, the defendant was convicted of aiding and abetting the illegal disposal of hazardous waste in violation of the Resource Conservation Recovery Act (RCRA). What had the defendant done? While Director of Public Works for the town of Ocean Shores, Washington, he had authorized the disposal of leftover road paint by burial on property adjoining the town's sewage treatment plant. After testing, the Environmental Protection Agency ("EPA") determined that the paint fell within the class of hazardous waste for which the EPA requires a disposal permit. Hoflin's defense was that he did not know the town lacked such a permit and that, therefore, the trial judge was required to instruct the jury that to convict Hoflin it had to find that he knew either that the town lacked the requisite permit or was acting in violation of one. Rejecting this claim, the Ninth Circuit found that the statute need not be read to require knowledge of the lack of a permit.

On a policy level, such a decision can be defended if one reads the burial of excess paint in *Hoflin* to be conduct equivalent to the possession of hand grenades in *Freed*. Yet, common sense tells us that the average citizen knows hand grenades are dangerous (and therefore presumptively regulated), but has no similar reaction to disposing of ordinary paint, which the average person has encountered and used much of his or her life. Burying paint becomes "hazardous" only once we apply that label to it, not from ordinary human experience. In short, the presumption that danger-invites-regulation is reasonable in one case, but not in the other.

Ultimately, the only factor truly suggesting "blameworthy" conduct on the defendant's part was the knowledge (or lack thereof) that an EPA permit was lacking. Thus, the mental element that the *Hoflin* court read out of the statute was the lone connection between "blameworthiness" and the criminal sanction. In contrast, a defendant in possession of a quantity of hand grenades is at least presumptively involved in "blameworthy" conduct simply based on possession. The line between *Freed* and *Liparota* then is not simply the presence or absence of a threat to the public safety, but the existence of factors corroborating blameworthiness in one and their absence in the other. [T]he immediate point is that because many regulatory statutes involve conduct creating some threat to the public safety, a theory may be on the verge of judicial acceptance that effectively severs this linkage between blameworthiness and criminal punishment. . . .

Public concern about a newly perceived social problem—the environment, worker safety, child neglect, etc.—seems to trigger a recurring social response: namely, an almost reflexive resort to criminal prosecution, either through the enactment of new legislation or the use of old standby theories that have great elasticity. Increasingly, criminal liability may be imposed based only on negligence or even on a strict liability basis. The premise appears to be that if a problem is important enough, the partial elimination of mens rea and the use of vicarious responsibility are justified. No doubt, the criminal sanction does provide additional deterrence, but what are the costs of resorting to strict liability and vicarious responsibility as instruments of social control? [O]ne aspect of this problem deserves special mention in view of the apparent escalation of public welfare offenses into felonies.

If the disposal of toxic wastes, securities fraud, the filling-in of wetlands, the failure to conduct aircraft maintenance, and the causing of workplace injuries become crimes that can be regularly indicted on the basis of negligence or less, society as a whole may be made safer, but a substantial population of the American workforce (both at white collar and blue collar levels) becomes potentially entangled with the criminal law. Today, most individuals can plan their affairs so as to avoid any realistic risk of coming within a zone where criminal sanctions might apply to their conduct. Few individuals have reason to fear prosecution for murder, robbery, rape, extortion or any of the other traditional common law crimes. Even the more contemporary, white collar crimes—price fixing, bribery, insider trading, etc.—can be easily avoided by those who wish to minimize their risk of criminal liability. At most, these statutes pose problems for individuals who wish to approach the line but who find that no bright line exists. In contrast, modern industrial society inevitably creates toxic wastes that must be disposed of by someone. Similarly, workplace injuries are, to a degree, inevitable. As a result, some individuals must engage in legitimate professional activities that are regulated by criminal sanctions; to this extent, they become unavoidably "entangled" with the criminal law. That is, they cannot plan their affairs so as to be free from the risk that a retrospective evaluation of their conduct, often under the uncertain standard of negligence, will find that they fell short of the legally mandated standard. Ultimately, if the new trend toward greater use of public welfare offenses continues, it will mean a more pervasive use of the criminal sanction, a use that intrudes further into the mainstream of American life and into the everyday life of its citizens than has ever been attempted before.

- Is criminal law the proper vehicle to punish violations of complex environmental laws?
- Does it concern you a person can be convicted of a felony even if he/she does not possess an intent to violate the law?
- Consider below the views of the former chief of the Environmental Crimes Section at the United States Department of Justice regarding the line between civil and criminal environmental violations.

- Do there need to be legislative modifications to environmental criminal statutes, or is prosecutorial discretion an adequate safeguard between civil and criminal violations?

David M. Uhlmann, Prosecutorial Discretion and Environmental Crime
38 Harv. Envtl. L. Rev. 159 (2014)

In January 1991, just four weeks after joining the Justice Department's Environmental Crimes Section as an entry-level attorney, I traveled to New Orleans to attend an environmental enforcement conference. The conference was attended by hundreds of criminal prosecutors and civil attorneys from the Justice Department, as well as enforcement officials from the Environmental Protection Agency ("EPA"). . . .

Attorney General Richard "Dick" Thornburgh delivered the keynote address at the 1991 Environmental Law Conference, which was an encouraging show of support for environmental enforcement efforts from the perspective of a newly minted environmental crimes prosecutor. The Attorney General heralded the Administration's commitment to environmental protection and decried environmental crime with sweeping rhetorical flourish, describing its perpetrators as:

> offenders who do some of the dirtiest work ever done to human health and the quality of life. They illicitly trade in sludge, refuse, waste, and other pollutants, and they pursue their noxious concealments only for the sake of gain. Everywhere—on our land, in our water, even in the air we breathe—they leave their touch of filth.

In the Attorney General's formulation, environmental criminals were "dirty white-collar criminals" who scarred precious natural resources, lied about their misconduct, and did so for pecuniary gain. On this account, there could be little question about which environmental violations warranted criminal prosecution. These violations caused great harm ("some of the dirtiest work ever done to human health and the environment") and were committed by dishonest defendants motivated by greed ("they pursue their noxious concealments only for the sake of gain").

Later the same day, the conference featured a panel discussion entitled "What Makes An Environmental Case Criminal?" At the time, I thought this could not be a serious question when confronting the filth, deceit, and greed excoriated by the country's top law enforcement official in his keynote address. If corporations and individuals were ravaging the Earth for monetary gain and hiding their dirty deeds with deceptive conduct like midnight dumping and doctored records, their violations would be criminal and should result in prosecution.

Yet, as I would learn at the 1991 conference and in the years to follow, the Attorney General was describing the easy cases, at least in terms of which violations should be prosecuted criminally. The environmental laws create a complex regulatory system affecting a wide range of economic activity in the United States. The Resource Conservation and Recovery Act ("RCRA") establishes a cradle-to-grave regulatory scheme for hazardous wastes; the Clean

Water Act ("CWA") regulates all discharges of pollutants into waters of the United States; and the Clean Air Act ("CAA") imposes limits on all air pollutants that could endanger public health and welfare. As with any complex regulatory scheme, there are significant disparities in the seriousness of environmental violations. Some involve devastating pollution, evacuation of communities, or deliberate efforts to mislead regulators. Others may be de minimis violations or isolated events that occur notwithstanding a robust compliance program.

Given the wide range of potential environmental violations, it might have been preferable for Congress to specify which environmental violations could result in criminal prosecution. Instead, . . . Congress made only limited distinctions between acts that could result in criminal, civil, or administrative enforcement. Even the most technical violation of the environmental laws theoretically could result in criminal prosecution if the defendant acted with the mental state specified by the statute. Mental state is not required for civil or administrative violations, but the additional proof required for criminal prosecution often does little to differentiate between criminal, civil, and administrative violations. In most cases, the government must show only that the defendant acted knowingly. In other words, the government must show defendants know they are engaging in the conduct that is a violation of the law; the government is not required to show that defendants know they are breaking the environmental laws. Indeed, in some cases, the government is required to prove only that the defendant acted negligently; in other cases, the government is not required to show any mental state at all.

If the same violation often could give rise to criminal, civil, or administrative enforcement—and if mental state requirements only preclude criminal enforcement for a small subset of violations—what determines which environmental violations result in criminal prosecution? The answer is the exercise of prosecutorial discretion, which exists in all areas of the criminal law, but assumes a particularly critical role in environmental cases because so much conduct falls within the criminal provisions of the environmental laws. Critics of environmental criminal enforcement argue that Congress gave too much discretion to prosecutors or, even worse from their perspective, to EPA enforcement officials. They note that whether a case is prosecuted criminally may be determined by nothing more substantive than whether the case originates with a criminal investigator or with one of their civil or administrative counterparts within the Agency. Even supporters of criminal enforcement acknowledge that prosecutorial discretion is broad under the environmental laws. But they insist that it is no greater than in other areas of economic or regulatory crime and that Congress properly relied on the good sense of prosecutors, the wisdom of judges, and the judgment of juries to determine when violators of the environmental laws should be convicted of criminal activity.

I see no merit in debating whether prosecutorial discretion is broad under the environmental laws—it clearly is—and I concede that it may be disquieting in a nation predicated on the rule of law that we depend so much on individual prosecutors to determine what conduct should be criminally prosecuted. I also acknowledge that the extent of prosecutorial discretion under the environmental laws may raise uncertainty in the regulated community about which environmental violations will result in criminal prosecution. On the other hand, our criminal justice system always relies to some degree upon the exercise of prosecutorial discretion to determine which violations will be prosecuted criminally. To evaluate whether prosecutors have too much discretion—and to address claims that the environmental laws criminalize too much conduct—we need to know more about the circumstances under which environmental prosecutors exercise their discretion to seek criminal charges for violations.

As a general matter, our understanding of prosecutorial discretion is limited, both because it is broad and unreviewable and also because prosecutors are never required to state publicly what factors prompted them to pursue criminal charges. Of course, prosecutors should only bring charges if there is sufficient evidence to prove each element of the offense beyond a reasonable doubt. But the exercise of prosecutorial discretion, particularly in the federal system where most environmental crimes are prosecuted, involves more than a rote analysis of whether the law and the facts allow prosecution. Prosecutors have limited resources and want to reserve criminal prosecution for cases that have jury appeal and advance the prosecutor's obligation to do justice. Whether a case has these attributes often depends upon the presence of aggravating factors beyond statutory elements.

For environmental crimes, . . . prosecutors should exercise their discretion to reserve criminal enforcement for cases with one or more of the following aggravating factors: (1) significant environmental harm or public health effects; (2) deceptive or misleading conduct; (3) operating outside the regulatory system; or (4) repetitive violations. Limiting criminal enforcement to cases with one or more of these aggravating factors would preclude prosecution for technical or de minimis violations and provide greater clarity about which environmental violations might result in criminal charges. The presence of one or more of these factors also would delineate an appropriate role for criminal prosecution in the environmental regulatory scheme by limiting criminal prosecution to cases involving substantial harm or risk of harm or to cases in which the conduct involves the type of deliberate misconduct we consider criminal in other contexts as well.

My views about prosecutorial discretion for environmental crime draw on my experience serving for seventeen years as a federal environmental crimes prosecutor, including seven as Chief of the Environmental Crimes Section when I was responsible for approving all charging decisions in cases brought by my office. The factors track what EPA has identified as significant in its exercise of investigative discretion and draw from the Principles of Federal Prosecution that govern all criminal cases brought by the Justice Department. But my former office does not handle all cases prosecuted under the federal environmental laws—the remainder are prosecuted by United States Attorneys—and the office does not require the presence of any specific aggravating factors to justify criminal charges.

I therefore created the Environmental Crimes Project to analyze the extent to which the aggravating factors I had identified as normatively desirable were present in recent prosecutions. Over a three-year period, with research assistance from 120 students at the University of Michigan Law School, we reviewed all cases investigated by EPA from 2005-2010. To ensure a representative dataset, we focused on defendants charged in federal court with pollution crime or related Title 18 offenses. We conducted our review based on court documents for over 600 cases involving nearly 900 defendants. In addition to analyzing the aggravating factors, we also compiled data regarding the types of defendants charged, the judicial districts and EPA regions involved, the statutes charged, and the outcomes of the cases. In the process, we developed a comprehensive database of information about pollution cases investigated by EPA from 2005-2010 that resulted in federal criminal charges.

Based on our research, I have determined that one or more aggravating factors were present in 96% of environmental criminal prosecutions from 2005-2010. This finding supports at least two significant conclusions. First, in exercising their discretion to bring criminal charges, prosecutors almost always focus on violations that include one or more of the aggravating factors I have identified. Second, violations that do not include one of those aggravating factors are not likely to be prosecuted criminally. I cannot say whether these aggravating factors will trigger criminal prosecution; declined cases are not public, so we do not have a control group of cases where prosecutors decided not to pursue criminal charges. Nor could we create a comparison group of civil matters, because civil cases involve notice pleading and most are resolved by consent decrees that do not identify whether there were aggravating factors. Indeed, I would expect that civil and administrative cases also involve at least significant harm and repetitive violations (deceptive or misleading conduct, in my experience, is likely to result in a referral for criminal enforcement). Nonetheless, my finding that criminal enforcement is reserved for cases involving at least one of the aggravating factors I have identified should provide greater clarity about the role of environmental criminal enforcement and reduce uncertainty in the regulated community about which environmental violations might lead to criminal charges.

- Do you agree with Professor Uhlmann that environmental criminal violations should only be pursued if one of the four aggravating factors is present?
- If so, is relying on prosecutorial discretion adequate to ensure that the truly "criminal" environmental violations are treated as such?
- Should Congress codify these criteria to limit prosecutorial discretion, or is relying on prosecutorial discretion an adequate safeguard against over-criminalizing civil violations?

CHAPTER 2

PROSECUTORIAL DISCRETION AND CHARGING

Given the importance of prosecutorial discretion in environmental crimes, knowing how that discretion should be and actually is exercised is important to representing the government, victims, and clients who may be the target of an environmental investigation. Although a prosecutor has a great deal of discretion, it is not unlimited. First, before a prosecutor is even presented with a potential environmental case, the EPA, USFWS, or NOAA Fisheries must investigate the matter. Given the limited resources of each agency, individual agents have discretion over whether and what to investigate. Second, assuming that a matter is deemed worthy of investigation and is presented to a prosecutor, the Department of Justice has issued several important guidelines that a prosecutor must consider before seeking charges in environmental cases. Finally, although the prosecutor has a great deal of discretion in determining which charges to seek, the prosecutor does not make the final charging decision. Instead, the United States Constitution tasks the grand jury with actually charging all felony crimes.[1] Consequently, this section discusses the guidelines that a prosecutor should follow in determining whether to seek an indictment from the grand jury and the role and rules that apply to grand juries. Each exercise of discretion is discussed below.

A. INVESTIGATORY DISCRETION

Criminal environmental investigatory resources are quite limited. In August 2017, EPA-CID had only 147 special agents working throughout the nation.[2] Special agents for the USFWS and NOAA are considerably fewer than 147 combined. Consequently, criminal investigatory resources are already strained. Additionally, due to the complexity of environmental crime, investigating

---

[1] A defendant may waive the right to indictment by a grand jury. However, that usually occurs only if the United States and the putative defendant have reached an agreement before the prosecutor seeks a grand jury indictment.

[2] Eric Katz, *EPA Has Slashed Its Criminal Investigation Division in Half*, Government Executive (Aug. 24, 2017), https://www.govexec.com/management/2017/08/epa-has-slashed-its-criminal-investigation-division-half/140509/.

potential violations takes a great deal of time and resources. For example, investigating whether a company is tampering with equipment that measures the amount of pollutants coming out of the company's incinerator requires an EPA-CID special agent to pour over thousands of pages of documents and interview dozens of employees and executives, among many other things. With the small number of special agents and the investment of time and limited resources that each investigation can require, special agents are spread very thin. Consequently, special agents in the environmental crimes arena cannot possibly investigate every environmental violation that the administrative or civil enforcers discover. Instead, EPA-CID and other environmental enforcement agencies must spend their severely limited resources looking for the environmental violations that have the greatest impact in terms of deterrence. To assist EPA-CID special agents determine which cases to investigate, the EPA issued the following memorandum in January 1994.

Environmental Protection Agency: The Exercise of Investigative Discretion
(Jan. 12, 1994)

I. Introduction
. . . In an effort to maximize our limited criminal resources, this guidance sets out the specific factors that distinguish cases meriting criminal investigation from those more appropriately pursued under administrative or civil judicial authorities. Indeed, the Office of Criminal Enforcement has an obligation to the American public, to our colleagues throughout EPA, the regulated community, Congress, and the media to instill confidence that EPA's criminal program has the proper mechanisms in place to ensure the discriminate use of the powerful law enforcement authority entrusted to us.

II. Legislative Intent Regarding Case Selection
The criminal provisions of the environmental laws are the most powerful enforcement tools available to EPA. Congressional intent underlying the environmental criminal provisions is unequivocal: criminal enforcement authority should target the most significant and egregious violators.

The Pollution Prosecution Act of 1990 recognized the importance of a strong national environmental criminal enforcement program and mandates additional resources necessary for the criminal program to fulfill its statutory mission. The sponsors of the Act recognized that EPA had long been in the posture of reacting to serious violations only after harm was done, primarily due to limited resources. Senator Joseph I. Lieberman (Conn.), one of the co-sponsors of the Act, explained that as a result of limited resources, ". . . few cases are the product of reasoned or targeted focus on suspected wrongdoing." He also expressed his hope that with the Act's provision of additional Special Agents, ". . . EPA would be able to bring cases that would have greater deterrent value than those currently being brought."

Further illustrative of Congressional intent that the most serious of violations should be addressed by criminal enforcement authority is the legislative history concerning the enhanced criminal provisions of RCRA:

[The criminal provisions were] intended to prevent abuses of the permit system by those who obtain and then knowingly disregard them. It [RCRA 3008(d)] is not aimed at punishing minor or technical variations from permit regulations or conditions if the facility operator is acting responsibility. The Department of Justice has exercised its prosecutorial discretion responsibly under similar provisions in other statutes and the conferees assume that, in light of the upgrading of the penalties from misdemeanor to felony, similar care will be used in deciding when a particular permit violation may warrant criminal prosecution under this Act.

H.R. Conf. Rep. No. 1444, 96th Cong., 2d Sess. 37, reprinted in 1980 U.S. Code Cong. & Admin. News 5036.

While EPA has doubled its Special Agent corps since passage of the Pollution Prosecution Act, and has achieved a presence in nearly all federal judicial districts, it is unlikely that OCE will ever be large enough in size to fully defeat the ever-expanding universe of environmental crime. Rather, OCE must maximize its presence and impact through discerning case-selection, and then proceed with investigations that advance EPA's overall goal of regulatory compliance and punishing criminal wrongdoing.

III. Case Selection Process

The case selection process is designed to identify misconduct worthy of criminal investigation. The case selection process is not an effort to establish legal sufficiency for prosecution. Rather, the process by which potential cases are analyzed under the case selection criteria will serve as an affirmative indication that OCE has purposefully directed its investigative resources toward deserving cases.

This is not to suggest that all cases meeting the case selection criteria will proceed to prosecution. Indeed, the exercise of investigative discretion must be clearly distinguished from the exercise of prosecutorial discretion. The employment of OCE's investigative discretion to dedicate its investigative authority is, however, a critical precursor to the prosecutorial discretion later exercised by the Department of Justice.

At the conclusion of the case selection process, OCE should be able to articulate the basis of its decision to pursue a criminal investigation, based on the case selection criteria. Conversely, cases that do not ultimately meet the criteria to proceed criminally, should be systematically referred back to the Agency's civil enforcement office for appropriate administrative or civil judicial action, or to a state or local prosecutor.

IV. Case Selection Criteria

The criminal case selection process will be guided by two general measures—significant environmental harm and culpable conduct.

A. Significant Environmental Harm

The measure of significant environmental harm should be broadly construed to include the presence of actual harm, as well as the threat of significant harm, to the environment or human health. The following factors serve as indicators that a potential case will meet the measure of significant environmental harm.

Factor 1. Actual harm will be demonstrated by an illegal discharge, release or emission that has an identifiable and significant harmful impact on human health or the environment. This measure will generally be self-evident at the time of case selection.

Factor 2. The threat of significant harm to the environment or human health may be demonstrated by an actual or threatened discharge, release or emission. This factor may not be as readily evident, and must be assessed in light of all the facts available at the time of case selection.

Factor 3. Failure to report an actual discharge, release or emission within the context of Factors 1 or 2 will serve as an additional factor favoring criminal investigation. While the failure to report, alone, may be a criminal violation, our investigative resources should generally be targeted toward those cases in which the failure to report is coupled with actual or threatened environmental harm.

Factor 4. When certain illegal conduct appears to represent a trend or common attitude within the regulated community, criminal investigation may provide a significant deterrent effect incommensurate with its singular environmental impact. While the single violation being considered may have a relatively insignificant impact on human health or the environment, such violations, if multiplied by the numbers in a cross-section of the regulated community, would result in significant environmental harm.

B. Culpable Conduct

The measure of culpable conduct is not necessarily an assessment of criminal intent, particularly since criminal intent will not always be readily evident at the time of case selection. Culpable conduct, however, may be indicated at the time of case selection by several factors.

Factor 1. History of repeated violations.

While a history of repeated violations is not a prerequisite to a criminal investigation, a potential target's compliance record should always be carefully examined. When repeated enforcement activities or actions, whether by EPA, or other federal, state and local enforcement authorities, have failed to bring a violator into compliance, criminal investigation may be warranted. Clearly, a history of repeated violations will enhance the government's capacity to prove that a violator was aware of environmental regulatory requirements, had actual notice of violations and then acted in deliberate disregard of those requirements.

Factor 2. Deliberate misconduct resulting in violation.

Although the environmental statutes do not require proof of specific intent, evidence, either direct or circumstantial, that a violation was deliberate will be a major factor indicating that criminal investigation is warranted.

Factor 3. Concealment of misconduct or falsification of required records.

In the arena of self-reporting, EPA must be able to rely on data received from the regulated community. If submitted data are false, EPA is prevented from effectively carrying out its mandate. Accordingly, conduct indicating the falsification of data will always serve as the basis for serious consideration to proceed with a criminal investigation.

Factor 4. Tampering with monitoring or control equipment.
The overt act of tampering with monitoring or control equipment leads to the certain production of false data that appears to be otherwise accurate. The consequent submission of false data threatens the basic integrity of EPA's data and, in turn, the scientific validity of EPA's regulatory decisions. Such an assault on the regulatory infrastructure calls for the enforcement leverage of criminal investigation.

Factor 5. Business operation of pollution-related activities without a permit, license, manifest or other required documentation.
Many of the laws and regulations within EPA's jurisdiction focus on inherently dangerous and strictly regulated business operations. EPA's criminal enforcement resources should clearly pursue those violators who choose to ignore environmental regulatory requirements altogether and operate completely outside of EPA's regulatory scheme.

V. Additional Consideration When Investigating Corporations
While the factors under measures IV.A and B, above, apply equally to both individual and corporate targets, several additional considerations should be taken into account when the potential target is a corporation.

In a criminal environmental investigation, OCE should always investigate individual employees and their corporate employers who may be culpable. A corporation is, by law, responsible for the criminal act of its officers and employees who act within the scope of their employment and in furtherance of the purposes of the corporation. Whether the corporate officer or employee personally commits the act, or directs, aids, or counsels other employees to do so is inconsequential to the issue of corporate culpability.

Corporate culpability may also be indicated when a company performs an environmental compliance or management audit, and then knowingly fails to promptly remedy the noncompliance and correct any harm done. On the other hand, EPA policy strongly encourages self-monitoring, self-disclosure, and self-correction. When self-auditing has been conducted (followed up by prompt remediation of the noncompliance and any resulting harm) and full, complete disclosure has occurred, the company's constructive activities should be considered as mitigating factors in EPA's exercise of investigative discretion. Therefore, a violation that is voluntarily revealed and fully and promptly remedied as part of a corporation's systematic and comprehensive self-evaluation program generally will not be a candidate for the expenditure of scarce criminal investigative resources.

VI. Other Case Selection Considerations
EPA has a full range of enforcement tools available—administrative, civil-judicial, and criminal. There is universal consensus that less flagrant violations with lesser environmental consequences should be addressed through administrative or civil monetary penalties and remedial orders, while the most

serious environmental violations ought to be investigated criminally. The challenge in practice is to correctly distinguish the latter cases from the former. . . .

VII. Conclusion

The manner in which we govern ourselves in the use of EPA's most powerful enforcement tool is critical to the effective and reliable performance of our responsibilities, and will shape the reputation of this program for years to come. We must conduct ourselves in keeping with these principles which ensure the prudent and proper execution of the powerful law enforcement authorities entrusted to us.

- Do the realities of limited environmental investigatory resources and these guidelines on criminal investigatory resources provide a meaningful response to scholars, like Professor Coffee and others, who are concerned about the purported ease of charging mere administrative or civil offenses as criminal offenses?

B. PROSECUTORIAL DISCRETION

After the environmental law enforcement agency decides to investigate an environmental violation as an environmental crime and refers the matter to the DOJ for prosecution, the prosecutor must consider several factors in determining whether criminal prosecution is warranted. These guiding principles are found in several sources. Chief among those sources, however, is the United States Attorney's Manual (USAM). Title 9 of the USAM provides the DOJ's policy on criminal matters. Sections 9-27 and 9-28 are entitled "Principles of Federal Prosecution" and "Principles of Federal Prosecution of Business Organizations" respectively. In addition to considering these two USAM sections, environmental crimes prosecutors also consider the guidelines from § 5-11 of the USAM, which deals specifically with environmental crimes.

Justice Manual: Principles of Federal Prosecution
(Updated Sept. 2018)

9-27.200—Initiating and Declining Prosecution—Probable Cause Requirement

If the attorney for the government concludes that there is probable cause to believe that a person has committed a federal offense within his/her jurisdiction, he/she should consider whether to:

1. Request or conduct further investigation;
2. Commence or recommend prosecution;
3. Decline prosecution and refer the matter for prosecutorial consideration in another jurisdiction;
4. Decline prosecution and commence or recommend pretrial diversion or other non-criminal disposition; or
5. Decline prosecution without taking other action.

Comment. USAM 9-27.200 sets forth the courses of action available to the attorney for the government once he/she concludes that there is probable cause to believe that a person has committed a federal offense within his/her jurisdiction. The probable cause standard is the same standard required for the issuance of an arrest warrant or a summons upon a complaint (see Fed. R. Crim. P. 4(a)), and for a magistrate's decision to hold a defendant to answer in the district court (see Fed. R. Crim. P. 5.1(a)), and is the minimal requirement for indictment by a grand jury. See *Branzburg v. Hayes*, 408 U.S. 665, 686 (1972). This is, of course, a threshold consideration only. Merely because this requirement can be met in a given case does not automatically warrant prosecution; further investigation may instead be warranted, and the prosecutor should still take into account all relevant considerations, including those described in the following provisions, in deciding upon his/her course of action. On the other hand, failure to meet the minimal requirement of probable cause is an absolute bar to initiating a federal prosecution, and in some circumstances may preclude reference to other prosecuting authorities or recourse to non-criminal sanctions or other measures as well.

9-27.220—Grounds for Commencing or Declining Prosecution

SEEMS COUNTER TO IDEALS OF JUSTICE

The attorney for the government should commence or recommend federal prosecution if he/she believes that the person's conduct constitutes a federal offense, and that the admissible evidence will probably be sufficient to obtain and sustain a conviction, unless (1) the prosecution would serve no substantial federal interest; (2) the person is subject to effective prosecution in another jurisdiction; or (3) there exists an adequate non-criminal alternative to prosecution.

Comment. Evidence sufficient to sustain a conviction is required under Rule 29(a) of the Federal Rules of Criminal Procedure, to avoid a judgment of acquittal. Moreover, both as a matter of fundamental fairness and in the interest of the efficient administration of justice, no prosecution should be initiated against any person unless the attorney for the government believes that the admissible evidence is sufficient to obtain and sustain a guilty verdict by an unbiased trier of fact. . . .

However, the attorney for the government's belief that a person's conduct constitutes a federal offense and that the admissible evidence will probably be sufficient to obtain and sustain a conviction is not sufficient standing by itself to commence or recommend prosecution. The prosecution must also serve a substantial federal interest, and the prosecutor must assess whether, in his/her judgment, the person is subject to effective prosecution in another jurisdiction; and whether there exists an adequate non-criminal alternative to prosecution. It is left to the judgment of the attorney for the government to determine whether these circumstances exist.

9-27.230—Initiating and Declining Charges—Substantial Federal Interest

In determining whether prosecution should be declined because no substantial federal interest would be served by prosecution, the attorney for the government should weigh all relevant considerations, including:

1. Federal law enforcement priorities, including any federal law enforcement initiatives or operations aimed at accomplishing those priorities;
2. The nature and seriousness of the offense;
3. The deterrent effect of prosecution;
4. The person's culpability in connection with the offense;
5. The person's history with respect to criminal activity;

6. The person's willingness to cooperate in the investigation or prosecution of others;

7. The interests of any victims; and

8. The probable sentence or other consequences if the person is convicted.

Comment. The list of relevant considerations is not intended to be all-inclusive. Moreover, not all of the factors will be applicable to every case, and in any particular case one factor may deserve more weight than it might in another case.

1. Federal Law Enforcement Priorities. Federal law enforcement resources are not sufficient to permit prosecution of every alleged offense over which federal jurisdiction exists. Accordingly, in the interest of allocating its limited resources so as to achieve an effective nationwide law enforcement program, from time to time the Attorney General may establish national investigative and prosecutorial priorities. These priorities are designed to focus federal law enforcement efforts on those matters within the federal jurisdiction that are most deserving of federal attention and are most likely to be handled effectively at the federal level, rather than state or local level. . . . In addition, individual United States Attorneys are required to establish their own priorities (in consultation with law enforcement authorities), within the national priorities, in order to concentrate their resources on problems of particular local or regional significance. The Attorney General and individual United States Attorneys may implement specific federal law enforcement initiatives and operations designed at accomplishing those priorities.

2. Nature and Seriousness of Offense. It is important that limited federal resources not be wasted in prosecuting inconsequential cases or cases in which the violation is only technical. Thus, in determining whether a substantial federal interest exists that requires prosecution, the attorney for the government should consider the nature and seriousness of the offense involved. A number of factors may be relevant to this consideration. One factor that is obviously of primary importance is the actual or potential impact of the offense on the community and on the victim(s). The nature and seriousness of the offense may also include a consideration of national security interests.

The impact of an offense on the community in which it is committed can be measured in several ways: in terms of economic harm done to community interests; in terms of physical danger to the citizens or damage to public property; and in terms of erosion of the inhabitants' peace of mind and sense of security. In assessing the seriousness of the offense in these terms, the prosecutor may properly weigh such questions as whether the violation is technical or relatively inconsequential in nature and what the public attitude may be toward prosecution under the circumstances of the case. The public may be indifferent, or even opposed, to enforcement of the controlling statute whether on substantive grounds, or because of a history of nonenforcement, or because the offense involves essentially a minor matter of private concern and the victim is not interested in having it pursued. On the other hand, the nature and circumstances of the offense, the identity of the offender or the victim, or the attendant publicity, may be such as to create strong public sentiment in favor of prosecution. While public interest, or lack thereof, deserves the prosecutor's careful attention, it should not be used to justify a decision to prosecute, or to take other action, that is not supported on other grounds. Public and professional responsibility sometimes will require the choosing of a particularly unpopular course.

3. Deterrent Effect of Prosecution. Deterrence of criminal conduct, whether it be criminal activity generally or a specific type of criminal conduct, is one of the primary goals of the criminal law. This purpose should be kept in mind, particularly when deciding whether a prosecution is warranted for an offense that appears to be relatively minor; some offenses, although seemingly not of great importance by themselves, if commonly committed would have a substantial cumulative impact on the community.

4. The Person's Culpability. Although a prosecutor may have sufficient evidence of guilt, it is nevertheless appropriate for him/her to give consideration to the degree of the person's culpability in connection with the offense, both in the abstract and in comparison with any others involved in the offense. If, for example, the person was a relatively minor participant in a criminal enterprise conducted by others, or his/her motive was non-criminal, and no other factors require prosecution, the prosecutor might reasonably conclude that some course other than prosecution would be appropriate.

5. The Person's Criminal History. If a person is known to have a prior conviction or is reasonably believed to have engaged in criminal activity at an earlier time, this should be considered in determining whether to commence or recommend federal prosecution. In this connection particular attention should be given to the nature of the person's prior criminal involvement, when it occurred, its relationship, if any, to the present offense, and whether he/she previously avoided prosecution as a result of an agreement not to prosecute in return for cooperation or as a result of an order compelling his/her testimony. By the same token, a person's lack of prior criminal involvement or his/her previous cooperation with the law enforcement officials should be given due consideration in appropriate cases.

6. The Person's Willingness to Cooperate. A person's willingness to cooperate in the investigation or prosecution of others is another appropriate consideration in the determination whether a federal prosecution should be undertaken. Generally speaking, a willingness to cooperate should not by itself relieve a person of criminal liability. There may be some cases, however, in which the value of a person's cooperation clearly outweighs the federal interest in prosecuting him/her. These matters are discussed more fully below, in connection with plea agreements and non-prosecution agreements in return for cooperation.

7. The Person's Personal Circumstances. In some cases, the personal circumstances of an accused may be relevant in determining whether to prosecute or to take other action. Some circumstances particular to the accused, such as extreme youth, advanced age, or mental or physical impairment, may suggest that prosecution is not the most appropriate response to his/her offense; other circumstances, such as the fact that the accused occupied a position of trust or responsibility which he/she violated in committing the offense, might weigh in favor of prosecution.

8. The Interests of Any Victims. It is also important to consider the economic, physical, and psychological impact of the offense, and subsequent prosecution, on any victims. In this connection, it is appropriate for the prosecutor to take into account such matters as the seriousness of the harm inflicted and the victim's desire

for prosecution. Prosecutors may solicit the victim's views on the filing of charges through a general conversation without reference to any particular defendant or charges. . . .

9. The Probable Sentence or Other Consequence. In assessing the strength of the federal interest in prosecution, the attorney for the government should consider the sentence, or other consequence, that is likely to be imposed if prosecution is successful, and whether such a sentence or other consequence would justify the time and effort of prosecution. . . .

Just as there are factors that are appropriate to consider in determining whether a substantial federal interest would be served by prosecution in a particular case, there are also considerations that deserve no weight and should not influence the decision . . . , such as the time and resources already expended in federal investigation of the case. No amount of investigative effort warrants commencing a federal prosecution that is not fully justified on other grounds.

9-27.300—Selecting Charges—Charging Most Serious Offenses

Once the decision to prosecute has been made, the attorney for the government should charge and pursue the most serious, readily provable offenses. By definition, the most serious offenses are those that carry the most substantial guidelines sentence, including mandatory minimum sentences.

However, there will be circumstances in which good judgment would lead a prosecutor to conclude that a strict application of the above charging policy is not warranted. In that case, prosecutors should carefully consider whether an exception may be justified. Consistent with longstanding Department of Justice policy, any decision to vary from the policy must be approved by a United States Attorney or Assistant Attorney General, or a supervisor designated by the United States Attorney or Assistant Attorney General, and the reasons must be documented in the file. . . .

Comment. Once it has been determined to commence prosecution, either by filing a complaint or an information, or by seeking an indictment from the grand jury, the attorney for the government must determine what charges to file or recommend. When the conduct in question consists of a single criminal act, or when there is only one applicable statute, this is not a difficult task. Typically, however, a defendant will have committed more than one criminal act and his/her conduct may be prosecuted under more than one statute. Moreover, the selection of charges may be complicated further by the fact that different statutes have different proof requirements and provide substantially different penalties. In such cases, considerable care is required to ensure selection of the proper charge or charges. In addition to reviewing the concerns that prompted the decision to prosecute in the first instance, particular attention should be given to the need to ensure that the prosecution will be both fair and effective.

At the outset, the attorney for the government should bear in mind that he/she will have to introduce at trial admissible evidence sufficient to obtain and sustain a conviction, or else the government will suffer a dismissal, or a reversal on appeal. For this reason, he/she should not include in an information, or recommend in an indictment, charges that he/she cannot reasonably expect to prove beyond a reasonable doubt by legally sufficient and admissible evidence at trial. . . .

Justice Manual: Principles of Federal Prosecution of Business Organizations
(Updated Sept. 2018)

9-28.010—Foundational Principles of Corporate Prosecution

The prosecution of corporate crime is a high priority for the Department of Justice. By investigating allegations of wrongdoing and bringing charges where appropriate for criminal misconduct, the Department promotes critical public interests. These interests include, among other things: (1) protecting the integrity of our economic and capital markets by enforcing the rule of law; (2) protecting consumers, investors, and business entities against competitors who gain unfair advantage by violating the law; (3) preventing violations of environmental laws; and (4) discouraging business practices that would permit or promote unlawful conduct at the expense of the public interest.

One of the most effective ways to combat corporate misconduct is by holding accountable all individuals who engage in wrongdoing. Such accountability deters future illegal activity, incentivizes changes in corporate behavior, ensures that the proper parties are held responsible for their actions, and promotes the public's confidence in our justice system.

Prosecutors should focus on wrongdoing by individuals from the very beginning of any investigation of corporate misconduct. By focusing on building cases against individual wrongdoers, we accomplish multiple goals. First, we increase our ability to identify the full extent of corporate misconduct. Because a corporation only acts through individuals, investigating the conduct of individuals is the most efficient and effective way to determine the facts and the extent of any corporate misconduct. Second, a focus on individuals increases the likelihood that those with knowledge of the corporate misconduct will be identified and provide information about the individuals involved, at any level of an organization. Third, we maximize the likelihood that the final resolution will include charges against culpable individuals and not just the corporation.

9-28.100—Duties of Federal Prosecutors and Duties of Corporate Leaders

Corporate directors and officers owe a fiduciary duty to a corporation's shareholders (the corporation's true owners) and they owe duties of honest dealing to the investing public and consumers in connection with the corporation's regulatory filings and public statements. A prosecutor's duty to enforce the law requires the investigation and prosecution of criminal wrongdoing if it is discovered. In carrying out this mission with the diligence and resolve necessary to vindicate the important public interests discussed above, prosecutors should be mindful of the common cause we share with responsible corporate leaders who seek to promote trust and confidence. Prosecutors should also be mindful that confidence in the Department is affected both by the results we achieve and by the real and perceived ways in which we achieve them. Thus, the manner in which we do our job as prosecutors—including the professionalism and civility we demonstrate, our willingness to secure the facts in a manner that encourages corporate compliance and self-regulation, and also our appreciation that corporate prosecutions can harm blameless investors, employees, and others—affects public perception of our mission. Federal prosecutors must maintain public confidence in the way in which we exercise our charging discretion. This endeavor requires the thoughtful analysis of all facts and circumstances presented in a given case.

9-28.200—General Considerations of Corporate Liability

A. General Principle: Corporations should not be treated leniently because of their artificial nature nor should they be subject to harsher treatment. Vigorous enforcement of the criminal laws against corporate wrongdoers, where appropriate, results in great benefits for law enforcement and the public, particularly in the area of white collar crime. Indicting corporations for wrongdoing enables the government to be a force for positive change of corporate culture, and a force to prevent, discover, and punish serious crimes.

B. **Comment**: In all cases involving corporate wrongdoing, prosecutors should consider the factors discussed in these guidelines. In doing so, prosecutors should be aware of the public benefits that can flow from indicting a corporation in appropriate cases. For instance, corporations are likely to take immediate remedial steps when one is indicted for criminal misconduct that is pervasive throughout a particular industry, and thus an indictment can provide a unique opportunity for deterrence on a broad scale. In addition, a corporate indictment may result in specific deterrence by changing the culture of the indicted corporation and the behavior of its employees. Finally, certain crimes that carry with them a substantial risk of great public harm—e.g., environmental crimes or sweeping financial frauds—may be committed by a business entity, and there may therefore be a substantial federal interest in indicting a corporation under such circumstances.

In certain instances, it may be appropriate to resolve a corporate criminal case by means other than indictment. Non-prosecution and deferred prosecution agreements, for example, occupy an important middle ground between declining prosecution and obtaining the conviction of a corporation. . . .

Prosecutors have substantial latitude in determining when, whom, how, and even whether to prosecute for violations of federal criminal law. In exercising that discretion, prosecutors should consider the following statements of principles that summarize the considerations they should weigh and the practices they should follow in discharging their prosecutorial responsibilities. Prosecutors should ensure that the general purposes of the criminal law—appropriate punishment for the defendant, deterrence of further criminal conduct by the defendant, deterrence of criminal conduct by others, protection of the public from dangerous and fraudulent conduct, rehabilitation, and restitution for victims—are adequately met, taking into account the special nature of the corporate "person."

9-28.210—Focus on Individual Wrongdoers

A. General Principle: Prosecution of a corporation is not a substitute for the prosecution of criminally culpable individuals within or without the corporation. Because a corporation can act only through individuals, imposition of individual criminal liability may provide the strongest deterrent against future corporate wrongdoing. Provable individual culpability should be pursued, particularly if it relates to high-level corporate officers, even in the face of an offer of a corporate guilty plea or some other disposition of the charges against the corporation, including a deferred prosecution or non-prosecution agreement, or a civil resolution. In other words, regardless of the ultimate corporate disposition, a separate evaluation must be made with respect to potentially liable individuals.

B. **Comment**: It is important early in the corporate investigation to identify the responsible individuals and determine the nature and extent of their misconduct. Prosecutors should not allow delays in the corporate investigation to undermine the Department's ability to pursue potentially culpable individuals. . . .

9-28.300—Factors to Be Considered

A. General Principle: Generally, prosecutors apply the same factors in determining whether to charge a corporation as they do with respect to individuals. Thus, the prosecutor must weigh all of the factors normally considered in the sound exercise of prosecutorial judgment: the sufficiency of the evidence; the likelihood of success at trial; the probable deterrent, rehabilitative, and other consequences of conviction; and the adequacy of noncriminal approaches. See id. However, due to the nature of the corporate "person," some additional factors are present. In conducting an investigation, determining whether to bring charges, and negotiating plea or other agreements, prosecutors should consider the following factors in reaching a decision as to the proper treatment of a corporate target:

1. the nature and seriousness of the offense, including the risk of harm to the public, and applicable policies and priorities, if any, governing the prosecution of corporations for particular categories of crime;

2. the pervasiveness of wrongdoing within the corporation, including the complicity in, or the condoning of, the wrongdoing by corporate management;

3. the corporation's history of similar misconduct, including prior criminal, civil, and regulatory enforcement actions against it;

4. the corporation's willingness to cooperate in the investigation of its agents;

5. the existence and effectiveness of the corporation's pre-existing compliance program;

6. the corporation's timely and voluntary disclosure of wrongdoing;

7. the corporation's remedial actions, including any efforts to implement an effective corporate compliance program or to improve an existing one, to replace responsible management, to discipline or terminate wrongdoers, to pay restitution, and to cooperate with the relevant government agencies;

8. collateral consequences, including whether there is disproportionate harm to shareholders, pension holders, employees, and others not proven personally culpable, as well as impact on the public arising from the prosecution;

9. the adequacy of remedies such as civil or regulatory enforcement actions; and

10. the adequacy of the prosecution of individuals responsible for the corporation's malfeasance.

B. **Comment**: The factors listed in this section are intended to be illustrative of those that should be evaluated and are not an exhaustive list of potentially relevant considerations. Some of these factors may not apply to specific cases, and in some cases one factor may override all others. For example, the nature and seriousness of the offense may be such as to warrant prosecution regardless of the other factors. In most cases, however, no single factor will be dispositive. In addition, national law enforcement policies in various enforcement areas may require that more or less weight be given to certain of these factors than to others.

Of course, prosecutors must exercise their thoughtful and pragmatic judgment in applying and balancing these factors, so as to achieve a fair and just outcome and promote respect for the law.

9-28.500—Pervasiveness of Wrongdoing Within the Corporation

A. General Principle: A corporation can only act through natural persons, and it is therefore held responsible for the acts of such persons fairly attributable to it. Charging a corporation for even minor misconduct may be appropriate where the wrongdoing was pervasive and was undertaken by a large number of employees, or by all the employees in a particular role within the corporation, or was condoned by upper management. On the other hand, it may not be appropriate to impose liability upon a corporation, particularly one with a robust compliance program in place, under a strict respondeat superior theory for the single isolated act of a rogue employee. There is, of course, a wide spectrum between these two extremes, and a prosecutor should exercise sound discretion in evaluating the pervasiveness of wrongdoing within a corporation.

B. **Comment**: Of these factors, the most important is the role and conduct of management. Although acts of even low-level employees may result in criminal liability, a corporation is directed by its management and management is responsible for a corporate culture in which criminal conduct is either discouraged or tacitly encouraged.

9-28.600—The Corporation's Past History

A. General Principle: Prosecutors may consider a corporation's history of similar conduct, including prior criminal, civil, and regulatory enforcement actions against it, in determining whether to bring criminal charges and how best to resolve cases.

B. **Comment**: A corporation, like a natural person, is expected to learn from its mistakes. A history of similar misconduct may be probative of a corporate culture that encouraged, or at least condoned, such misdeeds, regardless of any compliance programs. Criminal prosecution of a corporation may be particularly appropriate where the corporation previously had been subject to non-criminal guidance, warnings, or sanctions, or previous criminal charges, and it either had not taken adequate action to prevent future unlawful conduct or had continued to engage in the misconduct in spite of the warnings or enforcement actions taken against it. The corporate structure itself (e.g., the creation or existence of subsidiaries or operating divisions) is not dispositive in this analysis, and enforcement actions taken against the corporation or any of its divisions, subsidiaries, and affiliates may be considered, if germane. See USSG § 8C2.5(c), cmt. (n. 6).

9-28.800—Corporate Compliance Programs

A. General Principle: Compliance programs are established by corporate management to prevent and detect misconduct and to ensure that corporate activities are conducted in accordance with applicable criminal and civil laws, regulations, and rules. The Department encourages such corporate self-policing, including voluntary disclosures to the government of any problems that a corporation discovers on its own. However, the existence of a compliance program is not sufficient, in and of itself, to justify not charging a corporation for criminal misconduct undertaken by its officers, directors, employees, or agents. In addition, the nature of some crimes . . . may be such that national law enforcement policies mandate prosecutions of corporations notwithstanding the existence of a compliance program.

B. **Comment**: The existence of a corporate compliance program, even one that specifically prohibited the very conduct in question, does not absolve the corporation from criminal liability under the doctrine of *respondeat superior.*

While the Department recognizes that no compliance program can ever prevent all criminal activity by a corporation's employees, the critical factors in evaluating any program are whether the program is adequately designed for maximum effectiveness in preventing and detecting wrongdoing by employees and whether corporate management is enforcing the program or is tacitly encouraging or pressuring employees to engage in misconduct to achieve business objectives. . . .

Prosecutors should therefore attempt to determine whether a corporation's compliance program is merely a "paper program" or whether it was designed, implemented, reviewed, and revised, as appropriate, in an effective manner. In addition, prosecutors should determine whether the corporation has provided for a staff sufficient to audit, document, analyze, and utilize the results of the corporation's compliance efforts. Prosecutors also should determine whether the corporation's employees are adequately informed about the compliance program and are convinced of the corporation's commitment to it. This will enable the prosecutor to make an informed decision as to whether the corporation has adopted and implemented a truly effective compliance program that, when consistent with other federal law enforcement policies, may result in a decision to charge only the corporation's employees and agents or to mitigate charges or sanctions against the corporation.

9-28.1200—Civil or Regulatory Alternatives

A. General Principle: Prosecutors should consider whether non-criminal alternatives would adequately deter, punish, and rehabilitate a corporation that has engaged in wrongful conduct. In evaluating the adequacy of non-criminal alternatives to prosecution—e.g., civil or regulatory enforcement actions—the prosecutor should consider all relevant factors, including:

1. the sanctions available under the alternative means of disposition;
2. the likelihood that an effective sanction will be imposed; and
3. the effect of non-criminal disposition on federal law enforcement interests.

Factors in Decisions on Criminal Prosecutions for Environmental Violations in the Context of Significant Voluntary Compliance or Disclosure Efforts by the Violator
(July 1, 1991)

I. Introduction

It is the policy of the Department of Justice to encourage self-auditing, self-policing and voluntary disclosure of environmental violations by the regulated community by indicating that these activities are viewed as mitigating factors in the Department's exercise of criminal environmental enforcement discretion. This document is intended to describe the factors that the Department of Justice considers in deciding whether to bring a criminal prosecution for a violation of an environmental statute, so that such prosecutions do not create a disincentive to or undermine the goal of encouraging critical self-auditing, self-policing, and voluntary disclosure. It is designed to give federal prosecutors direction concerning the exercise of prosecutorial discretion in environmental criminal cases and to ensure that such discretion is exercised consistently nationwide. It is also intended to give the regulated community a sense of how the federal government exercises its criminal prosecutorial discretion with respect to such factors as the defendant's voluntary disclosure of violations, cooperation with the government in investigating the violations, use of environmental audits and other procedures to ensure compliance with all applicable environmental laws and regulations, and use of measures to remedy expeditiously and completely any violations and the harms caused thereby.

This guidance and the examples contained herein provide a framework for the determination of whether a particular case presents the type of circumstances in which lenience would be appropriate.

II. Factors to Be Considered

Where the law and evidence would otherwise be sufficient for prosecution, the attorney for the Department should consider the factors contained herein, to the extent they are applicable, along with any other relevant factors, in determining whether and how to prosecute. It must be emphasized that these are examples of the types of factors which could be relevant. They do not constitute a definitive recipe or checklist of requirements. They merely illustrate some of the types of information which is relevant to our exercise of prosecutorial discretion.

It is unlikely that any one factor will be dispositive in any given case. All relevant factors are considered and given the weight deemed appropriate in the particular case.

A. Voluntary Disclosure

The attorney for the Department should consider whether the person (1) made a voluntary, timely and complete disclosure of the matter under investigation. Consideration should be given to whether the person came forward promptly after discovering the noncompliance, and to the quantity and quality of information provided. Particular consideration should be given to whether the disclosure substantially aided the government's investigatory process, and whether it occurred before a law enforcement or regulatory authority (federal, state or local authority) had already obtained knowledge regarding noncompliance. A disclosure is not considered to be "voluntary" if that disclosure is already specifically required by law, regulation, or permit.

B. Cooperation

The attorney for the Department should consider the degree and timeliness of cooperation by the person. Full and prompt cooperation is essential, whether in the context of a voluntary disclosure or after the government has independently learned of a violation. Consideration should be given to the violator's willingness to make all relevant information (including the complete results of any internal or external investigation and the names of all potential witnesses) available to government investigators and prosecutors. Consideration should also be given to the extent and quality of the violator's assistance to the government's investigation.

C. Preventative Measures and Compliance Programs

The attorney for the Department should consider the existence and scope of any regularized, intensive, and comprehensive environmental compliance program; such a program may include an environmental compliance or management audit. Particular consideration should be given to whether the compliance or audit program includes sufficient measures to identify and prevent future noncompliance, and whether the program was adopted in good faith in a timely manner.

Compliance programs may vary but the following questions should be asked in evaluating any program: Was there a strong institutional policy to comply with all environmental requirements? Had safeguards beyond those required by existing law been developed and implemented to prevent noncompliance from occurring? Were there regular procedures, including internal or external compliance and management audits, to evaluate, detect, prevent and remedy circumstances like those that led to the noncompliance? Were there procedures and safeguards to ensure the integrity of any audit conducted? Did the audit evaluate all sources of pollution (i.e., all media), including the possibility of cross-media transfers of pollutants? Were the auditor's recommendations implemented in a timely fashion? Were adequate resources committed to the auditing program and to implementing its recommendations? Was environmental compliance a standard by which employee and corporate departmental performance was judged?

D. Additional Factors Which May Be Relevant

1. Pervasiveness of Noncompliance

Pervasive noncompliance may indicate systemic or repeated participation in or condonation of criminal behavior. It may also indicate the lack of a meaningful compliance program. In evaluating this factor, the attorney for the Department should consider, among other things, the number and level of employees participating in the unlawful activities and the obviousness, seriousness, duration, history, and frequency of noncompliance.

2. Internal Disciplinary Action

Effective internal disciplinary action is crucial to any compliance program. The attorney for the Department should consider whether there was an effective system of discipline for employees who violated company environmental compliance policies. Did the disciplinary system establish an awareness in other employees that unlawful conduct would not be condoned?

3. Subsequent Compliance Efforts

The attorney for the Department should consider the extent of any efforts to remedy any ongoing noncompliance. The promptness and completeness of any action taken to remove the source of the noncompliance and to lessen the environmental harm resulting from the noncompliance should be considered.

Considerable weight should be given to prompt, good-faith efforts to reach environmental compliance agreements with federal or state authorities, or both. Full compliance with such agreements should be a factor in any decision whether to prosecute.

- Do all of these factors bearing on prosecutorial discretion guide it and curtail it, or do they merely allow a prosecutor to justify whatever decision she/he makes?
- Specific to environmental crimes, why do the Federal Principles of Prosecution repeatedly insist that a prosecutor identify culpable individuals and seek charges against them even when investigating a corporate entity?
- Do you agree that prosecuting corporations can have a force-multiplier effect in terms of the change that such a prosecution can have on an entire industry?
- Assuming that corporate prosecution can have such an effect, is it a valid factor to consider when determining whether to seek criminal sanctions against a corporate entity as opposed to administrative or civil penalties?

C. THE FEDERAL GRAND JURY

The first right mentioned within the Fifth Amendment to the United States Constitution is: "No person shall be held to answer for a capital, or otherwise infamous crime, unless on a presentment or indictment of a Grand Jury. . . ." The United States Supreme Court has held that all crimes punishable by a prison stay are "infamous."[3] Thus, the Constitution captures a major function of the federal grand jury, which is to charge felony crimes while protecting individual citizens from "hasty, malicious, and oppressive persecution."[4] In addition to determining whether to charge "infamous crime[s]," the grand jury's powers include broad investigatory functions. The United States Supreme Court has repeatedly recognized that "[t]he grand jury occupies a unique role in our criminal justice system. It is an investigatory body charged with the responsibility of determining whether or not a crime has been committed. Unlike this Court, whose jurisdiction is predicated on a specific case or controversy, the grand jury 'can investigate merely on suspicion that the law is being violated, or even just because it wants assurance that it is not.'"[5] The nature and composition of the federal grand jury is introduced below, followed by a brief discussion of the grand jury's investigatory and charging powers. Given that this is not a class on federal criminal procedure

---

[3] *Mackin v. United States*, 117 U.S. 348, 350-52 (1886).

[4] *Wood v. Georgia*, 370 U.S. 375, 390 (1962); *see also Branzburg v. Hayes*, 408 U.S. 665, 686-87 (1972). The United States Attorney has the authority to charge misdemeanor crimes by way of a misdemeanor information instead of through indictment by the grand jury. Fed. R. Crim. P. 7, 58.

[5] *United States v. R. Enterprises*, 498 U.S. 292, 297 (1991).

or grand jury practice, the intent of discussing grand jury practice is to consider whether it provides a check on prosecutorial discretion or whether it is merely a "rubber stamp" on prosecutorial actions.[6]

1. The Nature and Composition of the Grand Jury

Under federal statute and the Federal Rules of Criminal Procedure, a grand jury consists of no fewer than 16 but no more than 23 citizens who are selected to participate as grand jurors for a term of approximately 18 months.[7] Congress requires these grand jurors to be "selected at random from a fair cross section of the community in the district or division wherein the court convenes."[8] Grand jury empanelment is presided over by either a federal district court or magistrate judge.

Although a federal judge presides over grand jury empanelment, the grand jury is neither part of the judiciary nor of the executive branches.[9] Some have even referred to the grand jury as the "fourth branch" of government.[10] Because the grand jury is independent of the prosecution, a federal prosecutor's function in the grand jury is one of a legal adviser and an advocate that seeks to convince the jurors to issue an indictment. The grand jury is not subject to the adversarial process because no one other than the prosecutor, any witness testifying before the grand jury, the court reporter, and the grand jurors themselves are even allowed to be present in the grand jury.[11]

Also, because the grand jury is not part of the judicial branch, no judge participates in or presides over the presentations that prosecutors make to the grand jury. Neither the judiciary nor the prosecution is present when the grand jury deliberates and votes on whether to issue an indictment.[12] In fact, what occurs before the grand jury is subject to strict secrecy, which precludes even the judiciary from knowing what matters are occurring before the grand jury unless the matter disclosed to the judiciary is covered by an exception to the secrecy rules.[13]

Instead of presiding over the grand jury's day-to-day functions, the court's role is limited to empaneling the grand jury and instructing the grand jurors of their duty to follow the law. The court then designates a foreperson, a deputy foreperson,

---

[6] *United States v. Navarro-Vargas*, 408 F.3d 1184, 1196 (9th Cir. 2005) (quotations and citations omitted).

[7] 18 U.S.C. § 3321; Fed. R. Crim. P. 6(a), (g) (grand jurors may serve for a term of 18 months or fewer but may be extended to up to 36 months of service by court order).

[8] 28 U.S.C. § 1861.

[9] *United States v. Williams*, 504 U.S. 36, 47 (1992) ("[T]he grand jury is mentioned in the Bill of Rights, but not in the body of the Constitution. It has not been textually assigned, therefore, to any of the branches described in the first three Articles. It 'is a constitutional fixture in its own right.'" (quoting *United States v. Chanen*, 549 F.2d 1306, 1312 (9th Cir. 1977))).

[10] John F. Decker, *Legislating New Federalism: The Call for Grand Jury Reform in the States*, 58 Okla. L. Rev. 341, 350 (Fall 2005).

[11] Fed. R. Crim. P. 6(d)(1).

[12] Fed. R. Crim. P. 6(d)(2).

[13] Fed. R. Crim. P. 6(e).

and a secretary.[14] The foreperson and the deputy are tasked with keeping track of the number of jurors voting in favor of indictment on each case that the DOJ presents.[15] The foreperson or deputy foreperson "returns" all of the indictments issued during a particular grand jury session to a magistrate judge for filing with the clerk of the court, which spawns the issuance of any arrest warrants or criminal summonses of the newly indicted defendants.[16]

2. The Grand Jury's Investigatory Powers

Because the grand jury is tasked with making an independent determination of whether to issue an indictment (also called "a true bill"), the Supreme Court has recognized that the grand jury has broad investigatory powers.[17] One of the chief ways that the grand jury is able to investigate is through its subpoena power. A grand jury subpoena can be served upon anyone and can be for documents and/or testimony. Although the grand jury can instruct a prosecutor to issue a grand jury subpoena, prosecutors typically issue the subpoenas in the name of the grand jury. Before issuing a subpoena, the prosecution need not make any preliminary showing of relevance or reasonableness.[18] The Supreme Court has stated that where "a subpoena is challenged on relevancy grounds, the motion to quash must be denied unless the district court determines that there is *no reasonable possibility* that the category of materials the Government seeks will produce information relevant to the general subject of the grand jury's investigation."[19] Although broad, grand jury subpoenas can neither eclipse substantive privileges to which a person is entitled nor supplant the requirement for the government to obtain a search warrant.

3. The Grand Jury's Indictment Authority

As both a legal adviser to the grand jury and as an advocate on behalf of the United States, the prosecutor may, but is not required to, provide legal advice to the grand jury.[20] However, the prosecutor should not provide facts to the jury in

---

[14] Fed. R. Crim. P. 6(c).

[15] *Id.*

[16] Fed. R. Crim. P. 6(f).

[17] *United States v. R. Enterprises, Inc.*, 498 U.S. 292, 297 (1991) ("As a necessary consequence of its investigatory function, the grand jury paints with a broad brush. A grand jury investigation is not fully carried out until every available clue has been run down and all witnesses examined in every proper way to find if a crime has been committed.") (citations and quotations omitted)).

[18] *See, e.g., Doe v. DiGenova*, 779 F.2d 74, 80 (D.C. Cir. 1985) ("The United States Attorney's Office has considerable latitude in issuing [grand jury] subpoenas. It has been held that the government is not required to make a preliminary showing of reasonableness or relevancy before issuing a subpoena.").

[19] *R. Enterprises, Inc.*, 498 U.S. at 301.

[20] *United States v. Lopez-Lopez*, 282 F.3d 1, 9 (1st Cir. 2002); *United States v. Wiseman*, 172 F.3d 1196, 1205 (10th Cir. 1999) (prosecutor did not improperly testify in the grand jury when she explained the interstate commerce element).

the form of testimony.[21] Instead, the prosecutor should call witnesses to provide the evidence that the grand jury needs to decide whether to indict. However, although the policy of the DOJ is to require prosecutors to present exculpatory evidence to the grand jury, the Supreme Court has held that the Constitution does not require it.[22] Unlike a petit jury during a trial, grand jurors may ask questions of any witnesses appearing before them. The prosecutor, as a legal adviser, may advise the grand jury not to ask a question if it is improper. However, the grand jury is free to decide whether to ignore the prosecutor's legal advice and ask the question anyway. Once the grand jury has heard the evidence presented, it will excuse the witness, the prosecutor, and the court reporter so that it can deliberate.[23] If a majority of the grand jurors find probable cause that the targets of the investigation have committed the crimes charged in the indictment, then the grand jury votes to issue a "true bill," which imposes charges upon the newly indicted defendant. There is no appeal from a grand jury indictment, and also no opportunity to challenge probable cause during a preliminary hearing before a federal magistrate or district court judge.[24] Even after issuing an indictment, the grand jury retains the authority to continue investigating and to request the prosecution to investigate others that may not have been part of the indictment.

United States v. Navarro-Vargas
408 F.3d 1184 (9th Cir. 2005)

BYBEE, Circuit Judge

[When the grand jury was empaneled, the district court provided instructions to guide grand jury deliberations as to whether probable cause existed to indict. After receiving this charge, the grand jury indicted the defendants for various drug-related offenses. After the defendants' convictions, they challenged the constitutionality of the grand jury instructions.]

I. FACTS AND PROCEEDINGS BELOW
. . . In each case the district court instructed the grand jury using the model charge recommended by the Judicial Conference of the United States. The grand jury charge included the following explanations and instructions (for convenience we have numbered the paragraphs):

> 1. The purpose of a Grand Jury is to determine whether there is sufficient evidence to justify a formal accusation against a person. If law enforcement officials were not required to submit to an impartial Grand Jury proof of guilt as to a proposed charge against a person suspected of having committed a crime, they would be free to arrest and bring to trial a suspect no matter how little evidence existed to support the charge.

---

[21] *United States v. Tulk*, 171 F.3d 596, 598 (8th Cir. 1999).

[22] *Williams*, 504 U.S. at 45-47.

[23] Fed. R. Crim. P. 6(d)(2).

[24] Fed. R. Crim. P. 5.1.

2. As members of the Grand Jury, you in a very real sense stand between the government and the accused. It is your duty to see to it that indictments are returned only against those whom you find probable cause to believe are guilty and to see to it that the innocent are not compelled to go to trial.

3. You cannot judge the wisdom of the criminal laws enacted by Congress, that is, whether or not there should or should not be a federal law designating certain activity as criminal. That is to be determined by Congress and not by you. Furthermore, when deciding whether or not to indict, you should not be concerned about punishment in the event of conviction. Judges alone determine punishment.

4. [Y]our task is to determine whether the government's evidence as presented to you is sufficient to cause you to conclude that there is probable cause to believe that the accused is guilty of the offense charged. To put it another way, you should vote to indict where the evidence presented to you is sufficiently strong to warrant a reasonable person's believing that the accused is probably guilty of the offense with which the accused is charged.

5. It is extremely important for you to realize that under the United States Constitution, the grand jury is independent of the United States Attorney and is not an arm or agent of the Federal Bureau of Investigation, the Drug Enforcement Administration, the Internal Revenue Service, or any governmental agency charged with prosecuting a crime. There has been some criticism of the institution of the Grand Jury for supposedly acting as a mere rubber stamp, approving prosecutions that are brought before it by governmental representatives. However, as a practical matter, you must work closely with the government attorneys. The United States Attorney and his Assistant United States Attorneys will provide you with important service in helping you to find your way when confronted with complex legal problems. It is entirely proper that you should receive this assistance. If past experience is any indication of what to expect in the future, then you can expect candor, honesty, and good faith in matters presented by the government attorneys.

Navarro-Vargas and Leon-Jasso contend that the grand jury's independence was compromised when it was instructed in paragraphs [3], [4], and [5] that it "should vote to indict" the accused in each case in which it believed probable cause exists, that it could not "judge the wisdom of the criminal laws enacted by Congress," and that government counsel would use "candor, honesty, and good faith." The Appellants argue that this error is structural and requires dismissal of the indictment.

II. CONSTITUTIONALITY OF THE GRAND JURY INSTRUCTIONS

The Grand Jury Clause of the Fifth Amendment provides that "[n]o person shall be held to answer for a capital, or otherwise infamous crime, unless on a presentment or indictment of a Grand Jury, except in cases arising in the land or naval forces, or in the Militia, when in actual service in time of War or public danger." The Clause is remarkably plain in its restrictions. It is also notable for what it does not say. The Clause presupposes much about grand juries. It does not prescribe the number of jurors. It does not limit the grand jury's function to returning or refusing to return indictments. It does not state whether a person appearing before the grand jury may be accompanied by counsel, whether the rules of evidence apply, or whether its proceedings may be disclosed for any purposes. The text of the Fifth Amendment simply provides for the right to indictment by a grand jury and does not explain how the grand jury is to fulfill this constitutional role. Either such details were assumed by the framers of the Bill of Rights or they decided to leave such details to Congress, the Executive, and the Judiciary. Congress, in fact, has provided for rules to govern grand jury proceedings.

The Court has observed that the grand jury is an "English institution, brought to this country by the early colonists and incorporated into the Constitution by the Founders. There is every reason to believe that our constitutional grand jury was intended to operate substantially like its English progenitor." Because the Constitution presumes a role for the grand jury, the Fifth Amendment must be linked to the grand jury's origins. We review briefly the history of the grand jury to understand its function and something of why "[h]istorically, this body has been regarded as a primary security to the innocent against hasty, malicious and oppressive persecution . . . [and] stand[s] between the accuser and the accused." . . .

A. The Historical Role of Grand Jury

1. The Early English Grand Jury: Quasi-Prosecutor

The modern grand jury is a direct descendant of the English grand jury first employed more than 800 years ago. Its origins belie its modern role as intermediary between the people and their government. The earliest grand juries were the tool of the Crown. In 1164, anxious to consolidate power held by the church and feudal barons, King Henry II signed the Constitutions of Clarendon, which created a jury "to charge all laity who were to be tried in ecclesiastical courts. Two years later he established the Assize of Clarendon, which was composed of twelve men who would 'present' those suspected of crimes to the royal courts." These acts reasserted the King's power over his subjects and filled his coffers with the proceeds from chattels confiscated after conviction.

During its first hundred years, the grand jury did not function as a shield to protect the accused, but as a sword to be wielded on behalf of the Crown. Indeed, the grand jury was "oppressive and much feared by the common people" because of its "unfettered power" and because the King would "manipulate the grand juries through suggestive instructions and fines levied against grand juries that failed to reach their quota of accusations." In this sense, the English grand jury was somewhat like a quasi-prosecutor for the King. Indeed, grand juries were expected to bring charges based on their own knowledge, as well as consider charges brought by prosecutors. A grand jury-initiated charge was a "presentment," while an "indictment" was prepared by the prosecutor and laid before the jury. The distinction between presentment and indictment is reflected in the text of our Fifth Amendment.

The first real evidence of the grand jury acting as a shield to protect the accused was in 1681 when two London grand juries refused to indict the Earl of Shaftesbury and his follower Stephen Colledge, the political enemies of King Charles II. The King wanted them held over for public proceedings before the grand jury, but the grand jury insisted on conducting its inquiry in private. Given its powerful influence, the Crown expected a quick indictment pursuant to its charges. However, the grand jury returned the equivalent of a no-bill [i.e., declined to indict] in the matter, defying the Crown's will both in holding private proceedings and in its ultimate decision not to indict.

2. The Colonial Grand Jury: Quasi-Legislative, Quasi-Administrative

American colonists adopted the grand jury as integral to the common law system. . . . In America, the institution gained broad powers to propose legislation and perform various administrative tasks. Grand juries "exercised broad, unorthodox powers," inspecting roads, jails, and other public buildings; monitoring public works expenditures, construction and maintenance; proposing new legislation; and criticizing poor administration. The colonial grand jury still performed a quasi-prosecutorial role by accusing individuals suspected of crimes, but colonial grand juries demonstrated greater independence than their English counterparts, due in part to the relatively weak position of colonial governments. With their expanding quasi-legislative and quasi-administrative roles, grand juries acquired greater popularity because they were regarded as more representative of the people. "Through presentments and other customary reports, the American grand jury in effect enjoyed a roving commission to ferret out official malfeasance or self-dealing of any sort and bring it to the attention of the public at large," becoming, as James Wilson put it, a "'great channel of communication, between those who make and administer the laws, and those for whom the laws are made and administered.'"

While Colonial grand juries continued to serve as accusatory bodies, they occasionally refused to return indictments in high-profile cases. The most celebrated example in American history is that of John Peter Zenger, a newspaper publisher charged with libel after criticizing the Governor of New York. Based on the jury instructions, it seems clear that Zenger was guilty of the crime of libel. Nevertheless, three grand juries refused to indict not because of insufficient evidence but rather because the jurors were politically opposed to the prosecutions.

As the Revolutionary War drew closer, the grand jury became popular "at least as much from its success as a political weapon as from its role in the criminal justice system." Colonial grand juries publicly called for boycotts of British goods, condemned British rule, criticized the use of the tea tax to pay British officials' salaries, and indicted British soldiers for breaking and entering into the homes of private citizens. Where the king's grand juries had once colluded with the king's prosecutors, in pre-Revolutionary America, colonial grand juries resisted the king's representatives in America. The historical division of authority between grand juries and prosecutors became a fissure exposing the political division between the colonists and their king. Grand jurors, selected from the public, frustrated prosecutors loyal to the king by refusing to indict those charged under unpopular laws imposed by the Crown, often on the urging of colonial judges. Grand jury presentments served an additional function during this time: they became "excellent mediums of propaganda" as grand juries issued "stinging denunciations of Great Britain and stirring defenses of their rights as Englishmen." In their presentments, colonial grand juries reported on matters of public interest and criticized public agencies or officials.

Despite the apparent popularity of these acts of defiance, when the original colonies drafted their first state constitutions between 1776 and 1790, only three states guaranteed the right to a grand jury in their constitution. Following the adoption of the U.S. Constitution, however, eight of the thirteen original states recommended an amendment to ensure the right to a federal grand jury. In early debates over the ratification of the Constitution, before the Bill of Rights had been written, some feared that "there is no provision . . . to prevent the attorney-general from filing information against any person, whether he is indicted by the grand jury or not; in consequence of which the most innocent person in the commonwealth may be taken by virtue of a warrant issued in consequence of such information. . . ." Because of this fear, the Grand Jury Clause, located in the Fifth Amendment, was adopted with little debate or discussion.

3. The Post-Revolutionary and Nineteenth Century Grand Jury: Screening Function

As they had in colonial times, nineteenth century grand juries occasionally asserted their independence by refusing to indict under unpopular laws, even when the grand jury was instructed to indict if the facts satisfied the law. Prominently, grand juries in Kentucky and Mississippi refused to indict former Vice President Aaron Burr, although he was finally indicted in Virginia; refused to indict Americans who aided French privateers in violation of the Neutrality Proclamation of 1793; and resisted indicting those accused of violating the controversial Alien and Sedition Acts. Throughout the nineteenth century, courts continued to recognize the necessity of secrecy in grand jury proceedings. This secrecy allowed grand juries to independently determine whether to indict, despite a judge's instructions.

In many post-revolution cases, judges instructed the jurors to enforce federal laws, even if the jury thought the laws unjust or unconstitutional. Justice Chase instructed a Philadelphia grand jury that until a law is repealed, even if it is unconstitutional, every citizen has a duty to "submit to it." Similarly, Chief Justice Jay explained that a grand juror, just like a judge, must apply the law of the land even if it is a subject of heated public debate as the duty to enforce the law must override "individual scruples and misgivings." Duty to submit to the laws was a common theme among grand jury charges contemporaneous with the adoption of the Bill of Rights.

The conflict between Federalists and Republicans over the Alien and Sedition Acts proved particularly nettlesome and may be illuminating because it follows so closely on the adoption of the Bill of Rights. "From the first, the new federal judges regarded their addresses to grand juries as excellent opportunities to deliver political orations. Though grand jury charges originated for the purpose of instructing the jurors in their duties, judges had long used them as a means of disseminating political propaganda." Federalist judges, supporters of President

John Adams and defenders of the Alien and Sedition Acts, took advantage of their right to instruct juries and "impress upon grand jurors the necessity for the strict enforcement of federal laws." In a politically charged speech before a grand inquest, Chief Justice Francis Dana of Massachusetts denounced Jefferson and the Democratic Republican Candidates for Congress as "apostles of atheism and anarchy, bloodshed and plunder." On the other hand, Republican judges, taking a "slap at partisan federal judges[,]" advised juries that their proper place was "as a strong barrier between the supreme power of the government and the citizens," rather than as an instrument of the state. Nevertheless, these "partisan harangues . . . did not stampede jurymen into returning indiscriminate indictments on political grounds. Instead, jurors often reacted against the heated charges and refused to indict."

The political potential in the screening function of the grand jury was also manifest during the Civil War era. Prior to the war, Southern grand juries readily indicted those involved in crimes related to abolition of the slave trade, while Northern grand juries were slow to indict those charged with violations of the fugitive slave laws. Following the Civil War, Southern grand juries frustrated enforcement of Reconstruction-era laws by refusing to indict Ku Klux Klan members and others accused of committing crimes against newly-freed blacks. "During the Reconstruction period, the grand jury served as a principal weapon of Southern whites in their struggle against radical Republicans and Negro rights."

4. The Modern Grand Jury

By the twentieth century, dramatic confrontations between prosecutors and jurors in grand jury proceedings had become rare. Currently, grand jurors no longer perform any other function but to investigate crimes and screen indictments, and they tend to indict in the overwhelming number of cases brought by prosecutors. Because of this, many criticize the modern grand jury as no more than a "rubber stamp" for the prosecutor. "Day in and day out, the grand jury affirms what the prosecutor calls upon it to affirm—investigating as it is led, ignoring what it is never advised to notice, failing to indict or indicting as the prosecutor 'submits' that it should." Or, as the Supreme Court of New York so colorfully put it: "[M]any lawyers and judges have expressed skepticism concerning the power of the Grand Jury. This skepticism was best summarized by the Chief Judge of this state in 1985 when he publicly stated that a Grand Jury would indict a 'ham sandwich.'"

As the grand jury's tendency to indict has become more pronounced, some commentators claim that the modern grand jury has lost its independence. . . . Against this criticism, the Supreme Court has steadfastly insisted that the grand jury remains as a shield against unfounded prosecutions. . . .

B. The Structural Role of the Grand Jury

The grand jury belongs to no branch of government, but is a "constitutional fixture in its own right." Although no branch may control the grand jury, each branch enjoys some power to direct or check the grand jury's actions. "[T]radition and the dynamics of the constitutional scheme of separation of powers define a limited function for both court and prosecutor in their dealings with the grand jury." The Fifth Amendment's guarantee to indictment by a grand jury "presupposes an investigative body 'acting independently of either prosecuting attorney or judge' whose mission is to clear the innocent, no less than to bring to trial those who may be guilty." Thus,

> the grand jury has been accorded wide latitude to inquire into violations of criminal law. No judge presides to monitor its proceedings. It deliberates in secret and may determine alone the course of its inquiry. The grand jury may compel the production of evidence or the testimony of witnesses as it considers appropriate, and its operation generally is unrestrained by the technical procedural and evidentiary rules governing the conduct of criminal trials.

The grand jury does not belong to the judicial branch, but it is "subject to the supervision of a judge" in some respects. The court summons the grand jury and ensures that it is properly constituted. The district court may extend the grand jury's service or discharge it. The grand jury may subpoena testimony, but it depends on the judiciary for enforcement, and the court may decline enforcement and quash the subpoena. The grand jury may be "clothed with great independence in many areas, but it remains an appendage of the court, powerless to perform its investigative functions without the court's aid, because powerless itself to compel the testimony of witnesses."

On the other hand, the grand jury, while not within the executive branch, shares investigative duties with federal prosecutors. Indeed, in some respects, the grand jury has even broader latitude than prosecutors. Grand jurors "may act on tips, rumors, evidence offered by the prosecutor, or their own personal knowledge" in making its decisions. The privilege of acting on "their own personal knowledge" is, of course, a vestige of the earliest grand juries, which were expected to bring their own charges, and it is reflected in the Fifth Amendment's reference to "presentment."

Grand juries and prosecutors serve as a check on one another. The grand jury, acting on its own information, may return a presentment, may request that the prosecutor prepare an indictment, or may review an indictment submitted by the prosecutor. The prosecutor has no obligation to prosecute the presentment, to sign the return of an indictment, or even to prosecute an indictment properly returned. Similarly, the grand jury has no obligation to prepare a presentment or to return an indictment drafted by the prosecutor. The grand jury thus determines not only whether probable cause exists, but also whether to "charge a greater offense or a lesser offense; numerous counts or a single count; and perhaps most significant of all, a capital offense or a noncapital offense—all on the basis of the same facts." And, significantly, the grand jury may refuse to return an indictment even "where a conviction can be obtained."

The grand jury's discretion—its independence—lies in two important characteristics: the absolute secrecy surrounding its deliberations and vote and the unreviewability of its decisions. At least since the seventeenth century, the grand jury has deliberated in secret, and neither the judge nor the prosecutor may question the grand jury's findings, conclusions, or motives. In fact, the 1974 version of the Federal Handbook for Grand Jurors notes that "[t]he secrecy imposed upon grand jurors is a major source of protection for them." . . . Today, . . .

grand jurors may not disclose their deliberations or vote, on penalty of imprisonment.

The grand jury's decision to indict or not is unreviewable in any forum; its decision is final. It is true that the district court may convene another grand jury and the prosecutor may seek another indictment, but there is no check on the grand jury's refusal or failure to return an indictment. Like other officers of the court, the grand jury enjoys absolute immunity from civil or criminal suit for its acts, which prevents any inquiry into the grand jury's motivations. It is the fact that its judgments are unreviewable and its deliberations unknowable that gives the grand jury its independence.

Indeed, the grand jury is uniquely unaccountable; grand jurors are insulated from public oversight in ways that no other government instrumentality is. Judges must issue their decisions on the public record; prosecutors must inform the accused of the nature of the charges and conduct a public trial. Decisions by judges and prosecutors are subject to review and public criticism; and, in extreme cases, judges and executive officers may be impeached for their decisions and, if convicted, removed from office. Grand juries are not subject to these constraints. . . .

C. Appellants' Objections to the Model Instructions

With this in mind, we turn to the Appellants' arguments. They challenge three instructions that in their view "demean" the grand jury's historical responsibility. Appellants do not ask us to rewrite the instructions in any particular way, but they suggest that no instruction would be better than an incorrect instruction. We consider each challenged instruction in turn.

1. "The Wisdom of the Criminal Laws"

. . . Appellants contend that this passage unconstitutionally misinstructs the grand jury as to its role and function. They assert that no authority supports the district court's decision to circumscribe the subject matter of the grand jurors' inquiries and deliberations. According to Appellants, this limitation "run[s] counter to the whole history of the grand jury institution, in which laymen conduct their inquiries unfettered by technical rules." In addition, Appellants argue that federal courts have limited powers to fashion rules of grand jury procedure and that they cannot use this power to reshape the grand jury institution, "substantially altering the traditional relationships between the prosecutor, the constituting court, and the grand jury itself." They further contend that since the grand jury has the power to charge greater or lesser offenses, it can surely judge the wisdom of a particular law in determining whether to indict. Appellants submit that this faulty instruction constitutes structural error requiring dismissal of the indictment.

We first wish to observe that the instruction is not contrary to any long-standing historical practice surrounding the grand jury. We know of no English or American practice to advise grand juries that they may stand in judgment of the wisdom of the laws before them. Indeed, there is strong evidence to support the current instruction. . . .

2. "Should" Indict If Probable Cause Is Found

. . . Appellants claim that this passage is unconstitutional because it instructs grand jurors that they "should" indict if they find probable cause, but does not explain that they can refuse to indict even if they find probable cause. . . .

This instruction does not violate the grand jury's independence. The language of the model charge does not state that the jury "must" or "shall" indict, but merely that it "should" indict if it finds probable cause. As a matter of pure semantics, it does not "eliminate discretion on the part of the grand jurors," leaving room for the grand jury to dismiss even if it finds probable cause.

Even assuming that the grand jury should exercise something akin to prosecutorial discretion, the instruction does not infringe upon that discretion. The analogy that the Court recognized between the grand jury and the prosecutor is useful for understanding the source of both the grand jury's and prosecutor's discretion. Under Article II, § 3, the president "shall take Care that the Laws be faithfully executed." That duty can be delegated to subordinates, including the attorney general and the U.S. attorneys serving in each judicial district. U.S. attorneys, operating with limited resources, are literally incapable of seeing that each and every federal law is executed. . . .

Notwithstanding Article II's instruction to take care that the laws are faithfully executed, the president and those who represent him have broad independence in their prosecutorial decisions. The president's independence arises not out of any constitutional direction to exercise prosecutorial discretion, prosecutorial nullification, or substantive constitutional review, but out of the lack of any check on the president's ability to do so. The president operates virtually without check on decisions not to charge violations. There are, of course, long-term checks on the president. Congress has broad powers of inquiry and may, if necessary, impeach a president for his decisions. In extreme cases, courts may make judgments about selective prosecutions that violate the promise of due process or equal protection of the laws. The people have a check by bringing political pressure on the president and, if the president seeks a second term, to offer a referendum vote at the ballot box on the president's judgment in enforcing the laws.

In this respect, the grand jury has even greater powers of nonprosecution than the executive because there is, literally, no check on a grand jury's decision not to return an indictment. The grand jury has no accountability at the ballot box, before Congress, the President, or the courts. The grand jury's duty to follow the Constitution is no less than the President's duty to take care that the laws are faithfully executed. It is the grand jury's position in the constitutional scheme that gives it its independence, not any instructions that a court might offer.

Even though the terms "purpose" and "task" are singular, conveying that the grand jury has one purpose, these instructions do not undermine the grand jury's purpose. . . .

3. The "Candor, Honesty, and Good Faith" of Government Attorneys

. . . Appellants claim that this vote of confidence by the judge to the honesty of the government attorneys further undermines the independence of the grand jury. They argue that the grand jury is told to independently evaluate probable cause but that this independence is diluted by this instruction that encourages deference to prosecutors.

We also reject this final contention and hold that although this passage may include unnecessary language, it does not violate the Constitution. The "candor, honesty, and good faith" language, when read in the context of the instructions as a whole, does not violate the constitutional relationship between the prosecutor and grand jury. The contested passage may be surplusage, but it is not unprecedented. Apparently, these laudatory comments about the prosecutor have been included in grand jury materials for some time. The instructions balance the praise for the government's attorney by informing the grand jurors that some have criticized the grand jury as a "mere rubber stamp" to the prosecution and reminding them that the grand jury is "independent of the United States Attorney[.]"

. . . The U.S. attorney is not testifying, but is presenting the testimony of others. The phrase is not vouching for the prosecutor, but is closer to advising the grand jury of the presumption of regularity and good faith that the branches of government ordinarily afford each other.

Again, the question before us is whether this language is unconstitutional, not whether it is overly deferential or unnecessary. This passage would be problematic if it misinstructed the grand jury that it was an agent of the U.S. attorney and not an independent body acting as a check to the prosecutor's power. However, it does not do this. . . .

IV. CONCLUSION

For the foregoing reasons, the decision of the district court denying Appellants' motion to dismiss their indictments is AFFIRMED.

HAWKINS, Circuit Judge, with whom Circuit Judges PREGERSON, WARDLAW, W. FLETCHER, and BERZON join, dissenting.

The majority tells us that a constitutionally created institution, designed precisely to filter prosecutorial desire through citizen judgment, must give way to the unbridled exercise of prosecutorial discretion. The majority arrives at this remarkable conclusion by relying principally upon British history and the use of the grand jury in England prior to King George III. Yet the presence of the grand jury in our constitutional system is a uniquely American institution, born out of concern for unchecked government power and the experience of American colonists that led them to separate themselves from the very history the majority embraces.

A. IMPROPERLY LIMITING GRAND JURORS TO PROBABLE CAUSE DETERMINATION

The instructions begin by telling the grand jurors that what would follow outlines their responsibilities. This prefatory emphasis is significant because the instructions go on to explain that "the purpose of the Grand Jury is to determine whether there is sufficient evidence to justify a formal accusation against a person." A grand juror paying close attention would conclude that the purpose of the grand jury is singular and that its discretion is constrained by the instruction. . . .

The majority discounts the admonishment "should," arguing that it is distinct from "must" or "shall." Even "[a]s a matter of pure semantics," the majority is incorrect to say that the use of the word "should" preserves the grand jury's discretion. The word "should" is used "to express a duty [or] obligation." The "should" and "shall" distinction is a lawyer's distinction, not a difference most lay people sitting as grand jurors would be likely to understand. The instruction's use of the word "should" is most likely to be understood as imposing an inflexible "duty or obligation" on grand jurors, and thus to circumscribe the grand jury's constitutional independence.

This "should" admonishment is at odds with the grand jury's broad independent role. As the Supreme Court held . . . "[t]he grand jury does not determine only that probable cause exists to believe that a defendant committed a crime, or that it does not."

The grand jury's defining feature is its independence. The Fifth Amendment deliberately inserts a group of citizens between the government's desire to bring serious criminal charges and its ability to actually do so. "It is a constitutional fixture in its own right[,] . . . belong[ing] to no branch of the institutional Government, serving as a kind of buffer or referee between the Government and the people." Indeed, "the Fifth Amendment's 'constitutional guarantee presupposes an investigative body acting independently of either [the] prosecuting attorney or judge.'" The history of the adoption of the grand jury requirement in the Bill of Rights underscores its independent role, and its independence was noted by courts at the founding of the Republic.

B. LIMITING GRAND JURY'S PROTECTIVE ROLE

The grand jury's independence serves not only in the determination of probable cause, as these grand juries were instructed, but also to protect the accused from the other branches of government by acting as the "conscience of the community." . . .

The significance of this second—and potentially protective—role should not be understated. . . . [T]he Supreme Court said:

> By refusing to indict, the grand jury has the unchallengeable power to defend the innocent from government oppression by unjust prosecution. And it has the equally unchallengeable power to shield the guilty, should the whims of the jurors or their conscious or subconscious response to community pressures induce twelve or more jurors to give sanctuary to the guilty.

Though grand jurors undoubtedly possess these powers, and the majority so acknowledges, the jurors in this case were misled by the instructions given to them, told that their powers were restricted to probable cause. This necessarily compromises their independence. Further eroding the powers described in [Supreme Court opinions], the instructions admonish grand jurors:

> You cannot judge the wisdom of the criminal laws enacted by Congress, that is, whether or not there should or should not be a federal law designating certain activity as criminal. That is to be determined by Congress and not by you. Furthermore, when deciding whether or not to indict, you should not be concerned about punishment in the event of conviction. Judges alone determine punishment.

This instruction improperly limits the jurors' discretion regarding the proper scope of application of federal criminal law, as well as matters of sentencing. . . .

C. PRAISING THE GOVERNMENT ATTORNEYS

Further invading the independence of the grand jury was the court's instruction that it could expect "candor, honesty, and good faith in matters presented by the government attorneys." In Leon-Jasso's case, the judge also told the grand jurors that the prosecutors were "wonderful public servants." What these instructions do not tell grand jurors is that prosecutors are free to deprive the grand jurors of exculpatory evidence, to provide unconstitutionally seized evidence, and to present evidence otherwise inadmissible at trial. How independent can a grand jury be when they are told how wonderful the prosecutors are? The majority concedes that the "candor, honesty, and good faith" instruction is "unnecessary language," but attempts to justify its constitutionality by demonstrating that this language has been included for some time and claiming that the laudatory remarks do not threaten the constitutional relationship between the prosecutor and grand jury. Appellants, however, have the better argument: the grand jury's independence is diluted by this instruction, which encourages deference to prosecutors. By undermining the grand jury's independence, this part of the grand jury instruction is also unconstitutional. . . .

Because the defendants here were convicted after their grand juries were erroneously instructed, and because the erroneous instructions constituted a substantial impediment to the regular functioning of the grand jury as envisioned by the Constitution, I would reverse the convictions, dismiss these indictments, and allow the government to re-present evidence to a grand jury properly instructed as to its independent role.

- After reviewing the functioning of the grand jury, its relationship to the judiciary, and the role of the prosecution in grand jury proceedings, do you think the grand jury provides a check against prosecutorial discretion?
- Given the complexity of environmental crime prosecutions, do you think that the complexity inures to the prosecution's benefit or to the target's?
- Because some environmental laws can be very unpopular in various locations at various times, does that inure to the prosecution's benefit or to the target's when it comes to the grand jury's secret deliberations?
- After reviewing the limited resources on environmental investigation, the guidelines on investigative and prosecutorial discretion, and the purported independence of the grand jury, do you believe that prosecutorial discretion plays too large of a role in environmental crimes, or is it sufficiently mitigated from sweeping in conduct that is not otherwise "criminal" in nature?
- With this background in mind, the next chapter explores the mens rea that Congress requires the United States to prove to either a grand jury or to a petit jury to warrant criminal charges or a criminal conviction, respectively.

CHAPTER 3

MENS REA IN ENVIRONMENTAL CRIMES

Whether an actor possesses the requisite "evil mind" (i.e., mens rea) is the distinguishing factor between criminal acts that can be pursued and punished through the exclusive exercise of the executive branch's authority and acts that are pursued and punished through civil litigation, which can be brought by private parties independent of the executive branch of the government. Consider the following illustrations.

ILLUSTRATION A: A rancher sees an animal off in the distance and says to his colleague, "There's no way that wolf is going to take my sheep." The colleague points out that the law prohibits the rancher from shooting a wolf. The rancher says that he could care less what the law says, then raises his rifle and shoots the animal dead. Upon verification at the kill site, the rancher confirms that the deceased animal is indeed a gray wolf, the killing of which the Endangered Species Act prohibits.

ILLUSTRATION B: Assume the same facts, but this time the rancher says to his colleague, "I'm not sure if that's a coyote or a gray wolf, but either way, I need to kill it before it kills my sheep." The rancher then shoots and kills the animal, arrives at the kill site, and realizes that it is a gray wolf.

ILLUSTRATION C: Assume that the same rancher upon seeing the animal off in the distance says to his colleague, "That coyote is the biggest one I have ever seen." He then shoots the animal, arrives at the kill site, and realizes that it is a gray wolf.

ILLUSTRATION D: Assume the same facts, but this time the animal appears to him to be a coyote, which is legal to kill under both state and federal law. In an attempt to protect his sheep, he shoots the animal he believes to be a coyote. However, upon arriving at the kill site, he realizes that the coyote is really a gray wolf.

The following sections will discuss the hierarchy of mens rea in federal environmental crimes: (1) willful, (2) knowing, (3) negligent, and (4) strict liability. Throughout the following discussion, consider which of the four above-mentioned illustrations arguably fits with each of the four mens rea standards.

A. WILLFUL

Typically, ignorance of the law is no excuse for criminal liability.[1] However, where Congress has imposed a "willful" mens rea, ignorance of the law is an absolute defense to criminal liability. In fact, in order for the prosecution to prevail, it must convince the fact finder (i.e., the jury or, in the case of a bench trial, the judge) beyond a reasonable doubt that the defendant knew what he/she was doing was unlawful, but that the defendant did it anyway. If the defendant is able to show that he/she possessed even an unreasonable but sincere belief that his/her conduct was lawful, then the defendant must be acquitted.

United States v. Henderson
243 F.3d 1168 (9th Cir. 2001)

GRABER, Circuit Judge:

Defendant Gerald Henderson appeals his conviction under 43 U.S.C. § 1733(a) for violations of . . . a regulation promulgated by the Bureau of Land Management (BLM). Defendant contends that the magistrate judge committed reversible error when he failed to instruct the jury that 43 U.S.C. § 1733 is a "specific intent" offense, requiring the prosecution to prove that Defendant knew that his conduct was unlawful. We agree with Defendant that 43 U.S.C. § 1733 is a specific-intent offense. However, because the magistrate judge's failure to give Defendant's requested instruction was harmless error, we affirm the conviction.

FACTUAL AND PROCEDURAL BACKGROUND

On February 2, 1998, Defendant was observed digging an open trench on public land administered by the BLM at Farrar Gulch in Arizona. A field inspection of the land by a BLM employee on February 4, 1998, revealed a travel trailer, heavy equipment, building materials, an open trench, and barriers constructed from boulders. On February 5, 1998, BLM agents served Defendant with a Notice of Immediate Suspension, directing him to remove all equipment and barriers and to fill all trenches within five days. It also ordered him to cease residential occupancy of the land within two days. The BLM conducted another field inspection on February 10, 1998. It discovered that Defendant had not complied with the suspension notice. On February 11, 1998, Defendant met with BLM agents to request additional time to comply with the suspension, but declined to accept the BLM's conditions for additional time. The BLM investigated the land again on February 16. By that time, Defendant had removed his trailer and personal belongings; the trench, barriers, and equipment remained, however. By February 25, Defendant had removed all equipment and had vacated the land, leaving the trench and the barriers. The BLM incurred $1,491.26 in costs for filling the trench and removing the barriers left by Defendant, plus additional costs for replacing vegetation that he destroyed.

Based on the foregoing events, a misdemeanor complaint was filed in the District of Arizona. It alleged multiple violations of 43 U.S.C. § 1733(a).

---

[1] *See, e.g., United States v. Nelson*, 712 F.3d 498, 508 (11th Cir. 2013).

At his jury trial, Defendant requested the following jury instruction on the "willfulness" element in 43 U.S.C. § 1733(a): "Wilfulness is to commit an act willfully, which is 'voluntary and purposeful and . . . committed with the specific intent to do or fail to do what [defendant] knows is unlawful.'" The magistrate judge declined to give Defendant's proposed instruction, instead instructing the jury that "[t]he word 'willfully' means that a person knowingly and intentionally committed the acts which constitute the offenses charged."

The jury found Defendant guilty under 43 U.S.C. § 1733(a). . . .

Defendant filed a motion for a new trial with the magistrate judge. The magistrate judge then sentenced Defendant to a term of three years' probation, a fine of $1,000, restitution of $2,786.26 to the BLM, and a special assessment of $25.00. Defendant filed a notice of appeal to the district court before the magistrate judge could rule on the motion for a new trial.

The district court heard Defendant's appeal. It affirmed from the bench with respect to the magistrate judge's jury instruction on willfulness. The court also concluded that Defendant's motion for a new trial was not before the court and, at any rate, was mooted by Defendant's filing of a notice of appeal. Defendant timely filed an appeal in this court.

ANALYSIS
1. The Instruction on the Element of Willfulness
We review de novo whether a jury instruction misstated an element of a statutory crime. If it did, we reverse a defendant's conviction unless the misstatement was harmless beyond a reasonable doubt.

A. There Was Error
Title 43 U.S.C. § 1733(a) authorizes the Secretary of the Interior to promulgate regulations in order to enforce the statutes governing the management of public lands. Section 1733(a) also authorizes the Secretary to enforce the regulations through criminal sanctions:

> The Secretary shall issue regulations necessary to implement the provisions of this Act with respect to the management, use, and protection of the public lands, including the property located thereon. Any person who knowingly and willfully violates any such regulation which is lawfully issued pursuant to this Act shall be fined no more than $1,000 or imprisoned no more than twelve months, or both. Any person charged with violation of such regulation may be tried and sentenced by any United States magistrate judge designated for that purpose by the court by which he was appointed, in the same manner and subject to the same conditions and limitations as provided for in [18 U.S.C. § 3401].

Chapter 43 C.F.R. part 3715 is one set of regulations promulgated under § 1733. Those regulations govern the occupancy of public lands for mining purposes. . . .

It is clear from the text of 43 U.S.C. § 1733(a) that the government must show that violations of BLM regulations were committed "knowingly and willfully" before a court can impose criminal liability on a defendant. We conclude that Congress' use of the word "willfully" compels the prosecution to establish that

Defendant was aware that the conduct in question was unlawful in order to sustain a conviction under that statute.

The Supreme Court has recognized that "[t]he word 'willfully' is sometimes said to be 'a word of many meanings' whose construction is often dependent on the context in which it appears." Often, in the criminal context, "in order to establish a 'willful' violation of a statute, 'the Government must prove that the defendant acted with knowledge that his conduct was unlawful.'" In particular, proof of knowledge of unlawfulness is required when the criminal conduct is contained in a regulation instead of in a statute, and when the conduct punished is not obviously unlawful, creating a "danger of ensnaring individuals engaged in apparently innocent conduct."

[The Supreme] Court held that the word "willfully" in 18 U.S.C. § 924(a)(1)(D), the provision penalizing violations of the statutes regulating the use and sale of firearms, required a showing that the defendant knew that his conduct was unlawful. The Court rejected the defendant's argument that the prosecution was required to prove that he had knowledge of the specific statutory provision that he was charged with violating, holding that the following instruction on "wilfully" was sufficient:

> A person acts willfully if he acts intentionally and purposely and with the intent to do something the law forbids, that is, with the bad purpose to disobey or to disregard the law. Now, the person need not be aware of the specific law or rule that his conduct may be violating. But he must act with the intent to do something that the law forbids.

[The Supreme Court also] held that the use of the word "willfully" in 31 U.S.C. § 5322(a), a provision penalizing violations of the currency-reporting statutes and regulations, created a specific-intent offense requiring proof of violation of a known legal duty. The statute provided: "'A person willfully violating this subchapter or a regulation prescribed under this subchapter shall be fined not more than $250,000, or [imprisoned] for not more than five years, or both.'" The Court reasoned that the lower courts' interpretation of "willfully" as requiring the government to prove only "defendant's knowledge of the banks' reporting obligation and his attempt to evade that obligation, but [the government] did not have to prove defendant knew the structuring was unlawful," rendered the word "willfully" mere "surplusage." The Court cautioned: "Judges should hesitate so to treat statutory terms in any setting, and resistance should be heightened when the words describe an element of a criminal offense." The Court further reasoned that, without the requirement of specific intent to engage in conduct known to be illegal, individuals engaged in structured transactions that were not obviously illegal would be subject to criminal liability: "[W]e are unpersuaded by the argument that structuring is so obviously 'evil' or inherently 'bad' that the 'willfulness' requirement is satisfied irrespective of the defendant's knowledge of the illegality of structuring."

This court, too, has addressed the question whether violations of regulations enforced under a statute criminalizing "willful" violations are specific-intent offenses. [W]e held that violations of the regulations governing the import and export of munitions were specific-intent offenses, requiring proof that a defendant was aware of the unlawfulness of the conduct. Subsection (c) of 22 U.S.C. § 1934 (repealed 1976), which governed the imposition of criminal penalties for violations of the regulations, provided that "[a]ny person who willfully violates any provision of this section or rule or regulation issued under this section . . . shall upon conviction be fined not more than $25,000 or imprisoned not more than two years, or both." Two reasons supported our conclusion that Congress' use of the word "willfully" created a requirement to prove specific intent. "First, the statute prohibits exportation of items listed by administrative regulation, not by the statute itself." Second, our review of the regulations demonstrated that they prohibited conduct that was not obviously illegal: "[I]tems might be exported or imported innocently. Under such circumstances, it appears likely that Congress would have wanted to require a voluntary, intentional violation of a known legal duty not to export such items before predicating criminal liability."

In this case, Congress' use of the word "willfully" similarly suggests that violations of BLM regulations enforced under 43 U.S.C § 1733(a) are specific-intent offenses. First, . . . the conduct penalized by the statute is listed not in the statute, but in administrative regulations. Second, . . . some of the regulations bar conduct that is not obviously illegal, such as the restriction on "searching for buried treasure." Because it is not obvious that such conduct would subject an individual to criminal liability, it seems "likely that Congress would have wanted to require a voluntary, intentional violation of a known legal duty" as a predicate to criminal liability.

Additionally, the magistrate judge's definition of "willfully" reads the term out of the statute. . . . As discussed above, 43 U.S.C. § 1733(a) authorizes criminal punishment for those who "knowingly and willfully" violate BLM regulations. In general, "knowingly" means that the prosecution must prove that the defendant possessed "knowledge of the facts that constitute the offense." That definition of "knowingly" is nearly identical to the magistrate judge's instruction on the meaning of "willfully": "'willfully' means that a person knowingly and intentionally committed the acts which constitute the offenses charged." Consequently, it renders the word "willfully" surplusage.

. . . We hold that the court erred by not giving Defendant's requested instruction.

B. The Error Was Harmless Beyond a Reasonable Doubt

Nevertheless, we affirm Defendant's conviction. Our review of the record shows that the magistrate judge's error was harmless beyond a reasonable doubt. [The court found that the BLM had personally given defendant so much notice that what he was doing was unlawful that even though the jury was improperly instructed, the prosecution had proven beyond a reasonable doubt that defendant knew what he was doing was wrong.]

CONCLUSION

The magistrate judge erred when he failed to instruct the jury that the government was required to prove that Defendant was aware of the unlawfulness of his conduct in order to convict him under 43 U.S.C. § 1733. However, because the error was harmless beyond a reasonable doubt, we affirm Defendant's conviction. . . .

AFFIRMED.

- As mentioned in Chapter 1, and as will be discussed in great detail below, most environmental crimes do not require the prosecution to prove that the violation was willful. Instead, in most cases, the government must only establish that the violation was done knowingly. Given that many environmental criminal violations encompass the enforcement of regulations and involve conduct that the accused may not know is unlawful, does the knowing standard violate the Supreme Court's holdings in other cases that such violations carry a willful mens rea?

- Under the Clean Air Act, which will be discussed in far greater detail below, Congress established a dual willful and knowing mens rea for the same crime based on the role that the alleged offender plays in the corporation. For those whom the Clean Air Act considers "senior management personnel," the prosecution need only prove a knowing mens rea. However, for those who are not deemed "senior management personnel" under the Clean Air Act, the prosecution must prove a willful mens rea. Is this distinction fair?

United States v. Hairston
819 F.2d 971 (10th Cir. 1987)

McKAY, Circuit Judge

Richard P. Hairston was found guilty by a jury of three counts of willfully failing to file income tax returns for the years 1980, 1981, and 1982 in violation of 26 U.S.C. § 7203.

I.

The record shows that Mr. Hairston filed income tax returns for the years 1973 through 1976, inclusive. In the spring of 1976, his 1975 tax return was audited, and Mr. Hairston was required to pay an additional $465 in taxes. Mr. Hairston then began purchasing literature published by, and attending tax seminars . . . with the so-called "tax protest movement" who claim that the sixteenth amendment was never properly ratified and that filing tax returns is completely voluntary. He even attended some criminal trials of those charged with failure to file and visited acquaintances imprisoned on tax-related charges. On several occasions, he freely voiced his views that the tax laws were illegal and unconstitutional.

In the years 1977, 1978, 1979, and 1980, Mr. Hairston filed returns completed with only the words "object," "self-incrimination," or "none." He filed no returns in 1981 and 1982. He received numerous registered letters from the Internal Revenue Service informing him of his obligation to file a return and the possibility of criminal liability for failure to comply. In the years 1980, 1981, and 1982, Mr. Hairston submitted thirty-one withholding certificates commonly known as "W-4s" on which he claimed to be exempt from withholding requirements.

Mr. Hairston's defense at trial was that he did not file due to a bona fide misunderstanding as to his legal duty to file a return. A good faith misunderstanding of the duty to file a return can negate the willfulness element of a failure-to-file charge. We have held that "a subjective standard is appropriately applied in assessing a defendant's claimed belief that the law did not require that he file a return." Mr. Hairston claimed that the seminars he attended and literature he read caused him to believe that filing a return was voluntary and that he was under no legal duty to file.

II.

On appeal, Mr. Hairston first argues that the trial court erred in failing to admit into evidence the tax protest literature upon which he ostensibly relied in forming his belief that he was under no legal obligation to file. The court allowed Mr. Hairston to testify extensively with respect to the seminars he attended and tax literature he purchased "that might have led him to make a mistake." Titles were quoted, passages were read, and the thrust of the materials were summarized. In fact, the majority of Mr. Hairston's testimony pertained to the various materials and his interpretation of them, and Mr. Hairston was the sole defense witness. Nearly the entire closing argument was devoted to this defense.

The literature dealt exhaustively with the constitutionality of the tax laws. Because a good faith disagreement with the laws or good faith belief that they are unconstitutional provides no defense, the court found that the materials themselves might mislead or confuse the jury and disallowed them under Fed. R. Evid. 403.

The critical inquiry for the jury was whether Mr. Hairston subjectively believed that he did not need to file under the law's requirements. Because his subjective belief was central, direct testimony from Mr. Hairston regarding the effect these seminars and publications had on his understanding of the tax law filing requirements was more probative of his proffered defense than the publications themselves. The court did not prevent Mr. Hairston from mounting a defense . . . but rather exercised its discretion regarding the form in which such evidence should be admitted so as to minimize jury confusion. The defense theory was argued, and the jury had the testimonial evidence to consider. We hold that the trial court did not abuse its discretion in prohibiting the documentary evidence offered by defendant. . . .

AFFIRMED.

- Although the jury did not believe Mr. Hairston's claim that he subjectively misunderstood the legal requirement to file a tax return, Mr. Hairston was allowed to present that defense to the jury. Had the jury believed that Mr. Hairston truly did not understand the requirement to file a tax return, it should have acquitted him. If a subjective, albeit unreasonable, belief of what the law allows is sufficient to defend against criminal charges, what challenges would exist in obtaining a conviction on a complex environmental crime if willfulness were the standard?
- Should willfulness be the standard for those discharging pollutants into a river from a point source without a permit? Why?
- Should willfulness be the standard for those discharging pollutants into a river from a point source in excess of the effluent limitations in their permit? Why?

- Whereas the Clean Air Act imposes a different mens rea based on the managerial level of the defendant, the Clean Water Act does not. Thus, a non-managerial employee who is aware that he/she is discharging a pollutant into the waters of the United States without or in violation of permit can be held criminally liable even if he/she was commanded to do so by a superior and had no idea that the conduct was unlawful. Should the Clean Water Act include the same dual mens rea as the Clean Air Act?

B. KNOWING

As mentioned previously, the majority of environmental crimes impose a "knowing" mens rea. However, "'[k]nowingly' may convey any number of meanings."[2] For example, the Clean Water Act imposes criminal liability upon anyone who, among other things, "knowingly" discharges a pollutant from a point source into waters of the United States without or in violation of a permit.[3] Does this mean that the prosecution must show the defendant knew that:

- Her/his action constitutes a "discharge" under the Clean Water Act?
- The substance discharged is a "pollutant" under the Clean Water Act?
- The pollutant was discharged from what the Clean Water Act deems to be a "point source"?
- The pollutant was discharged into what the Clean Water Act deems "waters of the United States"?
- The defendant knew that she/he needed a permit to discharge a pollutant into water and that defendant knew that she/he did not have one? or
- The defendant knew that the permit allowed a certain amount of discharges into water but that the discharges the defendant caused exceeded the permit limit?

If the prosecution must establish beyond a reasonable doubt that "knowing" applies to factual, legal, and jurisdictional elements, one can quickly see how difficult obtaining a conviction under the Clean Water Act would be. To illustrate what type of knowledge the prosecution must show in a criminal prosecution, the next sections discuss the differences between knowledge of the facts, knowledge of jurisdictional requirements, and knowledge of the law. Thereafter, two surrogates to prove knowledge known as willful blindness and collective knowledge are discussed.

---

[2] *Freeman United Coal Mining Co. v. Federal Mine Safety & Health Rev. Comm'n*, 108 F.3d 358, 363 (D.C. Cir. 1997).
[3] 33 U.S.C. § 1319(c)(2)(A).

1. Knowledge of the Facts

United States v. Ahmad
101 F.3d 386 (5th Cir. 1996)

JERRY E. SMITH, Circuit Judge

Attique Ahmad appeals his conviction of, and sentence for, criminal violations of the Clean Water Act ("CWA"). Concluding that the district court erred in its instructions to the jury, we reverse and remand.

I.

This case arises from the discharge of a large quantity of gasoline into the sewers of Conroe, Texas, in January 1994. In 1992, Ahmad purchased the "Spin-N-Market No. 12," a combination convenience store and gas station located at the intersection of Second and Lewis Streets in Conroe. The Spin-N-Market has two gasoline pumps, each of which is fed by an 8000-gallon underground gasoline tank. Some time after Ahmad bought the station, he discovered that one of the tanks, which held high-octane gasoline, was leaking. This did not pose an immediate hazard, because the leak was at the top of the tank; gasoline could not seep out. The leak did, however, allow water to enter into the tank and contaminate the gas. Because water is heavier than gas, the water sank to the bottom of the tank, and because the tank was pumped from the bottom, Ahmad was unable to sell from it.

In October 1993, Ahmad hired CTT Environmental Services ("CTT"), a tank testing company, to examine the tank. CTT determined that it contained approximately 800 gallons of water, and the rest mostly gasoline. Jewel McCoy, a CTT employee, testified that she told Ahmad that the leak could not be repaired until the tank was completely emptied, which CTT offered to do for 65¢ per gallon plus $65 per hour of labor. After McCoy gave Ahmad this estimate, he inquired whether he could empty the tank himself. She replied that it would be dangerous and illegal to do so. On her testimony, he responded, "Well, if I don't get caught, what then?"

On January 25, 1994, Ahmad rented a hand-held motorized water pump from a local hardware store, telling a hardware store employee that he was planning to use it to remove water from his backyard. Victor Fonseca, however, identified Ahmad and the pump and testified that he had seen Ahmad pumping gasoline into the street. Oscar Alvarez stated that he had seen Ahmad and another person discharging gasoline into a manhole. Tereso Uribe testified that he had confronted Ahmad and asked him what was going on, to which Ahmad responded that he was simply removing the water from the tank.

In all, 5,220 gallons of fluid were pumped from the leaky tank, of which approximately 4,690 gallons were gasoline. Some of the gas-water mixture ran down Lewis Street and some into the manhole in front of the store.

The gasoline discharged onto Lewis Street went a few hundred feet along the curb to Third Street, where it entered a storm drain and the storm sewer system and flowed through a pipe that eventually empties into Possum Creek. When city officials discovered the next day that there was gasoline in Possum Creek, several vacuum trucks were required to decontaminate it. Possum Creek feeds into the San Jacinto River, which eventually flows into Lake Houston.

The gasoline that Ahmad discharged into the manhole went a different route: It flowed through the sanitary sewer system and eventually entered the city sewage treatment plant. On January 26, employees at the treatment plant discovered a 1,000-gallon pool of gasoline in one of the intake ponds. To avoid shutting down the plant altogether, they diverted the pool of gasoline and all incoming liquid into a 5,000,000-gallon emergency lagoon.

The plant supervisor ordered that non-essential personnel be evacuated from the plant and called firefighters and a hazardous materials crew to the scene. The Conroe fire department determined the gasoline was creating a risk of explosion and ordered that two nearby schools be evacuated. Although no one was injured as a result of the discharge, fire officials testified at trial that Ahmad had created a "tremendous explosion hazard" that could have led to "hundreds, if not thousands, of deaths and injuries" and millions of dollars of property damage.

By 9:00 a.m. on January 26, investigators had traced the source of the gasoline back to the manhole directly in front of the Spin-N-Market. Their suspicions were confirmed when they noticed a strong odor of gasoline and saw signs of corrosion on the asphalt surrounding the manhole. The investigators questioned Ahmad, who at first denied having operated a pump the previous night. Soon, however, his story changed: He admitted to having used a pump but denied having pumped anything from his tanks.

Ahmad was indicted for three violations of the CWA: knowingly discharging a pollutant from a point source into a navigable water of the United States without a permit, in violation of 33 U.S.C. §§ 1311(a) and 1319(c)(2)(A) (count one); knowingly operating a source in violation of a pretreatment standard, in violation of 33 U.S.C. §§ 1317(d) and 1319(c)(2)(A) (count two); and knowingly placing another person in imminent danger of death or serious bodily injury by discharging a pollutant, in violation of 33 U.S.C. § 1319(c)(3) (count three). At trial, Ahmad did not dispute that he had discharged gasoline from the tank or that eventually it had found its way to Possum Creek and the sewage treatment plant. Instead, he contended that his discharge of the gasoline was not "knowing," because he had believed he was discharging water.

. . . The jury found Ahmad guilty on counts one and two and deadlocked on count three.

II.

Ahmad argues that the district court improperly instructed the jury on the mens rea required for counts one and two. The instruction on count one stated in relevant part:

> For you to find Mr. Ahmad guilty of this crime, you must be convinced that the government has proved each of the following beyond a reasonable doubt:
> (1) That on or about the date set forth in the indictment,
> (2) the defendant knowingly discharged
> (3) a pollutant
> (4) from a point source

(5) into the navigable waters of the United States

(6) without a permit to do so.

On count two, the court instructed the jury:

> In order to prove the defendant guilty of the offense charged in Count 2 of the indictment, the government must prove beyond a reasonable doubt each of the following elements:
> (1) That on or about the date set forth in the indictment
> (2) the defendant,
> (3) who was the owner or operator of a source,
> (4) knowingly operated that source by discharging into a public sewer system or publicly owned treatment works
> (5) a pollutant that created a fire or explosion hazard in that public sewer system or publicly owned treatment works.

Ahmad contends that the jury should have been instructed that the statutory mens rea—knowledge—was required as to each element of the offenses, rather than only with regard to discharge or the operation of a source. . . .

The language of the CWA is less than pellucid. Title 33 U.S.C. § 1319(c)(2)(A) says that "any person who knowingly violates" any of a number of other sections of the CWA commits a felony. One of the provisions that § 1319(c)(2)(A) makes it unlawful to violate is § 1311(a), which, when read together with a series of definitions in § 1362, prohibits the addition of any pollutant to navigable waters from a "point source." That was the crime charged in count one. Section 1319(c)(2)(A) also criminalizes violations of § 1317(d), which prohibits the operation of any "source" in a way that contravenes any effluent standard, prohibition, or pretreatment standard. That was the crime charged in count two.

The principal issue is to which elements of the offense the modifier "knowingly" applies. The matter is complicated somewhat by the fact that the phrase "knowingly violates" appears in a different section of the CWA from the language defining the elements of the offenses. Ahmad argues that within this context, "knowingly violates" should be read to require him knowingly to have acted with regard to each element of the offenses. The government, in contrast, contends that "knowingly violates" requires it to prove only that Ahmad knew the nature of his acts and that he performed them intentionally. Particularly at issue is whether "knowingly" applies to the element of the discharge's being a pollutant, for Ahmad's main theory at trial was that he thought he was discharging water, not gasoline.

The Supreme Court has spoken to this issue in broad terms. In *United States v. X-Citement Video, Inc.*, 513 U.S. 64 (1994), the Court read "knowingly" to apply to each element of a child pornography offense, notwithstanding its conclusion that under the "most natural grammatical reading" of the statute it should apply only to the element of having transported, shipped, received, distributed, or reproduced the material at issue. The Court also reaffirmed the long-held view that "the presumption in favor of a scienter requirement should apply to each of the statutory elements which criminalize otherwise innocent conduct."

Although *X-Citement Video* is the Court's most recent pronouncement on this subject, it is not the first. In *Staples v. United States*, 511 U.S. 600, 619–20 (1994), the Court found that the statutes criminalizing knowing possession of a machinegun, 26 U.S.C. §§ 5845(a)(6) and 5861(d), require that defendants know not only that they possess a firearm but that it actually is a machinegun. Thus, an awareness of the features of the gun—specifically, the features that make it an automatic weapon—is a necessary element of the offense. More generally, the Court also made plain that statutory crimes carrying severe penalties are presumed to require that a defendant know the facts that make his conduct illegal.

Our own precedents are in the same vein. In *United States v. Baytank (Houston), Inc.*, 934 F.2d 599, 613 (5th Cir. 1991), we concluded that a conviction for knowing and improper storage of hazardous wastes under 42 U.S.C. § 6928(d)(2)(A) requires "that the defendant know[ ] factually what he is doing—storing, what is being stored, and that what is being stored factually has the potential for harm to others or the environment, and that he has no permit. . . ." This is directly analogous to the interpretation of the CWA that Ahmad urges upon us. Indeed, we find it eminently sensible that the phrase "knowingly violates" in § 1319(c)(2)(A), when referring to other provisions that define the elements of the offenses § 1319 creates, should uniformly require knowledge as to each of those elements rather than only one or two. To hold otherwise would require an explanation as to why some elements should be treated differently from others, which neither the parties nor the caselaw seems able to provide.

In support of its interpretation of the CWA, the government cites cases from other circuits. We find these decisions both inapposite and unpersuasive on the point for which they are cited. In *United States v. Hopkins*, 53 F.3d 533, 537–41 (2d Cir. 1995), the court held that the government need not demonstrate that a § 1319(c)(2)(A) defendant knew his acts were illegal. The illegality of the defendant's actions is not an element of the offense, however. In *United States v. Weitzenhoff*, 35 F.3d 1275 (9th Cir. 1994), the court similarly was concerned almost exclusively with whether the language of the CWA creates a mistake-of-law defense. Both cases are easily distinguishable, for neither directly addresses mistake of fact [n]or the statutory construction issues raised by Ahmad.

The government also protests that CWA violations fall into the judicially-created exception for "public welfare offenses," under which some regulatory crimes have been held not to require a showing of mens rea. On its face, the CWA certainly does appear to implicate public welfare.

As recent cases have emphasized, however, the public welfare offense exception is narrow. The *Staples* Court, for example, held that the statute prohibiting the possession of machineguns fell outside the exception, notwithstanding the fact that "[t]ypically, our cases recognizing such offenses involve statutes that regulate potentially harmful or injurious items."

Though gasoline is a "potentially harmful or injurious item," it is certainly no more so than are machineguns. Rather, *Staples* held, the key to the public welfare offense analysis is whether "dispensing with mens rea would require the defendant to have knowledge only of traditionally lawful conduct." The CWA offenses of which Ahmad was convicted have precisely this characteristic, for if knowledge is not required as to the nature of the substance discharged, one who honestly and reasonably believes he is discharging water may find himself guilty of a felony if the substance turns out to be something else.

The fact that violations of § 1319(c)(2)(A) are felonies punishable by years in federal prison confirms our view that they do not fall within the public welfare offense exception. As the *Staples* Court noted, public welfare offenses have virtually always been crimes punishable by relatively light penalties such as fines or short jail sentences, rather than substantial terms of imprisonment. Serious felonies, in contrast, should not fall within the exception "absent a clear statement from Congress that mens rea is not required." Following *Staples*, we hold that the offenses charged in counts one and two are not public welfare offenses and that the usual presumption of a mens rea requirement applies. With the exception of purely jurisdictional elements, the mens rea of knowledge applies to each element of the crimes.

Finally, the government argues that the instructions, considered as a whole, adequately conveyed to the jury the message that Ahmad had to have known that what he was discharging was gasoline in order for the jury to find him guilty. We disagree.

At best, the jury charge made it uncertain to which elements "knowingly" applied. At worst, and considerably more likely, it indicated that only the element of discharge need be knowing. The instructions listed each element on a separate line, with the word "knowingly" present only in the line corresponding to the element that something was discharged. That the district court included a one-sentence summary of each count in which "knowingly" was present did not cure the error.

The obvious inference for the jury was that knowledge was required only as to the fact that something was discharged, and not as to any other fact. In effect, with regard to the other elements of the crimes, the instructions implied that the requisite mens rea was strict liability rather than knowledge.

. . . Because the charge effectively withdrew from the jury's consideration facts that it should have been permitted to find or not find, this error requires reversal.

IV.

. . . The convictions are REVERSED and the case REMANDED.

- Do you agree with the court's statement that the Clean Water Act is not a public welfare offense?
- As you will see more amply in the next chapter, when courts are confronted with a criminal violation that is deemed a "public welfare offense," then courts presume that the defendant has certain knowledge about what he/she is doing because of the highly regulated nature of the substances with which the defendant is working. Does working with large storage tanks of gasoline include working with a highly regulated substance?
- Given the strong smell of gasoline, is it reasonable to believe that Mr. Ahmad truly thought that he was discharging water into the storm drain?

United States v. Kelley Technical Coatings, Inc.
157 F.3d 432 (6th Cir. 1998)

BELL, District Judge[4]

Defendants Kelley Technical Coatings, Inc. ("Kelley") and Arthur Sumner were convicted of knowingly storing and disposing of hazardous waste without a permit in violation of the Resource Conservation and Recovery Act ("RCRA"). The District Court sentenced Kelley to pay a fine of $225,000, and sentenced Sumner to 21 months' imprisonment and a fine of $5000.

Kelley and Sumner appeal their convictions, and Sumner also appeals his sentence.

I.

Kelley is an industrial paint manufacturing company which operates two plants in Louisville, Kentucky. At all relevant times Arthur Sumner was the Vice President in charge of manufacturing operations for Kelley. In this role Sumner oversaw the manufacturing process at both plants, including the storage and disposal of hazardous wastes. He was also responsible for environmental regulatory compliance, and submitted the necessary paperwork to the state environmental authorities to register Kelley as a generator of hazardous waste.

Kelley generated substantial quantities of hazardous wastes in its manufacturing process, including spent solvents, such as toluene, ethyl benzene, xylene, and methyl ethyl ketone; excess and unusable paint, paint resins, and other paint ingredients which contained, among other things, toxic heavy metals such as chromium, lead, cadmium, and nickel; and paint sludge. Kelley accumulated hundreds of drums of these waste materials and stored them in drums behind Plant Two. During the period covered by the indictment Kelley never applied for a permit to store or dispose of its hazardous wastes on-site.

At the time of the July 1992 inspection by the Kentucky Department of Environmental Protection there were between 600 and 1000 drums behind Plant Two. The drums had been stored on-site for more than 90 days, and in some cases for many years. Some of the drums had rusted and were leaking on the ground.

Between 1986 and 1989, Sumner had arranged for a licensed hazardous waste disposal company to remove and dispose of some of the drums containing hazardous wastes. From late 1989 to July 1992, however, no drums of hazardous waste were shipped off-site. Instead, in an effort to save money, Kelley contracted with a hazardous waste disposal company to come on site and drain the liquids from the drums. After the bulk of the hazardous wastes were drained off, employees were directed to pour off any rainwater that had collected into the drums onto the ground and to consolidate the remaining residue into one drum. The consolidation process resulted in the spilling of hazardous substances onto the ground. Although Sumner claimed that some of the material was kept on site because it might be reused, he acknowledged that Kelley generated waste at a far greater rate than it was used.

---

[4] Judge Bell was sitting on the Sixth Circuit by designation.

II.

Kelley and Sumner challenge their convictions on the basis that the jury was improperly instructed on the mens rea required for conviction under the RCRA statute. . . .

Defendants were convicted of knowingly storing and disposing of hazardous wastes in violation of 42 U.S.C.A. § 6928(d)(2)(A). The statute provides for the imposition of criminal penalties against any person who "(2) knowingly treats, stores, or disposes of any hazardous waste identified or listed under this subchapter—(A) without a permit under this subchapter. . . ."

With respect to the storage count, the trial court instructed the jury as follows:

> Each individual defendant can be found guilty as to Count Two of the indictment only if all of the following facts are proved beyond a reasonable doubt with respect to that defendant.
>
> First, that on or about January 1, 1986 through September 29, 1992, the defendant knowingly stored material on the premises of Kelley Plant Two for a period exceeding 90 days.
>
> Second, that the material was hazardous waste.
>
> Third, that the defendant did not have a permit to store hazardous waste.
>
> Fourth, that the defendant knew that the material was waste and that it had the potential to be harmful to others or to the environment.

The trial court gave an identical instruction as to the disposal charge in Count III, except for the insertion of "disposed of" for "stored". . . . The trial court further instructed that "the United States is not required to prove that the defendant knew that the material was listed or identified by law as hazardous waste or that he was required to obtain a permit before storing or disposing of material."

A.

Defendants contend that the district court erred because it failed to instruct the jury that they could not convict unless they found the Defendants "knowingly" violated the law. Defendants contend that the jury should have been instructed that they could not convict unless they determined that Defendants knew that the material in question was regulated hazardous waste and knew that a permit was required.

Defendants' "knowledge of illegality" argument has been rejected by this court. This argument has also been rejected by every other court of appeals that has considered the issue.

[T]his court addressed the specific issue of whether the government should be required to prove the defendant knew a permit was required in order to convict a defendant for violating 42 U.S.C. § 6928(d). Based upon statutory construction, this court concluded that Section 6928(d)(2)(A) does not require knowledge of the permit requirement. Section 6928(d)(2)(A) requires knowing treatment, knowing storage, or knowing disposal of hazardous waste. It also requires proof that the treatment, or storage, or disposal was done without a permit. "It does not require that the person charged have known that a permit was required, and that knowledge is not relevant."

Notwithstanding [that] decision, Defendants contend that *Liparota v. United States*, 471 U.S. 419 (1985), requires knowledge of illegality. In *Liparota* the Supreme Court held that "in a prosecution for violation of § 2024(b)(1), the Government must prove that the defendant knew that his acquisition or possession of food stamps was in a manner unauthorized by statute or regulations."

Defendants' argument based upon *Liparota* was considered and rejected. . . . This court distinguished the food stamp statute from those statutes where Congress has rendered criminal a type of conduct that a reasonable person should know is subject to stringent public regulation and may seriously threaten the community's health or safety. In contrast to food stamp regulations, "persons involved in hazardous waste handling have every reason to be aware that their activities are regulated by law."

Defendants direct this court's attention to two Supreme Court decisions . . . *United States v. X-Citement Video*, 513 U.S. 64 (1994), and *Staples v. United States*, 511 U.S. 600. . . .

Neither *X-Citement Video* nor *Staples*, indicate that . . . there was any error in the jury instructions given in this case. Neither of the Supreme Court cases cited by Defendants construed the mens rea requirements of RCRA or any other environmental statute. *Staples* involved the mens rea requirement under a federal firearm registration statute, 26 U.S.C. § 5861(d). The Supreme Court held the statute required proof that the defendant knew of the characteristics of his weapon that made it a "firearm" under the Act. . . .

X-Citement Video involved the mens rea requirements under a child pornography statute, 18 U.S.C. § 2252(a). The Supreme Court required proof that the defendant knew his sexually explicit mailing pictured minors because "the age of the performers is the crucial element separating legal innocence from wrongful conduct."

In *United States v. Ahmad*, 101 F.3d 386 (5th Cir. 1996), the Fifth Circuit applied *Staples* and *X-Citement Video* to a prosecution under Clean Water Act . . . and struck down a jury instruction that failed to require that the defendant know that the substance he discharged was a pollutant. The defendant's primary defense in *Ahmad* was that he thought he was discharging water, not gasoline.

Staples, *X-Citement Video*, and *Ahmad* focused on the requirement that the government prove the defendant's knowledge of particular facts—i.e., that the firearm was capable of firing automatically, that the subject of the pornographic depiction was a minor child, or that the substance discharged was a pollutant. None of these cases held that knowledge of the law or regulatory requirements was an element of the offense.

In *United States v. Hopkins*, 53 F.3d 533, 540 (2nd Cir. 1995), the Second Circuit rejected the defendant's reliance on *Staples* for the proposition that for a conviction under the Clean Water Act the government was required to prove that the defendant knew his conduct violated the law or a regulatory permit. The Second Circuit noted that although the Court in *Staples* held that the defendant could not properly be convicted unless the government proved that he knew the nature of his acts, the Court in no way suggested that the government had the burden of proving that the defendant also knew that his acts violated the law.

The instructions given in this case were consistent with *Staples* and *X-Citement Video*. They required the government to prove the defendant's knowledge of the storage or disposal, the defendant's knowledge that the material was waste, and the defendant's knowledge that it had the potential to be harmful to others or to the environment. The instructions adequately required that the defendant have knowledge of the facts that made the conduct a crime. . . .

VI.

Having found no reversible error in the trial proceedings or the sentencing, we AFFIRM the convictions of Defendants Kelley and Sumner. . . .

- Based on *Ahmad* and *Kelly Technical Coatings*, does the prosecution need to prove the defendant's knowledge as to each element of the Clean Water Act and RCRA or just the "factual" elements?
- Is knowing whether a substance qualifies as a "pollutant" under the Clean Water Act a "factual" element or a "legal" element?
- If proving knowledge that something is a "pollutant" is "legal knowledge," then what is the difference between "knowing" and "willful"?
- Under the Endangered Species Act (ESA), a person may be prosecuted for a misdemeanor for, among other things, "knowingly" taking a threatened or endangered species without a permit. 16 U.S.C. § 1540(b). Must the prosecution prove that the defendant knew that the animal being taken was threatened or endangered or just that the defendant was intending to take the animal, which happened to be a threatened or endangered species?
  - o In *United States v. McKittrick*, 142 F.3d 1170 (9th Cir. 1998), the Court of Appeals for the Ninth Circuit affirmed a jury instruction that required the prosecution to prove only that the defendant intended to take an animal, but, unfortunately for the defendant, the taken animal was protected under the ESA.
  - o On appeal to the United States Supreme Court, the Solicitor General of the United States determined that the jury instruction was in error and that the prosecution must prove that the defendant knew the species that he/she took but not that taking that animal is illegal. This became known as the McKittrick Policy.
  - o On June 21, 2017, Judge Bury of the District of Arizona invalidated the McKittrick Policy, holding that the DOJ abdicated its statutory responsibility under the ESA. *WildEarth Guardians v. United States Dep't of Justice*, 283 F. Supp. 3d 783 (D. Ariz. 2017).
  - o On October 28, 2018, the Court of Appeals for the Ninth Circuit reversed the District of Arizona because plaintiffs lacked standing. *WildEarth Guardians v. U.S. Dep't of Justice*, Nos. 17-16677, -16678, -16679, 2018 WL 5278941 (9th Cir. Oct. 23, 2018).
- Are you more persuaded by the Solicitor General's interpretation of what knowing means under the ESA or by Judge Bury's interpretation?

2. Knowledge of Jurisdictional Facts

United States v. Cooper
482 F.3d 658 (4th Cir. 2007)

WILKINSON, Circuit Judge:

D.J. Cooper was convicted by a jury on nine counts of knowingly discharging a pollutant from a point source into waters of the United States, in violation of the . . . Clean Water Act ("CWA" or "the Act"). He claims that the district court should have granted an acquittal for lack of sufficient evidence, in part because the government failed to prove Cooper knew that he was discharging pollutants into waters of the United States. Because the district court did not err, and because the CWA does not require the government to establish Cooper's knowledge as to the jurisdictional status of the waters he affected, we affirm the judgment of the district court.

I.

. . . Defendant Cooper has been operating a sewage lagoon at his trailer park in Bedford County, Virginia, since 1967. In recent times the lagoon has served as the only method of human waste disposal for twenty-two of the trailers in the park. The lagoon treats sewage according to the following process: Solid materials settle to the bottom of the lagoon, while the fluid level rises until it reaches an overflow structure in the middle of the lagoon, from which it flows through a pipe into a chlorine contact tank. In the tank, an electric pump dispenses a solution of water and granular chlorine, which mixes with the sewage. The chlorinated fluid then flows through a discharge pipe, down a channel of a few feet, and thence into a small creek.

The creek into which the treated sewage flows is a tributary of Sandy Creek, which is in turn a tributary of the Roanoke River. . . . There is no dispute that, as a tributary of an interstate water, the small creek into which the lagoon discharges constitutes a water of the United States.

Cooper's permit [under the Clean Water Act] regulated discharge from the lagoon in a number of ways. . . .

Between 1993 and 1998, DEQ recorded over 300 violations of the permit, including excessive levels of Kjeldahl nitrogen, chlorine, and suspended solids and impermissibly low levels of oxygen in the creek. In response, DEQ took enforcement action which culminated in a 1998 Consent Order. . . .

After the Consent Order, discharges from the lagoon continued to violate the permit. DEQ inspections of the creek found a strong sewage smell, decreased oxygen levels, dark solids, and a proliferation of bloodworms, pollution-tolerant organisms that thrive in low-oxygen environments like that provided by raw sewage.

In August 2000, Cooper violated the 1998 Consent Order. . . .

In March 2002, Cooper's discharge permit expired with Cooper having failed to file the necessary paperwork to receive a new permit. . . . In response, in October 2002 the State Water Control Board canceled the Consent Order, and DEQ notified Cooper that he was no longer operating with a valid discharge permit.

Nevertheless, discharges from the lagoon into the creek continued. . . .

In late 2003, the U.S. Environmental Protection Agency's Criminal Investigation Division ("CID") began to investigate discharges from the lagoon. . . .

On October 29, 2003, in an interview with CID Special Agent Matthew Goers, Cooper admitted that he was discharging from the lagoon into the creek without a permit and that DEQ had notified him that these discharges were in violation of the VPDES program. Cooper acknowledged that he might go to jail. He told Goers that he had hired an attorney to fight on his behalf and stated, "I'm going to fight as long as God gives me the power to fight."

On October 21, 2004, Cooper was indicted on thirteen felony counts of knowingly discharging a pollutant into waters of the United States without a permit, in violation of 33 U.S.C. §§ 1311(a) and 1319(c)(2)(A). . . .

After a three-day jury trial, on April 28, 2005 the jury found Cooper guilty on nine counts. The district court sentenced Cooper to 27 months' imprisonment, plus a $30,000 fine for each count of conviction, resulting in a total fine of $270,000. Defendant appeals. . . .

III.

Cooper argues that the government failed to prove that Cooper knew the waters into which he discharged pollutants "were a tributary of a navigable water, or adjacent to a navigable water, or had a significant nexus to a navigable water." The premise of this claim is that, under 33 U.S.C. §§ 1311(a) and 1319(c)(2)(A), the government had to prove that Cooper was aware of the facts that establish the federal government's jurisdiction over the water for purposes of the CWA. For the reasons explained below, we reject this contention.

A.

Cooper was convicted of knowingly discharging a pollutant without a permit from a point source to navigable waters, which are defined as waters of the United States. "Waters of the United States" in this statutory scheme operates as a jurisdictional element. A jurisdictional element of a federal offense states the basis of Congress' power to regulate the conduct at issue: its "primary purpose is to identify the factor that makes the [conduct] an appropriate subject for federal concern." Without a jurisdictional basis for its exercise of its authority, Congress would be acting beyond its enumerated powers under Article I, Section 8 of the Constitution. "Waters of the United States" in the CWA is a classic jurisdictional element, which situates Congress' authority to enact the statute in "its traditional jurisdiction over waters that were or had been navigable in fact or which could reasonably be so made."

It is well settled that mens rea requirements typically do not extend to the jurisdictional elements of a crime—that "the existence of the fact that confers federal jurisdiction need not be one in the mind of the actor at the time he perpetrates the act made criminal by the federal statute." This court has long recognized this principle in construing jurisdictional elements of federal criminal statutes.

Congress legislates against this well-established backdrop, aware that jurisdictional elements generally assert federal jurisdiction but do not create additional statutory elements as to which defendants must have formed the appropriate mens rea in order to have broken the law.

In *United States v. Feola*, the Supreme Court recognized that it is possible, in exceptional circumstances, that Congress might intend for a jurisdictional element to have both a jurisdictional and substantive component, rather than being "jurisdictional only." The Court also suggested that the primary authority in answering this question is the intent of Congress as expressed in the statute itself. We thus turn to consider whether Congress has expressed an intention that "waters of the United States" in this case serve more than a jurisdictional function.

B.

Of the four other circuits to have considered the scope of "knowingly" in § 1319(c)(2)(A), three have not extended it to "waters of the United States." The Fifth Circuit has held that "knowingly" applies to each element of the offense "[w]ith the exception of purely jurisdictional elements," without stating explicitly whether "waters of the United States" constitutes such a purely jurisdictional element.

The CWA offers every reason to conclude that the term "waters of the United States" as it operates in this case is "nothing more than the jurisdictional peg on which Congress based federal jurisdiction." . . .

The question, then, is whether Congress intended for the term "knowingly" in § 1319(c)(2)(A) to extend, via § 1311(a), to "navigable waters" in § 1362(12), and thus to "waters of the United States" in § 1362(7), with the result that the government must prove that Cooper was aware of the facts connecting the small creek to the regulatory definition of "waters of the United States." To say the least, the statute's string of provisions hardly compels such a reading. If Congress meant to overcome the customary understanding that mens rea requirements do not attach to jurisdictional elements, it would have spoken much more clearly to that effect.

The stated purposes of the Act provide further support for this view. As articulated by Congress, the principal goal of the Act is "to restore and maintain the chemical, physical, and biological integrity of the Nation's waters." 33 U.S.C. § 1251(a). This purpose would be severely undermined if polluters could only be prosecuted for knowingly polluting the nation's waters when the government could prove they were aware of the facts conferring federal jurisdiction. Such a blanket rule would be absurd in many cases, including the present one. Cooper's deliberate discharge of human sewage into running waters is exhaustively recorded. He knew he was discharging sewage into them, he knew his treatment facilities were inadequate, and he knew he was acting without a permit. It seems unlikely that Congress intended for culpability in such an instance to turn upon whether the defendant was aware of the jurisdictional nexus of these acts, any more than, for example, Congress intended conviction of a felon-in-possession offense to turn upon the defendant's knowledge of the interstate travels of a firearm.

This conclusion squares with the Supreme Court's analysis of congressional intent as to jurisdictional elements in *Feola*. In that case, the Court considered 18 U.S.C. § 111, proscribing assault of a federal officer. The Court recognized the "federal officer" requirement as a jurisdiction-conferring element and went on to consider whether it also functioned as a substantive element of the offense—that is, whether Congress intended for the statute to punish only those defendants who were aware that their victims were federal officers. The Court concluded that Congress intended for the statute both to deter conduct intended to obstruct federal law enforcement activities and to protect federal law enforcement officers to the fullest extent possible. Given the statute's clear aims, the Court said, it "cannot be construed as embodying an unexpressed requirement that an assailant be aware that his victim is a federal officer. All the statute requires is an intent to assault, not an intent to assault a federal officer."

Just as Congress in 18 U.S.C. § 111 intended to "accord[ ] maximum protection to federal officers," id., so Congress in the CWA clearly intended to provide strong protection to the nation's water-ways. To attach a mens rea to the jurisdictional element would as surely undermine Congress' intent here as it would have in *Feola*. We cannot broadly exempt environmental crimes from the longstanding rule that mens rea requirements do not pertain to jurisdictional facts. Such a blanket exception would not only be astonishingly broad, but it would also suggest without objective basis that separate and less stringent rules apply to environmental harms. Finding in the CWA a broad exception to the general rule would be tantamount to assuming that Congress, in creating criminal penalties for environmental degradation, did not really mean what it said. . . .

In sum, the creek's status as a "water of the United States" is simply a jurisdictional fact, the objective truth of which the government must establish but the defendant's knowledge of which it need not prove. The language of the relevant statutes[,] . . . the congressional intent that text plainly reflects, as well as relevant precedent, all require this conclusion. . . .

The judgment of the district court is hereby AFFIRMED.

- Should the prosecution have to prove that the defendant knew that his/her discharge of a pollutant was into a "water of the United States"? Why or why not?
- Is the reasoning in *Ahmad* or *Cooper* more persuasive?

3. Knowledge of the Law

Liparota v. United States
471 U.S. 419 (1985)

Justice BRENNAN delivered the opinion of the Court.

The federal statute governing food stamp fraud provides that "whoever knowingly uses, transfers, acquires, alters, or possesses coupons or authorization cards in any manner not authorized by [the statute] or the regulations" is subject to a fine and imprisonment. 78 Stat. 708, as amended, 7 U.S.C. § 2024(b)(1). The question presented is whether in a prosecution under this provision the Government must prove that the defendant knew that he was acting in a manner not authorized by statute or regulations.

I

Petitioner Frank Liparota was the co-owner with his brother of Moon's Sandwich Shop in Chicago, Illinois. He was indicted for acquiring and possessing food stamps in violation of § 2024(b)(1). The Department of Agriculture had not authorized petitioner's restaurant to accept food stamps. At trial, the Government proved that petitioner on three occasions purchased food stamps from an undercover Department of Agriculture agent for substantially less than their face value. On the first occasion, the agent informed petitioner that she had $195 worth of food stamps to sell. The agent then accepted petitioner's offer of $150 and consummated the transaction in a back room of the restaurant with petitioner's brother. A similar transaction occurred one week later, in which the agent sold $500 worth of coupons for $350. Approximately one month later, petitioner bought $500 worth of food stamps from the agent for $300.

In submitting the case to the jury, the District Court rejected petitioner's proposed "specific intent" instruction, which would have instructed the jury that the Government must prove that "the defendant knowingly did an act which the law forbids, purposely intending to violate the law." Concluding that "[t]his is not a specific intent crime" but rather a "knowledge case," the District Court instead instructed the jury as follows:

> "When the word 'knowingly' is used in these instructions, it means that the Defendant realized what he was doing, and was aware of the nature of his conduct, and did not act through ignorance, mistake, or accident. Knowledge may be proved by defendant's conduct and by all of the facts and circumstances surrounding the case."

The District Court also instructed that the Government had to prove that "the Defendant acquired and possessed food stamp coupons for cash in a manner not authorized by federal statute or regulations" and that "the Defendant knowingly and wilfully acquired the food stamps." Petitioner objected that this instruction required the jury to find merely that he knew that he was acquiring or possessing food stamps; he argued that the statute should be construed instead to reach only "people who knew that they were acting unlawfully." The judge did not alter or supplement his instructions, and the jury returned a verdict of guilty.

Petitioner appealed his conviction to the Court of Appeals for the Seventh Circuit, arguing that the District Court erred in refusing to instruct the jury that "specific intent" is required in a prosecution under 7 U.S.C. § 2024(b)(1). The Court of Appeals rejected petitioner's arguments. Because this decision conflicted with recent decisions of three other Courts of Appeals, we granted certiorari. We reverse.

II

The controversy between the parties concerns the mental state, if any, that the Government must show in proving that petitioner acted "in any manner not authorized by [the statute] or the regulations." The Government argues that petitioner violated the statute if he knew that he acquired or possessed food stamps and if in fact that acquisition or possession was in a manner not authorized by statute or regulations. According to the Government, no mens rea, or "evil-meaning mind," is necessary for conviction. Petitioner claims that the Government's interpretation, by dispensing with mens rea, dispenses with the only morally blameworthy element in the definition of the crime. To avoid this allegedly untoward result, he claims that an individual violates the statute if he knows that he has acquired or possessed food stamps and if he also knows that he has done so in an unauthorized manner. Our task is to determine which meaning Congress intended.

The definition of the elements of a criminal offense is entrusted to the legislature, particularly in the case of federal crimes, which are solely creatures of statute. With respect to the element at issue in this case, however, Congress has not explicitly spelled out the mental state required. Although Congress certainly intended by use of the word "knowingly" to require some mental state with respect to some element of the crime defined in § 2024(b)(1), the interpretations proffered by both parties accord with congressional intent to this extent. Beyond this, the words themselves provide little guidance. Either interpretation would accord with ordinary usage. The legislative history of the statute contains nothing that would clarify the congressional purpose on this point.

Absent indication of contrary purpose in the language or legislative history of the statute, we believe that § 2024(b)(1) requires a showing that the defendant knew his conduct to be unauthorized by statute or regulations. "The contention that an injury can amount to a crime only when inflicted by intention is no provincial or transient notion. It is as universal and persistent in mature systems of law as belief in freedom of the human will and a consequent ability and duty of the normal individual to choose between good and evil." Thus, in *United States v. United States Gypsum Co.*, 438 U.S. 422, 438 (1978), we noted that "[c]ertainly far more than the simple omission of the appropriate phrase from the statutory definition is necessary to justify dispensing with an intent requirement" and that criminal offenses requiring no mens rea have a "generally disfavored status." Similarly, in this case, the failure of Congress explicitly and unambiguously to indicate whether mens rea is required does not signal a departure from this background assumption of our criminal law.

This construction is particularly appropriate where, as here, to interpret the statute otherwise would be to criminalize a broad range of apparently innocent conduct. For instance, § 2024(b)(1) declares it criminal to use, transfer, acquire, alter, or possess food stamps in any manner not authorized by statute or regulations. The statute provides further that "[c]oupons issued to eligible households shall be used by them only to purchase food in retail food stores which have been approved for participation in the food stamp program at prices prevailing in such stores." 7 U.S.C. § 2016(b); *see also* 7 CFR § 274.10(a) (1985). This seems to be the only authorized use. A strict reading of the statute with no knowledge-of-illegality requirement would thus render criminal a food stamp recipient who, for example, used stamps to purchase food from a store that, unknown to him, charged higher than normal prices to food stamp program participants. Such a reading would also render criminal a nonrecipient of food stamps who "possessed" stamps because he was mistakenly sent them through the mail due to administrative error, "altered" them by tearing them up, and "transferred" them by throwing them away. Of course, Congress could have intended that this broad range of conduct be made illegal, perhaps with the understanding that prosecutors would exercise their discretion to avoid such harsh results. However, given the paucity of material suggesting that Congress did so intend, we are reluctant to adopt such a sweeping interpretation.

In addition, requiring mens rea is in keeping with our longstanding recognition of the principle that "ambiguity concerning the ambit of criminal statutes should be resolved in favor of lenity." Application of the rule of lenity ensures that criminal statutes will provide fair warning concerning conduct rendered illegal and strikes the appropriate balance between the legislature, the prosecutor, and the court in defining criminal liability. Although the rule of lenity is not to be applied where to do so would conflict with the implied or expressed intent of Congress, it provides a time-honored interpretive guideline when the congressional purpose is unclear. In the instant case, the rule directly supports petitioner's contention that the Government must prove knowledge of illegality to convict him under § 2024(b)(1).

The Government argues, however, that a comparison between § 2024(b)(1) and its companion, § 2024(c), demonstrates a congressional purpose not to require proof of the defendant's knowledge of illegality in a § 2024(b)(1) prosecution. Section 2024(c) is directed primarily at stores authorized to accept food stamps from program participants. It provides that "[w]hoever presents, or causes to be presented, coupons for payment or redemption . . . knowing the same to have been received, transferred, or used in any manner in violation of [the statute] or the regulations" is subject to fine and imprisonment. The Government contrasts this language with that of § 2024(b)(1), in which the word "knowingly" is placed differently: "whoever knowingly uses, transfers. . . ." Since § 2024(c) undeniably requires a knowledge of illegality, the suggested inference is that the difference in wording and structure between the two sections indicates that § 2024(b)(1) does not.

The Government urges that this distinction between the mental state required for a § 2024(c) violation and that required for a § 2024(b)(1) violation is a sensible one. Absent a requirement of mens rea, a grocer presenting food stamps for payment might be criminally liable under § 2024(c) even if his customer or employees have illegally procured or transferred the stamps without the grocer's knowledge. Requiring knowledge of illegality in a § 2024(c) prosecution is allegedly necessary to avoid this kind of vicarious, and non-fault-based, criminal liability. Since the offense defined in § 2024(b)(1)—using, transferring, acquiring, altering, or possessing food stamps in an unauthorized manner—does not involve this possibility of vicarious liability, argues the Government, Congress had no reason to impose a similar knowledge of illegality requirement in that section.

We do not find this argument persuasive. The difference in wording between § 2024(b)(1) and § 2024(c) is too slender a reed to support the attempted distinction, for if the Government's argument were accepted, it would lead to the demise of the very distinction that Congress is said to have desired. According to the Government, Congress did intend a knowledge of illegality requirement in § 2024(c), while it did not intend such a requirement in § 2024(b)(1). Anyone who has violated § 2024(c) has "present[ed], or caus[ed] to be presented, coupons for payment or redemption" in an unauthorized manner. Such a person would seemingly have also "use[d], transfer[red], acquir[ed], alter[ed], or possess[ed]" the coupons in a similarly unauthorized manner, and thus to have violated § 2024(b)(1). It follows that the Government will be able to prosecute any violator of § 2024(c) under § 2024(b)(1) as well. If only § 2024(c)—and not § 2024(b)(1)—required the Government to prove knowledge of illegality, the result would be that the Government could always avoid proving knowledge of illegality in food stamp fraud cases, simply by bringing its prosecutions under § 2024(b)(1). If Congress wanted to require the Government to prove knowledge of illegality in some, but not all, food stamp fraud cases, it thus chose a peculiar way to do so.

For similar reasons, the Government's arguments that Congress could have had a plausible reason to require knowledge of illegality in prosecutions under § 2024(c), but not § 2024(b)(1), are equally unpersuasive. Grocers are participants in the food stamp program who have had the benefit of an extensive informational campaign concerning the authorized use and handling of food stamps. Yet the Government would have to prove knowledge of illegality when prosecuting such grocers, while it would have no such burden when prosecuting third parties who may well have had no opportunity to acquaint themselves with the rules governing food stamps. It is not immediately obvious that Congress would have been so concerned about imposing strict liability on grocers, while it had no similar concerns about imposing strict liability on nonparticipants in the program. Our point once again is not that Congress could not have chosen to enact a statute along these lines, for there are no doubt policy arguments on both sides of the question as to whether such a statute would have been desirable. Rather, we conclude that the policy underlying such a construction is neither so obvious nor so compelling that we must assume, in the absence of any discussion of this issue in the legislative history, that Congress did enact such a statute.

[T]he Government contends that the § 2024(b)(1) offense is a "public welfare" offense, which the Court defined in *Morissette v. United States*, 342 U.S., at 252–253, to "depend on no mental element but consist only of forbidden acts or omissions." Yet the offense at issue here differs substantially from those "public welfare offenses" we have previously recognized. In most previous instances, Congress has rendered criminal a type of conduct that a reasonable person should know is subject to stringent public regulation and may seriously threaten the community's health or safety. Thus, in *United States v. Freed*, 401 U.S. 601 (1971), we examined the federal statute making it illegal to receive or possess an unregistered firearm. In holding that the Government did not have to prove that the recipient of unregistered hand grenades knew that they were unregistered, we noted that "one would hardly be surprised to learn that possession of hand grenades is not an innocent act." Similarly, in *United States v. Dotterweich*, 320 U.S. 277, 284 (1943), the Court held that a corporate officer could violate the Food, Drug, and Cosmetic Act when his firm shipped adulterated and misbranded drugs, even "though consciousness of wrongdoing be totally wanting." The distinctions between these cases and the instant case are clear. A food stamp can hardly be compared to a hand grenade, nor can the unauthorized acquisition or possession of food stamps be compared to the selling of adulterated drugs, as in *Dotterweich*.

III

We hold that in a prosecution for violation of § 2024(b)(1), the Government must prove that the defendant knew that his acquisition or possession of food stamps was in a manner unauthorized by statute or regulations. This holding does not put an unduly heavy burden on the Government in prosecuting violators of § 2024(b)(1). To prove that petitioner knew that his acquisition or possession of food stamps was unauthorized, for example, the Government need not show that he had knowledge of specific regulations governing food stamp acquisition or possession. Nor must the Government introduce any extraordinary evidence that would conclusively demonstrate petitioner's state of mind. Rather, as in any other criminal prosecution requiring mens rea, the Government may prove by reference to facts and circumstances surrounding the case that petitioner knew that his conduct was unauthorized or illegal.

Reversed.

Justice WHITE, with whom THE CHIEF JUSTICE joins, dissenting.

Forsaking reliance on either the language or the history of § 2024(b)(1), the majority bases its result on the absence of an explicit rejection of the general principle that criminal liability requires not only an actus reus, but a mens rea. In my view, the result below is in fact supported by the statute's language and its history, and it is the majority that has ignored general principles of criminal liability.

I

The Court views the statutory problem here as being how far down the sentence the term "knowingly" travels. Accepting for the moment that if "knowingly" does extend to the "in any manner" language today's holding would be correct—a position with which I take issue below—I doubt that it gets that far. The "in any manner" language is separated from the litany of verbs to which "knowingly" is directly connected by the intervening nouns. We considered an identically phrased statute last Term in *United States v. Yermian*, 468 U.S. 63 (1984). The predecessor to the statute at issue in that case provided: "'[W]hoever shall knowingly and willfully . . . make . . . any false or fraudulent statements or representations . . . in any matter within the jurisdiction of any department or agency of the United States . . . shall be fined.'" We found that under the "most natural reading" of the statute, "knowingly and willfully" applied only to the making of false or fraudulent statements and not to the fact of jurisdiction. By the same token, the "most natural reading" of § 2024(b)(1) is that "knowingly" modifies only the verbs to which it is attached.

In any event, I think that the premise of this approach is mistaken. Even accepting that "knowingly" does extend through the sentence, or at least that we should read § 2024(b)(1) as if it does, the statute does not mean what the Court says it does. Rather, it requires only that the defendant be aware of the relevant aspects of his conduct. A requirement that the defendant know that he is acting in a particular manner, coupled with the fact that that manner is forbidden, does not establish a defense of ignorance of the law. It creates only a defense of ignorance or mistake of fact. Knowingly to do something that is unauthorized by law is not the same as doing something knowing that it is unauthorized by law.

This point is demonstrated by the hypothetical statute referred to by the majority, which punishes one who "knowingly sells a security without a permit." Even if "knowingly" does reach "without a permit," I would think that a defendant who knew that he did not have a permit, though not that a permit was required, could be convicted.

Section 2024(b)(1) is an identical statute, except that instead of detailing the various legal requirements, it incorporates them by proscribing use of coupons "in any manner not authorized" by law. This shorthand approach to drafting does not transform knowledge of illegality into an element of the crime. As written, §

2024(b)(1) is substantively no different than if it had been broken down into a collection of specific provisions making crimes of particular improper uses. For example, food stamps cannot be used to purchase tobacco. The statute might have said, *inter alia*, that anyone "who knowingly uses coupons to purchase cigarettes" commits a crime. Under no plausible reading could a defendant then be acquitted because he did not know cigarettes are not "eligible food." But in fact, that is exactly what § 2024(b)(1) does say; it just does not write it out longhand.

The Court's opinion provides another illustration of the general point: someone who used food stamps to purchase groceries at inflated prices without realizing he was overcharged. I agree that such a person may not be convicted, but not for the reason given by the majority. The purchaser did not "knowingly" use the stamps in the proscribed manner, for he was unaware of the circumstances of the transaction that made it illegal.

The majority and I would part company in result as well as rationale if the purchaser knew he was charged higher than normal prices but not that overcharging is prohibited. In such a case, he would have been aware of the nature of his actions, and therefore the purchase would have been "knowing." I would hold that such a mental state satisfies the statute. Under the Court's holding, as I understand it, that person could not be convicted because he did not know that his conduct was illegal.

Much has been made of the comparison between § 2024(b)(1) and § 2024(c). The Government, like the court below, argues that the express requirement of knowing illegality in subsection (c) supports an inference that the absence of such a provision in subsection (b)(1) was intentional. While I disagree with the majority's refutation of this argument, I view most of this discussion as beside the point. The Government's premise seems to me mistaken. Subsection (c) does not impose a requirement of knowing illegality. The provision is much like statutes that forbid the receipt or sale of stolen goods. Just as those statutes generally require knowledge that the goods were stolen, so § 2024(c) requires knowledge of the past impropriety. But receipt-of-stolen-goods statutes do not require that the defendant know that receipt itself is illegal, and similarly § 2024(c) plainly does not require that the defendant know that it is illegal to present coupons that have been improperly used in the past. It is not inconceivable that someone presenting such coupons—again, like someone buying stolen goods—would think that his conduct was above-board despite the preceding illegality. But that belief, however sincere, would not be a defense. In short, because § 2024(c) does not require that the defendant know that the conduct for which he is being prosecuted was illegal, it does not create an ignorance-of-the-law defense.

I therefore cannot draw the Government's suggested inference. The two provisions are nonetheless fruitfully compared. What matters is not their difference, but their similarity. Neither contains any indication that "knowledge of the law defining the offense [is] an element of the offense." A requirement of knowing illegality should not be read into either provision.

I do agree with the Government that when Congress wants to include a knowledge-of-illegality requirement in a statute it knows how to do so, even though I do not consider subsection (c) an example. Other provisions of the United States Code explicitly include a requirement of familiarity with the law defining the offense—indeed, in places where, under the majority's analysis, it is entirely superfluous.

Finally, the lower court's reading of the statute is consistent with the legislative history. As the majority points out, the history provides little to go on. Significantly, however, the brief discussions of this provision in the relevant congressional Reports do not mention any requirement of knowing illegality. To the contrary, when the Food Stamp Act was rewritten in 1977, the House Report noted that "[a]ny unauthorized use, transfer, acquisition, alteration, or possession of food stamps . . . may be prosecuted under" § 2024(b)(1). H.R. Rep. No. 95–464, p. 376 (1977), U.S. Code Cong. & Admin. News p. 2305.

II

SLIPPERY SLOPE

The broad principles of the Court's opinion are easy to live with in a case such as this. But the application of its reasoning might not always be so benign. For example, § 2024(b)(1) is little different from the basic federal prohibition on the manufacture and distribution of controlled substances. Title 21 U.S.C. § 841(a) provides:

> "Except as authorized by this subchapter, it shall be unlawful for any person knowingly or intentionally—
> "(1) to manufacture, distribute, or dispense, or possess with intent to manufacture, distribute or dispense, a controlled substance. . . ."

I am sure that the Members of the majority would agree that a defendant charged under this provision could not defend on the ground that he did not realize his manufacture was unauthorized or that the particular substance was controlled. On the other hand, it would be a defense if he could prove he thought the substance was something other than what it was. By the same token, I think, someone in petitioner's position should not be heard to say that he did not know his purchase of food stamps was unauthorized, though he may certainly argue that he did not know he was buying food stamps. I would not stretch the term "knowingly" to require awareness of the absence of statutory authority in either of these provisions. . . .

IV

I wholly agree that "[t]he contention that an injury can amount to a crime only when inflicted by intention is no provincial or transient notion." But the holding of the court below is not at all inconsistent with that longstanding and important principle. Petitioner's conduct was intentional; the jury found that petitioner "realized what he was doing, and was aware of the nature of his conduct, and did not act through ignorance, mistake, or accident." Whether he knew which regulation he violated is beside the point.

- According to the Supreme Court in *Liparota*, the term "knowingly" in the Food Stamp Fraud statute required the prosecution to prove that the defendant was aware that the law prohibited his/her conduct because not imposing such a requirement on the prosecution could criminalize innocent conduct. As you will see throughout this course, the "knowing" mens rea is often applied to conduct that is otherwise innocent but still violative of environmental laws.

- For example, suppose a person engages in conduct that violates the terms of a permit under the Clean Water Act but is totally unaware that his/her conduct was against the law. Under the Clean Water Act's knowing standard, such a person would be guilty of a felony. *United States v. Weitzenhoff*, 35 F.3d 1275 (9th Cir. 1993).
- Similarly, a person who sells taxidermized owls over the internet may have no idea that he/she is violating the Migratory Bird Treaty Act's felony prohibition against knowingly selling a migratory bird. However, courts have found that ignorance of the law is no defense. *United States v. Pitrone*, 115 F.3d 1 (1st Cir. 1997).
- If a mens rea of "knowing" does not require the prosecution to prove that the defendant knew that what he/she was doing was wrong under the Clean Water Act and Migratory Bird Treaty Act, among many other statutes, why did the "knowing" mens rea in *Liparota* require the prosecution to prove that the defendant knew his actions were unlawful?
- Because of *Liparota*, a common theme in nearly all arguments regarding the meaning of "knowingly" in environmental crimes statutes focuses on whether *Liparota* applies or whether the court should interpret "knowingly" to mean that the defendant did not have to know that his/her conduct was unlawful.

United States v. Sinskey
119 F.3d 712 (8th Cir. 1997)

MORRIS SHEPPARD ARNOLD, Circuit Judge.

The defendants appeal their convictions for criminal violations of the Clean Water Act. We affirm the judgments of the trial court.

I.

In the early 1990s, Timothy Sinskey and Wayne Kumm were, respectively, the plant manager and plant engineer at John Morrell & Co. ("Morrell"), a large meat-packing plant in Sioux Falls, South Dakota. The meat-packing process created a large amount of wastewater, some of which Morrell piped to a municipal treatment plant and the rest of which it treated at its own wastewater treatment plant ("WWTP"). After treating wastewater at the WWTP, Morrell would discharge it into the Big Sioux River.

One of the WWTP's functions was to reduce the amount of ammonia nitrogen in the wastewater discharged into the river, and the Environmental Protection Agency ("EPA") required Morrell to limit that amount to levels specified in a permit issued under the Clean Water Act ("CWA"). As well as specifying the acceptable levels of ammonia nitrogen, the permit also required Morrell to perform weekly a series of tests to monitor the amounts of ammonia nitrogen in the discharged water and to file monthly with the EPA a set of reports concerning those results.

In the spring of 1991, Morrell doubled the number of hogs that it slaughtered and processed at the Sioux Falls plant. The resulting increase in wastewater caused the level of ammonia nitrate in the discharged water to be above that allowed by the CWA permit. Ron Greenwood and Barry Milbauer, the manager and assistant manager, respectively, of the WWTP, manipulated the testing process in two ways so that Morrell would appear not to violate its permit. In the first technique, which the parties frequently refer to as "flow manipulation" or the "flow game," Morrell would discharge extremely low levels of water (and thus low levels of ammonia nitrogen) early in the week, when Greenwood and Milbauer would perform the required tests. After the tests had been performed, Morrell would discharge an exceedingly high level of water (and high levels of ammonia nitrogen) later in the week. The tests would therefore not accurately reflect the overall levels of ammonia nitrogen in the discharged water. In addition to manipulating the flow, Greenwood and Milbauer also engaged in what the parties call "selective sampling," that is, they performed more than the number of tests required by the EPA but reported only the tests showing acceptable levels of ammonia nitrogen. When manipulating the flow and selective sampling failed to yield the required number of tests showing acceptable levels of ammonia nitrogen, the two simply falsified the test results and the monthly EPA reports, which Sinskey then signed and sent to the EPA. Morrell submitted false reports for every month but one from August, 1991, to December, 1992.

As a result of their participation in these activities, Sinskey and Kumm were charged with a variety of CWA violations. After a three-week trial, a jury found Sinskey guilty of eleven of the thirty counts with which he was charged, and Kumm guilty of one of the seventeen counts with which he was charged. In particular, the jury found both Sinskey and Kumm guilty of knowingly rendering inaccurate a monitoring method required to be maintained under the CWA . . . and Sinskey guilty of knowingly discharging a pollutant into waters of the United States in amounts exceeding CWA permit limitations. Each appeals his conviction.

II.

. . . The trial court gave an instruction, which it incorporated into several substantive charges, that in order for the jury to find Sinskey guilty of acting "knowingly," the proof had to show that he was "aware of the nature of his acts, perform[ed] them intentionally, and [did] not act or fail to act through ignorance, mistake, or accident." The instructions also told the jury that the government was not required to prove that Sinskey knew that his acts violated the CWA or permits issued under that act. Sinskey contests these instructions as applied to 33 U.S.C. § 1319(c)(2)(A), arguing that because the adverb "knowingly" immediately precedes the verb "violates," the government must prove that he knew that his conduct violated either the CWA or the NPDES permit. We disagree.

Although our court has not yet decided whether 33 U.S.C. § 1319(c)(2)(A) requires the government to prove that a defendant knew that he or she was violating either the CWA or the relevant NPDES permit when he or she acted, we are guided in answering this question by the generally accepted construction of the word "knowingly" in criminal statutes, by the CWA's legislative history, and by the decisions of the other courts of appeals that have addressed this issue. In construing other statutes with similar language and structure, that is, statutes in which one provision punishes the "knowing violation" of another provision that defines the illegal conduct, we have repeatedly held that the word "knowingly" modifies the acts constituting the underlying conduct.

CHAPTER 3: MENS REA IN ENVIRONMENTAL CRIMES | 79

In *Farrell*, for example, we discussed 18 U.S.C. § 924(a)(2), which penalizes anyone who "knowingly violates" § 922(o)(1), which in turn prohibits the transfer or possession of a machine gun. In construing the word "knowingly," we held that it applied only to the conduct proscribed in § 922(o)(1), that is, the act of transferring or possessing a machine gun, and not to the illegal nature of those actions. A conviction under § 924(a)(2) therefore did not require proof that the defendant knew that his actions violated the law.

We see no reason to depart from that commonly accepted construction in this case, and we therefore believe that in 33 U.S.C. § 1319(c)(2)(A), the word "knowingly" applies to the underlying conduct prohibited by the statute. Untangling the statutory provisions discussed above in order to define precisely the relevant underlying conduct, however, is not a little difficult. At first glance, the conduct in question might appear to be violating a permit limitation, which would imply that § 1319(c)(2)(A) requires proof that the defendant knew of the permit limitation and knew that he or she was violating it. To violate a permit limitation, however, one must engage in the conduct prohibited by that limitation. The permit is, in essence, another layer of regulation in the nature of a law, in this case, a law that applies only to Morrell. We therefore believe that the underlying conduct of which Sinskey must have had knowledge is the conduct that is prohibited by the permit, for example, that Morrell's discharges of ammonia nitrates were higher than one part per million in the summer of 1992. Given this interpretation of the statute, the government was not required to prove that Sinskey knew that his acts violated either the CWA or the NPDES permit, but merely that he was aware of the conduct that resulted in the permit's violation. . . .

The act's legislative history, moreover, supports our view of the mens rea required for conviction under 33 U.S.C. § 1319(c)(2)(A). In 1987, Congress amended the act, in part to increase deterrence by strengthening the criminal sanctions for its violation. To that end, Congress changed the term "willfully" to "knowingly" in that section of the act dealing with intentional violations. Although Congress did not explicitly discuss this change, it may logically be viewed as an effort to reduce the mens rea necessary for a conviction, as the word "willfully" generally connotes acting with the knowledge that one's conduct violates the law, while the word "knowingly" normally means acting with an awareness of one's actions.

Our confidence in this interpretation is increased by decisions of the only other appellate courts to analyze the precise issue presented here.

Contrary to the defendants' assertions, moreover, *United States v. Ahmad*, 101 F.3d 386 (5th Cir. 1996), is inapposite. In *Ahmad*, 101 F.3d at 388, a convenience store owner pumped out an underground gasoline storage tank into which some water had leaked, discharging gasoline into city sewer systems and nearby creeks in violation of 33 U.S.C. § 1319(c)(2)(A). At trial, the defendant asserted that he thought that he was discharging water, and that the statute's requirement that he act knowingly required that the government prove not only that he knew that he was discharging something, but also that he knew that he was discharging gasoline. The Fifth Circuit agreed, holding that a defendant does not violate the statute unless he or she acts knowingly with regard to each element of an offense. *Ahmad*, however, involved a classic mistake-of-fact defense, and is not applicable to a mistake-of-law defense such as that asserted by Sinskey and Kumm. . . .

For the foregoing reasons, we affirm the convictions in all respects.

- Is it fair that a person can be charged with and convicted of violating the Clean Water Act or Clean Air Act for violating a permit even if he/she does not know what the permit allows or that the discharges in question violate it?

- Consider the dissent in *United States v. Weitzenhoff*, 35 F.3d 1275 (9th Cir. 1993), which involved the defendant's conviction for discharging sewage in violation of a permit:

> The harm our mistaken decision may do is not necessarily limited to Clean Water Act cases. Dilution of the traditional requirement of a criminal state of mind, and application of the criminal law to innocent conduct, reduces the moral authority of our system of criminal law. If we use prison to achieve social goals regardless of the moral innocence of those we incarcerate, then imprisonment loses its moral opprobrium and our criminal law becomes morally arbitrary.
>
> We have now made felons of a large number of innocent people doing socially valuable work. They are innocent, because the one thing which makes their conduct felonious is something they do not know. It is we, and not Congress, who have made them felons. The statute, read in an ordinary way, does not. If we are fortunate, sewer plant workers around the circuit will continue to perform their vitally important work despite our decision. If they knew they risk three years in prison, some might decide that their pay, though sufficient inducement for processing the public's wastes, is not enough to risk prison for doing their jobs. We have decided that they should go to prison if, unbeknownst to them, their plant discharges exceed permit limits. Likewise for power plant operators who discharge warm water into rivers near their plants, and for all sorts of other dischargers in public and private life. If they know they are discharging into water, have a permit for the discharges, think they are conforming to their permits, but unknowingly violate their permit conditions, into prison they go with the violent criminals. . . .
>
> In this case, the defendants, sewage plant operators, had a permit to discharge sewage into the ocean, but exceeded the permit limitations. The legal issue for the panel was what knowledge would turn innocently or negligently violating a permit into "knowingly" violating a permit. Were the plant operators felons if they knew they were discharging sewage, but did not know that they were violating their permit? Or did they also have to know they were violating their permit? Ordinary English

grammar, common sense, and precedent, all compel the latter construction.

As the panel opinion states the facts, these two defendants were literally "midnight dumpers." They managed a sewer plant and told their employees to dump 436,000 pounds of sewage into the ocean, mostly at night, fouling a nearby beach. Their conduct, as set out in the panel opinion, suggests that they must have known they were violating their National Pollution Discharge Elimination System (NPDES) permit. But we cannot decide the case on that basis, because the jury did not. The court instructed the jury that the government did not have to prove the defendants knew their conduct was unlawful, and refused to instruct the jury that a mistaken belief that the discharge was authorized by the permit would be a defense. Because of the way the jury was instructed, its verdict is consistent with the proposition that the defendants honestly and reasonably believed that their NPDES permit authorized the discharges.

This proposition could be true. NPDES permits are often difficult to understand and obey. The EPA had licensed the defendants' plant to discharge 976 pounds of waste per day, or about 409,920 pounds over the fourteen months covered by the indictment, into the ocean. The wrongful conduct was not discharging waste into the ocean. That was socially desirable conduct by which the defendants protected the people of their city from sewage-borne disease and earned their pay. The wrongful conduct was violating the NPDES permit by discharging 26,000 more pounds of waste than the permit authorized during the fourteen months. Whether these defendants were innocent or not, in the sense of knowing that they were exceeding their permit limitation, the panel's holding will make innocence irrelevant in other permit violation cases where the defendants had no idea that they were exceeding permit limits. The only thing they have to know to be guilty is that they were dumping sewage into the ocean, yet that was a lawful activity expressly authorized by their federal permit.

- If the courts were to require knowledge of the permit requirements, would the mens rea still be "knowingly" or would it become "willfully"?
- Which construction of "knowingly" is more in keeping with Congress's intent for enacting criminal provisions in the Clean Water Act?

4. Willful Blindness

Courts throughout the nation recognize that knowledge can be established even where the defendant has purposely tried to avoid gaining any. For example, assume that Thomas is the manager of an automobile repair shop. One of the repair shop's specialties is repairing car radiators. However, radiators in need of repair usually carry a great deal of heavy metals mixed in with fluid that is so toxic that it should not be introduced into the sewer system. When Thomas obtained his sewer connection for his repair shop, he signed a permit the stipulations of which prohibited, among other things, the introduction of radiator waste into the sewer system. The industrial sewer permit that the city issued to Thomas is part of a pretreatment program governed by the Clean Water Act. After repairing a few radiators, the collection drum for the radiator fluid was near capacity. Because the radiator fluid was hazardous, it needed to be disposed of through a permitted facility, which, Thomas knew, was very costly. One of Thomas's employees asks what he should do with the full drum of radiator fluid. Thomas says, "I don't care. Do what you need to do to dispose of it." The employee then dumps the entire drum down the toilet in the employee bathroom and sends it into the local sewer system. When Thomas goes into the employee bathroom, he notices that the toilet bowl has streaks of color that appear to match the color of the toxic radiator fluid. But Thomas does not ask his employee what he did with the radiator fluid, and, when another one of the employees tries to bring up the subject, Thomas cuts him off and says, "I don't need to know as long as you've taken care of it." Each Friday before Thomas leaves the shop, he sees that the radiator collection drum is full, and when he returns on Monday, it is empty.

After the city sewer plant experienced several toxicity problems with its wastewater, it began looking for the source of the problem. Samples taken from the wastewater at the sewer plant during the toxicity exceedances reveal a high concentration of heavy metals. The city that runs the sewer system begins working backwards through the sewer by taking samples at various manholes. Through the process of elimination, the city determines that the manhole nearest Thomas's repair shop contains significant evidence of the very metals that were causing problems at the sewer plant along with fluid that appears to be antifreeze. Investigators speak to Thomas about whether he is dumping radiator fluids into the sewer system. Thomas states that he had no idea what was happening with the waste radiator fluids. He simply told his employees to dispose of them, and, of course, he meant that they should do it legally because he would never ask them to violate the law.

Suppose that the city takes this investigation to the United States Attorney's Office to determine whether Thomas and his business could be charged with knowingly violating a requirement imposed by a pretreatment program under the Clean Water Act. The evidence shows that the permit barred radiator waste from being introduced into the sewer, and the chemical samples clearly show that radiator waste was unlawfully introduced from Thomas's shop. The issue is whether Thomas knowingly engaged in the unlawful behavior. To analyze whether Thomas acted "knowingly," consider the following case.

United States v. Wasserson
418 F.3d 225 (3d Cir. 2005)

McKEE, Circuit Judge.

We are asked to review the district court's grant of the defendant's motion for judgment of acquittal on Count Three of an indictment charging Gary Wasserson with causing, and aiding and abetting, the disposal of hazardous waste without a permit in violation of the Resource Conservation and Recovery Act. For the reasons that follow, we will reverse.

I. FACTUAL BACKGROUND

Gary Wasserson was the president and chief executive officer of Sterling Supply Company, located in Philadelphia, Pennsylvania. Sterling supplied commercial laundry and dry cleaning products. . . . Sterling had a warehouse in Philadelphia where it stored cleaning products consisting of cleaners, soaps and detergents, as well as equipment and business records. When Sterling went out of business in 1994, the warehouse contained hundreds of containers of chemicals, including napthene, acetone and perchloroethylene.

After Wasserson closed Sterling in 1994, he began selling off remaining inventory. In 1999, Wasserson met with Samuel Graboyes. Sterling had sold Graboyes dry cleaning supplies in 1995, and Wasserson offered to give Graboyes some of the remaining supplies free of charge. Graboyes declined the offer and told Wasserson to contact a hazardous waste hauling company to dispose of the remaining supplies. Wasserson replied by telling Graboyes that he had already contacted such companies, but that it was costly to have them dispose of the remaining inventory.

Charles Hughes was a Sterling employee from 1980 through 1994. His job involved transporting Sterling's inventory and products, first in a box truck and later in a tractor-trailer. . . . Wasserson claimed that he put Hughes in charge of Sterling's warehouse and that he (Wasserson) rarely visited it.

According to the government, in August of 1999, Wasserson asked Hughes to hire someone to remove the remaining materials at Sterling's warehouse. The material included scrap metal, wooden pallets, debris and hundreds of containers of chemicals. The government further claimed that Hughes had no experience in transporting or disposing of hazardous waste and no knowledge of the Resource Conservation and Recovery Act ("RCRA"). . . . In response to Wasserson's request, Hughes consulted the yellow pages and found a company named, "Davis Rubbish Removal" under the heading, "Rubbish & Garbage Removal." Hughes then proceeded to contact Charles Davis, a rubbish removal contractor who had no environmental experience. The government claims that Wasserson never communicated directly with Davis about the removal. Rather, Wasserson telephoned Davis's receptionist and dictated a contract. That contract gave Davis responsibility for properly disposing of the chemicals at a "legal dumpsite." In turn, Davis hired a disposal company called, "Will-Haul, Inc.," to provide dumpsters, remove them once filled, and dispose of their contents. . . .

Hughes telephoned Wasserson and told him that Davis was willing to remove the hazardous waste as well as the trash, that Davis said he would handle the waste properly, and that Davis said he had "been doing this for year[s]." Wasserson claimed to have told Hughes that Davis could only remove the waste if it would be handled properly. Wasserson purportedly insisted that this requirement be put in writing. . . .

Davis then arranged to have empty dumpsters delivered to the warehouse. Davis planned to fill them with trash and hazardous waste and send them to the Girard Point Transfer Station, a municipal solid waste transfer station in Philadelphia. However, the first dumpster that was to be used contained a sticker that read, "No Hazardous Chemicals." Since Davis knew that the drums contained hazardous waste, he contacted a different company, "Will-Haul, Inc.," which delivered dumpsters that did not contain any such stickers. Davis testified that he told Will-Haul's proprietor, Carlos Rivera, about the hazardous nature of the cleaners and chemicals, and that Rivera agreed to take them. Rivera testified that [it] has been in the waste business for 31 years.

Hughes helped Davis load the drums and trash into the dumpsters, while Davis and his employees focused on collecting the scrap metal. Hughes, believing that the drums were being transported to a location where they would be sorted and transferred to their ultimate destinations, shrink-wrapped them to avoid leaks and spills. Hughes kept drums that were not in pristine condition. Hughes left labels on the drums that bore the Sterling name and address and disclosed their contents.

On September 7, 1999, Rivera picked up a dumpster at Sterling's warehouse that contained hazardous waste and transported it to the Girard Point Transfer Station. However, when Rivera dumped the load onto the floor at Girard Point he saw the drums containing hazardous materials. Rivera knew the drums could not be accepted at the transfer station. Indeed, he had told Davis that he would not accept drums. However, the transfer station operator loaded the drums into a landfill-bound truck. The contents of the dumpster were commingled with other trash, loaded into a container and transported to Modern Landfill, a solid waste landfill in York, Pennsylvania, that did not have a permit to receive hazardous waste.

When the container was unloaded at the landfill, employees recognized an organic, paint-like odor coming from containers with Sterling labels on them. Landfill employees immediately shut down the affected part of the landfill and isolated the area. Thereafter, environmental specialists discovered that the drums were filled with hazardous waste.

Later that same day, a representative from the Pennsylvania Department of Environmental Protection ("PaDEP") arrived at Sterling's warehouse and alerted Hughes to the problem. Wasserson was contacted and arrived at the warehouse later that evening. Wasserson claimed that because most of the chemical drums had never left the warehouse, he personally undertook to have them properly removed from the premises.

. . . [N]o one informed Davis or Will-Haul that the drums and containers contained hazardous waste and therefore had to be transported to, and disposed of at, a permitted facility pursuant to the RCRA. Neither Girard Point nor Modern Landfill had a hazardous waste permit. The government claimed that neither Wasserson nor Davis nor Will-Haul complied with the RCRA. According to the government, that Act requires that persons possessing hazardous waste must prepare a manifest identifying the waste, properly transport the waste to a RCRA-permitted hazardous waste disposal facility, and dispose of the waste only at such a facility.

At trial, Wasserson stipulated that he knew that a manifest must accompany hazardous waste when shipped for disposal; that a facility that receives the hazardous waste must have a permit; and that hazardous waste may properly be disposed of only at a facility that has obtained a permit from either the Environmental Protection Agency or the Commonwealth of Pennsylvania. Wasserson also stipulated that he knew that the materials being disposed of were hazardous wastes.

II. DISTRICT COURT PROCEEDINGS

Wasserson was indicted by a federal grand jury and charged with three counts of violating the RCRA: causing, and aiding and abetting, the transportation of hazardous waste without a manifest . . . causing, and aiding and abetting, the transportation of hazardous waste to facilities which were not authorized to store or dispose of hazardous waste . . . and causing, and aiding and abetting, the disposal of hazardous waste without a permit. . . .

A jury convicted Wasserson of all three counts at the end of a three-day trial. Thereafter, Wasserson . . . moved for a judgment of acquittal on Count Three, arguing that 42 U.S.C. § 6928(d)(2)(A) only applied to owners and operators of disposal facilities, and that he could therefore not be convicted of violating that statute. . . .

The district court granted Wasserson's motion [for] judgment of acquittal on Count Three. . . .

The government moved for reconsideration of the judgment of acquittal on Count Three. . . . The district court disagreed, and this appeal followed.

III. DISCUSSION

. . . The government bottomed its aiding and abetting theory on the premise of Wassersons' willful blindness in handling the disposal of the hazardous waste. "A willful blindness instruction is often described as sounding in deliberate ignorance." "Such instructions must be tailored . . . to avoid the implication that a defendant may be convicted simply because he or she should have known of facts of which he or she was unaware." "Willful blindness is not to be equated with negligence or lack of due care, for willful blindness is a subjective state of mind that is deemed to satisfy a scienter requirement of knowledge." "The instruction must make clear that the defendant himself was subjectively aware of the high probability of the fact in question, and not merely that a reasonable man would have been aware of the probability."

Our review of the evidence in the light most favorable to the government leads us to conclude that there was clearly sufficient evidence for a reasonable jury to find that Wasserson was willfully blind to the ultimate destination of his hazardous waste.

Wasserson had owned Sterling since about 1980, and was actively involved in running the business. Although Sterling ceased operations around 1993 or 1994, Wasserson kept the warehouse. Wasserson knew the warehouse contained dry cleaning products, and Wasserson concedes that he knew the products constituted hazardous waste.

Wasserson also knew the requirements for handling hazardous waste and, particularly for handling hazardous dry cleaning chemicals. From about mid-1989 through 1990, Wasserson employed an environmental consultant, Michael Tatch, to advise him on a number of regulatory matters, including transporting hazardous waste. At one point, Wasserson was interested in expanding his business into hauling hazardous waste from dry cleaners. At another point, Wasserson asked Tatch about becoming a disposal facility, and Tatch reviewed the requirements for generators, haulers and disposers of hazardous waste with Wasserson.

Tatch also instructed Wasserson about the importance of manifests and their relevance to the regulatory framework governing hazardous waste. He told Wasserson that generators were required to manifest their waste, and that transporters had to sign those manifests and pass them along to those who took possession as well as to state agencies. Tatch described the information that a manifest must contain. He specifically covered the obligation of a generator of waste to provide a manifest if it generates more than 220 pounds of waste, and he advised Wasserson that it is the generator's responsibility to ensure that any waste leaving the generator's control has a properly completed and signed manifest.

Thus, as Wasserson stipulated, he knew that a completed manifest must accompany any hazardous waste shipped for disposal; that hazardous waste may only be transported to a facility that has a proper permit; and that a facility that disposes of hazardous waste must also have a proper permit to do so. Significantly for our purposes, Wasserson also knew that the proper disposal of hazardous waste was expensive.

Wasserson asked Hughes, his intermediary and employee, to find someone to clean out the trash in the warehouse. When Hughes reported back to Wasserson that Davis would clear everything out, including the hazardous wastes, Wasserson told Hughes to get it in writing because he did not want any problems.

In contrast to Wasserson's knowledge about the requirements for handling hazardous waste, Hughes knew nothing about hazardous waste disposal. Hughes had worked for Wasserson at Sterling from about 1980 as a truck or tractor-trailer driver making deliveries of dry cleaning supplies. Before Wasserson hired him, Hughes had also been a truck driver. After Sterling closed in 1993 or 1994, Hughes was Wasserson's chauffer for a few years. He also undertook various assignments for Wasserson, such as general clean-up of the warehouse, and helping load trucks for people interested in any of the goods at the warehouse. One of these assignments included hiring someone to get rid of the trash in the warehouse.

Before he hired Davis, Hughes had never been involved in disposing of Sterling's supply of hazardous waste. He knew nothing about the legal and technical requirements for a manifest. All that he did know was that if a manifest was needed on a job he drove, it was provided by "the office upstairs." Hughes did not participate in preparing any manifests. It was only after Davis disposed of the hazardous waste that Hughes first saw a manifest, which had been provided by a company called, "Onyx" that was eventually hired to perform a proper clean-up of the warehouse.

Given this evidence, Wasserson's level of knowledge about the legal requirements for handling hazardous waste, and Hughes's lack of knowledge; a jury could reasonably infer that Wasserson's failure to make proper inquiry and to provide a proper manifest were tantamount to willful blindness to the ultimate destination and disposal of the waste. Wasserson did not ask Davis, and Hughes did not even know to ask Davis, about the essential requirements for the proper transport and disposal of Sterling's hazardous waste. Wasserson did communicate directly with Davis's company, but only to ensure that Davis agreed to assume responsibility for the waste. Wasserson spoke to Davis's secretary, dictated those terms to her, and had her read them back to him and fax him the signed agreement. Thus, the jury could have believed that for the $13,000 he paid to Davis, Wasserson thought he could wash his hands of the trash, debris, and hazardous waste in his warehouse, and leave Davis "holding the bag."

As Wasserson knew, the warehouse that Davis agreed to clean was quite large, and the amount of debris and waste was significant. The areas to be cleaned included about 125 multi-drawer filing cabinets full of old papers and trash, plastic pipe, long crates, old machinery, old safes, about 500 multiple tier racks and three "huge" filters; and then there was the hazardous waste. A reasonable jury could conclude from this evidence that Wasserson's only concern regarding the hazardous waste was shifting legal responsibility to Davis.

Accordingly, it was reasonable for the jury to conclude that Wasserson knew that the hazardous wastes might well be disposed of at an unpermitted facility, or at least that he was willfully blind to that eventuality.

For all of these reasons, we find that there is more than sufficient evidence to support the unlawful disposal conviction. Accordingly, we will reverse the district court's order granting judgment of acquittal on Count Three and reinstate the jury's verdict of guilty.

- Was Wasserson guilty because of what he knew or what he should have known?
- In *Global-Tech Apps., Inc. v. SEB S.A.*, 563 U.S. 754, 769 (2011), which was a case of patent infringement, the United States Supreme Court stated that to prove willful blindness: "(1) the defendant must subjectively believe that there is a high probability that a fact exists and (2) the defendant must take deliberate actions to avoid learning the fact." The Court further stated that this test "give[s] willful blindness an appropriately limited scope that surpasses recklessness and negligence. Under this formulation, a willfully blind defendant is one who takes deliberate actions to avoid confirming a high probability of wrongdoing and who can almost be said to have actually known the critical facts."
- Based on *Wasserson* and *Global-Tech*, would you seek an indictment against Thomas, in the example above, with a knowing violation of the Clean Water Act?
- If you were representing Thomas and trying to convince prosecutors not to seek an indictment against your client, what would you argue about whether Thomas knowingly violated the Clean Water Act?

5. Collective Knowledge

As the DOJ's Principles of Federal Prosecution of Business Organizations repeatedly stated in the previous chapter, in addition to individuals, business entities may be held accountable for criminal violations. Because a business organization does not have its own mind and will, it only "knows" and "does" as much as its officers and employees know and do. As business organizations increase in size and complexity, employees and employee groups become increasingly specialized and may know little or nothing about what happens one or two steps removed from their contribution to production. As knowledge and authority become more specialized and compartmentalized, significant legal violations can occur without any one person knowing about them, which can result in significant harm. For instances such as these, courts have recognized a theory of knowledge that aggregates what all of the employees of a business organization know and imputes all of it to the business entity. Consider the following example.

United States v. Pacific Gas & Electric Co.
No. 14-CR-00175-TEH, 2015 WL 9460313 (N.D. Cal. 2015)

THELTON E. HENDERSON, United States District Judge

This matter came before the Court on October 19, 2015 for a hearing on Defendant Pacific Gas & Electric ("PG&E")'s Motion to Dismiss for Erroneous Legal Instructions to the Grand Jury. . . . [T]he Court now DENIES PG&E's motion, for the reasons set forth below.

BACKGROUND

On September 9, 2010, a gas line owned and operated by PG&E ruptured, causing a fire that killed 8 people and injured 58 others. The fire damaged 108 homes, 38 of which were completely destroyed. On July 30, 2014, a grand jury returned a superseding indictment ("Indictment") charging PG&E with 28 counts, including 27 counts of violating the minimum federal safety standards for the transportation of natural gas by pipeline ("Pipeline Safety Act"), as set forth in 49 C.F.R. § 192 ("Section 192"). "Knowing and willful" violations of these standards are criminalized under 49 U.S.C. § 60123 ("Section 60123"). . . .

DISCUSSION

PG&E now moves to dismiss all 27 Pipeline Safety Act counts of the Indictment, as well as the Indictment's Alternative Fines Act Sentencing Allegation. PG&E argues that because the prosecutor gave the grand jury erroneous legal instructions on both the intent requirement for violations of the Section 192 (Counts 2-28) . . . "[o]ne cannot conclude that the grand jury actually found probable cause the defendant committed a crime under the laws of the United States," and the only appropriate remedy is dismissal. The Government argues that the prosecutor's collective intent instructions were correct. . . .

II. The Intent Instructions on Counts 2-28 Were Not in Error

PG&E argues that "the government repeatedly told the grand jury that it could charge the defendant [for violations of Section 192] based on a 'collective knowledge' theory of intent," and that such instruction was erroneous because "this theory of criminal liability has never been applied in the Ninth Circuit." Specifically, PG&E challenges the following instruction from April 1, 2014, the day the grand jury returned the original indictment:

> It's the idea that you are imputing to a company the actions of all of its employees to get to the state of showing the company willfully violated the law. . . . The idea being that the company, not any individual, but the company through the actions of all of its employees, that that—that liability imputes to the company.

Section 60123's mens rea requirement has two prongs: The statute criminalizes violations of Section 192 only if they are both knowing and willful. PG&E focuses its argument on the "willful" prong,[5] and for good reason. There is ample persuasive precedent and widespread acceptance of legal treatises that define a "collective knowledge" theory to prove that a corporate defendant acted "knowingly." The leading case, out of the First Circuit, is *United States v. Bank of New England*, 821 F.2d 844 (1st Cir. 1987). There, the court held that "[a] collective knowledge instruction is entirely appropriate in the context of corporate criminal liability." 821 F.2d at 856. Likewise, the Restatement (Third) of Agency provides that "[o]rganizations are treated as possessing the collective knowledge of their employees and other agents, when that knowledge is material to the agents' duties. . . ." Restatement (Third) of Agency § 5.03 (Am. Law Inst. 2006). The focus of this motion has therefore rightfully been placed on aggregation of "intent," i.e. the "willful" prong, and its relationship to the aggregation of "knowledge," i.e. the "knowing" prong.

The Ninth Circuit has not addressed the question of whether a "collective intent" theory may be used to prove that a corporate defendant acted "willfully" in violating a criminal statute. . . .

To that end, the Government has offered *United States v. T.I.M.E.-D.C., Inc.*, 381 F. Supp. 730 (W.D. Va. 1974), in which the court approved a collective corporate knowledge theory to prove both the knowing and willful prongs of a criminal statute. In *T.I.M.E.*, a corporate defendant was charged with violating federal regulations related to interstate motor carriers. A criminal violation of these regulations required the government to prove a "knowing and willful violation of any of the [relevant] regulations." The court first upheld the government's use of the collective corporate knowledge doctrine to prove the knowing prong: "[K]nowledge acquired by employees within the scope of their employment is imputed to the corporation. . . . [T]he corporation is considered to have acquired the collective knowledge of its employees and is held responsible for their failure to act accordingly." Then, as to the willful prong, the court explained that the very fact that the corporate defendant had corporate knowledge, but declined to act on that knowledge, was sufficient evidence that the corporation acted "willfully":

> The Company had an affirmative responsibility not to 'require or permit' drivers to operate their vehicles while impaired. Cognizant of the situation—for, as previously noted, the Company is held responsible for the knowledge acquired by its various employees—it adopted a more or less 'hands-off' attitude towards

---

[5] PG&E argued that "'[c]ollective knowledge,' at most, could be used to prove what its name implies—knowledge. It cannot be used to prove a corporation's specific intent, i.e., the 'willful' prong." *Id.* *3 n.2.

> compliance with the regulation and, in effect, left adherence
> almost entirely the responsibility of its drivers.

Accordingly, the court held "that the Government has established beyond a reasonable doubt that the Company did 'willfully' disregard its duty under" the relevant regulations.

PG&E urges this Court to reject *T.I.M.E.* and instead follow what it contends is "[a] long line of courts since *Bank of New England*" that have found that "'[c]ollective knowledge' . . . cannot be used to prove a corporation's specific intent, i.e., the 'willful' prong." However, the cases PG&E cites are distinguishable. In both cases, the plaintiffs attempted to establish a collective state of mind by piecing together knowledge of individual employees. In *Kern*, for example, a buyer of crude oil sued to recover from the seller, and the seller counterclaimed for breach of contract. 792 F.2d at 1380. The seller argued that where the buyer's accounting department knew the price that was paid to the seller, and the buyer's legal department knew the contractual ceiling on price, the buyer's employees collectively knew of both facts, which rendered the buyer's overpayment knowing and voluntary. Id. at 1386-87. In *First Equity Corp.*, investors brought a fraud claim against Standard & Poor's for an incorrect bond description printed in one of the company's publications. 690 F. Supp. at 257. Plaintiffs attempted to prove the required mens rea—recklessness—"by pointing out alleged inconsistencies in the understandings held by various people at Standard & Poor's," as a demonstration that Standard and Poor's recklessly "had no understanding as to the meaning of the description when it was published." Id. at 259. Here, by contrast, the prosecutor did not ask the grand jury to aggregate innocent pieces of information from various employees across PG&E to construct a single "knowing and willful" transaction. Instead, the prosecutor invited the grand jury to consider whether PG&E's employees' individual knowledge and disregarding of the company's Section 192 duties rendered the company liable for "knowingly and willfully" violating those duties.

The Ninth Circuit recognized a distinction between these two kinds of reasoning in *Kern* itself, citing *T.I.M.E.*:

> [Seller] also cites [*T.I.M.E.*], in which the court held that a
> corporation could be held criminally responsible for the collective
> knowledge of its employees. The corporation had a duty to insure
> that its drivers obeyed a federal regulation. Various employees
> had notice of facts that, taken together, revealed that the drivers
> were violating the regulation. The holding that the corporation
> was charged with knowledge of the violations was thus based on
> the corporation's legal duty to prevent the violations. Such a duty
> is not present in this case.

792 F.2d at 1387. In so doing, the Ninth Circuit impliedly agreed that where a corporation has a legal duty to prevent violations, and the knowledge of that corporation's employees collectively demonstrates a failure to discharge that duty, the corporation can be said to have "willfully" disregarded that duty. *See T.I.M.E.*, 381 F. Supp. at 741.

In this case, as in *T.I.M.E.*, PG&E is legally obligated to follow safety regulations set forth by the federal government. This is the closest factual and legal comparison that either party has offered the Court to consider in understanding the mens rea requirement in Section 60123. Accordingly, the Court adopts the reasoning in *T.I.M.E.*, rendering correct the legal instructions PG&E is challenging on Counts 2-28 in this motion. These legal instructions therefore cannot be the basis for a dismissal. . . .

- How are the requirements for the collective knowledge theory different when they are applied to a willful mens rea compared to a knowing mens rea?
- Does that distinction make logical sense?
- However, as one court has observed,

> Both commentators and later decisions have undermined the force of *Bank of New England*'s collective knowledge doctrine. *See, e.g.*, Thomas A. Hagemann & Joseph Grinstein, The Mythology of Aggregate Corporate Knowledge: A Deconstruction, 65 Geo. Wash. L. Rev. 210, 226–36 (1997) (collecting and describing cases). In particular, Hagemann and Grinstein have persuasively described *Bank of New England*'s holding as a gloss on criminal culpability and willful blindness: "[b]efore courts will collectivize knowledge, they will first demand a showing that corporations deliberately attempted somehow to compartmentalize or avoid inculpatory information." *Id*. at 237–38. Moreover, later decisions, including those applying the actual malice standard to corporations, have shied from applying the collective knowledge doctrine to culpable states of mind. For instance, in *First Equity Corp. of Florida v. Standard & Poor's Corp.*, 690 F. Supp. 256 (S.D.N.Y. 1988) (Mukasey, J.) aff'd, 869 F.2d 175 (2d Cir. 1989), a defamation case in which the actual malice standard was at issue, the court held, "While it is not disputed that a corporation may be charged with the collective knowledge of its employees, it does not follow that the corporation may be deemed to have a culpable state of mind when that state of mind is possessed by no single employee." 690 F. Supp. at 260. The *First Equity* court cited the Ninth Circuit's decision in *Kern Oil & Refining Co. v. Tenneco Oil Co.*, 792 F.2d 1380 (9th Cir. 1986) for support. There, this Circuit declined to find that a corporation made "knowing and voluntary payments" where one corporate department knew the actual price, one department knew the contract price, but no department knew both prices. *See Kern Oil*, 792 F.2d at 1387. And these decisions all accord with *Reed v. Nw. Pub. Co.*, 530 N.E.2d 474 (Ill. 1988), in which the Illinois

Supreme Court blocked the plaintiff's attempt to "circumvent the [actual-malice] requirement . . . by pooling all of the information arguably within the knowledge of various employees and imputing all of that knowledge to the corporate defendant to establish that the corporate defendant acted with actual malice."

These holdings make sense. Principally, they guard against a court-led expansion of criminal and civil liability. As Hagemann and Grinstein argue, the collective knowledge doctrine conflates "knowing" culpability with "negligent" culpability, at least when applied to corporate wrongdoing. *See* Hagemann and Grinstein, *supra*, at 238–41. For instance, the collective knowledge doctrine favors liability where various corporate agents have different pieces of information, but the corporation was negligent in compiling these pieces of information. *See id.* But then liability is premised on negligence, not on the "intentional" conduct that is at the heart of the higher levels of mens rea, knowing and willful conduct. *See* Model Penal Code § 2 .02(2).

Ginena v. Alaska Airlines, Inc., No. 2:04CV01304, 2013 WL 3155306, at *7 (D. Nev. June 19, 2013).

- Do you agree that pooling all employees' knowledge and imputing it to the business entity blurs the line between knowing and negligent conduct, which, in turn, allows companies to be charged with felonies to the detriment of the shareholders?

- Not surprisingly, other scholars disagree with the Hagemann and Grinstein view on which the District of Nevada relied. Alexander F. Sarch, *Beyond Willful Ignorance*, 88 U. Colo. L. Rev. 97, 152-68 (2017). The development of the collective knowledge theory will be the subject of continuing litigation.

C. CRIMINAL NEGLIGENCE

Whereas under a willful or knowing standard, the prosecution must prove that the defendant subjectively had the requisite state of mind to commit a crime, negligence allows for criminal liability where the defendant violated an objective standard by deviating from a standard of care. Thus, criminal liability may be imposed if the person violated the objective standard regardless of whether he/she was subjectively aware of it. Although a person may be criminally liable for negligence, the crimes associated with this mens rea are misdemeanors.[6]

---

[6] *See, e.g.*, 16 U.S.C. § 3373(d)(2) (imposing misdemeanor where person engaged in prohibited action when "in the exercise of due care" the defendant "should know that the fish or wildlife or plants were taken, possessed, transported, or sold in violation of . . . any underlying law or treaty"); 33 U.S.C. § 1319(c)(1) (imposing misdemeanor where person negligently violates the Clean Water Act).

United States v. Ortiz
427 F.3d 1278 (10th Cir. 2005)

LUCERO, Circuit Judge

After a jury convicted David Ortiz of violating the Clean Water Act by negligently discharging a pollutant into the Colorado River, the district court entered a judgment of acquittal. The court ruled as a matter of law that an individual is not guilty of negligently discharging a pollutant unless he knows that the pollutant's path terminates in protected water. This conclusion is at odds with the plain language of the Clean Water Act, which criminalizes any act of ordinary negligence that leads to the discharge of a pollutant into the navigable waters of the United States. We therefore REVERSE the district court's judgment of acquittal.

I

. . . Chemical Specialties, Inc. operates a propylene glycol distillation facility in Grand Junction, Colorado where David Ortiz served as the Grand Junction facility's operations manager and sole employee. The process of distilling propylene glycol, an airplane wing de-icing fluid, produces significant amounts of wastewater. At the optimum mixture, the distillation of 1,000 gallons of used propylene glycol generates 500 gallons of industrial wastewater. Propylene glycol distillation enterprises typically discharge such wastewater to a municipal waste treatment plant for processing. Chemical Specialties, however, specifically declined to obtain a permit to discharge its industrial wastewater to Grand Junction's pretreatment plant and instead represented to city officials that it would ship all of its wastewater to a nearby business.

Grand Junction currently operates a bifurcated sewage system consisting of a wastewater treatment plant fed by numerous sanitary sewer lines and a storm water drainage system that collects rain water and distributes it into the Colorado River. Prior to the early 1990s, the city maintained a combined sewer line directing both waste and rain water to the treatment plant. In segregating its combined line into sanitary sewer lines and storm drains after the early 1990s, Grand Junction overlooked sewer service line connections in the area near Chemical Specialties, with the effect that since the early 1990s all sanitary discharges from Chemical Specialties and surrounding businesses flowed into a storm drain that discharged into the Colorado River.

In late April 2002, the city received a complaint of a noxious odor near the Colorado River, and subsequent investigation revealed a black substance accompanied by a pungent odor described as being reminiscent of onions pouring from a storm drain outfall and seeping into the river. City employees traced the malodorous black substance upstream along the storm drain and took samples en route. The samples were found to contain propylene glycol and propionaldehyde, a breakdown constituent of propylene glycol.

On May 1st, a city official accompanied by an employee of the Colorado Department of Public Health and Environment met with Ortiz at Chemical Specialties. After informing Ortiz that they were investigating the source of an unusual odor downstream from Chemical Specialties, Ortiz insisted that he sent all of his wastewater to a nearby business. Six days later, after discovering more of the black discharge downstream from Chemical Specialties and none upstream, the two officials returned and told Ortiz that the substance appeared to be coming from his facility. Specifically, they told Ortiz that black fine material reeking like onions was spilling into the Colorado River, that the officials had traced it through the storm drain, and that it seemed to be emanating from Chemical Specialties. They asked Ortiz if the facility had discharged any wastewater. Again, Ortiz said no. Dubious, the officials sought and received permission to inspect the facility, whereupon they observed significant amounts of water on the bathroom floor and several hoses and pumps lying nearby. On inspection of the grounds behind the facility, the officials detected the same onion odor. They also observed a large canvas bag containing a black granular substance, which Ortiz identified as carbon used in the distillation process.

During a follow-up investigation on May 29th, a city employee collected samples from the storm drain downstream from Chemical Specialties and from a pool of water below the storm drain flapper gate. Analysis revealed propylene glycol in the samples. Because earlier investigation had ruled out surrounding businesses as the likely source of the discharges, officials turned their attention exclusively to Chemical Specialties. On June 6th, a city employee conducted a test that conclusively demonstrated a connection between the toilet in Chemical Specialties and the storm sewer. The city employee informed Ortiz that the toilet was definitely connected to the storm drain and instructed Ortiz not to discharge anything down the toilet or sink. In their words, officials "shut the water off" at Chemical Specialties and arranged for a portable toilet and handwash station to be delivered to the facility.

On June 18th, two EPA special agents were dispatched to Chemical Specialties where they discovered a tanker truck spewing a liquid with "a fermenting type of smell that comes off of [wet onions]" onto the ground at the facility. The agents then walked to the nearby storm drain outfall where yet again a black liquid with the stench of rotten onions was observed pouring into the Colorado River. Although the storm drain downstream from Chemical Specialties had the same smell, immediately upstream from the facility the storm drain was dry and odorless. Returning to Chemical Specialties, the agents interviewed Ortiz who informed them that the leaking tanker contained propylene glycol that Ortiz intended to process. Ortiz stated that he was the sole employee of Chemical Specialties, and volunteered that he was the only person with a key to the facility. When asked if he had ever discharged pollutants through the toilet, Ortiz refused to answer. City investigators again observed puddles of water on the bathroom floor and hoses lying nearby, and noted that water supply to the toilet had been turned back on and the toilet was operational.

On submission of the case to a federal grand jury, a superseding indictment was returned charging Ortiz with two violations of the Clean Water Act ("CWA"): (1) negligently discharging chemical pollutants from a point source (a storm drain) into waters of the United States (the Colorado River) without a permit on May 29, 2002 and (2) knowingly discharging chemical pollutants from a point source into waters of the United States without a permit on June 18, 2002. Having been convicted on both counts on trial to a jury, Ortiz filed a motion for judgment of acquittal. The district court denied the motion as to Count Two but granted it as to Count One, finding: "There is no evidence that the defendant had any awareness that the toilet was not connected to a sanitary sewer line before June 6, 2002. While the first count of the Superseding Indictment charges a negligent discharge, the defendant could not be guilty on that discharge in the absence of his knowledge that using the toilet would result in the discharge . . . to the river." . . . Ortiz received a sentence of twelve months' imprisonment. The government appeals the judgment of acquittal on Count One. . . .

. . . The CWA prohibits the discharge of any pollutant into the navigable waters of the United States without a National Pollution Discharge Elimination System ("NPDES") permit. To enforce strict compliance with its terms, the CWA provides penalties not only for individuals who knowingly violate the statute, 33 U.S.C. § 1319(c)(2)(A), but also for any person who negligently discharges a pollutant in derogation of the NPDES. 33 U.S.C. § 1319(c)(1)(A) ("any person who negligently violates [section 1311] shall be punished"). As the court below properly instructed the jury, an individual commits a crime by (1) negligently, (2) discharging, (3) a pollutant, (4) from a point source, (5) into the navigable waters of the United States, (6) without a permit.

In granting Ortiz's motion for a judgment of acquittal of negligent discharge, the district court found that "the defendant could not be guilty on that discharge in the absence of his knowledge that using the toilet would result in the discharge . . . to the river." On appeal, the government argues that the court improperly imposed a mens rea requirement, and effectively conflated the elements required for a negligent discharge conviction under § 1319(c)(1)(A) and a knowing discharge conviction under § 1319(c)(2)(A). It continues with the assertion that the CWA does not saddle the government with the burden of proving that a defendant knew that waste traversed some boustrophedonic path and ended in a navigable stream. Ortiz does not dispute that ordinary negligence suffices to establish a negligent discharge. . . . Rather, Ortiz characterizes the court's judgment of acquittal as resting on the recognition "that one cannot be negligent, that is, flout a known risk, without being aware of what that risk is." Because Ortiz claims that he had no reason to suspect on May 29th that his toilet was connected to the storm drain, he argues that he cannot have been negligent in flushing dangerous chemicals down his toilet.

Even though the CWA does not define the term "negligently," we can easily determine what the government must prove to obtain a conviction under § 1319(c)(1)(A) by applying straightforward principles of statutory interpretation. We begin with the plain language of the statute. . . .

Section 1319(c)(1)(A) imposes punishment upon "any person who negligently violates" certain enumerated sections of the CWA. Those enumerated sections include § 1311(a), which states that "the discharge of any pollutant by any person shall be unlawful" except "as in compliance with this section and sections 302, 306, 307, 318, 402, and 404 of this Act." To determine what "negligently" means in this statutory context, we "start with the assumption that the legislative purpose is expressed by the ordinary meaning of the words used." In its ordinary usage, "negligently" means a failure to exercise the degree of care that someone of ordinary prudence would have exercised in the same circumstance. Under the statute's plain language, an individual violates the CWA by failing to exercise the degree of care that someone of ordinary prudence would have exercised in the same circumstance, and, in so doing, discharges any pollutant into United States waters without an NPDES permit. Thus, contrary to the district court's reading, the CWA does not require proof that a defendant knew that a discharge would enter United States waters.

. . . If Ortiz failed to exercise the degree of care that someone of ordinary prudence would have exercised in the same circumstance and, in so doing, discharged a pollutant into the Colorado River without a permit to do so, then he violated § 1319(c)(1)(A). Ortiz does not dispute on appeal that on May 29, 2002 he discharged some amount of propylene glycol wastewater down the toilet at Chemical Specialties. He does not deny that the wastewater flowed into the Colorado River and does not claim to have a permit to discharge untreated propylene glycol wastewater into the river. He argues, however, that when dumping the propylene glycol wastewater down the toilet, he was not acting negligently. We disagree.

In viewing the evidence in the light most favorable to the government, we have little trouble concluding that a reasonable jury could have found that Ortiz violated § 1319(c)(1)(A). Prior to May 29th, investigators told Ortiz that they had traced a black discharge with a strong onion odor from the Colorado River, up the storm drain, to the Chemical Specialties facility, and questioned him about how he was disposing of wastewater. The government presented evidence that prior to these conversations, Ortiz was dumping propylene glycol wastewater (a black substance with a strong onion odor) down the toilet. A reasonable jury could have well found that Ortiz acted negligently on May 29th when, after being alerted by investigators, he again dumped propylene glycol wastewater into the toilet. Because a reasonable jury could have found beyond a reasonable doubt that Ortiz committed a violation of § 1319(c)(1)(A) on May 29, 2002, we reverse the district court's judgment of acquittal on Count One of the superceding indictment.

- Does the fact that ordinary negligence under the Clean Water Act is sufficient to impose criminal liability give support to Professor Coffee's argument that the line between civil and criminal liability is being blurred?
- What is the difference between a "negligent" state of mind and a "knowing" state of mind?
- Why did the United States charge Ortiz with both negligently violating the Clean Water Act and knowingly doing so?
- What evidence would you look for to determine whether a discharge was negligent versus knowing?
- If ordinary negligence is the standard of criminal liability, then what role, if any, should the traditional tort principle of foreseeability play in the analysis?
- Would you find a defense to negligence more persuasive if the defendant were to argue that he could not have reasonably foreseen that the business's toilet would be connected to a storm drain, which discharges directly into a river, instead of to a municipal sewer system, to which toilets are typically connected?

D. STRICT LIABILITY

In addition to "negligence," some misdemeanor crimes use a strict liability standard. For example, the Migratory Bird Treaty Act (MBTA) contains a misdemeanor for anyone who "violates" its provisions. 16 U.S.C. § 707. A person can violate the MBTA if he/she "at any time, by any means or in any manner," pursues, hunts, takes, captures, kills "any migratory bird." 16 U.S.C. § 703. Because the misdemeanor provisions of the MBTA do not contain a mental state, many courts have held those provisions to provide a strict liability crime where merely having a dead migratory bird is sufficient for criminal liability. Consider the contours of strict liability under the MBTA for industry in the following case.

United States v. Corrow
119 F.3d 769 (10th Cir. 1997)

JOHN C. PORFILIO, Circuit Judge.

This appeal raises issues of first impression in this Circuit under . . . the Migratory Bird Treaty Act, 16 U.S.C. §§ 701–712 (MBTA). Richard Nelson Corrow . . . invites us to read a scienter requirement into § 703 of the MBTA to vitiate the government's proof he possessed protected bird feathers. Failing these propositions, he attacks the sufficiency of the evidence supporting his . . . conviction. We affirm.

I. BACKGROUND

On December 9, 1994, Mr. Corrow arrived at the Albuquerque airport en route to Santa Fe carrying one large suitcase, one small suitcase, and a cardboard box. . . . Agents [who were there to meet Mr. Corrow for an undercover buy] found the two suitcases Mr. Corrow had carried . . . one holding Navajo religious objects, small bundles, herbs, mini prayer sticks, and other artifacts adorned with eagle feathers. Another suitcase contained eagle feathers rolled inside several cloth bundles, Yei B'Chei dance aprons, and five headdress pieces made of eagle and owl feathers. . . .

The government subsequently charged Mr. Corrow in a two-count indictment, Count one for trafficking in Native American cultural items; and Count two for selling Golden Eagle, Great Horned Owl, and Buteoine Hawk feathers protected by the MBTA. . . . [T]he jury convicted Mr. Corrow of illegal trafficking in cultural items, Count one, but acquitted him of Count two, selling protected feathers, instead finding him guilty of committing the lesser included offense, possession of protected feathers. . . . The district court . . . sentenced him to two concurrent five-year probationary terms and one hundred hours of community service. . . .

III. MBTA

Under 16 U.S.C. § 703, it is

> unlawful at any time, by any means or in any manner to . . . possess, offer for sale, sell . . . any migratory bird, any part . . . or any product, which consists, or is composed in whole or in part, of any such bird or any part . . . included in the terms of the conventions

between the United States and Great Britain for the protection of migratory birds. . . .

Since its enactment, the majority of courts considering misdemeanor violations under § 703 of the MBTA have treated these offenses as strict liability crimes, eliminating proof of scienter from the government's case. Although we have not previously so held, we now join those Circuits which hold misdemeanor violations under § 703 are strict liability crimes. *See United States v. Smith*, 29 F.3d 270, 273 (7th Cir. 1994); *United States v. Engler*, 806 F.2d 425, 431 (3d Cir. 1986); *United States v. Chandler*, 753 F.2d 360, 363 (4th Cir. 1985); *United States v. Catlett*, 747 F.2d 1102, 1105 (6th Cir. 1984); *United States v. Wood*, 437 F.2d 91 (9th Cir. 1971); *Rogers v. United States*, 367 F.2d 998, 1001 (8th Cir. 1966); *contra, United States v. Delahoussaye*, 573 F.2d 910, 913 (5th Cir. 1978). Simply stated, then, "it is not necessary to prove that a defendant violated the Migratory Bird Treaty Act with specific intent or guilty knowledge." *United States v. Manning*, 787 F.2d 431, 435 n. 4 (8th Cir. 1986).

Nonetheless, Mr. Corrow invites us to read a scienter requirement into the MBTA to satisfy the due process concerns implicit in all criminal statutes. However, the plain language of § 703 renders simple possession of protected feathers unlawful ("it shall be unlawful"). Like other regulatory acts where the penalties are small and there is "no grave harm to an offender's reputation," *Engler*, 806 F.2d at 432, conduct alone is sufficient.

Here, in fact, the district court instructed the jury it must find Mr. Corrow knowingly possessed Golden Eagle and Great-Horned Owl feathers. In rejecting his motion for judgment of acquittal on Count two, the district court pointed to the photographs of the Yei B'Chei Mr. Corrow gave to East-West, the feathers found in his suitcase, and testimony of an F.B.I. agent indicating Mr. Corrow's awareness of the illegal trade in protected feathers. Under our announced position, this evidence abundantly satisfied § 703. We therefore affirm the district court's denial of the motion for judgment of acquittal and hold the evidence was sufficient to permit a rational jury to find Mr. Corrow possessed protected bird feathers whether he did so knowingly or not.

We therefore AFFIRM the judgment of the district court.

- Is it fair to hold a person strictly liable for a crime for possessing a feather of a migratory bird when the person does not even know what the feather is, much less that it is protected?

- Consider a company that operates numerous wind-power turbines, which, on occasion, kill migratory birds. Should they be held strictly liable for killing protected migratory birds and bald and golden eagles? As shown in Chapter 8, the courts disagree.

CHAPTER 4

THEORIES OF LIABILITY FOR INDIVIDUALS AND ORGANIZATIONS

In 1993, movie director Fred Schepisi produced a suspense film entitled *Six Degrees of Separation*,[1] which was based on the theory that any person on the planet can be connected to any other person on the planet through a chain of acquaintances of no more than five intermediaries. The common law, like Schepisi's movie, recognized this phenomenon and characterized potential criminal actors in terms of their degree of separation from the criminal act itself. For example, under the common law, the person who actually performed the disposal of hazardous waste without a permit was the "principal in the first degree." The person who ordered the principal in the first degree to do the criminal act but did not physically assist in its performance could be the "principal in the second degree." The executive who ordered the principal in the second degree to take care of the hazardous waste problem as cheaply as possible without filling out any paperwork could be the "principal in the third degree." As principals, each could be subject to criminal liability. Beyond principal liability, the common law also recognized that those who entered into a conspiracy could be held responsible for the acts of others in the conspiracy even if each person in the conspiracy did not actually do the act. Unlike Schepisi's film, however, the common law did not claim that every person on the planet was within six acquaintances of every crime.

The common law also recognized that the entities for which the principals and coconspirators worked could be held liable for their employees' actions. This concept is known as *respondeat superior*, the literal translation of which means, "the man higher up must answer." The obvious hope of recognizing this type of liability is that the threat of liability will encourage the organization to police itself of criminal conduct and eradicate it instead of profit from it.

In modernity, Congress has retained vestiges of these common law theories of liability and has added its own flourishes. Because all of these liability concepts

---

[1] *Six Degrees of Separation*, https://www.imdb.com/title/tt0108149/ (last accessed July 24, 2018).

are important to environmental criminal enforcement, they are discussed below. Accordingly, this chapter first explores the theories of individual liability, followed by a discussion of *respondeat superior* liability.

A. THEORIES OF INDIVIDUAL LIABILITY

The prosecution and defense of modern environmental crime chiefly involves three major theories of liability: principal, conspirator, and responsible corporate officer. How each theory functions in criminal enforcement is discussed in order below.

1. Principal Liability

Instead of worrying about whether someone is a principal in the first, second, or other degree, as the common law required, Congress simplified the inquiry in 18 U.S.C. § 2, which succinctly provides:

> (a) Whoever commits an offense against the United States or aids, abets, counsels, commands, induces or procures its commission, is punishable as a principal.

> (b) Whoever willfully causes an act to be done which if directly performed by him or another would be an offense against the United States, is punishable as a principal.

Thus, a person may be a principal who is subject to criminal liability if he/she: (1) actually commits the offense; (2) aids, abets, counsels, commands, induces, or procures its commission; or (3) willfully causes another to perform an act that would be criminal if the person causing the act did it him/herself. To aid and abet a crime under 18 U.S.C. § 2(a), the person aiding and abetting must desire to participate in the crime to bring it about. However, under 18 U.S.C. § 2(b), the person actually committing the criminal act may have no idea that he/she is engaged in a criminal act, but the person who willfully caused the innocent person to do the criminal act is liable as a principal. Consider the following example.

Case Study: Spearmint Smuggling

Terra DeYoung operates a very successful essential oils business, producing products that people use as air fresheners as well as for many clinically unsubstantiated medical benefits. To make the essential oils, Terra uses plants from all over the globe. In one of her most popular essential oil blends, Terra requires a spearmint plant that grows only in Switzerland. Recently, the Swiss government became concerned that this unique plant was going to become endangered due to commercial exploitation. Consequently, the Swiss government enacted a law that precluded commercial trade in the spearmint plant and listed the species in Appendix III of the Convention on International Trade in Endangered Species (CITES). As a signatory to CITES, the United States honors Switzerland's prohibition on the commercial trade of the spearmint plant and will not allow it into the United States. Terra is upset with this change in the law and decides that she needs to get the spearmint into her oil factory in the United States or else she is going to lose a great deal of money. Under 18 U.S.C. § 545, "[w]hoever fraudulently or knowingly imports or brings into the United States, any merchandise contrary to law . . . knowing the same to have been imported or brought into the United States contrary to law—[s]hall be fined under this title or imprisoned not more than 20 years, or both."

- Suppose that Terra hides some protected spearmint plants in her luggage, goes through customs, and does not declare that she has the plants. As she is exiting customs, a K-9 from the United States Department of Agriculture hits as Terra walks by with her spearmint-containing luggage. Can Terra be charged with smuggling?

- Suppose that Terra tells her vice-president, Jerry, with whom Terra travels, about the change in the law and asks Jerry to carry some protected spearmint plants in his luggage. Jerry states in a text to Terra that he thinks that the change in the law is "stupid" and that he can understand why she is upset. Jerry puts the spearmint plants in his luggage, goes through customs in the United States, and, on the way out of customs, the K-9 hits as Jerry walks by with his luggage. Can Jerry be charged with smuggling? Can Terra?

- Suppose that Terra does not tell Jerry about the law change and, instead, just asks if he would mind taking "this package" back to the United States. Jerry, who neither knows about the package's contents nor the law change in the United States and Switzerland, goes through customs in the United States, and, on the way out of customs, the K-9 hits as Jerry walks by with his luggage. Can Jerry be charged with smuggling? Can Terra?

United States v. Wasserson
418 F.3d 225 (3d Cir. 2005)

McKEE, Circuit Judge.
[The factual background for this case appeared in the previous chapter. Recall that Gary Wasserson was the president of a company that supplied commercial laundry and dry cleaning products to dry cleaners in Pennsylvania, Virginia, and Maryland. He went out of business and knew that his leftover products needed to be disposed of as hazardous waste, which was quite expensive. Wasserson hired Davis to haul and dispose of the hazardous waste, dictated the terms of the deal, and knew that Davis was going to dispose of the waste unlawfully. Davis disposed of the hazardous waste in a municipal landfill that did not know the waste was hazardous. The state of Pennsylvania learned of the disposal and investigated. The grand jury issued a three-count indictment against Wasserson for violating RCRA by: (1) causing, and aiding and abetting the transportation of hazardous waste without a manifest; (2) causing, and aiding and abetting the transportation of hazardous waste to facilities not authorized to dispose of hazardous waste; and (3) causing, and aiding and abetting the disposal of hazardous waste without a permit. At trial, the jury convicted Wasserson on all three counts. However, the trial court granted Mr. Wasserson's motion for a new trial on counts 1 and 2 and, in addition,

acquitted Wasserson as a matter of law on counts 1-3. This appeal followed regarding the motion of acquittal.]

. . . Wasserson was convicted of violating each of these subsections. But the district court granted Wasserson's motion for judgment of acquittal on Count Three, holding that one who generates hazardous waste cannot be convicted under § 6928(d)(2)(A) without actually disposing of it.

On appeal, the government contends that any or all of the separate RCRA offenses enumerated under § 6928(d), including the prohibition on unlawful disposal, can give rise to aiding and abetting liability under 18 U.S.C. § 2. We agree. 18 U.S.C. § 2 provides:

> (a) Whoever commits an offense against the United States or aids, abets, counsels, commands, induces or procures its commission, is punishable as a principal.
>
> (b) Whoever willfully causes an act to be done which if directly performed by him or another would be an offense against the United States, is punishable as a principal.

We have previously explained that every "indictment must be read as if 18 U.S.C. § 2 were embodied in each count." Accordingly, the "indictment need not specifically charge aiding and abetting in order to support a conviction for aiding and abetting."

> The general rule is that in order to convict a defendant of aiding and abetting the commission of a substantive offense, the proof must establish that the crime in question was committed by someone and that the person charged as an aider and abettor, aided and abetted in its commission. It is not a prerequisite to the conviction of the aider and abettor that the principal be tried and convicted or in fact even be identified. Each participant in an illegal venture is required to stand on his own two feet. An individual may be indicted for commission of a substantive crime by proof showing him to be an aider and abettor.

Here, the government specifically charged Wasserson as both a principal and an aider and abetter under 42 U.S.C. §§ 6928(d)(1), (d)(2)(A), and (d)(5). . . .

Wasserson nevertheless contends that the text and structure of the statute impliedly foreclose aiding and abetting liability for unlawful disposal under subsection (d)(2)(A). This is so, according to Wasserson, because subsection (d)(2)(A) does not expressly address those who "cause" the unlawful disposal— whereas the preceding subsection, § 6928(d)(1), penalizes anyone "who knowingly transports or *causes to be transported* any hazardous waste . . . to a facility which does not have a permit." (emphasis added). Wasserson contends that, by mentioning causation liability in subsection (d)(1) but omitting it from subsection (d)(2)(A), Congress must have intended to penalize under (d)(2)(A) only the actual disposer of the hazardous waste and not one who causes, aids or abets the disposal.

We cannot accept this argument without ignoring the fundamental doctrine of vicarious liability embodied in 18 U.S.C. § 2. In 1948, Congress amended that statute by adding subsection (b). Subsection (b), in turn, was further amended in 1951.

> The House report explaining this 1948 provision instructed that the purpose of § 2(b) was to permit the deletion from criminal provisions of words such as "causes or procures" and to remove any doubt that the legislature intended that one who causes the commission of an indispensable element of an offense against the United States by an innocent agent or instrumentality be guilty as a principal. This provision was in accord with Supreme Court decisions in *Ruthenberg v. United States*, and *United States v. Giles*[.]
>
> * * *
>
> In the Senate Report accompanying the proposed amendment it was explained that the section: [i]ntended to clarify and make certain the intent to punish aiders and abettors regardless of the fact that they may be incapable of committing the specific violation which they are charged to have aided and abetted. . . .

It is well-settled that 18 U.S.C. § 2 applies to the entire federal criminal code unless Congress clearly provides to the contrary. The omission of causation language from § 6928(d)(2)(A) is insufficient to indicate a clear Congressional intent to override the plain language of 18 U.S.C. § 2. Accordingly, we must recognize aiding and abetting liability under subsection (d)(2)(A). . . .

In explaining its order granting judgment of acquittal, the district court . . . explained that Congress' intent [was] that "one who merely generates but does not carry out the disposal of hazardous waste does not incur liability under subsection (d)(2)(A)." However . . . the issue here is not whether one who is guilty of generating hazardous waste must, of necessity, also be guilty of illegally disposing of it in violation of § 6928(d)(2)(A). Rather, the government concedes that disposal is a separate crime from transportation, and that it must prove both beyond a reasonable doubt to sustain convictions under the applicable subsections. The issue here is whether Wasserson can be convicted of the illegal disposal if he did not himself dispose of the hazardous waste. If the elements of aiding and abetting the principal offense are established beyond a reasonable doubt, then it is clear that he can be convicted. . . .

The government bottomed its aiding and abetting theory on the premise of Wasserson's willful blindness in handling the disposal of the hazardous waste. [Recall that the *Wasserson* court found sufficient evidence that Wasserson had knowledge that his hazardous waste would not be disposed of properly because he willfully blinded himself to the location where the hazardous waste would be disposed of. Based on Wasserson's knowledge and what he did to get others to do his dirty work, his conviction for aiding and abetting disposal of the hazardous waste was affirmed.]

- Do you think it's fair that the person who aided, abetted, or willfully commanded the criminal act to occur can be convicted even if the person who actually committed the crime is not even indicted?
- Why do you think 18 U.S.C. § 2 allows this to happen?

- How much involvement must a person have in the criminal act to be guilty of the crime under 18 U.S.C. § 2?
  - In *United States v. Whitney*, 229 F.3d 1296 (10th Cir. 2000), the defendant, Mr. Whitney, was indicted and stood trial for aiding and abetting the intimidation of an African-American family regarding their housing rights. In affirming the defendant's conviction, the Tenth Circuit observed that:

    > [p]articipation in the criminal venture may be established by circumstantial evidence and the level of participation may be of "relatively slight moment." Further, [o]ne may become an accomplice . . . by words or gestures of encouragement, or by providing others with the plan for the crime. Conduct of the defendant or special circumstances may justify an inference that the defendant has associated himself with the criminal objective.

  - Because "the government presented evidence that Mr. Whitney used racial epithets when referring to [his neighbors], and discussed cross burning as a symbol of hatred towards African-Americans on the afternoon prior to [Mr. Whitney's associates actually burning a cross on the neighbors' lawn]," the court held that "[a] juror could reasonably find these were 'words or gestures of encouragement.'" Additionally, the court relied on disputed testimony that Mr. Whitney had been the one to come up with the idea of burning the cross on his neighbor's lawn even though he did not participate in the actual cross burning.

- Unlike conspiracy, which is discussed next, the prosecution does not need to establish an agreement between the aider and abettor and the person(s) who actually commit the crime. Consider this statement in *United States v. Torres*, 809 F.2d 429, 433 (7th Cir. 1987):

  MENS REA

  > [I]t is not necessary that the [aider or abettor] have knowledge of the particular means the principal in the crime uses to carry out the criminal activity. Accordingly, criminal liability under the aider or abettor statute results from the existence of "a community of intent between the [aider and abettor] and the [principal]"; an aider or abettor is "liable for any criminal act which in the ordinary course of things was the natural or probable consequence of the crime that he advised or commanded, although such consequences may not have been intended by him."

- Under the standards articulated in *Whitney* and *Torres*, assume that Terra sends an email to Jerry complaining that the new laws regarding the protected spearmint plant in Switzerland and the United States were "stupid," and that they should haul out as much of the plant as they could just "to stick it to the environmentally psychotic bureaucrats of both countries." However, unknown to Terra, Jerry fills his suitcase with the protected spearmint plant and gets caught with it after passing through customs in the United States. Jerry shows the Immigration and Customs Enforcement and Department of Agriculture agents Terra's email as he is being questioned in the airport. When later questioned by Immigration and Customs Enforcement agents, Terra says that she "really didn't mean it" because she was just letting off some steam about how a government decision could so quickly cost her so much money. Could a jury properly find that Terra aided and abetted Jerry's smuggling?

2. Conspirator Liability

As you learned in your Criminal Law class, under the common law, agreeing with another person to commit a crime and engaging in an overt act (which may be a perfectly legal act) to bring about the object of the conspiracy is actually a crime by itself. Congress captured this in 18 U.S.C. § 371, which provides:

> If two or more persons conspire either to commit any offense against the United States, or to defraud the United States, or any agency thereof in any manner or for any purpose, and one or more of such persons do any act to effect the object of the conspiracy, each shall be fined under this title or imprisoned not more than five years, or both.

> If, however, the offense, the commission of which is the object of the conspiracy, is a misdemeanor only, the punishment for such conspiracy shall not exceed the maximum punishment provided for such misdemeanor.

Any crime in the United States Code counts as an "offense against the United States."[2] Consider these requirements as you read the case below.

United States v. Wells
873 F.3d 1241 (10th Cir. 2017)

HOLMES, Circuit Judge.

Recapture Canyon lies just east of Blanding in Southeastern Utah and runs south of Recapture Dam and U.S. Highway 191 along a creek. The Bureau of Land Management ("BLM") closed an area of Recapture Canyon to all-terrain vehicles ("ATVs") in 2007, to prevent soil damage and the spoliation of archeological resources near the trail. Frustrated with what had been billed as a temporary closure—and against a backdrop of simmering tensions between federal land management agencies and some residents of Southeastern Utah—in 2014, certain individuals planned an ATV ride to protest the BLM's closure order.

---

[2] *See, e.g., United States v. Brave Thunder*, 445 F.3d 1062, 1065 (8th Cir. 2006) ("[Defendants] both allege that their conspiracy convictions cannot stand because there was no evidence that there was a conspiracy involving the United States. This argument is based on a misreading of the statute and of the indictment. . . .").

The ride took place in May 2014. Defendant-Appellant Phil Lyman, a County Commissioner for San Juan County, was a major promoter of the ride. He was charged along with Defendant-Appellant Monte Wells in a misdemeanor criminal information with operating ATVs on lands closed to such use by the BLM and conspiring to do so. Mr. Wells owned a small business and ran a website entitled The PetroGlyph that reported on issues of local concern in San Juan County, especially issues relating to public lands.

Following a trial, a jury found both men guilty of the charged offenses. The district court sentenced them to terms of probation and brief terms of imprisonment. They were also ordered to pay restitution for the costs of assessing and repairing the damage that the protest ride caused to the land.

On appeal, Messrs. Lyman and Wells (collectively, "Defendants-Appellants") bring a variety of challenges to their convictions and the restitution order. . . . Because none of Defendants-Appellants' arguments are grounds for reversal of the district court's judgment . . . we affirm.

I. BACKGROUND & PROCEDURAL HISTORY

San Juan County, located in the southeastern corner of Utah, is home to significant swaths of public lands managed by the BLM. Among these, just east of the town of Blanding, is Recapture Canyon. In 2007, the BLM closed to ATVs part of Recapture Canyon because of potential damage to the soil and archaeological sites. See Notice of Closure of Public Lands to Off-Highway Vehicle (OHV) Use. This was intended to be a temporary order, but as of 2014, the order was still in place. The perceived delay in reopening the area strained already tense relations between the BLM and some local citizens.

Upset at the delay in reopening the portion of Recapture Canyon to ATV traffic, County Commissioner Phil Lyman organized a protest ride on ATVs into the closed portion of the Canyon. He was assisted in this by Monte Wells, who ran a website called The PetroGlyph that reported on local news of interest, particularly issues related to public lands. Mr. Wells interviewed Mr. Lyman on video and reposted Mr. Lyman's Facebook posts inviting others to the protest ride. Despite strong warnings from the BLM that criminal and civil penalties would be enforced against anyone riding an ATV in the closed section of the Canyon, the ride took place on May 10, 2014. Undisputed photographic evidence taken from within the closed area shows that Mr. Lyman and Mr. Wells rode ATVs in the protest that day.

A point of geography that requires some explanation for a full understanding of the case is that the northernmost part of the closed area of Recapture Canyon has a road where the local water district has a right-of-way to access and attend to the maintenance needs of a pipeline running from the reservoir to the north. The protest entered the closed area of Recapture Canyon on this road. To the south is a turn-around point where that road and the water district's right-of-way ends, but a trail continues further south, along which lies the majority of the archaeological and cultural resources that the BLM sought to protect. Mr. Lyman and Mr. Wells claim to have turned around at this point. Ferd Johnson, a representative of the local water district, testified that he had consented to a request by Mr. Lyman to use the water district's right-of-way for the protest. However, the parties stipulated that the scope of the right-of-way was limited to the purposes of "operating and maintaining a pipeline."

After an investigation, which included an assessment of the damages, the government filed a superseding criminal information charging Defendants-Appellants with riding ATVs on lands closed to ATVs and with conspiracy to do the same. . . . They timely appealed. . . .

C. Mr. Wells's Insufficiency of the Evidence Claim

Mr. Wells argues essentially that the government failed to introduce sufficient evidence that he was acting as a coconspirator rather than as a journalist. . . . Here, the relevant crime is a conspiracy, under 18 U.S.C. § 371, to violate the BLM's 2007 closure order.

"A conviction of conspiracy under 18 U.S.C. § 371 requires: (1) an agreement, (2) to break the law, (3) an overt act, (4) in furtherance of the conspiracy's object, and (5) proof that the defendant wilfully entered the conspiracy." Here, Mr. Wells appears to challenge the sufficiency of the evidence on the element of the existence of an agreement, insofar as he claims to have been acting as a journalist rather than a coconspirator.

The evidence presented by the government, however, was sufficient for a jury to find beyond a reasonable doubt that Mr. Wells acted not merely as a journalist reporting on issues important to his local community, but as a coconspirator who agreed with Mr. Lyman to ride a portion of the closed Recapture Canyon trail on ATVs. More specifically, Mr. Wells reposted Mr. Lyman's advertisements of the ATV protest ride, often adding flourishes of his own that suggested active support for and agreement with the planned ride on the closed portion of Recapture Canyon.

For example, the government's trial exhibit 73 is largely a reposting of an announcement by Mr. Lyman, but with the addition of the text "Show your support click 'Like' and Share!" and a large, iconic image of Uncle Sam pointing at the reader and stating "We Need You!!!" That posting further states: "It is only motorized machines that are deemed unfit (by the BLM) for these trails. I for one plan to be riding an ATV, carefully and respectfully, on these well established trails which have existed in this canyon for many many many years."

In a video interview of Mr. Lyman conducted by Mr. Wells, in addition to generally agreeing with Mr. Lyman's plans and reasons for the protest ride, Mr. Wells twice implies that he has agreed to ride on the trail with Mr. Lyman. Taken together with the evidence showing that Mr. Wells in fact rode the closed portion of the trail on an ATV, the jury could infer that Mr. Wells knowingly and voluntarily agreed with Mr. Lyman to ride ATVs in the closed portion of Recapture Canyon. The evidence presented was legally sufficient to sustain a conviction for conspiracy. . . .

E. Restitution

The district court ordered Mr. Lyman to pay approximately $96,000 in restitution, of which the court ruled Mr. Wells was jointly and severally responsible for $48,000. Mr. Wells principally challenges the restitution order on two grounds: (1) it includes harms that are not recoverable as restitution because they were not caused by the conspiracy and its underlying conduct, and (2) it includes amounts that are not legally cognizable as actual loss or supported by the evidence. Mr. Lyman appears to make a similar argument regarding causation and also attacks the court's fact finding. . . .

1. Causation

Under the Mandatory Victims Restitution Act ("MVRA"), which undisputedly governs the restitution analysis here, restitution shall be ordered for an offense causing damage to property by either returning property, or if

> impossible, impracticable, or inadequate, pay[ing] an amount equal to . . . the greater of . . . the value of the property on the date of the damage . . . or . . . the value of the property on the date of sentencing, less . . . the value (as of the date the property is returned) of any part of the property that is returned.

18 U.S.C. § 3663A(b)(1). The MVRA requires courts to order a defendant to pay restitution to a "victim" of the offense. No party disputes that the United States can constitute a "victim" under the MVRA. However, the question here is for what alleged harms can the United States properly recover restitution, and the answer to that question requires an inquiry into causation.

The MVRA's definition of "victim" provides:

> [T]he term 'victim' means a person directly and proximately harmed as a result of the commission of an offense for which restitution may be ordered including, in the case of an offense that involves as an element a scheme, conspiracy, or pattern of criminal activity, any person directly harmed by the defendant's criminal conduct in the course of the scheme, conspiracy, or pattern. . . .

18 U.S.C. § 3663A(a)(2).

In *United States v. Speakman*, we held that this language actually "sets forth two separate ways an individual [or entity, like the United States] can be a victim under the MVRA": first, the government may show that the victim was "directly and proximately harmed as a result of" the offense; and second, if a scheme, conspiracy, or pattern of criminal activity is "an element" of the crime at issue, the government may instead demonstrate that the victim was "directly harmed by the defendant's criminal conduct in the course of the scheme, conspiracy, or pattern of criminal activity."

Notably, "[t]he first clause [of the statute] also 'includ[es]' the second," and thus all harms contemplated by the statute must be "directly and proximately" caused and also must be "the result of the commission of the offense." However, the way a person can be shown to be a "victim" under the first clause is "in some ways broader [than the second clause] because it requires only that the individual be harmed 'as a result of' the defendant's offense, and not 'in the course of' the offense." "It thus follows that an individual could be deemed a victim by meeting the first criteria only, and not the second." Consequently, even if a defendant was convicted of an offense involving a scheme, conspiracy, or pattern element—quite apart from the "in the course of" criterion—the government's evidence could still establish that a person suffered injuries making them a "victim" by proving under the first clause that the harms at issue were "as a result of" the offense.

In addressing Defendants-Appellants' causation challenge, we elect to focus on whether the government has carried its burden under the first method. Like the second, this method is governed by the overarching direct-and-proximate standard. In *Speakman*, we observed "that phrase 'directly and proximately' uses the conjunctive 'and,' which indicates that direct harm and proximate harm have separate meanings." And discerning these separate meanings to relate to, respectively, "but-for" and "proximate" causation, the *Speakman* court held that "the government must show both that the defendant's conduct is the 'but-for' cause of the individual's [or entity's] harm and that the defendant 'proximately' caused the harm." The general meanings of but-for and proximate causation are well-known in the law.

But, more specifically, in the restitution context, the Supreme Court has opined that "[t]he basic question that a proximate cause requirement presents is 'whether the harm alleged has a sufficiently close connection to the conduct' at issue." *Robers v. United States*, 134 S. Ct. 1854. And answering this question generally entails an inquiry into the foreseeability of the harm. "As Justice O'Connor has noted 'proximate cause principles inject a foreseeability element into [a] statute.'" *Burkholder*, 816 F.3d at 613 (alteration in original).

Turning to the parties' arguments, with respect to but-for causation, the government's principal contention was that the conspiracy and its underlying conduct was the but-for cause of "motorized damage to archeological, riparian, and upland soil resources in the closed area." We conclude that the government presented ample evidence from which the district court could find by a preponderance of the evidence that this was so. The court did not clearly err in this regard.

Notably, the government introduced photos of the area taken before the ride and photos taken two days after it; the latter supported its contentions of motorized damage. Furthermore, prior to the restitution hearing, Chief Ranger Moore offered an affidavit that the trail camera had taken photos of about thirty-two "motorized vehicles"; though overexposed, the court could readily infer from these photos that multiple riders traveled through the area in Recapture Canyon that the BLM had closed to ATV users at the time of the protest ride and caused significant motorized damage. Thus, we conclude that the government's proof satisfied but-for causation.

As for proximate causation, "[w]here there are causes in addition to the offense conduct that appear to have contributed to the harm suffered by the victims of the offense, the issue is raised as to whether the defendant bears the risk of all the harm or whether the chain of causation was in effect broken by the intervening cause, resulting in less harm for which the defendant would be held liable in restitution." Thus, we reasoned in *Speakman* that the proximate cause requirement is satisfied "if either there are no intervening causes, or, if there are any such causes, if those causes are directly related to the defendant's offense." The direct-relation requirement means that the intervening cause must not be "too attenuated . . . so that it would be unjust to hold . . . responsible" the defendants.

Mr. Wells and Mr. Lyman argue that the government did not establish proximate causation because "the scope of the alleged conspiracy ended at the turnaround on the Pipeline Road," they personally never traveled beyond that turnaround; and most of the damage occurred beyond it. In effect, Defendants-Appellants argue that if any damage occurred at all, it was due to riders other than them who were not coconspirators and whose conduct should not otherwise be attributed to them. In effect, they reason that those other riders who continued riding south of the Pipeline Road should be viewed as an intervening cause, breaking the chain of proximate causation.

However, even if we assume *arguendo*, following the logic of Defendants-Appellants' argument, that the southbound riders were an intervening cause, we still reject their ultimate conclusion. We determine that the government has established proximate causation. Specifically, we conclude that this purported intervening cause was directly related to the offense conduct—that is, the conspiracy—and thus a proper predicate for the establishment of proximate causation. In this regard, Defendants-Appellants' focus on the ostensible termination of the conspiracy is misguided. As we made clear in *Speakman*, in the analogous context of a fraudulent scheme, intervening causes may still be directly related to the offense conduct for purposes of proximate causation "well after the conclusion" of that offense conduct.

In other words, even if we assume arguendo that those who rode south beyond the Pipeline Road turnaround exceeded the conspiracy's scope and were not coconspirators, their conduct could still be deemed directly related to that conspiracy. These riders initiated their ride in closed portions of Recapture Canyon "directly in response to," Defendants-Appellants' conspiratorial efforts, as the district court put it, to "organize a protest ride in closed areas in Recapture Canyon. And, as the court further observed, the geography of the area made it entirely foreseeable that the riders would continue south beyond the turnaround, even if the object of the conspiracy had been attained. . . . In other words, that riders who had come to ride on closed trails within Recapture Canyon as part of an unlawful conspiracy that Defendants-Appellants promoted might ride on trails beyond those on which the Defendants-Appellants themselves chose to ride and beyond those within the ostensible scope of the conspiracy is the kind of intervening cause that has "a direct relationship that is not too attenuated from" the conspiracy—especially when one of these trails provided the most convenient route back to a residential city. Accordingly, we conclude that the government's evidence established proximate causation.

In sum, the district court did not err in ruling that Defendants-Appellants were responsible for paying restitution to the United States for damages stemming directly and proximately from Defendants-Appellants' unlawful conspiracy to conduct a protest ride in closed portions of Recapture Canyon.

- What evidence showed that Mr. Wells had made an agreement with Mr. Lyman to commit a crime?
- Was aiding and abetting also an argument available to the prosecution?
- As the *Wells* court recognized, a conspirator may be held liable for the acts of conspirators unless those acts exceed the scope of the conspiracy or the time in which the conspirator was part of the conspiracy. Why did the court affirm the restitution award that the court imposed on the defendants when the court assumed that others, who were acting outside the ostensible scope of the conspiracy, caused the damage?
- Would restitution for the acts of others have been available had conspiracy not been charged?

3. Responsible Corporate Officer

Former President Dwight D. Eisenhower once said: "Leadership consists of nothing but taking responsibility for everything that goes wrong and giving your subordinates credit for everything that goes well." [3] Although President Eisenhower did not have the criminal law in mind when he made this comment about leadership, Congress had this idea in mind when it created the "responsible corporate officer" doctrine. Under this criminal law doctrine, a corporate officer can be held criminally responsible for the actions of subordinates where the officer knows about unlawful conduct, has the authority to stop it, but fails to do so. Consider the application of this doctrine under the following cases.

United States v. Park
421 U.S. 658 (1975)

Mr. Chief Justice BURGER delivered the opinion of the Court.

We granted certiorari to consider whether the jury instructions in the prosecution of a corporate officer under s 301(k) of the Federal Food, Drug, and Cosmetic Act were appropriate under *United States v. Dotterweich*, 320 U.S. 277 (1943).

Acme Markets, Inc., is a national retail food chain with approximately 36,000 employees, 874 retail outlets, 12 general warehouses, and four special warehouses. Its headquarters, including the office of the president, respondent Park, who is chief executive officer of the corporation, are located in Philadelphia, Pa. In a five-count information filed in the United States District Court for the District of Maryland, the Government charged Acme and respondent with violations of the Federal Food, Drug and Cosmetic Act. Each count of the information alleged that the defendants had received food that had been shipped in interstate commerce and that, while the food was being held for sale in Acme's Baltimore warehouse following shipment in interstate commerce, they caused it to be held in a building accessible to rodents and to be exposed to contamination by rodents. These acts were alleged to have resulted in the food's being adulterated within the meaning of [and] in violation of the Food and Drug Act.

Acme pleaded guilty to each count of the information. Respondent pleaded not guilty. The evidence at trial demonstrated that in April 1970 the Food and Drug Administration (FDA) advised respondent by letter of insanitary conditions in Acme's Philadelphia warehouse. In 1971 the FDA found that similar conditions existed in the firm's Baltimore warehouse. An FDA consumer safety officer testified concerning evidence of rodent infestation and other insanitary conditions discovered during a 12-day inspection of the Baltimore warehouse in November and December 1971. He also related that a second inspection of the warehouse had been conducted in March 1972. On that occasion the inspectors found that there had been improvement in the sanitary conditions, but that 'there was still evidence of rodent activity in the building and in the warehouses and we found some rodent-contaminated lots of food items.'

[3] Edgar F. Puryear, Jr., *Nineteen Stars: A Study of Military Character and Leadership* (Presidio Press, 2003).

The Government also presented testimony by the Chief of Compliance of the FDA's Baltimore office, who informed respondent by letter of the conditions at the Baltimore warehouse after the first inspection. There was testimony by Acme's Baltimore division vice president, who had responded to the letter on behalf of Acme and respondent and who described the steps taken to remedy the insanitary conditions discovered by both inspections. The Government's final witness, Acme's vice president for legal affairs and assistant secretary, identified respondent as the president and chief executive officer of the company and read a bylaw prescribing the duties of the chief executive officer. He testified that respondent functioned by delegating 'normal operating duties,' including sanitation, but that he retained 'certain things, which are the big, broad, principles of the operation of the company,' and had 'the responsibility of seeing that they all work together.'

At the close of the Government's case in chief, respondent moved for a judgment of acquittal on the ground that 'the evidence in chief has shown that Mr. Park is not personally concerned in this Food and Drug violation.' The trial judge denied the motion, stating that *United States v. Dotterweich*, 320 U.S. 277 (1943), was controlling.

Respondent was the only defense witness. He testified that, although all of Acme's employees were in a sense under his general direction, the company had an 'organizational structure for responsibilities for certain functions' according to which different phases of its operation were 'assigned to individuals who, in turn, have staff and departments under them.' He identified those individuals responsible for sanitation, and related that upon receipt of the January 1972 FDA letter, he had conferred with the vice president for legal affairs, who informed him that the Baltimore division vice president 'was investigating the situation immediately and would be taking corrective action and would be preparing a summary of the corrective action to reply to the letter.' Respondent stated that he did not 'believe there was anything (he) could have done more constructively than what (he) found was being done.'

On cross-examination, respondent conceded that providing sanitary conditions for food offered for sale to the public was something that he was 'responsible for in the entire operation of the company,' and he stated that it was one of many phases of the company that he assigned to 'dependable subordinates.' Respondent was asked about and, over the objections of his counsel, admitted receiving, the April 1970 letter addressed to him from the FDA regarding insanitary conditions at Acme's Philadelphia warehouse. He acknowledged that, with the exception of the division vice president, the same individuals had responsibility for sanitation in both Baltimore and Philadelphia. Finally, in response to questions concerning the Philadelphia and Baltimore incidents, respondent admitted that the Baltimore problem indicated the system for handling sanitation 'wasn't working perfectly' and that as Acme's chief executive officer he was responsible for 'any result which occurs in our company.'

At the close of the evidence, respondent's renewed motion for a judgment of acquittal was denied. . . . The jury found respondent guilty on all counts of the information, and he was subsequently sentenced to pay a fine of $50 on each count.

The Court of Appeals reversed the conviction and remanded for a new trial. That court viewed the Government as arguing 'that the conviction may be predicated solely upon a showing that . . . (respondent) was the President of the offending corporation,' and it stated that as 'a general proposition, some act of commission or omission is an essential element of every crime.' It reasoned that, although our decision in *United States v. Dotterweich*, 320 U.S. at 281, had construed the statutory provisions under which respondent was tried to dispense with the traditional element of 'awareness of some wrongdoing,' the Court had not construed them as dispensing with the element of 'wrongful action.' The Court of Appeals concluded that the trial judge's instructions "might well have left the jury with the erroneous impression that Park could be found guilty in the absence of 'wrongful action' on his part," and that proof of this element was required by due process. It held, with one dissent, that the instructions did not 'correctly state the law of the case,' and directed that on retrial the jury be instructed as to 'wrongful action,' which might be 'gross negligence and inattention in discharging . . . corporate duties and obligations or any of a host of other acts of commission or omission which would "cause" the contamination of food.' . . .

We granted certiorari because of an apparent conflict among the Courts of Appeals with respect to the standard of liability of corporate officers under the Federal Food, Drug, and Cosmetic Act as construed in *United States v. Dotterweich*, and because of the importance of the question to the Government's enforcement program. We reverse.

I

The question presented by the Government's petition for certiorari in *United States v. Dotterweich*, and the focus of this Court's opinion, was whether 'the manager of a corporation, as well as the corporation itself, may be prosecuted under the Federal Food, Drug, and Cosmetic Act of 1938 for the introduction of misbranded and adulterated articles into interstate commerce.' In *Dotterweich*, a jury had disagreed as to the corporation, a jobber purchasing drugs from manufacturers and shipping them in interstate commerce under its own label, but had convicted Dotterweich, the corporation's president and general manager. The Court of Appeals reversed the conviction on the ground that only the drug dealer, whether corporation or individual, was subject to the criminal provisions of the Act, and that where the dealer was a corporation, an individual connected therewith might be held personally only if he was operating the corporation 'as his "alter ego."'

In reversing the judgment of the Court of Appeals and reinstating Dotterweich's conviction, this Court looked to the purposes of the Act and noted that they 'touch phases of the lives and health of the people which, in the circumstances of modern industrialism, are largely beyond self-protection.' It observed that the Act is of 'a now familiar type' which 'dispenses with the conventional requirement for criminal conduct-awareness of some wrongdoing. In the interest of the larger good it puts the burden of acting at hazard upon a person otherwise innocent but standing in responsible relation to a public danger.'

Central to the Court's conclusion that individuals other than proprietors are subject to the criminal provisions of the Act was the reality that 'the only way in which a corporation can act is through the individuals who act on its behalf.' The Court also noted that corporate officers had been subject to criminal liability under the Federal Food and Drugs Act of 1906, and it observed that a contrary result under the 1938 legislation would be incompatible with the expressed intent of Congress to 'enlarge and stiffen the penal net' and to discourage a view of the Act's criminal penalties as a 'license fee for the conduct of an illegitimate business.'

At the same time, however, the Court was aware of the concern which was the motivating factor in the Court of Appeals' decision, that literal enforcement 'might operate too harshly by sweeping within its condemnation any person however remotely entangled in the proscribed shipment.' A limiting principle, in the form of 'settled doctrines of criminal law' defining those who 'are responsible for the commission of a misdemeanor,' was available. In this context, the Court concluded, those doctrines dictated that the offense was committed 'by all who . . . have . . . a responsible share in the furtherance of the transaction which the statute outlaws.'

The Court recognized that, because the Act dispenses with the need to prove 'consciousness of wrongdoing,' it may result in hardship even as applied to those who share 'responsibility in the business process resulting in' a violation. It regarded as 'too treacherous' an attempt 'to define or even to indicate by way of illustration the class of employees which stands in such a responsible relation.' The question of responsibility, the Court said, depends 'on the evidence produced at the trial and its submission—assuming the evidence warrants it—to the jury under appropriate guidance.' The Court added: 'In such matters the good sense of prosecutors, the wise guidance of trial judges, and the ultimate judgment of juries must be trusted.' Id., at 284-285.

II

The rule that corporate employees who have 'a responsible share in the furtherance of the transaction which the statute outlaws' are subject to the criminal provisions of the Act was not formulated in a vacuum. Cases under the Federal Food and Drugs Act of 1906 reflected the view both that knowledge or intent were not required to be proved in prosecutions under its criminal provisions, and that responsible corporate agents could be subjected to the liability thereby imposed. Moreover, the principle had been recognized that a corporate agent, through whose act, default, or omission the corporation committed a crime, was himself guilty individually of that crime. The principle had been applied whether or not the crime required 'consciousness of wrongdoing,' and it had been applied not only to those corporate agents who themselves committed the criminal act, but also to those who by virtue of their managerial positions or other similar relation to the actor could be deemed responsible for its commission.

In the latter class of cases, the liability of managerial officers did not depend on their knowledge of, or personal participation in, the act made criminal by the statute. Rather, where the statute under which they were prosecuted dispensed with 'consciousness of wrongdoing,' an omission or failure to act was deemed a sufficient basis for a responsible corporate agent's liability. It was enough in such cases that, by virtue of the relationship he bore to the corporation, the agent had the power to prevent the act complained of.

The rationale of the interpretation given the Act in *Dotterweich*, as holding criminally accountable the persons whose failure to exercise the authority and supervisory responsibility reposed in them by the business organization resulted in the violation complained of, has been confirmed in our subsequent cases. Thus, the Court has reaffirmed the proposition that 'the public interest in the purity of its food is so great as to warrant the imposition of the highest standard of care on distributors.' In order to make 'distributors of food the strictest censors of their merchandise,' the Act punishes 'neglect where the law requires care, or inaction where it imposes a duty.' 'The accused, if he does not will the violation, usually is in a position to prevent it with no more care than society might reasonably expect and no more exertion than it might reasonably exact from one who assumed his responsibilities.' Similarly, in cases decided after *Dotterweich*, the Courts of Appeals have recognized that those corporate agents vested with the responsibility, and power commensurate with that responsibility, to devise whatever measures are necessary to ensure compliance with the Act bear a 'responsible relationship' to, or have a 'responsible share' in, violations.

Thus *Dotterweich* and the cases which have followed reveal that in providing sanctions which reach and touch the individuals who execute the corporate mission—and this is by no means necessarily confined to a single corporate agent or employee—the Act imposes not only a positive duty to seek out and remedy violations when they occur but also, and primarily, a duty to implement measures that will insure that violations will not occur. The requirements of foresight and vigilance imposed on responsible corporate agents are beyond question demanding, and perhaps onerous, but they are no more stringent than the public has a right to expect of those who voluntarily assume positions of authority in business enterprises whose services and products affect the health and well-being of the public that supports them.

The Act does not, as we observed in *Dotterweich*, make criminal liability turn on 'awareness of some wrongdoing' or 'conscious fraud.' The duty imposed by Congress on responsible corporate agents is, we emphasize, one that requires the highest standard of foresight and vigilance, but the Act, in its criminal aspect, does not require that which is objectively impossible. The theory upon which responsible corporate agents are held criminally accountable for 'causing' violations of the Act permits a claim that a defendant was 'powerless' to prevent or correct the violation to 'be raised defensively at a trial on the merits.' If such a claim is made, the defendant has the burden of coming forward with evidence, but this does not alter the Government's ultimate burden of proving beyond a reasonable doubt the defendant's guilt, including his power, in light of the duty imposed by the Act, to prevent or correct the prohibited condition. Congress has seen fit to enforce the accountability of responsible corporate agents dealing with products which may affect the health of consumers by penal sanctions cast in rigorous terms, and the obligation of the courts is to give them effect so long as they do not violate the Constitution.

III

We cannot agree with the Court of Appeals that it was incumbent upon the District Court to instruct the jury that the Government had the burden of establishing 'wrongful action' in the sense in which the Court of Appeals used that phrase. The concept of a 'responsible relationship' to, or a 'responsible share' in, a violation of the Act indeed imports some measure of blameworthiness; but it is equally clear that the Government establishes a prima facie case when it introduces evidence sufficient to warrant a finding by the trier of the facts that the defendant had, by reason of his position in the corporation, responsibility and authority either to prevent in the first instance, or promptly to correct, the violation complained of, and that he failed to do so. The failure thus to fulfill the duty imposed by the interaction of the corporate agent's authority and the statute furnishes a sufficient causal link. The considerations which prompted the imposition of this duty, and the scope of the duty, provide the measure of culpability.

Turning to the jury charge in this case, it is of course arguable that isolated parts can be read as intimating that a finding of guilt could be predicated solely on respondent's corporate position. But this is not the way we review jury instructions, because 'a single instruction to a jury may not be judged in artificial isolation, but must be viewed in the context of the overall charge.'

Reading the entire charge satisfies us that the jury's attention was adequately focused on the issue of respondent's authority with respect to the conditions that formed the basis of the alleged violations. Viewed as a whole, the charge did not permit the jury to find guilt solely on the basis of respondent's position in the corporation; rather, it fairly advised the jury that to find guilt it must find respondent 'had a responsible relation to the situation,' and 'by virtue of his position . . . had . . . authority and responsibility' to deal with the situation. The situation referred to could only be 'food . . . held in unsanitary conditions in a warehouse with the result that it consisted, in part, of filth or . . . may have been contaminated with filth.'

Moreover, in reviewing jury instructions, our task is also to view the charge itself as part of the whole trial. 'Often isolated statements taken from the charge, seemingly prejudicial on their face, are not so when considered in the context of the entire record of the trial.' The record in this case reveals that the jury could not have failed to be aware that the main issue for determination was not respondent's position in the corporate hierarchy, but rather his accountability, because of the responsibility and authority of his position, for the conditions which gave rise to the charges against him.

We conclude that, viewed as a whole and in the context of the trial, the charge was not misleading and contained an adequate statement of the law to guide the jury's determination. Although it would have been better to give an instruction more precisely relating the legal issue to the facts of the case, we cannot say that the failure to provide the amplification requested by respondent was an abuse of discretion. Finally, we note that there was no request for an instruction that the Government was required to prove beyond a reasonable doubt that respondent was not without the power or capacity to affect the conditions which founded the charges in the information. In light of the evidence adduced at trial, we find no basis to conclude that the failure of the trial court to give such an instruction sua sponte was plain error or a defect affecting substantial rights.

IV

Our conclusion that the Court of Appeals erred in its reading of the jury charge suggests as well our disagreement with that court concerning the admissibility of evidence demonstrating that respondent was advised by the FDA in 1970 of insanitary conditions in Acme's Philadelphia warehouse. We are satisfied that the Act imposes the highest standard of care and permits conviction of responsible corporate officials who, in light of this standard of care, have the power to prevent or correct violations of its provisions. Implicit in the Court's admonition that 'the ultimate judgment of juries must be trusted,' *United States v. Dotterweich*, 320 U.S., at 285, however, is the realization that they may demand more than corporate bylaws to find culpability.

Respondent testified in his defense that he had employed a system in which he relied upon his subordinates, and that he was ultimately responsible for this system. He testified further that he had found these subordinates to be 'dependable' and had 'great confidence' in them. By this and other testimony respondent evidently sought to persuade the jury that, as the president of a large corporation, he had no choice but to delegate duties to those in whom he reposed confidence, that he had no reason to suspect his subordinates were failing to insure compliance with the Act, and that, once violations were unearthed, acting through those subordinates he did everything possible to correct them.

Although we need not decide whether this testimony would have entitled respondent to an instruction as to his lack of power, had he requested it, the testimony clearly created the 'need' for rebuttal evidence. That evidence was not offered to show that respondent had a propensity to commit criminal acts or that the crime charged had been committed; its purpose was to demonstrate that respondent was on notice that he could not rely on his system of delegation to subordinates to prevent or correct insanitary conditions at Acme's warehouses, and that he must have been aware of the deficiencies of this system before the Baltimore violations were discovered. The evidence was therefore relevant since it served to rebut respondent's defense that he had justifiably relied upon subordinates to handle sanitation matters. And, particularly in light of the difficult task of juries in prosecutions under the Act, we conclude that its relevance and persuasiveness outweighed any prejudicial effect.

Reversed.

Mr. Justice STEWART, with whom Mr. Justice MARSHALL and Mr. Justice POWELL join, dissenting.

Although agreeing with much of what is said in the Court's opinion, I dissent from the opinion and judgment, because the jury instructions in this case were not consistent with the law as the Court today expounds it.

As I understand the Court's opinion, it holds that in order to sustain a conviction under § 301(k) of the Federal Food, Drug, and Cosmetic Act the prosecution must at least show that by reason of an individual's corporate position and responsibilities, he had a duty to use care to maintain the physical integrity of the corporation's food products. A jury may then draw the inference that when the good is found to be in such condition as to violate the statute's prohibitions, that condition was 'caused' by a breach of the standard of care imposed upon the responsible official. This is the language of negligence, and I agree with it.

To affirm this conviction, however, the Court must approve the instructions given to the members of the jury who were entrusted with determining whether the respondent was innocent or guilty. Those instructions did not conform to the standards that the Court itself sets out today.

The trial judge instructed the jury to find Park guilty if it found beyond a reasonable doubt that Park 'had a responsible relation to the situation. . . . The issue is, in this case, whether the Defendant, John R. Park, by virtue of his position in the company, had a position of authority and responsibility in the situation out of which these charges arose.' Requiring, as it did, a verdict of guilty upon a finding of 'responsibility,' this instruction standing alone could have been construed as a direction to convict if the jury found Park 'responsible' for the condition in the sense that his position as chief executive officer gave him formal responsibility within the structure of the corporation. But the trial judge went on specifically to caution the jury not to attach such a meaning to his instruction, saying that 'the fact that the Defendant is pres(id)ent and is a chief executive officer of the Acme Markets does not require a finding of guilt.' 'Responsibility' as used by the trial judge therefore had whatever meaning the jury in its unguided discretion chose to give it.

The instructions, therefore, expressed nothing more than a tautology. They told the jury: 'You must find the defendant guilty if you find that he is to be held accountable for this adulterated food.' In other words: 'You must find the defendant guilty if you conclude that he is guilty.' The trial judge recognized the infirmities in these instructions, but he reluctantly concluded that he was required to give such a charge under *United States v. Dotterweich*, 320 U.S. 277, which, he thought, in declining to define 'responsible relation' had declined to specify the minimum standard of liability for criminal guilt. . . .

To be sure, 'the day (is) long past when (courts) . . . parsed instructions and engaged in nice semantic distinctions,' But this Court has never before abandoned the view that jury instructions must contain a statement of the applicable law sufficiently precise to enable the jury to be guided by something other than its rough notions of social justice. And while it might be argued that the issue before the jury in this case was a 'mixed' question of both law and fact, this has never meant that a jury is to be left wholly at sea, without any guidance as to the standard of conduct the law requires. The instructions given by the trial court in this case, it must be emphasized, were a virtual nullity, a mere authorization to convict if the jury thought it appropriate. Such instructions—regardless of the blameworthiness of the defendant's conduct, regardless of the social value of the Food, Drug, and Cosmetic Act, and regardless of the importance of convicting those who violate it—have no place in our jurisprudence.

We deal here with a criminal conviction, not a civil forfeiture. It is true that the crime was but a misdemeanor and the penalty in this case light. But under the statute even a first conviction can result in imprisonment for a year, and a subsequent offense is a felony carrying a punishment of up to three years in prison. So the standardless conviction approved today can serve in another case tomorrow to support a felony conviction and a substantial prison sentence. However highly the Court may regard the social objectives of the Food, Drug, and Cosmetic Act, that regard cannot serve to justify a criminal conviction so wholly alien to fundamental principles of our law.

For these reasons, I cannot join the Court in affirming Park's criminal conviction.

- Was Park's conviction really "standardless," as the dissent says? What is required to convict a responsible corporate officer of a crime?
- The *Park* majority and the dissent seem to take solace in the fact that the responsible corporate officer doctrine was applied to a misdemeanor conviction. Could this same reasoning be used to justify a felony conviction? Why or why not?

United States v. Iverson
162 F.3d 1015 (9th Cir. 1998)

GRABER, Circuit Judge:

A jury convicted defendant of four counts of violating federal water pollution law, as embodied in the Clean Water Act (CWA), the Washington Administrative Code (WAC), and the City of Olympia's Municipal Code (Olympia code). . . . We are not persuaded by any of defendant's arguments and, thus, we affirm his convictions.

BACKGROUND

A. Summary of Facts

. . . Defendant was a founder of CH2O, Inc., and served as the company's President and Chairman of the Board. CH2O blends chemicals to create numerous products, including acid cleaners and heavy-duty alkaline compounds. The company ships the blended chemicals to its customers in drums.

CH2O asked its customers to return the drums so that it could reuse them. Although customers returned the drums, they often did not clean them sufficiently. Thus, the drums still contained chemical residue. Before CH2O could reuse the drums, it had to remove that residue.

To remove the residue, CH2O instituted a drum-cleaning operation, which in turn generated wastewater. In the early to mid-1980s, defendant approached the manager of the local sewer authority to see whether the sewer authority would accept the company's wastewater. The sewer authority refused, because the wastewater "did not meet the parameters we had set for accepting industrial waste. It had too high of a metal content." Thereafter, defendant and the general manager of CH2O made two other attempts to convince the sewer authority to accept the wastewater. Both times, it refused.

Beginning in about 1985, defendant personally discharged the wastewater and ordered employees of CH2O to discharge the wastewater in three places: (1) on the plant's property, (2) through a sewer drain at an apartment complex that defendant owned, and (3) through a sewer drain at defendant's home. (The plant did not have sewer access.) Those discharges continued until about 1988, when CH2O hired Bill Brady.

Brady initially paid a waste disposal company to dispose of the wastewater. Those efforts cost the company thousands of dollars each month. Beginning in late 1991, CH2O stopped its drum-cleaning operation and, instead, shipped the drums to a professional outside contractor for cleaning.

In April 1992, CH2O fired Brady. Around that same time, defendant bought a warehouse in Olympia. Unlike the CH2O plant, the warehouse had sewer access. After the purchase, CH2O restarted its drum-cleaning operation at the warehouse and disposed of its wastewater through the sewer. CH2O obtained neither a permit nor permission to make these discharges. The drum-cleaning operation continued until the summer of 1995, when CH2O learned that it was under investigation for discharging pollutants into the sewer.

A few months before CH2O restarted its drum-cleaning operation, defendant announced his "official" retirement from CH2O. Thereafter, he continued to receive money from CH2O, to conduct business at the company's facilities, and to give orders to employees. Moreover, the company continued to list him as the president in documents that it filed with the state, and the employee who was responsible for running the day-to-day aspects of the drum-cleaning operation testified that he reported to defendant.

During the four years of the operation at the warehouse, defendant was sometimes present when drums were cleaned. During those occasions, defendant was close enough to see and smell the waste.

In some instances, defendant informed employees that he had obtained a permit for the drum-cleaning operation and that the operation was on the "up and up." At other times, however, defendant told employees that, if they got caught, the company would receive only a slap on the wrist.

B. Procedural History

On September 18, 1997, a grand jury filed a superseding indictment, charging defendant with violating the CWA, the WAC, and the Olympia code. Count 1 charged defendant with conspiracy to violate those codes. Counts 2 through 4 charged defendant with violating the CWA and the WAC in 1992, 1993, and 1994. Each count represented a different year. Count 5 charged defendant with violating all three laws in 1995.

After an eight-day trial, the jury found defendant guilty on all counts. Thereafter, the district court sentenced defendant to one year in custody, three years of supervised release, and a $75,000 fine. This timely appeal ensued.

STATUTORY BACKGROUND

As noted, the jury convicted defendant of violating the CWA, the WAC, and the Olympia code. The WAC and the Olympia code are not, by themselves, federal offenses. However, the CWA allows states to administer water pretreatment programs. If the Environmental Protection Agency (EPA) approves a state's regulations, violations of those regulations are treated as federal criminal offenses. On September 30, 1986, the EPA approved the WAC. 51 F.R. 36806.

Similarly, the CWA requires publicly owned treatment works (POTW) to create their own regulatory programs. Those local regulations are deemed pretreatment standards under the CWA. In 1994, the City of Olympia approved its regulatory code. Thus, its provisions state federal offenses. . . .

RESPONSIBLE CORPORATE OFFICER

. . . The district court instructed the jury that it could find defendant liable under the CWA as a "responsible corporate officer" if it found, beyond a reasonable doubt:

> 1. That the defendant had knowledge of the fact that pollutants were being discharged to the sewer system by employees of CH2O, Inc.;
> 2. That the defendant had the authority and capacity to prevent the discharge of pollutants to the sewer system; and
> 3. That the defendant failed to prevent the on-going discharge of pollutants to the sewer system.

Defendant argues that the district court misinterpreted the scope of "responsible corporate officer" liability. Specifically, defendant suggests that a corporate officer is "responsible" only when the officer in fact exercises control over the activity causing the discharge or has an express corporate duty to oversee the activity. We have not previously interpreted the scope of "responsible corporate officer" liability under the CWA. We do so now and reject defendant's narrow interpretation.

"When interpreting a statute, this court looks first to the words that Congress used." The CWA holds criminally liable "any person who . . . knowingly violates" its provisions. The CWA defines the term "person" to include "any responsible corporate officer." However, the CWA does not define the term "responsible corporate officer."

When a statute does not define a term, we generally interpret that term by employing the ordinary, contemporary, and common meaning of the words that Congress used. As pertinent here, the word "responsible" means "answerable" or "involving a degree of accountability." Webster's Third New Int'l Dictionary 1935 (unabridged ed. 1993). Using that meaning, "any corporate officer" who is "answerable" or "accountable" for the unlawful discharge is liable under the CWA.

The history of "responsible corporate officer" liability supports the foregoing construction. The "responsible corporate officer" doctrine originated in a Supreme Court case interpreting the Federal Food, Drug, and Cosmetic Act (FFDCA), *United States v. Dotterweich*, 320 U.S. 277 (1943).

In *Dotterweich*, the president and the general manager of a corporation each argued that he was not a "person" as that term is defined in the FFDCA. The Court disagreed, holding that "[t]he offense is committed . . . by all who do have such a responsible share in the furtherance of the transaction which the statute outlaws." The Court refused to define the boundaries of the doctrine, however, leaving the question for district courts and juries.

Because Congress used a similar definition of the term "person" in the CWA, we can presume that Congress intended that the principles of *Dotterweich* apply under the CWA. Under *Dotterweich*, whether defendant had sufficient "responsibility" over the discharges to be criminally liable would be a question for the jury.

After Congress initially enacted the CWA in 1972, the Supreme Court further defined the scope of the "responsible corporate officer" doctrine under the FFDCA. In *United States v. Park*, 421 U.S. 658 (1975), a corporate president argued that he could not be "responsible" under *Dotterweich*, because he had delegated decision-making control over the activity in question to a subordinate. The Court rejected that argument, holding that

> the Government establishes a prima facie case when it introduces evidence sufficient to warrant a finding by the trier of the facts that the defendant had, by reasons of his position in the corporation, responsibility and authority either to prevent in the first instance or promptly to correct, the violation complained of, and that he failed to do so.

Id. at 673–74. Stated another way, the question for the jury is whether the corporate officer had "authority with respect to the conditions that formed the basis of the alleged violations." The Court did not, however, require the corporate officer actually to exercise any authority over the activity.

In 1987, after the Supreme Court decided *Park*, Congress revised and replaced the criminal provisions of the CWA. (Most importantly, Congress made a violation of the CWA a felony, rather than a misdemeanor.) In replacing the criminal provisions of the CWA, Congress made no changes to its "responsible corporate officer" provision. That being so, we can presume that Congress intended for *Park*'s refinement of the "responsible corporate officer" doctrine to apply under the CWA. . . .

Taken together, the wording of the CWA, the Supreme Court's interpretations of the "responsible corporate officer" doctrine, and this court's interpretation of similar statutory requirements establish the contours of the "responsible corporate officer" doctrine under the CWA. Under the CWA, a person is a "responsible corporate officer" if the person has authority to exercise control over the corporation's activity that is causing the discharges. There is no requirement that the officer in fact exercise such authority or that the corporation expressly vest a duty in the officer to oversee the activity.

E. Underlying Violation of the CWA

Defendant also argues that the "responsible corporate officer" instruction allowed the jury to convict him without finding a violation of the CWA. Defendant's focus is too narrow. The relevant inquiry is whether the instructions as a whole are misleading or inadequate. The district court first instructed the jury that, as to all five counts, the government had to prove that:

> 1. During on or about the dates charged in the indictment, the defendant knowingly caused a pollutant to be discharged to a publicly owned treatment works;
> 2. The discharges were made in violation of a federal or state pretreatment standard, or [for count 5] a requirement of the City of Olympia code; and
> 3. The defendant knew that the material discharged was a pollutant, that is, that it consisted of chemical waste or industrial waste.

The court also told the jury that, "[i]n addition to a defendant who discharges or causes the discharge of pollutants directly [Requirement 1 in the instruction above], the Clean Water Act also holds accountable 'responsible corporate officers.'" Read together with the previous instruction, the "responsible corporate officer" instruction relieved the government only of having to prove that defendant personally discharged or caused the discharge of a pollutant. The government still had to prove that the discharges violated the law and that defendant knew that the discharges were pollutants. Thus, read as a whole, the instructions were not erroneous in the manner that defendant asserts. . . .

AFFIRMED.

- What was the statutory construction rationale for applying the responsible corporate officer doctrine to felony charges under the Clean Water Act?
- What are the policy reasons for applying the responsible corporate officer doctrine to the Clean Water Act's felony provisions?

- Do principles of fundamental fairness argue against applying the responsible corporate officer doctrine to felony crimes? Why or why not?

B. CORPORATE LIABILITY

The liability of a corporation for the acts of its employees is well established in criminal enforcement. The United States Supreme Court recognized in *New York Central & Hudson River R.R. Co. v. United States*, 212 U.S. 481, 494-95 (1909), that a corporation could be held criminally liable for the actions of its agents. It reasoned:

> It is now well established that in actions for tort the corporation may be held responsible for damages for the acts of its agent within the scope of his employment.
>
> And this is the rule when the act is done by the agent in the course of his employment, although done wantonly or recklessly or against the express orders of the principal. In such cases the liability is not imputed because the principal actually participates in the malice or fraud, but [liability is imputed] because the act is done for the benefit of the principal, while the agent is acting within the scope of his employment in the business of the principal.
>
> A corporation is held responsible for acts not within the agent's corporate powers strictly construed, but which the agent has assumed to perform for the corporation when employing the corporate powers actually authorized, and in such cases there need be no written authority under seal or vote of the corporation in order to constitute the agency or to authorize the act. . . .
>
> We see no valid objection in law, and every reason in public policy, why the corporation, which profits by the transaction, and can only act through its agents and officers, shall be held punishable by fine because of the knowledge and intent of its agents to whom it has intrusted authority to act in the subject-matter . . . and whose knowledge and purposes may well be attributed to the corporation for which the agents act. While the law should have regard to the rights of all, and to those of corporations no less than to those of individuals, it cannot shut its eyes to the fact that the great majority of business transactions in modern times are conducted through these bodies . . . and to give them immunity from all punishment because of the old and exploded doctrine that a corporation cannot commit a crime would virtually take away the only means of effectually controlling the subject-matter and correcting the abuses aimed at.

As the Supreme Court stated, to prove corporate liability, the prosecution must show that agent was acting: (1) within the scope of his/her authority, and (2) for the benefit of the corporation. Consider the following cases regarding these two principles.

1. Scope of Authority

United States v. Hilton Hotels Corp.
467 F.2d 1000 (9th Cir. 1972)

BROWNING, Circuit Judge:

. . . Operators of hotels, restaurants, hotel and restaurant supply companies, and other businesses in Portland, Oregon, organized an association to attract conventions to their city. To finance the association, members were asked to make contributions in predetermined amounts. Companies selling supplies to hotels were asked to contribute an amount equal to one per cent of their sales to hotel members. To aid collections, hotel members, including appellant, agreed to give preferential treatment to suppliers who paid their assessments, and to curtail purchases from those who did not.

I

The jury was instructed that such an agreement by the hotel members, if proven, would be a per se violation of the Sherman Act. Appellant argues that this was error.

. . . [A]ppellant requested certain instructions bearing upon the criminal liability of a corporation for the unauthorized acts of its agents. These requests were rejected by the trial court. The court instructed the jury that a corporation is liable for the acts and statements of its agents "within the scope of their employment," defined to mean "in the corporation's behalf in performance of the agent's general line of work," including "not only that which has been authorized by the corporation, but also that which outsiders could reasonably assume the agent would have authority to do." The court added: "A corporation is responsible for acts and statements of its agents, done or made within the scope of their employment, even though their conduct may be contrary to their actual instructions or contrary to the corporation's stated policies."

Appellant objects only to the court's concluding statement.

Congress may constitutionally impose criminal liability upon a business entity for acts or omissions of its agents within the scope of their employment. Such liability may attach without proof that the conduct was within the agent's actual authority, and even though it may have been contrary to express instructions. . . .

Despite the fact that "the doctrine of corporate criminal responsibility for the acts of the officers was not well established in 1890", the Act expressly applies to corporate entities. The preoccupation of Congress with corporate liability was only emphasized by the adoption in 1914 of section 14 of the Clayton Act to reaffirm and emphasize that such liability was not exclusive, and that corporate agents also were subject to punishment if they authorized, ordered, or participated in the acts constituting the violation.

Criminal liability for the acts of agents is more readily imposed under a statute directed at the prohibited act itself, one that does not make specific intent an element of the offense. The Sherman Act is aimed at consequences. Specific intent is not an element of any offense under the Act except attempt to monopolize under section 2, and conscious wrongdoing is not an element of that offense. The

Sherman Act is violated if "a restraint of trade or monopoly results as the consequence of a defendant's conduct or business arrangements."

The breadth and critical character of the public interests protected by the Sherman Act, and the gravity of the threat to those interests that led to the enactment of the statute, support a construction holding business organizations accountable, as a general rule, for violations of the Act by their employees in the course of their businesses. In enacting the Sherman Act, "Congress was passing drastic legislation to remedy a threatening danger to the public welfare. . . ."

With such important public interests at stake, it is reasonable to assume that Congress intended to impose liability upon business entities for the acts of those to whom they choose to delegate the conduct of their affairs, thus stimulating a maximum effort by owners and managers to assure adherence by such agents to the requirements of the Act.

Legal commentators have argued forcefully that it is inappropriate and ineffective to impose criminal liability upon a corporation, as distinguished from the human agents who actually perform the unlawful acts. But it is the legislative judgment that controls, and "the great mass of legislation calling for corporate criminal liability suggests a widespread belief on the part of legislators that such liability is necessary to effectuate regulatory policy." Moreover, the strenuous efforts of corporate defendants to avoid conviction, particularly under the Sherman Act, strongly suggests that Congress is justified in its judgment that exposure of the corporate entity to potential conviction may provide a substantial spur to corporate action to prevent violations by employees.

Because of the nature of Sherman Act offenses and the context in which they normally occur, the factors that militate against allowing a corporation to disown the criminal acts of its agents apply with special force to Sherman Act violations.

Sherman Act violations are commercial offenses. They are usually motivated by a desire to enhance profits. They commonly involve large, complex, and highly decentralized corporate business enterprises, and intricate business processes, practices, and arrangements. More often than not they also involve basic policy decisions, and must be implemented over an extended period of time.

Complex business structures, characterized by decentralization and delegation of authority, commonly adopted by corporations for business purposes, make it difficult to identify the particular corporate agents responsible for Sherman Act violations. At the same time, it is generally true that high management officials, for whose conduct the corporate directors and stockholders are the most clearly responsible, are likely to have participated in the policy decisions underlying Sherman Act violations, or at least to have become aware of them.

Violations of the Sherman Act are a likely consequence of the pressure to maximize profits that is commonly imposed by corporate owners upon managing agents and, in turn, upon lesser employees. In the face of that pressure, generalized directions to obey the Sherman Act, with the probable effect of foregoing profits, are the least likely to be taken seriously. And if a violation of the Sherman Act occurs, the corporation, and not the individual agents, will have realized the profits from the illegal activity.

In sum, identification of the particular agents responsible for a Sherman Act violation is especially difficult, and their conviction and punishment is peculiarly ineffective as a deterrent. At the same time, conviction and punishment of the business entity itself is likely to be both appropriate and effective.

For these reasons we conclude that as a general rule a corporation is liable under the Sherman Act for the acts of its agents in the scope of their employment, even though contrary to general corporate policy and express instructions to the agent. . . .

Affirmed.

- What did the court find were the policy reasons for enacting the Sherman Act?
- How did those policy reasons factor into the court's interpretation of corporate liability?
- Do environmental statutes have the same or similar policy reasons as the Sherman Act for their existence?
- Does the fact that Congress included "corporations" in the definition of "person" in the Clean Water Act, Clean Air Act, RCRA, the Endangered Species Act, and the Lacey Act, among others, show that Congress intended to hold corporations liable for the acts of their employees?
- Is it fair to hold a company criminally liable for the acts of its subordinates even when those employees disobey the rules and procedures of the company?
- Should the law impose at least a negligence standard on companies whose employees commit crimes within the scope of their employment or should the standard be strict liability? V.S. Khanna, *Is the Notion of Corporate Fault a Faulty Notion?: The Case of Corporate Mens Rea,* 79 B.U. L. Rev. 355 (1999).

2. Benefit of the Corporation

United States v. Gold
743 F.2d 800 (11th Cir. 1984)

VANCE, Circuit Judge:

The appellants in this case . . . were convicted in the United States District Court for the Middle District of Florida on charges of conspiracy and defrauding the government through the filing of false Medicare claims. . . .

I. STATEMENT OF FACTS . . .

Opti-Center, Inc. was a Georgia corporation engaged in selling retail eyewear that began doing business in Florida's Tampa Bay area in 1976. Opti-Center had a lease arrangement with Montgomery Ward and operated as the "Montgomery Ward Optical Department" in eight of its stores in and around Tampa. Except for a brief interval in 1980, Columbus optometrist Dr. Donald Gold was the President and majority shareholder of Opti-Center from its inception until its sale to the U.S. Vision Company in 1981. Patricia Warren was Regional Manager for the eight Tampa Bay area stores, with responsibilities that included hiring and firing of personnel, training, coordination, scheduling, and monitoring of inventory. Sue

Conway was an optician who started out as the manager of the Opti-Center unit at the East Lake Square Mall in 1978; she was later promoted to the position of district manager in charge of the Dale Mabry unit and two other stores. Gary Highsmith was another optician who joined Opti-Center in April 1980 and became the manager of Opti-Center's Lakeland store.

The evidence presented at the trial established that Dr. Gold was a hard-driving businessman who carefully supervised almost every detail of Opti-Center's operations. . . .

Dr. Gold followed through on these initial instructions by making occasional inspection tours of his individual stores. Gilbert [an employee] recalled that Dr. Gold would usually stop by four or five times a year. He was often accompanied by Patricia Warren, who in her capacity as regional manager made frequent inspection visits. On these occasions, Gilbert reported, they would quiz the opticians and other salespersons on the use of the sales tract and observe their handling of potential customers. If an employee's knowledge of the sales tract appeared defective, he would be sent home with orders not to return until he had committed it to memory. Dr. Gold and Warren also instructed their salespersons not to wait for potential customers to enter the optical department, but to aggressively seek them out by approaching shoppers as they were passing through the store aisles nearby. Gilbert estimated that "nine out of ten people we sold glasses to were people that were not thinking about buying glasses when they walked into Montgomery Wards'." Dr. Gold's obsessive concern for the bottom line was also reflected by his practice of calling the stores at the end of each day to inquire about the sales figures. Gilbert testified that Warren usually called each of the stores three or four times a day as well, and the store manager would be harshly reprimanded and told to do better if sales were down.

The pressure that Dr. Gold put upon Opti-Center employees to generate ever-increasing sales figures gradually led the company and its personnel into illegal activity. Opti-Center's slide into criminality began in the summer of 1979. Gilbert had been transferred to the Opti-Center unit at Clearwater, where he found that it was often difficult to make sales because the senior citizens who made up most of the store's clientele were usually unable to pay the full purchase price in cash. Gilbert discussed this problem with Warren and suggested that it would be easier to make sales if the company changed its policy against accepting claims on assignment. Dr. Gold approved the change, and the sales figures of the Clearwater store improved dramatically.

One of the principal growth areas at the Clearwater unit was cataract glasses. At some point in the autumn of 1979, Gilbert sold a pair of cataract sunglasses on assignment to a customer who had purchased a pair of regular cataract glasses from him shortly before. When Blue Cross subsequently paid on the assignment, Gilbert realized that he could boost his sales figures by urging customers who came into the store to purchase regular cataract glasses to acquire a pair of cataract sunglasses at the same time. There was a slight hitch, however: Blue Cross proved unwilling to pay for more than one pair of glasses when two pairs were submitted on the same claim form. Warren and Gilbert conferred about this problem, concluded that the computer at Blue Cross was misreading the claim form, and decided to start submitting two separate forms with different dates for the two pairs of glasses. This practice of falsifying one of the dates seemed to take care of the problem, and Opti-Center had no further difficulties collecting from Blue Cross on each pair of glasses.

Because these simultaneous sales of both regular and dark-tinted cataract glasses—known as "double-cataract" sales by company employees—could bring in as much as $450 from a single sale, they soon became a major focus of Gilbert's business. . . .

Nevertheless, Gilbert continued making double cataract sales and soon ventured into other fraudulent practices as well. In addition to spacing out the sales dates on the 1490 forms, Gilbert began changing the prices on glasses that cost the same amount in order to make them appear different from one another. Then he began billing Medicare for more expensive lenses than he had actually provided a customer—such as charging Medicare for bifocal lenses when he had in fact supplied the customer with less expensive single-vision lenses. On some occasions when he had merely changed the lenses within a customer's existing frames, Gilbert billed Medicare for both the lenses and a pair of frames. He also charged Medicare for the cost of mistakes and re-doing lenses that proved unsatisfactory to customers. Gilbert's initiative and productivity were duly rewarded by Opti-Center with several raises before he left the company in the autumn of 1980.

The techniques that Gilbert had pioneered gradually infected the other Opti-Center stores in the Tampa area as Dr. Gold and Warren put pressure on other employees to emulate Gilbert's success. . . .

In the autumn of 1981, the Department of Health and Human Services commenced an investigation into Opti-Center's Medicare billing practices under the direction of Special Agent Frank Cioffi. This investigation ultimately resulted in the indictment and conviction of Dr. Gold, [and] Opti-Center, Inc [among others].

2. Opti-Center

Opti-Center similarly challenges the instruction employed by the district court on the issue of corporate liability. The relevant portion of the charge read as follows:

> To find a corporate defendant guilty, you must find beyond a reasonable doubt that all the essential elements in the offense as set forth in these instructions are present to the corporation in the form of acts or omissions of its agents, which were performed within the scope of their employment. Whether the agents' acts or omissions were committed within the scope of their employment is a question of fact. To be acting within his employment, the agent first must have intended that his act would have produced some benefit to the corporation or some benefit to himself and the corporation second.

Opti-Center's complaint concerns the final sentence cited above, which it asserts is an erroneous statement of the law under *Standard Oil Co. v. United States*, 307 F.2d 120 (5th Cir. 1962). Opti-Center asserts that the district court erred by not adopting its proposed instructions . . . which highlighted the holding in *Standard Oil* that "the purpose to benefit the corporation is decisive in terms of equating the agent's action with that of the corporation." To the extent that Opti-Center's requested instructions implied that an agent had to be acting for the exclusive benefit of the corporation for corporate liability to exist, however, they clearly misstate the law. The court in *Standard Oil* was faced with the question of whether a corporation could be held liable in a case where the criminal acts of its employees "not only did not benefit the employer, but in some instances, at least, result[ed] in a theft of its property." In this case, in contrast, the criminal acts of Opti-Center employees redounded to the benefit of both the corporation (which received the revenues generated by the improper claims) and its employees (who received bonuses based on their sales volume). The district court here therefore faced the question of how to treat the actions of employees who could be simultaneously pursuing both their own interests and those of their corporate employer—a situation which is markedly different from that which faced the *Standard Oil* court. The language employed by the district court here is clearly supported by Prosser's statement that "in general the servant's conduct is within the scope of his employment if it is of the kind he is employed to perform, occurs substantially within the authorized limits of time and space, and is actuated, at least in part, by a purpose to serve the master." Because the charge utilized by the district court both accurately stated the law and properly reflected the distinct facts of this case, we must reject the argument advanced by Opti-Center.

- In the *Gold* case, benefiting the company was merely a means to the end of benefiting the individuals. Should the fact that these employees were benefitting the business only as a means to benefit themselves be relevant in determining whether to hold the corporation liable for the criminal acts of its employees?
- If the fraudulent scheme in *Gold* would have turned out to be a loss to the corporation instead of a huge gain, would corporate liability still be legally valid? Why or why not?[4]
- What level of employee needs to commit the crime in order to subject the company to criminal liability? Must the employee be a manager? What about an entry-level mail room worker?[5]

Although corporate liability has been well established for well over a century, it has been and is still the subject of great debate with many diverse approaches to fix the perceived problems that many see with the current state of the law. Consider the views of former United States Attorney for the Southern District of New York, Preet Bharara, regarding his view of the current state of corporate liability and the viable options to reform it.

---

[4] *United States v. Automated Med. Labs, Inc.*, 770 F.2d 399, 407 (4th Cir. 1985) (holding that business need not profit from employee's criminal act to be convicted under *respondeat superior* liability).

[5] *Standard Oil Co. of Tex. v. United States*, 307 F.2d 120, 127 (5th Cir. 1962) ("[T]he corporation may be criminally bound by the acts of subordinate, even menial employees.").

Preet Bharara, *Corporations Cry Uncle and Their Employees Cry Foul: Rethinking Prosecutorial Pressure on Corporate Defendants*
44 Am. Crim. L. Rev. 53 (2007)

In . . . *United States v. Stein*, a federal judge sharply rebuked the government for, among other things, coercing accounting giant KPMG into interfering with its employees' Sixth Amendment right to counsel and Fifth Amendment right against self-incrimination. In a June 2006 opinion, the court wrote that the government, by virtue of the threat of prosecution, had "held the proverbial gun to [KPMG's] head." . . .

This Article attempts to place the current debate in better jurisprudential perspective and proposes that, notwithstanding the KPMG case, efforts to reduce the risk of prosecutorial excess are, in the long run, better directed at the source of prosecutors' leverage rather than at their conduct. Thus, this Article explains that the "proverbial gun"—though wielded by prosecutors—was licensed and loaded by a century of Supreme Court jurisprudence that has encouraged prosecutors to take dead aim, not just at the individual miscreants responsible for corporate crime, but at the business organizations that employed and arguably enabled them. The courts have obligingly stocked the federal prosecutor's arsenal with legal doctrines whose effect has been to expose business organizations to maximum criminal liability. During the same period, courts have depleted the corporation's available defenses, so that today a business entity faces indictment and almost certain conviction if there is so much as one low-level criminal actor in the organization. This legal state of affairs has been decried by virtually every commentator who has thought to study it.

The literature to date, therefore, reflects two separate but related ongoing debates. One, gaining steam for the better part of only the last decade and culminating in *Stein*, focuses narrowly on perceived prosecutorial excesses in obtaining cooperation from corporations as allegedly encouraged by coercive Justice Department guidelines. The other debate, raging for the better part of the last century, centers more generally on the proper scope of corporate criminal liability.

Participants in the first debate direct virtually all of their attention to the use (and perceived misuse) of prosecutorial discretion, with little discussion of the salutary effect a narrower liability rule might have on the exercise of that discretion. It is, one supposes, easier to lament today's overreaching prosecutors than yesterday's rule-expanding judges. Meanwhile, participants in the second debate seldom consider how their proposals for change might affect the exercise of prosecutorial discretion and whether that effect further militates in favor of the particular proposal. Thus, while many scholars have suggested that the corporate criminal liability rules should be narrowed (or eliminated altogether), none of these proposals is grounded on the premise that a narrower rule would serve as a more reasonable check on the risks of prosecutorial overreaching against corporations and interference with individual defendants' rights and privileges. Indeed, there is little sustained and serious examination of the likelihood and desirability of reining in prosecutorial power through a tightening of the standards for corporate criminal liability rules. . . .

One need not delve too deeply into the literature to discover that the basic rule of corporate criminal liability has few friends. That rule—a vicarious liability principle borrowed wholesale from tort law—states that a business organization is criminally liable for the illegal acts of any of its agents so long as those actions were within the scope of his duties and were intended, even only in part, to benefit the corporation. One writer famously derided the principle of corporate criminal liability with resort to a horticultural metaphor: "Many weeds have grown on the acre of jurisprudence which has been allotted to the criminal law. Among these weeds is . . . corporate criminal liability. . . . Nobody bred it, nobody cultivated it, nobody planted it. It just grew." Another appears to have borrowed from astrophysics, calling the jumbled jurisprudence relating to corporate criminal liability "the blackest hole in the theory of corporate criminal law."

. . . On one point, however, there is virtually unanimous agreement: corporate criminal liability is extremely broad. The implications for that breadth are profound, as it vests prosecutors with extraordinary discretion to threaten not just individual malefactors, but the corporations that employ them. On one hand, that discretion gives prosecutors unparalleled ability to identify and prevent corporate crime, whose effects can be devastating to large numbers of people. On the other hand, such vast discretion can threaten the functioning of entire industries and subject work forces the size of cities to unemployment as a collateral consequence of a prosecutor's choice simply to do what the law permits.

At various moments, the Supreme Court has had opportunities to restrain the expansion of corporate criminal liability, or at least uphold checks on the discretion and tools used by prosecutors. Those moments have mostly gone unseized. . . .

Thus, in the present day, the basic rule of respondeat superior announced in *New York Central*, combined with the doctrine of collective knowledge, has come to mean the following: A corporation is criminally liable even if the criminal conduct is undertaken without the knowledge of top management; the criminal activity was performed by a low level employee; the primary purpose was to benefit only the miscreant employee; there was no actual benefit to the corporation; the criminal acts were performed in direct violation of instructions from the company; there is a rigorous compliance program in place; no single individual had the requisite intent or knowledge sufficient to violate the law; it is never possible to identify the actual employee or agent responsible for the crime; or the offending employees are all acquitted of the same offense.

Accordingly, under these longstanding rules, a multinational corporation may theoretically be indicted, convicted, and perhaps put out of business based on the alleged criminal activity of a single, low-level, rogue employee who was acting without the knowledge of any executive or director, in violation of well-publicized procedures, practices, and instructions of the company. And the corporation's conviction will stand even if the rogue worker is himself acquitted of wrongdoing. Although in practice . . . prosecutors rarely indict corporations, the risk of overreaching is real. . . . [The article then discusses the long-standing judicial authority stating that corporations lack a right against self-incrimination under the Fifth Amendment of the Constitution and how courts have ruled that the government can subpoena one-person-owned companies to obtain records that will incriminate the owner without violating the Fifth Amendment.] . . .

As an initial matter, one proposed reform, the elimination of all criminal liability for business entities, would completely eviscerate prosecutors' leverage against corporations to obtain incriminating information about individual miscreants. Such an extreme proposal fails to comport with the widespread view that corporations, as entities, can be blameworthy in at least certain circumstances, and a purely civil liability regime in which corporations will have less incentive to self-police is not ideal, as many writers have argued. Accordingly, any proposal to eliminate all criminal liability for corporations, apart from other failings, gives corporations an unsatisfactorily free hand, merely transferring to business entities the leverage that prosecutors now enjoy. In any event, given overwhelming public, Congressional, and judicial support for the idea of corporate criminal liability, its elimination has little possibility of gaining acceptance in the foreseeable future.

Three other approaches—which can be loosely termed the corporate culture, Model Penal Code ("MPC"), and corporate compliance approaches—offer more promise for our purposes. First, the corporate culture approach to tightening the rules of liability is typified in an influential article by Pamela Bucy. Her approach builds on the substantial literature exposing the incoherence of a criminal liability system that renders artificial persons indictable without any proof that the entity . . . had the requisite mens rea to be criminally culpable. Bucy overcomes the difficulties of attributing mens rea and assigning blame to a soulless, artificial entity by developing a corporate "ethos" theory, in which the "ethos" of the firm serves as a reasonable substitute for mental state, and by which prosecutors, juries, judges, and the public can identify the blameworthiness of the corporation.

Criticisms of this approach are manifold. Critics contend, among other things, that the inherent amorphousness of "corporate ethos" renders a clear liability standard unattainable. . . . Moreover, Bucy's proposal may unduly increase the government's burdens of litigation and discovery. . . .

A second potential method of tightening the broad corporate criminal liability rule—which would require Congressional action—is reflected in the American Law Institute's approach in the Model Penal Code ("MPC"). . . . The MPC approach sprang in part from concern over the rash of inconsistent verdicts in which juries convicted the corporation while acquitting individual defendants under the vicarious liability rule. It purports to limit the breadth of the vicarious liability rule largely by calling for criminal liability only where felony crimes requiring intent were "authorized, requested, commanded, [or] performed . . . by a high managerial agent acting in behalf of the corporation within the scope of his office or employment." . . .

. . . Some commentators find that the MPC approach retains much of the flawed nature of the vicarious liability rule without offering much improvement. Moreover, it is suggested that the MPC approach, where followed, has had the undesirable effect of "afford[ing] organizations protection from criminal liability for acts of deliberate indifference by high managerial agents." . . .

Finally, a number of proposals, which might be grouped under the rubric of corporate compliance, contain some of the attributes of both the corporate ethos and MPC approaches. The central feature of the compliance policy approach is the availability to an indicted corporation of some consideration at trial for the existence of a corporate compliance program designed to police misconduct and prevent wrongdoing. Such consideration is, in most circumstances, unavailable under current law and often identified as one of the most egregious excesses of the current liability standard. Thus, . . . many courts have excluded as irrelevant any evidence of a compliance program from the jury.

Th[is] approach[], too, [is] no stranger[] to criticisms. Chief among them is the risk that the creation of a compliance program affirmative defense will allow companies to immunize themselves from liability by simply establishing such programs. . . . Recognizing that "the threat of liability under respondeat superior also provides an important deterrent," institution of a compliance program defense risks creating a system of under-deterrence. . . .

[T]he compliance approach may hold the most promise for a number of reasons. First, it . . . provides more guidance than the corporate culture approach, as the concreteness of a compliance program seems more likely to influence the prosecutor-corporation dynamic than an amorphous corporate culture paradigm. Second, . . . it may transfer some of the power from "unaccountable" prosecutors to a judge and jury to determine questions relating to the relevance, aggressiveness, and efficacy of a corporate compliance program. Over time, moreover, courts can be expected to develop more detailed parameters regarding the necessary features of a compliance program. This will ultimately provide better notice and guidance to corporations attempting to develop such programs and to those corporations that become targets, which are trying to decide whether to cooperate and how much to give up in doing so. . . .

- Why do you think that courts have been so quick to both expand corporate criminal liability and limit corporate defenses over the years?
- Do you think that courts have gone too far?
- Does this place too much power in the hands of the prosecutor?
- If corporate liability and prosecutorial discretion are too broad, what can be done to fix the problem?

CHAPTER 5

WATER POLLUTION

Protecting the nation's water resources from pollutants that would create navigation and health hazards has concerned Congress since the late nineteenth century. In 1899, Congress enacted the Rivers and Harbors Act, which, among other things, established misdemeanor offenses for obstructing navigable waters and for depositing refuse in navigable waters or along their banks. This law is still used today. For example, as discussed further below, the Clean Water Act (i.e., 33 U.S.C. § 1344) prohibits a person from depositing fill and dredged spoil into waters of the United States. However, § 1344 does not regulate dredging navigable waters of the United States themselves. Instead, Congress left that issue to § 403 of the Rivers and Harbors Act of 1899. Specifically, § 403 provides:

> The creation of any obstruction not affirmatively authorized by Congress, to the navigable capacity of any of the waters of the United States is prohibited . . . and it shall not be lawful to excavate or fill, or in any manner to alter or modify the course, location, condition, or capacity of, any port, roadstead, haven, harbor, canal, lake, harbor or refuge, or inclosure within the limits of any breakwater, or of the channel of any navigable water of the United States, unless the work has been recommended by the Chief of Engineers and authorized by the Secretary of the Army prior to beginning the same.

To impose criminal penalties for violating this provision, Congress further provided that "[e]very person and every corporation that shall violate [§ 403, among others] . . . shall be deemed guilty of a misdemeanor, and on conviction thereof shall be punished by a fine . . . or by imprisonment (in the case of a natural person) not exceeding one year, or by both. . . ." 33 U.S.C. § 406. What are the elements of this offense? Is this a strict liability offense or does the prosecution have to prove a particular mens rea?

In one potential answer to the latter question, the Eastern District of Michigan stated that the United States must prove that a defendant knowingly violated § 403 even though, on its face, there is no mens rea mentioned. *United States v. Commodore Club, Inc.*, 418 F. Supp. 311, 319-20 (E.D. Mich. 1976). In that case, the court reasoned that strict liability was not a proper standard because it did not believe that "the lack of explicit words of scienter from § 403 compels the deduction that no scienter element is required. If an offense carries a requirement of specific intent, proper words of scienter must be found in the statute; however, scienter may be that of general intent and it is common for codified common law and statutory offenses requiring general intent to omit reference to that element." Based on what you have learned about mens rea, is this a reasonable conclusion?

Additionally, the Rivers and Harbors Act of 1899 prohibited depositing refuse into navigable waters or along their banks. Specifically, Congress provided:

> It shall not be lawful to throw, discharge, or deposit, or cause, suffer, or procure to be thrown, discharged, or deposited either from or out of any ship, barge, or other floating craft of any kind, or from the shore, wharf, manufacturing establishment, or mill of any kind, any refuse matter of any kind or description whatever other than that flowing from streets and sewers and passing therefrom in a liquid state, into any navigable water of the United States, or into any tributary of any navigable water from which the same shall float or be washed into such navigable water; and it shall not be lawful to deposit, or cause, suffer, or procure to be deposited material of any kind in any place on the bank of any navigable water, or on the bank of any tributary of any navigable water, where the same shall be liable to be washed into such navigable water, either by ordinary or high tides, or by storms or floods, or otherwise, whereby navigation shall or may be impeded or obstructed. . . .

33 U.S.C. § 407. Congress further stated that violating § 407, among other sections, is a misdemeanor punished by a "fine up to $25,000 per day or by imprisonment . . . not less than thirty days nor more than one year, or both [with] one half of said fine to be paid to the person or persons giving information which shall lead to conviction." 33 U.S.C. § 411. What are the elements of this offense? What is the requisite mens rea? Is there a difference between this misdemeanor provision and the one in § 403 and § 406?

Unlike the Eastern District of Michigan in *Commodore Club*, numerous courts have held that violating § 407 is a strict liability offense. For example, in *United States v. White Fuel Corp.*, 498 F.2d 619, 622-24 (1st Cir. 1974), the defendant, White Fuel Corp., operated a tank farm in part of the Boston harbor, which, obviously, is a navigable water of the United States. The Coast Guard found oil in the water of the cove, and White Fuel

> immediately undertook to clean up the oil and to trace its source. Although at first an oil-water separator and later a leaky pipe were suspected, experts called in by White Fuel finally determined that the oil was seeping from an immense accumulation (approximately half a million gallons) which had gathered under White Fuel's property. White Fuel concedes, and the court found, that it owned the oil, which continued to seep into the cove throughout the summer of 1972 even though White Fuel worked diligently to drain or divert the accumulation. By September it was successful and seepage had ceased. As part of its clean-up efforts,

and to prevent the oil from spreading, White Fuel had installed booms across the mouth of the cove. There was testimony that on occasion these booms were tended improperly, so that some of the oil drifted out into the channel.

The district court found that the seepage was a violation of the Refuse Act and imposed a $1,000 fine. The court denied White Fuel's motion for judgment of acquittal and, ruling that intent or scienter is irrelevant to guilt, also denied White Fuel's offer to present evidence that it had not known of the underground deposit, had not appreciated its hazards, and had acted diligently when the deposit became known. The court held that White Fuel's only defense would be to show that third parties caused the oil seepage- that 'this oil escaped from a source other than that under the control of the defendant'. White Fuel contends that the government was required to prove scienter or at least negligence as part of its case, and that the court erred by precluding the proffered defense.

Id. at 621.

The First Circuit agreed with the district court insofar as no mens rea was required. The court reasoned:

In the seventy-five years since enactment, no court to our knowledge has held that there must be proof of scienter; to the contrary, the Refuse Act has commonly been termed a strict liability statute. The offense falls within the category of public welfare offenses which

'are not in the nature of positive aggressions or invasions, with which the common law so often dealt, but are in the nature of neglect where the law requires care, or inaction where it imposes a duty. . . . The accused, if he does not will the violation, usually is in a position to prevent it with no more care than society might reasonably expect and no more exertion than it might reasonably exact from one who assumed his responsibilities.' *Morissette v. United States*, 342 U.S. 246, 255-56 (1952).

We do not accept White Fuel's further argument that if the government need not prove scienter it must at least prove negligence. Actually, merely by showing that White Fuel's oil escaped into public waters, the government presented facts from which negligence could be inferred. The real issue is not the government's prima facie case, which was sufficient by any standard, but whether due care—lack of negligence—is available as a defense. In the [Clean Water Act], Congress imposed criminal penalties only upon any person who 'willfully or negligently' violates its prohibitions, but provided civil penalties for all violations. In the Refuse Act, on the other hand, Congress made no such distinction. . . . The dominant purpose is to require people to exercise whatever diligence they must to keep refuse out of public waters. Given this aim, we are disinclined to invent defenses beyond those necessary to ensure a defendant constitutional due process. Specifically we reject the existence of any generalized 'due care' defense that would allow a polluter to avoid conviction on the ground that he took precautions conforming to industry-wide or commonly accepted standards.

Id. at 622.

Ironically, the courts in *White Fuel* and *Commodore Club* relied on the same Supreme Court decision to reach opposite conclusions regarding whether the prosecution must prove mens rea or whether each offense is strict liability. Does it make sense to require a knowing mens rea for violations of § 403 but to allow strict liability for violations of § 407? Given the strict liability component of the Rivers and Harbors Act, it remains a viable part of criminal enforcement against water pollution. In fact, when the United States prosecuted Exxon for the catastrophic oil spill from the *Exxon Valdez*, the company pled guilty to violations of the Rivers and Harbors Act. Another reason that the Rivers and Harbors Act remains a viable enforcement mechanism is because Congress increased fines for all crimes in the Alternative Fines Act, 18 U.S.C. § 3571, which made violations of the Rivers and Harbors Act far more expensive.

Although Congress's work in 1899 provided and still provides a useful tool for combating water pollution, it was inadequate for at least three reasons. First, enforcement of the Act was sparse, which resulted in direct discharges of pollutants with impunity into waters of the United States. These discharges led to iconic photos such as the Cuyahoga River in Cleveland, Ohio catching fire. This happened 13 times on the Cuyahoga River alone between the 1860s and the late twentieth century.[1] Sadly, this was not the only waterway that was that heavily polluted in the United States.

Second, the Rivers and Harbors Act of 1899 did not regulate sewage discharges into waters of the United States. In fact, the Act specifically excluded liquid "flowing from streets and sewers" as refuse, which entirely exempted those discharges from regulation. Given the vast amount of waste that our modern sewer and storm-drain systems handle and discharge into waters of the United States, exempting them from regulation ignores a major source of water pollution.

Finally, the minimal fines for dredging and filling wetlands did not serve as an adequate deterrent to the destruction of ecologically important wetlands. The new construction that occurred on these newly filled in wetlands then increased the population in the area and, consequently, the load on sewers, storm drains, and, waters of the United States. To address these issues, Congress enacted the Federal Water Pollution Control Act (a.k.a. the Clean Water Act) in 1972. 33 U.S.C. §§ 1251 et seq.

To strengthen enforcement of these regulatory systems, Congress eventually enacted felony criminal provisions to address all three: direct discharges into waters of the United States; publicly owned treatment works (i.e., sewer systems);

---

[1] For more information on this hot topic, see Julie Grant, *How a Burning River Helped Create the Clean Water Act*, The Allegheny Front (Apr. 21, 2017), https://www.alleghenyfront.org/how-a-burning-river-helped-create-the-clean-water-act/.

and wetlands. Congress imposed a maximum of a three-year prison term and substantial fines for a first offense, with double prison times and fines for a second offense. 33 U.S.C. § 1319(c)(2)(B). Additionally, Congress was aware that violations of those three provisions could, at times, inflict significant injury or death on the public. Consequently, Congress established the crime of knowing endangerment, which carried up to 15 years in prison and a $1 million fine for the first conviction. 33 U.S.C. § 1319(c)(3)(A). Finally, in the new criminal provisions of the Clean Water Act, Congress knew that there would be those who would attempt to cheat the Clean Water Act's ample regulatory system. Therefore, Congress enacted felony provisions carrying up to two years in prison and hefty fines to punish those who falsify or tamper with the information gathering on which the enforcement system depends. 33 U.S.C. § 1319(c)(4). Each of these five criminal categories is discussed below.

A. DIRECT DISCHARGES

For our purposes, the phrase "direct discharge" refers to pollutants that are added to water without first traversing a sewer or other pretreatment system. For example, direct discharges include a septic tank vacuum truck dumping its contents directly into a river or a chemical waste pipe from a factory discharging directly into the ocean. In either instance, there are pollutants going directly from their source into water. The Clean Water Act established a significant regulatory system to address direct discharges. Specifically, Congress established the National Pollution Discharge Elimination System (NPDES), which required those directly discharging pollutants into the waters of the United States from a point source to first obtain a permit either from the EPA directly or from a state to which the EPA had delegated permitting authority. In fact, Congress prohibited "the discharge of any pollutant" unless that "person" has an NPDES permit or an equivalent permit from a state to which the EPA has delegated permitting authority. 33 U.S.C. § 1311(a). Both NPDES and EPA-authorized state permits are federally enforceable. 33 U.S.C. § 1319(c)(1)(A), (2)(A). The criminal provisions of the Clean Water Act penalize "any person who negligently" or "knowingly" violates 33 U.S.C. § 1311, among other sections. 33 U.S.C. § 1319(c)(1), (2).

To determine whether a violation of § 1311(a) has occurred—to say nothing of whether the violation was "negligent" or "knowing"—the statutory definitions matter greatly. Congress defined "person" broadly to include "an individual, corporation, partnership, association, State, municipality, commission, or political subdivision of a State, or any interstate body." 33 U.S.C. § 1362(5). To determine whether one of the entities defined as a "person" actually discharged pollutants, courts look to 33 U.S.C. § 1362(12), which provides:

> The term "discharge of a pollutant" and the term "discharge of pollutants" each means (A) any addition of any *pollutant* to *navigable waters* from any *point source*, (B) any addition of any *pollutant* to the waters of the contiguous zone or the ocean from any *point source* other than a vessel or other floating craft.

(Emphasis added.) The definition of "discharge of a pollutant" reflects the complexity of environmental law because in order to understand it, one must consult additional definitions within the statute. To figure out whether there has been a "discharge of a pollutant," one must first determine whether the material that was "added" into a water body is a "pollutant" that emanated from a "point source" and that the water body the pollutant ended up in is "navigable." Each of these terms have a life of their own. If a discharge of a pollutant has occurred, then § 1311 has been violated if the discharge was done without or in violation of an NPDES permit or its EPA-approved state equivalent. Recall that for criminal enforcement purposes, in addition to establishing all of these elements, the central issue will be whether the defendant acted "knowingly" or "negligently." Each of these issues are addressed in greater detail below.

1. Pollutant

The Clean Water Act defines "pollutant" as: "dredged spoil, solid waste, incinerator residue, sewage, garbage, sewage sludge, munitions, chemical wastes, biological materials, radioactive materials, heat, wrecked or discarded equipment, rock, sand, cellar dirt and industrial, municipal, and agricultural waste discharged into water." 33 U.S.C. § 1362(6). Although the definition of the term "pollutant" includes many categories,[2] it is restrictive because, unlike the definition of "point source," the definition of "pollutant" does not contain the phrase "including but not limited to." Consequently, any material alleged to be added to water must fall within one of the categories listed in the aforementioned definition (e.g., solid waste, heat, etc.) in order to qualify as a pollutant under the statute. Recognizing this limitation is important in criminal enforcement because an indictment, misdemeanor information, and jury instructions should make clear that the pollutant alleged to have been discharged falls into one of the aforementioned statutory categories.

For example, suppose that a riverboat crew on the Ohio River maintains trash barrels on the boat to collect the daily garbage that the crew generates. Every two or three days, the crew burns the garbage within the trash barrels and empties their charred contents into the Ohio River. Is the burned material from the trash barrels a "pollutant"? If so, which category of pollutant is it? If you represent the United States, how would you phrase the charge in an indictment for the grand jury to consider?

2. Point Source

The term "point source" is defined in the Clean Water Act as "any discernible, confined and discrete conveyance, *including but not limited to* any pipe, ditch, channel, tunnel, conduit, well, discrete fissure, container, rolling stock, concentrated animal feeding operation, or vessel or other floating craft, from which pollutants are or may be discharged." 33 U.S.C. § 1362(14) (emphasis added).

---

[2] *United States v. M/G Trans. Servs., Inc.*, 173 F.3d 584, 590 (6th Cir. 1999) ("The term 'pollutant' is . . . very broadly defined in the Clean Water Act.").

Given that this definition is not restrictive like "pollutant," courts have concluded that the definition of "'point source' was designed to further the [Clean Water Act] scheme by embracing the broadest possible definition of any identifiable conveyance. . . ."[3] For example, courts have held that bulldozers and backhoes are point sources under the Clean Water Act. *Avoyelles Sportsmen's League, Inc. v. Marsh*, 715 F.2d 897, 923-25 (5th Cir. 1983); *United States v. Weisman*, 489 F. Supp. 1331, 1337 (M.D. Fla. 1980) ("[I]t is clear that . . . bulldozers and dump trucks are point sources."). However, not all courts have interpreted this definition so broadly.

United States v. Plaza Health Laboratories, Inc.
3 F.3d 643 (2d Cir. 1993)

GEORGE C. PRATT, Circuit Judge:

Defendant Geronimo Villegas appeals from a judgment . . . convicting him of two counts of knowingly discharging pollutants into the Hudson River in violation of the Clean Water Act ("CWA"). *See* 33 U.S.C. §§ 1311 and 1319(c)(2). . . .

FACTS AND BACKGROUND

Villegas was co-owner and vice president of Plaza Health Laboratories, Inc., a blood-testing laboratory in Brooklyn, New York. On at least two occasions between April and September 1988, Villegas loaded containers of numerous vials of human blood generated from his business into his personal car, and drove to his residence at the Admirals Walk Condominium in Edgewater, New Jersey. Once at his condominium complex, Villegas removed the containers from his car and carried them to the edge of the Hudson River. On one occasion he carried two containers of the vials to the bulkhead that separates his condominium complex from the river, and placed them at low tide within a crevice in the bulkhead that was below the high-water line.

On May 26, 1988, a group of eighth graders on a field trip at the Alice Austin House in Staten Island, New York, discovered numerous glass vials containing human blood along the shore. Some of the vials had washed up on the shore; many were still in the water. Some were cracked, although most remained sealed with stoppers in solid-plastic containers or ziplock bags. Fortunately, no one was injured. That afternoon, New York City workers recovered approximately 70 vials from the area.

On September 25, 1988, a maintenance worker employed by the Admirals Walk Condominium discovered a plastic container holding blood vials wedged between rocks in the bulkhead. New Jersey authorities retrieved numerous blood vials from the bulkhead later that day.

Ten of the retrieved vials contained blood infected with the hepatitis-B virus. All of the vials recovered were eventually traced to Plaza Health Laboratories.

Based upon the May 1988 discovery of vials, Plaza Health Laboratories and Villegas were indicted on May 16, 1989, on two counts each of violating §§ 1319(c)(2) and (3) of the Clean Water Act. A superseding indictment charged both

[3] *United States v. Earth Sciences, Inc.*, 599 F.2d 368, 373 (10th Cir. 1979).

defendants with two additional CWA counts based upon the vials found in September 1988. . . .

Counts II and IV of the superseding indictment charged Villegas with knowingly discharging pollutants from a "point source" without a permit. *See* 33 U.S.C. §§ 1311(a), 1319(c)(2). [The other counts charged Villegas with knowingly endangering others, which will be discussed later.] On January 31, 1991, following a trial before Judge Korman, the jury found Villegas guilty. . . .

Renewing a motion made at trial, Villegas moved for a judgment of acquittal on all counts under rule 29 of the Federal Rules of Criminal Procedure. . . . The district judge denied the motion on counts II and IV, rejecting arguments that the act did not envision a human being as a "point source".

Judge Korman sentenced Villegas on counts II and IV to two concurrent terms of twelve months' imprisonment, one year of supervised release, and a $100 special assessment. Execution of the sentence was stayed pending this appeal.

Villegas contends that one element of the CWA crime, knowingly discharging pollutants from a "point source", was not established in his case. He argues that the definition of "point source", 33 U.S.C. § 1362(14), does not include discharges that result from the individual acts of human beings. Raising primarily questions of legislative intent and statutory construction, Villegas argues that at best, the term "point source" is ambiguous as applied to him, and that the rule of lenity should result in reversal of his convictions. . . .

DISCUSSION

Because "discharge from a point source" is an essential element of a "knowing" violation . . . [w]e therefore consider the "point source" issue first.

A. Navigating the Clean Water Act

The basic prohibition on discharge of pollutants is in 33 U.S.C. § 1311(a), which states:

> Except as in compliance with this section and sections 1312, 1316, 1317, 1328, 1342, and 1344 of this title, the discharge of any pollutant by any person shall be unlawful.

Id.

The largest exception to this seemingly absolute rule is found in 33 U.S.C. § 1342, which establishes the CWA's national pollutant discharge elimination system, or NPDES:

> (a) Permits for discharge of pollutants
> (1) Except as provided in sections 1328 [aquaculture] and 1344 of this title [dredge and fill permits], the Administrator may, after opportunity for public hearing, issue a permit for the discharge of any pollutant * * * notwithstanding section 1311(a) of this title, upon condition that such discharge will meet * * * all applicable requirements under sections 1311, 1312, 1316, 1317, 1318, and 1343 of this title * * *.

33 U.S.C. § 1342(a).

Reading § 1311(a), the basic prohibition, and § 1342(a)(1), the permit section, together, we can identify the basic rule, our rhumb line to clean waters, that, absent a permit, "the discharge of any pollutant by any person" is unlawful. 33 U.S.C. § 1311(a).

We must then adjust our rhumb line by reference to two key definitions—"pollutant" and "discharge". "Pollutant" is defined, in part, as "biological materials * * * discharged into water." 33 U.S.C. § 1362(6). "Discharge", in turn, is "any addition of any pollutant to navigable waters from any point source * * *." 33 U.S.C. § 1362(12).

As applied to the facts of this case, then, the defendant "added" a "pollutant" (human blood in glass vials) to "navigable waters" (the Hudson River), and he did so without a permit. The issue, therefore, is whether his conduct constituted a "discharge", and that in turn depends on whether the addition of the blood to the Hudson River waters was "from any point source".

For this final course adjustment in our navigation, we look again to the statute.

> (14) The term "point source" means any discernible, confined and discrete conveyance, including but not limited to any pipe, ditch, channel, tunnel, conduit, well, discrete fissure, container, rolling stock, concentrated animal feeding operation, or vessel or other floating craft, from which pollutants are or may be discharged. This term does not include agricultural stormwater discharges and return flows from irrigated agriculture.

33 U.S.C. § 1362(14).

During and after Villegas's trial, Judge Korman labored over how to define "point source" in this case. At one point he observed that the image of a human being is not "conjured up" by congress's definition of "point source". Ultimately, he never defined the "point source" element but he did charge the jury:

> Removing pollutants from a container, and a vehicle is a container, parked next to a navigable body of water and physically throwing the pollutant into the water constitutes a discharge from a point source.

In ruling on Villegas's rule 29 motion, however, Judge Korman held that the element "point source" may reasonably be read

> to include any discrete and identifiable conduit—*including a human being*—designated to collect or discharge pollutants produced in the course of a waste-generating activity. (emphasis added).

As the parties have presented the issue to us in their briefs and at oral argument, the question is "whether a human being can be a point source". Both sides focus on the district court's conclusion in its rule 29 memorandum that, among other things, the requisite "point source" here could be Villegas himself.

Significantly, the jury was never clearly instructed on this legal theory, and the instruction actually given bordered on an improper removal of the determination of an essential element of the crime from the jury's consideration. Serious problems might be presented by the government's attempt to justify Judge Korman's post-verdict definitional efforts as an alternate theory upon which to uphold Villegas's convictions.

However, far more fundamental than any error in jury instructions is the problem highlighted by the district court's analytical struggle to find somewhere in the Villegas transaction a "discernible, confined and discrete conveyance". Simply put, that problem is that this statute was never designed to address the random, individual polluter like Villegas.

To determine the scope of the CWA's "point source" definition, we first consider the language and structure of the act itself. If the language is not plain, an excursion into legislative history and context may prove fruitful. Judicial interpretations of the term can be instructive as well, as may be interpretive statements by the agency in charge of implementing the statute. If we conclude after this analysis that the statute is ambiguous as applied to Villegas, then the rule of lenity may apply.

1. Language and Structure of Act

Human beings are not among the enumerated items that may be a "point source". Although by its terms the definition of "point source" is nonexclusive, the words used to define the term and the examples given ("pipe, ditch, channel, tunnel, conduit, well, discrete fissure", etc.) evoke images of physical structures and instrumentalities that systematically act as a means of conveying pollutants from an industrial source to navigable waterways.

In addition, if every discharge involving humans were to be considered a "discharge from a point source", the statute's lengthy definition of "point source" would have been unnecessary. It is elemental that Congress does not add unnecessary words to statutes. Had Congress intended to punish any human being who polluted navigational waters, it could readily have said: "any person who places pollutants in navigable waters without a permit is guilty of a crime."

The Clean Water Act generally targets industrial and municipal sources of pollutants, as is evident from a perusal of its many sections. Consistent with this focus, the term "point source" is used throughout the statute, but invariably in sentences referencing industrial or municipal discharges. *See, e.g.,* 33 U.S.C. § 1311 (referring to "owner or operator" of point source); § 1311(e) (requiring that effluent limitations established under the Act "be applied to all point sources of discharge"); § 1311(g)(2) (allows an "owner or operator of a point source" to apply to EPA for modification of its limitations requirements); § 1342(f) (referring to classes, categories, types, and sizes of point sources); § 1314(b)(4)(B) (denoting "best conventional pollutant control technology measures and practices" applicable to any point source within particular category or class); § 1316 ("any point source * * * which is constructed as to meet all applicable standards of performance"); § 1318(a) (administrator shall require owner or operator of any point source to install, use and maintain monitoring equipment or methods); and § 1318(c) (states may develop procedures for inspection, monitoring, and entry with respect to point sources located in state).

This emphasis was sensible, as "[i]ndustrial and municipal point sources were the worst and most obvious offenders of surface water quality. They were also the easiest to address because their loadings emerge from a discrete point such as the end of a pipe."

Finally on this point, we assume that Congress did not intend the awkward meaning that would result if we were to read "human being" into the definition of "point source". Section 1362(12)(A) defines "discharge of a pollutant" as "any addition of any pollutant to navigable waters from any point source". Enhanced by this definition, § 1311(a) reads in effect "the addition of any pollutant to navigable waters *from any point source by any person* shall be unlawful" (emphasis added). But were a human being to be included within the definition of "point source", the prohibition would then read: "the addition of any pollutant to navigable waters from any person by any person shall be unlawful", and this simply makes no sense. As the statute stands today, the term "point source" is comprehensible only if it is held to the context of industrial and municipal discharges.

2. Legislative History and Context

The broad remedial purpose of the CWA is to "restore and maintain the chemical, physical, and biological integrity of the Nation's waters". 33 U.S.C. § 1251(a). The narrow questions posed by this case, however, may not be resolved merely by simple reference to this admirable goal. . . .

The legislative history of the CWA, while providing little insight into the meaning of "point source", confirms the act's focus on industrial polluters. Congress required NPDES permits of those who discharge from a "point source". The term "point source", introduced to the act in 1972, was intended to function as a means of identifying industrial polluters—generally a difficult task because pollutants quickly disperse throughout the subject waters. The senate report for the 1972 amendments explains:

> In order to further clarify the scope of the regulatory procedures in the Act the Committee had added a definition of point source to distinguish between control requirements where there are specific confined conveyances, such as pipes, and control requirements which are imposed to control runoff. The control of pollutants from runoff is applied pursuant to section 209 and the authority resides in the State or other local agency.

S. Rep. No. 92-414, reprinted in 1972 U.S.C.C.A.N. 3668, 3744.

Senator Robert Dole added his comments to the committee report:

> Most of the problems of agricultural pollution deal with non-point sources. Very simply, a non-point source of pollution is one that does not confine its polluting discharge to one fairly specific outlet, such as a sewer pipe, a drainage ditch or a conduit; thus, a feedlot would be considered to be a non-point source as would pesticides and fertilizers.

Id. at 3760 (supplemental views).

We find no suggestion either in the act itself or in the history of its passage that Congress intended the CWA to impose criminal liability on an individual for the myriad, random acts of human waste disposal, for example, a passerby who flings a candy wrapper into the Hudson River, or a urinating swimmer. Discussions during the passage of the 1972 amendments indicate that Congress had bigger fish to fry.

The 1972 congress modeled the NPDES, its aggressive new permitting program, after the Rivers and Harbors Act of 1899 ("RHA"; known also as the Refuse Act. The CWA's focus on transporting pollutants to navigable waters via the "point source" mechanism represented a departure from the RHA's more general approach:

> It shall not be lawful to throw, discharge, or deposit * * * any refuse matter of any kind or description whatever other than that flowing from streets and sewers and passing therefrom in a liquid state, into any navigable water of the United States * * *.

33 U.S.C. § 407.

Unlike §§ 1311 and 1319(c)(2) of the CWA, the RHA's relevant criminal provision, 33 U.S.C. § 411, has been held to provide for strict liability, and the most severe criminal penalty is a misdemeanor. *United States v. White Fuel Corp.*, 498 F.2d 619, 622 (1st Cir. 1974). Accordingly, we view with skepticism the government's contention that we should broadly construe the greatly magnified penal provisions of the CWA based upon RHA cases that did so in the context of strict-liability and misdemeanor penalties.

3. Caselaw

Our search for the meaning of "point source" brings us next to judicial constructions of the term.

The "point source" element was clearly established in the few CWA criminal decisions under § 1319(c) that are reported.

With the exception of *Oxford Royal Mushroom*, the cases that have interpreted "point source" have done so in civil-penalty or licensing settings, where greater flexibility of interpretation to further remedial legislative purposes is permitted, and the rule of lenity does not protect a defendant against statutory ambiguities. *See, e.g., Avoyelles Sportsmen's League, Inc. v. Marsh*, 715 F.2d 897, 922 (5th Cir. 1983) ("point source" includes bulldozing equipment that discharged dredged materials onto wetland).

For example, our circuit recently held in *Dague v. City of Burlington*, a civil-penalty case, that a discharge of pollutant-laden leachate into a culvert leading to navigable waters was through a "point source". 935 F.2d 1343, 1354–55 (2d Cir. 1991), rev'd in part on other grounds, 505 U.S. 557 (1992). But in *Dague*, unlike in this case, the city's discharge involved a culvert, one of the specifically enumerated examples of a "point source" set forth in § 1362(14). *Dague* thus presented a classic "point source" discharge.

The government relies on broad dicta in another civil case, *United States v. Earth Sciences, Inc.*, 599 F.2d 368, 373 (10th Cir. 1979), in which the court held "[t]he concept of a point source was designed to further this [permit regulatory] scheme by embracing the broadest possible definition of any identifiable conveyance from which pollutants might enter the waters of the United States." We do not find this *Earth Sciences* dicta persuasive here, however, because that court found a "point source" in a ditch used in the mining operation—certainly not a far leap when "ditch" also is an expressly listed example of a "point source". We cannot, however, make the further leap of writing "human being" into the statutory language without doing violence to the language and structure of the CWA.

4. Regulatory Structure

Finally, not even the EPA's regulations support the government's broad assertion that a human being may be a "point source". The EPA stresses that the discharge be "through pipes, sewers, or other conveyances". . . . This definition includes additions of pollutants into waters of the United States from: surface runoff which is collected or channelled by man; discharges through pipes, sewers, or other conveyances owned by a State, municipality, or other person which do not lead to a treatment works; and discharges through pipes, sewers, or other conveyances, leading into privately owned treatment works. This term does not include an addition of pollutants by any "indirect discharger."

In sum, although Congress had the ability to so provide, § 1362(14) of the CWA does not expressly recognize a human being as a "point source"; nor does the act make structural sense when one incorporates a human being into that definition. The legislative history of the act adds no light to the muddy depths of this issue, and cases urging a broad interpretation of the definition in the civil-penalty context do not persuade us to do so here, where congress has imposed heavy criminal sanctions. Adopting the government's suggested flexibility for the definition would effectively read the "point source" element of the crime out of the statute, and not even the EPA has extended the term "point source" as far as is urged here.

We accordingly conclude that the term "point source" as applied to a human being is at best ambiguous.

B. Rule of Lenity

In criminal prosecutions the rule of lenity requires that ambiguities in the statute be resolved in the defendant's favor. In other words, we cannot add to the statute what Congress did not provide. "[B]efore a man can be punished as a criminal under the Federal law his case must be 'plainly and unmistakably' within the provisions of some statute."

Since the government's reading of the statute in this case founders on our inability to discern the "obvious intention of the legislature", to include a human being as a "point source", we conclude that the criminal provisions of the CWA did not clearly proscribe Villegas's conduct and did not accord him fair warning of the sanctions the law placed on that conduct. Under the rule of lenity, therefore, the prosecutions against him must be dismissed. . . .

CONCLUSION

The Clean Water Act targets industrial and municipal production of pollutants. Its criminal provisions do not reach actions such as those done by Villegas, despite their heinous character. While we might think it desirable to punish such an obviously wrong act, we must nevertheless ensure that we apply the statute as Congress wrote it, giving Villegas the benefit of the substantial ambiguity in its meaning. . . .

Compelled by the rule of lenity, we reverse Villegas's judgment of conviction and remand with a direction to dismiss the indictment.

- Does the fact that both § 1311 and § 1319(c) (i.e., the criminal provisions enforcing § 1311) apply to a "person"—which, by definition, includes "an individual"—undermine the Second Circuit's analysis that a "person" cannot be a point source? Why or why not?
- Suppose a person dropped a container of a toxin into the Hudson River that was so lethal that it killed thousands of aquatic species for miles downstream. Under the Second Circuit's analysis, would a Clean Water Act prosecution be out of the question under § 1311?

3. Navigable Waters

Even assuming that a person has added a "pollutant" into water from a "point source," that pollution still does not constitute a "discharge of a pollutant" under the Clean Water Act unless the receiving water body was "navigable." Here, the Clean Water Act's definition is less helpful because it defines "navigable water" simply as "the waters of the United States." 33 U.S.C. § 1362(7). The United States Supreme Court attempted to provide some guidance on this definition arising from a criminal prosecution under the Clean Water Act. Read the case below to determine whether the Supreme Court succeeded in clarifying this definition. Although the Supreme Court's decision dealt with the wetlands provisions of the Clean Water Act, the Court's opinion affects this definition for direct discharges too.

United States v. Rapanos
547 U.S. 715 (2006)

Justice SCALIA announced the judgment of the Court and delivered an opinion, in which THE CHIEF JUSTICE, Justice THOMAS, and Justice ALITO join.

In April 1989, petitioner John A. Rapanos backfilled wetlands on a parcel of land in Michigan that he owned and sought to develop. This parcel included 54 acres of land with sometimes-saturated soil conditions. The nearest body of navigable water was 11 to 20 miles away. 339 F.3d 447, 449 (C.A.6 2003) (*Rapanos I*). Regulators had informed Mr. Rapanos that his saturated fields were "waters of the United States," 33 U.S.C. § 1362(7), that could not be filled without a permit. Twelve years of criminal and civil litigation ensued.

The burden of federal regulation on those who would deposit fill material in locations denominated "waters of the United States" is not trivial. In deciding whether to grant or deny a permit, the U.S. Army Corps of Engineers (Corps) exercises the discretion of an enlightened despot, relying on such factors as "economics," "aesthetics," "recreation," and "in general, the needs and welfare of the people," 33 CFR § 320.4(a) (2004). The average applicant for an individual permit spends 788 days and $271,596 in completing the process, and the average applicant for a nationwide permit spends 313 days and $28,915—not counting costs of mitigation or design changes. "[O]ver $1.7 billion is spent each year by the private and public sectors obtaining wetlands permits." These costs cannot be avoided, because the Clean Water Act "impose[s] criminal liability," as well as steep civil fines, "on a broad range of ordinary industrial and commercial activities." *Hanousek v. United States*, 528 U.S. 1102, 1103 (2000) (THOMAS, J., dissenting from denial of certiorari). In this litigation, for example, for backfilling his own wet fields, Mr. Rapanos faced 63 months in prison and hundreds of thousands of dollars in criminal and civil fines. *See United States v. Rapanos*, 235 F.3d 256, 260 (C.A.6 2000).

The enforcement proceedings against Mr. Rapanos are a small part of the immense expansion of federal regulation of land use that has occurred under the Clean Water Act—without any change in the governing statute—during the past five Presidential administrations. In the last three decades, the Corps and the Environmental Protection Agency (EPA) have interpreted their jurisdiction over "the waters of the United States" to cover 270-to-300 million acres of swampy lands in the United States—including half of Alaska and an area the size of California in the lower 48 States. And that was just the beginning. The Corps has also asserted jurisdiction over virtually any parcel of land containing a channel or conduit—whether man-made or natural, broad or narrow, permanent or ephemeral—through which rainwater or drainage may occasionally or intermittently flow. On this view, the federally regulated "waters of the United States" include storm drains, roadside ditches, ripples of sand in the desert that may contain water once a year, and lands that are covered by floodwaters once every 100 years. Because they include the land containing storm sewers and desert washes, the statutory "waters of the United States" engulf entire cities and immense arid wastelands. In fact, the entire land area of the United States lies in some drainage basin, and an endless network of visible channels furrows the entire surface, containing water ephemerally wherever the rain falls. Any plot of land containing such a channel may potentially be regulated as a "water of the United States."

I

Congress passed the Clean Water Act (CWA or Act) in 1972. The Act's stated objective is "to restore and maintain the chemical, physical, and biological integrity of the Nation's waters." The Act also states that "[i]t is the policy of Congress to recognize, preserve, and protect the primary responsibilities and rights of States to prevent, reduce, and eliminate pollution, to plan the development and use (including restoration, preservation, and enhancement) of land and water resources, and to consult with the Administrator in the exercise of his authority under this chapter." § 1251(b).

One of the statute's principal provisions is 33 U.S.C. § 1311(a), which provides that "the discharge of any pollutant by any person shall be unlawful." "The discharge of a pollutant" is defined broadly to include "any addition of any pollutant to navigable waters from any point source," § 1362(12), and "pollutant" is defined broadly to include not only traditional contaminants but also solids such as "dredged spoil, . . . rock, sand, [and] cellar dirt," § 1362(6). And, most relevant here, the CWA defines "navigable waters" as "the waters of the United States, including the territorial seas." § 1362(7).

The Act also provides certain exceptions to its prohibition of "the discharge of any pollutant by any person." § 1311(a). Section 1342(a) authorizes the Administrator of the EPA to "issue a permit for the discharge of any pollutant, . . . notwithstanding section 1311(a) of this title." Section 1344 authorizes the Secretary of the Army, acting through the Corps, to "issue permits . . . for the discharge of dredged or fill material into the navigable waters at specified disposal sites." § 1344(a), (d). It is the discharge of "dredged or fill material"—which, unlike traditional water pollutants, are solids that do not readily wash downstream—that we consider today.

For a century prior to the CWA, we had interpreted the phrase "navigable waters of the United States" in the Act's predecessor statutes to refer to interstate waters that are "navigable in fact" or readily susceptible of being rendered so. After a District Court enjoined these regulations as too narrow, the Corps adopted a far broader definition. The Corps' new regulations deliberately sought to extend the definition of "the waters of the United States" to the outer limits of Congress's commerce power.

The Corps' current regulations interpret "the waters of the United States" to include, in addition to traditional interstate navigable waters, "[a]ll interstate waters including interstate wetlands," "[a]ll other waters such as intrastate lakes, rivers, streams (including intermittent streams), mudflats, sandflats, wetlands, sloughs, prairie potholes, wet meadows, playa lakes, or natural ponds, the use, degradation or destruction of which could affect interstate or foreign commerce," "[t]ributaries of [such] waters," and "[w]etlands adjacent to [such] waters [and tributaries] (other than waters that are themselves wetlands)". The regulation defines "adjacent" wetlands as those "bordering, contiguous [to], or neighboring" waters of the United States. It specifically provides that "[w]etlands separated from other waters of the United States by man-made dikes or barriers, natural river berms, beach dunes and the like are 'adjacent wetlands.'"

We first addressed the proper interpretation of 33 U.S.C. § 1362(7)'s phrase "the waters of the United States" in *United States v. Riverside Bayview Homes, Inc.*, 474 U.S. 121 (1985). That case concerned a wetland that "was adjacent to a body of navigable water," because "the area characterized by saturated soil conditions and wetland vegetation extended beyond the boundary of respondent's property to . . . a navigable waterway." Noting that "the transition from water to solid ground is not necessarily or even typically an abrupt one," and that "the Corps must necessarily choose some point at which water ends and land begins," 474 U.S. at 132, we upheld the Corps' interpretation of "the waters of the United States" to include wetlands that "actually abut[ted] on" traditional navigable waters. *Id.* at 135.

Following our decision in *Riverside Bayview*, the Corps adopted increasingly broad interpretations of its own regulations under the Act. For example, in 1986, to "clarify" the reach of its jurisdiction, the Corps announced the so-called "Migratory Bird Rule," which purported to extend its jurisdiction to any intrastate waters "[w]hich are or would be used as habitat" by migratory birds. In addition, the Corps interpreted its own regulations to include "ephemeral streams" and "drainage ditches" as "tributaries". . . . This interpretation extended "the waters of the United States" to virtually any land feature over which rainwater or drainage passes and leaves a visible mark—even if only "the presence of litter and debris."

[L]ower courts upheld the application of this expansive definition of "tributaries" to such entities as storm sewers that contained flow to covered waters during heavy rainfall and dry arroyos connected to remote waters through the flow of groundwater over "centuries."

In *SWANCC*, we considered the application of the Corps' "Migratory Bird Rule" to "an abandoned sand and gravel pit in northern Illinois." 531 U.S. at 162. Observing that "[i]t was the significant nexus between the wetlands and 'navigable waters' that informed our reading of the CWA in *Riverside Bayview*," id. at 167, we held that *Riverside Bayview* did not establish "that the jurisdiction of the Corps extends to ponds that are not adjacent to open water," 531 U.S. at 168 (emphasis deleted). On the contrary, we held that "nonnavigable, isolated, intrastate waters"—which, unlike the wetlands at issue in *Riverside Bayview*, did not "actually abu[t] on a navigable waterway"—were not included as "waters of the United States."

Following our decision in *SWANCC*, the Corps did not significantly revise its theory of federal jurisdiction under § 1344(a). The Corps provided notice of a proposed rulemaking in light of *SWANCC*, but ultimately did not amend its published regulations. Because *SWANCC* did not directly address tributaries, the Corps notified its field staff that they "should continue to assert jurisdiction over traditional navigable waters . . . and, generally speaking, their tributary systems (and adjacent wetlands)." In addition, because *SWANCC* did not overrule *Riverside Bayview*, the Corps continues to assert jurisdiction over waters "'neighboring'" traditional navigable waters and their tributaries.

Even after *SWANCC*, the lower courts have continued to uphold the Corps' sweeping assertions of jurisdiction over ephemeral channels and drains as "tributaries." For example, courts have held that jurisdictional "tributaries" include the "intermittent flow of surface water through approximately 2.4 miles of natural streams and manmade ditches; a "roadside ditch" whose water took "a winding, thirty-two-mile path to the Chesapeake Bay"; irrigation ditches and drains that intermittently connect to covered waters; and (most implausibly of all) the "washes and arroyos" of an "arid development site," located in the middle of the desert, through which "water courses . . . during periods of heavy rain."

These judicial constructions of "tributaries" are not outliers. Rather, they reflect the breadth of the Corps' determinations in the field. The Corps' enforcement practices vary somewhat from district to district because "the definitions used to make jurisdictional determinations" are deliberately left "vague." But district offices of the Corps have treated, as "waters of the United States," such typically dry land features as "arroyos, coulees, and washes," as well as other "channels that might have little water flow in a given year." They have also applied that definition to such man-made, intermittently flowing features as "drain tiles, storm drains systems, and culverts."

In addition to "tributaries," the Corps and the lower courts have also continued to define "adjacent" wetlands broadly after *SWANCC*. For example, some of the Corps' district offices have concluded that wetlands are "adjacent" to covered waters if they are hydrologically connected "through directional sheet flow during storm events," or if they lie within the "100-year floodplain" of a body of water— that is, they are connected to the navigable water by flooding, on average, once every 100 years. Others have concluded that presence within 200 feet of a tributary automatically renders a wetland "adjacent" and jurisdictional. And the Corps has successfully defended such theories of "adjacency" in the courts, even after *SWANCC*'s excision of "isolated" waters and wetlands from the Act's coverage. One court has held since *SWANCC* that wetlands separated from flood control channels by 70-foot-wide berms, atop which ran maintenance roads, had a "significant nexus" to covered waters because, inter alia, they lay "within the 100 year floodplain of tidal waters." In one of the cases before us today, the Sixth Circuit held, in agreement with "[t]he majority of courts," that "while a hydrological connection between the non-navigable and navigable waters is required, there is no 'direct abutment' requirement" under *SWANCC* for "'adjacency.'" 376 F.3d 629, 639 (2004) (*Rapanos II*). And even the most insubstantial hydrologic connection may be held to constitute a "significant nexus." One court distinguished *SWANCC* on the ground that "a molecule of water residing in one of these pits or ponds [in *SWANCC*] could not mix with molecules from other bodies of water"—whereas, in the case before it, "water molecules currently present in the wetlands will inevitably flow towards and mix with water from connecting bodies," and "[a] drop of rainwater landing in the Site is certain to intermingle with water from the [nearby river]."

II

In these consolidated cases, we consider whether four Michigan wetlands, which lie near ditches or man-made drains that eventually empty into traditional navigable waters, constitute "waters of the United States" within the meaning of the Act. [T]he Rapanos and their affiliated businesses deposited fill material without a permit into wetlands on three sites near Midland, Michigan: the "Salzburg site," the "Hines Road site," and the "Pine River site." The wetlands at the Salzburg site are connected to a man-made drain, which drains into Hoppler Creek, which flows into the Kawkawlin River, which empties into Saginaw Bay and Lake Huron. The wetlands at the Hines Road site are connected to something called the "Rose Drain," which has a surface connection to the Tittabawassee River. And the wetlands at the Pine River site have a surface connection to the Pine River, which flows into Lake Huron. It is not clear whether the connections between these wetlands and the nearby drains and ditches are continuous or intermittent, or whether the nearby drains and ditches contain continuous or merely occasional flows of water.

The United States brought civil enforcement proceedings against the Rapanos petitioners. The District Court found that the three described wetlands were "within federal jurisdiction" because they were "'adjacent to other waters of the United States,'" and held petitioners liable for violations of the CWA at those sites. On appeal, the United States Court of Appeals for the Sixth Circuit affirmed, holding that there was federal jurisdiction over the wetlands at all three sites because "there were hydrological connections between all three sites and corresponding adjacent tributaries of navigable waters."

. . . We granted certiorari . . . to decide whether these wetlands constitute "waters of the United States" under the Act, and if so, whether the Act is constitutional.

III

The Rapanos petitioners contend that the terms "navigable waters" and "waters of the United States" in the Act must be limited to the traditional definition of *The Daniel Ball*, which required that the "waters" be navigable in fact, or susceptible of being rendered so. See 10 Wall., at 563. But this definition cannot be applied wholesale to the CWA. The Act uses the phrase "navigable waters" as a defined term, and the definition is simply "the waters of the United States." 33 U.S.C. § 1362(7). Moreover, the Act provides, in certain circumstances, for the substitution of state for federal jurisdiction over "navigable waters . . . other than those waters which are presently used, or are susceptible to use in their natural condition or by reasonable improvement as a means to transport interstate or foreign commerce . . . including wetlands adjacent thereto." § 1344(g)(1). This provision shows that the Act's term "navigable waters" includes something more than traditional navigable waters. We have twice stated that the meaning of "navigable waters" in the Act is broader than the traditional understanding of that term, *SWANCC*, 531 U.S. at 167; *Riverside Bayview*, 474 U.S. at 133. We have also emphasized, however, that the qualifier "navigable" is not devoid of significance.

We need not decide the precise extent to which the qualifiers "navigable" and "of the United States" restrict the coverage of the Act. Whatever the scope of these qualifiers, the CWA authorizes federal jurisdiction only over "waters." 33 U.S.C. § 1362(7). The only natural definition of the term "waters," our prior and subsequent judicial constructions of it, clear evidence from other provisions of the statute, and this Court's canons of construction all confirm that "the waters of the United States" in § 1362(7) cannot bear the expansive meaning that the Corps would give it.

The Corps' expansive approach might be arguable if the CWA defined "navigable waters" as "water of the United States." But "the waters of the United States" is something else. The use of the definite article ("the") and the plural number ("waters") shows plainly that § 1362(7) does not refer to water in general. In this form, "the waters" refers more narrowly to water "[a]s found in streams and bodies forming geographical features such as oceans, rivers, [and] lakes," or "the flowing or moving masses, as of waves or floods, making up such streams or bodies." Webster's New International Dictionary 2882 (2d ed. 1954) (hereinafter Webster's Second). On this definition, "the waters of the United States" include only relatively permanent, standing or flowing bodies of water. The definition refers to water as found in "streams," "oceans," "rivers," "lakes," and "bodies" of water "forming geographical features." All of these terms connote continuously present, fixed bodies of water, as opposed to ordinarily dry channels through which water occasionally or intermittently flows. Even the least substantial of the definition's terms, namely, "streams," connotes a continuous flow of water in a permanent channel—especially when used in company with other terms such as "rivers," "lakes," and "oceans." None of these terms encompasses transitory puddles or ephemeral flows of water. . . .

In addition, the Act's use of the traditional phrase "navigable waters" (the defined term) further confirms that it confers jurisdiction only over relatively permanent bodies of water. The Act adopted that traditional term from its predecessor statutes. On the traditional understanding, "navigable waters" included only discrete bodies of water. For example, in *The Daniel Ball*, we used the terms "waters" and "rivers" interchangeably. And in *Appalachian Electric*, we consistently referred to the "navigable waters" as "waterways." 311 U.S. at 407–409. Plainly, because such "waters" had to be navigable in fact or susceptible of being rendered so, the term did not include ephemeral flows. . . .

Our subsequent interpretation of the phrase "the waters of the United States" in the CWA likewise confirms this limitation of its scope. In *Riverside Bayview*, we stated that the phrase in the Act referred primarily to "rivers, streams, and other hydrographic features more conventionally identifiable as 'waters'" than the wetlands adjacent to such features. We thus echoed the dictionary definition of "waters" as referring to "streams and bodies *forming geographical features* such as oceans, rivers, [and] lakes." Webster's Second 2882 (emphasis added). Though we upheld in that case the inclusion of wetlands abutting such a "hydrographic featur[e]"—principally due to the difficulty of drawing any clear boundary between the two—nowhere did we suggest that "the waters of the United States" should be expanded to include, in their own right, entities other than "hydrographic features more conventionally identifiable as 'waters,'" Likewise, in both *Riverside Bayview* and *SWANCC*, we repeatedly described the "navigable waters" covered by the Act as "open water" and "open waters." Under no rational interpretation are typically dry channels described as "open waters."

Most significant of all, the CWA itself categorizes the channels and conduits that typically carry intermittent flows of water separately from "navigable waters," by including them in the definition of "'point source.'" The Act defines "'point source'" as "any discernible, confined and discrete conveyance, including but not limited to any pipe, ditch, channel, tunnel, conduit, well, discrete fissure, container, rolling stock, concentrated animal feeding operation, or vessel or other floating craft, from which pollutants are or may be discharged." 33 U.S.C. § 1362(14). It also defines "'discharge of a pollutant'" as "any addition of any pollutant to navigable waters from any point source." The definitions thus conceive of "point sources" and "navigable waters" as separate and distinct categories. The definition of "discharge" would make little sense if the two categories were significantly overlapping. The separate classification of "ditch[es], channel[s], and conduit[s]"—which are terms ordinarily used to describe the watercourses through which intermittent waters typically flow—shows that these are, by and large, not "waters of the United States."

. . . Even if the phrase "the waters of the United States" were ambiguous as applied to intermittent flows, our own canons of construction would establish that the Corps' interpretation of the statute is impermissible. As we noted in *SWANCC*, the Government's expansive interpretation would "result in a significant impingement of the States' traditional and primary power over land and water use." 531 U.S. at 174. Regulation of land use, as through the issuance of the development permits sought by petitioners in both of these cases, is a quintessential state and local power. The extensive federal jurisdiction urged by the Government would authorize the Corps to function as a de facto regulator of immense stretches of intrastate land—an authority the agency has shown its willingness to exercise with the scope of discretion that would befit a local zoning board. We ordinarily expect a "clear and manifest" statement from Congress to authorize an unprecedented intrusion into traditional state authority. The phrase "the waters of the United States" hardly qualifies.

Likewise, just as we noted in *SWANCC*, the Corps' interpretation stretches the outer limits of Congress's commerce power and raises difficult questions about the ultimate scope of that power. Even if the term "the waters of the United States" were ambiguous as applied to channels that sometimes host ephemeral flows of water (which it is not), we would expect a clearer statement from Congress to authorize an agency theory of jurisdiction that presses the envelope of constitutional validity.

In sum, on its only plausible interpretation, the phrase "the waters of the United States" includes only those relatively permanent, standing or continuously flowing bodies of water "forming geographic features" that are described in ordinary parlance as "streams[,] . . . oceans, rivers, [and] lakes." *See* Webster's Second 2882. The phrase does not include channels through which water flows intermittently or ephemerally, or channels that periodically provide drainage for rainfall. The Corps' expansive interpretation of the "the waters of the United States" is thus not "based on a permissible construction of the statute." *Chevron U.S.A. Inc. v. Natural Resources Defense Council, Inc.*, 467 U.S. 837, 843 (1984). . . .

V

Respondents and their amici urge that such restrictions on the scope of "navigable waters" will frustrate enforcement against traditional water polluters under 33 U.S.C. §§ 1311 and 1342. Because the same definition of "navigable waters" applies to the entire statute, respondents contend that water polluters will be able to evade the permitting requirement of § 1342(a) simply by discharging their pollutants into noncovered intermittent watercourses that lie upstream of covered waters.

That is not so. Though we do not decide this issue, there is no reason to suppose that our construction today significantly affects the enforcement of § 1342, inasmuch as lower courts applying § 1342 have not characterized intermittent channels as "waters of the United States." The Act does not forbid the "addition of any pollutant directly to navigable waters from any point source," but rather the "addition of any pollutant *to* navigable waters." § 1362(12)(A) (emphasis added); § 1311(a). Thus, from the time of the CWA's enactment, lower courts have held that the discharge into intermittent channels of any pollutant that naturally washes downstream likely violates § 1311(a), even if the pollutants discharged from a point source do not emit "directly into" covered waters, but pass "through conveyances" in between.

In fact, many courts have held that such upstream, intermittently flowing channels themselves constitute "point sources" under the Act. The definition of "point source" includes "any pipe, ditch, channel, tunnel, conduit, well, discrete fissure, container, rolling stock, concentrated animal feeding operation, or vessel or other floating craft, from which pollutants are or may be discharged." We have held that the Act "makes plain that a point source need not be the original source of the pollutant; it need only convey the pollutant to 'navigable waters.'" *South Fla. Water Management Dist. v. Miccosukee Tribe*, 541 U.S. 95, 105 (2004). . . .

VI

In an opinion long on praise of environmental protection and notably short on analysis of the statutory text and structure, the dissent would hold that "the waters of the United States" include any wetlands "adjacent" (no matter how broadly defined) to "tributaries" (again, no matter how broadly defined) of traditional navigable waters. For legal support of its policy-laden conclusion, the dissent relies exclusively on two sources: "[o]ur unanimous opinion in *Riverside Bayview*," and "Congress' deliberate acquiescence in the Corps' regulations in 1977." Each of these is demonstrably inadequate to support the apparently limitless scope that the dissent would permit the Corps to give to the Act.

A

The dissent's assertion that *Riverside Bayview* "squarely controls these cases," is wholly implausible. First, *Riverside Bayview* could not possibly support the dissent's acceptance of the Corps' inclusion of dry beds as "tributaries," because the definition of tributaries was not at issue in that case. *Riverside Bayview* addressed only the Act's inclusion of wetlands abutting navigable-in-fact waters, and said nothing at all about what non-navigable tributaries the Act might also cover. . . .

B

Absent a plausible ground in our case law for its sweeping position, the dissent relies heavily on "Congress' deliberate acquiescence in the Corps' regulations in noting that "[w]e found [this acquiescence] significant in *Riverside Bayview*," and even "acknowledged in *SWANCC*" that we had done so. . . .

Congress takes no governmental action except by legislation. What the dissent refers to as "Congress' deliberate acquiescence" should more appropriately be called Congress's failure to express any opinion. We have no idea whether the Members' failure to act in 1977 was attributable to their belief that the Corps' regulations were correct, or rather to their belief that the courts would eliminate any excesses, or indeed simply to their unwillingness to confront the environmental lobby. To be sure, we have sometimes relied on congressional acquiescence when there is evidence that Congress considered and rejected the "precise issue" presented before the Court. However, "[a]bsent such overwhelming evidence of acquiescence, we are loath to replace the plain text and original understanding of a statute with an amended agency interpretation." . . .

VII

Justice KENNEDY's opinion concludes that our reading of the Act "is inconsistent with its text, structure, and purpose." His own opinion, however, leaves the Act's "text" and "structure" virtually unaddressed, and rests its case upon an interpretation of the phrase "significant nexus," which appears in one of our opinions.

To begin with, Justice KENNEDY's reading of "significant nexus" bears no easily recognizable relation to either the case that used it (*SWANCC*) or to the earlier case that that case purported to be interpreting (*Riverside Bayview*). To establish a "significant nexus," Justice KENNEDY would require the Corps to "establish . . . on a case-by-case basis" that wetlands adjacent to nonnavigable tributaries "significantly affect the chemical, physical, and biological integrity of other covered waters more readily understood as 'navigable.'" This standard certainly does not come from *Riverside Bayview*, which explicitly rejected such case-by-case determinations of ecological significance for the jurisdictional question whether a wetland is covered, holding instead that all physically connected wetlands are covered. It is true enough that one reason for accepting that physical-connection criterion was the likelihood that a physically connected wetland would have an ecological effect upon the adjacent waters. But case-by-case determination of ecological effect was not the test. Likewise, that test cannot be derived from *SWANCC*'s characterization of *Riverside Bayview*, which emphasized that the wetlands which possessed a "significant nexus" in that earlier case "actually abutted on a navigable waterway," and which specifically rejected the argument that physically unconnected ponds could be included based on their ecological connection to covered waters. In fact, Justice KENNEDY acknowledges that neither *Riverside Bayview* nor *SWANCC* required, for wetlands abutting navigable-in-fact waters, the case-by-case ecological determination that he proposes for wetlands that neighbor nonnavigable tributaries. Thus, Justice KENNEDY misreads *SWANCC*'s "significant nexus" statement as mischaracterizing *Riverside Bayview* to adopt a case-by-case test of ecological significance; and then transfers that standard to a context that *Riverside Bayview* expressly declined to address (namely, wetlands nearby non-navigable tributaries); while all the time conceding that this standard does not apply in the context that *Riverside Bayview* did address (wetlands abutting navigable waterways). Truly, this is "turtles all the way down." . . .

Only by ignoring the text of the statute and by assuming that the phrase of *SWANCC* ("significant nexus") can properly be interpreted in isolation from that text does Justice KENNEDY reach the conclusion he has arrived at. Instead of limiting its meaning by reference to the text it was applying, he purports to do so by reference to what he calls the "purpose" of the statute. Its purpose is to clean up the waters of the United States, and therefore anything that might "significantly affect" the purity of those waters bears a "significant nexus" to those waters, and thus (he never says this, but the text of the statute demands that he mean it) is those waters. This is the familiar tactic of substituting the purpose of the statute for its text, freeing the Court to write a different statute that achieves the same purpose. To begin with, as we have discussed earlier, clean water is not the only purpose of the statute. So is the preservation of primary state responsibility for ordinary land-use decisions. 33 U.S.C. § 1251(b). Justice KENNEDY's test takes no account of this purpose. More fundamentally, however, the test simply rewrites the statute, using for that purpose the gimmick of "significant nexus." It would have been an easy matter for Congress to give the Corps jurisdiction over all wetlands (or, for that matter, all dry lands) that "significantly affect the chemical, physical, and biological integrity of" waters of the United States. It did not do that, but instead explicitly limited jurisdiction to "waters of the United States." . . .

VIII

Because the Sixth Circuit applied the wrong standard to determine if these wetlands are covered "waters of the United States," and because of the paucity of the record in both of these cases, the lower courts should determine, in the first instance, whether the ditches or drains near each wetland are "waters" in the ordinary sense of containing a relatively permanent flow; and (if they are) whether the wetlands in question are "adjacent" to these "waters" in the sense of possessing a continuous surface connection that creates the boundary-drawing problem we addressed in *Riverside Bayview*.

    * * *

We vacate the judgments of the Sixth Circuit in both No. 04-1034 and No. 04-1384, and remand both cases for further proceedings.

It is so ordered.

[Concurring opinion by Chief Justice ROBERTS omitted].

Justice KENNEDY, concurring in the judgment.

These consolidated cases require the Court to decide whether the term "navigable waters" in the Clean Water Act extends to wetlands that do not contain and are not adjacent to waters that are navigable in fact. In *Solid Waste Agency of Northern Cook Cty. v. Army Corps of Engineers*, 531 U.S. 159 (2001) (*SWANCC*), the Court held, under the circumstances presented there, that to constitute "'navigable waters'" under the Act, a water or wetland must possess a "significant nexus" to waters that are or were navigable in fact or that could reasonably be so made. Id. at 167. In the instant cases neither the plurality opinion nor the dissent by Justice STEVENS chooses to apply this test; and though the Court of Appeals recognized the test's applicability, it did not consider all the factors necessary to determine whether the lands in question had, or did not have, the requisite nexus. In my view the cases ought to be remanded to the Court of Appeals for proper consideration of the nexus requirement.

I

Although both the plurality opinion and the dissent by Justice STEVENS (hereinafter the dissent) discuss the background of these cases in some detail, a further discussion of the relevant statutes, regulations, and facts may clarify the analysis suggested here.

A

The "objective" of the Clean Water Act (or Act) is "to restore and maintain the chemical, physical, and biological integrity of the Nation's waters." 33 U.S.C. § 1251(a). To that end, the statute, among other things, prohibits "the discharge of any pollutant by any person" except as provided in the Act. § 1311(a). As relevant here, the term "discharge of a pollutant" means "any addition of any pollutant to navigable waters from any point source." § 1362(12). . . .

The statutory term to be interpreted and applied in the two instant cases is the term "navigable waters." The outcome turns on whether that phrase reasonably describes certain Michigan wetlands the Corps seeks to regulate. Under the Act "[t]he term 'navigable waters' means the waters of the United States, including the territorial seas." In a regulation the Corps has construed the term "waters of the United States" to include not only waters susceptible to use in interstate commerce—the traditional understanding of the term "navigable waters of the United States," but also tributaries of those waters and, of particular relevance here, wetlands adjacent to those waters or their tributaries. . . .

II

... The plurality's opinion begins from a correct premise. As the plurality points out, and as *Riverside Bayview* holds, in enacting the Clean Water Act Congress intended to regulate at least some waters that are not navigable in the traditional sense. This conclusion is supported by "the evident breadth of congressional concern for protection of water quality and aquatic ecosystems." It is further compelled by statutory text, for the text is explicit in extending the coverage of the Act to some nonnavigable waters. . . .

From this reasonable beginning the plurality proceeds to impose two limitations on the Act; but these limitations, it is here submitted, are without support in the language and purposes of the Act or in our cases interpreting it. First, because the dictionary defines "waters" to mean "water '[a]s found in streams and bodies forming geographical features such as oceans, rivers, [and] lakes,' or 'the flowing or moving masses, as of waves or floods, making up such streams or bodies,'" (quoting Webster's New International Dictionary 2882 (2d ed. 1954) (hereinafter Webster's Second)), the plurality would conclude that the phrase "navigable waters" permits Corps and EPA jurisdiction only over "relatively permanent, standing or flowing bodies of water," a category that in the plurality's view includes "seasonal" rivers, that is, rivers that carry water continuously except during "dry months," but not intermittent or ephemeral streams. Second, the plurality asserts that wetlands fall within the Act only if they bear "a continuous surface connection to bodies that are 'waters of the United States' in their own right"—waters, that is, that satisfy the plurality's requirement of permanent standing water or continuous flow.

The plurality's first requirement—permanent standing water or continuous flow, at least for a period of "some months," makes little practical sense in a statute concerned with downstream water quality. The merest trickle, if continuous, would count as a "water" subject to federal regulation, while torrents thundering at irregular intervals through otherwise dry channels would not. Though the plurality seems to presume that such irregular flows are too insignificant to be of concern in a statute focused on "waters," that may not always be true. Areas in the western parts of the Nation provide some examples. The Los Angeles River, for instance, ordinarily carries only a trickle of water and often looks more like a dry roadway than a river. Yet it periodically releases water volumes so powerful and destructive that it has been encased in concrete and steel over a length of some 50 miles. Though this particular waterway might satisfy the plurality's test, it is illustrative of what often-dry watercourses can become when rain waters flow.

To be sure, Congress could draw a line to exclude irregular waterways, but nothing in the statute suggests it has done so. Quite the opposite, a full reading of the dictionary definition precludes the plurality's emphasis on permanence: The term "waters" may mean "flood or inundation," Webster's Second 2882, events that are impermanent by definition. Thus, although of course the Act's use of the adjective "navigable" indicates a focus on waterways rather than floods, Congress' use of "waters" instead of "water," does not necessarily carry the connotation of "relatively permanent, standing or flowing bodies of water". . . . In any event, even granting the plurality's preferred definition—that "waters" means "water '[a]s found in streams and bodies forming geographical features such as oceans, rivers, [and] lakes,'" the dissent is correct to observe that an intermittent flow can constitute a stream, in the sense of "'[a] current or course of water or other fluid, flowing on the earth,'" (quoting Webster's Second 2493), while it is flowing. It follows that the Corps can reasonably interpret the Act to cover the paths of such impermanent streams. . . .

Also incorrect is the plurality's attempt to draw support from the statutory definition of "point source" as "any discernible, confined and discrete conveyance, including but not limited to any pipe, ditch, channel, tunnel, conduit, well, discrete fissure, container, rolling stock, concentrated animal feeding operation, or vessel or other floating craft, from which pollutants are or may be discharged." This definition is central to the Act's regulatory structure, for the term "discharge of a pollutant" is defined in relevant part to mean "any addition of any pollutant to navigable waters from any point source," § 1362(12). Interpreting the point-source definition, the plurality presumes, first, that the point-source examples describe "watercourses through which intermittent waters typically flow," and second, that point sources and navigable waters are "separate and distinct categories." From this the plurality concludes, by a sort of negative inference, that navigable waters may not be intermittent. The conclusion is unsound. Nothing in the point-source definition requires an intermittent flow. Polluted water could flow night and day from a pipe, channel, or conduit and yet still qualify as a point source; any contrary conclusion would likely exclude, among other things, effluent streams from sewage treatment plants. As a result, even were the statute read to require continuity of flow for navigable waters, certain water-bodies could conceivably constitute both a point source and a water. At any rate, as the dissent observes, the fact that point sources may carry continuous flow undermines the plurality's conclusion that covered "waters" under the Act may not be discontinuous.

The plurality's second limitation—exclusion of wetlands lacking a continuous surface connection to other jurisdictional waters—is also unpersuasive. To begin with, the plurality is wrong to suggest that wetlands are "indistinguishable" from waters to which they bear a surface connection. Even if the precise boundary may be imprecise, a bog or swamp is different from a river. The question is what circumstances permit a bog, swamp, or other nonnavigable wetland to constitute a "navigable water" under the Act—as § 1344(g)(1), if nothing else, indicates is sometimes possible. . . .

B

While the plurality reads nonexistent requirements into the Act, the dissent reads a central requirement out—namely, the requirement that the word "navigable" in "navigable waters" be given some importance. Although the Court has held that the statute's language invokes Congress' traditional authority over waters navigable in fact or susceptible of being made so, the dissent would permit federal regulation whenever wetlands lie alongside a ditch or drain, however remote and insubstantial, that eventually may flow into traditional navigable waters. The deference owed to the Corps' interpretation of the statute does not extend so far.

Congress' choice of words creates difficulties, for the Act contemplates regulation of certain "navigable waters" that are not in fact navigable. Nevertheless, the word "navigable" in the Act must be given some effect. Thus, in *SWANCC* the Court rejected the Corps' assertion of jurisdiction over isolated ponds and mudflats bearing no evident connection to navigable-in-fact waters. And in *Riverside*

Bayview, while the Court indicated that "the term 'navigable' as used in the Act is of limited import," it relied, in upholding jurisdiction, on the Corps' judgment that "wetlands adjacent to lakes, rivers, streams, and other bodies of water may function as integral parts of the aquatic environment even when the moisture creating the wetlands does not find its source in the adjacent bodies of water." The implication, of course, was that wetlands' status as "integral parts of the aquatic environment"—that is, their significant nexus with navigable waters—was what established the Corps' jurisdiction over them as waters of the United States.

Consistent with *SWANCC* and *Riverside Bayview* and with the need to give the term "navigable" some meaning, the Corps' jurisdiction over wetlands depends upon the existence of a significant nexus between the wetlands in question and navigable waters in the traditional sense. The required nexus must be assessed in terms of the statute's goals and purposes. Congress enacted the law to "restore and maintain the chemical, physical, and biological integrity of the Nation's waters," and it pursued that objective by restricting dumping and filling in "navigable waters," §§ 1311(a), 1362(12). With respect to wetlands, the rationale for Clean Water Act regulation is, as the Corps has recognized, that wetlands can perform critical functions related to the integrity of other waters—functions such as pollutant trapping, flood control, and runoff storage. Accordingly, wetlands possess the requisite nexus, and thus come within the statutory phrase "navigable waters," if the wetlands, either alone or in combination with similarly situated lands in the region, significantly affect the chemical, physical, and biological integrity of other covered waters more readily understood as "navigable." When, in contrast, wetlands' effects on water quality are speculative or insubstantial, they fall outside the zone fairly encompassed by the statutory term "navigable waters." . . .

When the Corps seeks to regulate wetlands adjacent to navigable-in-fact waters, it may rely on adjacency to establish its jurisdiction. Absent more specific regulations, however, the Corps must establish a significant nexus on a case-by-case basis when it seeks to regulate wetlands based on adjacency to nonnavigable tributaries. Given the potential overbreadth of the Corps' regulations, this showing is necessary to avoid unreasonable applications of the statute. Where an adequate nexus is established for a particular wetland, it may be permissible, as a matter of administrative convenience or necessity, to presume covered status for other comparable wetlands in the region. That issue, however, is neither raised by these facts nor addressed by any agency regulation that accommodates the nexus requirement outlined here.

Justice STEVENS, with whom Justice SOUTER, Justice GINSBURG, and Justice BREYER join, dissenting.

. . . The broader question is whether regulations that have protected the quality of our waters for decades, that were implicitly approved by Congress, and that have been repeatedly enforced in case after case, must now be revised in light of the creative criticisms voiced by the plurality and Justice KENNEDY today. Rejecting more than 30 years of practice by the Army Corps, the plurality disregards the nature of the congressional delegation to the agency and the technical and complex character of the issues at stake. Justice KENNEDY similarly fails to defer sufficiently to the Corps, though his approach is far more faithful to our precedents and to principles of statutory interpretation than is the plurality's.

In my view, the proper analysis is straightforward. The Army Corps has determined that wetlands adjacent to tributaries of traditionally navigable waters preserve the quality of our Nation's waters by, among other things, providing habitat for aquatic animals, keeping excessive sediment and toxic pollutants out of adjacent waters, and reducing downstream flooding by absorbing water at times of high flow. The Corps' resulting decision to treat these wetlands as encompassed within the term "waters of the United States" is a quintessential example of the Executive's reasonable interpretation of a statutory provision.

Our unanimous decision in *United States v. Riverside Bayview Homes, Inc.*, 474 U.S. 121 (1985), was faithful to our duty to respect the work product of the Legislative and Executive Branches of our Government. Today's judicial amendment of the Clean Water Act is not. . . .

II

Our unanimous opinion in *Riverside Bayview* squarely controls these cases. . . .

Contrary to the plurality's revisionist reading today, *Riverside Bayview* nowhere implied that our approval of "adjacent" wetlands was contingent upon an understanding that "adjacent" means having a "continuous surface connection" between the wetland and its neighboring creek." Instead, we acknowledged that the Corps defined "adjacent" as including wetlands "'that form the border of or are in reasonable proximity to other waters'" and found that the Corps reasonably concluded that adjacent wetlands are part of the waters of the United States. . . .

In closing, we emphasized that the scope of the Corps' asserted jurisdiction over wetlands had been specifically brought to Congress' attention in 1977, that Congress had rejected an amendment that would have narrowed that jurisdiction, and that even proponents of the amendment would not have removed wetlands altogether from the definition of "waters of the United States." . . .

III

. . . Most importantly, the plurality disregards the fundamental significance of the Clean Water Act. As then-Justice Rehnquist explained when writing for the Court in 1981, the Act was "not merely another law" but rather was "viewed by Congress as a 'total restructuring' and 'complete rewriting' of the existing water pollution legislation." "Congress' intent in enacting the [Act] was clearly to establish an all-encompassing program of water pollution regulation," and "[t]he most casual perusal of the legislative history demonstrates that . . . views on the comprehensive nature of the legislation were practically universal." The Corps has concluded that it must regulate pollutants at the time they enter ditches or streams with ordinary high-water marks—whether perennial, intermittent, or ephemeral—in order to properly control water pollution. Because there is ambiguity in the phrase "waters of the United States" and because interpreting it broadly to cover such ditches and streams advances the purpose of the Act, the Corps' approach should command our deference. Intermittent streams can carry pollutants just as perennial streams can, and their regulation may prove as important for flood control purposes. The inclusion of all identifiable tributaries that ultimately drain into large bodies of water within the mantle of federal protection is surely wise.

The plurality's second statutory invention is as arbitrary as its first. Trivializing the significance of changing conditions in wetlands environments, the plurality imposes a separate requirement that "the wetland has a continuous surface connection" with its abutting waterway such that it is "difficult to determine where the 'water' ends and the 'wetland' begins." An "intermittent, physically remote hydrologic connection" between the wetland and other waters is not enough. Under this view, wetlands that border traditionally navigable waters or their tributaries and perform the essential function of soaking up overflow waters during hurricane season—thus reducing flooding downstream—can be filled in by developers with impunity, as long as the wetlands lack a surface connection with the adjacent waterway the rest of the year. . . .

The plurality goes on, however, to define "'adjacent to'" as meaning "with a continuous surface connection to" other water. It is unclear how the plurality reached this conclusion, though it plainly neglected to consult a dictionary. Even its preferred Webster's Second defines the term as "[l]ying near, close, or contiguous; neighboring; bordering on" and acknowledges that "[o]bjects are ADJACENT when they lie close to each other, but not necessarily in actual contact." Webster's Second 32 (emphasis added); see also Webster's Third 26. In any event, the proper question is not how the plurality would define "adjacent," but whether the Corps' definition is reasonable.

The Corps defines "adjacent" as "bordering, contiguous, or neighboring," and specifies that "[w]etlands separated from other waters of the United States by man-made dikes or barriers, natural river berms, beach dunes and the like are 'adjacent wetlands.'" This definition is plainly reasonable, both on its face and in terms of the purposes of the Act. While wetlands that are physically separated from other waters may perform less valuable functions, this is a matter for the Corps to evaluate in its permitting decisions. . . .

IV

While I generally agree with Parts I and II-A of Justice KENNEDY's opinion, I do not share his view that we should replace regulatory standards that have been in place for over 30 years with a judicially crafted rule distilled from the term "significant nexus" as used in *SWANCC*. To the extent that our passing use of this term has become a statutory requirement, it is categorically satisfied as to wetlands adjacent to navigable waters or their tributaries. . . .

. . . I think it clear that wetlands adjacent to tributaries of navigable waters generally have a "significant nexus" with the traditionally navigable waters downstream. Unlike the "nonnavigable, isolated, intrastate waters" in *SWANCC*, these wetlands can obviously have a cumulative effect on downstream water flow by releasing waters at times of low flow or by keeping waters back at times of high flow. This logical connection alone gives the wetlands the "limited" connection to traditionally navigable waters that is all the statute requires, and disproves Justice KENNEDY's claim that my approach gives no meaning to the word "'navigable'". . . .

Justice KENNEDY's "significant-nexus" test will probably not do much to diminish the number of wetlands covered by the Act in the long run. Justice KENNEDY himself recognizes that the records in both cases contain evidence that "should permit the establishment of a significant nexus," and it seems likely that evidence would support similar findings as to most (if not all) wetlands adjacent to tributaries of navigable waters. But Justice KENNEDY's approach will have the effect of creating additional work for all concerned parties. Developers wishing to fill wetlands adjacent to ephemeral or intermittent tributaries of traditionally navigable waters will have no certain way of knowing whether they need to get § 404 permits or not. And the Corps will have to make case-by-case (or category-by-category) jurisdictional determinations, which will inevitably increase the time and resources spent processing permit applications. These problems are precisely the ones that *Riverside Bayview*'s deferential approach avoided. Unlike Justice KENNEDY, I see no reason to change *Riverside Bayview*'s approach—and every reason to continue to defer to the Executive's sensible, bright-line rule.

V

. . . The [Clean Water] Act has largely succeeded in restoring the quality of our Nation's waters. Where the Cuyahoga River was once coated with industrial waste, "[t]oday, that location is lined with restaurants and pleasure boat slips." By curtailing the Corps' jurisdiction of more than 30 years, the plurality needlessly jeopardizes the quality of our waters. In doing so, the plurality disregards the deference it owes the Executive, the congressional acquiescence in the Executive's position that we recognized in *Riverside Bayview*, and its own obligation to interpret laws rather than to make them. While Justice KENNEDY's approach has far fewer faults, nonetheless it also fails to give proper deference to the agencies entrusted by Congress to implement the Clean Water Act.

I would affirm the judgments in both cases, and respectfully dissent from the decision of five Members of this Court to vacate and remand. I close, however, by noting an unusual feature of the Court's judgments in these cases. It has been our practice in a case coming to us from a lower federal court to enter a judgment commanding that court to conduct any further proceedings pursuant to a specific mandate. That prior practice has, on occasion, made it necessary for Justices to join a judgment that did not conform to their own views. In these cases, however, while both the plurality and Justice KENNEDY agree that there must be a remand for further proceedings, their respective opinions define different tests to be applied on remand. Given that all four Justices who have joined this opinion would uphold the Corps' jurisdiction in both of these cases—and in all other cases in which either the plurality's or Justice KENNEDY's test is satisfied—on remand each of the judgments should be reinstated if either of those tests is met.

[Dissenting opinion of Justice BREYER omitted].

- Given that there was no majority decision telling lower courts which standard to apply on remand, which standard should lower courts apply: the "significant surface-connection test" of the plurality or the "substantial nexus test" that Justice Kennedy endorsed? The dissent agreed that either test would be sufficient to sustain Rapanos's conviction on remand. If you were the prosecutor, what would you argue on remand? What evidence would you look for?
- Since *Rapanos*, litigation has arisen challenging whether a discharge of a pollutant can even be regulated under an NPDES permit claiming that the body of water into which the discharge is occurring is not "waters of the United States." Consequently, in any prosecution for direct

discharges, the prosecution and the defense must consider whether the receiving water constitutes "waters of the United States."

- Not surprisingly, the Courts of Appeals have split as to which test they will accept for proving the element of "navigable waters." The First Circuit has held that *either* the plurality's or Justice Kennedy's approach will suffice. *United States v. Charles Johnson*, 467 F.3d 56 (1st Cir. 2006). However, other circuits have held that Justice Kennedy's standard is the sole basis for establishing jurisdiction under the Clean Water Act. *United States v. McWane*, 505 F.3d 1208 (11th Cir. 2008). Some courts have punted on the issue. *United States v. Lucas*, 516 F.3d 316 (5th Cir. 2008). However, at this point, no circuit has adopted solely the plurality's test.

- Recall that, for criminal enforcement purposes, "navigable waters" constitutes a jurisdictional element under which the prosecution does not need to show that the defendant had knowledge (under the "knowingly" mens rea). However, remember that the Fifth Circuit stated in *Ahmad* that the "knowingly" mens rea applies to all elements. Assuming that this is true, what does *Rapanos* do to the prosecution's ability to establish that a defendant knew that the waters into which the discharge occurred were "waters of the United States"?

4. Mens Rea and the Permit Requirement

If a person, as defined under the Clean Water Act, has discharged a pollutant without or in violation of an NPDES permit or its state equivalent, then to apply criminal sanctions, the issue is whether this violation was done "knowingly," in the case of the Clean Water Act's felony provision, or "negligently," in the case of a misdemeanor. 33 U.S.C. § 1319(c)(2) (felony provision); 33 U.S.C. § 1319(c)(1) (misdemeanor provisions). As discussed in previous chapters, courts have struggled with whether the term "knowingly" applies to all the elements of the offense or whether it applies only to the act of discharging a pollutant. *Compare United States v. Ahmad*, 101 F.3d 386 (5th Cir. 1996), *and United States v. Kelley Technical Coatings, Inc.*, 157 F.3d 432 (6th Cir. 1998). Additionally, all courts agree that the prosecution does not need to prove under a knowing mens rea that the defendant knew that he/she was violating the law but must prove that the defendant knew of the facts necessary to complete the offense. Is the non-existence of a permit a fact or knowledge of the law? Are the limitations in a permit a fact of which the defendant must have knowledge or is it a legal question?

United States v. Weitzenhoff
35 F.3d 1275 (9th Cir. 1993)

FLETCHER, Circuit Judge:
Michael H. Weitzenhoff and Thomas W. Mariani, who managed the East Honolulu Community Services Sewage Treatment Plant, appeal their convictions for violations of the Clean Water Act ("CWA"), 33 U.S.C. §§ 1251 et seq.,

contending that 1) the district court misconstrued the word "knowingly" under section 1319(c)(2) of the CWA. . . .

We affirm the convictions and sentence.

FACTS AND PROCEDURAL HISTORY

In 1988 and 1989 Weitzenhoff was the manager and Mariani the assistant manager of the East Honolulu Community Services Sewage Treatment Plant ("the plant"), located not far from Sandy Beach, a popular swimming and surfing beach on Oahu. The plant is designed to treat some 4 million gallons of residential wastewater each day by removing the solids and other harmful pollutants from the sewage so that the resulting effluent can be safely discharged into the ocean. The plant operates under a permit issued pursuant to the National Pollution Discharge Elimination System ("NPDES"), which established the limits on the Total Suspended Solids ("TSS") and Biochemical Oxygen Demand ("BOD")—indicators of the solid and organic matter, respectively, in the effluent discharged at Sandy Beach. During the period in question, the permit limited the discharge of both the TSS and BOD to an average of 976 pounds per day over a 30-day period. It also imposed monitoring and sampling requirements on the plant's management.

The sewage treatment process that was overseen by Weitzenhoff and Mariani began with the removal of large inorganic items such as rags and coffee grounds from the incoming wastewater as it flowed through metal screens and a grit chamber at the head of the plant. The wastewater then entered large tanks known as primary clarifiers, where a portion of the organic solids settled to the bottom of the tanks. The solid material which settled in the primary clarifiers, known as primary sludge, was pumped to separate tanks, known as anaerobic digesters, to be further processed. Those solids that did not settle continued on to aeration basins, which contained microorganisms to feed on and remove the solids and other organic pollutants in the waste stream.

From the aeration basins the mixture flowed into final clarifiers, where the microorganisms settled out, producing a mixture that sank to the bottom of the clarifiers called activated sludge. The clarified stream then passed through a chlorine contact chamber, where the plant's sampling apparatus was, and emptied into the plant's outfall, a long underground pipe which discharged the plant's effluent into the ocean through diffusers 1,100 to 1,400 feet from shore (the "Sandy Beach outfall").

Meanwhile, the activated sludge that had settled in the final clarifiers was pumped from the bottom of the clarifiers. A certain portion was returned to the aeration basins, while the remainder, known as waste activated sludge ("WAS"), was pumped to WAS holding tanks. From the holding tanks, the WAS could either be returned to other phases of the treatment process or hauled away to a different sewage treatment facility.

From March 1987 through March 1988, the excess WAS generated by the plant was hauled away to another treatment plant, the Sand Island Facility. In March 1988, certain improvements were made to the East Honolulu plant and the hauling was discontinued. Within a few weeks, however, the plant began experiencing a buildup of excess WAS. Rather than have the excess WAS hauled away as before, however, Weitzenhoff and Mariani instructed two employees at the plant to dispose of it on a regular basis by pumping it from the storage tanks directly into the outfall, that is, directly into the ocean. The WAS thereby bypassed the plant's effluent sampler so that the samples taken and reported to Hawaii's Department of Health ("DOH") and the EPA did not reflect its discharge.

The evidence produced by the government at trial showed that WAS was discharged directly into the ocean from the plant on about 40 separate occasions from April 1988 to June 1989, resulting in some 436,000 pounds of pollutant solids being discharged into the ocean, and that the discharges violated the plant's 30-day average effluent limit under the permit for most of the months during which they occurred. Most of the WAS discharges occurred during the night, and none was reported to the DOH or EPA. DOH inspectors contacted the plant on several occasions in 1988 in response to complaints by lifeguards at Sandy Beach that sewage was being emitted from the outfall, but Weitzenhoff and Mariani repeatedly denied that there was any problem at the plant. In one letter responding to a DOH inquiry in October 1988, Mariani stated that "the debris that was reported could not have been from the East Honolulu Wastewater Treatment facility, as our records of effluent quality up to this time will substantiate." One of the plant employees who participated in the dumping operation testified that Weitzenhoff instructed him not to say anything about the discharges, because if they all stuck together and did not reveal anything, "they [couldn't] do anything to us."

Following an FBI investigation, Weitzenhoff and Mariani were charged in a thirty-one-count indictment with conspiracy and substantive violations of the Clean Water Act ("CWA"). At trial, Weitzenhoff and Mariani admitted having authorized the discharges, but claimed that their actions were justified under their interpretation of the NPDES permit. The jury found them guilty of six of the thirty-one counts.

Weitzenhoff was sentenced to twenty-one months and Mariani thirty-three months imprisonment. Each filed a timely notice of appeal.

DISCUSSION

A. Intent Requirement

Section 1311(a) of the CWA prohibits the discharge of pollutants into navigable waters without an NPDES permit. 33 U.S.C. § 1311(a). Section 1319(c)(2) makes it a felony offense to "knowingly violate [ ] section 1311, 1312, 1316, 1317, 1318, 1321(b)(3), 1328, or 1345 . . . or any permit condition or limitation implementing any of such sections in a permit issued under section 1342."

Prior to trial, the district court construed "knowingly" in section 1319(c)(2) as requiring only that Weitzenhoff and Mariani were aware that they were discharging the pollutants in question, not that they knew they were violating the terms of the statute or permit. According to appellants, the district court erred in its interpretation of the CWA and in instructing the jury that "the government is not required to prove that the defendant knew that his act or omissions were unlawful," as well as in rejecting their proposed instruction based on the defense that they mistakenly believed their conduct was authorized by the permit. Apparently, no court of appeals has confronted the issue raised by appellants. . . .

As with certain other criminal statutes that employ the term "knowingly," it is not apparent from the face of the statute whether "knowingly" means a knowing violation of the law or simply knowing conduct that is violative of the law. We turn, then, to the legislative history of the provision at issue to ascertain what Congress intended.

In 1987, Congress substantially amended the CWA, elevating the penalties for violations of the Act. Increased penalties were considered necessary to deter would-be polluters. With the 1987 amendments, Congress substituted "knowingly" for the earlier intent requirement of "willfully" that appeared in the predecessor to section 1319(c)(2). The Senate report accompanying the legislation explains that the changes in the penalty provisions were to ensure that "[c]riminal liability shall . . . attach to any person who is not in compliance with all applicable Federal, State and local requirements and permits and causes a POTW [publicly owned treatment works] to violate any effluent limitation or condition in any permit issued to the treatment works." *Id.* Similarly, the report accompanying the House version of the bill, which contained parallel provisions for enhancement of penalties, states that the proposed amendments were to "provide penalties for dischargers or individuals who knowingly or negligently violate or cause the violation of certain of the Act's requirements." Because they speak in terms of "causing" a violation, the congressional explanations of the new penalty provisions strongly suggest that criminal sanctions are to be imposed on an individual who knowingly engages in conduct that results in a permit violation, regardless of whether the polluter is cognizant of the requirements or even the existence of the permit.

Our conclusion that "knowingly" does not refer to the legal violation is fortified by decisions interpreting analogous public welfare statutes. The leading case in this area is *United States v. International Minerals & Chem. Corp.*, 402 U.S. 558 (1971). In *International Minerals*, the Supreme Court construed a statute which made it a crime to "knowingly violate[ ] any . . . regulation" promulgated by the ICC pursuant to 18 U.S.C. § 834(a), a provision authorizing the agency to formulate regulations for the safe transport of corrosive liquids. The Court held that the term "knowingly" referred to the acts made criminal rather than a violation of the regulation, and that "regulation" was a shorthand designation for the specific acts or omissions contemplated by the act. "[W]here . . . dangerous or deleterious devices or products or obnoxious waste materials are involved, the probability of regulation is so great that anyone who is aware that he is in possession of them or dealing with them must be presumed to be aware of the regulation."

This court followed *International Minerals* in *United States v. Hoflin*, 880 F.2d 1033 (9th Cir. 1989), when it held that knowledge of the absence of a permit is not an element of the offense defined by 42 U.S.C. § 6928(d)(2)(A), part of the Resource Conservation and Recovery Act ("RCRA"). *Id.* at 1039. "There can be little question that RCRA's purposes, like those of the Food and Drug Act, '. . . touch phases of the lives and health of people which, in the circumstances of modern industrialism, are largely beyond self-protection.'" *Id.* at 1038 (quoting *United States v. Dotterweich*, 320 U.S. 277, 280 (1943) (construing Food, Drug and Cosmetic Act)). Other courts have also followed *International Minerals* by similarly construing the knowledge requirement in statutes that regulate deleterious devices or obnoxious waste materials.

Appellants seek to rely on the Supreme Court's decision in *Liparota v. United States*, 471 U.S. 419 (1985), to support their alternative reading of the intent requirement. *Liparota* concerned 7 U.S.C. § 2024(b)(1), which provides that anyone who "knowingly uses, transfers, acquires, alters, or possesses [food stamp] coupons or authorization cards in any manner not authorized by [the statute] or regulations" is subject to a fine or imprisonment. The Court, noting that the conduct at issue did not constitute a public welfare offense, distinguished the *International Minerals* line of cases and held that the government must prove the defendant knew that his acquisition or possession of food stamps was in a manner unauthorized by statute or regulations.

Subsequent to the filing of the original opinion in this case, the Supreme Court decided two cases which Weitzenhoff contends call our analysis into question. *See Ratzlaf v. United States*, 510 U.S. 135 (1994); *Staples v. United States*, 511 U.S. 600 (1994). We disagree.

The statute in *Ratzlaf* does not deal with a public welfare offense, but rather with violations of the banking statutes. The Court construed the term "willfully" in the anti-structuring provisions of the Bank Secrecy Act to require both that the defendant knew he was structuring transactions to avoid reporting requirements and that he knew his acts were unlawful. The Court recognized that the money structuring provisions are not directed at conduct which a reasonable person necessarily should know is subject to strict public regulation and that the structuring offense applied to all persons with more than $10,000, many of whom could be engaged in structuring for innocent reasons. In contrast, parties such as Weitzenhoff are closely regulated and are discharging waste materials that affect public health. The *International Minerals* rationale requires that we impute to these parties knowledge of their operating permit. This was recognized by the Court in *Staples*.

The specific holding in *Staples* was that the government is required to prove that a defendant charged with possession of a machine gun knew that the weapon he possessed had the characteristics that brought it within the statutory definition of a machinegun. But the Court took pains to contrast the gun laws to other regulatory regimes, specifically those regulations that govern the handling of "obnoxious waste materials." It noted that the mere innocent ownership of guns is not a public welfare offense. The Court focused on the long tradition of widespread gun ownership in this country and, recognizing that approximately 50% of American homes contain a firearm, acknowledged that mere ownership of a gun is not sufficient to place people on notice that the act of owning an unregistered firearm is not innocent under the law.

Staples thus explicitly contrasted the mere possession of guns to public welfare offenses, which include statutes that regulate "'dangerous or deleterious devices or products or obnoxious waste materials,'" and confirmed the continued vitality of statutes covering public welfare offenses, which "regulate potentially harmful or injurious items" and place a defendant on notice that he is dealing with a device or a substance "that places him in 'responsible relation to a public danger.'" "[I]n such cases Congress intended to place the burden on the defendant to ascertain at his peril whether [his conduct] comes within the inhibition of the statute."

Unlike "[g]uns [which] in general are not 'deleterious devices or products or obnoxious waste materials,' that put their owners on notice that they stand 'in responsible relation to a public danger[,]' the dumping of sewage and other pollutants into our nation's waters is precisely the type of activity that puts the discharger on notice that his acts may pose a public danger. Like other public welfare offenses that regulate the discharge of pollutants into the air, the disposal of hazardous wastes, the undocumented shipping of acids, and the use of pesticides on our food, the improper and excessive discharge of sewage causes cholera, hepatitis, and other serious illnesses, and can have serious repercussions for public health and welfare.

The criminal provisions of the CWA are clearly designed to protect the public at large from the potentially dire consequences of water pollution, and as such fall within the category of public welfare legislation. *International Minerals* rather than *Liparota* controls the case at hand. The government did not need to prove that Weitzenhoff and Mariani knew that their acts violated the permit or the CWA. . . .

- The *Weitzenhoff* court stated that the Clean Water Act violations of which the defendants were convicted were public welfare offenses that defendants knew were heavily regulated. Therefore, the prosecution was not required to prove "knowledge" of the permit. Conversely, the *Ahmad* court stated that the defendant's actions in violation of the Clean Water Act were not public welfare offenses and, therefore, the prosecution was required to prove knowledge as to all elements but those that were clearly jurisdictional. What are the arguments in support of each court's respective position?
- Which court's reasoning is more persuasive?

B. PUBLICLY OWNED TREATMENT WORKS

Considering all of the foul things that go into sewers, the public good that has come out of having them is rather ironic. Indeed, nineteenth-century poet John Ruskin once said: "A good sewer . . . is far nobler and a far holier thing than the most admired Madonna ever painted."[4] Although difficult to fathom for those of us who take sewers for granted, Ruskin's effusive praise may have stemmed from his familiarity with water-borne illness, like cholera, which killed thousands in London, England, among many other places. Ruskin was a contemporary of Dr. John Snow, who was able to show that the deadly London cholera outbreaks were tied to people drawing their water from a "sewage-contaminated part of the River Thames."[5] The subsequent development and use of reliable sewer systems made outbreaks of cholera and other water-borne diseases a thing of the past for those areas fortunate enough to have such systems.

Not surprisingly, the importance of sewer systems—especially publicly owned treatment works ("POTWs")—in protecting public health is something that Congress recognized in the Clean Water Act. Instead of merely setting aspirational standards, Congress put its money where its collective mouth was by creating an enormous financing system for the construction of new and the improvement of existing sewer systems and water treatment plants. 33 U.S.C. §§ 1281 et seq. Congress then enacted three different provisions, which provide criminal sanctions

[4] John Ruskin, as quoted in Anthony Wohl, *Endangered Lives: Public Health in Victorian Britain* 101 (Harvard University Press, 1983).
[5] Steven J. Burian, Stephen J. Nix, Robert E. Pitt & S. Rocky Durrans, *Urban Wastewater Management in the United States: Past, Present, and Future*, J. Urban Tech. 33, 40 (Dec. 2000).

through the misdemeanor and felony provisions of 33 U.S.C. § 1319(c) for those who put POTWs and other types of sewer systems at risk. First, Congress provided criminal penalties for violating pretreatment standards. Second, Congress allowed local POTWs to impose requirements separate from the pretreatment standards, which may be criminally enforced in federal court. Finally, Congress imposed a catchall criminal provision for anyone who introduces a pollutant into a "sewer system or [POTW]" that the person knew or reasonably should have known could cause personal injury or property damage. Each criminal provision is discussed below.

1. Pretreatment Standards

To protect its massive national investment in POTWs, Congress required the EPA to promulgate pretreatment standards. 33 U.S.C. § 1317. These pretreatment standards that EPA promulgated into the Code of Federal Regulations fall into three general categories: (1) general prohibitions; (2) specific prohibitions; and (3) categorial standards. 40 C.F.R. § 403.5 (general and specific prohibitions); 40 C.F.R. Parts 405-471 (categorical standards).

In terms of criminal enforcement for these pretreatment standards, Congress provided that "[a]fter the effective date of any . . . pretreatment standard promulgated under this section, it shall be unlawful for any owner or operator of any source to operate any source in violation of any such . . . pretreatment standard." 33 U.S.C. § 1317(d). Congress then assessed misdemeanor and felony crimes for anyone who violates § 1317 negligently or knowingly, respectively. 33 U.S.C. § 1319(c)(1)(A), (c)(2)(A). Thus, to prove a criminal violation of these pretreatment standards—whether a general prohibition, a specific prohibition, or a categorial standard—the prosecution must establish that (1) an owner or operator operated a source (2) in violation of a pretreatment standard (3) after the pretreatment standard's effective date, and (4) the owner or operator acted negligently or knowingly.

a. Owner and Operator of a Source

Given the definition-centric nature of environmental statutes, including the Clean Water Act, it is somewhat surprising that neither the Act nor its implementing regulations define the terms "owner," "operator," or "source." Where, as here, the Clean Water Act does not define those terms, courts interpret them "consistent with their ordinary meaning . . . at the time Congress enacted the statute. *Wis. Cent. Ltd. v. United States*, 138 S. Ct. 2067, 2070 (2018). According to the dictionary, an "owner" means "one who has the legal or rightful title to something."[6] Additionally, "operator" means "one who operates (i.e., performs a function; to produce an appropriate effect)."[7] Finally, the term "source" means "a point of origin."[8]

---

[6] *Owner*, https://www.merriam-webster.com/dictionary/owner (last visited Aug. 15, 2018).
[7] *Operator*, https://www.merriam-webster.com/dictionary/operator, and *Operates*, https://www.merriam-webster.com/dictionary/operates (last visited Aug. 15, 2018).
[8] *Source*, https://www.merriam-webster.com/dictionary/source (last visited Aug. 15, 2018).

Assume that instead of being charged with discharging vials of blood into the Hudson River without a permit from a point source, the defendant in *United States v. Plaza Health Laboratories, Inc.*, 3 F.3d 643 (2d Cir. 1993), was charged with violating a pretreatment standard by discharging vials of blood into the local POTW. Assuming that discharging vials of blood into a POTW violates a pretreatment standard after its effective date, would the defendant be deemed an owner or operator of a source? What is the source? What would the defense argue against the prosecution's claims?

b. In Violation of Pretreatment Standards

Pretreatment standards are classified as general, specific, and categorial. Given the industry-specific nature of categorial standards and their complexity, the remainder of this section focuses instead on the general and specific pretreatment standards. Although general and specific prohibitions are very much related, one way to distinguish them is to think of general prohibitions as protecting the operations of the POTW by precluding anything that causes certain effects at the POTW whereas specific prohibitions apply to specific types of pollutants entering the POTW in order to protect the infrastructure of the POTW system.

i. General Prohibitions

As stated above, general prohibitions do not specifically regulate what can go into the POTW but rather preclude the introduction of any pollutant that causes disruption of the POTW's normal operations. Specifically, under 40 C.F.R. § 403.5(a), "[a] user may not introduce into a POTW any pollutant(s) which cause Pass Through or Interference." The term "Pass Through"

> means a Discharge which exits the POTW into waters of the United States in quantities or concentrations which, alone or in conjunction with a discharge or discharges from other sources, is a cause of a violation of any requirement of the POTW's NPDES permit (including an increase in the magnitude or duration of a violation).

40 C.F.R. § 403.3(p). When used in the context of POTWs, the term "Discharge" means "the introduction of pollutants into a POTW from any non-domestic source. . . ." 40 C.F.R. § 403.3(i). The term "pollutant" carries its definition under the Clean Water Act. 40 C.F.R. § 403.3(a), 40 C.F.R. § 401.11(f). Thus, to violate the general prohibition against pass throughs, an owner or operator of a source must introduce into the POTW a non-domestic discharge of a pollutant, by itself or in conjunction with other discharges, that causes the pollutant to pass through the POTW untreated into waters of the United States, which causes the POTW to violate its NPDES or state-equivalent permit.

Similarly, an "Interference" means that a discharge of a pollutant into the POTW, which by itself or in conjunction with other discharges from other sources,

> (1) Inhibits or disrupts the POTW, its treatment processes or operations, or its sludge processes, use or disposal; *and*

CHAPTER 5: WATER POLLUTION

(2) Therefore is a cause of a violation of any requirement of the POTW's NPDES permit (including an increase in the magnitude or duration of a violation) or of the prevention of sewage sludge use or disposal in compliance with [the Clean Water Act, RCRA, applicable State regulations, the Clean Air Act, the Toxic Substances Control Act, and the Marine Protection, Research and Sanctuaries Act].

40 C.F.R. § 403.3(k) (emphasis added). Thus, to prove an Interference, the prosecution must show that the owner or operator of the source introduced a pollutant into the POTW that disrupted or contributed to the disruption of its treatment process and caused it to violate an NPDES permit or other statute listed in the regulation. The contribution to the Pass Through or Interference does not need to be a "significant contribution." *Ark. Poultry Fed'n v. U.S. Envtl. Protection Agency*, 852 F.2d 324, 328 (8th Cir. 1988).

Case Study: Dirty Trucks

Wayne Daggett owned and operated a company called Dirty Trucks, which made a powerful truck-wash solution containing a high percentage of sulfuric acid that removed cement and other stubborn substances from construction vehicles. Dirty Trucks would make the solution in its shop, deliver a 55-gallon drum to the customer, and collect the nearly empty 55-gallon drum that the customer had used. The used drums were "nearly empty" because the pumps used to remove the truck-wash solution would never be able to extract all of it from the drum. Instead, the pump would leave approximately 1-2 gallons of solution at the bottom. When he returned the drums to the shop at Dirty Trucks, Daggett ordered his employees to discharge the residual solution into the drain, which emptied into the local POTW.

Before an industrial user like Dirty Trucks connects to the POTW's system, the industrial user must fill out a form stating what the industrial user will discharge into the POTW's system. The POTW reviews the discharged materials and determines whether it will require the industrial user to pretreat its wastewater before discharging it into the POTW's system. Before filling out the form, Daggett spoke with the POTW representative, who said that the POTW was concerned about corrosive chemicals being introduced into the sewer. Therefore, the POTW representative said, industrial users discharging acidic pollutants would have to pretreat their wastewater before discharging into the POTW's system. After hearing this and knowing how expensive a pretreatment system would be, Daggett omitted sulfuric acid from his response to the POTW's survey.

Although Daggett had been discharging the residual truck-wash solution into the sewer for many months, on three occasions, the POTW had a massive influx of suds coming into its water treatment area. The sudsy wastewater entered the POTW's treatment system and was closely monitored as it went through the treatment process. At the end of the process, the POTW tests the toxicity of its treated effluent by allowing it to flow into a tank with many small fish. When the sudsy batch of water entered the fish test tank, the vast majority of the fish died. The wastewater then was discharged from the POTW into the Laverkin River, which flows all year. The POTW's NPDES permit precludes it from discharging toxic water into the navigable river. Samples of the toxic water show that it has a high sulfuric acid content.

After the third time this sudsy event occurred, the POTW conducted an investigation to determine the source of the chemicals that caused the suds and post-treatment toxic water. After following the sulfuric acid trail up the POTW's system and after reviewing the businesses' forms as to what they discharge, the POTW determined that the source of the problem discharge was Dirty Trucks. During an administrative inspection of Dirty Trucks, the inspector sees all of the drums of sulfuric acid stored on the property and knows, through other inspections, that no other business on that branch of the POTW's sewer system uses sulfuric acid in any of its processes.

The POTW contacts EPA-CID, which, after investigation, refers the case to the United States Attorney's Office to determine whether to seek an indictment. What is the likelihood of succeeding on a prosecution for violating the general prohibitions? Against whom would charges be brought? Is there any other evidence that you, either as a prosecutor or defense attorney, would want to know before making any litigation decisions?

ii. Specific Prohibitions

As the term indicates, specific prohibitions are pretreatment standards that preclude certain types of pollutants from being introduced into the sewer system because of the deleterious effect that those pollutants have, or in some cases may have, on the sewer system's infrastructure. Federally enforceable specific prohibitions come in two forms: (1) EPA's regulations, and (2) local POTWs. Under the second type of specific prohibition, the Clean Water Act allows for federal criminal enforcement of exclusively local laws pertaining to POTWs.

EPA's Specific Prohibitions
40 C.F.R. § 403.5(b)

(b) *Specific prohibitions.* In addition, the following pollutants shall not be introduced into a POTW:

(1) Pollutants which create a fire or explosion hazard in the POTW, including, but not limited to, wastestreams with a closed cup flashpoint of less than 140 degrees Fahrenheit or 60 degrees Centigrade using the test methods specified in 40 CFR 261.21;

(2) Pollutants which will cause corrosive structural damage to the POTW, but in no case Discharges with pH lower than 5.0, unless the works is specifically designed to accommodate such Discharges;

(3) Solid or viscous pollutants in amounts which will cause obstruction to the flow in the POTW resulting in Interference;

(4) Any pollutant, including oxygen demanding pollutants (BOD, etc.) released in a Discharge at a flow rate and/or pollutant concentration which will cause Interference with the POTW.

(5) Heat in amounts which will inhibit biological activity in the POTW resulting in Interference, but in no case heat in such quantities that the temperature

at the POTW Treatment Plant exceeds 40°C (104°F) unless the Approval Authority, upon request of the POTW, approves alternate temperature limits.

(6) Petroleum oil, nonbiodegradable cutting oil, or products of mineral oil origin in amounts that will cause interference or pass through;

(7) Pollutants which result in the presence of toxic gases, vapors, or fumes within the POTW in a quantity that may cause acute worker health and safety problems;

(8) Any trucked or hauled pollutants, except at discharge points designated by the POTW.

- Notice that to prove a violation of the first specific prohibition, the prosecution need only prove that the discharge of the pollutant created a "hazard" of fire or explosion, not an actual fire or explosion.
- The second, third, fourth, and sixth prohibitions all preclude the introduction of "pollutants that will cause" a specified type of harm. However, the prosecution need not prove actual harm to establish a violation.
- The second and fifth specific prohibitions each have two tiers. In the second prohibition, the prosecution must show either: (1) that the owner and operator discharged a corrosive pollutant that "will cause corrosive structural damage," or (2) that the pH of the discharge is lower than 5.0 and that the POTW is not "specifically designed to accommodate such Discharges." 40 C.F.R. § 403.5(b)(2). The fifth prohibition precludes the discharge of: (1) heat in amounts that "will inhibit" biological activity to the point of causing an interference, or (2) that the discharge exceeds 40°C (104°F) when measured at the POTW and that the POTW did not authorize discharges to exceed 40°C (104°F).
- Notice how these specific prohibitions are related to but independent from the general prohibitions discussed above.

United States v. Hajduk
370 F. Supp. 2d 1103 (D. Colo. 2005)

BABCOCK, Chief Judge.

The Grand Jury returned a second superseding indictment against Defendants on March 10, 2005. The second superseding indictment contains 19 substantive counts relating to criminal violations of the Clean Water Act ("CWA") and Resource Conservation and Recovery Act ("RCRA"). Defendants . . . move to dismiss Count 18 . . . or in the alternative, for a bill of particulars. . . . The parties submitted these motions on their papers.

I. BACKGROUND

Defendant Albert David Hajduk is the plant manager of Defendant Luxury Wheels O.E. Plating, Inc., of Grand Junction, Colorado. Luxury Wheels electroplates automobile wheels with chrome, and has done so since 1993. In the course of its operations, it generates hazardous wastes that are regulated under state and federal law.

Luxury Wheels was issued a wastewater discharge permit under CWA, 33 U.S.C. § 1251 et seq., which allowed it to discharge specified wastes into Grand Junction's Persigo Publicly Owned Treatment Works ("POTW").

Defendants contend that Luxury Wheels "did its best to comply with these permits although it would be the first to concede that its history of compliance is not perfect." Prior to the events forming the basis for the second superseding indictment, Luxury Wheels had been cited infrequently for discharge violations throughout its existence.

The wheel-plating operation involves the following elements. First, wheels are subjected to heated and pressurized chemical washes, corrosive baths, rinse tanks, and metal baths to layer and build up the wheels' surfaces with chromium, nickel, copper, and zinc. Second, an on-site wastewater treatment system pre-treats industrial waste waters. This system consists of a pH-neutralization tank; a clarification tank that removes heavy metals by polymer/flocculent adhesion and gravity; a settling tank where the liquid and particles further separate; a filter press, where the flocculent is made into solid filter cakes; and a final collection tank. Finally, a storage outbuilding separate from the plating line holds waste waters for on-site treatment or before sending it off-site to hazardous-waste handlers.

In November 2003, following administrative hearings conducted by Persigo, Luxury Wheels applied for a "zero-discharge" permit. It ceased all industrial discharges at that time, and suspended plating operations until a new closed-loop treatment system was installed in February 2004. It has been operating under the zero-discharge permit since December 2003, so that currently no wastes from plating operations are discharged into the POTW.

The second superseding indictment in this case followed investigative activity beginning in the fall of 2001, including secret sampling by Persigo and criminal investigators from the Environmental Protection Agency, who operated under a court-authorized search warrant. The second superseding indictment alleges nineteen counts: . . . the eighteenth and nineteenth counts are for negligent violation of the CWA. . . .

Defendants do not argue that their compliance with the environmental laws was perfect or even adequate. They do contend, however, that their actions were not criminal.

II. DISCUSSION . . .

Defendant, Luxury Wheels, moves to dismiss Count 18. . . . It argues that the government "does not allege, as it must, that any such discharge from Luxury Wheels caused pass through to the POTW, or interference at the POTW." Count 18 states: "On or about July 25, 2002, in the State and District of Colorado, defendant LUXURY WHEELS did negligently discharge, or cause to be discharged, pollutants, namely, industrial wastewater, which contributed toxic gases, vapors or fumes within the POTW in quantities that caused acute worker health and/or safety problems, all in violation of [Title 33 U.S.C. § 1319(c)(1)(A); 40 C.F.R. part 403.5(b)(7); and 18 U.S.C. § 2]."

40 C.F.R. part 403.5(a)(1) states: "(a)(1) General prohibitions. A User may not introduce into a POTW any pollutant(s) which cause Pass Through or Interference. These general prohibitions and the specific prohibitions in paragraph (b) of this section apply to each User introducing pollutants into a POTW whether or not the

User is subject to other National Pretreatment Standards or any national, State, or local Pretreatment Requirements."

40 C.F.R. part 403.5(b)(7) states: "(b) . . . the following pollutants shall not be introduced into a POTW: . . . (7) Pollutants which result in the presence of toxic gases, vapors, or fumes within the POTW in a quantity that may cause acute worker health and safety problems."

The government contends that Defendants misread the 403.5(b)(7) requirements. While 403.5(a) provides a "catch-all" as to any industrial user's discharges that cause "pass through" or "interference," part 403.5(b) specifically identifies types of discharges that, the government says, "inherently interfere" with POTWs. This is one reason, it contends, that alleging Defendants' discharges "passed through" or "interfered" with the POTW is unnecessary. I note that the second superseding indictment includes language not present in the first two indictments: "within the POTW." If there was any question when Defendants originally filed their motion (before the second superseding indictment) whether the government's allegation in Count [18] incorporated the "pass through" or "interference" language, the phrase "within the POTW" in what is now Count 18 necessarily alleges that Defendants' unlawful discharges somehow affected the POTW.

That said, my reading of the regulations demonstrates that 403.5(a) and 403.5(b) are distinct. 403.5(a) considers "any pollutant(s) which cause Pass Through or Interference." 403.5(b) considers specifically categorized pollutants "in addition" to those listed in 403.5(a) whether or not they cause pass through or interference. This is clear because some of 403.5(b)'s listed pollutant categories are described specifically as causing interference with the POTW, while other listed pollutant categories are described with no reference whatsoever to pass through or interference. For example, consider the subsections of 403.5(b).

"(1) Pollutants which create a fire or explosion hazard in the POTW, including, but not limited to, wastestreams with a closed-cup flashpoint of less than 140 degrees Fahrenheit or 60 degrees Centigrade using the test methods specified in 40 CFR 261.21." This has nothing to do with "pass through" or "interference." The concern is fire or explosion hazards.

"(2) Pollutants which will cause corrosive structural damage to the POTW, but in no case Discharges with pH lower than 5.0, unless the works is specifically designed to accommodate such Discharges." The concern here is the acidic properties of some pollutants.

"(3) Solid or viscous pollutants in amounts which will cause obstruction to the flow in the POTW resulting in Interference." Here, "interference" is the explicit concern.

"(4) Any pollutant, including oxygen demanding pollutants (BOD, etc.) released in a Discharge at a flow rate and/or pollutant concentration which will cause Interference with the POTW." Here, interference is specific.

"(5) Heat in amounts which will inhibit biological activity in the POTW resulting in Interference, but in no case heat in such quantities that the temperature at the POTW Treatment Plant exceeds 40 C (104 F) unless the Approval Authority, upon request of the POTW, approves alternate temperature limits." Here, both heat and, explicitly, interference, are the foci.

"(6) Petroleum oil, nonbiodegradable cutting oil, or products of mineral oil origin in amounts that will cause interference or pass through." Both pass-through and interference are explicit.

"(7) Pollutants which result in the presence of toxic gases, vapors, or fumes within the POTW in a quantity that may cause acute worker health and safety problems." This is the section upon which the government has alleged Count 18. It has absolutely no connection within the context of these subsections to either "pass through" or "interference."

"(8) Any trucked or hauled pollutants, except at discharge points designated by the POTW." Again, there is no connection to "pass through" or "interference."

The regulations specify "interference" or "pass through" when such is required to make a discharge prohibited. They do not require "interference" or "pass through" when the inherent nature of the discharge interferes with the POTW in some other way, such as through explosion, radiated heat, acid content, or detrimental effects on worker health. Moreover, "[w]here Congress includes particular language in one section of a statute but omits it in another section of the same Act, it is generally presumed that Congress acts intentionally and purposely in the disparate inclusion or exclusion." In this case, the EPA promulgated the regulations at issue. Nonetheless, the same basic presumption of statutory interpretation applies to an agency's use of specific language in one part of a regulation but not in another. I conclude Count 18 is not "surplusage," and I deny Defendant's motion to dismiss it.

- If the general prohibitions already preclude both Pass Through and Interference, how would you interpret the specific prohibitions against the introduction of pollutants that "will cause" interference or pass through? If all Interference and Pass Through are precluded in the general prohibitions, would it be surplusage to interpret "will cause" to require a showing of Interference or Pass Through in the specific prohibitions?

Affirmative Defenses to the General and Some Specific Prohibitions
40 C.F.R. § 403.5(a)(2)

(2) Affirmative Defenses. A User shall have an affirmative defense in any action brought against it alleging a violation of the general prohibitions established in paragraph (a)(1) of this section and the specific prohibitions in paragraphs (b)(3), (b)(4), (b)(5), (b)(6), and (b)(7) of this section where the User can demonstrate that:

(i) It did not know or have reason to know that its Discharge, alone or in conjunction with a discharge or discharges from other sources, would cause Pass Through or Interference; and

(ii)(A) A local limit designed to prevent Pass Through and/or Interference, as the case may be, was developed in accordance with paragraph (c) of this section for each pollutant in the User's Discharge that caused Pass Through or Interference, and the User was in compliance with each such local limit directly prior to and during the Pass Through or Interference; or

(B) If a local limit designed to prevent Pass Through and/or Interference, as the case may be, has not been developed in accordance with paragraph (c) of this section for the pollutant(s) that caused the Pass Through or Interference, the User's

Discharge directly prior to and during the Pass Through or Interference did not change substantially in nature or constituents from the User's prior discharge activity when the POTW was regularly in compliance with the POTW's NPDES permit requirements and, in the case of Interference, applicable requirements for sewage sludge use or disposal.

- Notice that the affirmative defense to charges for violating the general and most specific prohibitions in EPA's regulations have two parts: (1) the defendant must show that it neither knew nor had reason to know that its discharges would cause a Pass Through or Interference; *and* (2) either that the local POTW rules allowed for the discharge *or* that prior discharges did not change from past practices.
- If you were prosecuting or defending a case involving EPA's general and specific prohibitions, what evidence would you look for to either preclude or establish these affirmative defenses?
- If you were counsel for a POTW, what information would you want to distribute to all non-domestic users on your sewer system to preclude anyone from being able to use this affirmative defense in either a civil or criminal action?

POTW Specific Prohibitions
40 C.F.R. § 403.5(c), (d)

(c) When specific limits must be developed by POTW.

(1) Each POTW developing a POTW Pretreatment Program pursuant to § 403.8 shall develop and enforce specific limits to implement the prohibitions listed in paragraphs (a)(1) and (b) of this section. Each POTW with an approved pretreatment program shall continue to develop these limits as necessary and effectively enforce such limits.

(2) All other POTW's shall, in cases where pollutants contributed by User(s) result in Interference or Pass-Through, and such violation is likely to recur, develop and enforce specific effluent limits for Industrial User(s), and all other users, as appropriate, which, together with appropriate changes in the POTW Treatment Plant's facilities or operation, are necessary to ensure renewed and continued compliance with the POTW's NPDES permit or sludge use or disposal practices.

(3) Specific effluent limits shall not be developed and enforced without individual notice to persons or groups who have requested such notice and an opportunity to respond.

(4) POTWs may develop Best Management Practices (BMPs) to implement paragraphs (c)(1) and (c)(2) of this section. Such BMPs shall be considered local limits and Pretreatment Standards for the purposes of this part and section 307(d) of the Act.

(d) Local limits. Where specific prohibitions or limits on pollutants or pollutant parameters are developed by a POTW in accordance with paragraph (c) above, such limits shall be deemed Pretreatment Standards for the purposes of section 307(d) of the Act.

- These provisions allow POTWs to learn from the Pass Throughs or Interferences that have occurred at the POTW and to impose effluent limitations and prohibitions upon industrial users, which are deemed "Pretreatment Standards" under the Clean Water Act and, therefore, are federally enforceable.

United States v. Iverson
162 F.3d 1015 (9th Cir. 1998)

GRABER, Circuit Judge:

A jury convicted defendant of four counts of violating federal water pollution law, as embodied in the Clean Water Act (CWA), the Washington Administrative Code (WAC), and the City of Olympia's Municipal Code (Olympia code). The jury also convicted defendant of one count of conspiring to violate the WAC or the CWA. Defendant appeals, arguing that: (1) the district court misinterpreted the CWA, the WAC, and the Olympia code; (2) those provisions are unconstitutionally vague. . . . We are not persuaded by any of defendant's arguments and, thus, we affirm his convictions.

BACKGROUND
A. Summary of Facts

[Recall from page 119 that the defendant was the president of a chemical company that made a powerful chemical cleaning agent. After the drums of cleaning agent were returned from the customer, they were cleaned out before they could be used again. Defendant repeatedly asked the POTW for permission to discharge the residual cleaning agent into the sewer, but the POTW refused because the metal content of the discharge was too high. Undaunted, the defendant discharged and ordered others to discharge the residual chemical agent down the toilet at the plant or at his or employees' residences.]

B. Procedural History

On September 18, 1997, a grand jury filed a superseding indictment, charging defendant with violating the CWA, the WAC, and the Olympia code. Count 1 charged defendant with conspiracy to violate those codes. Counts 2 through 4 charged defendant with violating the CWA and the WAC in 1992, 1993, and 1994. Each count represented a different year. Count 5 charged defendant with violating all three laws in 1995.

After an eight-day trial, the jury found defendant guilty on all counts. Thereafter, the district court sentenced defendant to one year in custody, three years of supervised release, and a $75,000 fine. This timely appeal ensued.

STATUTORY BACKGROUND

As noted, the jury convicted defendant of violating the CWA, the WAC, and the Olympia code. The WAC and the Olympia code are not, by themselves, federal offenses. However, the CWA allows states to administer water pretreatment programs. 33 U.S.C. § 1342(b). If the Environmental Protection Agency (EPA) approves a state's regulations, violations of those regulations are treated as federal criminal offenses. 33 U.S.C. § 1319(c)(2). On September 30, 1986, the EPA approved the WAC.

Similarly, the CWA requires publicly owned treatment works (POTW) to create their own regulatory programs. 40 C.F.R. § 403.5(c). Those local regulations are deemed pretreatment standards under the CWA. 40 C.F.R. § 403.5(d). In 1994, the City of Olympia approved its regulatory code. Thus, its provisions state federal offenses. 33 U.S.C. § 1319(c)(2).

INTERPRETATION OF THE CWA, THE WAC, AND THE OLYMPIA CODE

Defendant argues that: (1) the district court's jury instructions incorrectly stated elements of his charged offenses, (2) the district court erred by limiting the testimony of his expert witness, and (3) the district court erred by denying his motion for acquittal. Although labeled as three separate challenges, defendant bases all three claims of error on the premise that the WAC and the Olympia code allow discharges of industrial waste that do not affect the water. We disagree.

. . .

B. Analysis

The district court held that the WAC and the Olympia code prohibit discharges of hauled or trucked industrial waste, regardless of the effect of those discharges on the water. Relying first on the Olympia code's definition of "pollutant," defendant argues that the district court erred. The Olympia code defines "pollutant" as

> any substance discharged into the POTW which if discharged directly would alter the chemical, physical, biological or radiological integrity of the water of the state. This includes, but is not limited to the priority pollutants listed in 40 CFR Part 403.1.

Olympia Municipal Code § 13.20.20.2.

Although the Olympia code does define "pollutant" based on the effect of the discharge, the Olympia code also expressly provides that, if state standards are more stringent, then state law applies under the Olympia code itself:

> State requirements and limitations on discharges to the POTW shall be met by all users which are subject to such standards in any instances in which they are more stringent than federal requirements and limitations, or those in this chapter or other applicable ordinances.

Olympia Municipal Code § 13.20.490. Defendant argues that the foregoing incorporation by reference is unimportant, because state law also measures discharges based on their effect on the water. Specifically, the WAC allows

> [d]ischarges to municipal sewerage systems of wastes from industrial or commercial sources whose wastewater is similar in character and strength to normal domestic wastewater: Provided, That such discharges do not have the potential to adversely affect performance of the system. Examples of this type of discharge

> sources may include hotels, restaurants, laundries and food preparation establishments.

Wash. Admin. Code § 173-216-050(1)(d).

However, subsection (2) of that provision of the WAC states that, notwithstanding subsection (1)(d), "[a] permit is required for any source subject to pretreatment standards promulgated under section 307 of FWPCA [Federal Water Pollution Control Act] unless exempted under subsections (1)(b) and (c) of this section." Wash. Admin. Code § 173-216-050(2). Further, the next section of the WAC lists discharges that always are prohibited, including "[t]he discharge into a municipal sewerage of substances prohibited from such discharge by section 307 of FWPCA." Wash. Admin. Code § 173-216-060(2)(a). Pursuant to section 307 of the FWPCA, as amended by the CWA, the EPA has prohibited the discharge of "[a]ny trucked or hauled pollutants, except at discharge points designated by the POTW." 40 C.F.R. § 403.5(b)(8). The CWA defines "pollutant" to include any "industrial . . . waste discharged into water." See 33 U.S.C. § 1362(6) (so providing). When all its provisions are read together, the CWA prohibits the discharge of "any trucked or hauled industrial waste except at discharge points designated by the POTW."

Because the WAC and the Olympia code incorporate the federal standard by reference, they also prohibit the discharge of "any trucked or hauled industrial waste except at discharge points designated by the POTW." That incorporation is not surprising, because the CWA prohibits "any State or political subdivision thereof" from adopting

> an effluent limitation, or other limitation, effluent standard, prohibition, pretreatment standard, or standard of performance which is less stringent than the effluent limitation, or other limitation, effluent standard, prohibition, pretreatment standard, or standard of performance under this chapter.

33 U.S.C. § 1370. Accordingly, the CWA, the WAC, and the Olympia code prohibit the discharge of hauled or trucked industrial waste except at a discharge point designated by the POTW.

Here, defendant discharged hauled or trucked industrial waste at a point not designated by the POTW. Defendant thereby violated the CWA, the WAC, and the Olympia code irrespective of any effect that his discharges had on the water. . . .

- Should the fact that no appreciable environmental harm occurred be a defense to criminal liability under the Clean Water Act?
- Should environmental harm be a factor at sentencing?
- Violations of most local ordinances do not carry the risk of federal criminal charges. What are the policy reasons for making a federal criminal case out of violating local ordinances regarding POTWs?

2. POTW Requirements

The Clean Water Act also allows for federal civil and criminal enforcement of any "requirements" of approved local pretreatment programs. Specifically, 33 U.S.C. § 1342 authorizes the EPA to establish a state program to administer

NPDES permits. Included within those state-issued permits, Congress required provisions to account for discharges from POTWs. 33 U.S.C. § 1342(b)(8). EPA's regulations grant POTWs the authority to impose requirements on industrial users of the sewer system to ensure that the POTW meets its own permit obligations. 40 C.F.R. § 403.3(t). Indeed, the term "Pretreatment Requirements" includes "any substantive or procedural requirement related to Pretreatment, other than a National Pretreatment Standard, imposed on an Industrial User." 40 C.F.R. § 403.3(t). Thus, "Pretreatment Requirements" under the Clean Water Act are exclusively local, but they can be federally enforced. Notice, however, that whereas the prohibitions are enforced under 33 U.S.C. § 1319's reliance on 33 U.S.C. § 1317, enforcement of the POTW's requirements relies on 33 U.S.C. § 1342. These local Pretreatment Requirements are typically found in permitting programs that POTWs conduct with their industrial users.

Case Study: Big Gold

"Big Gold" is a precious metal refining operation in a large city and has permission to use the city's POTW. However, as a condition precedent to discharging its industrial wastewater into the POTW, Big Gold must sign an industrial-user discharge permit, which the local POTW administers to ensure its own compliance with its NPDES permit. This POTW-issued permit imposes a requirement on Big Gold to pretreat its wastewater before discharging into the POTW. To ensure that Big Gold lives up to its pretreatment obligations, the POTW's permit imposes effluent limitations on Big Gold's wastewater by limiting the maximum discharge of selenium in the wastewater to 50 parts per million per hour. Big Gold's manager, Doug Makleroy, wants to increase production and believes that the POTW's selenium limit is far too low. However, instead of either talking to the POTW to seek an increase in the selenium limit or filing a civil lawsuit against the POTW in state court challenging the low selenium effluent limitation, Makleroy decides to increase production and to hide the amount of selenium in the wastewater when the POTW comes by to conduct its testing by running clean water from a culinary connection into the wastewater during tests. The POTW gets suspicious because the samples seem "too clean," and, therefore, comes by when Makleroy is not around and finds that Big Gold is greatly exceeding the POTW's selenium limit. The POTW notifies EPA-CID, which learns about Makleroy's decision to increase production and to hide the actual wastewater discharges by interviewing current and former employees. Thinking that violating what he calls the "podunk POTW permit" was only going to result in a small fine from the city, Makleroy is very surprised to learn that the United States Attorney's Office is reviewing the case for federal criminal prosecution. Big Gold's counsel sits down to talk with the Assistant United States Attorney assigned to the case and argues that this is "not a federal case, much less a federal criminal case. It should be handled as an administrative or civil action by the POTW in state court." You are the Assistant United States Attorney assigned to the case. How would you respond to Big Gold's attorney? Would you seek charges? Why or why not? If you would seek charges, against whom would you seek them?[9]

---

[9] *See United States v. Johnson-Matthey, PLC*, 2:06-CR-169 DB (D. Utah 2006).

3. The POTW and Sewer System Catchall

In addition to general prohibitions, specific prohibitions (both EPA's and the POTW's), and the POTW's "requirements," Congress included a catchall provision to protect POTWs and other types of "sewer systems." Specifically, 33 U.S.C. § 1319(c)(1)(B) and (c)(2)(B) impose criminal penalties on "[a]ny person who"

> negligently [or knowingly] introduces into a sewer system or into a publicly owned treatment works any pollutant or hazardous substance which such person knew or reasonably should have known could cause personal injury or property damage or, other than in compliance with all applicable Federal, State, or local requirements or permits, which causes such treatment works to violate any effluent limitation or condition in any permit issued to the treatment works under section 1342 of this title by the Administrator or a State[.]

Notice how this provision applies not only to POTWs but also to a "sewer system." This is an important provision because in the United States, there are many privately owned sewer systems and many of those connect to POTWs. The term "hazardous substance" is defined in 33 U.S.C. § 1319(c)(7) and includes substances deemed hazardous under numerous statutes. The prosecution must also prove that the hazardous substance or pollutant "could cause" injury to either people or property or actually "causes" the sewer system or POTW to violate its NPDES or state-equivalent permit.

The mens rea required to prove this charge is complex. The introduction of the pollutant must be done either negligently or knowingly. However, in addition to proving mens rea for the act of pollutant introduction, the prosecution must also show either that the defendant knew that the pollutant "could cause" injury or that the defendant "reasonably should have known." The latter standard is based on negligence, but if the discharge of a qualifying pollutant was done knowingly, it would support a felony conviction. Consider the following example.

Case Study: Bad Bio-diesel in the Sewer

Dan McTavish is the president of Renewable Fuels, LLC, which claims to be an environmentally friendly company because it makes a renewable-energy bio-diesel fuel for cars and trucks. Renewable Fuels collects grease from local restaurants, hauls it to its facility, puts the grease through a chemical process, and eventually generates bio-diesel. However, because Renewable Fuels has inadequate testing procedures for the grease that it receives from local restaurants, it sometimes finds after going through the chemical process that its bio-diesel does not work because it has too many impurities. Paying to dispose of the unusable bio-diesel is very expensive and is cutting into already tight profit margins. So, to save money, McTavish orders his employees to dispose of the defective bio-diesel batches into the sewer system to which Renewable Fuels is connected. Renewable Fuels is not connected to a POTW, but a private sewer system that is owned and operated by the local business owner association, which manages the industrial park in which Renewable Fuels has its facility. The private sewer system has several hundred yards of pipe and uses a lift station to pump the effluent uphill to additional pipes, which eventually connect to the local POTW. The POTW's system delivers the effluent from the private sewer system to the public treatment works, which then discharges the effluent into a navigable waterway.

About 30 minutes after discharging a bad batch of bio-diesel into the sewer, McTavish sees the owners of the industrial park opening the manhole cover over the lift station a few hundred feet away from Renewable Fuels' facility. He hears the workers say that there is this thick goo that has gummed up the pump and that it will have to be replaced. The workers go into each business upstream from the lift station to see if any of them had discharged anything matching the description of what had gummed up the lift station pump. McTavish denies knowing anything about it. Nevertheless, he continues to discharge bad batches of bio-diesel into the sewer. The pump breaks down two more times, and the same greasy substance is the cause.

A few months later, businesses upstream from the lift station are complaining that their sewers are backed up. The industrial park owners open up the manhole and see that this greasy, fatty substance has coated the pipes and, as with an artery, has clogged them. After trying in vain to auger the material from the pipes, the industrial park owners determine that the only solution is to dig up the pipes and replace them. After this expenditure, the industrial park owners are furious. They hire the POTW to use a robot to go through the sewer pipes upstream from the lift station to see if it can spot the source of the mess in the pipes. The robot's camera shows that the greatest concentration of this substance comes from Renewable Fuels' outfall. The POTW contacts the local police department, which calls in EPA-CID. EPA-CID interviews former and current employees and learns that McTavish ordered bad batches of bio-diesel to be introduced into the sewer. McTavish agrees to talk to EPA-CID with counsel present and says that he never ordered any of his workers to discharge bio-diesel into the sewer. He concedes, however, that he was aware that some of his workers may have done it, but that he never addressed it with them.

EPA-CID refers the case to the United States Attorney's Office, which decides it needs help from the Department of Justice's Environmental Crimes Section. Assume you are a trial attorney in the Environmental Crimes Section. Would you seek charges from the grand jury? If so, which and against whom?[10] If you were a defense attorney trying to convince the Department of Justice not to seek an indictment, which arguments would you make?

C. WETLANDS

As scientific knowledge about wetlands has increased, so has our understanding of their importance to society, not to mention the ecosystem generally. For example, wetlands are believed to play a significant role in reducing

---

[10] See United States v. Barnett, Jr., 2:12-CR-378 (D. Utah 2012).

storm surge during hurricanes,[11] providing critical habitat for threatened and endangered species,[12] providing habitat for migratory birds[13] and fish,[14] supporting boreal forest health,[15] and providing resources to communities in developing countries,[16] just to name a few. Although Congress did not fully understand the importance of wetlands, it knew enough to enact a significant regulatory scheme in the Clean Water Act to protect wetlands from unpermitted intrusions.

In 33 U.S.C. § 1344, Congress created a permit program administered by the Army Corps of Engineers ("the Corps"). Section 1344 authorizes the Corps to "issue permits . . . for the discharge of dredged or fill material into the navigable waters at specified disposal sites." 33 U.S.C. § 1344(a). Although the Corps administers the wetlands permitting program, EPA retains a veto authority over issued permits. 33 U.S.C. § 1344(c). EPA-CID, instead of the Corps, is the criminal investigative body for alleged wetlands violations. Also, the Corps may delegate permitting authority to an approved state entity, 33 U.S.C. § 1344(a), but only two states have availed themselves of this permitting authority.

Even though § 1344 is well known to pertain to wetlands, Congress never saw fit to use that term. Instead, Congress mentioned only dredging and filling material into "navigable waters" because dredging and filling occurs in water bodies other than wetlands. Recall that the Clean Water Act defines "navigable waters" as the unhelpful phrase "waters of the United States." 33 U.S.C. § 1362(7). Although the Clean Water Act does not mention "wetlands" as being "waters of the United States," the EPA's regulatory definition of "waters of the United States" does. 40 C.F.R. § 401.11(l)(3)(iv).

Similar to the NPDES program, the Clean Water Act enforces dredge and fill permits for wetlands and other water bodies under 33 U.S.C. § 1311, which provides, "[e]xcept as in compliance with . . . 33 U.S.C. § 1344 . . . the discharge of any pollutant by any person shall be unlawful." Criminal enforcement of these permits occurs because 33 U.S.C. § 1319(c)(1) and (2) each establish criminal penalties for negligent or knowing violations, respectively, of § 1311 regardless of whether the Corps or a state has authority to issue a permit.

Because § 1311 is the statute through which criminal enforcement is authorized, the elements of proving a violation of § 1344's dredge and fill

---

[11] Ty V. Wamsley, Mary A. Cialone, Jane M. Smith, John H. Atkinson & Julie D. Rosati, *The Potential of Wetlands in Reducing Storm Surge*, 37 Ocean Eng'g 59-68 (2010).

[12] Environmental Protection Agency, *Why Are Wetlands Important?*, https://www.epa.gov/wetlands/why-are-wetlands-important ("More than one-third of the United States' threatened and endangered species live only in wetlands and nearly half use wetlands at some point in their lives.").

[13] *See, e.g.,* Hong Yang, Mingguo Ma, Julian R. Thompson & Roger J. Fowler, *Protect Coastal Wetlands in China to Save Endangered Migratory Birds*, E5491 (July 2017) (part of Proceedings of the National Academy of Sciences of the United States of America).

[14] Environmental Protection Agency, *supra* note 12 ("Most commercial and game fish breed and raise their young in coastal marshes and estuaries.").

[15] Vincent L. St. Louis, John W.M. Rudd, Carol A. Kelly, Ken G. Beaty, Nicholas S. Bloom & Robert J. Flett, *Importance of Wetlands as Sources of Methyl Mercury to Boreal Forest Ecosystems*, 51 Canadian J. Fisheries & Aquatic Species 1065 (1994).

[16] M.J. Silvius, M. Oneka & A. Verhagen, *Wetlands: Lifeline for People at the Edge*, 25 Physics and Chemistry of the Earth Part B, 645 (2000).

provisions require the prosecution to establish that the defendant engaged in the "discharge of any pollutant." 33 U.S.C. § 1311(a). Consequently, as with direct-discharge violations, the prosecution must prove that a person discharged a pollutant without a permit. To "discharge a pollutant," the prosecution must show that the substance discharged falls within one of the categories of "pollutant," that the pollutant came from a point source, and entered into waters of the United States without or in violation of a permit under § 1344. Of course, in addition to all of this, the prosecution must establish the requisite negligent or knowing mens rea. Currently, however, the question that looms over nearly every prosecution under the Clean Water Act for wetlands is which jurisdictional test must be established post-*Rapanos*. *See, e.g., United States v. Robertson*, 875 F.3d 1281 (9th Cir. 2017) (discussing at length the differences within and among the circuits in terms of which is the appropriate jurisdictional test to prove "navigable waters" under the Clean Water Act). Consider the following example.

Case Study: Shovel Party in Illinois

Alf lives in a rural part of Illinois where he owns several acres of land. The Kaskaskia River runs near his property. During the Kaskaskia River's high-water season, a meadow within his property floods to between four and six inches of water every year. The meadow stays flooded for about four months. However, after that time, the meadow becomes dry. This ephemeral wet meadow is centrally located to some of Alf's most fertile fields. To more conveniently work his fields, Alf wants to build an equipment garage in the wet meadow area. When Alf tells one of his neighbors about the plan to build an equipment garage on the meadow, his neighbor tells Alf to be careful. The neighbor claims to have heard that if a person uses heavy equipment to fill in a wet meadow, "the federal government environmental cops will come looking for you." Alf, not wanting to draw any unnecessary attention to his building activities, decides that he is going to invite all of his family and friends to have a "shovel party" in which they will simply hand shovel trenches in the meadow, install drainage pipes, and then, over time, will shovel clean fill dirt into the meadow to build a foundation for the new equipment garage. Myrtle, who has a long-running feud with Alf, sees him doing this and decides that she is going to call the "environmental cops" on Alf. She calls the EPA, which comes out and investigates. Assume you work for EPA-CID as a Regional Criminal Enforcement Counsel, which advises the EPA-CID agents on legal matters. What is your recommendation as to whether to refer this matter to the Department of Justice? Why?

D. KNOWING ENDANGERMENT

In 1987, Congress added a "knowing endangerment" provision to the Clean Water Act, which it patterned after a similar provision that Congress enacted years before in the Resource Conservation and Recovery Act. 42 U.S.C. § 6928(e), (f). The Clean Water Act's "knowing endangerment" provision first requires the prosecution to prove a violation of one of several enumerated Clean Water Act sections. 33 U.S.C. § 1319(c)(3)(A). The predicate offenses for knowing endangerment include: discharging pollutants without or in violation of an NPDES (or state equivalent) permit; pretreatment violations (prohibitions and categories but not "requirements"); and discharging pollutants without or in violation of a dredge and fill permit from the Army Corps of Engineers, among many others. After proving one of the predicate offenses, the prosecution must also establish that in the course of violating it, the defendant knew at the time that his/her action placed another in danger of imminent death or serious bodily injury.

However, because this is environmental law, it cannot be that simple. To prove that the defendant knew that his conduct placed another in imminent danger of death or serious bodily injury, Congress requires the prosecution to prove that the defendant possessed "actual awareness or actual belief" that his/her action placed the victim in danger of death or serious injury. Although actual awareness or belief is required, Congress recognized that willful blindness would suffice. 33 U.S.C. § 1319(c)(3)(B)(i).

Additionally, Congress provided affirmative defenses to the knowing endangerment charge. If the defendant can show "by a preponderance of the evidence" that the victim consented and that the danger presented stems from the "reasonably foreseeable hazards of an occupation, a business, or a profession" or was the result of "medical treatment" or "scientific experimentation conducted by professionally approved methods" and that the victim was "made aware of the risks known prior to giving consent," then the defendant should be acquitted of a knowing endangerment charge. 33 U.S.C. § 1319(c)(3)(B)(ii).

If convicted of knowing endangerment, Congress provided a maximum sentence of 15 years in prison and a fine of not more than $1,000,000.00. If a defendant is twice convicted of knowing endangerment, then the penalties double. 33 U.S.C. § 1319(c)(3)(A).

Consider how the Court of Appeals for the First Circuit applied the Clean Water Act's knowing endangerment provision to a violation in which the defendants' employees were endangered by the pollutants that they were discharging into the POTW.

United States v. Borowski
977 F.2d 27 (1st Cir. 1992)

HORNBY, District Judge.

Congress enacted the Clean Water Act "to restore and maintain the chemical, physical, and biological integrity of the Nation's waters." 33 U.S.C. § 1251 (1988). As one means of improving water quality, Congress ordered the Environmental Protection Agency (EPA) to design pretreatment standards for industrial waste discharges into publicly-owned treatment works. 33 U.S.C. § 1317(b). Under the Act, someone who knowingly violates these standards and knows that he or she thereby places another person in imminent danger of death or serious injury commits a felony. 33 U.S.C. § 1319(c)(3). Does this criminal sanction apply when the imminent danger is not to people at the publicly-owned treatment works, municipal sewers or other downstream locations affected by the illegal discharge, but rather to employees handling the pollutants on the premises from which the illegal discharge originates? We hold that it does not.

FACTS

The defendant John Borowski was the President and owner of Borjohn Optical Technology, Inc. and Galaxie Laboratory, Inc. ("Borjohn"). Borjohn operated a manufacturing facility in Burlington, Massachusetts, producing optical mirrors for use in aerospace guidance and sighting systems.

Borjohn used various rinses, dips and nickel plating baths to plate nickel onto its mirrors. When a mirror was improperly plated, Borjohn used a nitric acid bath to strip the nickel off. From time to time the nickel plating solutions and nitric acid stripping baths had to be replaced.

Borjohn disposed of its spent nickel plating baths and nitric acid baths by crudely dumping them directly into plating room sinks, without any form of pretreatment. Those sinks drained immediately into Borjohn's underground pipes which, at the property border line, fed into the Burlington municipal sewer system and from there into the Massachusetts Water Resource Authority's treatment works. Because the pollutants were ultimately discharged into a publicly-owned treatment works, Borjohn was subject to the EPA's pretreatment regulations. The EPA regulations prohibited nickel discharges into the publicly-owned treatment works in amounts exceeding 3.98 milligrams per liter and also prohibited concentrations of nitric acid discharges into the publicly-owned treatment works if they had a pH balance of less than 5. See 40 C.F.R. §§ 433.17(a), § 403.5(b)(2) (1991). [These are categorical standards.] The nickel and nitric acid baths Borjohn discharged greatly exceeded these pretreatment standards.

According to medical experts, enormous health concerns are associated with exposure to nitric acid and nickel in the amounts involved here. Contact with the chemicals causes severe allergic reactions, chemical burns, serious skin disorders such as rashes and dermatitis, and cancer. Inhalation of nickel vapors and nitric acid fumes can cause breathing problems, nasal bleeding and serious damage to a person's respiratory tract. Various Borjohn employees testified to symptoms consistent with these health problems. Employees testified to having had "daily nose bleeds," headaches, chest pains, breathing difficulties, dizziness, rashes and blisters.

Repeated employee exposure to the chemicals was unavoidable. In discharging the spent nickel plating baths and nitric acid baths, for instance, Borjohn employees were told to bail out the harmful solutions by hand using a plastic bucket or a portable pump. Once a tank was nearly empty it was tipped over the edge of the sink and a scoop or small cup was used to scoop out any remaining solution. The employees were required to scrape the sides and bottom of nickel baths to extricate a layer of nickel byproduct called "extraneous plate out." Sometimes employees were told to dump "hot" nitric acid solutions into the sinks. This created an "alka seltzer" like appearance on the surface of the sink. Employees testified that the nickel and nitric acid solutions sometimes splashed and spilled directly onto their skins. Indeed, one employee complained that he was always "wet" with the solution and at times was scalded by the chemicals.

The protective gear available to Borjohn employees was grossly inadequate to protect them against exposure. Moreover, the nickel waste discharges produced "nickel mists or vapors" and the nitric acid disposal gave off "reddish-brown fumes." Ventilation at the plating room was seriously deficient and no suitable respirator was provided to the employees.

Borjohn and Borowski knew that their practices created serious health risks to the employees. Borowski was in charge of the plating room, participated in the disposal practices and personally ordered Borjohn employees to do likewise. The original containers carrying the nickel and nitric acid had warning labels about the dangers of contact with the substances. The defendants routinely received Material Safety Data Sheets from the chemical suppliers warning of the dangers associated with exposure. Borowski and Borjohn were also aware that their disposal practices violated the EPA's pretreatment regulations. Borjohn employees complained to Borowski about the dangers of their disposal practices and about the numerous health problems they were experiencing.

On April 4, 1990, Borjohn and Borowski were indicted on two counts (one for nickel and one for nitric acid) of violating the Federal Clean Water Act's knowing endangerment felony provision, 33 U.S.C. § 1319(c)(3). The indictment alleged that from February 5, 1987, to July, 1988, Borjohn and Borowski knowingly discharged the contents of nickel plating baths and nitric acid baths into Burlington's sewer system and the Massachusetts Water Resource Authority's publicly-owned treatment works; that these baths contained nickel and nitric acid in amounts exceeding the EPA's pretreatment standards, 40 C.F.R. §§ 433.17(a), 403.5(b)(2); and that Borjohn and Borowski knew at the time that they were thereby placing Borjohn employees in imminent danger of death or serious bodily injury. Borjohn and Borowski moved to dismiss the indictment on the same ground as is at issue here. That motion, along with a later motion for acquittal, was denied. On May 23, 1990, after 18 days of trial, a jury returned guilty verdicts against both defendants on both counts. The United States Attorney presented no evidence of danger to anyone other than Borjohn employees.

DISCUSSION

Section 1317(b) of the Clean Water Act directs the EPA to promulgate pretreatment standards for pollutants going into publicly-owned treatment works. Subsection (d) prohibits the owner or operator of any source (a term that includes Borjohn and Borowski) from violating these standards. Section 1319(c)(3)(A) provides that anyone who "knowingly violates section . . . 1317 . . . and who knows at that time that he thereby places another person in imminent danger of death or serious bodily injury" is guilty of a felony.

We assume for purposes of this appeal that both defendants knowingly violated § 1317 and knew of the dangers to the Borjohn employees. It is undisputed that Borjohn employees were placed in imminent danger of serious bodily injury during their employment and that some of this danger occurred at the time of dumping chemical solutions into sinks that ultimately led to a publicly-owned treatment works. The question is whether the defendants, in knowingly violating § 1317, knew that they "thereby" placed the employees in imminent danger.

There is no single correct answer to this semantic puzzle. In one sense, it can be said that the knowing violation "thereby" placed the employees in danger. After all, the defendants knew that the sinks were connected to the publicly-owned sewer and treatment works and that the wastes would therefore illegally proceed without interruption to the publicly-owned treatment works. They also knew that the employees' actions in performing the dumping as instructed placed them in imminent danger. Arguably, therefore, through the knowing violation the defendants "thereby" endangered the employees. On the other hand, there could be no violation unless the wastes ultimately ended up in a publicly-owned sewer and treatment works. But the risks and dangers to these employees would have been the same if the plugs had always remained in the sinks so that no discharge to the publicly-owned treatment works (and therefore no § 1317 violation) ever occurred. The danger to the employees was inherent in their handling of the various chemical solutions, solutions that were part of the defendant's manufacturing process. They would have been subject to the identical hazards had they been dumping the chemicals into drums or other containers for appropriate treatment under the Act. In that respect, therefore, although the defendants knew that their employees were placed in imminent danger, that danger was not caused by the knowing violation of § 1317.

Since semantic analysis alone is insufficient, how is this puzzle to be resolved? Several factors assist us. First, the purpose of the statute is clear. The Clean Water Act is not a statute designed to provide protection to industrial employees who work with hazardous substances. Instead, section 1251(a) states: "The objective of this Act is to restore and maintain the chemical, physical, and biological integrity of the Nation's waters." The EPA is directed to promulgate pretreatment standards only so as to "prevent the discharge of any pollutant" that will pass through publicly-owned treatment works, interfere with the works, be incompatible with the works, 33 U.S.C. § 1317(b), or otherwise violate effluent standards for the works. 33 U.S.C. § 1317(c). The EPA regulations reflect this same focus of concern on publicly-owned treatment works. The regulations' goals are:

> (a) To prevent the introduction of pollutants into POTWs which will interfere with the operation of a POTW, including interference with its use or disposal of municipal sludge;
> (b) To prevent the introduction of pollutants into POTWs which will pass through the treatment works or otherwise be incompatible with such works; and
> (c) To improve opportunities to recycle and reclaim municipal and industrial wastewaters and sludges.

40 C.F.R. § 403.2.6. One can read the entire statute and regulations in vain for any protection mechanism for industrial employees who work with wastes at the point of discharge. Instead, other laws deal with industrial employee health and safety. The Occupational Safety and Health Act (OSHA) is the best known. 29 U.S.C. §§ 651 et seq. (1988 & Supp. II 1990). It carries extensive remedial provisions, including administrative steps by which unsafe employer practices can be halted on short notice. See, e.g., 29 U.S.C. §§ 657–59, 662, 666. To be sure, it does not carry criminal penalties for unsafe practices unless a death occurs, see 29 U.S.C. § 666, but the sanction of its fines and the administrative remedies available to OSHA are well known throughout the industrial workplace.

Second, Congress has passed a separate law dealing with the general handling, treatment and storage of hazardous substances. Specifically, the Resource Conservation and Recovery Act (RCRA) is a cradle-to-grave statute providing a full range of remedies designed to protect both health and the environment. See 42 U.S.C. § 6902 (1988). The Clean Water Act, on the other hand, is not directed at the handling of pollutants. Indeed, under the Clean Water Act, if the publicly-owned treatment works were itself capable of removing the nickel and acid from Borjohn's discharges (thereby satisfying Clean Water Act goals), the works could seek to avoid the prohibition placed on Borjohn's discharge, 33 U.S.C. § 1317(b)(1)—yet the health hazard to the employees would obviously remain the same. Moreover, unlike the Clean Water Act, RCRA exhibits explicit concern for industrial health. It has a provision specifically requiring the EPA to provide information about employee hazards to the Secretary of Labor and OSHA for OSHA enforcement purposes. 42 U.S.C. § 6971(f). The Clean Water Act exhibits no equivalent concern for workplace dangers. 33 U.S.C. § 1367 (employee protection provisions limited to remedies against retaliation).

Finally, the well-known rule of lenity in applying criminal statutes applies here. Where there is ambiguity in a criminal statute, the ambiguity is to be construed in favor of the defendant. Our initial semantic exercise reveals the ambiguity in this statute.

These three factors lead us to conclude that a knowing endangerment prosecution cannot be premised upon danger that occurs before the pollutant reaches a publicly-owned sewer or treatment works. Section 1319(c)(3)(A) therefore does not apply to the defendants' conduct as set forth in this indictment.

The United States Attorney argues that only under his interpretation of the statute does a separate provision of the Act have any meaning. We must, of course, interpret a statute so as to give effect to all its terms. We therefore examine this argument. Section 1319(c)(3)(B)(ii) provides that it is a defense to prosecution if the charged conduct "was consented to by the person endangered and . . . the danger and conduct charged were reasonably foreseeable hazards" of a particular business, occupation or profession. The United States Attorney argues that the only people who could be "endangered" and yet consent to such hazards are employees of an illegal discharger. Thus, the United States Attorney concludes that the statute envisions criminal liability for the illegal discharger who endangers his employees. We find the premise to be faulty. In the course of ordinary industrial activity, illegal discharges will undoubtedly occur from time to time (human or mechanical failure) that the industrial manufacturer or other entity physically cannot correct or halt immediately. Such an entity, if it is also a good citizen, will inform the publicly-owned treatment works of the discharge so that any corrective steps possible can be taken downstream. These publicly-owned treatment works may then hire professional consultants to advise the publicly-owned treatment works how to handle these fully disclosed but illegal discharges until they are corrected or halted. These "downstream" actors—consciously and freely dealing with illegal substances after they have reached the publicly-owned sewers or treatment works—are legitimate subjects for the affirmative defense and give it appropriate content. The section does not, therefore, require us to give section 1319 the reading the United States Attorney urges, a reading that is inconsistent with the overall thrust of the Clean Water Act.

CONCLUSION

The endangered persons on whom this prosecution is based had no connection to the publicly owned treatment works or municipal sewers, but were endangered solely as a result of their employment activities at their private place of employment prior to any illegal discharge reaching the public sewer or works. The defendants' conduct here was utterly reprehensible and may have violated any number of other criminal laws, but it did not violate the knowing endangerment provision of the Clean Water Act.

Accordingly, the judgments of conviction are VACATED; judgments of acquittal shall be entered for both defendants on both counts.

- Did the *Borowski* court read the Clean Water Act correctly? Is there anything in the statutory language of § 1319(c)(3) that indicates that only "downstream" victims are covered by the knowing endangerment provision?
- The knowing endangerment provision of the Clean Water Act requires the presence of at least two people. First, there is the "person" who actually commits the crime of knowingly violating the Clean Water Act. Second, there must be "another person" who is endangered by the illegal actions of the "person" committing the crime. Given that the workers were the ones actually discharging the nickel solution into the sewer unlawfully, could they be "another person" under the statute? Does it matter that their supervisor was the defendant instead of them?
- Do you agree that this statute is ambiguous enough to warrant the rule of lenity? Do you really think that the statute was so ambiguous that it did not put the defendant on notice that if he endangered his employees in the course of committing a violation of the pretreatment standards, then he would be prosecuted for knowing endangerment?

E. DISHONEST ACTS

Although the Clean Water Act establishes a significant administrative regulatory regime to protect the nation's water resources, the EPA and its state delegates are unable to monitor all regulated parties in real time. Even if the regulated parties actually have monitoring equipment, the EPA or the state regulatory entity still has to come visit the regulated party to determine whether equipment is functioning and to determine whether the entity is in compliance with the law. Thus, ensuring environmental compliance depends upon the honesty of the regulated entities. If a regulated party is able to violate the Clean Water Act and then hide that fact from regulators, then that business has a competitive advantage over other entities that are going through the expense of complying with the law. To preclude this unfair competitive advantage and to incentivize honesty with regulators, Congress included a provision in the Clean Water Act that heavily penalizes lying to regulators or manipulating testing equipment. This provision reads as follows:

> Any person who knowingly makes any false material statement, representation, or certification in any application, record, report, plan, or other document filed or required to be maintained under this chapter or who knowingly falsifies, tampers with, or renders inaccurate any monitoring device or method required to be maintained under this chapter, shall upon conviction, be punished by a fine of not more than $10,000, or by imprisonment for not

more than 2 years, or by both. If a conviction of a person is for a violation committed after a first conviction of such person under this paragraph, punishment shall be by a fine of not more than $20,000 per day of violation, or by imprisonment of not more than 4 years, or by both.

33 U.S.C. § 1319(c)(4). Observe how the Court of Appeals for the Eighth Circuit interpreted this provision below.

United States v. Sinskey
119 F.3d 712 (8th Cir. 1997)

MORRIS SHEPPARD ARNOLD, Circuit Judge.

[Recall from Chapter 4 that the defendants, Timothy Sinskey and Wayne Kumm, were the plant manager and plant engineer of John Morell & Co. ("Morell"), which was a meat-packing plant in South Dakota. As part of the meat-packing process, Morell piped some of its wastewater to the POTW, but, for the rest, Morell had to pretreat it on-site at its wastewater treatment plant ("WWTP") and then discharge it directly into the Big Sioux River. As you learned above, to discharge a pollutant into the Big Sioux River from a point source, Morell had to first obtain an NPDES (or state equivalent) permit. This permit required Morell to perform weekly tests for ammonia nitrogen in the wastewater that it discharged into the river so that Morell did not exceed the permit's limitation on that pollutant.]

In the spring of 1991, Morrell doubled the number of hogs that it slaughtered and processed at the Sioux Falls plant. The resulting increase in wastewater caused the level of ammonia nitrate in the discharged water to be above that allowed by the CWA permit. Ron Greenwood and Barry Milbauer, the manager and assistant manager, respectively, of the WWTP, manipulated the testing process in two ways so that Morrell would appear not to violate its permit. In the first technique, which the parties frequently refer to as "flow manipulation" or the "flow game," Morrell would discharge extremely low levels of water (and thus low levels of ammonia nitrogen) early in the week, when Greenwood and Milbauer would perform the required tests. After the tests had been performed, Morrell would discharge an exceedingly high level of water (and high levels of ammonia nitrogen) later in the week. The tests would therefore not accurately reflect the overall levels of ammonia nitrogen in the discharged water. In addition to manipulating the flow, Greenwood and Milbauer also engaged in what the parties call "selective sampling," that is, they performed more than the number of tests required by the EPA but reported only the tests showing acceptable levels of ammonia nitrogen. When manipulating the flow and selective sampling failed to yield the required number of tests showing acceptable levels of ammonia nitrogen, the two simply falsified the test results and the monthly EPA reports, which Sinskey then signed and sent to the EPA. Morrell submitted false reports for every month but one from August, 1991, to December, 1992.

As a result of their participation in these activities, Sinskey and Kumm were charged with a variety of CWA violations. After a three-week trial, a jury found Sinskey guilty of eleven of the thirty counts with which he was charged, and Kumm guilty of one of the seventeen counts with which he was charged. In particular, the jury found both Sinskey and Kumm guilty of knowingly rendering inaccurate a monitoring method required to be maintained under the CWA, in violation of 33 U.S.C. § 1319(c)(4). . . .

III

Kumm attacks his conviction for violating 33 U.S.C. § 1319(c)(4) on a number of grounds, first among them the sufficiency of the government's evidence. Kumm claims that the government's evidence established only that he failed to stop others from rendering inaccurate Morrell's monitoring methods, not that he affirmatively participated in the deceit either directly or by aiding and abetting those who did. As Kumm correctly argues, to convict him of aiding and abetting the monitoring scheme, the government must prove more than his mere association with, and knowledge of the activities of, Greenwood, Milbauer, and Sinskey. Instead, the government must show that Kumm associated himself with the misleading monitoring scheme, participated in it "as something [he] wished to bring about," and acted in such a way as to ensure its success. Encouraging the perpetrators of a crime in their efforts to effect that crime is therefore aiding and abetting the commission of a crime.

After a careful review of the record in the light most favorable to the jury's verdict, we believe that the evidence against Kumm, although hardly overwhelming, is not so weak that no reasonable juror could have convicted him. In particular, we believe that the evidence supports a verdict that he aided and abetted the misleading monitoring scheme by encouraging Greenwood to render Morrell's monitoring methods inaccurate and by discouraging him from complaining about it to others at the WWTP.

Kumm once reassured a worried Greenwood, for example, "not to worry about [the violations] because if we did get caught, Morrell's had enough lawyers and lobbyists that it wouldn't be a problem." Although Kumm knew of Greenwood's illegal activities, moreover, he praised Greenwood on employee evaluations and even recommended that Greenwood receive a raise. When Greenwood began complaining about the violations and campaigning for physical improvements at the WWTP to decrease future violations, Kumm silenced him. At a meeting of the plant's mechanical department, for example, Kumm told Greenwood that "[n]ow is not the time or the place to discuss those matters" when Greenwood raised the subject of the violations. Lastly, although Greenwood would "rant and rave" to Kumm several times a week about the permit violations and about getting the WWTP fixed, Kumm responded only by submitting to Morrell headquarters routine requests for future improvements that were similar to previous requests that had already been denied. We believe that these affirmative acts constitute sufficient evidence to support Kumm's conviction.

Kumm challenges the jury instructions on several grounds. . . . Kumm asserts that the essence of the government's case was his failure to report the violations and to intervene to stop their continuation, that he had no such duties, and that the trial court therefore abused its discretion when it refused to give an instruction to the jury that Kumm had no affirmative legal duty to report violations of the CWA permits or to intervene to prevent them. Though such an instruction would certainly have been appropriate, after a careful review of the record we see no abuse of discretion in the trial court's decision not to give the requested instruction, for the following reasons.

Contrary to Kumm's assertions, the government's case did not focus solely on Kumm's role as a supervisor and his failure to report the violations or to intervene. We note at the outset of this discussion that Kumm was neither charged with, nor convicted of, a failure to report CWA permit violations. Instead, he was charged with, and convicted of, "render[ing] inaccurate" the monitoring methods required under Morrell's CWA permit. Kumm argues, however, that the testimony of several witnesses and certain portions of the government's closing argument so emphasized his supervisory status and his inaction, that they led the jury to convict him for being an innocent bystander who merely failed to report the violations or to intervene. After a careful review of the statements at issue, in their full context, we disagree.

As we indicated above, the government sufficiently proved that Kumm actively encouraged the flow manipulation and selective sampling, thereby affirmatively participating in the misleading monitoring scheme. Presenting evidence that Kumm was a supervisor, that is, that he was in a position capable of giving rewards and reassurances, was but a necessary part of showing how he was able to encourage Greenwood. Likewise, testimony that Kumm neither reported nor interfered with the permit violations was consistent with the government's claim that Kumm was encouraging illegal activity. Contrary to Kumm's assertions, this evidence did not merely tend to show that Kumm violated some supposed duty to report permit violations; it tended instead to prove acts of concealment on Kumm's part that allowed the selective sampling scheme effectively to camouflage Morrell's violations.

Nor do we find reversible error in the prosecutor's closing argument. As Kumm points out, the prosecutor did, at times, argue that Sinskey and Kumm had "a duty" or "an obligation" to "protect the river" or "make sure that the plant operated in compliance with the law." In the context of the full closing argument, however, we believe that these statements refer not to legal duties, but rather to the duties of his job. And while the prosecutor did refer to what Kumm did not do, such as not reporting the violations and not interfering with them, these references were always, as a rhetorical device, juxtaposed against what Kumm did do. In context, we do not believe that these statements suggested to the jury that it could convict Kumm solely for the failure to report permit violations or the failure to intervene to stop them.

We do, however, believe that the prosecutor misstated the law when he told the jury, with respect to the violation of 33 U.S.C. § 1319(c)(4), that if "these two gentlemen knew that the selective sampling and the flow game was going on, they are guilty." We note, though, not only that this statement was not objected to either during or after the argument in question, but also that we believe that the jury instructions sufficiently cured whatever unfair prejudice this statement may have created. The trial court told the jury that it had to "follow the law as stated in these instructions," that it had to "follow my instructions on the law, even if you thought the law was different," and that "[i]t would be a violation of your sworn duty to base your verdict upon any rules of law other than the ones given you in these instructions." The instructions relevant to § 1319(c)(4) defined accurately the elements of a violation of it and the elements of aiding and abetting, including the necessity that a defendant act knowingly. The aiding and abetting instructions, moreover, correctly told the jury that a defendant's mere presence at a crime scene or his mere association with the perpetrators of a violation was insufficient to prove that the defendant aided and abetted the commission of an offense.

- How would reliance on the Clean Water Act's responsible corporate officer doctrine address the error that the prosecutor made at oral argument? 33 U.S.C. § 1319(c)(6).
- Based on *Sinskey*, what must a person do to violate the false statements provisions of the Clean Water Act?
- Is forgetting to conduct a required test a violation of 33 U.S.C. § 1319(c)(4)? How about being in hurry and not following testing procedures?

CHAPTER 6

AIR POLLUTION

As American industry kicked into high gear, so did air pollution. To address this problem, Congress authorized the Surgeon General to study the issue in 1955 and appropriated funds to "support research, training, and demonstration projects, and to provide technical assistance to state and local governments attempting to abate pollution."[1] Five years later, Congress tasked the Surgeon General with studying the health hazards arising from motor vehicle emissions.[2] In 1963, Congress intervened more directly by enacting the "Clean Air Act," which authorized the federal government to expand its air pollution research, to make air pollution reduction grants to the states, and to allow for direct federal intervention to combat interstate air pollution in limited circumstances.[3] Congress amended the new Clean Air Act in 1965 and again in 1966 to increase federal control over motor vehicle emissions.[4]

In 1967, Congress passed the Air Quality Act, which reiterated the state-driven focus of controlling air pollution while simultaneously increasing the federal role in supervising and enforcing air pollution control measures.[5] However, this new act did very little to set any deadlines for the states to attain the air quality standards that they deemed necessary.

Because progress with state implementation to improve air quality was too slow for Congress's liking, it stopped using the carrot of grant money to encourage states to act and instead decided to employ the metaphorical stick.[6] In 1970, Congress significantly amended the Clean Air Act by changing the origin of clean air policymaking from states to the federal government. Although recognizing that "[e]ach state shall have the primary responsibility for assuring air quality" within its entire geographic area, the 1970 amendments established federally created air quality programs in which the states would participate and, in some cases, directly regulate upon federal approval.[7] These federally created programs included: (1) National Ambient Air Quality Standards (NAAQS); (2) New Source Review and New Source Performance Standards, 42 U.S.C. § 7411; and (3) National

---

[1] *Train v. Natural Res. Def. Council, Inc.*, 421 U.S. 60, 63 (1975).
[2] *Id.*
[3] *Id.* (citing 77 Stat. 392).
[4] *Id.* at 64.
[5] *Id.*
[6] *Id.*
[7] *Id.*

Emission Standards for Hazardous Air Pollutants (NESHAP), which was amended in 1977 and again in 1990, 42 U.S.C. § 7412.

In addition to significantly amending the hazardous pollutants program of the Clean Air Act, Congress's 1990 amendments also created three new programs to control air pollution in the United States: (4) acid deposition control, 42 U.S.C. §§ 7651 to 7651o; (5) provisions to protect stratospheric ozone (as opposed to ground-level O_3), 42 U.S.C. §§ 7671 to 7671q; and (6) Title V, which established a new permitting program that was modeled after the NPDES permit under the Clean Water Act. *Compare* 42 U.S.C. § 7661a *and* 33 U.S.C. § 1342.

The 1990 amendments to the Clean Air Act also increased the criminal consequences for violators by adding felony provisions for violations associated with each of the six above-referenced program areas, among others. 42 U.S.C. § 7413(c)(1). Similar to the Clean Water Act, Congress also imposed felony provisions for dishonest acts related to Clean Air Act requirements, 42 U.S.C. § 7413(c)(2), and adopted the "responsible corporate officer" provision of the Clean Water Act. 42 U.S.C. § 7413(c)(6).

However, in a departure from the Clean Water Act, Congress's 1990 amendments to the Clean Air Act imposed a peculiar mens rea standard, which is entirely dependent upon the violator's position within the organization that committed the criminal act. 42 U.S.C. § 7413(h). Because of the centrality of the mens rea requirements to criminal enforcement of the Clean Air Act, they will be discussed first. Following the discussion of mens rea, the remainder of the chapter will discuss possible crimes in each of the six Clean Air Act program categories, recognizing, however, that there is not a separate discussion of the acid deposition control program because that program is enforced through Title V permits. 42 U.S.C. § 7651g(a). Although criminal enforcement is possible under each of these six program categories, some are rarely, if ever, criminally enforced. Consequently, those programs that are rarely, if ever, criminally enforced, will only be discussed briefly below. The remaining discussion will, instead, spend more time on those provisions that are more common to criminal enforcement.

A. THE DUAL MENS REA

Unlike any other environmental criminal statute, the Clean Air Act imposes a mens rea requirement that is specific to the position of the defendant within the organization in which the violation occurred. Section 7413(c)(1) and (c)(2) both provide that "[a]ny person" who knowingly violates the enumerated statutes, in the case of § 7413(c)(1), or knowingly commits any act of dishonesty, in the case of § 7413(c)(2), will be imprisoned up to five years or two years, respectively. 42 U.S.C. § 7413(c)(1), (2). However, § 7413(h) provides in relevant part:

> Except in the case of knowing and willful violations, for purposes of subsection (c)(4) of this section, the term "a person" shall not include an employee who is carrying out his normal activities and who is not a part of senior management personnel or a corporate officer. Except in the case of knowing and willful violations, for purposes of paragraphs (1), (2), (3), and (5) of subsection (c) of this section the term "a person" shall not include an employee who

is carrying out his normal activities and who is acting under orders
from the employer.

42 U.S.C. § 7413(h). In other words, if the person who committed the criminal act under the Clean Air Act is "part of senior management personnel or a corporate officer," then the mens rea is "knowing." However, if the violator is not "part of senior management personnel or a corporate officer," then the mens rea is "knowing and willful."

United States v. Fern
155 F.3d 1318 (11th Cir. 1998)

HATCHETT, Chief Judge. . . .

FACTS

The events leading up to Fern's indictment and eventual convictions began on October 3, 1993. Early that morning, a fire partially damaged the Monte Carlo Oceanfront Resort Hotel, a thirteen-story building on Miami Beach. The Monte Carlo was insured for up to two million dollars under a fire loss policy the Lexington Insurance Company issued. Under the fire loss policy, Lexington agreed to pay for asbestos removal and contamination at the Monte Carlo, but only if the asbestos-related contamination occurred as a result of a fire.

Shortly after the fire, Waquar Ahmed Khan, the president of the company that owned the Monte Carlo, contracted with Fern to determine whether the Monte Carlo's conference room and suites were contaminated with asbestos as a result of the fire. At the time, Fern owned an asbestos testing and consulting firm known as Air Environmental Research Services (AER). Fern then orchestrated a fraudulent scheme to (1) convince Lexington that the Monte Carlo was contaminated thoroughly with asbestos; and (2) profit from a bogus asbestos abatement project at the Monte Carlo.

The scheme unfolded, in part, as follows. Fern directed the Monte Carlo project manager, Jerry Joyner, to take a piece of "Mag Block"—a material containing chalky, crushable asbestos—from a crawl space at the Monte Carlo. Fern then directed Jerry Joyner to take some "hot" air samples from the Monte Carlo using the Mag Block to spike the samples. (In total, Jerry Joyner spiked over twenty samples, often in the presence of Fern, Fern's wife or other AER employees.) After Jerry Joyner spiked the samples, he labeled some of them—at Fern's request—as if they came from the Monte Carlo's pipe-chases. Fern made this request in order to support a claim of asbestos contamination within the entire Monte Carlo resort.

After receiving test results from the spiked air samples, Fern's company, AER, proceeded to prepare an emergency action plan detailing a proposed asbestos abatement project for the Monte Carlo. Neither Fern nor AER was licensed to conduct asbestos abatement or removal work. Consequently, Fern needed to list the name of an authorized asbestos abatement company on the asbestos abatement project paperwork required under 42 U.S.C. § 7413, a provision of the Clean Air Act.

On October 13, 1993, Fern, or one of his employees, filed the first of three Ten-Day Notices completed during the course of the proposed Monte Carlo asbestos abatement project. This Ten-Day Notice—as well as subsequent notices filed on December 14, 1993, and April 4, 1994—contained false responses indicating that a company named Action Systems Unlimited, Inc., was responsible for the asbestos abatement project at the Monte Carlo, and that Judy Joyner—Jerry Joyner's sister-in-law and the president of Action Systems—was the on-site supervisor. The Ten-Day Notice also contained Judy Joyner's forged signature on the notice lines indicating that the information on the notice was correct and that an appropriately trained individual would be on-site at the Monte Carlo during the asbestos abatement project. The first and third Ten-Day Notices also contain references to Judy Joyner's Florida asbestos removal license number.

Neither Judy Joyner nor Action Systems ever did any work at the Monte Carlo. Moreover, Judy Joyner testified at trial that she never authorized anyone to sign her name, use Action Systems's name or use her asbestos removal license number on a Ten-Day Notice for the Monte Carlo asbestos abatement project. Nevertheless, Fern instructed Jerry Joyner to tell anyone who inquired that he worked for Action Systems and that Action Systems was the actual asbestos removal contractor at the Monte Carlo.

At trial, two officials with the Metropolitan Dade County Department of Environmental Resources Management (DERM) testified about the significance of the Ten-Day Notices. According to Hugh Wong, chief of DERM's Air Pollution Control section, Ten-Day Notices are federally required notices that provide information on sites so that regulators can make sure that work is going to be done properly. Wong testified that he "absolutely" relied on the information contained in Ten-Day Notices and that it is important for the information to be accurate. Wong also indicated that DERM uses the information in Ten-Day Notices to determine if the contractor is certified or not, and stated that "if we have not inspected that contractor's work before, we try and target the inspections [to that contractor]." Ray Gordon, a DERM asbestos supervisor, testified that before employees in his office input information from Ten-Day Notices into their computers, they check to make sure that the contractor has a license number noted on the Notice and that the contractor is familiar to them. According to Gordon, the only way DERM officials can know if the individual removing asbestos is properly trained is "if they have the appropriate license."

In addition to submitting false Ten-Day Notices, Fern, and/or AER, also filed documents representing that the contents of the Monte Carlo (e.g., room furnishings and equipment) had to be destroyed because of asbestos contamination. In actuality, Fern gave away, sold or kept most of the Monte Carlo's furnishings and equipment.

Ultimately, Fern submitted a bill for over five hundred thousand dollars to the Monte Carlo for the cost of the bogus asbestos abatement project. The bill was converted into a proof-of-loss and submitted to Lexington via the mail. At trial, Daniel Corbeil, a former co-owner of Action Systems, testified that Fern bragged to him about how he fooled Lexington with spiked samples and with the Action Systems license.

In 1994, the Environmental Protection Agency (EPA) started investigating Fern's work at the Monte Carlo. Jerry Joyner and other AER employees cooperated with the EPA. Jerry Joyner played a critical role in the investigation; he taped his conversations with Fern. During those conversations, Fern offered Jerry Joyner ten thousand dollars to mislead investigators and told him to lie to the grand jury.

PROCEDURAL HISTORY
A grand jury indicted Fern on June 16, 1994, charging him with one count of witness intimidation. The government obtained a superseding indictment from the grand jury on August 12, 1994, charging Fern with eight other counts: three counts of making false statements, four counts of mail fraud and one count of witness tampering.

Fern's first trial began on November 28, 1994. Prior to the testimony of the government's first witness, Fern moved to dismiss the three false statement counts of the indictment for failure to allege essential elements of the charged crime. Fern argued that the indictment was insufficient because it did not allege that the statements were made willfully or that the statements were material. Fern also argued that the indictment did not inform him of the specific statements that were allegedly false. The district court denied Fern's motion and allowed the government to proceed with its presentation of evidence on all counts of the indictment.

ISSUES
Fern raises six issues on appeal. We find each unpersuasive and address . . . whether the superseding indictment contained sufficient information to sustain the three false statement counts against Fern. . . .

DISCUSSION . . .
"A criminal conviction will not be upheld if the indictment upon which it is based does not set forth the essential elements of the offense." This rule serves two functions. First, it puts the defendant on notice of "the nature and cause of the accusation as required by the Sixth Amendment of the Constitution. Second, it fulfills the Fifth Amendment's indictment requirement, ensuring that a grand jury only return an indictment when it finds probable cause to support all the necessary elements of the crime." The law does not, however, require that an indictment track the statutory language. If an indictment specifically refers to the statute on which the charge was based, the reference to the statutory language adequately informs the defendant of the charge. Similarly, if the facts alleged in the indictment warrant an inference that the jury found probable cause to support all the necessary elements of the charge, the indictment is not fatally deficient on Fifth Amendment grounds.

Counts I-III of the superseding indictment charged that Fern, on three separate dates, "did knowingly make false statements on the Notification of Demolition and Renovation form filed, and required to be maintained, pursuant to the Clean Air Act . . . in violation of Title 42, United States Code, Section 7413(c)(2)." Fern contends that these counts of the indictment are insufficient because they . . . fail to state expressly that "willfulness" and "materiality" are elements of a Clean Air Act false statement offense. . . .

Fern's contention regarding the failure to allege "willfulness" is meritless because "willfulness" is not an essential element of an offense under the relevant provision of section 7413(c)(2). Section 7413(c)(2)(A) makes it a crime for any person to "knowingly" make a false material statement in a document required to be filed or maintained. 42 U.S.C. § 7413(c)(2)(A). The plain language of the statute does not require a showing of willfulness, and we decline Fern's invitation to read willfulness into the statute via the language of section 7413(h) of the Clean Air Act. [Footnote 10 of the opinion says: "Section 7413(h) provides in part that certain lower-level employees will not be held liable for some Clean Air Act violations unless their actions are 'knowing and willful.' 42 U.S.C. § 7413(h). Even if section 7413(h) applied in this case—and we do not hold that it does—Fern would not be covered under it because, at the relevant time, he was the president of AER, not a lower-level employee."]

CONCLUSION

For the foregoing reasons, we affirm Daniel Fern's convictions.

AFFIRMED.

- How might knowing a potential defendant's position within the offending company affect prosecutorial discretion in terms of whether to bring charges against that person?
- Why would knowing the individual defendant's position in the company be important before seeking an indictment from a grand jury?
- What evidence would you look for to prove that a person was in "senior management" of the organization whose employees violated the Clean Air Act?
- What do you think Congress was attempting to do by creating this dual mens rea under the Clean Air Act?

B. NATIONAL AMBIENT AIR QUALITY STANDARDS

Congress tasked the EPA with publishing national air quality standards for the "ambient air," which the EPA defined as "that portion of the atmosphere, external to buildings, to which the general public has access." 40 C.F.R. § 50.1(e). Congress required the EPA's national standards to consist of primary NAAQS and secondary NAAQS. Primary NAAQS are those that the EPA determines necessary to protect public health, whereas secondary NAAQS are those designed to "protect the public welfare from any known or anticipated adverse effects associated with the presence of such air pollutant in the ambient air." 42 U.S.C. § 7409.

The EPA promulgated NAAQS for what are known as "criteria pollutants." 42 U.S.C. § 7408(a)(2). Currently, there are six criteria pollutants: sulfur dioxide (SO_2), nitrogen dioxide (NO_2), lead (Pb), carbon monoxide (CO), particulate matter (PM), and ground-level ozone (O_3).

- Sulfur oxides can adversely affect breathing in children, the elderly, and those who suffer from asthma. SO_x can also react with other particles in the air to create acid rain and can contribute to haze that affects visibility.[8]

---

[8] Environmental Protection Agency, *Sulfur Dioxide Basics*, https://www.epa.gov/so2-pollution/sulfur-dioxide-basics.

- Nitrous oxides can irritate the human respiratory system, especially for those with respiratory conditions such as asthma. Similar to SO_2, NO_2 can also react with other chemicals to form acid rain and can contribute to haze. NO_2 can also adversely impact coastal waters.[9]
- Upon exposure to Pb, the human body mistakes it for a nutrient and stores it in the bones. Depending upon the level of exposure along with the sensitivity of the exposed body, Pb can adversely affect the nervous system, kidney function, the immune system, the reproductive system, and the cardiovascular system. Young children exposed to Pb in high enough quantities may also experience learning disabilities. The adverse effects of Pb upon wildlife includes decreased growth and reproductive rates in addition to neurological effects.[10]
- CO reduces the amount of oxygen that the human blood stream can transport. When oxygen is diminished to vital organs like the heart and the brain, a person may suffer a range of symptoms from dizziness to death, depending upon the level of exposure. CO exposure can aggravate symptoms for those with heart disease.[11]
- The EPA regulates PM of 10 or fewer micrometers in size. PM measuring fewer than 10 micrometers can cause breathing problems while PM measuring fewer than 2.5 micrometers contributes to haze and reduced visibility.[12]
- Although O_3 high up in the atmosphere is important to protecting the Earth, when O_3 is found in the lower atmosphere, especially near ground level, it can have harmful effects on human health.[13] Ground-level O_3 can cause breathing difficulty in children, the elderly, and those who suffer from asthma, bronchitis, and emphysema. Additionally, ground-level O_3 can adversely impact the growth of vegetation.[14]

The limits set under the NAAQS apply all over the nation regardless of whether the area is remote and relatively unpopulated (e.g., Great Basin National Park in Nevada) or a heavily populated, sprawling metropolis (e.g., Los Angeles, California). Although the NAAQS set national limits for the amount of each pollutant that is allowed to be present in the ambient air for a given geographic area, the NAAQS themselves are neither civilly nor criminally enforceable. In

[9] Environmental Protection Agency, *Basic Information About NO2*, https://www.epa.gov/no2-pollution/basic-information-about-no2#Effects.
[10] Environmental Protection Agency, *Basic Information About Lead Air Pollution*, https://www.epa.gov/lead-air-pollution/basic-information-about-lead-air-pollution#health.
[11] Environmental Protection Agency, *Basic Information About Carbon Monoxide Outdoor Air Pollution*, https://www.epa.gov/co-pollution/basic-information-about-carbon-monoxide-co-outdoor-air-pollution#Effects.
[12] Environmental Protection Agency, *Particulate Matter Basics*, https://www.epa.gov/pm-pollution/particulate-matter-pm-basics#effects.
[13] Environmental Protection Agency, *Basic Information About Ozone*, https://www.epa.gov/ozone-pollution/basic-information-about-ozone#what%20 where%20how.
[14] Environmental Protection Agency, *Basic Information About Ozone*, https://www.epa.gov/ozone-pollution/basic-information-about-ozone#effects.

other words, Congress did not authorize the Department of Justice to file a civil action or criminal charges against an entity for exceeding the NAAQS. Instead of directly enforcing the NAAQS, enforcement arises out of the programs that attempt to help states remain in or to attain compliance with the NAAQS.

To set forth the programs to remain in or to attain compliance with the NAAQS, the 1970 Clean Air Act amendments required every state to create and have the EPA approve a State Implementation Plan (SIP). 42 U.S.C. § 7410. The requirements for a SIP take up 511 pages in the Code of Federal Regulations. 40 C.F.R. Part 51 (2017). Among these many requirements, SIPs allow for the creation of standards for new sources, motor vehicle inspection requirements, and permits for individual pollution sources with specific emissions limits for certain pollutants.

SIP requirements can be criminally enforced under 42 U.S.C. § 7413(c)(1). However, federal criminal enforcement of the SIP is rare for two reasons. First, federal criminal enforcement of the SIP can only occur "during any period of federally assumed enforcement or more than 30 days after" notifying the violator and the state with an EPA-approved Clean Air program that the violator is not in compliance with a specific SIP provision. If the violation continues any time after the 30-day notice requirement, then a criminal action may be commenced for violating the SIP after the 30-day notice period. However, "federally assumed enforcement" is rare, and notifying the state and the violator of the criminal violation usually remedies the problem or gives violators notice that they are being investigated, which leads to missing evidence and makes proving a "knowing" violation very difficult.

Second, as a practical matter, most of the requirements that may be found in a SIP are usually independent requirements in other parts of the Clean Air Act and, therefore, can be enforced under those other Clean Air Act provisions, which are free from the 30-day notice requirement. Therefore, prosecutors are likely to rely on other sections of the Clean Air Act instead of the SIP provisions.

C. NEW SOURCE REVIEW

The 1970 Clean Air Act amendments sought to assist those areas that were in non-attainment status with the NAAQS to reach attainment status by getting regulatorily involved in the planning, construction, and subsequent operation of new "major stationary sources" of air pollution and major modifications to "major stationary sources." This regulation took the form of a permitting regime that new and major modified major stationary sources of air pollution would have to obtain from the EPA or the EPA-approved state entity before construction and operation of the new or modified major stationary source could begin. 42 U.S.C. §§ 7479, 7502(c)(5), 7602(j). Although Congress required this program to be included in every SIP, the enforcement of the pre-construction permits required under the Clean Air Act can be enforced independently of the SIP.

In the 1977 amendments, Congress became concerned that those areas that were in attainment with the NAAQS would fall into non-attainment. To prevent such a backward step, Congress created the "Prevention of Significant Deterioration of Air Quality" (PSD) program. Under this program, Congress followed the permitting regime from the 1970 amendments for new and modified major stationary sources. Although Congress implemented a pre-construction permitting regime for new and modified major stationary sources in both non-attainment and PSD areas, the requirements for when a permit is required are different for each type of area.

In non-attainment areas, what constitutes a "major stationary source"—and, therefore, is subject to the pre-construction permitting regime—depends on the source's location, its emissions, and the criteria pollutant that is not in compliance with the NAAQS. The term "source" does not refer to one smokestack, for example, but the entire facility. *Chevron, U.S.A., Inc. v. Nat'l Res. Def. Council*, 467 U.S. 837, 840 (1984). If the "source" emits or has the potential to emit more than 100 tons per year of any pollutant regulated under the New Source Review regime, then it is a "major stationary source." 42 U.S.C. § 7602(j); 40 C.F.R. § 51.165(a)(1)(iv). However, if the area in which the source operates is in an "extreme" nonattainment area or emits less than 100 tons per year of certain regulated pollutants, then emitting or having the potential to emit fewer than 100 tons per year will make the stationary source "major." 40 C.F.R. § 51.165(a)(1)(iv)(A)(1).

For PSD areas, a "major stationary source" emits or has the potential to emit 100 tons per year of any criteria pollutant or 250 tons per year of any pollutant regulated under the New Source Review standards. 40 C.F.R. § 52.21(b)(1). Thus, any new source meeting this criterion is required to obtain a pre-construction permit.

Additionally, any "major modification" will trigger the pre-construction permit requirements for both non-attainment and PSD areas. In both non-attainment and PSD areas, a "major modification" means "any physical change in or change in the method of operation of a major stationary source that would result in" a "significant emissions increase" of a regulated New Source Review pollutant and a significant net increase in emissions of that pollutant. 40 C.F.R. §§ 51.165(a)(1)(v)(A), 52.21(b)(2). Thus, if a source makes a modification to one part of its operation that results in an emission increase of a regulated pollutant but is able to reduce emission of that pollutant elsewhere in the operation, then the modification may not be deemed "major." But, if there is an emissions increase of the regulated pollutant and a net increase of that pollutant from the entire source, then the operator of that source is required to obtain a pre-construction permit. These permits will impose technology-based standards upon the new or modified source such as "Reasonably Available Control Technology" (RACT) in non-attainment areas or "Best Available Control Technology" (BACT) in PSD areas.

Criminal enforcement for the pre-construction permit regime is through 42 U.S.C. § 7413(c)(1), which imposes a felony upon "[a]ny person who knowingly violates . . . section 7475(a) . . . (relating to preconstruction requirements). . . ." Also, recall that the mens rea for this provision may be "knowing and willful" if the violator is neither an officer of the company or in senior management. 42 U.S.C. § 7413(h). Although the Clean Air Act imposes criminal liability for violating the pre-construction permit requirements, enforcement is difficult for two reasons. First, the PSD regulations are only triggered if and when the . . . operator (the person with an incentive to avoid the program) voluntarily "self-reports" by applying for a preconstruction permit. There is no mechanism—other than post-hoc litigation—by which environmental regulators are empowered to trigger the PSD and BACT requirements. In other words, the PSD program is somewhat reliant on the proverbial fox to guard the henhouse.

If the operator determines (rightly or wrongly) that a pre-construction PSD permit is not necessary for a particular modification of the plant, no specific action is required on anyone's part—the operator simply continues to run the plant as usual. The statutory and regulatory mechanisms for implementing pollution controls are not triggered. No pre-construction permit is issued by which operating conditions may be established. . . . The process to determine BACT case-by-case at the facility does not occur.

United States v. EME Homer City Generation, L.P., 823 F. Supp. 2d 274, 283-84 (W.D. Pa. 2011). Thus, detecting that a major stationary source has engaged in activity that triggers the pre-construction permit requirement is difficult given that the EPA or approved state agency may only find out about the change if the regulated entity applies for a pre-construction permit.

Second, if the EPA or appropriate state entity discovers the new source or the major modification of an existing one, proving the requisite criminal intent may be challenging due to complexity of the regulations. In fact, given the complexity of the pre-construction permit regime, proving the crime may require proving "willful" intent instead of merely "knowing." For example, suppose that the EPA is made aware that a power plant modified part of its coal-burning operation three years ago. Upon further investigation, it discovers that the change actually resulted in a significant increase in both the emission of a regulated pollutant and an increase of the pollutant from the entire source. However, the power plant argues that its studies and data all showed at the time that the modification would not cause such an increase or that the power plant would be able to reduce emissions elsewhere in the source to zero out the increase in pollution from the new or modified existing source. In the face of such a defense, the prosecution would have to prove that the company knew that its change would require a permit but it chose not to obtain one. Knowing what the law requires but choosing to violate it is "willful" not "knowing." Thus, proving a criminal violation for not obtaining a permit is challenging.

Further, even if a pre-construction permit is applied for and issued, proving that a source knowingly violated that permit can be difficult as well. For example, permit language can often be ambiguous, and the permit provisions may be highly technical, which can lead to understandable confusion about what is required. In such circumstances, criminal enforcement is extremely challenging because the difficulty of proving permit violation is exacerbated by proving that the violation was done knowingly (or even willfully if the violator was not a manager or officer of the company). Given the difficulty of proving criminal liability under this permitting regime, prosecutors often look elsewhere in the Clean Air Act for criminal provisions that are easier to establish, which may explain why there are no reported cases regarding criminal enforcement of the pre-construction permit regime.

D. NEW SOURCE PERFORMANCE STANDARDS

In addition to requiring a permit system prior to constructing a new source or modifying existing major stationary sources, Congress attempted to tackle the air pollution problem from stationary sources by imposing new standards upon them. Consistent with the Clean Air Act's complexity, the definitions of "new source" and "modification" under the New Source Performance Standards (NSPS) regulatory regime are slightly, but significantly, different from those same definitions under the New Source Review standards. For example, under NSPS, the term "new source" means the "construction or modification" of any stationary source "which is commenced after the publication of regulations prescribing a standard of performance" that is applicable to that particular source. 42 U.S.C. § 7411(a)(2). Similarly, the term "modification" includes "any physical change in, or change in the method of operation of, a stationary source which increases the amount of any air pollutant emitted by such source *or* which results in the emission of any air pollutant not previously emitted." 42 U.S.C. § 7411(a)(4). Thus, instead of following the New Source Review definition of a "modification" by basing it solely on the amount of a regulated pollutant that may emerge from the modified source, a "modification" under NSPS includes the increase of any pollutant or emission of a new pollutant. The EPA promulgated 75 source categories in 40 C.F.R. Part 60. Most of the NSPS limits are given in numerical standards.

For example, consider the NSPS standards for "municipal waste combustor metals, acid gases, organics, and nitrogen oxides." Among other standards, the EPA required the following for all "Large Municipal Waste Combustors That Are Constructed on or Before September 20, 1994." 40 C.F.R. Part 60 subpart Cb.

> Before April 28, 2009, the emission limit for cadmium contained in the gases discharged to the atmosphere from a designated facility is 40 micrograms per dry standard cubic meter, corrected to 7 percent oxygen. On and after April 28, 2009, the emission limit for cadmium contained in the gases discharged to the atmosphere from a designated facility is 35 micrograms per dry standard cubic meter, corrected to 7 percent oxygen.

40 C.F.R. § 60.33b(a)(2)(i). As in other parts of the Clean Air Act, a state plan to enforce the NSPS must incorporate the limitations set forth in 40 C.F.R. Part 60, but the state may make those limitations more restrictive than the EPA's limits.

However, where a specific, numerical standard "is not feasible," the Clean Air Act provides that the NSPS for a given category can be expressed through a "standard of performance," which may include "a design, equipment, work practice, or operational standard, or combination thereof." 42 U.S.C. § 7411(h)(1). For example, for oil and gas wells that engage in hydraulic fracturing, 40 C.F.R. § 60.5365a(a)(1), the EPA allows an equipment or work practice standard as an alternative to numerical limits for volatile organic compounds if the well operator can show that by using particular equipment or by performing a job a certain way, it results in fewer emissions of volatile organic compounds.

To determine whether an operator is complying with the NSPS, the EPA has also indicated which tests should be performed for each category. 42 U.S.C. Part 60 appendices. In addition to these tests, the EPA allows enforcement "based exclusively on any credible evidence, without the need to rely on any data from a particular reference test." Credible Evidence Revisions, 62 Fed. Reg. 8,314 (Feb. 24, 1997). Thus, non-compliance with the NSPS limitations can be determined by the EPA-approved tests or by any credible evidence, including the source's own studies.

Criminal enforcement of the NSPS is also done through 42 U.S.C. § 7413(c)(1), which imposes a felony on "[a]ny person who knowingly violates any . . . requirement or prohibition of section 7411(e) of this title (relating to new source performance standards). . . ." Because § 7411(e) applies to "any owner of operator," the prosecution must establish that the defendant is "an owner or operator" of the source. Section 7411(a)(5) defines "owner or operator" as "any person who owns, leases, operates, controls, or supervises a stationary source." 42 U.S.C. § 7411(a)(5). Consider the following example to determine how these principles apply to criminal enforcement.

Case Study: Incinerators in the World's Biggest Little City

Barry is the plant manager for a large incinerator in Reno, Nevada with which the city of Reno, and other municipalities, contract to incinerate their municipal waste. This incinerator was manufactured in 1999, and the EPA NSPS regulations for that incinerator were promulgated in 1994. The state of Nevada's regulations regarding emissions of cadmium are no more stringent than the EPA's regulations for NSPS. Barry's company charges its customers by the ton for the municipal waste Barry's company burns. Barry knows that the more waste his company incinerates, the more money his company makes. Consequently, Barry constantly reminds his subordinate managers that they need to make sure that they are getting as much waste into the incinerator as possible. In fact, Barry bases the bonuses of his subordinate managers on the production totals for the incinerator each quarter. Rod, Barry's environmental compliance contractor, comes to Barry with news that internal tests show that they are exceeding the NSPS for cadmium by 20 micrograms when they incinerate waste at a rate above 4,300 pounds per hour. Consequently, Rod recommends to Barry that he limit production on the incinerator to 3,500 pounds per hour to make sure that the company not exceed the limit on cadmium. Barry thanks Rod for the information but then does nothing to pass along this information to his subordinate managers. Instead, Barry decides that he will reduce the hourly incineration rate to 3,500 when Rod returns next quarter to perform his tests. However, Rod never returns to perform tests because Barry never paid Rod for his work. Barry claims that Rod was incompetent and messed up the testing. Rod, now angry for being cheated out of his money and losing business because of Barry's claims, approaches the EPA to disclose that Barry is exceeding the NSPS for cadmium.

- Should this be a civil or criminal investigation? Why?
- If it should be a criminal investigation, who would you investigate?

- Would you seek an indictment? If so, against whom and for which charges?
- What potential defenses would the defendants have?
- What is the likelihood of success at trial for these charges?

E. NATIONAL EMISSION STANDARDS FOR HAZARDOUS POLLUTANTS

Although the amendments to the Clean Air Act in the 1970s sought to regulate hazardous air pollutants, Congress left it to the EPA to promulgate emissions standards or design, equipment, or work practice standards for each hazardous air pollutant that the EPA identified. 42 U.S.C. § 7412(e) (1977). However, by 1990, Congress had grown tired of waiting for the EPA to follow through. Consequently, Congress took matters into its collective hands by significantly amending § 7412 to identify 187 specific hazardous air pollutants and imposing very strict deadlines on the EPA to promulgate emission standards or design, equipment, or work practice standards for each of the identified pollutants. 42 U.S.C. § 7412(d) and (e). In the nearly 30 years from the enactment of the 1990 amendments, the EPA has managed to promulgate National Emissions Standards for Hazardous Air Pollutants (NESHAPs) for 145 hazardous pollutants. 40 C.F.R. Part 63. In addition to NESHAPs, Congress increased the penalties for those who, in releasing hazardous pollutants, knowingly or negligently endanger others. This section first discusses the most well-known and most often prosecuted NESHAP, which governs asbestos, followed by knowing and negligent endangerment.

1. NESHAP Enforcement: Asbestos

One of the first hazardous substances for which the EPA promulgated standards was asbestos. Air Pollution Prevention and Control, 36 Fed. Reg. 5,931 (March 31, 1971) (listing asbestos, beryllium, and mercury as hazardous air pollutants). "Asbestos is the name given to six minerals that occur naturally in the environment as bundles of fibers that can be separated into thin, durable threads for use in commercial and industrial applications."[15] Once regarded as a miracle substance that was used in insulation, ceiling tiles, roofing, and brake pads, to name a few uses, a subsequent study showed that asbestos was deadly when its fibers were inhaled. Asbestos is a known carcinogen (i.e., causes mesothelioma) and can cause non-cancerous lung disease (i.e., asbestosis) because inhaled fibers remain in the lungs and cause scarring and, therefore, lead to serious health problems.[16] In promulgating specific regulations for asbestos, the EPA could not find that asbestos was safe at any level of emission and, therefore, instead of providing a numerical limit for asbestos emission, the EPA imposed work practice standards. 40 C.F.R. Part 61 subpart M.

Non-compliance with the asbestos NESHAP is the most prosecuted violation under the Clean Air Act. Chief among the most often prosecuted work practice

---

[15]National Cancer Institute, *Asbestos Exposure and Cancer Risk*, www.cancer.gov/about-cancer/causes-prevention/risk/substances/asbestos/asbestos-fact-sheet.

[16] *Id.*

standards for asbestos deals with demolition and renovation. 40 C.F.R. § 61.145. The demolition and renovation asbestos NESHAP first requires an "owner or operator of a demolition or renovation activity" to first inspect the facility or part of the facility to be demolished to determine whether asbestos is present. 40 C.F.R. § 61.145(a). Under the NESHAP, the "owner or operator of a demolition or renovation activity" includes "any person who owns, leases, operates, controls, or supervises the facility being demolished or renovated" and "any person who owns, leases, operates, controls, or supervises the demolition or renovation operation." 40 C.F.R. § 61.142. If the inspection reveals the presence of both Regulated Asbestos Containing Material (RACM) or Asbestos Containing Materials (ACM) in a minimum quantity, then the owner or operator of the demolition or renovation activity must notify the EPA prior to starting activity. RACM includes "friable asbestos," which means any material consisting of at least 1 percent asbestos that can be crumbled or reduced to powder by mere hand pressure. 40 C.F.R. § 61.141. The owner or operator must also inform the EPA if the demolition or renovation activity encounters unanticipated conditions. 40 C.F.R. § 61.145(b). The NESHAP then explains the procedures that the owner and operator must follow to remove or to mitigate RACM and to ensure that ACM does not become RACM. Some of these procedures include ventilation systems, leak-tight wrapping, and wetting the RACM to prevent it from becoming airborne. 40 C.F.R. § 61.145(c)(6). The EPA promulgated another NESHAP specifically for the disposal of asbestos-containing waste. 40 C.F.R. § 61.150.

Similar to the previously discussed Clean Air Act provisions, criminal enforcement of the NESHAPs is through 42 U.S.C. § 7413(c)(1), which imposes a felony punishable up to five years in prison for "knowingly" violating § 7412. Section 7412(f)(4) prohibits the emission of a hazardous air pollutant contrary to any emission standard that the EPA promulgates. However, § 7412 regulates the actions of an "owner or operator," not their employees. *United States v. Burrell*, No. 96-1419 (3d Cir. Oct. 23, 1996) (unpublished). Thus, if an owner or operator of a demolition or renovation activity knowingly violates the inspection, notification, removal, or disposal provisions of the NESHAP, then he/she/it may be subjected to criminal liability. Consider the following examples.

United States v. Dipentino
242 F.3d 1090 (9th Cir. 2001)

DAVID R. THOMPSON, Circuit Judge:
Rocco Dipentino and Rafiq Ali appeal their convictions following their joint trial for improperly removing asbestos-containing materials from the Landmark Hotel and Casino in Las Vegas, Nevada, prior to its demolition, in violation of the Clean Air Act, 42 U.S.C. §§ 7412(f)(4) and (h), 7413(c)(1). . . .

The Las Vegas Convention and Visitors Authority ("Visitors Authority") hired Ab-Haz Environmental, Inc. ("Ab-Haz"), an asbestos-abatement consulting firm, to oversee the removal of asbestos-containing materials from the Landmark Hotel and Casino in Las Vegas, Nevada, prior to its demolition. Rafiq Ali was the president and sole proprietor of Ab-Haz; Rocco Dipentino was an industrial hygienist employed by Ab-Haz as the on-site inspector at the Landmark. Under the terms of its contract with the Visitors Authority, Ab-Haz was required to: (1)

survey the Landmark and identify the asbestos-containing materials that needed to be removed prior to demolition; (2) prepare specifications for how the asbestos removal job was to be performed; (3) assist the Visitors Authority in selecting an asbestos-removal contractor to remove the asbestos-containing materials; (4) serve as the Visitors Authority's on-site representative, providing day-to-day monitoring and oversight of the work to ensure that it was being performed in accordance with the law; and (5) inspect and certify that the site was free from asbestos following the completion of the asbestos-removal work.

The Clean Air Act classifies asbestos as a hazardous air pollutant. Emissions of hazardous air pollutants in violation of work practice standards promulgated by the Environment Protection Agency are prohibited. Under the work practice standard relevant to this case, an owner or operator of a demolition activity is required to remove all asbestos prior to demolition and must "[a]dequately wet the [asbestos-containing] material and ensure that it remains wet until collected and contained" in leak-tight containers for proper disposal. An owner or operator of a demolition activity who knowingly violates a work practice standard is subject to criminal penalties. An employee who is carrying out his or her normal activities and acting under orders from the employer is liable only for knowing and willful violations.

The grand jury for the District of Nevada returned a two-count indictment against Ab-Haz, Rafiq Ali, Rocco Dipentino, and a defendant who was later acquitted, Richard Lovelace, who was the on-site inspector of the asbestos-removal contractor hired by the Visitors Authority. Count 1 of the indictment charged the defendants with knowingly conspiring to violate the Clean Air Act by removing regulated asbestos-containing materials from surfaces in the Landmark without complying with the applicable work practice standards. Count 2, paragraph A ("Count 2 ¶ A") charged each defendant with knowingly violating the Clean Air Act by leaving scraped asbestos-containing debris on floors and other surfaces, where it was allowed to dry out, instead of placing the debris, while wet, into leak-proof containers for removal from the site. Count 2, paragraph B ("Count 2 ¶ B") charged each defendant with knowingly violating the Clean Air Act by causing asbestos-covered facility components to fall from the ceiling to the floor, rather than carefully lowering such components so as not to dislodge asbestos. One government inspector described the removal project as "the worst [asbestos] abatement job I've seen."

At the close of the government's case, the district court granted the defendants' motions for judgment of acquittal on Counts 1 and 2 ¶ B, but held that the government had produced sufficient evidence to support a conviction on Count 2 ¶ A. The jury convicted Ali and Dipentino on Count 2 ¶ A, but acquitted Lovelace. The district court sentenced Ali and Dipentino to five months' incarceration and five months of home detention, and fined Ali $3,000 and Dipentino $2,000. . . .

Dipentino asserts that the evidence was insufficient to support his conviction for violating the Clean Air Act. We reach this argument because if the evidence presented at trial was insufficient to support a conviction, the Double Jeopardy Clause would bar a retrial. "Sufficient evidence exists to support a conviction if, viewing the evidence in the light most favorable to the prosecution, any rational trier of fact could have found the essential elements of the crime beyond a reasonable doubt."

The Clean Air Act imposes criminal liability on an owner or operator if he or she knowingly violates the Act. The term "owner or operator" is defined under the asbestos regulations as "any person who owns, leases, operates, controls, or supervises the facility being demolished or renovated or any person who owns, leases, operates, controls or supervises the demolition or renovation operation, or both." In determining whether a person is an owner or operator within the meaning of the Clean Air Act, the question is whether the person "ha[d] significant or substantial or real control and supervision over [the] project."

The evidence established that Dipentino "ha[d] significant or substantial or real control and supervision" over the asbestos-abatement project at the Landmark and that he knowingly violated the relevant work practice standards charged in the indictment. The government presented evidence that Dipentino was employed by Ab-Haz as the Landmark's "on-site representative during the term of work"; that he was present at the site on a daily basis; that he performed inspections of areas that the asbestos-removal contractor had allegedly abated; that he prepared and signed final inspection reports certifying that rooms in the Landmark were clear of asbestos-containing material; and that he had the power to stop the asbestos-removal contractor's work for improper performance.

The government also presented evidence that Dipentino was licensed by the State of Nevada as an asbestos-abatement supervisor and consultant; that in support of his applications for those licenses, Dipentino certified that he had completed courses and training in environmental law requirements; that Dipentino co-authored with Rafiq Ali the asbestos survey of the Landmark, which revealed that the Landmark contained 328,000 square feet of asbestos-containing acoustical ceiling spray, 1250 linear feet of asbestos-containing fireproofing material on structural components such as beams, as well as asbestos-containing pipe insulation and other materials found throughout the facility; and that piles of asbestos-containing debris were discovered by inspectors after the Landmark abatement job was certified as completed. Although Dipentino argues that the jury could not reasonably have concluded that he knew, simply by looking, that the debris left to dry on the floors of the Landmark contained asbestos, the district court properly rejected this argument in a post-judgment order stating: "Knowledge that a debris pile contains asbestos, however, can also result from knowing the source and nature of the material in the debris pile. Plainly it can be concluded that a person knows a debris pile contains asbestos if that person knew that the debris pile was created from material that the person knew to contain asbestos." In sum, there was sufficient evidence to convict Dipentino.

- To prove a knowing violation, must the prosecution prove that the defendant knew that the material that was improperly removed was RACM?
- If so, is that a "knowing" mens rea or a "willful" mens rea?

United States v. San Diego Gas & Electric Co.
2007 WL 4326773 (S.D. Cal. Dec. 7, 2007)

DANA M. SABRAW, District Judge.

On August 22, 2007, Defendants San Diego Gas and Electric Company ("SDG & E"), Kyle Rheubottom, and David Joseph Williamson filed motions for acquittal and, in the alternative, for new trial under Rules 29 and 33 of the Federal Rules of Criminal Procedure. The motions were fully briefed by the parties, and argued on September 26, 2007. On October 4, 2007, the parties submitted supplemental briefing at the request of the Court regarding the admissibility of certain samples of asbestos containing materials and the test methodology employed to determine the asbestos content of those samples.

Defendants advanced numerous grounds in support of their motions. Two grounds merit relief. The admission of scientific test results regarding the asbestos content of certain samples of pipe wrap, combined with the manner in which such results were argued to the jury, warrants a new trial as to all Defendants on the asbestos NESHAP work practices counts.

I.

BACKGROUND

The facts are well known to the parties and thus, only facts relevant to the issues addressed in this Order are set forth below. Defendants SDG & E, Kyle Rheubottom, David Joseph Williamson, and Jacquelyn McHugh were among the first persons in the nation to be charged with criminal violations of asbestos NESHAP work practice standards promulgated by the Environmental Protection Agency ("EPA"). The Government alleged Defendants violated certain NESHAP work practice standards during the removal of over nine miles of asbestos-containing gas pipeline. The Government's case-in-chief included five counts: three work practices counts, one false statement count, and one conspiracy count. After the Government rested, the Court granted Defendants' Rule 29 motion and dismissed the conspiracy count as to all Defendants. The counts in the indictment were thereafter renumbered, and the jury was charged with deciding the remaining four counts.

Counts one through three charged Defendants with various violations of the asbestos NESHAP work practice standards, including failure to provide written notice of the removal of "regulated asbestos containing material" ("RACM") in advance of the start date of the renovation operation (count one), failure to adequately wet RACM (count two), and failure to contain RACM in leak tight containers (count three). The fourth count charged Defendants SDG & E and Williamson with making a false statement to federal authorities under 18 U.S.C. § 1001.

After a lengthy trial involving numerous novel issues of law, a jury found Defendant SDG & E guilty on all counts, and Defendants Rheubottom and Williamson guilty on count three (failure to contain RACM in leak tight containers). Defendants Rheubottom and Williamson were acquitted of the remaining work practices counts. The jury deadlocked as to Defendant Williamson on the false statement count, and Defendant McHugh was acquitted of the one work practice count with which she was charged: failure to provide written notice (count one).

The regulatory scheme promulgated by the EPA subjects the removal of certain "asbestos containing materials," or "ACM," to environmental oversight and regulation. Not all materials containing asbestos, and not all demolition projects, are regulated. To be "regulated," the material and project must exceed certain thresholds regarding project size and asbestos content. Pertinent to the present motion are the following requirements: (1) the quantity of asbestos content in the ACM must exceed 1% as determined by a designated test method (40 C.F.R. § 61.141); and (2) the ACM must be "friable," that is, the material may be crumbled by hand pressure creating dust, or if initially "nonfriable," the ACM must have a "high probability" of becoming friable due to acts of disturbance during the removal process. (Id.) If the ACM meets these and other standards not relevant here, it is deemed to be regulated asbestos containing material, or RACM, and subject to governmental oversight and regulation through the NESHAP work practices standards. Accordingly, as a threshold to criminal culpability, the Government must prove that the material under investigation is RACM, i.e., contains more than 1% asbestos and is friable or has a high probability of becoming friable. The central issue here is whether the Government properly proved that the pipe wrap in question contained more than 1% asbestos.

To prove the pipe wrap contained more than 1% asbestos, the Government presented eighteen samples of pipe wrap to the jury. Each sample was analyzed by a laboratory, and each laboratory was represented by a witness who testified before the jury about the test procedure used by the lab to determine asbestos content. All but five of the samples were destroyed after testing. Defendants' labs tested the five existing samples ("SD-1, 2, 3, 4 & 5"), and Defendants presented their own evidence reporting the results of those tests.

Throughout the litigation, both the test procedures used to determine asbestos content and the nature of the samples tested were the subject of intense debate. These disputes, which were novel and highly technical, were the subject of several pre-trial orders issued by the Court. In its first order, the Court held that where discrete layers of ACM are identified, each layer must be analyzed for asbestos content, and the results must then be combined to determine "an estimate of asbestos content for the whole sample." This test method has been referred to by the Court throughout this litigation as the "averaging test."

The Government initially charged and indicted Defendants with work practices violations based upon a different test, one in which only a single layer was tested for asbestos content. Using the "single layer" test method, the Government determined asbestos content by testing only the layer of pipe wrap that contained asbestos (and ignoring other non-asbestos containing layers). The Court held the single layer test method was not subject to rulemaking procedures as mandated by the Administrative Procedures Act and thus, the test could not be used in place of the averaging test. Because the Government relied upon single layer testing to indict Defendants, the Court dismissed the work practices counts. Thereafter, the Government re-indicted Defendants. . . .

During trial, Defendants moved to exclude most of the Government's scientific evidence on grounds that it conformed with neither the NESHAP regulations nor the Court's RACM Orders. The Government represented the tests were compliant with the pretrial orders. The Court ultimately concluded that its pretrial orders were clear, and any non-compliance by the laboratories would go to the weight rather than the admissibility of the evidence in question. The Court was satisfied that any nonconformity would be revealed during cross examination and the evidence—given its probative value—was not sufficiently confusing or prejudicial to warrant exclusion. On these grounds, the Court allowed the Government to present the evidence. . . .

III.
DISCUSSION
A. The NESHAP and the Court's Pretrial Orders

The NESHAP regulations describe the process for collecting and analyzing ACM to determine asbestos content. More specifically, the Court's RACM Orders describe the type of sample required for testing, and the test method for determining asbestos content where discrete strata are identified. These matters are discussed in more detail below.

1. Step One: Sampling

As discussed, the Court in its pretrial orders held that a "complete" sample must be used to determine asbestos content under the averaging test. After trial, Defendants refined their arguments on this issue.

Defendants now focus on Section 1.7.1 of the regulations, which provides in pertinent part, "[s]amples for analysis of asbestos content shall be taken in the manner prescribed in Reference 5. . . . If there are any questions about the representative nature of the sample, another sample should be requested before proceeding with the analysis." Reference 5 is a document entitled "Asbestos-Containing Materials in School Buildings: A Guidance Document." ("Guidance Document"). Under the heading "How to Take a Sample," the Guidance Document states, "a representative sample should be taken from within the material itself by penetrating the depth of the material with a sample container." (Guidance Document at 9). It further emphasizes, "be sure to penetrate any paint or protective coating and all the layers of the material." (Id. at 10). While this precise argument was not advanced pretrial by Defendants, it is entirely consistent with the Court's pretrial orders, with one significant difference: the sampling requirements set forth in Section 1.7.1 are not limited to the volumetric averaging test, but rather apply to all samples tested under any test methodology. The Court's RACM Orders, in response to the parties' briefings and arguments, focused only on proper sampling methods for testing by volumetric averaging.

The Government advances four principal arguments that a "representative" sample as described by Section 1.7.1 (and apparently a "whole" or "complete" sample as described in the RACM 1.5 Order) is not required. These arguments lack merit for the following reasons.

First, the Government argues the phrase "representative sample" as used in the EPA regulations refers only to a representative sample of the pipe wrap that an inspector was actually provided, regardless of whether the sample is representative of the pipe wrap as it existed on the pipe. The Government argues that were it otherwise, a sophisticated defendant that managed to clean up most of the ACM could make it impossible for the EPA to find a representative sample of the type described in the Guidance Document, and thus hamper the Government's ability to prosecute. Inspectors, according to the Government, should therefore be able to sample and test whatever material they find, regardless of whether it is a representative sample.

The regulations, however, clearly require a representative sample of ACM, not simply a sample representative of whatever material inspectors happen to find. Case law is consistent: "samples are receivable in evidence to show the quality or condition of the entire lot or mass from which they are taken. The prerequisites necessary to the admission in evidence of samples are that the mass should be substantially uniform with reference to the quality in question and that the sample portion should be of such a nature as to be fairly representative." In other words, if a sample is only representative of what inspectors encounter, it tells the fact finder nothing about the composition of the material as a whole, or, in this case, the pipe wrap on the pipe.

Further, the Government's argument that obtaining representative samples of the type required by the regulation could be difficult and sometimes impossible, thereby precluding prosecution, is purely theoretical. The Government not only could have collected representative samples from over nine miles of pipe wrap on the pipe, it did in fact collect such samples. The parties agree, for example, that SD-2 is a representative (or whole) sample of pipe wrap. In addition, even if regulatory authorities are precluded from obtaining a representative sample due to illicit cover-up efforts of an owner or operator of a renovation or demolition operation, otherwise inadmissible evidence does not become admissible on that basis alone.

Second, the Government argues the sampling methods set forth in the Guidance Document are intended for self-evaluation purposes, and are not required for compliance or admissibility in a criminal prosecution. Adopting this interpretation would subject owners and operators of demolition and renovation projects to arbitrary prosecution. If the Government is not required to test samples that are representative of the suspected ACM, a party's guilt or innocence would depend entirely upon the sample collected, no matter how contaminated or unrepresentative. The Government's proposed rule would permit the following situation: a company tests ACM using a representative sample, finds it is not RACM, and on that information, properly concludes there is no obligation to comply with the NESHAP requirements. Later, after demolition or renovation activities begin, the regulatory authorities retrieve and test bits and pieces from the project that may not be representative or whole samples. If such samples reveal high concentrations of asbestos, the company would be subject to criminal prosecution for asbestos NESHAP violations even when the ACM, based upon a representative sample, is not RACM. Such a result would violate basic principles of due process, which "require[ ] legislatures to set reasonably clear guidelines for law enforcement officials and triers of fact in order to prevent arbitrary and discriminatory enforcement" of the law.

Third, the Government argues it understood the phrase "whole sample" as used by the Court in its Order to require that the whole sample collected be tested in its entirety, not, as Defendants argue, that the sample itself be a whole or representative section of pipe wrap. This argument is contrary to the record. . . . The Court inquired of the Government whether it had any whole samples, i.e., samples that "contained all the layers, albeit not intact." The Government responded, "SD-2 does contain all of the layers of the material." Clearly, it was understood by the parties that a "whole sample" meant an all-layers sample.

Fourth, the Government argues the sampling procedure outlined in the Guidance Document only applies to the sampling of "friable" material, so if material is non-friable on the pipe, no representative samples must be collected. The regulation itself belies this argument. . . .

Accordingly, in order to establish threshold quantities of asbestos (1% or more) to support a finding of RACM and criminal prosecution, the Government must base its showing upon a representative sample. If a sample is not representative, it is inadmissible for purposes of proving asbestos content of the ACM (pipe wrap) as a whole. The determination that a representative sample is a foundational prerequisite to admitting test results significantly impacts this case, as many non-representative samples were admitted into evidence and considered by the jury.

2. Step Two: Testing

Once a representative sample is collected, it must be tested by a sanctioned laboratory in accordance with the NESHAP regulations. In addition to collecting a representative sample under Section 1.7.1, the regulations set forth a number of steps to testing, including but not limited to, averaging when discrete strata are identified (1.7.2.1), sample preparation (1.7.2.2), fiber identification (1.7.2.3), and quantification (1.7.2.4).

In simple terms, after a sample is prepared and fibers are identified, the fibers must be quantified. The proper method of quantification depends upon whether discrete layers are found during the sample preparation step. If discrete layers are not identified, the Government argues the quantity of asbestos in a homogenized sample or representative sub-sample ("pinch mounts") represents the quantity of asbestos in the entire sample, and the analysis is complete. This method of testing was not briefed by the parties, and the Court did not determine whether any of the samples complied with these test procedures. Conversely, as discussed, where discrete strata are identified, volumetric averaging is employed.

B. The Government's Samples

Of the eighteen samples offered by the Government and admitted in evidence, twelve are described by both parties as "debris" or "waste" collected from the CRC Evans stripping machine and nearby dumpsters. ("Debris Samples"). The Debris Samples are not representative. . . .

C. Admissibility of Non-Representative Samples and Test Methodologies Other Than Volumetric Averaging . . .

While the test results from non-representative samples are relevant to whether the pipe wrap is friable, their probative value on the issue of whether the pipe wrap contained more than 1% asbestos was—with the benefit of hindsight—substantially outweighed by undue prejudice and confusion of issues. This is particularly so given the highly technical and scientific nature of the testimony. It is axiomatic that expert testimony can be "quite misleading because of the difficulty in evaluating it." Therefore, courts "in weighing possible prejudice against probative force under Rule 403 . . . exercise[ ] more control over experts than over lay witnesses." The Government presented the jury with eighteen samples, all of which contained over 1% asbestos (some as high as 60%). The evidence overwhelmingly indicated that the pipe wrap contained more than 1% asbestos, despite strenuous Defense argument that nearly all of the samples did not comply with the regulatory requirements. . . .

The admission of both non-representative samples and samples tested under methods of debatable validity, combined with the manner in which such results were argued to the jury, caused unfair prejudice and confusion of issues. Defendants presented substantial evidence regarding SD-2 (the only sample the Government demonstrated was representative), calling into question the accuracy of the Government's volumetric averaging test results. Such evidence preponderated sufficiently against the verdict that the Court is persuaded a serious miscarriage of justice occurred. For these reasons, the Court sets aside the convictions on the asbestos NESHAP counts, and grants a new trial.

- Based on this ruling, what would happen if the EPA happened upon piles of pipe insulation after a pipe-stripping activity and not all of the layers of asbestos were still intact in the debris piles? Samples from the debris piles show that portions of the insulation contained much more than 1 percent asbestos. Is the United States, therefore, unable to bring either a civil or a criminal case against the owner or operator because it cannot piece together the order of the layers of insulation for purposes of taking the average of the asbestos content?
- Is this consistent with what Congress was trying to accomplish through the NESHAPs?

2. Knowing and Negligent Endangerment

In further recognition of the danger that hazardous air pollutants create, Congress imposed additional criminal penalties on those who negligently or knowingly release one of the specified hazardous air pollutants into the outdoor air and, by so doing, negligently or knowingly place another person "in imminent danger of death or serious bodily injury." 42 U.S.C. § 7413(c)(4), (5). The Clean Air Act is unique in that Congress imposed misdemeanor liability for negligent endangerment. Similar to the Clean Water Act and RCRA, Congress imposed up to 15 years' imprisonment for those whose releases of hazardous air pollutants result in knowing endangerment.

Unlike many of the criminal provisions in the Clean Air Act, which require the violator to be an "owner or operator," the negligent and knowing endangerment provisions allow "any person" to be liable. However, recall that 42 U.S.C. § 7413(h) provides that the mens rea for "a person" is "knowing and willful" if he/she is either carrying out his/her "normal activities and who is not part of senior management" or is "carrying out his normal activities and who is acting under orders from the employer." Thus, negligent and knowing endangerment will carry a "knowing and willful" mens rea for those workers who are doing their jobs and are not part of senior management (for negligent endangerment) or are carrying out their normal activities under their employer's direction (for knowing endangerment). Given the high standard, it is not surprising that, as of this writing, there have been no known convictions or guilty pleas for knowing endangerment under the Clean Air Act. However, there have been several guilty pleas for negligent endangerment. Consider the following negligent endangerment case.

United States v. Hamilton
2:11-CR-00130 (W.D. La. 2011), ECF No. 1

Bill of Information
THE UNITED STATES ATTORNEY CHARGES:

Count 1
On or about August 22, 2005, through on or about December 31, 2005, and specifically including September 11, 2005, and October 15, 2005, in the Western District of Louisiana, the defendant, BYRON HAMILTON, negligently released and caused the release into the ambient air hazardous air pollutants that were listed pursuant to 42 U.S.C. § 7412 (to wit: benzene, ethylbenzene, toluene, and xylene) and an extremely hazardous substance listed pursuant to 42 U.S.C. § 11002(a)(2) (to wit: hydrogen sulfide) which at the time of the releases negligently placed other persons in imminent danger of death or serious bodily injury. All in violation of 42 U.S.C. § 7413(c)(4).

Count 2
On or about January 1, 2006, through on or about December 31, 2006, in the Western District of Louisiana, the defendant, BYRON HAMILTON, negligently released and caused the release into the ambient air hazardous air pollutants that were listed pursuant to 42 U.S.C. § 7412 (to wit: benzene, ethylbenzene, toluene, and xylene) and an extremely hazardous substance listed pursuant to 42 U.S.C. § 11002(a)(2) (to wit: hydrogen sulfide) which at the time of the releases negligently placed other persons in imminent danger of death or serious bodily injury. All in violation of 42 U.S.C. § 7413(c)(4). . . .

United States v. Hamilton
2:11-CR-00130 (W.D. La. 2011), ECF No. 8

PLEA AGREEMENT
A. INTRODUCTION
1. Pursuant to Federal Rule of Criminal Procedure 11(c)(1)(C), this document contains the complete plea agreement between the United States (the "Government," meaning exclusively the U.S. Attorney's Office for the Western District of Louisiana and the U.S. Department of Justice's Environmental Crimes Section) and BYRON HAMILTON (the "Defendant"). . . .

B. THE DEFENDANT'S OBLIGATIONS
1. BYRON HAMILTON shall waive Grand Jury presentment of an indictment of the charges filed in this case and appear in open court and plead guilty to the two count Bill of Information pending in this case. Counts 1-2 charge negligent endangerment violations of the Clean Air Act, 42 U.S.C. § 7412(c)(4). In pleading guilty, the Defendant admits that with respect to each of Counts 1-2,

he negligently released and caused to be released into the ambient air a hazardous air pollutant and extremely hazardous substance and at the time negligent placed other persons in imminent danger of death or serious bodily injury. Defendant agrees that the Joint Factual Statement is a true and accurate statement of his criminal conduct. . . .

JOINT FACTUAL STATEMENT

The United States of America and Defendant, Byron Hamilton ("Defendant"), hereby agree that this Joint Factual Statement is a true and accurate statement of the Defendant's criminal conduct, that it provides a sufficient basis for the Defendant's pleas of guilt to the charges in the above-captioned matter and as set forth in the Plea Agreement signed this same day, and had this matter proceeded to trial, the United States would have proven the facts contained in this Joint Factual Statement beyond a reasonable doubt.

1. Defendant Byron Hamilton served as the Vice President and General Manager of Pelican Refining Company ("PRC") from approximately January 2005 to the present. At all relevant times, PRC operated the Pelican Refinery, a crude oil and asphalt refining facility located in Lake Charles, Louisiana. . . . The highest level managers at the facility, including two refinery managers, reported directly to Hamilton. . . . The Defendant was a responsible corporate officer and acknowledges that he is guilty of the charged conduct by virtue of his knowledge, position, and authority. . . .

5. In 2005 and 2006, the Pelican Refinery processed "sour" crude supplied by its owners that had high concentrations of hydrogen sulfide, also known as "H2S." H2S is a highly toxic and flammable gas inherent in sour crude refining. H2S is classified as an "extremely hazardous substance" pursuant to 42 U.S.C. § 11002(a)(2). Louisiana has classified hydrogen sulfide as a Class III toxic air pollutant (acute and chronic toxin). H2S is colorless and flammable. It has a characteristic odor of "rotten eggs" at low concentrations. Refinery workers reported smelling H2S as well as having their personal H2S monitors "go off" from time-to-time. PRC had no procedure to record, track, report, or mitigate H2S releases. At higher concentrations, H2S paralyzes the sense of smell so that its odor is no longer perceived. At very high concentrations it paralyzes the respiratory center of the brain so that the exposed individual stops breathing, and loses consciousness and dies unless removed from exposure and is resuscitated. Crude oil also contains benzene, toluene, ethylbenzene, and xylene (collectively "BTEX") which are listed hazardous air pollutants and extremely hazardous substances. . . .

6. The Pelican Refinery stored crude oil in tanks with floating roofs that go up and down with the volume of the petroleum inside and which have seals around the perimeter. The purpose of the [roof] is to prevent pollutants including volatile organic compounds and H2S from escaping. At the time, the refinery was purchased by PRC, tank 110-16 had a failed roof. . . . [The refinery manager was notified by the owner] that oil would be arriving at the facility and directed that it should be placed in tank 110-16 since other tanks were in use with oil supplied by the other owner. The refinery manager refused to do so on the grounds that the roof had failed and that it would be unlawful. The refinery manager resigned. . . . On or about October 13, 2005 . . . PRC introduce[d] and caused the introduction and storage of sour crude oil . . . into tank 110-16 in violation of the Clean Air Act

because [the roof had failed]. . . . Hamilton was notified of the failure at the time. . . . Employees suggested to Hamilton that the oil be removed from the tank by offloading it onto barges. Hamilton, knowing the expense of ordering barges would not be approved by the owners, refused and told the employees that he would not pay for barges. . . . The release of H2S and BTEX into the ambient air resulted in an imminent danger of death of serious bodily injury to employees at the facility. . . .

[Paragraphs 7-16 recount other instances of H2S and BTEX escaping into the atmosphere from other areas of the source that were in disrepair, which caused adverse health effects in the surrounding neighborhood and among workers.]

- Does this guilty plea admitting endangerment of workers as a factual basis for conviction cut against the court's ruling in *United States v. Borowski*, 977 F.2d 27 (1st Cir. 1992), which held that, under the Clean Water Act's knowing endangerment provision, workers who performed the activity resulting in the unlawful emission are not protected?
- When does "negligent" endangerment become "knowing" endangerment? In other words, if a manager is repeatedly told that extremely hazardous substances are being emitted and, yet, the manager does nothing about it, does there come a point when negligent endangerment becomes knowing endangerment?

F. ATMOSPHERIC OZONE PROTECTION

In 1987, the United States and several other nations signed the Montreal Protocol on Substances that Deplete the Ozone Layer.[17] This protocol focused on reducing the production, consumption, and emission of ozone-depleting substances such as chlorofluorocarbons (CFCs) and halons, among others. CFCs and halons have been used as refrigerants in cooling systems and fire-suppression systems, among many other uses. The United States implemented this protocol in the 1990 amendments to the Clean Air Act. 42 U.S.C. §§ 7671 to 7671q. Pursuant to the protocol, Congress, as implemented through the EPA's regulations, used a "divide and prohibit" policy. First, Congress divided the substances designated as ozone-depleting (ODSs) into two categories: Class I and Class II ODSs. Congress phased out domestic production and importation of Class I ODSs (i.e., halons) on January 1, 1994. Congress followed up by phasing out production and importation of Class II ODSs over time. For example, the production and importation of certain CFCs were phased out by January 1, 1996, while others will be phased out by 2020 followed by a final, all-CFC ban by 2030. After each of these respective dates, production or importation of Class I and II ODSs are prohibited unless a person has obtained certain allowances under the law. Criminal enforcement of these bans is generally done through the smuggling provisions of 18 U.S.C. §§ 542 and 545, which will be discussed in Chapter 9.

In addition to regulating production and importation of ODSs, the 1990 amendments also imposed stiff criminal penalties for knowingly venting any Class

[17] Montreal Protocol on Substances that Deplete the Ozone Layer (with annex), Sept. 16, 1987, https://treaties.un.org/doc/publication/unts/volume%201522/volume-1522-i-26369-english.pdf.

I or Class II substance used as a refrigerant. 42 U.S.C. § 7671g(c). Currently, the Clean Air Act prohibits "any person" from knowingly venting or knowingly releasing or disposing of "any class I or class II substance used as a refrigerant . . . in a manner which permits such substance to enter the environment" unless the amount released is "de minimus" and is done in "good faith attempts to recapture and recycle or safely dispose" of such substances. 42 U.S.C. § 7671g(c)(1). Additionally, the Clean Air Act prohibits the "venting, release, or disposal of any substitute substance for a class I or class II substance by any person maintaining, servicing, repairing, or disposing of an appliance or industrial process refrigeration." 42 U.S.C. § 7671g(c)(2). The term "appliance" includes "any air conditioner, refrigerator, chiller, or freezer." *Id.* Criminal enforcement of this prohibition is done through 42 U.S.C. § 7413(c)(1), which imposes a felony for knowingly violating these provisions, among others. Consider the following example.

Case Study: Air Conditioner Theft Gone Wrong

Alexander Morrissette and his buddy, Randall Wimpey, were looking for a little extra money. Instead of robbing a bank or selling drugs, they decided to steal aluminum-copper coils from functioning air-conditioner units around the city, extract the copper, and sell it to a smelter that was paying good money for copper. Morrissette stole 12 aluminum-copper coils from 12 functioning, commercial air conditioning units at a pharmacy in Monroe, Georgia. Wimpey followed suit by stealing coils from another building in the city. Because the air conditioning units from which these men stole the air conditioner coils were functioning, they released a Class II refrigerant from each unit. Unfortunately for both of them, Wimpey was caught when he tried to rob the coil from his assigned air conditioner unit. Wimpey sang like a canary and told police about his agreement with Morrissette.[18]

- As a prosecutor, which charges related to the Clean Air Act would you seek?
- Would the "knowing and willful" mens rea of 42 U.S.C. § 7413(h) apply to Morrissette and Wimpey? Why or why not?
- If "knowing" were the appropriate mens rea, on which evidence would you rely to establish guilt?
- If the "knowing and willful" mens rea applies to them, is there sufficient evidence to obtain a conviction beyond a reasonable doubt?

G. TITLE V PERMITS

In the 1990 amendments, Congress decided to include a permitting system in the Clean Air Act that was as expansive as the Clean Water Act's. Consequently, whereas New Source Review, NSPS, and NESHAPs regulate specified pollutants, the Clean Air Act's Title V permits allow for the regulation of any air pollutant (including NAAQS pollutants such as sulfur dioxides and nitrogen oxides, which

---

[18] Based on *United States v. Morrissette*, 579 Fed. App'x 916 (11th Cir. Sept. 16, 2014).

contribute to acid deposition, among other pollution problems). Although these Title V permits issued by a state can be federally enforced, the state permit can specifically exclude them from federal enforcement. 40 C.F.R. § 70.6(b)(2).

Title V allows the EPA or state-approved agency to use permits to link together all of the various Clean Air Act programs. For example, Title V permits can be issued to: any source required to obtain a pre-construction permit under the New Source Review program; any "major stationary source" or "major emitting facility" under the NSPS and NESHAP programs; any "affected source" under the Acid Deposition Control program; and any other source designated under EPA regulations. 42 U.S.C. §§ 7661(1) and (2), 7661a(a). Similar to NPDES permits under the Clean Water Act, Title V permits allow the EPA or authorized state agency to impose numerical emission limitations on polluters. The permit may also require monitoring and testing requirements in addition to imposing requirements from the SIP. Section 7661a(a) prohibits "any person" from violating any requirement of a Title V permit.

To encourage compliance with Title V, Congress provided "shield" provisions for those who apply for and obtain a permit. If a regulated entity is complying with its Title V permit, then the entity "shall be deemed in compliance with" the Clean Air Act. 42 U.S.C. § 7661c(f). The EPA also promulgated regulations that provide an "application shield" for a regulated entity when it applies for a permit. This "application shield" precludes the government from seeking an enforcement action against the entity for operating without a Title V permit. 40 C.F.R. § 70.7. This shield lasts until the EPA or approved state entity approves or rejects the requested permit. 40 C.F.R. §§ 70.5(a)(2), 70.7(a)(4).

United States v. Tonawanda Coke Corporation
Case No. 10-CR-219S, 2014 WL 1053729 (W.D.N.Y. Mar. 13, 2014)

WILLIAM M. SKRETNY, Chief Judge.
I. INTRODUCTION
On March 28, 2013, a jury convicted Defendant Tonawanda Coke Corporation ("TCC") and its manager of environmental control, Defendant Mark L. Kamholz, of violating environmental laws. . . . Defendants now move for judgments of acquittal pursuant to Rule 29 of the Federal Rules of Criminal Procedure or, alternatively, for a new trial pursuant to Rule 33. For the reasons discussed below, Defendants' motion is denied.

II. BACKGROUND
TCC is a merchant by-product coke facility that has been in operation since 1978. Coke is used in the steel-mill and foundry industries as an additive in the steel-making process. It is produced through the prolonged heating of bituminous coal in sealed ovens at high temperatures. During the heating process, volatile materials are driven from the coal and removed from the ovens as coke oven gas, which is then sent through a by-product recovery system and reused or sold. One by-product of coke oven gas is coal tar sludge, which can be reused by adding it to coal before the coal is loaded into the coke ovens. Because of the potential impact

coke production has on the environment, the industry is regulated by federal and state statutes and regulations.

On July 29, 2010, a federal grand jury returned an indictment against TCC and Kamholz, charging them with committing environmental crimes and obstructing justice in the course of operating the coke facility. . . .

Counts 1-15 of the trial indictment charged Defendants with violating the Clean Air Act ("CAA"), 42 U.S.C. § 7413(c)(1), from 2005 through 2009, by operating a stationary source of air pollution (i.e., TCC) in violation of its CAA permit. In particular, Counts 1-5 charged Defendants with emitting coke oven gas from a pressure relief valve in the by-products department at TCC. Counts 6-10 charged Defendants with operating the western quench tower (quench tower 1) at TCC without a baffle system.[19] . . .

Trial began on February 26, 2013, and concluded on March 28, 2013. Upon the close of the government's proof, this Court denied Defendants' Rule 29 motions. Defendants then presented a defense case and the government presented a brief rebuttal witness. The jury subsequently found TCC and Kamholz guilty on Counts 1-5, 9, 11-15, and 17-19. . . . It also acquitted both TCC and Kamholz on Counts 6-8 and 10. Following the verdict, Defendants filed the instant motion for judgments of acquittal or, alternatively, for a new trial.

III. DISCUSSION

A. Defendants' Rule 29 Motion

1. Rule 29 of the Federal Rules of Criminal Procedure

Under Rule 29(a), a court must, upon a defendant's motion, "enter a judgment of acquittal of any offense for which the evidence is insufficient to sustain a conviction." A defendant may move for a judgment of acquittal after the government closes its evidence, after the close of all evidence, or after the jury has returned its verdict and been discharged. A defendant may also renew a previously denied Rule 29 motion, so long as renewal occurs within 14 days after the guilty verdict or discharge of the jury, whichever is later. . . .

A defendant challenging the sufficiency of the evidence bears a heavy burden. "In evaluating whether the evidence was sufficient to convict a defendant, [a reviewing court] consider[s] all of the evidence, both direct and circumstantial, 'in the light most favorable to the government, crediting every inference that the jury might have drawn in favor of the government.'"

When considering the trial evidence, "the court must be careful to avoid usurping the role of the jury." The court may not "substitute its own determination of . . . the weight of the evidence and the reasonable inferences to be drawn for that of the jury." Determining the witnesses' credibility falls strictly within the province of the jury.

---

[19] [Fn. 1] Quenching is the process of cooling hot incandescent coke with water. A quench tower is any structure in which hot incandescent coke is deluged or quenched with water. Quenching begins when a quench car enters the quench tower and ends when it exits. Baffles are pollution control devices used to disrupt or deflect particulate emissions rising from the quench tower as a result of the quenching process, and are typically constructed of wood, steel, or plastic.

A judgment of acquittal is warranted only if the court concludes that the evidence is non-existent or so meager that no rational trier of fact could find the defendant guilty beyond a reasonable doubt. . . .

2. Clean Air Act Counts

a. Counts 1-5

Defendants maintain that they are entitled to a judgment of acquittal on Counts 1-5 because no reasonable juror could have found that Condition 4 of TCC's Title V operating permit applied to operation of the pressure relief valve in the by-products area. Specifically, Defendants argue that the pressure relief valve is an emission "point," not an emission "source."

Counts 1-5 charged Defendants with violating TCC's Title V permit requirements "by emitting coke oven gas from a pressure relief valve in the by-products department, an unpermitted emission source." Consistent with New York law, this Court instructed the jury that "emission source" is defined as any apparatus, contrivance, or machine capable of causing emission of any air contaminant to the outdoor atmosphere, including any appurtenant exhaust system, air cleaning device. It further instructed the jury that "emission point" is defined as any conduit, chimney, duct, vent, flue, stack, or opening of any kind through which air contaminants are emitted to the outdoor atmosphere.

Whether the pressure relief valve is an "emission source" or "emission point" is a question of fact for the jury. By its verdict, the jury concluded that the pressure relief valve was an "emission source." This is a reasonable determination supported by the trial evidence. Two of the government's expert witnesses—Al Carlacci and Larry Sitzman—testified that the terms "emission source" and "emission point" are synonymous and often used interchangeably. Carlacci also testified that Defendants' operation of the pressure relief valve violated TCC's Title V permit, the fair inference being that the pressure relief valve was an "emission source."

Defendants also argue that they are entitled to a judgment of acquittal on Counts 1-5 because there was insufficient proof that the pressure relief valve was subject to permitting requirements at the time it was constructed or modified. Defendants maintain that the government failed to offer evidence concerning the dates of construction or modification of the pressure relief valve, yet they concede that Sitzman testified that the pressure relief valve was a "process" that was modified each time it was adjusted, such that condition 4 of the Title V permit would apply. Defendants' argument also fails to consider that several witnesses testified that the pressure relief valve had been in a different location before the current pressure relief valve was constructed. This testimony, along with the testimony establishing that the pressure relief valve was occasionally adjusted such that it was modified consistent with Sitzman's testimony, supports the jury's verdict that Defendants violated the Title V permit.

Consequently, viewing all of the evidence in the government's favor, this Court finds that the evidence was sufficient to sustain the convictions on Counts 1-5. . . .

- Recall that the rule of lenity applies in criminal cases where there is ambiguity as to what the law requires. Should the rule of lenity have been applied if the terms in the Title V permit regard the pressure relief valve as an "emission source" or an "emission point," which was a distinction that may have had regulatory significance?

- How important is having a clearly written permit in criminally enforcing Title V permits?
- Do you see a potential role for experts in determining whether the requirements of a Title V permit are written clearly enough to be criminally enforceable?
- Is this level of complexity reasonable for criminal enforcement?

H. DISHONEST ACTS

Similar to the Clean Water Act, the Clean Air Act also imposes criminal penalties upon those who knowingly make materially false statements or omissions from required documents, records, and reports under the Clean Air Act. 42 U.S.C. § 7413(c)(2). However, unlike the Clean Water Act, the Clean Air Act uses a dual mens rea for dishonest acts depending upon the defendant's position in the organization. 42 U.S.C. § 7413(c)(2), (h). Thus, if a low-level employee is responsible for the dishonest act, then the prosecution must prove that the employee acted knowingly and willfully, whereas a senior official need only act "knowingly" to violate the provisions regarding dishonest acts. The term "material" means that the false statement or omission "will have a tendency to influence action or inaction by the EPA," not that the false statement or omission actually did have such influence. S. Rep. No. 101-228, 101st Cong., 2d Sess. 363 (1989). Additionally, consistent with the Clean Water Act, the Clean Air Act imposes a felony for tampering with monitoring devices and test methods. 42 U.S.C. § 7413(c)(2).

United States v. Fern
155 F.3d 1318 (11th Cir. 1998)

HATCHETT, Chief Judge:
[Recall that on October 3, 1993 a fire partially damaged the Monte Carlo Oceanfront Resort Hotel, a 13-story building on Miami Beach. Shortly after the fire, Waquar Ahmed Khan, the president of the company that owned the Monte Carlo, contracted with Fern, who owned as asbestos consulting company, to determine whether the Monte Carlo's conference room and suites were contaminated with asbestos as a result of the fire. Fern then orchestrated a fraudulent scheme to (1) show that the Monte Carlo was contaminated with asbestos; and (2) profit from a bogus asbestos abatement project at the Monte Carlo. Fern provided false samples to govern regulators showing asbestos in the hotel and provided false representations in the required pre-demolition notices ("Ten-Day Notices") to the government that the company he had hired to "abate" the fake asbestos was licensed for asbestos removal.

Fern was tried for various offenses, including making false statements under the Clean Air Act. At trial, two officials with the Metropolitan Dade County Department of Environmental Resources Management (DERM) testified about the significance of the notices that Fern provided to the government. The officials testified that they "absolutely" relied on the information contained in the notices that Fern provided and that it is important for the information to be accurate. The officials also indicated that DERM uses the information in notices to determine if the contractor is certified or not. A jury convicted Fern for making false statements, among many other charges. Fern appealed.]

B. Sufficiency of the Indictment

"A criminal conviction will not be upheld if the indictment upon which it is based does not set forth the essential elements of the offense." . . .

Counts I-III of the superseding indictment charged that Fern, on three separate dates, "did knowingly make false statements on the Notification of Demolition and Renovation form filed, and required to be maintained, pursuant to the Clean Air Act . . . in violation of Title 42, United States Code, Section 7413(c)(2)." Fern contends that these counts of the indictment are insufficient because they (1) fail to state expressly that . . . "materiality" are elements of a Clean Air Act false statement offense, and (2) fail to identify adequately the particular false statements Fern made. . . .

Fern's contention regarding the indictment's failure to allege "materiality" is more substantial, but still unpersuasive. Fern contends correctly that the indictment does not mention the word "material," and that a false statement must be a "material" statement to constitute a violation under the Clean Air Act. The indictment does, however, specifically reference "Title 42, United States Code, Section 7413(c)(2)." Fern contends that this reference is insufficiently specific to put him on notice that he allegedly violated section 7413(c)(2)(A). We find the omission of a reference to subsection (A) harmless.

The indictment charged Fern with making a "false statement." The only provision within section 7413(c)(2) that could even potentially concern "false statements" is subsection (A) which begins with the following words: "makes any false material statement." 42 U.S.C. § 7413(c)(2)(A). Subsection (B) of section 7413(c)(2) refers to failures to notify or report under the Clean Air Act, and subsection (C) refers to prohibited acts with "any monitoring device or method." 42 U.S.C. § 7413(c)(2)(B), (C). Because Fern could not read section 7413(c)(2) and conclude that he was charged with a violation of anything but section 7413(c)(2)(A), we reject his claim that the indictment failed to notify him of the charges that he had to defend. . . .

At trial, the district court instructed the jury as follows:

> Title 42, United States Code, section 7413(c)(2)(A) makes it a federal crime to knowingly make any false material statement, representation or certification in any notice, report or other document required to be filed or maintained pursuant to the Clean Air Act. The defendant can be found guilty of that offense only if all of the following facts are proved beyond a reasonable doubt:
> First: The defendant was the owner or operator of the facility being renovated.
> Second: That the combined amount of regulated asbestos-containing material stripped, removed, dislodged, cut, drilled or

similarly disturbed was at least 260 linear feet on pipes or 160 square feet on other facility components.

Third: That the notifications of demolition and renovation were filed as required under the Clean Air Act.

Fourth: That the defendant knowingly made a false material statement in the notification.

Fifth: That the defendant knew the statement was false at the time the notification was submitted.

The 10-day notices of renovation and demolition in this case are documents which are required to be filed and maintained pursuant to the Clean Air Act.

You are further instructed that the Court has already determined that the statements in this case were material. And I find that the statement that Action Systems was the contractor who was to remove the asbestos is a material statement, and that the signature of Judy Joyner was a material representation. That is a fact question for you to determine. You determine on the evidence whether it was authorized, as argued by the defendant, or was not authorized, as argued by the government.

The district court later clarified the last portion of the instruction, stating that "[t]he Government must prove beyond a reasonable doubt, in order to find the defendant guilty of those three counts concerning that statement, that that statement was false, that [the signature of] Judy Joyner was not authorized." In addition, the district court instructed the jury that "[t]he word 'knowingly,' as that term has been used . . . in the instructions, means that the act was done voluntarily and intentionally and not because of mistake or accident."

[The court evaluated whether the United States had proven "materiality" beyond a reasonable doubt.] First, . . . DERM officials Wong and Gordon testified that they "absolutely" relied on the information contained in Ten-Day Notices and that the "only" way DERM officials can know if the individual removing asbestos is properly trained is if they have the appropriate license. On cross-examination, Curry Joyner, a witness that Fern called, engaged in the following exchange:

Prosecutor: Now, it's important on the ten-day notices that there be a signature at the bottom, you testified?

Joyner: Yeah, you should always sign them.

Prosecutor: In fact, you said that was important, even if Donald Duck's name was on it?

Joyner: Right, as long as you make the notification and it gets to D.E.R.M. that in ten days from now there will be a job starting.

Prosecutor: Mr. Joyner, why didn't you sign your name? Why didn't you sign Curry Joyner?

Joyner: Because it's her license. I just signed her name.

Prosecutor: If Donald Duck could sign, couldn't Curry Joyner?

Joyner: Well, I mean, okay—well, if Donald Duck could write Judy Joyner, he could write Judy Joyner.

Curry Joyner went on to testify that "we couldn't have done the [Monte Carlo] job without her [Judy Joyner] license." Both prosecution and defense witnesses thus firmly established the materiality of the name signed on the signature line of Ten-Day Notices, demonstrating beyond doubt that materiality was not a genuine factually disputed issue in this case.

Second, we believe the jury necessarily credited the foregoing testimony establishing the materiality of the false statements when it rejected Fern's two-pronged defense theory. That defense theory was that Judy Joyner's forged signature was authorized, and that no evidence showed beyond a reasonable doubt that "Dan Fern submitted the form; that Dan Fern knowingly made any false statements on that form . . . [; and] that the form was submitted for any improper purpose." When the jury found that the signature was not authorized and was knowingly forged—forged "voluntarily and intentionally and not because of mistake or accident," i.e., forged for an improper reason—it necessarily found that the signature was forged because Fern believed Judy Joyner's signature might positively influence DERM officials in the exercise of their regulatory oversight duties. If the jury had not so concluded it would have characterized the false signature as a "mistake or accident" and acquitted Fern. . . .

CONCLUSION
For the foregoing reasons, we affirm Daniel Fern's convictions.

In light of *Fern*, consider the following example:

Case Study: Big Pipe and SO₂

Dan McDermit is the manager of a cast-iron pipe factory called Big Pipe, which uses an enormous incinerator as part of its operations. Big Pipe's incinerator is regulated under a Title V permit, which requires yearly testing to determine whether the incinerator is complying with the permit's emissions limitation for sulfur oxides. The Title V permit specifies that stack tests should be done when Big Pipe's incinerator is engaged in "normal operations." Based on Big Pipe's own internal testing, McDermit is aware that when certain substances are burned in the incinerator, Big Pipe greatly exceeds the Title V permit's sulfur oxide limitations. Consequently, when the time comes to perform the yearly stack test, McDermit specifically precludes his employees from placing any of the substances into the incinerator that he knows will exceed the sulfur dioxide limitation. Instead, McDermit orders his employees to only incinerate other items, which are also part of Big Pipe's normal incinerator process, but will not violate the sulfur dioxide limitations. Based on this method, Big Pipe passes the yearly stack test. As required by the Title V permit, McDermit must certify under the penalty of perjury that the stack test was performed under "normal operations." McDermit certifies the stack test was conducted under "normal operations" but never discloses that he specifically instructed his employees not to burn certain substances during the stack test. An employee who did not feel right about what McDermit had requested tells EPA-CID about what McDermit has been doing during stack testing. What is the likelihood of obtaining a conviction under 42 U.S.C. § 7413(c)(2)?

CHAPTER 7

HAZARDOUS WASTES AND SUBSTANCES

In the minds of many members of the public, the concept of hazardous substances sparks fear due to the mystery in which these substances are shrouded.[1] However, the truth is that tens of thousands of hazardous substances are used every day in the United States to produce the goods on which society relies. Many of these substances have never been tested by government entities to determine which, if any, exposure level humans may safely tolerate. Frank R. Lautenberg Chemical Safety for the 21st Century Act, Pub. L. No. 114-182 (2016).[2] In addition to the all-too-often unknown risks of the chemicals that society uses every day, there are risks associated with exposure to the hazardous waste products that are created when once valuable hazardous materials are no longer useful. For example, disposing of old cell phones, tablets, televisions, and computers as society upgrades to new ones each year results in 20-50 million tons of toxic waste annually, which creates horrendous consequences around the world.[3]

Given the ubiquity of hazardous substances, Congress has enacted numerous statutes that created many regulatory regimes for the generation, testing, transportation, use, storage, treatment, and disposal of hazardous materials. Although administrative and civil penalties are the chief enforcement mechanism for hazardous substances, criminal enforcement has a more modest, albeit significant, presence in the enforcement world. Criminal enforcement regarding hazardous substances most often focuses around: (A) the cradle to grave handling of hazardous wastes under the Resource Conservation and Recovery Act (RCRA); (B) failure to notify the proper authorities when hazardous substances are released

---

[1] G. James Rubin, Richard Amlôt, Lisa Page, Julia Pearce & Simon Wessely, *Assessing Perceptions AbouT Hazardous Substances (PATHS): The PATHS Questionnaire*, 18 J. Health Psych. 1100-13 (2012).

[2] *See* Mark Scialla, *It Could Take Centuries for EPA to Test All the Unregulated Chemicals Under a New Landmark Bill*, PBS News Hour, https://www.pbs.org/newshour/science/it-could-take-centuries-for-epa-to-test-all-the-unregulated-chemicals-under-a-new-landmark-bill.

[3] Qingbin Song & Jinhui Li, *A Review on Human Health Consequences of Metals Exposure to e-Waste in China*, 196 Environmental Pollution 450-61 (2015).

into the environment under the Comprehensive Environmental Response, Compensation, and Liability Act (CERCLA); and (C) enforcing the approved use of specific pesticides under the Federal Insecticide, Fungicide, and Rodenticide Act (FIFRA). Criminal enforcement for each law is discussed below.

A. HAZARDOUS WASTE ENFORCEMENT

Although the Clean Water Act and the Clean Air Act regulated hazardous discharges and releases into the water and air, no statute regulated the disposal of hazardous waste upon land. Consequently, in 1976, Congress amended the Solid Waste Disposal Act of 1965 to include prohibitions against disposing of hazardous waste upon land. 42 U.S.C. § 6901(b)(3) (1976). Through RCRA, Congress enacted a broad and complicated regulatory regime that governs hazardous waste from "cradle to grave."[4] As far as criminal penalties were concerned, Congress's 1976 law initially established a misdemeanor offense with up to one year in prison for those who knowingly: (1) transported a hazardous waste to an unpermitted facility; (2) disposed of a hazardous waste without a permit; or (3) made any false statement in a document required to be maintained under RCRA. A felony conviction for these acts was available only upon the defendant's second conviction under RCRA, and, even then, the maximum incarceration period was two years. 42 U.S.C. § 6928(d) (1976). Fines were up to $25,000 per day of violation.

In the 1980s and again in 1990, Congress significantly amended RCRA. Congress kept the original three criminal acts from the 1976 version and greatly expanded the scope of criminal liability to include the knowing storage and treatment of hazardous waste without or in violation of a permit. Congress also criminalized knowingly transporting hazardous waste without a manifest, the unpermitted importation and exportation of hazardous waste, and added a knowing endangerment provision. 42 U.S.C. § 6928(d), (e) (1994). In addition to increasing the scope of criminal liability, Congress increased the criminal penalties to five years' imprisonment for those who knowingly transport hazardous waste to an unapproved facility and for those who dispose, treat, or store hazardous waste without or in violation of a permit or interim status. 42 U.S.C. § 6928(d). Penalties were also increased up to $50,000 per day of violation. Similar to the Clean Water Act and Clean Air Act, Congress established a 15-year felony for knowing endangerment with a fine of up to $1 million.

Because RCRA regulates hazardous *wastes* not hazardous *materials* generally, understanding what is required to prove the existence of a hazardous waste is essential to understanding and proving each of RCRA's criminal provisions. Consequently, the requirements to prove a hazardous waste are discussed first. Thereafter, the following four categories RCRA offenses are discussed: (1) storage, treatment, and disposal of hazardous waste without or in violation of a permit or interim status; (2) transporting hazardous waste in violation of law; (3) dishonest acts; and (4) knowing endangerment.

---

[4] *Chem. Waste Mgmt. v. Hunt*, 504 U.S. 334, 337 n.1 (1992).

1. Proving That a Material Is Hazardous Waste

To determine whether RCRA applies, the first and most complex question is whether the entity is dealing with a substance that is a "hazardous waste." RCRA defines a "hazardous waste" as "a solid waste, or combination of solid wastes" that have deleterious effects on human health or the environment. 42 U.S.C. § 6903(5). Thus, proving that the material at issue is a "hazardous waste" consists of two parts: (a) whether the material is a "solid waste," and (b) whether the material is sufficiently dangerous to be "hazardous."

a. Is the Material a Solid Waste?

Proving that a material is a "solid waste" is often one of the most complicated tasks under RCRA because of its dense, counterintuitive, and, often, tautological regulatory definitions. For starters, although a "hazardous waste" must be a "solid waste," the term "solid waste" does not require the material to actually be "solid." In fact, a "solid waste" can be solid, semisolid, liquid, or gas. 42 U.S.C. § 6903(27).

In any event, regardless of its state of solidity, the regulations define a "solid waste" as a "discarded material" that the regulations do not elsewhere exempt from RCRA. 40 C.F.R. § 261.2(a)(1). Certain substances that are exempt from the definition of "solid wastes" include domestic sewage, irrigation return flows, used and intact cathode ray tubes (in older televisions and computer monitors). 40 C.F.R. § 261.4(a). However, if the material at issue is not exempted from RCRA, the prosecution must show that the substance is a "discarded material." To meet that definition, the material must be "abandoned," "recycled," or "inherently waste-like." 40 C.F.R. § 261.2(a)(2). RCRA's regulations increase the level of complexity by defining the three terms in the definition of "discarded material."

A material is "abandoned" if it is "disposed of," "burned or incinerated," or "accumulated, stored, or treated (but not recycled) before or in lieu of being . . . disposed of, burned or incinerated," or is "sham recycled." 40 C.F.R. § 261.2(b). A material is a "solid waste" by being "recycled" if it is used in a manner constituting disposal, burned for energy recovery, reclaimed, or accumulated speculatively. 40 C.F.R. § 261.2(c). However, a material is not a "solid waste" when recycled if it is used in the industrial process from which it was produced or can be used as a substitute for commercial products. 40 C.F.R. § 261.2(e). Thus, under certain circumstances, a "recycled" material can be a solid waste, but under other circumstances, it is not. "Inherently waste-like materials" are defined as possessing certain characteristics that the EPA has determined make the material "inherently wastelike" (e.g., a material containing "a bromine concentration of at least 45%.") 42 C.F.R. § 261.2(d).

The complexity of these definitions is a major factor that the prosecution must consider before seeking an indictment. Indeed, by suggesting that the material may have value, the prosecution must be ready to convincingly and simply prove why the material at issue really is a "solid waste" under these confusing definitions. The "beyond a reasonable doubt standard" that the prosecution must prove in criminal cases was not built for taking a novel position as to whether a material is a "solid waste."

b. Is the Solid Waste Hazardous?

If a material is indeed a "solid waste," then the prosecution must prove that the substance manifests sufficient deleterious effects to be deemed "hazardous." RCRA provides two mechanisms by which a solid waste may be deemed "hazardous." First, EPA has promulgated four lists that contain specific substances in the Code of Federal Regulations that the EPA has deemed "hazardous."[5] If the solid waste at issue is on one of the four EPA lists, then it is a "hazardous waste." Hazardous wastes found on one of these four lists are commonly referred to as "listed wastes."

Second, for those solid wastes that are not be found on any of the EPA's lists, the EPA has promulgated regulations that allow the solid waste in question to be deemed "hazardous" if "a representative sample" of the material manifests at least one of four hazardous characteristics. The EPA's regulations specify the testing procedures and the parameters for when a sample is "representative." 40 C.F.R. § 261.20(c). Again, to meet the "beyond a reasonable doubt" standard, the prosecution must closely adhere to EPA's sampling and testing procedures. The four characteristics that render a representative sample of a solid waste as hazardous are: (1) Ignitability; (2) Corrosivity; (3) Reactivity; and (4) Toxicity. 40 C.F.R. §§ 261.21 to 261.24. The parameters for each characteristic are shown in the table below.

Characteristic	Properties
Ignitability	• A liquid that has a flash point of less than 60 degrees Celsius • A non-liquid capable of causing a fire under standard temperature and pressure that burns so vigorously and persistently as to create a hazard • An ignitable compressed gas • An oxidizer as defined by Department of Transportation regulations
Corrosivity	• A liquid with a pH of less than or equal to 2 or greater than or equal to 12.5 • A liquid that corrodes steel at a rate greater than 6.35 mm per year at a temperature of 55 degrees Celsius

---

[5] Whether a Freudian slip or an attempt at regulatory humor, the EPA's four lists are the F, K, U, P lists. 40 C.F.R. §§ 261.30 to 261.33.

Reactivity	• Normally unstable and readily undergoes violent change without detonating
	• Reacts violently with water
	• Forms potentially explosive mixtures with water, if subjected to a strong initiating force, is heated under confinement, or under standard temperature and pressure
	• When mixed with water, generates toxic gases in a quantity that endangers humans
Toxicity	• Found to contain a sufficient concentration of at least one specified substance in 40 C.F.R. § 261.24 after using the Toxicity Characteristic Leaching Procedure test (TCLP)

In addition to having listed and characteristic hazardous wastes, RCRA's regulations define the conditions under which a solid waste is hazardous if it is a listed waste that is mixed with other hazardous or non-hazardous substances. At first blush, the rule seems simple: if a listed hazardous waste is mixed with some other substance, then the resulting mixed substance is a hazardous waste. 40 C.F.R. § 261.3(a)(2)(iv). However, RCRA's seemingly simple rule has a major exception. If the listed substance is on one of EPA's four lists "solely because it exhibits one or more characteristics of ignitability, corrosivity, or reactivity" then, the resulting mixed substance is only a hazardous waste if it manifests "any characteristic of a hazardous waste." 40 C.F.R. § 261.3(g)(1), (2). Notice that if a solid waste is on one of EPA's four lists because of toxicity, then a hazardous waste is produced no matter what the listed, toxic waste is mixed with. However, if the listed hazardous waste is on one of EPA's four lists because of a characteristic other than toxicity, it will only create a hazardous waste when mixed with another substance if that resulting substance manifests a hazardous characteristic.

For example, suppose that a truck containing several thousand pounds of a listed hazardous waste has an accident on the side of the highway and spills a significant amount of the hazardous waste on soil dirt next to the highway. The listed hazardous waste spills on and mixes with the soil. If the listed hazardous waste was on one of the EPA's four lists solely because it was ignitable, corrosive, or reactive, then the mixture of the listed hazardous waste and the soil would be deemed hazardous waste only if a representative sample of the soil manifests a hazardous characteristic. However, if the listed hazardous waste was listed because of toxicity, then the soil/hazardous waste mixture is also deemed to be a hazardous waste, which must be transported, stored, or disposed of according to RCRA's provisions.

To add to the complexity of proving that a solid waste is "hazardous," certain substances are exempt from the definition of "hazardous waste" even if they manifest hazardous characteristics. Some examples of exempted "hazardous waste" are: household wastes coming from the garbage of residences, hotels, and motels; certain agricultural wastes; mining overburden; and specific drilling fluids, among others. 40 C.F.R. § 261.4(b). Additionally, if an industrial entity generates no more than 100 kilograms of a hazardous waste each month, then the hazardous waste that the entity produces may not be deemed "hazardous waste" and, therefore, not subject to RCRA at all if the waste is transported to an approved facility for treatment and disposal. 40 C.F.R. § 261.5(g)(3). Entities meeting these requirements are known as Conditionally Exempt Small Quantity Generators.

United States v. Richter
796 F.3d 1173 (10th Cir. 2015)

McHUGH, Circuit Judge.

This case arises out of Brandon Richter and Tor Olson's business selling electronic devices for export overseas. The government brought criminal charges against Mr. Richter and Mr. Olson for fraudulently obtaining the electronic devices they exported and for violating federal law governing the exportation of hazardous electronic waste. After a fifteen-day trial, the jury found them guilty of committing fraud and facilitating the illegal exportation of hazardous waste, and it also convicted Mr. Richter on a single count of obstruction of justice. On appeal, Mr. Richter and Mr. Olson raise a variety of legal and evidentiary challenges to these convictions. Exercising jurisdiction under 28 U.S.C. § 1291, we AFFIRM in part and REVERSE in part.

II. BACKGROUND
A. Factual History

Mr. Richter and Mr. Olson served, respectively, as the Chief Executive Officer and Vice President of Operations for Executive Recycling, Inc. (Executive), a waste removal and recycling business. The company, founded in 2004 by Mr. Richter, provided electronic waste removal and recycling services to various businesses, governments, and government entities in Colorado, Utah, and Nebraska. Specifically, the defendants promised potential customers that Executive would domestically recycle or destroy electronics that could not be resold and would do so in an environmentally friendly manner that complied with all environmental laws and regulations governing electronic waste.

Generally speaking, electronic waste, or e-waste, refers to used electronics such as computers, printers, keyboards, speakers, and phones that are destined for disposal or recycling. Proper disposal of these types of electronic devices, whether by resale, by destruction, or by reduction to raw materials that can be resold, is difficult and expensive because the devices contain toxic materials. For example, Cathode Ray Tubes (CRTs) are "the glass video display component of an electronic device, usually a computer or television monitor, and are known to contain lead." CRTs cannot be disposed of in a landfill because of the risk that the lead will leach into the soil.

Executive contracted to dispose of e-waste for a number of government and business entities in Colorado, including the City and County of Boulder, the City and County of Broomfield, the Denver Newspaper Agency, El Paso County, and the Jefferson County School District. The defendants promised these customers that any electronic devices delivered to Executive would not be shipped overseas, would be processed in the United States, and would be totally destroyed in compliance with all environmental laws.

Contrary to its promises, Executive sold many items for overseas export to Hong Kong and China. Between 2005 and 2008, Executive served as the exporter of record in over three hundred exports and received over $1.9 million from its top five brokers in exchange for used electronics. Of particular relevance, the company sold CRTs to brokers in China for eventual reuse or refurbishment as components in new monitors. Over a four-year period, Executive sold 142,917 CRTs to their top five overseas brokers.

One shipment to Hong Kong, the "GATU shipment," contained CRTs that were broken and did not work, and thus could not be reused. The GATU shipment was featured in an episode of a television news program, 60 Minutes, which called into question Executive's compliance with environmental statutes and regulations. The program also brought Executive to the attention of the authorities.

As a result, the Environmental Protection Agency (EPA), Immigration and Customs Enforcement (ICE), and the Colorado Attorney General's Office began investigating Executive. An EPA investigator asked Mr. Richter to supply records of Executive's shipments over a three-year period. In response, Mr. Richter provided only a handful of records. One was a record corresponding to the GATU shipment. The subsequent execution of a federal search warrant revealed more shipping records that Mr. Richter had not produced. Some of these documents, including the original record for the GATU shipment, had been shredded. Upon closer inspection, EPA investigators discovered that the GATU record previously produced by Mr. Richter had been altered before it was provided to the EPA.

B. Procedural History

In the United States District Court for the District of Colorado, the government charged Executive, Mr. Richter, and Mr. Olson with . . . one count of exporting hazardous waste in violation of the Resource Conservation and Recovery Act (RCRA), 42 U.S.C. § 6928(d); and one count of smuggling hazardous waste, in violation of 18 U.S.C. § 554 and the same RCRA provision. According to the government, the defendants violated environmental laws regulating hazardous waste when they exported the CRTs (both broken and intact) overseas, and their actions in shipping the CRTs overseas were contrary to the representations made to customers. . . .

The parties also raised pretrial motions concerning the jury instructions on the RCRA and smuggling charges. Both of these criminal charges were based on the government's allegations that the defendants had exported, and facilitated the export of, regulated "hazardous waste" in violation of federal law. The parties' disagreement with respect to the jury instructions focused on the proper definition of waste under Colorado law. The government argued the jury should be instructed on the relevant regulations, as well as the Colorado Department of Public Health and Environment's (the Department) guidance interpreting those regulations, while the defendants claimed only the regulation should be included in the jury instruction. The district court agreed with the government that the Department's interpretation of the regulation was "relevant to the jury's determination of whether the electronic materials at issue in this case were waste." It therefore adopted a waste instruction, which stated that a used electronic device or component becomes waste on the date that a recycler determines it cannot be resold, donated, repaired, refurbished, or reused for its original intended purpose.

At trial, the defendants continued to challenge the government's allegation that they violated the law by exporting hazardous waste. First, Mr. Richter and Mr. Olson asserted that even if broken CRTs are regulated waste, they did not know Executive's shipments contained broken CRTs. In support of this theory, Mr. Olson offered three e-mails as evidence that he was not responsible for loading CRTs into shipping containers and that he had taken measures to prevent Executive's employees from breaking CRTs while packing them for export. The district court sustained the government's hearsay objection to these e-mails, but allowed Mr. Olson to testify about their content.

Second, the defendants challenged the government's allegation that Executive's shipment of intact CRTs also violated the relevant environmental laws. According to the defendants, these CRTs could not constitute waste, even under the government's definition, because they were sold for reuse in new television monitors, which is a use consistent with the CRTs' original intended purpose. In rebuttal, the government offered testimony from Edward Smith, an employee of the Department, who claimed a CRT re-housed in another monitor is waste because the reuse requires "processing."

Following trial, the jury returned verdicts against Mr. Richter and Mr. Olson on six counts of wire fraud, one count of mail fraud, and one count of smuggling. It also found Mr. Richter guilty of obstructing justice based on his response to the EPA's request for documents. The district court sentenced Mr. Richter to thirty months' imprisonment, three years' supervised release, and ordered him to pay $70,144 in restitution. The court sentenced Mr. Olson to fourteen months' imprisonment, three years' supervised release, and ordered him to pay $17,536 in restitution. The defendants filed this timely appeal.

III. DISCUSSION

Mr. Richter and Mr. Olson raise several challenges to their convictions. First, they ask us to reverse their convictions for smuggling because the jury instruction defining waste was incorrect as a matter of law and violated their due process right to fair notice of criminal prohibitions. . . .

To resolve these issues, we first consider whether the district court correctly instructed the jury on the definition of waste under Colorado law. Our analysis of this question begins, as it must, with the relevant statutory framework, and then considers the impact of any valid regulations. Next, we interpret the relevant regulation, taking into account the legislative history, the consequences of the parties' suggested constructions, and the ends to be achieved by the regulation. Ultimately, we conclude the regulation is ambiguous and that Colorado courts would interpret the regulation in a manner consistent with the waste jury instruction, even in the absence of the Guidance Document. We therefore do not determine the level of deference, if any, appropriate to the Department's informal Guidance Document in this criminal enforcement action.

Having thus resolved the ambiguity in the regulation, we reject the defendants' argument that the rule of lenity dictates a contrary interpretation. Instead, we hold the Waste Instruction is a correct statement of Colorado law. We further conclude the defendants here had fair notice that, under Colorado law, electronic components become waste unless they are resold, donated, repaired, or refurbished for their original intended purpose. Accordingly, we reject their federal due process argument. . . .

A. The Validity of the Smuggling Conviction

We turn first to the defendants' smuggling conviction. The defendants were charged with, and convicted of, smuggling in violation of 18 U.S.C. § 554. Section 554(a) prescribes criminal penalties for fraudulently or knowingly exporting, attempting to export, or facilitating the transportation, concealment, or sale of "any merchandise, article, or object contrary to any law or regulation of the United States." The indictment alleges that defendants violated § 554 by facilitating the exportation of the CRTs contrary to RCRA, in particular 42 U.S.C. § 6928(d)(4) and (d)(6), which impose restrictions on the exportation of hazardous waste. The defendants' primary challenge is that the jury instruction defining waste for purposes of Colorado's regulatory scheme was erroneous and that, even if the instruction was correct, they lacked fair notice that this definition might be criminally enforced against them. Thus, the validity of the defendants' convictions for smuggling turns on whether the exportation of the CRTs in this case violated the requirements for the lawful exportation of hazardous waste. Accordingly, we begin our analysis of this issue by describing the applicable hazardous waste management framework, which is governed by RCRA and corresponding Colorado law. We then explain how the district court arrived at its waste instruction and proceed to address the defendants' challenges.

1. The Pertinent Legal Framework and the District Court's Jury Instruction

"RCRA is a comprehensive statute designed to reduce or eliminate the generation of hazardous waste and 'to minimize the present and future threat to human health and the environment' created by hazardous waste." The statute "empowers EPA to regulate hazardous wastes from cradle to grave, in accordance with [RCRA's] rigorous safeguards and waste management procedures." It imposes criminal penalties against a person who, among other things, knowingly exports "any hazardous waste" and "fails to file any record, application, manifest, report, or other document required to be maintained or filed," or knowingly exports "a hazardous waste" "without the consent of the receiving country" or in violation of an international agreement governing the export of hazardous waste. Thus, as is relevant here, RCRA makes it a crime to export hazardous waste without filing the proper notification of intent to export with the EPA or without the consent of the receiving country.

Although RCRA establishes a federal regulatory scheme for hazardous waste, it authorizes the EPA Administrator to approve state hazardous waste programs to operate "in lieu of" the federal scheme. 42 U.S.C. § 6926(b). But federal law sets a floor for state hazardous waste programs, and the Administrator can authorize a state program only if it is both "consistent with" and "equivalent to" the federal program. 42 U.S.C. § 6926(b). Thus, although states are free to impose requirements that "are more stringent than those imposed by" RCRA and its regulations, they may not impose standards less stringent than those federal standards. Id. § 6929.

When a state program is authorized under RCRA, federal regulations are displaced or supplanted by state regulations. But EPA retains the power under RCRA to pursue civil and criminal remedies for violations of the state program.

Consistent with RCRA's delegation of authority to the states, Colorado administers its own program, the Colorado Hazardous Waste Management Act (the Act). The Act's Solid Waste regulations generally mirror those of the federal scheme. Under the Act, as under RCRA, a material can be classified as a hazardous waste only if it is first classified as a waste. But the Act differs from the federal scheme in certain respects. For example, the federal program contains rules that expressly govern broken and used CRTs. Colorado, on the other hand, has not adopted the federal CRT rules and instead regulates the disposal of electronic devices and components, including CRTs, under its universal waste regulations.

Part 273.2(f)(3) of Colorado's waste regulations establish four ways by which an electronic device or component becomes a "waste": . . .

> (ii) A used electronic device destined for recycling becomes a waste on the date the recycler determines that the device cannot be resold, donated, repaired, or refurbished, or determines that he/she cannot directly reuse or sell useable parts from the device.
> (iii) An electronic component becomes a waste on the date the recycler determines that the component cannot be resold, donated, repaired, or refurbished, or determines that he/she cannot directly reuse the component. . . .

(hereinafter Part 273.2(f)(3)). Notably, under subsections (ii) and (iii) of this provision, the "waste" classification turns on whether the device or component can be "resold, donated, repaired, or refurbished," or whether a recycler "cannot directly reuse or sell useable parts from the device" or otherwise "directly reuse the component."

In March 2004, the Department issued a memorandum, made available on its website, clarifying "the hazardous waste regulations as they pertain to electronic waste recycling service providers doing business in Colorado." This Guidance Document specifically addressed how electronic waste recyclers should distinguish regulated "waste" from a "product"—such as an electronic device offered for resale—explaining:

> The definition of "product" also needs to be clarified. *For post-consumer electronic devices or components to be considered products, they must have reuse and/or resale value for their original intended purpose.* Examples include a computer monitor that is resold for continued use as a monitor, a computer CPU that is refurbished for continued use as a computer, or a computer chip that can be removed from one CPU and used to repair another for continued use as a computer.

Id. at 177 (emphasis added).

The district court included language from this Guidance Document in the Waste Jury Instruction, which stated, with our emphasis:

Electronic devices and electronic components can become a "waste" in four ways:

(1) A used electronic device destined for disposal becomes a waste on the date it is discarded;

(2) A used electronic device destined for recycling becomes a waste on the date the recycler determines that the device cannot be resold, donated, repaired or refurbished, or determines that he cannot directly reuse or sell useable parts from the device.

(3) An electronic component becomes a waste on the date the recycler determines that the component cannot be resold, donated, repaired, or refurbished, or determines that he cannot directly reuse the component.

(4) An unused electronic device becomes a waste on the date the handler decides to discard it.

For subparts (2) and (3) above, in order for an electronic device or electronic component to not be a waste, it must be resold, donated, repaired, reused or refurbished for its original intended purpose. For example, the following would not be considered a waste: (1) a computer monitor that is resold for continued use as a monitor, (2) a computer CPU that is refurbished for continued use as a computer, or (3) a computer chip that can be removed from one CPU and used to repair another for continued use as a computer.

On appeal, Mr. Richter and Mr. Olson challenge the correctness of the district court's inclusion of the "original intended purpose" requirement in the jury instruction defining hazardous waste. First, they argue the district court improperly deferred to the Department's interpretation of the waste regulation contained in the Guidance Document and that alternatively, even if deference were otherwise appropriate, the Department's interpretation of the regulation is not reasonable. Relatedly, they claim the rule of lenity prohibits interpreting the regulation to include an original intended purpose requirement. . . .

2. The Accuracy of the Waste Instruction

. . . Because Colorado administers its own hazardous waste program under RCRA, we apply Colorado law to ascertain the meaning of waste. Colorado, like RCRA, does not define "waste" by statute, so we look to Part 273.2(f)(3) of Colorado's waste regulations for a definition of this term. In construing a regulation, Colorado courts "apply those basic rules of interpretation which pertain to the construction of a statute." The primary goal of interpretation is to "give effect to the intent of the enacting body." Thus, Colorado courts "first look at the plain language of the regulation and interpret its terms in accordance with their commonly accepted meanings." Id. The courts "read the provisions of a regulation together, interpreting the regulation as a whole." If a regulation's language is unambiguous, Colorado courts "give effect to the plain and ordinary meaning of the section without resorting to other rules of statutory construction." Language is ambiguous when it is susceptible to multiple valid interpretations.

a. Plain Language

Part 273.2(f)(3)'s definition of waste is ambiguous because it is susceptible to multiple valid interpretations. Recall that the regulation provides that electronic devices and components are not waste so long as they can be "resold," "donated," "repaired," "refurbished," or "reuse[d]." The defendants have offered one permissible reading of the regulation. They argue that Part 273.2(f)(3) does not expressly include an original intended purpose requirement, and that the words "resold," "donated," "refurbished," and "reused" likewise do not mandate such a requirement. Thus, they interpret Part 273.2(f)(3) to mean that an electronic device or component that can be resold, donated, repaired, refurbished, or reused for any purpose is not waste.

Although the defendants' reading of the regulation may be permissible, the regulation can also be reasonably interpreted to include an original intended purpose requirement. Indeed, two of the words, "repair" and "refurbish," lend themselves most naturally to an interpretation that an item will retain its originally intended purpose. And there is nothing about any of the other three words, "resold," "donated," and "reused," that excludes an original intended purpose requirement. Therefore, these terms could also plausibly be read to carry a similar meaning. Thus, the interpretation adopted by the Department's Guidance Document that electronic devices and components are not waste so long as they can be resold, donated, repaired, refurbished, or reused for their original intended purpose is a second permissible reading of the regulation. Because the regulation here is susceptible to at least two valid interpretations, it is ambiguous. Therefore, we apply Colorado's normal tools of statutory construction to discern Part 273.2(f)(3)'s proper meaning.

b. Regulatory Context and Purpose

To resolve ambiguities, Colorado courts attempt to effectuate the underlying purpose of a regulatory scheme and, to that end, "may rely on other factors such as legislative history, the consequences of a given construction, and the end to be achieved by the statute." Considering the legislative purpose of the adoption of Colorado's waste management program generally, and the Department's responsibility to administer it consistently with that intent, the meaning of Part 273.2(f)(3) is apparent.

The Colorado General Assembly adopted the Act to "[e]stablish[ ] a state program of comprehensive regulation of hazardous waste management in lieu of the federal program" under RCRA. The General Assembly then charged the Department with the responsibility to administer that program, and authorized the Department to promulgate the regulations necessary to operate it in lieu of the federal program. To realize the General Assembly's intent, the state program had to be at least as protective of the environment as the federal RCRA regulations. The General Assembly expressly recognized this limitation and, by statute, ordered the Department to implement its hazardous waste control program in a manner that "[m]aintains program authorization by the federal government."

RCRA and its implementing regulations define hazardous wastes to include potentially toxic solid waste. And, subject to exceptions not relevant here, solid waste under federal law includes spent material that "has been used and as a result of contamination can no longer serve the purpose for which it was produced without processing." Thus, under RCRA, used electronic devices and components become waste when they can no longer be used for their original intended purpose. Colorado was therefore required to adopt a definition of waste at least as protective as the federal rule—one that requires the device or component to be classified as waste unless it can be resold, donated, repaired, refurbished, or reused for its original intended purpose.

The defendants' contrary interpretation would create a defect in Colorado's hazardous waste program by permitting conduct (here, resale, donation, repair, refurbishment, or reuse of electronic devices and components for any purpose) that falls below the environmental protections mandated by federal law. Because Colorado's hazardous waste program must be "consistent with" and "equivalent to" the federal program, such a defect would mean Colorado's program could no longer be authorized by the EPA. That outcome is contrary to the General Assembly's express goal and direction to the Department. Although there are two plausible readings of Part 273.2(f)(3), only the reading that classifies an electronic device as waste when it can no longer be resold, donated, repaired, refurbished, or reused for its original intended purpose "effectuate[s] the underlying purpose of [the] regulatory scheme," is consistent with the legislative history of the Act, and results in a construction that facilitates "the end to be achieved by the statute." Accordingly, we hold that Colorado would define waste consistently with the district court's instruction to the jury. . . .

For these reasons, we hold that under Colorado law, an electronic device or component becomes waste unless it is resold, donated, repaired, refurbished, or reused for its original intended purpose. Accordingly, the Waste Instruction was a correct statement of the applicable law.

- How was the prosecution able to show that the CRTs included in the defendants' shipments were a solid waste?
- Given how complicated the analysis for determining whether something is a "solid waste" can be, how can a member of the regulated public know when his/her electronic device becomes a "solid waste" that is subject to RCRA?
- Why were the shipments of CRTs for which the defendants were charged under RCRA from city and county governments instead of from households?

In addition to the complexity of proving that a substance is actually a "hazardous waste," RCRA uses a "knowing" mens rea. This has generated numerous cases regarding whether the prosecution must prove that the defendant knew that the substance at issue was, in fact, a hazardous waste. Consider the following case as to whether the prosecution must prove knowledge of the substance's hazardous nature.

United States v. Self
2 F.3d 1071 (10th Cir. 1993)

BALDOCK, Circuit Judge.

Defendant Steven M. Self appeals his convictions on four counts of violating the Resource Conservation and Recovery Act ("RCRA"). . . .

I.

The record reveals the following facts. In 1981, Defendant and Steven Miller formed EkoTek, Inc. . . . Defendant and Miller managed EkoTek on a day-to-day basis with Defendant primarily responsible for the financial aspects of the business, and Miller primarily responsible for the technical aspects.

The facility purchased by EkoTek was an authorized RCRA interim status treatment, storage and disposal facility. In 1981 and again in 1982, Defendant signed and submitted an updated part A RCRA permit application. In 1983, Defendant signed and submitted a part B RCRA permit application. By submitting the permit applications, EkoTek could continue operating as a treatment, storage and disposal facility under RCRA interim status, pending its RCRA permit approval. . . .

In April 1987, a representative of Southern California Gas Company ("SCGC"), met with Miller at EkoTek and discussed EkoTek disposing of SCGC's natural gas pipeline condensate. The parties agreed that the condensate was hazardous waste and should, therefore, be transported and handled under a RCRA manifest. Miller indicated that EkoTek could dispose of the natural gas condensate by burning it as fuel in EkoTek's onsite process heaters or boilers. SCGC subsequently contracted with and agreed to pay EkoTek "to transport, burn, and/or dispose of" natural gas condensate for $2.50 per gallon.

Shortly thereafter, an EkoTek tanker truck driver picked up a shipment of natural gas condensate from a SCGC facility in Los Angeles, California. The driver had been instructed by his supervisor to pick up the shipment and bring it back to EkoTek. As was his routine practice, the driver stopped at a gas station in Barstow, California, which was owned by Defendant, and telephoned his supervisor. On instructions from Defendant, the supervisor told the driver to leave the trailers containing the natural gas condensate at the gas station and return to Los Angeles to pick up an unrelated shipment. Defendant telephoned the gas station manager and instructed him to blend the natural gas condensate with gasoline in a 5-10% mixture and add an octane booster. The gasoline and condensate mixture was then sold to the public as automotive fuel. On Defendant's instructions, Miller told EkoTek's Refinery Operations Manager to sign the manifest to indicate that the natural gas condensate shipment had been received at EkoTek and to falsify EkoTek's operating log accordingly. A copy of the manifest was mailed to SCGC.

In early 1987, EkoTek began receiving fifty-five gallon drums of waste material from different sources. Defendant instructed an employee to store the drums in the south warehouse. When the south warehouse filled up, Defendant instructed the employee to store the drums in the east warehouse. The employee was also instructed by his immediate supervisor to scrape the "hazardous waste" label off of each drum, paint a number on the drum, and list it on an inventory sheet. In July 1987, the State of Utah, pursuant to its delegated RCRA authority, see 42 U.S.C. § 6926(b), granted EkoTek a RCRA permit which prohibited EkoTek from storing hazardous waste in the east warehouse. Defendant discussed this illegal storage practice with Miller. Defendant's office at EkoTek had a view of the doors to the east warehouse which were usually left open and through which stored fifty-five gallon drums were visible. On several occasions, Defendant ordered the doors to the east warehouse closed after being informed that inspectors would be at the facility.

Among the drums stored in the east warehouse were seventeen drums of waste from Avery Label and twelve drums of waste from Reynolds Metals both of which were shipped to EkoTek under RCRA manifests identifying the materials as hazardous wastes. Avery Label's manager of safety and environmental affairs testified that the waste sent to EkoTek was a mixture of ultraviolet curer ink waste, solvent ink waste, and cleaning solvent. Ultraviolet curer ink has a flash point exceeding 200° F and is, therefore, not considered hazardous due to ignitability. Solvent ink, on the other hand, has a flash point well below 140° F and is, therefore, considered hazardous due to ignitability. The Material Safety Data Sheets ("MSDS") for the type of solvent inks that Avery Label used in 1987 indicated that the solvent inks had a flash point of between 16° F and 116° F. According to the Avery Label representative, mixing solvent ink waste with ultraviolet curer ink waste does not raise the flash point because the vapors of the solvent ink waste, which determine its ignitability, rise to the top. In his opinion, the waste sent to EkoTek had a flash point of between 70°> F to 100°> F. The hazardous waste broker who had arranged for the disposal of the Avery Label waste personally observed the waste sent to EkoTek and recognized it as a solvent-based ink due to its smell.

The RCRA manifest which accompanied the shipment of the Reynolds Metals waste to EkoTek indicated that the material was a mixture of "MEK" (methyl ethyl ketone) and a spray residue. MEK is a listed hazardous waste, and it has a flash point of 23° F. The spray residue has a flash point of 100° F.

In April 1988, the hazardous waste broker responsible for shipping both the Avery Label and Reynolds Metals wastes to EkoTek visited the EkoTek facility after having been informed that drums of waste which he brokered had never been processed and were being illegally stored at the facility. By this time, EkoTek was no longer in business, and Petro Chemical Recycling, with which Defendant had no affiliation, had taken over operation of the facility. The broker observed "a lot of drums" being stored in the east warehouse, none of which were labeled but were crudely marked with a number. Using EkoTek's inventory sheet and recognizing the drums by their distinctive color, the broker identified the seventeen drums of Avery Label waste and the twelve drums of Reynolds Metals waste. He subsequently arranged for Marine Shale Processors to dispose of these as well as several other drums of waste. On documentation submitted to Marine Shale Processors, the broker indicated that the materials were from four types of waste streams, and he identified the material in twenty-four of the 128 barrels as "UV ink waste." Marine Shale Processors tested a sample from each of the four types of waste streams and determined that each type of identified waste had a flash point below 70°> F.

Defendant also claims that the district court's jury instruction concerning Defendant's knowledge that the material was hazardous waste was erroneous. The district court instructed the jury as follows:

> That on or about the dates alleged in the Indictment, the defendant knowingly stored or commanded and caused others to store hazardous waste. The defendant need have no specific knowledge of the particular hazardous characteristics of the material in question, only that it was hazardous waste and not a benign or innocuous material such as water.

Defendant objected to this instruction claiming that the instruction should require the jury to find that Defendant knew the waste was an identified or listed hazardous waste under RCRA. Defendant reasserts this same argument before us. . . .

Defendant points to the language of the statute which proscribes "*knowingly* . . . stor[ing] . . . any hazardous waste identified or listed under this subchapter . . . in *knowing violation* of any material condition or requirement of [a RCRA] permit." 42 U.S.C. § 6928(d)(2)(B) (emphasis added). According to Defendant, because the statute expressly requires knowledge that the storage violates the permit, and the permit only regulates RCRA hazardous waste, the statute necessarily requires proof of the defendant's knowledge that the material is hazardous waste identified or listed under RCRA.

Whether 42 U.S.C. § 6928(d)(2)(B) requires proof that the defendant knew the substance at issue was identified or listed hazardous waste under RCRA appears to be an issue of first impression. However, several circuits have given narrower constructions of the knowing requirement in other RCRA criminal provisions. The Fourth, Fifth and Eleventh Circuits have held that § 6928(d)(2)(A), which prohibits knowingly treating, storing or disposing of hazardous waste without a permit, does not require proof of the defendant's knowledge that the materials are listed or identified as hazardous waste under RCRA regulations. Similarly, the Eleventh Circuit has also held that § 6928(d)(1), which prohibits knowingly transporting hazardous waste to an unpermitted facility, does not require proof of the defendant's knowledge that the material was hazardous waste within the meaning of RCRA regulations. These circuits, as well as the Third and Ninth Circuits in the context of § 6928(d)(2)(A), have held that the government need only prove that Defendant knew the material was hazardous in that it was potentially harmful to persons or the environment.

These courts have generally relied on the Supreme Court's reasoning in *United States v. International Minerals & Chem. Corp.*, 402 U.S. 558, (1971). *International Minerals* involved a prosecution under 18 U.S.C. § 834(f) (repealed 1979) for knowingly violating an Interstate Commerce Commission regulation which required shipping papers to describe hazardous materials. The defendant argued that, because he was not aware of the particular regulation, he could not have knowingly violated it as required under the terms of the criminal statute. The Court held that the defendant's lack of knowledge of the regulation was no defense. The Court reasoned that "where . . . obnoxious waste materials are involved, the probability of regulation is so great that anyone who is aware that he is in possession of them or dealing with them must be presumed to be aware of the regulation." *Id.* at 565. Courts which have applied *International Minerals'* reasoning to the knowing requirement of RCRA's criminal provisions have generally reasoned that persons dealing with materials, which by their very nature are potentially dangerous, are presumed to know the regulatory status of the material, or that to permit a defendant to claim that he or she did not know the material was identified or listed as a RCRA hazardous waste would effectively approve of a mistake of law defense which is generally not viable in a criminal prosecution.

Notwithstanding *International Minerals'* reasoning and the application of this reasoning to the knowing requirement of RCRA's criminal provisions by every circuit that has addressed the issue, Defendant argues that we should follow the Supreme Court's reasoning in *Liparota v. United States*, 471 U.S. 419 (1985). In *Liparota*, the Supreme Court held that 7 U.S.C. § 2024(b)(1), which prohibited the knowing acquisition or possession of food stamps in any manner not authorized by the statute or regulations, required proof, not only of the defendant's knowledge of his acquisition or possession of the food stamps, but also of the defendant's knowledge that his possession or acquisition of the food stamps was not authorized by the regulation. *Liparota* does not control this case. The *Liparota* Court distinguished *International Minerals* because the statute at issue in *Liparota* did not involve "a type of conduct that a reasonable person should know is subject to stringent public regulation and may seriously threaten the community's health and safety." Given that RCRA is a public welfare statute which was designed "to protect human health and the environment," the *Liparota* Court's reasoning, in light of its recognized distinction of *International Minerals*, is inapposite.

We recognize that § 6928(d)(2)(B) requires proof that the storage was "in knowing violation" of the RCRA permit, and the RCRA permit only governs storage of RCRA hazardous waste. We do not believe, however, that this particular knowing requirement makes knowledge of the regulatory status of the material a prerequisite to conviction under § 6928(d)(2)(B). Rather, the second "knowing" requirement of § 6928(d)(2)(B) ensures that a good faith belief that a permit allows a particular manner of treatment, storage or disposal of hazardous waste, when in fact it does not, is a defense to a criminal charge. *See* H.R. Conf. Rep. No. 1444, 96th Cong., 2d Sess. 37 (1980), reprinted in 1980 U.S.C.C.A.N. 5019, 5036 ("This section is intended to prevent abuses of the permit system by those who obtain and then knowingly disregard them.") It does not eliminate the presumption, applicable to every other RCRA criminal provision and to regulatory statutes in general which concern dangerous substances, that persons handling such materials know of their regulatory status. Accordingly, Defendant's claim that the district court should have instructed the jury that it must find that Defendant knew the material at issue in count was identified or listed as hazardous waste under RCRA regulations is not persuasive.

On appeal, Defendant broadens his contention that the instruction was erroneous by arguing, not only that the instruction failed to require the government to prove that Defendant knew the material was RCRA hazardous waste, but also that it allowed the jury to convict merely by finding that Defendant knew the material was "not a benign or innocuous material such as water." Because Defendant did not raise this particular objection below, we review only for plain error.

While the government was not required to prove that Defendant knew that the material was identified or listed as hazardous waste under RCRA regulations, the government was required to prove that Defendant knew the material was hazardous in that it had the potential to be harmful to persons or the environment. Here, the district court's instruction specifically required the jury to find that Defendant knew the material was hazardous. However, the instruction did not define hazardous as having the potential to harm other persons or the environment, but merely told the jury that it meant a non-benign or non-innocuous material, and gave water as an example of a benign or innocuous material.

The Eleventh and Ninth Circuits have approved of an instruction regarding knowledge which requires the jury to find that "the defendant knew that the stored material had the potential to be harmful to others or to the environment, in other words, that it was not an innocuous substance like water." While we agree with this instruction and find it preferable to the instruction given in this case, the instruction here was not an erroneous statement of the law. The instruction specifically required the jury to find that Defendant knew the material was hazardous waste. Thus, it is unlike the erroneous instruction in *Dee* which required the jury to find only that Defendant knew the materials were chemicals without also requiring a finding that Defendant knew the materials were hazardous. As a result, even though the instruction in this case may have been incomplete by failing to inform the jury that Defendant must know the material had the potential to be harmful to others or the environment, this omission was not so obvious as to rise to the level of plain error. . . .

V.

Defendant's convictions on counts 1, 2, 3 and 7 are REVERSED. Defendant's convictions on counts 4 and 8 are AFFIRMED. The case is REMANDED to the district court for proceedings consistent with this opinion.

- What is the statutory basis for requiring the prosecution to prove that the defendant knew that the substance was "not innocuous like water" but not requiring proof that the defendant knew that the substance was actually hazardous?
- What is the purpose of requiring the prosecution to prove that the hazardous waste at issue was "not innocuous like water"?
- If you were deciding whether to prosecute a case against an individual for a hazardous waste violation under RCRA, what type of facts would you look for to prove that the defendant knew that the material was not innocuous like water?

2. Storage, Treatment, and Disposal of Hazardous Waste

RCRA imposes a felony punishable up to five years in prison for "any person" who "knowingly treats, stores, or disposes of any hazardous waste" without or in "knowing violation" of any material condition of a permit or interim status. 42 U.S.C. § 6928(d)(2). To understand criminal enforcement of § 6928(d)(2), the elements necessary to prove disposal, storage, and treatment are set forth below. Thereafter, this section discusses permits and interim status, followed by a discussion of RCRA's unique mens rea requirements for permit violations.

a. Disposal and Storage

RCRA prohibits the unpermitted disposal and storage of hazardous waste. Both of these terms are discussed together because understanding the definition of "disposal" is necessary to understand the definition of "storage." Under RCRA, the term "disposal" means:

> the discharge, deposit, injection, dumping, spilling, leaking, or placing of any solid waste or hazardous waste into or on any land or water *so that such solid waste or hazardous waste or any constituent thereof may enter the environment* or be emitted into the air or discharged into any waters, including ground waters.

42 U.S.C. § 6903(3) (emphasis added). As the emphasized language shows, the key issue to determining if a disposal has occurred is whether the person's action or failure to act placed the hazardous waste on or in land or water where it has the opportunity to enter the environment.

Although the definition of "disposal" is broad, *United States v. Waste Indus., Inc.*, 734 F.2d 159, 165 (4th Cir. 1984), it has its limitations. For example, to avoid duplication with the Clean Water Act, Congress defined "solid waste" to exclude "solid or dissolved material in domestic sewage" and "industrial discharges which are point sources subject to [Clean Water Act] permits." 42 U.S.C. § 6903(27). Thus, if disposal of a hazardous waste occurs under conditions that the Clean Water Act governs, then the Clean Water Act, not RCRA, applies to the discharge of the pollutant into the water of the United States. However, if the water into which a hazardous waste is disposed is not a water of the United States, then RCRA, not the Clean Water Act governs. *Pape v. Lake States Wood Preserving, Inc.*, 948 F. Supp. 967, 699 (W.D. Mich. 1995).

Knowing what "disposal" means under RCRA is important to understanding the definition of "storage." RCRA defines "storage" as "the containment of hazardous waste, either on a temporary basis or for a period of years, in such a manner as not to constitute disposal of such hazardous waste." 42 U.S.C. § 6903(33). In other words, if the hazardous waste is kept in such a way that it is not able to enter into the environment, then storage, not disposal, applies.

RCRA sets certain time limitations on how long hazardous waste may be stored without permit. For example, an entity that generates at least 1,000 kilograms of hazardous waste in a month is a "large quantity generator." 40 C.F.R. Part 262. A large quantity generator may store hazardous waste on site for up to 90 days if the generator follows certain labeling and safety requirements. 40 C.F.R. § 262.34(a). A "small quantity generator" generates between 100 and 1,000 kilograms of hazardous waste each month. 40 C.F.R. § 260.10. A small quantity generator may store hazardous waste on site for between 180 and 270 days depending upon how far away the storage, treatment, or disposal facility is located from the generator and assuming that the generator follows certain labeling and safety precautions. 40 C.F.R. § 262.34(d). Additionally, as shown in the previous section, an entity that generates fewer than 100 kilograms of hazardous waste per month and abides by certain disposal conditions is a "conditionally exempt small quantity generator" and is exempt from RCRA regulation. 40 C.F.R. § 261.5(a).

To illustrate the differences between "disposal" and "storage" consider the following.

Case Study: There's Gold in Them Thar Barrels

Sam Del Rio purchased a semi-trailer full of various wastes that were contained in dozens of plastic and metal drums. He purchased the trailer for the purpose of extracting precious metals from the contents of the drums. However, after not being as successful in extracting precious metals as he wished, he abandoned the trailer on the side of the road. The semi-trailer had numerous gaping holes in it, one large side door was open, and the contents of one of the barrels was spilling out of the trailer onto the ground. When a parking attendant discovered the trailer and saw some of the odd-colored contents spilling onto the ground, he called the fire department, who then saw that this was a hazmat situation and called the EPA. EPA responded to the trailer and cleaned it up. While doing so, EPA-CID performed representative sampling of the waste and found that it manifested the hazardous characteristic of toxicity. EPA-CID also sampled the contents that had spilled onto the ground from the semi-trailer and determined that the material was not hazardous. Could Sam be found guilty of knowingly storing or disposing of a hazardous waste or both?[6]

b. Treatment of Hazardous Waste

In addition to precluding the unlawful disposal and storage of hazardous waste, RCRA criminalizes its unlawful treatment. The term "treatment" means:

> any method, technique, or process, including neutralization, designed to change the physical, chemical, or biological character or composition of any hazardous waste so as to neutralize such waste or so as to render such waste nonhazardous, safer for transport, amenable for recovery, amenable for storage, or reduced in volume. Such term includes any activity or processing designed to change the physical form or chemical composition of hazardous waste so as to render it nonhazardous.

42 U.S.C. § 6903(34). To apply this definition, consider the above-referenced hypothetical involving Sam Del Rio. However, instead of leaving the drums of waste on the side of the road in a semi-trailer, assume that Del Rio incinerated the contents of the drums and then placed the incinerated remains of the waste in his municipal trash can for disposal at the local landfill. Incineration of the hazardous waste in the drums would be treatment because Del Rio is using a "method, technique, or process" (i.e., incineration) to "change the physical . . . character of any hazardous waste" to "reduce its volume" so that it can be disposed of. Applying these principles, consider the following.

---

[6] See United States v. Costa, Case No. 2:09CR744 (D. Utah 2010), ECF No. 24.

Case Study: Blame It on the Rain

Assume that Milli V'Nilli owns an electroplating shop that uses powerful chemical washes to make aluminum tire rims for cars and trucks look like chrome. The chemicals used in these metal washes can only be used 15 times before new chemicals have to be used to obtain the same shiny results. Assume that the spent chemicals have a pH of less than 1.5. V'Nilli takes the spent chemicals and dumps them down a metal grate that sits atop a 10-foot by 5-foot cement box that he installed in the ground. V'Nilli leaves the spent chemicals in the cement box so that rainfall and water runoff from his property goes through the grate and into the cement box to mix with the spent chemicals. After a couple of rain storms, V'Nilli pumps the remaining chemicals from the cement box and then dumps it onto the ground in the back of his electroplating business. Assume that V'Nilli does not have a permit of any kind regarding hazardous wastes. Assume that the state hazardous waste regulators inspect V'Nilli's shop, discover the foregoing, and tell V'Nilli that they may refer this for criminal prosecution for treatment of hazardous waste. V'Nilli calls you for legal advice after he received a call from EPA-CID. What would you tell him regarding the allegations that V'Nilli is treating hazardous waste?

c. Permits, Interim Status, and Mens Rea

Similar to the Clean Water Act and the Clean Air Act, permits under RCRA are issued by the EPA or through a state-run program that the EPA has approved to administer the RCRA program. 42 U.S.C. § 6925(a)-(d). The term "interim status" allows an applicant for a RCRA permit to act as if it has the permit even though the entity is awaiting final permit approval from the appropriate government agency. 42 U.S.C. § 6925(e). The EPA and state-issued permits and interim status are both federally enforceable.

As with the Clean Water Act and Clean Air Act, RCRA imposes a "knowing" standard for storing, treating, and disposing of a hazardous waste. Similar to these Acts, RCRA's knowing standard does not require an individual to know that a permit is required to store, treat, or dispose of a hazardous waste.

United States v. Laughlin
10 F.3d 961 (2d Cir. 1993)

MINER, Circuit Judge:

Defendant-appellant Harris Goldman appeals from a judgment of conviction and sentence entered in the United States District Court for the Northern District of New York (Munson, J.), after a jury trial, convicting him of knowingly disposing of hazardous waste without a permit, in violation of the Resource Conservation and Recovery Act of 1976. . . . The district court sentenced Goldman to concurrent prison terms of three-and-one-half years for the RCRA violation. . . . He was further ordered to pay restitution to the United States in the amount of $607,868. Goldman primarily contends on appeal that the district court delivered an improper charge to the jury regarding the RCRA . . . violations. For the reasons that follow, we affirm.

BACKGROUND

In 1983, GCL Tie & Treating, Inc. ("GCL") purchased a railroad tie treating business located in Sidney, New York from the Railcon Corporation ("Railcon"). GCL was owned by Goldman and his business partner, Thomas Cuevas.

The tie treatment process consisted of first placing untreated green ties into a large cylinder and then adding creosote. The creosote then was heated to boiling. As water and natural wood alcohols were drawn out by a vacuum process, the creosote penetrated the ties. The water, wood alcohols and some creosote, collectively referred to in the industry as "bolton water," would vaporize in the cylinder, where it was then drawn off and run through condensation coils. This mixture, consisting of twenty-five percent creosote, thereafter was placed in a heated evaporation tank. Once in this tank, the creosote quickly settled to the bottom due to its heavier weight, forming sludge. The water then was boiled off so that the remaining creosote sludge could be suctioned out and placed into storage for re-use in the treatment process.

Subsequent to 1983, GCL began having problems with its treatment process. As a result, excess creosote often became contaminated or spilled from the system. GCL supervisors regularly directed employees to dispose of the contaminated creosote by soaking it up with sawdust and dumping it in remote areas of the GCL property. GCL never had applied for a RCRA "TSD" (treatment, storage or disposal) permit and, therefore, neither the New York State Department of Environmental Conservation ("DEC") nor the United States Environmental Protection Agency ("EPA") was aware that GCL regularly handled, and disposed of, creosote.

On October 30, 1986, a large, accidental creosote spill occurred at GCL. Contrary to Goldman's instructions, this spill was reported to the DEC, which then began making periodic, pre-announced visits. With the exception of the October 30 spill, however, no regulatory agency had any knowledge or information of any other spill or disposal of creosote by GCL.

GCL began experiencing financial difficulties in 1987. Its problems were exacerbated when, early in June, GCL's boiler ceased to function properly. Without a properly functioning boiler, GCL could not recover the creosote sludge left over from the treatment process. GCL quickly began to run out of storage space for the bolton water, and GCL employees were directed to put the excess bolton water into a railroad tanker car that had recently delivered a shipment of new creosote. This tanker car remained on the GCL railroad spur and was used to store the bolton water generated by the treatment process.

During the time that the bolton water was being stored in the tanker car, Goldman became concerned over GCL's daily accrual of "demurrage" or rental charges for keeping the tanker car beyond its normal return date. After two weeks had passed with no resolution of the boiler problems, Goldman met with GCL Vice President of Operations and Plant Manager Ken Laughlin and a company consultant, Jack Thomas. The three discussed several methods of disposing of the bolton water, including: (1) returning the tanker car full of bolton water (approximately 22,000 gallons) to the creosote manufacturer, which would have proper disposal facilities available to it; (2) hiring a hazardous waste remover to cart away and properly dispose of the bolton water; and (3) pumping the bolton water into a truck and disposing of it by spraying it out of the back of the truck while it drove along dirt roads in Sidney. Goldman rejected the first two proposals as being too costly. He then proposed the spray truck scheme to Laughlin and Thomas, who both objected and informed Goldman that such a scheme would be illegal.

Shortly thereafter, Goldman began to demand repeatedly that Laughlin release the contents of the tanker car onto the ground. After Laughlin refused, Goldman informed him that he was going to release the creosote sludge himself. After one unsuccessful nocturnal attempt to release the creosote sludge, Goldman returned a second time, at approximately three o'clock in the morning, and successfully released the entire contents of the tanker car directly onto the ground.

The next morning, in the presence of GCL employees, Goldman admitted to Laughlin that he had dumped the creosote sludge, but told those present that they would be fired if the release was reported to the Government. Goldman then instructed Laughlin to hire an outside contractor to cover the contaminated soil with rock and gravel. This was done, no report was made to either the DEC or the EPA, and the spill was never mentioned during subsequent inspections.

Financial conditions at GCL continued to deteriorate, and on August 6, 1987, Railcon exercised its rights under a note it held from the 1983 sale and removed Goldman from operational control of GCL. Although Goldman remained an equity owner, he and the entire GCL board were removed as directors in August of 1987. GCL then filed for chapter 11 bankruptcy sometime in the autumn of 1987.

In December of 1987, Railcon President George Petti, informed by Laughlin of the June dumping, directed Laughlin to arrange for the contaminated soil to be excavated and removed. Approximately five hundred and twenty cubic yards of soil were recovered from the site where Goldman had released the creosote sludge. This soil was added to the pile of soil that was excavated after the spill in October of 1986.

GCL continued its financial slide and, by May of 1988, the entire facility was abandoned. Nothing was done to dispose of or safeguard either the tens of thousands of gallons of creosote left behind or the fifty-five gallon drums of hydrochloric acid and other hazardous chemicals that were abandoned. By the summer of 1988, the DEC learned that the site had been deserted and began piecing together details of its true condition. A criminal investigation ensued and, after detailed inspections were conducted, the facility was declared a federal Superfund site. On January 17, 1991, Goldman was arrested, pursuant to a warrant, in the Eastern District of New York. On December 11, 1991, Goldman was indicted for illegal disposal of hazardous waste, in violation of RCRA. . . .

During trial, Goldman testified on his own behalf and admitted that he knew GCL did not have a permit to dispose of hazardous waste; he knew that creosote sludge was a hazardous waste; he knew of the requirement to report the release of such material to the Government; he never reported any such release; and he knew that it was illegal to dump creosote sludge onto the ground. On September 4, 1992, a jury convicted Goldman on both counts. The district court sentenced Goldman to a prison term of forty-two months for the RCRA violation. . . . Goldman also was ordered to pay restitution to the United States in the amount of $607,868.

DISCUSSION

Goldman argues that (1) the district court erred when instructing the jury regarding the elements of the RCRA . . . ; [and] (2) there was insufficient evidence to support the jury's verdict[.] We are unpersuaded by any of Goldman's arguments and, therefore, uphold his conviction.

1. RCRA

Goldman argues that the district court improperly instructed the jury regarding the elements of the RCRA violation. He claims that the Government was required to prove, as essential elements of the violation, that he was aware of the RCRA regulations applicable to creosote sludge and knew GCL had not obtained a permit to dispose of the creosote sludge and that the district court's failure to so instruct the jury was error. It is axiomatic that in a criminal prosecution the Government must satisfy its burden of proof beyond a reasonable doubt for every essential element of the crime with which the defendant is charged. . . . Upon review, we conclude that the district court properly instructed the jury regarding the RCRA violation.

Goldman was convicted of violating 42 U.S.C. § 6928(d)(2)(A) which provides criminal penalties for:

> Any person who . . .
> (2) knowingly treats, stores, or disposes of any hazardous waste identified or listed under this subchapter—
> (A) without a permit under this subchapter. . . .

Appellant contends that the word "knowingly" applies not only to the prohibited act—treatment, storage, or disposal of a hazardous waste—but also to the fact that the hazardous waste has been identified or listed under RCRA and to the fact that a permit was lacking.

The district court instructed the jury that it had to find that the Government had proved the following elements beyond a reasonable doubt:

> (1) "the defendant knowingly disposed of or caused others to dispose of creosote sludge on or about the date set forth in the indictment";
> (2) "that pursuant to [RCRA], the creosote sludge was hazardous";
> (3) "the defendant knew creosote sludge had a potential to be harmful to others or the environment or, in other words, it was not a harmless substance like uncontaminated water"; and
> (4) "neither defendant nor GCL had obtained a permit or interim status which authorized the disposal of hazardous waste under [RCRA]."

Prior to delivering these instructions, the district court told the jury that creosote sludge was a hazardous waste as defined under RCRA. Appellant makes no objection to this aspect of the jury charge.

When knowledge is an element of a statute intended to regulate hazardous or dangerous substances, the Supreme Court has determined that the knowledge element is satisfied upon a showing that a defendant was aware that he was performing the proscribed acts; knowledge of regulatory requirements is not necessary. *See United States v. International Minerals & Chem. Corp.*, 402 U.S. 558, 563-65 (1971) (in prosecution for knowingly violating a hazardous materials regulation, Government was not required to prove that the defendant was aware of regulation, but only that he was aware of shipment of the hazardous materials.) "[W]here, as here . . . dangerous or deleterious devices or products or obnoxious waste materials are involved, the probability of regulation is so great that anyone who is aware that he is in possession of them or dealing with them must be presumed to be aware of the regulation." *International Minerals*, 402 U.S. at 565. In light of this precedent, particularly the presumption of awareness of regulation set forth in *International Minerals*, it is clear that section 6928(d)(2)(A) requires only that a defendant have a general awareness that he is performing acts proscribed by the statute. The district court did not err in declining to charge that the statute required knowledge that the creosote sludge was "identified or listed" under RCRA.

Although this Court never before has been presented with the question of whether 42 U.S.C. § 6928(d)(2)(A) requires that a defendant have knowledge of the lack of a permit for hazardous waste disposal, most of the courts of appeals that have addressed this issue have responded in the negative. *See, e.g., United States v. Dean*, 969 F.2d 187, 191 (6th Cir. 1992) ("[6928(d)(2)(A)] does not require that the person charged have known that a permit was required, and that knowledge is not relevant."); *United States v. Hoflin*, 880 F.2d 1033, 1037 (9th Cir. 1989) (expressly holding that knowledge of lack of permit is not an element of section 6928(d)(2)(A) offense); *see also United States v. Goldsmith*, 978 F.2d 643, 645-46 (11th Cir. 1992) (per curiam) (approving jury instruction which did not require knowledge of the absence of a permit); *United States v. Dee*, 912 F.2d 741, 745 (4th Cir. 1990) (Government need not prove that defendants knew that violation of RCRA was a crime nor did they need to know of existence of specific regulations or requirements); *but see United States v. Johnson & Towers, Inc.*, 741 F.2d 662, 667-68 (3d Cir. 1984) (stating in *dicta* that knowledge of the absence of a permit is required for conviction under section 6928(d)(2)(A)). Referring to the knowledge requirement, the panel in *Hoflin* stated, "[t]he statute is not ambiguous. On the contrary, '[t]he language is plain and the meaning is clear.'" *Hoflin*, 880 F.2d at 1037 (quoting *United States v. Patterson*, 820 F.2d 1524, 1526 (9th Cir. 1987)). It is also our perception that a defendant's knowledge that a permit is lacking is not an element of the offense defined by 42 U.S.C. § 6928(d)(2)(A). This conclusion is supported not only by the reasoning of *International Minerals* but also by the fact that the word "knowing" is included in paragraphs (B) and (C) of section 6928(d)(2) but notably omitted from paragraph (A), with which we are concerned. With respect to the mens rea required by section 6928(d)(2)(A), the Government need prove only that a defendant was aware of his act of disposing of a substance he knew was hazardous. Proof that a defendant was aware of the lack of a permit is not required. Accordingly, we hold that the district court properly instructed the jury concerning Goldman's violation of section 6928(d)(2)(A). . . .

The judgment of conviction is affirmed.

- What is the reasoning for not requiring the prosecution to prove that the defendant knew he/she needed a permit to store, dispose of, or treat hazardous waste?

- What are the similarities between the Clean Water Act, Clean Air Act, and RCRA's provisions for knowing violations where a permit is required?
- Does RCRA provide any textual difference for requiring knowledge that a permit is required?

Recall that the Clean Water Act and the Clean Air Act criminalize knowing violations of permits where the violator need not know the permit's provisions in order to be found guilty. *United States v. Weitzenhoff*, 35 F.3d 1275 (9th Cir. 1993). Unlike the Clean Water Act and the Clean Air Act, RCRA's criminal provision relating to permit and interim status violations includes an extra "knowing" element. Specifically, RCRA provides that "[a]ny person who . . . *knowingly* treats, stores, or disposes of any hazardous waste . . . *in knowing violation* of any material condition or requirement of such permit [or interim status] . . . shall, upon conviction, be subject to a fine . . . or imprisonment not to exceed . . . five years. . . ." 42 U.S.C. § 6928(d)(2), (3) (emphasis added). Thus, the prosecution must show that the defendant "knowingly" treated, stored, or disposed of a hazardous waste "in knowing violation" of a permit or interim status. *Self*, 2 F.3d at 1089-92.

This is an odd difference between RCRA and the Clean Water Act and the Clean Air Act because, as shown in the cases above, courts have repeatedly applied the reasoning of the Supreme Court's decision in *International Minerals*, which provided that "the probability of regulation is so great that anyone who is aware that he is in possession of them or dealing with them must be presumed to be aware of the regulation." *International Minerals*, 402 U.S. at 565. Therefore, knowing the permit requirements was not deemed to be an element of the crime of discharging a pollutant in violation of an NPDES permit, for example. It would seem, based on this reasoning, that a person storing, treating, or disposing of hazardous waste would be presumed to be aware of the permit's requirements and, if they are violated, then criminal liability should follow. However, Congress included "in knowing violation" of a permit or interim status in RCRA despite not including it in either the Clean Water Act or the Clean Air Act. This seems to produce the result of making prosecution of permit violations more difficult in the very arena in which a presumption of regulatory knowledge applies. Being able to show that the defendant knew the permit's requirements or willfully blinded him/herself to them is a factor that a prosecutor must take into consideration when deciding whether to charge such a count. Defense counsel for a would-be defendant would be well advised to use this factor to persuade a prosecutor not to seek such charges.

d. Transporting Hazardous Waste Contrary to Law

To maintain the "cradle to grave" regulatory system for hazardous waste, Congress required that all hazardous waste transportation be accompanied by a manifest. A manifest is a document that identifies "the quantity, composition, and the origin, routing, and destination of hazardous waste during its [off-site] transportation from the point of generation to the point of disposal, treatment, or storage." 42 U.S.C. § 6903(12). A generator creates the manifest; signs it; keeps a copy; gives a copy to the transporter, who also signs it; and, upon delivery of the hazardous waste shipment provides a copy of the manifest to the treatment, storage, or disposal facility ("TSD facility"). The TSD facility then signs the manifest and returns it to the generator. If the TSD facility fails to return a signed copy of the manifest to the generator within 45 days, then the generator must file an exception report with the EPA. 40 C.F.R. § 262.42(b). To show how serious it was about the manifest system, Congress imposed a two-year felony upon any person who "knowingly transports" or "causes to be transported" a hazardous waste "without a manifest." 42 U.S.C. § 6928(d)(5). Accordingly, generators and transporters alike who fail to adhere to the manifest requirement before transporting hazardous waste face the risk of a felony prosecution.

However, when it came to transporting hazardous waste, Congress was concerned that those manifest-less shipments represented something more than mere clerical neglect and were, instead, a sign that hazardous waste was being shipped so that it could be illegally treated, stored, or disposed of. Consequently, Congress imposed a five-year felony upon any person who "knowingly transports or causes to be transported any hazardous waste . . . to a facility which does not have a permit [or interim status] under [RCRA]." 42 U.S.C. § 6928(d)(1).

Similar to all of the other crimes that have been discussed thus far, it is essential to recognize which elements require a showing of the defendant's knowledge. Certainly, as discussed above, a person must be aware of the fact that he/she is transporting or causing to be transported a waste that is "not innocuous like water." But, must a person charged with the crime of transporting to an unpermitted facility also know that the facility to which he/she is delivering hazardous waste lacks a RCRA permit or interim status?

United States v. Hayes International Corp.
786 F.2d 1499 (11th Cir. 1986)

KRAVITCH, Circuit Judge:
The degree of knowledge necessary for a conviction under 42 U.S.C. § 6928(d)(1), unlawful transportation of hazardous waste, is the principal issue in this appeal. The district court granted judgments of acquittal notwithstanding the jury verdicts. The court held that the government had not presented sufficient evidence of knowledge to support convictions of Hayes International Corp. and L.H. Beasley. A decision of the district court setting aside a jury verdict of guilty is entitled to no deference, and we have conducted our own review of the evidence and find it sufficient. Accordingly, we reverse.

I. BACKGROUND
Hayes International Corp. (Hayes) operates an airplane refurbishing plant in Birmingham, Alabama. In the course of its business, Hayes generates certain waste products, two of which are relevant to this case. First, Hayes must drain fuel tanks of the planes on which it works. Second, Hayes paints the aircraft with spray guns and uses solvents to clean the paint guns and lines, thereby generating a mix of paint and solvents.

L.H. Beasley was the employee of Hayes responsible for disposal of hazardous wastes. In early 1981, Beasley orally agreed with Jack Hurt, an employee of

Performance Advantage, Inc., to dispose of certain wastes. Under the agreement, Performance Advantage would obtain from Hayes the valuable jet fuel drained from the planes; Performance Advantage would pay twenty cents per gallon for the jet fuel, and, at no charge, would remove other wastes from the Hayes plant including the mixture of paint and solvents. Performance Advantage was a recycler, and used the jet fuel to make marketable fuel. Wastes were transported from Hayes to Performance Advantage on eight occasions between January 1981 and March 1982.

Beginning in August 1982, government officials discovered drums of waste generated by Hayes and illegally disposed of by Performance Advantage. Approximately six hundred drums of waste were found, deposited among seven illegal disposal sites in Georgia and Alabama. The waste was the paint and solvent which Performance Advantage had removed from Hayes. Some of the drums were simply dumped in yards, while others were buried.

The prosecutions in this case were brought under the Resource Conservation and Recovery Act[, which] creates a cradle to grave regulatory scheme to ensure that hazardous wastes are properly disposed of. Generators of waste are required to identify hazardous wastes and use a manifest system to ensure that wastes are disposed of only in facilities possessing a permit. 42 U.S.C. § 6922(5). . . .

Beasley and Hayes each were convicted of eight counts of violating 42 U.S.C. § 6928(d)(1), which provides criminal sanctions for

> Any person who (1) knowingly transports any hazardous waste identified or listed under this subchapter to a facility which does not have a permit under section 6925 of this title.

Hayes' liability is based on the actions of Beasley. It is undisputed that Performance Advantage did not have a permit.

In their motion for judgment notwithstanding the verdict and on appeal, the appellees raise three basic theories of defense, and argue that the government's evidence was insufficient to refute any of them. First they contend that they did not commit any "knowing" violation because they misunderstood the regulations. Second, they contend that they did not "know" that Performance Advantage did not have a permit. Third, they contend that they did not commit a knowing violation because they believed that Performance Advantage was recycling the waste. Under the regulations in force at the time, characteristic hazardous waste was not regulated if it was "beneficially used or re-used [sic] or legitimately recycled or reclaimed." 40 C.F.R. § 261.6(a)(1), superseded effective July 5, 1985, 50 Fed. Reg. 665.

On appeal, the government argues that the first two defenses are legally insufficient, and that the jury could have rejected the third on the basis of the evidence. . . .

II. THE ELEMENTS OF A SECTION 6928(d) OFFENSE

Congress did not provide any guidance, either in the statute or the legislative history, concerning the meaning of "knowing" in section 6928(d). Indeed, Congress stated that it had "not sought to define 'knowing' for offenses under subsection (d); that process has been left to the courts under general principles." S. Rep. No. 172, 96th Cong., 2d Sess. 39 (1980), U.S. Code Cong. & Admin. News

1980, pp. 5019, 5038. In discerning the relevant general principles, we turn to a few examples from a long line of Supreme Court cases discussing the necessary elements of regulatory offenses.

Whether Knowledge of the Regulations Is Required

In certain cases, the Court has held that an offense requires no mental element, but simply requisite actions. In *United States v. Freed*, 401 U.S. 601 (1971), the defendant was charged with violating a statute making it unlawful "to receive or possess a firearm which is not registered to him." 401 U.S. at 607. The Court held that no element of scienter was necessary for conviction; a person need not even have known that the grenades were unregistered. The Court reasoned that the statute itself set forth no mental element, and that the statute was

> a regulatory measure in the interest of the public safety, which may well be premised on the theory that one would hardly be surprised to learn that possession of hand grenades is not an innocent act.

401 U.S. at 609. *See also United States v. Dotterweich*, 320 U.S. 277 (1943).

The Court has had greater difficulty with statutes in which Congress has created an offense of "knowingly violating a regulation." In *United States v. International Minerals & Chemical Corp.*, 402 U.S. 558 (1971), the defendant was charged with "knowingly" violating an I.C.C. regulation. The regulation prohibited shipping hazardous materials without showing them on the shipping papers. The Court held that knowledge of the regulation was not an element of the offense; the use of "knowingly" in the statute referred only to the defendant's knowledge that the materials being shipped were dangerous. The Court noted the general maxim that ignorance of the law is no excuse, but also reasoned that where

> obnoxious waste materials are involved, the probability of regulation is so great that anyone who is aware that he is in possession of them or dealing with them must be presumed to be aware of the regulation.

402 U.S. at 565. . . .

The Court reached a different result in a recent case involving food stamps, *Liparota v. United States*, 471 U.S. 419 (1985). The statute in *Liparota* provided punishment for anyone who "knowingly uses, transfers, acquires, alters, or possesses coupons or authorization cards in any manner not authorized by [the statute] or the regulations." The government argued that "knowingly" simply referred to knowledge of acquiring or possessing food stamps, and that the defendant need not have known the acquisition was in violation of the regulations. The Court disagreed, holding that knowledge of illegality was necessary. . . .

The appellees contend that our interpretation of section 6928(d)(1) should be controlled by *Liparota*. They argue that a violation of section 6928(d)(1) therefore requires knowledge of transportation, knowledge that the waste is a waste within the meaning of the statute, knowledge that disposal sites must have a permit, and knowledge that the site in question does not have a permit. In short, they contend that the defendants must have known that their actions violated the statute. . . .

We conclude that *Liparota* does not control this case. First, section 6928(d)(1) is not drafted in a manner which makes knowledge of illegality an element of the offense. The statute in *Liparota*, paraphrased, prohibited "knowing violation of a regulation," and reading a legal element into the offense therefore made linguistic sense. In addition, section 6928(d)(1) is undeniably a public welfare statute, involving a heavily regulated area with great ramifications for the public health and safety. As the Supreme Court has explained, it is completely fair and reasonable to charge those who choose to operate in such areas with knowledge of the regulatory provisions. Indeed, the reasonableness is borne out in this case, for the evidence at trial belied the appellees' profession of ignorance. Accordingly, in a prosecution under 42 U.S.C. § 6928(d)(1) it would be no defense to claim no knowledge that the paint waste was a hazardous waste within the meaning of the regulations; nor would it be a defense to argue ignorance of the permit requirement.

Whether Knowledge of the Permit Status Is Required

The government argues that the statute does not require knowledge of the permit status of the facility to which the wastes are transported. The Supreme Court has noted that statutes similarly drafted in the manner of section 6928(d) are linguistically ambiguous: it is impossible to tell how far down the sentence "knowingly" travels. In *Liparota*, as we discussed above, the Court held that "knowingly" travelled all the way down the sentence. In another recent case, however, the Court held that "knowingly" did not modify all elements of the crime at issue. *United States v. Yermian*, 468 U.S. 63 (1984) (statute forbidding knowingly making a false statement within the jurisdiction of a federal agency does not require actual knowledge of federal jurisdiction).

In this case, the congressional purpose indicates knowledge of the permit status is required. The precise wrong Congress intended to combat through section 6928(d) was transportation to an unlicensed facility. Removing the knowing requirement from this element would criminalize innocent conduct; for example, if the defendant reasonably believed that the site had a permit, but in fact had been misled by the people at the site. If Congress intended such a strict statute, it could have dropped the "knowingly" requirement. We also note that the statute is different than that in *Yermian*, where making a false statement would not be an innocent act regardless of whether the declarant knew the statement was to be submitted to a federal agency.

The government does not face an unacceptable burden of proof in proving that the defendant acted with knowledge of the permit status. Knowledge does not require certainty; a defendant acts knowingly if he is aware "'that that result is practically certain to follow from his conduct, whatever his desire may be as to that result.'" *United States v. United States Gypsum Co.*, 438 U.S. 422, 445 (1978). Moreover, in this regulatory context a defendant acts knowingly if he willfully fails to determine the permit status of the facility.

Moreover, the government may prove guilty knowledge with circumstantial evidence. In the context of the hazardous waste statutes, proving knowledge should not be difficult. The statute at issue here sets forth certain procedures transporters must follow to ensure that wastes are sent only to permit facilities. Transporters of waste presumably are aware of these procedures, and if a transporter does not follow the procedures, a juror may draw certain inferences. Where there is no evidence that those who took the waste asserted that they were properly licensed, the jurors may draw additional inferences. Jurors may also consider the circumstances and terms of the transaction. It is common knowledge that properly disposing of wastes is an expensive task, and if someone is willing to take away wastes at an unusual price or under unusual circumstances, then a juror can infer that the transporter knows the wastes are not being taken to a permit facility.

In sum, to convict under section 6928(d)(1), the jurors must find that the defendant knew what the waste was (here, a mixture of paint and solvent), and that the defendant knew the disposal site had no permit. Knowledge does not require certainty, and the jurors may draw inferences from all of the circumstances, including the existence of the regulatory scheme.

III. ANALYSIS . . .

The appellees' second defense is that the evidence was insufficient to show they knew that Performance Advantage did not have a permit. In considering the evidence, we view it in the light most favorable to the government, with all reasonable inferences drawn in favor of the jury's verdict. The evidence shows that Hayes was not following the regulatory procedure for manifesting waste sent to a permit site, from which the jury could have inferred that the appellees did not believe Performance Advantage had a permit. This inference is strengthened by Hayes' own documents, which set forth this requirement. Performance Advantage also was not charging to haul away the waste (although obviously they found the overall deal advantageous), and Beasley thought he had made a good deal; accordingly the terms were such as to raise suspicion. . . .

Based on all the above, the jury could have found beyond a reasonable doubt that appellees knew Performance Advantage did not have a permit.

. . . The judgments of acquittal notwithstanding the verdict as to both defendants are vacated. The case is remanded to the district court to enter judgment in accordance with the jury verdicts of guilty.

REVERSED and REMANDED.

- Why is knowing the regulatory status of the hazardous waste not an element of the offense but knowing the regulatory status of the TSD facility is an element? Is knowledge of legal status an example of the "knowing" mens rea or the "willful" mens rea?
- If hazardous wastes are so highly regulated that a jury is allowed to presume that the defendant knew that the material was dangerous, then why is a jury not allowed to presume that a hazardous waste generator is aware of the permit status of the facility to which he/she is sending hazardous waste?

3. Dishonest Acts

Similar to the Clean Water Act and Clean Air Act, RCRA imposes a two-year felony upon any person who "knowingly omits material information or makes any false material statement or representation in any application, label, manifest, record, report, permit, or other document filed, maintained, or used for purposes of compliance with regulations promulgated by the Administrator [] or by a State in the case of a State program . . . under [RCRA]." 42 U.S.C. § 6928(d)(3). Thus, the prosecution must prove that the omission or false statement was not an accident but was intentional. The prosecution must also show that the record that includes the omission or false statement was maintained for "purposes of compliance" with RCRA and its regulations even though RCRA may not require the document to be created or filed. Finally, the prosecution must prove that omission or false statement was "material." The term "material" means that the false statement or omission "has 'a natural tendency to influence, or [is] capable of influencing, the decision of the decisionmaking body to which it was addressed.'" *Neder v. United States*, 527 U.S. 1, 16 (1999) (citations omitted). However, unlike other RCRA crimes, § 6928(d)(3) does not require the prosecution to prove that a material is a hazardous waste. For example, if a person makes a false statement about a shipment of material with potential to be hazardous—which, if disclosed, would cause regulators to investigate the shipment further—then that false statement may still violate § 6928(d)(3). *Self*, 2 F.3d at 1083-84.

Whereas § 6928(d)(3) neither requires proof of hazardous waste nor that the records at issue are mandated under RCRA, Congress created § 6928(d)(4) to cover records for those who handle hazardous waste that RCRA requires to be filed or maintained. Specifically, § 6928(d)(4) provides a two-year felony for any person who

> knowingly generates, stores, treats, transports, disposes of, exports, or otherwise handles any hazardous waste . . . and who knowingly destroys, alters, conceals, or fails to file any record, application, manifest, report, or other document required to be maintained or filed for purposes of compliance with regulations promulgated by the Administrator (or by a State in the case of an authorized State program) under [RCRA].

42 U.S.C. § 6928(d)(4). To prove this offense, the prosecution must first establish that the defendant intentionally handled hazardous waste at some point from its metaphoric cradle to its metaphoric grave. Thereafter, the prosecution must show that the defendant intentionally failed to file a document or omitted or misrepresented information in any record that was required to be filed or maintained to comply with RCRA. Consider the following example.

Case Study: What's in the Storage Unit?

Steve Murray has a hobby of buying the contents of storage units where the former tenant's account is so overdue that the owner of the storage facility sells the unit's contents at an auction. Steve successfully bids on what he hopes is a promising storage unit because, as per auction rules, Steve is unaware what lies behind the storage unit door. When he opens the storage unit, he sees that it is filled with 55-gallon drums, some of which are leaking a weird, blue fluid. Steve calls a friend who works in a local chemical plant, and Steve's friend comes over to see Steve's new treasure. Steve's friend immediately recognizes the markings on the drums, the color of the fluid, and its smell as the waste from an electroplating operation. Steve's friend says, "I'm sorry, Steve. That stuff is hazardous waste because it is listed by the EPA." Naturally frustrated that he has now paid to own a problem that may cost him more money, Steve asks his friend what he should do. Steve's friend suggests that Steve get a U-Haul and take it to a local TSD. It will cost him some money, but it will be better than trying to get rid of it illegally. So, Steve loads a U-Haul and takes the load to a permitted TSD facility. When he arrives, the TSD facility asks if Steve has a hazardous waste manifest. Steve does not, but he looks online, finds one from another company for a load of who knows what, adjusts the number of drums so that it matches the number that he has, and gives it to the TSD facility. The TSD facility uses the manifest, accepts the drums, and disposes of them based on the contents of the manifest. However, because the chemicals on the manifest were very different than the ones actually in Steve's drums, the TSD's disposal method causes a massive fire that damages the facility. Thankfully, however, no one was injured. The TSD owner is irate and calls EPA-CID to investigate Steve. EPA-CID corroborates the foregoing facts. For what, if anything, may Steve be charged? May others be charged? If so, for what?

4. Knowing Endangerment

Similar to the Clean Water Act and the Clean Air Act, RCRA contains a "knowing endangerment" provision that imposes up 15 years in prison and a $1 million fine for any person who commits a predicate RCRA offense and "knows at the time that he thereby places another person in imminent danger of serious death or serious bodily injury." 42 U.S.C. § 6928(e). Section 6928(f)(1) and (2) define what the prosecution needs to prove to establish "knowing" under § 6928(e). However, how "imminent" must the "danger" be in order to meet that element?

United States v. Protext Industries, Inc.
874 F.2d 740 (10th Cir. 1989)

SAFFELS, District Judge.

This appeal was taken from the first criminal conviction under the "knowing endangerment" provision of the federal Resource Conservation and Recovery Act ("RCRA"), 42 U.S.C. § 6928(e), recently enacted by Congress. Appellant Protex Industries, Inc. ("Protex") appeals from its criminal conviction under that provision as well as from its other convictions under the RCRA.

Protex operated a drum recycling facility. It purchased used 55-gallon drums, many of which previously contained toxic chemicals. It cleaned and repainted the drums and used them to store and ship other products it manufactured.

The Environmental Protection Agency ("EPA") inspected Protex's facilities annually. One of these inspections was conducted on July 24, 1984, by a representative of the Colorado Department of Health under contract with the EPA. The Department of Health conducted the inspection pursuant to section 3012 of the RCRA, which requires each state to compile an inventory of sites at which hazardous waste has at any time been disposed of, treated or stored. . . .

On March 10 and 11, 1986, investigators from the EPA and the Federal Bureau of Investigation executed a search warrant at Protex's drum recycling facility. A federal grand jury later returned a nineteen count indictment against Protex, and Protex was convicted of sixteen of those nineteen counts.

Counts 17 through 19 of that indictment charged Protex with knowingly placing three of its employees in imminent danger of death or serious bodily injury as a result of its other alleged violations of the RCRA. The evidence showed that safety provisions for the employees in the drum recycling facility were woefully inadequate to protect the employees against the dangers of the toxic chemicals. Government experts testified that without these proper safety precautions, the employees were at an increased risk of suffering solvent poisoning. Solvent poisoning may cause psychoorganic syndrome, of which there are three types. Symptoms of Type 1 psychoorganic syndrome are disturbances in thinking, behavior and personality, and sleeping disorders. Type 1 is reversible quickly and goes away when exposure ends. Type 2 psychoorganic syndrome is divided into two categories, A and B. An individual suffering from Type 2-A suffers changes in personality and has difficulty controlling impulses; the individual engages in unplanned and unexpected behavior, lacks motivation, and usually experiences severe mood swings. If exposure to the toxic chemicals ends, an individual suffering from Type 2-A will eventually recover. An individual suffering from Type 2-B psychoorganic syndrome, however, will have additional, nonreversible symptoms, such as concentration problems, short and remote memory problems, decreased learning ability, and cognitive impairment. Finally, an individual suffering from Type 3 psychoorganic syndrome suffers a severe loss of learning capabilities, severe memory loss, severe psychiatric abnormalities and gross tremor. The government experts also testified that in addition to being at risk for psychoorganic syndrome, the employees suffered an increased risk of contracting cancer as a result of their extended exposure to the toxic chemicals.

The testimony of government experts further showed that two of the employees certainly had Type 2-A psychoorganic syndrome and may have had Type 2-B. The government expert testified that he could not demonstrate that the third employee was suffering from psychoorganic syndrome at the time he was examined, but pointed out that he might still have suffered from the syndrome and since recovered from its symptoms. Finally, the expert testified that all three individuals had an increased permanent and irreversible risk of developing cancer due to their prolonged exposure to the toxic chemicals.

Protex states three grounds for its appeal. It contends that the trial court rendered 42 U.S.C. § 6928(e) unconstitutionally vague as applied in two regards. First, it argues that the trial court erred in allowing the "knowing endangerment" counts to go to the jury, despite the alleged absence of any evidence showing the employees were placed in imminent danger of serious bodily injury as specifically defined by 42 U.S.C. § 6928(f)(6). Secondly, it contends the trial court rendered the section unconstitutionally vague as applied because it improperly instructed the jury that an individual was placed in "imminent danger" if it "could reasonably be expected" that the set of conditions would cause death or serious bodily injury. Defendant contends this language did not track the language of the statute and it unconstitutionally expanded it beyond the intent of Congress. . . .

I.

. . . Title 42, United States Code, Section 6928(e) provides that: "Any person who knowingly transports, treats, stores, disposes of, or exports any hazardous waste identified or listed under [the RCRA] in violation of [the criminal provisions of the RCRA] who knows at that time that he thereby places another person in imminent danger of death or serious bodily injury, shall [be guilty of an offense against the United States.]" Title 42, United States Code, Section 6928(f)(6) defines "serious bodily injury" as: (A) bodily injury which involves a substantial risk of death; (B) unconsciousness; (C) extreme physical pain; (D) protracted and obvious disfigurement; or (E) protracted loss or impairment of the function of a bodily member, organ, or mental faculty. Protex contends that the trial court rendered section 6928(e) unconstitutionally vague by expanding the definition of "serious bodily injury" beyond that set out in section 6928(f)(6). Protex states that if the employees were placed in any "danger" at all, it was a danger of developing Type 2-A psychoorganic syndrome, a condition which does not come within the scope of subparagraphs (A)-(E) of section 6928(f)(6). Protex also argues that the enhanced "risk" of contracting some indeterminate type of cancer at some unspecified time in the future is not sufficient to constitute "serious bodily injury."

Appellant's position demonstrates a callousness toward the severe physical effect the prolonged exposure to toxic chemicals may cause or has caused to the three former employees. There was evidence presented at trial to show that the three individuals not only had been in danger of serious bodily injury, but had in fact suffered serious bodily injury: Type 2-A and Type 2-B psychoorganic syndrome may cause an impairment of mental faculties.[7]

II.

Protex contends secondly that the statute was rendered unconstitutionally vague because in instructing the jury, the district court defined "imminent danger" as "the existence of a condition or combination of conditions which could reasonably be expected to cause death or serious bodily injury unless the condition is remedied." Protex contends this definition was in error, because in 42 U.S.C. § 6928(f)(1)(C), Congress referred to a "substantial certain[ty]" to cause death or serious bodily injury. Protex contends the use of the term "reasonable expectation," rather than the statutory term "substantial certainty," rendered the statute unconstitutionally vague as applied. . . .

In asserting its position on this point, Protex ignores the fact that the court indeed did instruct the jury in language directly derived from the statute. 42 U.S.C. § 6928(f)(1)(C) provides that "a person's state of mind is knowing with respect to . . . a result of his conduct, if he is aware or believes that his conduct is *substantially certain* to cause danger of death or serious bodily injury." (Emphasis added.) Thus, the "substantially certain" standard appears to define the mens rea necessary for commission of the crime, rather than the degree to which defendant's

[7] [Fn. 2] While Protex argues that the psychoorganic syndrome cannot be the basis for the serious bodily injury element here, because the syndrome was not defined by medical experts until after the investigation of Protex, Protex does not demonstrate that it was not known prior to that time that extended exposure to toxic chemicals could bring on certain impairments of mental faculties. Appellant's argument in this regard is rejected. The evidence presented at trial, viewed in a light most favorable to the government, was sufficient to show that the employees were in imminent danger of suffering "serious bodily injury" as that term is defined in 42 U.S.C. § 6928(f)(6). By submitting that evidence to the jury, the court did not render the statute unconstitutionally vague as applied, and appellant's argument is rejected.

conduct must be likely to cause death or serious bodily injury. And the court did quote directly from section 6928(f)(1)(C) in instructing the jury. Protex's contention that the term "substantial certainty," rather than the term "reasonable expectation," should have been used in defining "imminent danger" has no basis in the statutory language.

What Protex in fact seems to be contending is that in general, the statutory language and the legislative history indicate an intent on the part of Congress to narrowly restrict the incidences in which a party may be found guilty of "knowing endangerment," and to limit its application only to actions which cause the most severe physical injury. It uses the reference to the term "substantially certain" in 42 U.S.C. § 6928(f)(1)(C) merely as an example of this general intent.

The court need not address Congressional intent in this instance. We must keep in mind that defendant's argument is based on the void for vagueness doctrine. The essence of that doctrine is that a defendant must have advance notice that its contemplated conduct is forbidden. The court need only look at the statutory language, compare it with the instruction given by the district court, and conclude whether defendant was able to predict that its conduct would violate the RCRA. No complex analysis of legislative history is necessary for that inquiry.

Defendant is unable to articulate why it could have understood that the RCRA forbade it from placing its employees in a situation "substantially certain" to cause danger of death or serious bodily injury, but why it could not have understood that it should not place its employees in situations "reasonably expected" to cause death or serious bodily injury. The argument, premised on different parts of the statute, is unpersuasive as to lack of notice. The trial court's interpretation was not an unforeseeable expansion of a criminal statute that was narrow and precise, in violation of due process. The gist of the "knowing endangerment" provision of the RCRA is that a party will be criminally liable if, in violating other provisions of the RCRA, it places others in danger of great harm and it has knowledge of that danger. The district court conveyed this same idea to the jury in its instructions. The court rejects appellant's argument that it could not be aware that its behavior was prohibited by the "knowing endangerment" provision of the RCRA. . . .

Finding no error in the proceedings below, the judgment of the district court is AFFIRMED.

- How imminent must the danger of injury be to be criminally liable under § 6928(e)?
- How significant must the danger to another person be?
- Why do you think RCRA's imminent danger provision applies to employees who are placed in danger while working with hazardous waste but the Clean Water Act's imminent danger provisions did not protect employees who were working with pollutants that they discharged into the publicly owned treatment works? *See United States v. Borowski*, 977 F.2d 27 (1st Cir. 1992). Is there a difference between the Clean Water Act's and RCRA's knowing endangerment provisions that requires this outcome, or is one court simply wrong? If the former, then what is the statutory difference? If the latter, then which court is wrong and why?

B. RELEASES OF HAZARDOUS SUBSTANCES

In the wake of the horrendous environmental and human consequences arising from the hazardous waste buried by Hooker Chemical in Love Canal, New York, "Congress enacted CERCLA in 1980 to provide a comprehensive response to the problem of hazardous substance release." *Wickland Oil Terminals v. Asarco, Inc.*, 792 F.2d 887, 890 (9th Cir. 1986). CERCLA established a "Superfund" to which Congress appropriated approximately $1.6 billion to provide the federal government with "the tools necessary for a prompt and effective response" to clean up "releases" of "hazardous substances" into the "environment." *United States v. Reilly Tar & Chem. Corp.*, 546 F. Supp. 1100, 1112 (D. Minn. 1982). Notice that "hazardous substances" include more than just "hazardous wastes." As illustrated by the figure below, hazardous substances include materials that are brand new, not just those that are "discarded."

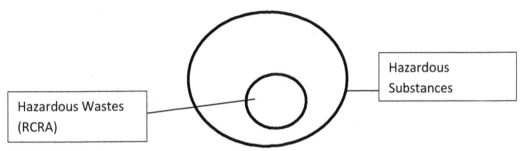

In addition to including the wide world of "hazardous substances" within CERCLA, Congress broadly defined "release" as "any spilling, leaking, pumping, pouring, emitting, emptying, discharging, injecting, escaping, leaching, dumping, or disposing into the environment (including the abandonment or discarding of barrels, containers, and other closed receptacles containing any hazardous substance or pollutant or contaminant). . . ." 42 U.S.C. § 9601(22). The term "hazardous substance" includes all those so designated by the Clean Water Act, Clean Air Act, RCRA, and CERCLA itself. 42 U.S.C. § 9601(14). To allow the EPA to effectively use its authority to clean up releases of hazardous substances, Congress created a National Response Center to which qualifying releases of hazardous substances must be reported. 42 U.S.C. § 9603. Congress also gave the EPA civil enforcement authorities broad authorization to enter private property to inspect and to remediate releases. 42 U.S.C. § 9604(e). These civil authorities can obtain a court order to enter and inspect premises if the property owner precludes them from entry. *Id.*; *In re Yoder's Slaughterhouse Site*, 519 F. Supp. 2d 574, 579-80 (D. Md. 2007). However, the purpose of the entry must be to comply with CERCLA and not as a ruse for criminal investigation by avoiding the process to obtain a criminal search warrant. If EPA's civil team finds evidence of a crime on the inspection site, their information can be used to establish probable cause so that EPA-CID can obtain a criminal search warrant to search for evidence of criminal violations.

In addition to empowering the EPA to remediate releases of hazardous substances, CERCLA casts a wide net of financial liability, which allows the federal government to recoup the money it expended to clean up hazardous substances from "potentially responsible parties" who had control over the hazardous materials and/or the land on which the release occurred. *Reilly Tar & Chem. Corp.*, 546 F. Supp. at 1112. Thus, CERCLA is chiefly devoted to establishing a significant and complex remediation and restitution scheme for releases of hazardous substances.

Despite its considerable size, CERCLA has few criminal provisions. Nevertheless, those provisions have proven to be useful and effective criminal enforcement tools. CERCLA's main criminal provision provides a three-year felony for any person "in charge of a" vessel or facility who fails to "immediately" notify the National Response Center that an unpermitted "release" of a "reportable quantity" of a "hazardous substance" has occurred. 42 U.S.C. § 9603(b). The terms "vessel" and "facility" are both broadly defined and encompass "any site or area where a hazardous substance has been deposited, stored, disposed of, or placed, or otherwise came to be located. . . ." 42 U.S.C. § 9601(9), (28).

United States v. Baytank, Inc.
934 F.2d 599 (5th Cir. 1991)

GARWOOD, Circuit Judge:

These consolidated appeals arise from the trial of a 37-count indictment against two corporations and nineteen individuals for violations of federal environmental laws in the operation of a chemical transfer and storage facility. At the conclusion of the proceedings in the district court, only one defendant, Baytank (Houston), Inc. (Baytank), stood convicted—and only on two counts. . . . The government . . . appeals the district court's order granting Baytank and the only three individual defendants whom the jury found guilty . . . new trials on various counts charging offenses under the Comprehensive Environmental Response, Compensation, and Liability Act of 1980 (CERCLA), 42 U.S.C. § 9603(b)(3). . . .

FACTS AND PROCEEDINGS BELOW

Baytank is a bulk liquid chemical transfer and storage facility located in Seabrook, Texas, near Houston. Baytank's principal function is to provide interim storage for customers transporting various chemicals. The three individual defendants before this Court are officers and employees of Baytank. Nordberg was executive vice president of Baytank, Johnsen was Baytank's safety manager and then its operations manager, and Gore was its technical manager.

This appeal concerns nine counts of the 37-count indictment. At the close of the government's case, the district court granted all defendants judgments of acquittal on all but eleven counts. The jury, at the conclusion of the four-week trial, returned guilty verdicts on nine of the eleven counts submitted. . . .

Count 29, brought under CERCLA, 42 U.S.C. § 9603(b)(3), alleges that the defendants failed to notify the National Response Center of an April 27, 1985 release of more than one hundred pounds of the hazardous chemical acrylonitrile. Under 42 U.S.C. § 9603(a), the National Response Center must be notified of the release of a hazardous substance in excess of the reportable quantity established by statute or regulation. The reportable quantity of acrylonitrile, established by regulation pursuant to 42 U.S.C. § 9602(a),12 is one hundred pounds. 40 C.F.R. § 302.4. . . .

At a motions hearing held following the trial, the district court set aside the jury's verdict, almost in its entirety. The district court . . . ordered new trials for all of the defendants on the remaining counts [including count 29] on which the jury had returned a guilty verdict. . . . The district court did not give any written statement of reasons or explanation for its action.

At sentencing, the district court fined Baytank $50,000. . . . The court refused to impose the mandatory $200 special assessment per count under 18 U.S.C. § 3013(a)(2)(B) on the ground that the law is a revenue-raising measure that originated in the Senate, and is therefore unconstitutional. . . .

DISCUSSION . . .

Count 29 charged that Baytank and Johnsen knowingly failed to timely report to the National Response Center an April 27, 1985 unpermitted "release" into "the environment" at the Baytank facility of a reportable quantity of a hazardous substance, namely over 100 pounds of acrylonitrile, contrary to § 9603(b)(3). . . . The government's evidence showed that some 4,000 pounds of acrylonitrile—a listed hazardous substance whose reportable quantity is 100 pounds—overflowed a Baytank tank on April 27, 1985, that several responsible personnel of Baytank knew about this spill the same day, but that it was not timely reported. The chemical spilled into the "tank bay," a moat-like area around the tank open to the atmosphere. The government's evidence also showed that within the first hour after the overflow some 1,800 pounds of the spilled chemical would have evaporated from the tank bay into the ambient air, and that the air containing this chemical traveled to the neighboring Celanese plant where employees noticed it and experienced resultant adverse effects. The district court instructed the jury that a reportable release into the environment included an "escaping" into the "ambient air," but that a release into a "contained structure . . . like tank bays" was not a release into the environment "unless you find that a reportable quantity of the chemical evaporated or otherwise traveled beyond the confines of the containment structure."

In granting a new trial the district court expressed doubt about the "level of proof" on count 29. The court noted that the testimony of the government's expert concerning the quantities that evaporated into the air was based on an assumption that 4,000 pounds had spilled into the tank bay, as to which latter amount the expert gave no opinion of his own. The district court found this "a serious defect" because the evidence of the quantity spilling into the tank bay was, in the court's view, mere "folk estimates" and "quantifications . . . in the industrial context where somebody scratches himself, looks at it, and says that's about X." However, Baytank's own written records show without contradiction that it contemporaneously estimated and subsequently reported to OSHA that "approximately 4,000 lbs." spilled on this occasion. A witness from the Celanese plant smelled the chemical there, looked for its cause, then shortly thereafter observed ongoing overflow ("like a curtain of liquid") from the Baytank tank at an estimated rate of 100 to 150 gallons a minute, with the spilling continuing until some 10 to 12 minutes had elapsed after the witness had first smelled it. Baytank written records reflect that the spilling went on for 15 minutes. Baytank records also reflect that three hours after the spill the ambient air in areas west and north of the tank bay contained respectively 400 and 800 parts per million of acrylonitrile, but that some eight hours after the spill that substance was not detectable in the ambient air at those same locations. Importantly, there was absolutely no evidence that the 4,000 pound figure was too high or was for any reason unreliable. Moreover, the 4,000 pound figure did not have to approach precision to sustain a finding that from it at least 100 pounds evaporated into the ambient air, as the government's expert stated that 1,800 pounds would evaporate in the first hour from the 4,000 pounds he assumed to have been spilled into the tank bay.

The evidence was clearly more than amply sufficient for the jury to conclude beyond a reasonable doubt that approximately 4,000 pounds spilled into the tank bay. The district court's determination that this undisputed and essentially unchallenged evidence was so weak as to justify a new trial is not supportable (and does not purport to be supported) by considerations of witness demeanor or trial atmospherics. We recognize the district court's especially broad discretion on these matters, but here we are driven to conclude that that discretion was clearly abused. . . .

The grant of new trial to Baytank on count 29 cannot stand. . . .

AFFIRMED in part; REVERSED and REMANDED in part; MANDAMUS GRANTED.

- Why was the spill of acrylonitrile into a moat around the tank a "release"?
- Did the evidence showing that the amount of acrylonitrile purportedly released into the environment met the "reportable quantity" element beyond a reasonable doubt? Why or why not?
- To avoid prosecution, how long of a time is allowed between knowing of a release and actual reporting? If the defendants had reported the spill within eight hours, would that create reasonable doubt as to whether the defendant "notified immediately" the National Response Center? What if it was one hour?

Given that this "failure to report" crime is phrased differently than the other crimes previously discussed, the mens rea for the crime may not be as obvious. After all, instead of stating that a person must "knowingly fail to report a release," CERCLA criminalizes the failure "to notify immediately the [National Response Center] as soon as [the defendant] has knowledge of such release." This means that the prosecution need not show an intent not to report; only that a report was not made after the defendant obtained knowledge of the release. Consider the Second Circuit's analysis.

United States v. Laughlin
10 F.3d 961 (2d Cir. 1993)

MINER, Circuit Judge:
[Recall that the defendants were convicted under RCRA for disposing of a hazardous waste (i.e., "bolton water" and sludge) without a permit. They were also convicted under CERCLA for failing to immediately report the releases of these hazardous substances. Reportable quantity was not an issue because of the significant volume of hazardous wastes that the defendants released. Instead, they argued that the evidence was insufficient to convict them under CERCLA because

the prosecution failed to prove that the defendants knew that their failure to report the releases violated CERCLA.]

. . . Goldman was charged with violating 42 U.S.C. § 9603(a), which provides, in pertinent part:

> Any person in charge of a . . . facility shall, as soon as he has knowledge of any release (other than a federally permitted release) of a hazardous substance from such . . . facility in quantities equal to or greater than those determined pursuant to section 9602 of this title, immediately notify the National Response Center . . . of such release.

42 U.S.C. § 9603(a).

The district court instructed the jury that it must find the Government had proven the following elements beyond a reasonable doubt:

> (1) "that there was a hazardous substance";
> (2) "that it was in an amount of equal to or greater than the reportable quantity";
> (3) "that it was released from a facility";
> (4) "that this release was other than a federally permitted release";
> (5) "that [the] defendant was a person in charge of the facility"; and
> (6) "that the defendant failed to give immediate notice to the National Response Center as soon as he had knowledge of that release."

Like RCRA, CERCLA is a regulatory scheme intended to protect the public health and safety. The reporting requirement at issue here insures the Government's ability to "move quickly to check the spread of a hazardous release." *United States v. Carr*, 880 F.2d 1550, 1552 (2d Cir. 1989). In accordance with our interpretation of "knowingly" in RCRA, we find that section 9603(a) does not demand knowledge of the regulatory requirements of CERCLA; it demands only that defendant be aware of his acts. *See United States v. Buckley*, 934 F.2d 84, 88 (6th Cir. 1991) (knowledge, as used in CERCLA, means only that the defendant is aware of his acts, rather than knowledge of the specific statute or legal requirements); *see also International Minerals*, 402 U.S. at 564-65 (defendant who is aware that his acts are harmful may be found guilty even though unaware of regulatory scheme). Accordingly, we conclude that the district court properly instructed the jury regarding the CERCLA violation.

- Why does the prosecution not have to prove that the defendant knew that he/she had an obligation to report the release?
- Why does the prosecution not have to prove that the defendant knew that the quantity of the released substance was "reportable"?

In addition to the crime of failing to immediately report a release of a reportable quantity of a hazardous substance, CERCLA includes a criminal provision that imposes a three-year felony for knowingly destroying, concealing, or falsifying any record respecting "the location, title, or condition of a facility, and the identity, characteristics, quantity, origin, or condition (including containerization and previous treatment) of any hazardous substances contained or deposited in a facility." 42 U.S.C. § 9603(d)(1). CERCLA imposes a document retention requirement on such documents of 50 years unless the EPA waives that requirement. 42 U.S.C. § 9604(d)(2). Consequently, criminal enforcement under CERCLA focuses chiefly on providing the government information necessary to properly respond to releases of hazardous substances. Knowing violations of these requirements can result in criminal penalties.

C. INSECTICIDES, FUNGICIDES, AND RODENTICIDES

Some of the hazardous substances on which society relies are specifically designed to kill things in the environment such as insects, fungi, and rodents. Indeed, without these substances, food supplies and public health would be at risk because insects and rodents, for example, are known vectors for disease.[8]

Although necessary to prevent disease and to protect our food supply, these killer chemical compounds also pose significant and, too often, unknown risks to human health and the environment. For example, Rachel Carson's landmark book *Silent Spring* (1962) raised a warning that highlighted the adverse and unintended consequences caused by the misuse of pesticides common to her time. Ms. Carson provided a strong case illustrating that the misuse of these pesticides was killing many bird species, and, once society was deprived of the birds' songs, a silent spring would follow.

For example, science has confirmed that the oft-used pesticide dichlorodiphenyltrichloroethane (DDT) was causing significant impact not only on birds but also on humans. Researchers learned that DDT caused cancer, birth defects, and endocrine disruption in animals and feared the same results in humans. They also found that DDT was not only killing insects, birds, and other animals directly exposed to it, but was also killing birds and other animals that fed on organisms that DDT had killed. Researchers determined that when humans eat animals that had preyed on animals or organisms killed by DDT, humans were exposed to DDT in high concentrations.[9] Given these tragic effects on human health and the environment, the United States banned the use of DDT in 1972.

These effects also prompted Congress to increase regulation on pesticides, fungicides, and rodenticides in 1972 by significantly amending the Federal Insecticide, Fungicide, and Rodenticide Act (FIFRA), 7 U.S.C. §§ 136-136y (2016). FIFRA is administered through the United States Environmental Protection Agency (EPA) and regulates the sale, distribution, and use of pesticides. FIFRA defines a "pesticide" as "(1) any substance or mixture of substances intended for preventing, destroying, repelling, or mitigating any pest, (2) any substance or mixture of substances intended for use as a plant regulator, defoliant,

---

[8] *See, e.g.,* Jeffrey M. Blazar, E. Kurt Lienau & Marc W. Allard, *Insects as Vectors of Foodborne Pathogenic Bacteria*, 4 Terrestrial Arthropod Revs. 5-16 (2011) (stating how insects "pose a serious health concern" in contributing to the estimated 76 million cases of foodborne illness each year worldwide).

[9] Kushik Jaga & Chandrabhan Dharmani, *Global Surveillance of DDT and DDE Levels in Human Tissues*, 16 Int'l J. Occupational Med. & Envtl. Health 7, 7-20 (2003).

or desiccant, and (3) any nitrogen stabilizer. . . ." 7 U.S.C. § 136(u). FIFRA's provisions can be divided into two general sections. First, FIFRA establishes a registration process that sets the legal parameters for the sale, distribution, and use of each registered pesticide along with the records that the applicant must maintain. Second, FIFRA provides for both civil and criminal enforcement. When discussing enforcement below, the focus is on criminal prosecution.

1. The Pesticide Registration Process[10]

The registration process is the cornerstone to FIFRA's regulatory scheme because, subject to narrow exceptions, FIFRA precludes any pesticide from being distributed or sold unless and until it is registered with the EPA. 7 U.S.C. § 136a(a). To register a pesticide, the applicant for registration must provide the EPA with several pieces of information. 7 U.S.C. § 136a. First, the applicant must provide the EPA with, among many other things, the pesticide's name, chemical formula, and all tests and data showing that the pesticide can be used for the purposes that the applicant proposes. 7 U.S.C. § 136a(c)(1).

Second, a registration application must include a request that the EPA classify the pesticide as "general use" or "restricted use." "General use" pesticides do not cause unreasonable adverse effects on the environment when applied for their registered uses, either as directed or in accordance with widespread and commonly recognized practice. 7 U.S.C. § 136a(d)(1)(B). These pesticides are available to and may be used by the general public without any specialized training or licensing. "Restricted use" pesticides, however, may cause unreasonable adverse effects to the environment, including injury to the applicator, if applied for their registered uses, either as directed or in accordance with widespread and commonly recognized practice. 7 U.S.C. § 136a(d)(1)(C). Given the risks that "restricted use" pesticides pose, they can only be applied by a "certified applicator" who has specialized training, has passed a pesticide licensing exam, and holds a valid license to apply the pesticide that is classified for restricted use. 7 U.S.C. § 136(e)(1). Most pesticide licensing programs are administered by state governments that have received delegated authority from the EPA. 7 U.S.C. §§ 136v, 136w-1, 136w-2.

Third, the applicant must ensure that the proper "labeling" for the pesticide is provided to the EPA. The "labeling" of a pesticide is not just the label on the pesticide container itself. 7 U.S.C. § 136(p). Instead, the "labeling" includes all of the literature accompanying the pesticide. This literature describes how, when, where, how much, and by whom the pesticide should be used and includes safety and first aid information. Once approved, the pesticide's "labeling" becomes the law for how that particular pesticide can be used.

Finally, to assist with enforcing the pesticide-specific law established during the registration process, Congress requires registrants, producers, and certified commercial applicators to keep records and reports about their pesticide activities.

---

[10] This section is derived from Jared C. Bennett, *The Soothsayer, Julius Caesar, and Modern-Day Ides: Why You Should Prosecute FIFRA Cases*, 59 Dep't Justice J. Fed. L. & Prac., July 2011, at 84, 85-86.

Id. §§ 136f, 136g, 136i-1. FIFRA and its implementing regulations empower the EPA to inspect the records of each entity to which the recordkeeping requirements apply. Consider the following hypothetical.

Jack is an accountant for a major accounting firm, but, in his spare time, he fancies himself as an inventor. As the season turns from fall to winter where Jack lives, he notices that spiders more frequently enter his home. This disgusts him, and he vows to find a solution. After a great deal of effort, trial, and error, Jack does just that: he creates a solution out of various household cleaners and some natural citrus oils that is effective at killing spiders. One day, a co-worker of Jack's is complaining about the spiders that she keeps finding in her home now that the temperatures are dropping. Jack tells her about this fantastic chemical solution he created and asks if she would like to try it out. Desperate for a solution, Jack's co-worker agrees to give it a try, and Jack gives her the mixture. Jack's co-worker informs Jack the next day that his magic solution did the trick and that Jack really should sell this. Excited about making some real money, Jack goes home, creates a website, and starts taking orders for his "Black Magic Spider Solution." Sales start off slowly and then really take off. However, one day, Jack receives a letter from the EPA telling Jack that he needs to immediately cease selling his product and that he needs to provide a whole host of information about the chemicals in his magic spider killer. Jack, infuriated that the government is trying to run him out of business, comes to you to seek your advice as to whether he should stop and whether he has to provide information about his secret formula, which Jack believes to be proprietary information. How would you advise Jack to proceed?

2. FIFRA's Enforcement Provisions[11]

FIFRA contains three types of criminal sanctions: (1) a felony; (2) a Class A misdemeanor; and (3) a Class C misdemeanor. First, FIFRA's criminal sanctions contain only one felony. 7 U.S.C. § 136*l*(b)(3). Specifically, FIFRA's lone felony provision applies to "[a]ny person, who, with intent to defraud, uses or reveals information relative to formulas of products acquired" during the registration process. 7 U.S.C. § 136*l*(b)(3). Persons that are convicted of this crime face up to three years in prison and a fine. 7 U.S.C. § 136*l*(b)(3); 18 U.S.C. § 3571. To prevail on this felony charge, the government must prove that a person, with intent to defraud, used or revealed information relative to formulas of products acquired under the registration process. Under FIFRA, the term "person" means "any individual, partnership, association, corporation, or any organized group of persons whether incorporated or not." 7 U.S.C. § 136(s). The element "with intent to defraud" means the same as in other Title 18 offenses. *See, e.g.*, 18 U.S.C. § 1341 (mail fraud). Specifically, the offender must act knowingly and with the intention or the purpose to deceive or to cheat. An "intent to defraud" is ordinarily accompanied by a desire or a purpose to bring about some gain or benefit to oneself or some other person or by a desire or a purpose to cause some loss to some

---

[11] This section is derived from Jared C. Bennett, *The Soothsayer, Julius Caesar, and Modern-Day Ides: Why You Should Prosecute FIFRA Cases*, 59 Dep't Justice J. Fed. L. & Prac., July 2011, at 84, 86-90.

person.[12] Finally, the government must prove that the offender used or revealed formulaic information obtained during the registration process.

Second, FIFRA provides for both a Class A misdemeanor and a Class C misdemeanor when the offender "knowingly violates" any provision of FIFRA. 7 U.S.C. § 136*l*(b)(1), (2). FIFRA's Class A misdemeanor includes up to one year in prison and a fine, 7 U.S.C. § 136*l*(b)(1), (2); 18 U.S.C. § 3571(b), whereas FIFRA's Class C misdemeanor penalty includes up to 30 days in jail and a much smaller fine.

To prove either misdemeanor violation under FIFRA, the prosecution must establish the offender's regulatory identity and that the offender knowingly violated a provision of FIFRA. 7 U.S.C. § 136*l*(b)(1), (2). Determining whether to charge the Class A or Class C misdemeanor depends entirely on the regulatory status of the offender. FIFRA's Class A misdemeanor applies only to a "registrant, applicant for registration, or producer" or a "commercial applicator of a restricted use pesticide" who "knowingly violates" any of the provisions of FIFRA discussed in the previous section. The Class C misdemeanor applies when a "private applicator or other person" (for example, someone who is not a "registrant, applicant for registration, or producer" or a "commercial applicator") "knowingly violates" any provision of FIFRA. Consequently, even if a "registrant, applicant for registration, or producer" or a "commercial applicator" were to knowingly violate the same provision of FIFRA as a "private applicator," the private applicator would be subject only to a Class C misdemeanor whereas the others would face a Class A misdemeanor. Thus, proving the regulatory status of the offender is critical to a FIFRA prosecution.

To establish the offender's regulatory identity for purposes of proving FIFRA's Class A misdemeanor, the prosecution must show that a "registrant, applicant for registration, or producer" or a "commercial applicator" is the offender. The term "registrant" means a "person who has registered any pesticide" under FIFRA. 7 U.S.C. § 136(y). An "applicant for registration" is a person who has applied to the EPA to register a pesticide. A "producer" means "the person who manufactures, prepares, compounds, propagates, or processes any pesticide or device or active ingredient used in producing a pesticide." 7 U.S.C. § 136(w). The term "commercial applicator" is a pesticide applicator "who uses or supervises the use of any [restricted use] pesticide" on property other than his own for compensation. 7 U.S.C. § 136(e)(3). The list of restricted use pesticides is found at 40 C.F.R. § 152.175.

To establish the offender's regulatory identity for the Class C misdemeanor under FIFRA, the government must show that the offender is a "private applicator" or other person who is not a "registrant, applicant for registration, or producer" or a "commercial applicator." 7 U.S.C. § 136*l*(b)(2). A "private applicator" is a person who is certified to apply restricted use pesticides for producing any agricultural commodity on land that the applicator or his employer owns or rents. The most obvious example of a "private applicator" is a farmer who is spraying pesticide on the crops that he is growing on land he owns or rents.

Once the government has established the regulatory identity of the offender, the next step, proving that the person "knowingly" violated a provision of FIFRA,

---

[12] Edward J. Devitt et al., 1 *Federal Jury Practice and Instructions* § 16.04 (4th ed. 1992).

is the same in both types of misdemeanors. Two of the most common criminally enforced FIFRA provisions involve the prohibition on selling an unregistered pesticide and using a pesticide in a manner inconsistent with its labeling. 7 U.S.C. §§ 136j(a)(1)(A); 136(a)(2)(G). Consider how the "knowing" mens rea under FIFRA is applied to the following labeling violation.

United States v. Corbin Farm Service
444 F. Supp. 510 (E.D. Cal. 1978)

MacBRIDE, Chief Judge.

Defendants are charged in a twelve-count information with misdemeanor violations of a Federal Insecticide, Fungicide and Rodenticide Act (FIFRA), 7 U.S.C.) 136 et seq., and . . . the alleged violations arise from the application of a registered pesticide to an alfalfa field and the subsequent death of a number of American widgeon, a water fowl protected under the [Migratory Bird Treaty Act]. Defendants have responded with a number of pretrial motions.

The defendants are Corbin Farm Service (CFS), a dealer and distributor of pesticides; John Richard Harris, a CFS employee who provided pesticide advice to farmers with the expectation that they would purchase from CFS; Patrick William Feeney, the owner of the alfalfa field; and Frank Harry Michaud, Jr., the licensed aerial operator who sprayed the field.

The twelve-count information alleges in Count 1 that CFS, through its agents and employees, violated FIFRA by causing a registered pesticide to be applied in a manner contrary to its labeling. Count 2 alleges that Harris, Feeney and Michaud also violated FIFRA by applying or causing the pesticide to be applied contrary to its labeling. . . .

Defendants attack the information on a number of points. This court will examine the challenge to the FIFRA counts first. . . .

MOTIONS TO DISMISS THE FIFRA COUNTS

Defendants CFS, Harris and Michaud move to dismiss the FIFRA counts on the ground that the statute and the label are unconstitutionally vague in that they fail to describe the proscribed conduct sufficiently to enable affected persons to know in advance the activities they may legally pursue. Section 136j(a)(2) (G) of FIFRA provides:

> (a) In general
> (2) It shall be unlawful for any person
> (G) to use any registered pesticide in a manner inconsistent with
> its labeling. . . .

The label on the pesticide applied to Feeney's field states in pertinent part:

> For water fowl protection do not apply . . . on fields where water
> fowl are known to repeatedly feed.

This quote from the label appears in the briefs of the United States and the defendants, not in the information. Since the parties agree on the quotation, this court will assume that it is correctly quoted. . . .

FIFRA provides that a manufacturer seeking registration of a pesticide must file a complete copy of the label with the EPA. 7 U.S.C. § 136a(c)(1)(C). The

Administrator of the EPA registers the pesticide if he determines that its label complies with the Act's requirements. Id. § 136a(c)(5)(B). If the label does not comply with the Act, the Administrator is required to deny registration. Id. § 136a(c)(6).

It is clear that the label itself was not enacted by Congress and is not entitled to the "strong presumptive validity" applicable to congressional action. The label was, however, examined by the Administrator under the procedures set forth by Congress. The label should be accorded a presumption of validity like that attaching to an administrative regulation adopted pursuant to power granted by Congress. It may be that the label, written as it was by a private manufacturer, should not be accorded the full measure of presumptive validity that would attach to a regulation prepared by the agency itself, but the Act requires the Administrator to examine such labels and determine their conformity to the Act. This court will not assume that the Administrator failed to carry out his responsibilities. Accordingly, this court will presume that the label is valid, giving substantially the same weight to that presumption as it would to a regulation.

Defendants attack the statute itself and the labeling on a number of grounds, each testing a particular word or phrase for vagueness. This court will examine each of these contentions seriatim, applying the vagueness doctrine. . . .

(1) "inconsistent with its labeling"

Defendant Michaud asserts that the FIFRA prohibition on the use of a pesticide "in a manner inconsistent with (its labeling)" is vague because of the word "inconsistent." It is difficult to discern the source of the asserted vagueness. Both Black's Law Dictionary and Webster's Dictionary define "inconsistent" to mean "contrary to" or "incompatible with." It is clear enough that, if one applies a pesticide in a way contrary to the directions on the label, one has violated the statute. The legislative history of this provision includes some discussion of the word "inconsistent."

> (I)t is the belief of the Committee that the use of the word "inconsistent" should be read and administered in a way so as to visit penalties only upon those individuals who have disregarded instructions on a label that would indicate to a man of ordinary intelligence that use not in accordance with such instructions might endanger the safety of others or the environment. Thus, for example, it would be expected that use of a general, unrestricted pesticide registered for use on enumerated household pests to exterminate a pest not specified on the label would not be inconsistent with the labeling. On the other hand, the use of even a general use pesticide in a manner inconsistent with a specified caution or restriction on the label should be considered inconsistent with the labeling.

S. Rep. No. 838, reprinted in 1972 U.S. Code Cong. & Admin. News pp. 3993, 4008. Defendants here are charged with a use inconsistent with a specific instruction on the label. This court finds no unconstitutional vagueness in the word "inconsistent."

Michaud also states that the word "inconsistent" is vague when viewed in the context of the "four different labels in a very short time span" that he asserts have been used on this pesticide. It may be that there have been a number of different labels on the particular pesticide and even that the application of the pesticide might have been consistent with one or more of the labels. Even if true, the different labels are irrelevant. The question is whether the application was inconsistent with the labeling on the particular container(s) of pesticide applied to the field in this case. If Michaud seeks to find vagueness in the existence of more than one label, he must provide evidence as to what each of the labels stated, when the labels were used, and whether the application was inconsistent with one label but consistent with another. In the absence of that evidence, this court finds no vagueness in the word "inconsistent.". . .

This court has considered the defendants' argument that the word "knowingly" in section 136*l* should be interpreted to increase the scienter requirement in this case. The argument is without merit. The penalty provisions of section 136*l* were drafted in a general fashion to encompass the wide variety of possible violations of FIFRA. Congress did not contemplate the conjunction of the word "knowingly" with a label direction including the word "known." Instead, Congress was enacting a general provision, using the word "knowingly" as it had in the context of other statutes creating *malum prohibitum* crimes. The word was used to reflect the requirement that general intent be proved in order to establish a violation.

Although no relevant case law exists construing this particular statute, it clearly falls within the framework of other regulatory statutes. In *United States v. International Minerals & Chem. Corp.*, 402 U.S. 558 (1971), the Court examined the mens rea requirements applicable to a violation of a regulation of the ICC charged under 18 U.S.C. § 834(f) which provides that whoever "knowingly violates any such regulation" is guilty of a crime. The Court held that knowledge of the facts is required, that is, a general intent to do the actions constituting the violation, but that a specific intent to violate the law or a knowledge of the regulation is not a necessary element of the crime. The Court stated:

> dangerous or deleterious devices or products or obnoxious waste materials are involved, (and) the probability of regulation is so great that anyone who is aware that he is in possession of them or dealing with them must be presumed to be aware of the regulation.

Id. at 1701-02. The mens rea requirement in the word "knowingly" would protect a person believing in good faith that he was dealing with distilled water rather than the corrosive liquids covered by the regulation. The same interpretation of the word "knowingly" has been applied in a number of other cases involving regulatory statutes and *malum prohibitum* crimes. It is clear that the word "knowingly" in section 136*l* should be interpreted in the same fashion; it requires proof that the defendants knew they were dealing with a pesticide when they sprayed the field or caused it to be sprayed.

The more difficult question is the interpretation of the word "known" in the label. Certain types of proof would clearly be sufficient. If the United States could show actual personal knowledge arising from the defendants' own frequent sightings of water fowl in the field, there would be no dispute as to the application of criminal penalties. The same result should apply to proof of their actual knowledge of other evidence of the birds' presence, such as duck damage to the field. Similarly, proof that the defendants knew that others believed that water fowl repeatedly fed in the field should be sufficient. Such actual knowledge of the beliefs of others would put the defendants on notice that water fowl were in the field with at least some frequency; in such a case, the defendants would act at their peril if they did not examine the field prior to spraying. Moreover, knowledge in this case cannot be limited to positive knowledge; it must include "the state of mind of one who does not possess positive knowledge only because he consciously avoided it." *United States v. Jewell*, 532 F.2d 697, 702 (9th Cir.) (en banc).

Given that the types of proof above are obviously sufficient to justify a conviction for use of the pesticide in a manner inconsistent with the instruction not to apply it where water fowl are known to feed repeatedly, the statute as it incorporates the label is not vague on its face. The United States seeks, however, to apply a broader construction of the word "known" to include knowledge by anyone, not necessarily including the individual defendants here. It is that construction which defendants assert would be unconstitutionally vague. The United States' interpretation goes too far; if the defendants reasonably believed that water fowl did not repeatedly feed in the field, then the fact that some other person unknown to the defendants believed that water fowl repeatedly fed in the field should not be a basis for conviction. The central concept is reasonableness. For example, in *United States v. Balint*, 258 U.S. 250, 252 (1922), the defendant appealed his conviction for sale of narcotics, claiming in part that he did not know what he was selling. The Court declared:

> where one deals with others and his mere negligence may be dangerous to them, as in selling diseased food or poison, the policy of the law may, in order to stimulate proper care, require the punishment of the negligent person though he be ignorant of the noxious character of what he sells.

The means were present whereby the defendants could determine whether water fowl had been feeding repeatedly in the field and an unreasonable failure to do so cannot free them from liability. However, a final ruling on the nature of the knowledge requirement in the word "known" as applied to these defendants must be deferred until after evidence has been received on the extent of their knowledge, their ability to determine the facts, and the reasonableness of their actions given the facts. Once that evidence has been taken, it can be determined whether the label's language would necessarily be vague as applied to these defendants under the circumstances in which they acted. It may be that the proof amassed by the United States will satisfy the standards discussed above as to the types of proof that would clearly be sufficient. If so, a ruling on the constitutionality of applying criminal penalties to persons with less knowledge would be unnecessary. At this point, it is sufficient to state that the knowledge requirement falls between the position argued by the United States and the position offered by defendant Michaud. . . .

- Do you see any due process or other constitutional arguments arising from being able to criminally enforce the provisions of a pesticide label that a private company wrote and the EPA approved?

- If a pesticide label is ambiguous in terms of what it requires, does the rule of lenity apply in a criminal prosecution of the pesticide applicator?

Although criminal enforcement of FIFRA has been an important tool to hold those accountable who fail to properly distribute, sell, or use these deadly substances, many feel that the penalties under FIFRA are backwards. After all, under FIFRA if a person knowingly mishandles proprietary information about a pesticide, then he/she could be guilty of a felony, but if a licensed pesticide applicator ignores the labeling and then injures or kills someone, then the crime is punished as a Class A misdemeanor. For example, consider the horrifying tragedy described in Chapter 1 of this text that resulted when a licensed pesticide applicator ignored the labeling of a powerful rodenticide called Fumitoxin, which caused the deaths of two little girls in Layton, Utah. Fumitoxin's EPA-approved labeling contained the following instruction, written in all capital letters: "THIS PRODUCT MUST NOT BE APPLIED INTO A BURROW SYSTEM THAT IS WITHIN 15 FEET (5 METERS) OF A RESIDENCE OR OTHER BUILDING THAT IS OR MAY BE OCCUPIED BY HUMANS AND/OR ANIMALS." Despite this clear warning, the applicator put more than double the amount of pesticide pellets allowed under the label against the foundation of the house of Nathan and Brenda Toone and their little children. As the family slept, the pesticide pellets came into contact with moisture in the soil, which created phosphine gas. The gas seeped into the Toone's home, wound its way up to the bedroom of the Toone's two youngest daughters, and, soon thereafter, ended their young lives.[13]

In FIFRA's 46 years of existence, many more sad stories have been lamented and, thereafter, prosecuted. Not surprisingly, there have been several congressional efforts over the years to increase FIFRA's penalties to include felonies. However, these efforts have proven unsuccessful. Consider the arguments and counterarguments below as to whether FIFRA warrants additional felony provisions.

Michael J. McClary & Jessica B. Goldstein, FIFRA at 40: The Need for Felonies for Pesticide Crimes
47 Envtl. L. Rptr. News & Analysis 10767 (Sept. 2017)

[O]ne of the first rationales opposing higher FIFRA penalties was that presented to Congress by Terminix in 1992. Terminix argued that commercial applicators of pesticides were (1) trained and certified users of pesticide products, and (2) end-users of pesticide products, "like 'do-it-yourselfers' and farmers." The underlying claim of the first argument seems to be that training and certification of commercial applicators made it unlikely that they would engage in criminal violations. However, the FIFRA crimes committed by Terminix in the U.S. Virgin Islands case disproved its own theory. Further refutation came from the crimes committed [where] trained and certified commercial applicators caused death or severe harm to children or adults through the knowing misapplication of pesticides.

---

[13] *United States v. Nocks*, 1:11CR0017 (D. Utah 2011); EPA Criminal Case File: Rebecca and Rachel Toone (Nov. 19, 2012), https://www.youtube.com/watch?v=XzAmkfRGFgc&feature=youtu.be.

Neither their training nor their certification deterred criminal behavior, but in fact made that behavior more inculpatory. Training and certification gave them the knowledge of the law that should have deterred their crimes.

Terminix's second argument appears to have been that commercial applicators should not be subject to higher misdemeanor penalties than private applicators, since commercial applicators are "end-users," just as are private applicators. However, as EPA's history of FIFRA enforcement demonstrates, pesticide misuse by a commercial applicator "end-user," by a farm "end-user," and by a do-it-yourself "end-user," have all resulted in sufficient harm or risk of harm to warrant felony penalties. Terminix's suggestion that commercial applicators be grouped with other end-users under the same penalty structure is not an argument for retaining inadequate misdemeanor penalties for FIFRA crimes committed by "end-users." Rather, it supports subjecting all end-users who commit FIFRA crimes to felony penalties. . . .

Another argument by a 1990s opponent of heightened FIFRA criminal penalties claimed that "knowing endangerment" of other people by pesticide misuse should not be subject to felony penalties if it occurred "on farms, or in homes or private institutions." [The National Agricultural Chemicals Association's (NACA)] concern seemed to be that such felony penalties would criminalize allegedly trivial misconduct, as NACA pointed to the prospect of prosecuting someone for violating a "standard label warning" on pesticide products that warns against using the product in a manner inconsistent with the labeling. NACA also feared that felony penalties might be "far beyond" the financial means of farmers.

None of these arguments are supported by the record of FIFRA criminal enforcement. Some of the most serious FIFRA criminal violations have been for misapplication of pesticides on farms, in homes, and in private institutions. . . . Moreover, FIFRA's pesticide label use instructions are not "standard" warnings, if by that is meant "commonplace" or "trivial." EPA-accepted pesticide labeling is specifically tailored to each pesticide, informs the user that it is illegal to use the pesticides contrary to the instructions, and is among the most significant protections FIFRA provides to non-licensed "end-users" like farmers, "do-it-yourselfers," and "private institutions." It provides the safety warnings and instructions that are specific to that pesticide and make application of such products safe for users and bystanders. To apply a pesticide contrary to its labeling is not to "violate" a trivial warning on a label, but is an act that jeopardizes the applicator and others, or the environment. . . .

Moreover, fears about the "financial means" of farmers or others to pay felony penalties have proven unfounded. In setting fines, judges routinely consider the ability of a defendant to pay the fine. . . .

NACA also argued that felony penalties should not apply to violations that do not involve injury, or to negligent rather than "intentional," "knowing," or repeat violations. NACA's argument that felony penalties should only apply if harm has occurred has been repeatedly and rightfully rejected by Congress in every federal environmental statute. . . . Title 18 makes false statements to the U.S. government a felony offense, and it sends the wrong and conflicting signal for FIFRA to have lesser penalties for false statements made to EPA regarding pesticides.

NACA's argument that felonies should not apply to "negligent" violations does not militate against FIFRA felony penalties. FIFRA felonies would not be based upon a "negligence" standard of mens rea, but instead involve "knowing" violations. A "knowing" mental standard for FIFRA felony penalties would be the same standard used in the felony provisions of almost all of the other federal environmental statutes. NACA acknowledged that "strong, meaningful authority" should exist to punish "intentional violators," but did not expressly argue that only "intentional violators," or those who willfully seek to break the law, should be subject to felonies. If that was NACA's suggestion, such a standard for FIFRA would again set a higher bar for FIFRA prosecutions than for most other environmental crimes, despite equally or more serious actual or potential harms from pesticide crimes.

Similarly, while NACA acknowledged that "repeat offenders" should be subject to "strong, meaningful" penalties, if it was thereby proposing to limit felony penalties to repeat offenders, it again was setting an unjustifiably higher—and unprecedented—bar for FIFRA prosecutions than for other environmental crimes. None of the other federal environmental statutes limit felony penalties to "repeat offenders." . . . Pesticide use instructions, and the ability to comply with them, are not so complex or difficult that fairness requires leniency for first-time knowing violators.

Other 1990s opponents of higher FIFRA penalties claimed that the need for, and "societal benefit" from, higher FIFRA penalties had not been shown, and that higher penalties would be enforcement overkill. The 20-year history of FIFRA cases discussed above, however, does demonstrate the need for, and "societal benefit" from, higher penalties. Deaths or injuries to children caused by pesticide misuse by commercial applicators occurred in [several cases]. Environmental harm and damage to animals and real property, and the environment, occurred in [several cases]. . . .

In addition, that history demonstrates the inadequacy of FIFRA's criminal penalties more than the inadequacy of official efforts to enforce the law. Criminal penalties of a few hundred or thousand dollars, or sentences of simple probation or a few months, in cases like those discussed above, will not deter individuals, small businesses, or megacorporations from evading FIFRA's requirements, when the possibility of either saving or earning higher amounts by not complying seems clear. . . .

[M]isdemeanors today are not enough. A misdemeanor should not be the maximum penalty when two little girls die due to an applicator's failure to take essential safety precautions as stated on the pesticide's label and instructions. A misdemeanor is insufficient when a whole family is hospitalized and suffers neurological damage from improper and illegal pesticide fumigation. A misdemeanor is insignificant to a multimillion-dollar corporation that continues to sell a misbranded pesticide, or misapplies pesticides, or lies to the government during the pesticide registration process. A misdemeanor does not deter a farmer who continues to spray pesticide on laboring farm workers, ignoring the pesticide label's warning and the health consequences. A misdemeanor is not enough for defendants attempting to cover up their crimes by making false statements to law enforcement, even though a young child lies in the hospital and doctors need to know the specific pesticide that poisoned him in order to treat him. Felony penalties for FIFRA crimes are needed today, more than ever.

- Why do you think felony provisions were enacted for Clean Water Act, Clean Air Act, and RCRA violations even though the vast majority of those violations do not result in death or serious bodily injury?
- Why has FIFRA been treated differently? Should it be? Why or why not?

CHAPTER 8

WILDLIFE OFFENSES

Worldwide, the illegal wildlife trade is estimated to be worth between $8 and $10 billion U.S. annually.[1] Over time, the wildlife trade has adversely affected species both large and small. For example, in the 1700s, North America was home to between 25 and 30 million American bison.[2] However, "by the late 1880s less than 100 [bison] remained wild in the Great Plains states."[3] More recently, the illegal wildlife trade is driving charismatic mega-fauna such as the tiger, African elephant, and black rhinoceros to their ultimate demise in the wild.[4] Additionally, smaller, less well-known species are also suffering the effects of the black market. Reptiles such as snakes, turtles, and tortoises are heavily traded for religious, alimentary, and pet purposes, which are rapidly driving them to extinction.[5] In fact, the illicit wildlife trade—in conjunction with many other human activities that are adversely affecting species' habitat—is causing what some scholars call "Earth's sixth major extinction event."[6] Humanity's ability to eliminate entire species off the face of the Earth is a historic reality and, sadly, may also be the future because humanity's desire for economic expedience seems to perpetually outweigh the long-term benefits of conservation and bio-diversity in human decisionmaking.

Given the reality of humanity's interactions with wildlife, nations have entered into international agreements to prohibit or substantially regulate wildlife trafficking. These international efforts have led to the creation of laws within the United States to disincentivize the international trade in animals by imposing criminal penalties upon those who improperly engage in that activity. These

---

[1] Angelo R. Mandimbihasina, Lance G. Woolaver, Lianne E. Woolaver, Lianne E. Concannon, E.J. Milner-Gulland, Richard E. Lewis, Andrew M.R. Terry, Niaraha Filazaha, Lydia L. Rabetafika & Richard P. Young, *The Illegal Pet Trade Is Driving Madagascar's Ploughshare Tortoise to Extinction*, Oryx: The International Journal of Conservation (online), Sept. 2018 at 1, https://doi.org/10.1017/S0030605317001880.

[2] M. Scott Taylor, *Buffalo Hunt: International Trade and the Virtual Extinction of the North American Bison*, 101 Am. Econ. Rev. 3162 (Dec. 2011).

[3] *Id.* at 3163.

[4] Mandimbihasina et al., *supra* note 1.

[5] *Id.*

[6] F. Stewart Chapin III, Erika S. Zavaleta, Valerie T. Eviner, Rosamond L. Naylor, Peter M. Viousek, Heather L. Reynolds, David U. Hooper, Sandra Lavorel, Osvaldo E. Sala, Sara E. Hobbie, Michelle C. Mack & Sandra Díaz, *Consequences of Changing Biodiversity*, 405 Nature 234-42 (2000).

numerous statutes include, among many others, the African Elephant Conservation Act, the Endangered Species Act's provisions enacting the Convention on the International Trade in Endangered Species, the Migratory Bird Treaty Act, the Lacey Act, and the Rhinoceros and Tiger Conservation Act of 1998.

In addition to the international trafficking of wildlife, Congress has also enacted criminal penalties to protect the substantial domestic wildlife resources in the United States. Examples include, among others, the Bald and Golden Eagle Protection Act, the Magnuson-Stevens Fishery Conservation and Management Act, the Endangered Species Act, the Lacey Act, and the Wild Free-Roaming Horses and Burros Act.

More recently, Congress has not only enacted statutes related to conservation and trade of wildlife, but has also become more involved in enacting criminal penalties against those who engage in acts of animal cruelty such as dog fighting. Criminal enterprises such as dog fighting and cockfighting account for billions of dollars in revenue. *See, e.g., United States v. Gibert*, 677 F.3d 613, 619-22 (4th Cir. 2012) (discussing impact of dog and cockfighting on interstate commerce) . Additionally, venues of animal fighting are often associated with drug trafficking. *United States v. Gibson*, 708 F.3d 1256, 1269 (11th Cir. 2013) (noting that defendants who dealt drugs became acquainted through dog fighting) ; *Jackson v. United States*, No. 16-3089, 2017 WL 3872403, at *1 (D.N.J. Sept. 5, 2017) (discussing evidence of drug trafficking and dog fighting at criminal defendant's home).

Although there are far too many wildlife and animal-related statutes in the United States Code to discuss here, the remainder of this chapter focuses on those laws that have become or are becoming the most relied upon weapons against wildlife trafficking and animal cruelty in the environmental prosecutorial arsenal: (1) the Lacey Act; (2) the Endangered Species Act; (3) the Migratory Bird Treaty Act; (4) the Bald and Golden Eagle Protection Act; and (5) the Animal Welfare Act.

A. THE LACEY ACT

The Lacey Act is one of the oldest wildlife protection statutes in the United States and has proven to be one of the most valuable tools in combating wildlife trafficking. The Lacey Act is named after its sponsor, Representative John Lacey, who sought to "aid in the restoration of [game birds and other wild birds] . . . where the same have become scarce or extinct, and also to regulate the introduction of American or foreign birds or animals in localities where they have not heretofore existed."[7] To accomplish these purposes, the Lacey Act provided "[t]hat it shall be unlawful for any person or persons to import into the United States any foreign wild animal or bird except under a special permit from the United States Department of Agriculture."[8] Additionally, the Lacey Act banned the importation of certain species into the United States and precluded those animals, dead or alive,

---

[7] Lacey Act, ch. 553, 31 Stat. 187, 188 (1900).
[8] *Id.*

from being shipped in the United States. Significantly, the Lacey Act also sought to stop the interstate poaching of wild game by precluding anyone from delivering to a common carrier a wild game animal that had been "killed in violation of the laws of the State, Territory, or District" where the killing occurred.[9]

Conserving some of these founding principles, the Lacey Act has been greatly expanded over the past 119 years to apply to all fish and wildlife (including their parts, eggs, and offspring) and plants that are taken or harvested in violation of federal, state, tribal, or foreign law. In terms of criminal enforcement, the Lacey Act contains both felony and misdemeanor crimes, which can be roughly divided into two categories: (1) trafficking crimes; and (2) labeling offenses. Each category of offense is discussed below.

1. Trafficking Offenses

The Lacey Act's trafficking offenses contain both a five-year felony and a misdemeanor crime. 16 U.S.C. § 3373(d). To prove either classification of crime, however, the prosecution must establish two steps: the prosecution must show: (1) that someone (although not necessarily the defendant) committed a predicate wildlife offense (civil or criminal) under federal,[10] state, tribal, or foreign law; and (2) that the defendant knowingly imported, exported, transported, sold, received, acquired, or purchased the fish, wildlife, or plant knowing (felony) or reasonably should have known (misdemeanor) that the fish, wildlife, or plant was "taken, possessed, transported, or sold" in violation of federal, state, tribal, or foreign law. 16 U.S.C. §§ 3373(d)(1), (2); 3372(a)(1), (2). If the charge is that a violation of state or foreign law occurred in the predicate offense, the defendant's conduct must involve interstate or foreign commerce for jurisdictional reasons. However, if the predicate wildlife violation involves federal or tribal law, interstate or foreign commerce is not necessary to prove the second part of the crime. For the felony trafficking offense that does not involve importing or exporting, the Lacey Act imposes one additional element: that the market value of the wildlife must exceed $350.

United States v. Cameron
888 F.2d 1279 (9th Cir. 1989)

ALDISERT, Circuit Judge:

The question for decision is whether violating regulations of the International Pacific Halibut Commission ("IPHC" or "Commission") is a proper basis for a criminal prosecution under the Lacey Act, 16 U.S.C. §§ 3372(a)(1), 3373(d)(1)(B). If so, we must then decide if promulgating a regulation limiting a day's catch to 20,000 lbs. exceeded the Commission's authority. We conclude that violating the regulation was a sufficient basis for the Lacey Act criminal prosecution here and that the Commission was duly authorized to promulgate the fish limit regulation. Accordingly, we will affirm the judgment of the district court in this appeal by

---

[9] *Id.*

[10] Certain federal wildlife laws are expressly exempt from being enforced under the Lacey Act. 16 U.S.C. § 3377.

Eugene B. Cameron from a judgment of sentence entered upon a guilty plea conditioned upon the resolution of the two issues presented to us. We will vacate only that portion of the sentence imposing a special assessment. . . .

I.

The Northern Pacific Halibut Fishery is regulated by the International Pacific Halibut Commission, pursuant to an international fishing treaty between the United States and Canada. Protocol Amending the Convention for the Preservation of the Halibut Fishery of the Northern Pacific Ocean and Bering Sea, United States-Canada, Mar. 29, 1979, 32 U.S.T. 2483 [hereinafter "Protocol"]. Regulations promulgated by the IPHC are adopted by the Secretary of Commerce, pursuant to The Northern Pacific Halibut Act of 1982, 16 U.S.C. §§ 773-773k. The Halibut Act makes it unlawful for anyone to violate any regulation adopted by the Secretary of Commerce. 16 U.S.C. §§ 773c(b)(1), 773e(a)(1). The Lacey Act, 16 U.S.C. §§ 3371-3378, federalizes the violation of most independent state, tribal and federal wildlife laws.

The Commission uses several regulatory mechanisms to preserve halibut fishing in Alaska. Included are the setting of overall catch limits. Protocol, at 2490. To do this effectively the IPHC separates the northern Pacific Ocean into eleven regulatory areas and sets limits on season openings, as well as on the size and quantity of halibut taken from these areas. See id. at 2491. Regulatory area 3A, is at issue in this case.

During 1987, area 3A was open for halibut fishing on three occasions: a 24-hour period from May 4 to May 5, a 24-hour period from June 1 to June 2, and a 24-hour period from September 30 to October 1. All vessels participating in the September 30 halibut opening were limited to a catch size of 20,000 lbs., regardless of the vessel's size or capacity. This regulation was adopted by the Secretary of Commerce and is codified at 50 C.F.R. § 301.9(c) (1987).

Cameron is a commercial fisherman in Alaska. During the September 30, 1987 halibut opening, Cameron caught 961 halibut, weighing 34,269 lbs., in regulatory area 3A. His catch was 14,269 lbs. over the area trip limit of 20,000 lbs. The catch was sold for $52,318.40 in Seldovia.

Cameron was charged with unlawfully acquiring and transporting halibut with a market value of more than $350 and knowingly intending to sell the illegally taken halibut, in violation of the Lacey Act. As stated before, he entered a guilty plea conditioned on the appeal of whether the Lacey Act applies to the Commission's regulations on catch limits, and whether the regulation was promulgated in excess of the Commission's authority. The court sentenced him to pay a substantial fine, to abstain from violating fishing laws, and to pay a special assessment of $25.00.

II.

Both issues presented turn on an interpretation of the international Protocol and two federal statutes. The Protocol provides in relevant part:

> [T]he [International Pacific Halibut] Commission, . . . may . . .
>   (a) divide the Convention waters into areas;

(b) establish one or more open or closed seasons as to each area;

(c) limit the size of fish and the quantity of the catch to be taken from each area within any season during which fishing is allowed. . . .

Protocol, at 2490-91. The Halibut Act provides:

It is unlawful—

(a) for any person subject to the jurisdiction of the United States—

(5) to ship, transport, offer for sale, sell, purchase, import, export or have custody, control or possession of, any fish taken or retained in violation of the Convention, this subchapter, or any regulation adopted under this subchapter. . . .

16 U.S.C. § 773e(a)(5).

Any person who is found by the Secretary, . . . to have committed an act prohibited by section 773e of this title shall be liable to the United States for a civil penalty. The amount of the civil penalty shall not exceed $25,000 for each violation.

16 U.S.C. § 773f(a).

A person is guilty of any (sic) [criminal] offense if he commits an act prohibited by section 773e(a)(2), (3), (4), or (6) of this title; or section 773e(b) of this title. . . .

16 U.S.C. § 773g(a). The Lacey Act provides:

It is unlawful for any person—

(1) to import, export, transport, sell, receive, acquire, or purchase any fish or wildlife or plant taken or possessed in violation of any law, treaty, or regulation of the United States or in violation of any Indian tribal law;

16 U.S.C. § 3372(a)(1).

Any person who—

(B) violates any provision of this chapter . . . by knowingly engaging in conduct that involves the sale or purchase of, the offer of sale or purchase of, or the intent to sell or purchase, fish or wildlife or plants with a market value in excess of $350, knowing that the fish or wildlife or plants were taken, possessed, transported, or sold in violation of, or in a manner unlawful under, any underlying law, treaty or regulation, shall be fined not more than $20,000, or imprisoned for not more than five years, or both.

16 U.S.C. § 3373(d)(1)(B).

III.

Cameron admits he committed the acts of which he is accused. He argues, however, that committing the acts was not a crime because his conduct was not subject to Lacey Act criminal prosecution. . . .

B.

Cameron next argues that the Lacey Act is not implicated when the underlying statute has stringent enforcement provisions because the Act was intended to bolster environmental laws with weak enforcement provisions. He emphasizes that the enforcement provisions of the Halibut Act are similar to, and as severe as, those of the Magnuson Fishery Management Act of 1976, an act not subject to the Lacey Act's criminal enforcement provisions. This argument does not persuade us for several reasons.

The argument ignores this court's discussion in *United States v. Doubleday*, 804 F.2d 1091 (9th Cir. 1986), *cert. denied*, 481 U.S. 1005 (1987). There, a fishing boat owner and operator fished for, caught and sold halibut from an unauthorized area in Alaskan waters. The question presented was whether the Magnuson Fishery Conservation and Management Act or the Lacey Act governed his conduct. We ruled that the Magnuson Act does not directly regulate halibut fishing and, therefore, the Lacey Act controlled. In so ruling, we implicitly upheld the application of the Lacey Act to conduct that is essentially the same as Cameron's. The *Doubleday* defendant transported halibut taken in violation of a regulation promulgated by the Halibut Commission and subsequently adopted by the Secretary of Commerce. Cameron is accused of the same type of conduct. See id. at 1092, 1094 n. 3 (in dicta, the court recognized that the Halibut Commission regulates halibut fishing).

Cameron is correct in noting that the enforcement provisions of the Magnuson Fishery Conservation and Management Act are similar to those of the Halibut Act. But, not all conduct regulated by the Magnuson Act is exempt from Lacey Act prosecution. Only activity regulated by a Magnuson fishery management plan is exempted. See id. at 1094. Therefore, there can be conduct regulated by the Magnuson Act that is also regulated by the Lacey Act. Also, in amending the Lacey Act in 1981, Congress chose to exempt portions of the Magnuson Act from its coverage. It did not choose to exempt portions of the predecessor statute of the Halibut Act, the Northern Pacific Halibut Act of 1937.

We concede that the enforcement provisions of the 1937 Halibut Act were much less stringent than those of the 1982 Act. But such a concession is irrelevant. The brute fact is that when Congress enacted the 1982 provisions, it did not exempt the Halibut Act from provisions of the Lacey Act. We must proceed on the assumption that Congress intended what would be exempt and what would not.

C.

Cameron next argues that the disclaimer provision of the Lacey Act, 16 U.S.C. § 3378(c)(1), precludes prosecution for conduct governed by the Halibut Act: "Nothing in this chapter shall be construed as (1) repealing, superceding, or modifying any provision of Federal law. . . ." He argues that if this court finds the Lacey Act governs his conduct, then the Lacey Act will be "superceding or modifying" the Halibut Act, a provision of federal law.

CHAPTER 8: WILDLIFE OFFENSES

We need not address this concept anew because we have previously interpreted a portion of the disclaimer provision of the Lacey Act, 16 U.S.C. § 3378(c)(2). *United States v. Sohappy*, 770 F.2d 816 (9th Cir. 1985), cert. denied, 477 U.S. 906 (1986). We believe that by analogy the same analysis applies here. In *Sohappy* a native American was prosecuted under the Lacey Act for violations of tribal fishing laws. The defendant argued that to enforce the Lacey Act against him for this conduct would be to violate the tribe's treaty reserved right to regulate fishing. He contended that this was prohibited by section 3378(c)(2) of the Lacey Act:

> Nothing in this chapter shall be construed as—
> (2) repealing, superceding, or modifying any right, privilege, or immunity granted, reserved, or established pursuant to treaty, statute, or executive order pertaining to any Indian tribe, band, or community. . . .

16 U.S.C. § 3378(c)(2). We held that the treaty did not reserve to the tribe exclusive jurisdiction to control fishing and that, therefore, the Lacey Act applied to defendant's conduct. The court recognized that the Lacey Act functions to create new offenses for trafficking in fish taken in violation of tribal law.

The disclaimer provision at issue in *Sohappy* is a subsection of the same Lacey Act section that Cameron argues exempts his conduct. 16 U.S.C. §§ 3378(c)(1), 3378(c)(2). Language of the two subsections of the disclaimer provision is similar, but not identical. The exemption pertaining to tribal law is broader than the exemption pertaining to federal law. But what is important about *Sohappy* is our court's recognition that two statutes can govern the same conduct, without running afoul of the disclaimer provision of the Lacey Act. *Sohappy* teaches that the Lacey Act and another statute or law, can govern identical conduct and yet have different enforcement provisions. The Lacey Act is not interpreted as "repealing, superceding, or modifying" the other law, unless the other law reserves exclusive control over the conduct at issue. Neither the Halibut Act nor the Protocol reserve exclusive control over halibut fishing.

This reading of *Sohappy* is consistent with Congressional intent. The Lacey Act was designed to strengthen and support existing wildlife laws. To fulfill its purpose, the Act must be applied to conduct that is also regulated by an existing treaty, state or federal law, regulation or tribal law. The grand purpose of fish, wildlife, and plant protection by the federal government would be severely dissipated by an exaggerated reading of the disclaimer provision.

D.

Finally, Cameron argues that because the Lacey Act and the Halibut Act are both penal statutes, and because ambiguity exists in the two statutes, the rule of lenity should apply. And if we apply the lenity doctrine, only the Halibut Act should control defendant's conduct. Although Cameron's authorities support his position, the argument must fail because the lenity rule comes into play only when ambiguity is present. We see no ambiguity here. The Halibut Act creates a civil penalty for the strict liability offense of transporting or selling halibut taken in violation of IPHC regulations. 16 U.S.C. § 773e(a)(5). The Lacey Act criminalizes the intentional violation of certain federal wildlife laws. 16 U.S.C. § 3372(a)(1). The two laws are not ambiguous.

Accordingly, we hold that a prosecution under the Lacey Act is authorized for a violation of a regulation of the Halibut Commission.

- The Halibut Act did not provide any criminal penalties at all; it only imposed civil penalties. Is it fair that the Lacey Act can take a civil statute and turn it into a felony?
- What is the policy reason for allowing a felony for anyone who knowingly imports, exports, sells, or acquires wildlife that was taken, possessed, transported, or sold in violation of a purely civil statute?

United States v. McNab
331 F.3d 1228 (11th Cir. 2003)

WILSON, Circuit Judge

David Henson McNab, Abner Schoenwetter, Robert D. Blandford, and Diane H. Huang (collectively the defendants) appeal the convictions and sentences they received after a jury found them guilty of conspiracy, smuggling, money laundering, and Lacey Act violations in connection with the importation, sale, and purchase of Caribbean spiny lobsters from Honduras. The defendants' main argument on appeal is that the district court erred in determining that the Honduran laws that served as the underlying basis of their convictions were valid and enforceable. The defendants contend that the Honduran laws were invalid, and, therefore, there was no violation of foreign law upon which to base their convictions.

The defendants' challenge to the validity of the Honduran laws requires us to undertake our own foreign law determination. Our task is complicated by conflicting representations from Honduran officials regarding the validity of the Honduran laws. Throughout the investigation and trial, Honduran officials offered support and assistance to the United States government, and both the government and the district court relied upon the Honduran officials' verification of the Honduran laws. Shortly after the defendants were convicted, the Honduran government reversed its position; it currently refutes the validity of the laws it previously verified. Therefore, we must decide whether our courts are bound by a foreign government's new representations regarding the validity of its laws when its new representations are issued only postconviction and directly contravene its original position upon which the government and our courts relied and the jury acted. This question is a matter of first impression in this Circuit and apparently the other circuits as well.

For the reasons set forth below, we affirm the defendants' convictions and sentences.

BACKGROUND

On February 3, 1999, agents of the National Marine Fisheries Service (NMFS) received an anonymous facsimile, which provided that McNab's cargo transport vessel, the M/V CARIBBEAN CLIPPER, would arrive in Bayou la Batre, Alabama on February 5, 1999, with a shipment of lobsters containing "undersized (3 & 4 oz) lobster tails, [which was] a violation of Honduran law." The facsimile further provided that Honduras prohibits the bulk exportation of lobsters and requires that lobsters be packed in boxes for export.

In response to the anonymous tip, NMFS agents consulted the Dirección General de Pesca y Acuicultura (DIGEPESCA) in Honduras regarding the legality of the lobster shipment referenced in the facsimile. The NMFS agents questioned whether the shipment violated the Lacey Act, which makes it unlawful to import into the United States "fish or wildlife [that has been] taken, possessed, transported, or sold in violation of . . . any foreign law." 16 U.S.C. § 3372(a)(2)(A). In three separate letters responding to the agents' inquiry, the director general of the DIGEPESCA described some of Honduras's fishing laws and confirmed that McNab's shipment "ha[d] been illegally transported in violation of the Fishing Law, the Industrial and Hygienic Sanitary Inspection Regulation for Fish Products and Resolution No. 030-95." The director general provided authentic copies of the applicable laws and stated that the DIGEPESCA was ready to support all efforts by the government to prosecute persons who violate the Lacey Act.

In early March of 1999 NMFS agents seized the lobster shipment that was referenced in the anonymous facsimile based upon the director general's assurances that the lobsters had been exported in violation of Honduran law. Over the next few months, NMFS agents communicated with Honduran officials about the Honduran laws and the legality of the seized lobster shipment. In June of 1999 NMFS special agents and an attorney in the United States National Oceanic and Atmospheric Administration Office of the General Counsel met with various Honduran officials from the Secretaria de Agricultura y Ganaderia (SAG) in Tegucigalpa, Honduras. The minister, the vice minister, the director of legal services, the director of legal affairs, the secretary general of the SAG, the director general of the DIGEPESCA, and the legal advisor for the Servicio Nacional de Sanidad Agropecuaria (SENASA) confirmed that the lobsters had been exported illegally without first being inspected and processed. Furthermore, the Honduran officials confirmed that there was a 5.5-inch size limit for lobster tails and that all catches had to be reported to Honduran authorities. The Honduran officials provided certified copies of the laws in question. In September of 1999 NMFS agents inspected the lobster shipment that had been seized earlier in the year. The inspection confirmed that the seized lobsters were packed in bulk plastic bags without being processed and revealed that a significant number had a tail length that was less than the 5.5 inches required by the Honduran size limit restriction. In addition, many of the lobsters were egg-bearing or had their eggs removed.

In March of 2000 two Honduran officials, a legal advisor in the Despacho Ministerial and a SAG legal advisor, traveled to Alabama to meet with government prosecutors and investigators. Both legal advisors provided written statements that cited Resolution 030-95 as a valid law regulating the lobster fishing industry. They also described the processing requirements mandated by Regulation 0008-93.4 They further explained that Honduras prohibits the harvesting of egg-bearing lobsters. Based upon the NMFS's investigation and the verification of the applicable foreign laws by the Honduran officials charged with regulating the lobster fishing industry, the government decided to prosecute the defendants for their roles in the illegal importing scheme. Subsequently, the grand jury returned a forty-seven-count second superseding indictment in September of 2000.

To determine the validity of the relevant Honduran laws, the district court conducted a pretrial hearing on foreign law in September of 2000. Most of the defendants' evidence at the hearing pertained to the validity of Resolution 030-95, which established a 5.5-inch size limit for lobsters. At the government's request, the minister of the SAG sent Secretary General Liliana Patricia Paz, the SAG's highest-ranking legal official, to testify at the foreign law hearing. Secretary General Paz testified as to the validity of various laws and confirmed that Resolution 030-95, Regulation 0008-93, and Article 70(3) of the Fishing Law were in effect and legally binding during the time period covered by the indictment. She also explained the means by which a Honduran citizen may seek the invalidation of a resolution in Honduras, and she testified that no such proceeding regarding Resolution 030-95 had been initiated at that time. Persuaded by the testimony of Secretary General Paz, the district court found that the government met its burden of establishing the validity of the Honduran laws that served as the predicates for the Lacey Act charges. Shortly after the foreign law hearing, a jury trial was conducted, and the defendants were found guilty on multiple counts. . . .

The defendants raise a number of issues in these consolidated appeals. First, they argue that the scope of the Lacey Act is limited to foreign statutes and that the Honduran resolutions and regulations listed in the indictment were used improperly as predicates for their convictions. Second, they contend that the district court's interpretation of the Honduran resolutions and regulations was erroneous and that the Honduran laws that served as predicates for the convictions were invalid. Third, McNab argues that the district court abused its discretion by excluding evidence at trial relating to his "knowledge" of Honduran law. Fourth, the defendants assert that the district court made several errors with respect to the jury instructions. Fifth, they contend that the jury's verdicts were based upon insufficient evidence. . . .

DISCUSSION
I. Scope of the Lacey Act
The first issue we address is whether the phrase "any foreign law" in the Lacey Act includes foreign regulations and other legally binding provisions that have the force and effect of law. The defendants argue that the phrase "any foreign law" should be read to mean foreign statutes and not foreign regulations or provisions that are legally binding. According to their argument, Resolution 030-95 and Regulation 0008-93 do not fall within the scope of the Lacey Act, because they are not statutes. They rely upon what they consider a distinction by Congress between "any law or regulation of any State" and "any foreign law." 16 U.S.C. § 3372(a)(2)(A). The defendants argue that by failing to include foreign regulations explicitly, Congress intended that only foreign statutes could serve as the basis for a foreign law Lacey Act violation. . . .

The Lacey Act provides that "[i]t is unlawful for any person . . . to import, export, transport, sell, receive, acquire, or purchase in interstate or foreign commerce . . . any fish or wildlife taken, possessed, transported, or sold in violation of any law or regulation of any State or in violation of any foreign law." 16 U.S.C. § 3372(a)(2)(A). The Act defines "law" as those "*laws* . . . which regulate the taking, possession, importation, exportation, transportation, or sale of fish or wildlife or plants." 16 U.S.C. § 3371(d) (emphasis added).

Unfortunately, the statutory definition defines the word "law" by using the word "laws." . . . Merriam Webster's Collegiate Dictionary provides several definitions of law, including "a binding custom or practice of a community: a rule of conduct or action prescribed or formally recognized as binding or enforced by a controlling authority" and "the whole body of such customs, practices, or rules." Under these broad definitions of the word "law," the phrase "any foreign law" incorporates the Honduran decrees and regulations at issue. . . .

In other words, the argument is that Congress specifically chose to limit domestic law to statutes and regulations, but specifically chose to use the language "any foreign law" to cover the wide varieties of laws in foreign countries.

The net result is that there are several reasonable ways to interpret the word "law" in the phrase "any foreign law." As a result of this ambiguity, we look beyond the language of the statute to determine legislative intent. We thus now look to the legislative history of the Lacey Act to ascertain Congress's intent. . . .

The Lacey Act was introduced by Representative John F. Lacey of Iowa in 1900. Representative Lacey recognized that individual states were unable to protect their wildlife, because their laws did not reach into neighboring states. Thus, he asserted that a federal law was necessary to outlaw the interstate traffic in wildlife illegally taken from their state of origin. By 1981 Congress recognized the need to strengthen the Lacey Act in response to "the massive illegal trade in fish, wildlife and plants." Congress thus amended the Lacey Act in 1981 "to correct . . . insufficiencies" in the Act and "to simplify administration and enforcement."

[T]he legislative history reflects that "the [main] thrust of Congress's intention in amending the Act was to expand its scope and enhance its deterrence effect." Indeed, Congress clearly stated that the amendments were meant to strengthen the existing wildlife protection laws and to "provide [the government] the tools needed to effectively control the massive illegal trade in fish, wildlife and plants." The Senate Report provided that the amendments "would allow the Federal Government to provide more adequate support for the full range of State, foreign and Federal laws that protect wildlife." The amendments were intended to "raise both the civil and criminal penalties of the current laws and target commercial violators and international traffickers." . . .

Our examination of the legislative history of the Lacey Act leads us to the conclusion that Congress by no means intended to limit the application of the Act by its adoption of the 1981 amendments. . . . We therefore conclude that regulations and other such legally binding provisions that foreign governments may promulgate to protect wildlife are encompassed by the phrase "any foreign law" in the Lacey Act.

As we have determined that the phrase "any foreign law" includes nonstatutory provisions such as Resolution 030-95 and Regulation 0008-93, we now turn to the defendants' argument that their convictions were based upon the district court's erroneous interpretation of foreign law.

II. Honduran Laws

The defendants contend that the Honduran laws that served as predicates for their convictions were invalid. Specifically, they argue that (1) Resolution 030-95, which established a 5.5-inch size limit for lobsters, never had the effect of law, because it was promulgated improperly and has been declared void by the

Honduran courts; (2) Regulation 0008-93, which established inspection and processing requirements for the lobster fishing industry, was repealed in 1995, prior to the time period covered by the indictment; and (3) Article 70(3), which prohibits the harvesting and destruction of lobster eggs, was misinterpreted by the district court and was repealed retroactively in 2001. . . .

In a Lacey Act prosecution, once the district court determines the validity of a foreign law during a given time period, it is up to the government to prove that the defendants knowingly violated those laws. The initial foreign law determination, however, is a question of law for the court. "The court, in determining foreign law, may consider any relevant material or source, including testimony, whether or not submitted by a party or admissible under the Federal Rules of Evidence." Among the most logical sources for the court to look to in its determination of foreign law are the foreign officials charged with enforcing the laws of their country. The district court, in the course of a Lacey Act prosecution, is entitled to rely upon such representations by foreign officials as to the validity of their government's laws. The court reasonably may assume that statements from foreign officials are a reliable and accurate source and may use such statements as a basis for its determination of the validity of foreign laws during a given time period.

When, however, a foreign government changes its original position regarding the validity of its laws after a defendant has been convicted, our courts are not required to revise their prior determinations of foreign law solely upon the basis of the foreign government's new position. There must be some finality with representations of foreign law by foreign governments. Given the inevitable political changes that take place in foreign governments, if courts were required to maintain compliance with a foreign government's position, we would be caught up in the endless task of redetermining foreign law.

In this case, the government solicited and received the assistance of the SAG and the DIGEPESCA during the investigation of the legality of the lobster shipments. From the earliest stages of the investigation until after the defendants were convicted, the statements from the SAG were consistent with the government's understanding of the laws. After the defendants were convicted, however, certain events in Honduras induced the Honduran government to refute its original statements. The newly issued statements and opinions of Honduran officials, however, do not persuade us that the district court erred in its determination that the Honduran laws at issue were valid and enforced during the time period covered by the indictment. . . .

Thus, we conclude that the postconviction shift in the Honduran government's position regarding the validity of its laws is not determinative as to whether the laws were valid at the time the lobsters were imported into the United States. . . .

CONCLUSION

Thus, we conclude that the Honduran laws used as the underlying predicates for the defendants' convictions fall within the scope of the Lacey Act and were valid and legally binding during the time period covered by the indictment. . . . We therefore AFFIRM the defendants' convictions and sentences.

FAY, Circuit Judge, dissenting:

The majority opinion is both thorough and scholarly in dealing with this complicated matter. With some hesitation, I most respectfully dissent from that portion of the majority opinion upholding the validity of Honduran Resolution 030-95. The theme of the majority opinion is that the government of Honduras has "shifted" its position. The question for determination is phrased as being complicated by the changed or new position of the Honduran government. The majority then decides this issue within the framework of whether or not we are free to follow the Honduran government's original position.

Try as I might, I simply cannot read this record that way. There was never unanimity nor agreement concerning the validity of Resolution 030-95. That question was hotly contested. But, throughout the course of this litigation, the resolution of that question was based upon the weight given by the trial judge to the evidence presented by the U.S. government during a pretrial hearing on foreign law. At that time, the Honduran courts had not ruled. Now they have.

It should come as no surprise to anyone that some of the "expert" witnesses were correct and some were wrong. Nor should we be surprised that it was the courts of Honduras which ultimately answered the question. That is the way it works in Honduras and in the United States of America. Simply stated, it is my position that we are bound by the rulings of the Honduran courts declaring Resolution 030-95 null and void. This being the case, the defendants' convictions must be reversed since one of the Honduran laws relied upon by the jury in finding guilt has now been found to be a nullity. . . .

Most reluctantly, I therefore dissent.

- Why did the majority continue to hold that a foreign law had been violated under the first step in the Lacey Act analysis when the Honduran courts later determined that the law that was allegedly violated was invalid?
- Does anything in the Lacey Act allow a United States federal court the ability to interpret foreign law contrary to the manner in which the foreign sovereign interprets its own law?
- What if the foreign sovereign interprets its law in a way that proscribes certain conduct but later interprets the law in a way that allows the conduct even though the law itself never changed? Should United States courts be required to abide by whichever meaning the foreign sovereign ascribes to its own laws even if the change is clearly erroneous or, possibly, based on corruption?

As shown above, the elements of a Lacey Act trafficking offense require proof of an underlying illegal act (civil or criminal) by someone who is not necessarily the defendant plus action by the defendant to knowingly import, export, transport, sell, purchase, or acquire the wildlife if the person knows (or should have known) that it was taken, possessed, transported, or sold in violation of law. Thus, the prosecution must show that the defendant's own act was done "knowingly" while "knowing" (or he should have known, in the case of the misdemeanor) that a prior civil or criminal illegal act was done. The knowing mens rea for the defendant's own act requires the prosecution to establish that he was aware of the facts that constitute the offense. *United States v. Fountain*, 277 F.3d 714, 717 (5th Cir. 2001). However, how much knowledge must a defendant have of the illegal nature of the predicate act of taking, possessing, transporting, or selling the wildlife prior to the defendant's knowing act?

United States v. Santillan
243 F.3d 1125 (9th Cir. 2001)

KLEINFELD, Circuit Judge:

Santillan was prosecuted under the Lacey Act for bringing ten baby parrots across the border from Tijuana. His appeal raises, among other issues, a significant question about the mens rea needed under the Lacey Act.

FACTS

Santillan was convicted of smuggling and importing wildlife in violation of the Lacey Act. Santillan owned a tropical fish store in Southern California. Returning home from a trip to Tijuana, he said he had nothing to declare. But actually, he had with him ten baby parrots packed in three paper bags stuffed under his car seats. When he was asked why he had not declared them, he said that he had had two beers a couple of hours before. He said he had bought the birds for $250 from a boy on Revolution Street in Tijuana, and would probably keep them rather than sell them. He admitted that he knew he was not allowed to bring the birds into the United States, but assumed that all that would happen if he got caught was that the birds would be seized. It turned out that he underestimated the aggressiveness of federal law enforcement on parrot importation. He was indicted and convicted of two felonies and put in jail for ten months.

ANALYSIS . . .

2. Lacey Act Mens Rea

Santillan challenges the sufficiency of the evidence, and argues that the jury instruction was erroneous on the required mental element of the Lacey Act. . . .

The Lacey Act count accused Santillan of importing wildlife in violation of a regulation that required him to complete and file a form. He reads the Act to require proof that he knew about this form requirement. There was no evidence at all that he knew anything about the form requirement so if he is right about the law, he would be entitled to acquittal on the felony Lacey Act count. The district judge instructed the jury that all Santillan had to know was that he knew he was importing wildlife and also knew that the wildlife was "possessed" in violation of law.

The regulation (of which, so far as the evidence shows, Santillan was entirely ignorant) says that wildlife importers must file a "Declaration for Importation or Exportation of Fish or Wildlife." The Lacey Act makes it unlawful to "import . . . any fish or wildlife or plant taken, possessed, transported, or sold in violation of any law, treaty, or regulation of the United States. . . ."

There are three provisions of law involved: (1) the regulation, which requires that wildlife importers file a "Declaration for Importation or Exportation of Fish or Wildlife"; (2) the provision of the Lacey Act which makes it unlawful to "import . . . any fish or wildlife or plant taken, possessed, transported, or sold in violation of any law, treaty, or regulation of the United States . . . "; and (3) The

Lacey Act provision setting out criminal penalties. The mens rea requirement is in the criminal penalty provision. That statute creates felony penalties for a "person who knowingly imports . . . wildlife . . . in violation . . . of this Act . . . knowing that the . . . wildlife [was] taken, possessed, transported or sold in violation" of law. . . .

We conclude that the Lacey Act does not require knowledge of the particular law violated by the possession or other predicate act, so long as the defendant knows of its unlawfulness. Careful examination of the text of the Lacey Act criminal provision shows that the felony provision requires two levels of knowledge. First, the defendant must be proved to have known that he was importing or exporting fish or wildlife. But that is not enough. Importation of fish or wildlife does not put a person in peril of strict liability for a Lacey Act felony conviction merely because it turns out that there was illegality, unknown to the importer, associated with its taking. To be guilty of the felony, the person must also know "that the fish or wildlife or plants were taken, possessed, transported, or sold in violation of, or in a manner unlawful under, any underlying law, treaty or regulation." This second requirement of knowledge is satisfied if the person knows that the possession, etc. was violative of any law, without regard to whether the person knows which law it violated.

The point of the second knowledge requirement is to assure that the violator is not strictly liable, but instead knows that the fish, wildlife or plants he imported was tainted by illegality. Thus the government does not satisfy its burden of proof merely by establishing that the defendant knew he was importing or exporting wildlife, and, unbeknownst to the defendant, there was some illegality associated with its taking. But it does satisfy its burden of proof if it establishes that the defendant knew that the wildlife was, for example, unlawfully taken, even if the defendant does not know precisely which law or regulation established the illegality of the taking.

The mens rea provisions in the Lacey Act are important "to separate wrongful conduct from 'otherwise innocent conduct.'" That objective does not require that the violator know all the details of the statutes and regulations that make the conduct unlawful. It suffices that he knows, not only that he is importing or exporting the animals, but also that the animals are tainted by a violation of some law associated with their taking, possession, transportation or sale. Here, there was sufficient evidence to show Santillan knew that what he did was unlawful: the parrots were concealed in the car, and Santillan admitted to the government agents that he knew importing the birds was illegal.

3. Lesser Included Offense

Santillan's third argument is that the district judge should have instructed the jury that it could convict him of a lesser included offense. The Lacey Act has a misdemeanor provision, in addition to the felony provision discussed in the previous section. The misdemeanor section criminalizes the same conduct, but instead of requiring knowledge that the fish, wildlife or plants are tainted by some violation of law, requires only that the violator "in the exercise of due care should know" that they are tainted. Thus the misdemeanant must have actual knowledge that he is importing or exporting the animals, etc., but need not know that they were taken or possessed illegally, so long as in the exercise of due care he should know.

Santillan requested a lesser included offense instruction. The prosecutor did not object to one. But the court declined to give it because the evidence, in the court's view, did not allow for it. We review this ruling for abuse of discretion.

The evidence established without contradiction that Santillan actually knew that importation of the baby parrots was against federal law, and expected them to be confiscated if he was caught. That evidence left no room for the possibility that he did not know that the birds were possessed against the law, but would have known had he exercised reasonable care. Santillan's argument comes back to the point that he did not know, though perhaps with reasonable care he might have learned, that the federal regulations required him to fill out a form. But as we explain above, the government had to prove only that he knew there was something illegal about possessing the birds, not that he knew precisely what statute or regulation tainted them.

AFFIRMED.

- What type of evidence would you look for to determine whether the defendant knew or should have known that the wildlife he/she imported, exported, transported, purchased, acquired, or sold was illegally taken, possessed, transported, or sold under some underlying wildlife law?

Consider the following example to determine whether a violation of the Lacey Act's trafficking provisions has occurred.

Case Study: Hunting Without Boundaries

Tommy Gorropolo has a state-issued permit to hunt elk. While hunting on state public land, he spots a large, trophy-sized elk. Before Tommy can get off a clean shot on the monster bull elk, it flees into the tribal trust lands for a Native American tribe, which the United States recognizes as such under federal law. Under an act of Congress, the federally recognized tribe is the governing authority over its tribal trust lands and has enacted laws that expressly preclude any non-tribal member from hunting or taking any wild game within the reservation. To remind hunters, the tribe posts "No Trespassing" signs along its boundary, which Tommy ignores as he pursues the trophy elk onto tribal land where he is able to deliver the killing shot. Tommy then calls his friend, who drives a large pickup onto tribal land to pick up the carcass of the immense elk. Tommy and his friend then attach Tommy's state hunting tag onto the elk's ear and transport the elk off the tribal land to a local taxidermist. Tommy tells his friend that if anyone asks where the elk was shot, they are going to say it was on private land. However, some locals hear about what Tommy did and call the local game warden who then calls the United States Fish and Wildlife Service's special agent to investigate, given that state law enforcement has no jurisdiction on tribal land.

- Has there been a violation of the Lacey Act?
- If so, is it a felony or a misdemeanor? Why?
- Do you need more information to make this determination? If so, what additional information do you require?

- What evidence would you use to show the value of the wildlife if you decided that a Lacey Act violation had occurred?
- Assuming that there is a Lacey Act offense here, who could be charged—Tommy, his friend, or both?

2. Labeling Offenses

In the Lacey Act, Congress recognized that those engaged in the illegal importation, exportation, or transportation of illegal wildlife have great incentive to mislabel their shipments. Accordingly, the Lacey Act includes a five-year felony for those who knowingly mislabel their wildlife shipments when they import or export wildlife, regardless of its value, or when they knowingly sell, purchase, offer to sell or purchase, or do any act with the intent to sell or purchase fish, wildlife, or plants whose value exceeds $350. 16 U.S.C. § 3373(d)(3)(A). If a mislabeling offense occurs and does not meet the elements of the felony, the Lacey Act imposes a misdemeanor for such an act. 16 U.S.C. § 3373(d)(3)(B). To "mislabel" a shipment of fish, wildlife, or plant, a person must "make or submit any false record, account, or label" that falsely identifies the fish, wildlife, or plant that has been or is intended to be imported, exported, transported, sold, or purchased in interstate or foreign commerce. 16 U.S.C. § 3373(d). Additionally, a 2008 amendment to the Lacey Act includes as a mislabeling offense the violation of requirements for those who import any plant species and fail to comply with importation declaration requirements for the plant shipment. Unlike the dishonesty offenses that were previously discussed in the Clean Water Act, Clean Air Act, or RCRA, the prosecution need not prove that the false statement was "material." *United States v. Fountain*, 277 F.3d 714, 717 (5th Cir. 2001). Moreover, because the Lacey Act provides that "[i]t is unlawful for any person to make *or* submit" a false record, the prosecution need not prove that the defendant actually submitted the false statement to any government authority. 16 U.S.C. § 3372(d); *United States v. Allemand*, 34 F.3d 923, 926-27 (10th Cir. 1994). Instead, the prosecution need only show that the document with the false statement was made in connection with "any fish, wildlife, or plant which has been or is intended to be" involved in foreign or interstate commerce. 16 U.S.C. § 3372(d)(1), (2).

Case Study: Expensive Trinkets

Suppose that Barbara goes on vacation to Zimbabwe where she acquires some ivory trinkets from a local street vendor. She is so excited about these pieces that she texts her friend a photo of the trinkets and writes, "Beautiful but forbidden artisanship in Zimbabwe. ☺" Because she is concerned that customs will find the ivory trinkets in her luggage at the airport, she sends them to her residence in Nebraska through FedEx. The FedEx paperwork requests that she provide a brief description of the items in the package, and Barbara writes "plastic knick-knacks." She carefully places the ivory trinkets in the FedEx box, affixes the label, and sends them off. However, when the FedEx shipment reaches the United States, an Immigration and Customs Enforcement (ICE) officer looks at the contents of Barbara's package, sees what appears to be ivory, and calls over the resident agent from the United States Fish and Wildlife Service (USFWS), who confirms that the "plastic knick-knacks" appear to be ivory. Subsequent testing at the USFWS lab proves it. By this time, Barbara is home from Zimbabwe and is wondering where her trinkets are. When she inputs her tracking number online, she sees that her package was held up by ICE. Shortly thereafter, a special agent from the USFWS shows up at Barbara's home to talk to her about her package. Barbara refuses to talk and, instead, gives the agent her attorney's phone number and says, "Talk to my lawyer." The special agent obtains a search warrant for Barbara's cell phone and encounters the text to her friend containing the photo of the trinkets and the message.

- Did Barbara commit a false labeling offense under the Lacey Act? If so, is the violation a misdemeanor or a felony?
- What defenses could Barbara argue at trial if she is charged?
- Is there sufficient evidence to prove the Lacey Act offense beyond a reasonable doubt?

B. THE ENDANGERED SPECIES ACT

In 1966, Congress enacted the Endangered Species Preservation Act.[11] This Act authorized the Secretary of the Interior to determine that a species is "regarded as threatened with extinction" when, "after consultation with the affected states," the Secretary finds that the species' "habitat is threated with destruction . . . or because of overexploitation, disease, predation, or because of other factors . . . its survival requires assistance." This Act allowed the Secretary to enter into agreements with states "for the administration and management of any area established for the conservation, protection, restoration, and propagation of endangered species of native fish and wildlife." Additionally, Congress prohibited anyone from "knowingly" injuring land set aside for species protection and from possessing or injuring endangered species themselves. Congress imposed a misdemeanor of up to six months' imprisonment for violations of the Act.

Three years later, Congress enacted the Endangered Species Conservation Act.[12] Among other changes, Congress precluded any person from importing wildlife that "the Secretary [of the Interior] has determined . . . to be threatened with worldwide extinction." Congress imposed a misdemeanor of up to a year in prison for violations of the Act. Thus, in both the 1966 and 1969 acts, Congress was concerned about domestic and international species that were threatened with extinction.

In 1973, the United States signed a multilateral treaty known as the Convention in International Trade of Endangered Species (CITES).[13] CITES required that each nation designate a government agency that would regulate the rules of the treaty by being the exclusive permitting authority for importing and exporting species governed under CITES. Member nations agreed not to accept any importation of CITES-covered species unless the proper permits from the

---

[11] Pub. L. No. 89-669, 80 Stat. 926 (1966).
[12] Pub. L. No. 91-135, 83 Stat. 275 (1969).
[13] 27 U.S.T. 1087 (entered into force July 1, 1975); available at https://www.cites.org/eng/disc/text.php

exporting nation's designated management authority were included with the wildlife shipment.

To determine which species were covered under CITES, the treaty signatories agreed to three lists of species that receive varying degrees of protection. For example, species listed in Appendix I of CITES are those that are threatened with extinction and can only be traded in exceptional circumstances (e.g., leopards, tigers, and gorillas). Appendix II species are those that will be confronted with extinction if commercialization of those species is not closely monitored and controlled (e.g., iguanas, certain species of turtles, most pythons). Appendix III allows a signatory nation to request assistance from other nations to protect a species that is important to that nation. For example, the United States has listed the alligator snapping turtle on Appendix III, which means that other nations have to ensure that the importation of that species is accompanied by the requisite paperwork from the United States Fish and Wildlife Service.

Given the international developments and the domestic need to designate and protect endangered and threatened species, Congress replaced the 1966 and 1969 acts with the Endangered Species Act of 1973. The Endangered Species Act created a mechanism for the Secretary of the Interior and the Secretary of Commerce to designate threatened and endangered species. 16 U.S.C. § 1533. Once designated as threatened or endangered, the "take" of such species is prohibited. 16 U.S.C. § 1538(a). The term "take" includes "to harass, harm, pursue, hunt, shoot, wound, kill, trap, capture, or collect to attempt to engage in any such conduct." 16 U.S.C. § 1532(19). The Act also required every agency of the federal government to consult with the United States Fish and Wildlife Service prior to permitting or undertaking any action over which the federal government had the requisite level of influence or control. 16 U.S.C. § 1536. As part of the Act, Congress also adopted CITES and designated the United States Fish and Wildlife Service as the United States' authority to administer the treaty. 16 U.S.C. §§ 1537, 1537a, 1538(c). This means that a violation of CITES is a violation of the Endangered Species Act. 16 U.S.C. § 1538(c). Additionally, the Endangered Species Act also provided a mechanism for determining exceptions to its prohibition against the take of threatened and endangered species. 16 U.S.C. § 1539.

In terms of enforcement, however, the Endangered Species Act did not change from its 1966 and 1969 predecessors. Unlike the Clean Water Act, Clean Air Act, and RCRA—whose criminal penalties have become more severe over time—the Endangered Species Act still imposes the 1969 act's one-year misdemeanor crime as the most severe punishment while allowing for the 1966 act's six-month misdemeanor for violations that are not severe enough to warrant the one-year misdemeanor offense. 16 U.S.C. § 1540(b)(1). However, in the 1973 version of the Act, Congress required a "wilfull" mens rea. In 1978, Congress changed the mens rea to "knowingly." H.R. Rep. No. 95-1625, at 26 (1978), reprinted in 1978 U.S.C.C.A.N. 9453, 9476. Today, the Endangered Species Act provides:

> Any person who knowingly violates any provision of this chapter,
> of any permit or certificate issued hereunder, or of any regulation
> issued in order to implement subsection (a)(1)(A), (B), (C), (D),
> (E), or (F); (a)(2)(A), (B), (C), or (D), (c), (d) (other than a

regulation relating to recordkeeping, or filing of reports), (f), or (g) of section 1538 of this title shall, upon conviction, be fined not more than $50,000 or imprisoned for not more than one year, or both. Any person who knowingly violates any provision of any other regulation issued under this chapter shall, upon conviction, be fined not more than $25,000 or imprisoned for not more than six months, or both.

16 U.S.C. § 1540(b)(1).

Although Congress followed many of the other environmental crimes previously discussed by imposing a "knowing" mens rea to violations of the Endangered Species Act, there has been significant debate over what that mens rea requires, especially when enforcing the prohibitions against the take of an endangered species. Consider the following saga over a gray wolf that Chad McKittrick killed in Montana.

United States v. McKittrick
142 F.3d 1170 (9th Cir. 1998)

SKOPIL, Senior Circuit Judge:

I.

The gray wolf, or Canis Lupus, is listed as endangered under the Endangered Species Act (ESA) throughout the coterminous United States, except in Minnesota, where it is listed as threatened. Gray wolf populations in Canada, however, are plentiful. Pursuant to ESA section 10(j), the Fish and Wildlife Service (FWS) captured Canadian gray wolves and released them in Yellowstone National Park as an "experimental population" designed to replenish wolves in Wyoming and parts of Montana and Idaho, where they had been all but eradicated by about 1930. One of these wolves migrated from Yellowstone to the Red Lodge, Montana area, where it had a fatal encounter with Chad McKittrick. After shooting and killing the wolf, McKittrick skinned and decapitated it, taking the hide and head to his home.

The government charged McKittrick with three counts: one, taking the wolf in violation of 16 U.S.C. §§ 1538(a)(1)(G), 1540(b)(1), and 50 C.F.R. § 17.84(i)(3); two, possessing the wolf in violation of 16 U.S.C. §§ 1538(a)(1)(G), 1540(b)(1), and 50 C.F.R. § 17.84(i)(5); and three, transporting the wolf in violation of the Lacey Act, 16 U.S.C. §§ 3372(a)(1), 3373(d)(2). Magistrate Judge Anderson conducted a trial and then sentenced McKittrick to six months' imprisonment after a jury convicted him on all counts. District Judge Shanstrom affirmed the conviction and sentence.

On appeal, McKittrick argues that . . . his taking of the wolf was not "knowing" because he did not realize what he was shooting. . . . We reject each of these challenges and affirm the conviction. . . .

II. . . .

C. Degree of Intent

McKittrick argues that a violation of ESA section 11 requires the government to prove that he knew he was shooting a wolf, and that the jury instructions misled the jury about the requisite intent. We review for an abuse of discretion whether the magistrate judge's "precise formulation" of the intent element was sufficient. . . .

The instructions were accurate. McKittrick need not have known he was shooting a wolf to "knowingly violate[ ]" the regulations protecting the experimental population. 16 U.S.C. § 1540(b)(1). In 1978, Congress changed the wording of section 11 to "reduce[ ] the standard for criminal violations from 'willfully' to 'knowingly.' " It did this to "make[ ] criminal violations of the act a general rather than a specific intent crime." As the magistrate judge recognized, the District of Montana had already decided the intent issue in the government's favor, holding on similar facts that "[t]he critical issue is whether the act was done knowingly, not whether the defendant recognized what he was shooting." The Fifth Circuit has reached the same conclusion in related situations. *See United States v. Nguyen*, 916 F.2d 1016, 1017-18 (5th Cir. 1990) (sustaining possession conviction did not require that defendant know animal's ESA-protected status); United States v. Ivey, 949 F.2d 759, 766 (5th Cir. 1991). The Eleventh Circuit has expressed its agreement with the reasoning of these cases in holding that an analogous provision of the African Elephant Conservation Act requires only general intent. *See United States v. Grigsby*, 111 F.3d 806, 817 (11th Cir. 1997). As these cases and the legislative history indicate, section 11 requires only that McKittrick knew he was shooting an animal, and that the animal turned out to be a protected gray wolf. . . .

- Is the Ninth Circuit's view of "knowing" when it comes to taking an endangered species consistent with the way "knowing" has been applied in other environmental crimes?
- Is knowing the identity of the species part of the facts that constitute the offense?
- Mr. McKittrick appealed the Ninth Circuit's decision to the United States Supreme Court. When the United States is involved in any appeal, especially to the Supreme Court, the Office of the Solicitor General of the United States within the Department of Justice reviews the case, which occurred with McKittrick's petition for a writ of certiorari. After review of McKittrick's petition regarding the proper mens rea, the Department of Justice issued the McKittrick Policy, which states that the United States must prove that the defendant knew the species that he/she was taking even if the defendant does not know that the species is threatened or endangered.[14]
- In 2017, WildEarth Guardians challenged the McKittrick Policy in the District of Arizona.

---

[14] Although the United States changed its position as to whether the defendant must know the species he/she is taking, McKittrick's conviction survived the change because McKittrick held onto the skin and head of the gray wolf even though he clearly knew at that point what species he possessed. The Endangered Species Act preludes the possession of an endangered or threatened species. 16 U.S.C. § 1538(a)(1)(D).

WildEarth Guardians v. United States Department of Justice
283 F. Supp. 3d 783 (D. Ariz. 2017)

Honorable DAVID C. BURY, United States District Judge

The Court grants in part and denies in part the Plaintiffs' Motion for Summary Judgment. The Court finds the McKittrick policy is arbitrary and capricious, an abuse of discretion and otherwise not in accordance with law in violation of the APA. Therefore, the Court grants summary judgment for Plaintiffs under the APA. . . .

A.

OVERVIEW: PROCEDURAL POSTURE OF THE CASE

"In *United States v. McKittrick*, 142 F.3d 1170, 1177 (9th Cir. 1998), the Ninth Circuit Court of Appeals determined that the knowledge element for the criminal misdemeanor offense of 'taking' an endangered species was: the defendant knew he was shooting an animal, and the animal shot was a Mexican wolf; 'McKittrick need not have known he was shooting a wolf to "knowingly violate[ ]" the regulation protecting the experimental population.' *Id.* According to the court, Congress changed the wording of 16 U.S.C. § 1540(b)(1) in 1978 from 'willfully' to 'knowingly,' making the offense a general rather than a specific intent crime." (Order (Doc. 30) at 1.)

McKittrick's conviction on this instruction was affirmed by the Ninth Circuit Court of Appeals, and he petitioned for a writ of certiorari. The government responded in relevant part that it would no longer use the knowledge instruction approved by the Ninth Circuit Court of Appeals in *McKittrick*. It agreed that the intent of Congress in 1978 was to make it clear that the statute only required proof of general, not specific, intent. Nevertheless, the government believed the jury instruction approved in *McKittrick* wrongly defined the mens rea required for a misdemeanor conviction under section 1540(b)(1). It reasoned the more analogous mens rea requirement was found in a public welfare offense for knowing violations of an Interstate Commerce regulation, which required drivers of motor vehicles transporting any explosive liquids or poisonous gasses to avoid, so far as practicable, driving into or through congested thoroughfares or places were crowds are assembled. . . .

The Supreme Court denied certiorari, and thereafter the Defendant, the Department of Justice (DOJ), notified all of its prosecuting attorneys to stop using and object to the jury instruction approved in *McKittrick*. In 1999, the DOJ distributed a memorandum instructing its prosecuting attorneys to request an instruction which requires the government to prove beyond a reasonable doubt that a defendant knew the biological identity of the animal taken was a wolf.

The Plaintiffs ask the Court to find that the DOJ has adopted an ultra vires agency policy, meaning that the DOJ has adopted an agency policy exceeding its statutory authority. . . .

Plaintiffs argue that the DOJ's adoption of the McKittrick policy violates the Administrative Procedures Act (APA) because it is "arbitrary, capricious, an abuse of discretion, or otherwise not in accordance with law." 5 U.S.C. §§ 702, 706(2)(A). To prove its APA claim, the Plaintiffs charge that the DOJ's adoption of the McKittrick policy is a complete abdication of its prosecutorial discretion as established under the law set out in the ESA and *United States v. McKittrick*, 142 F.3d 1170, 1177 (9th Cir. 1998). Additionally, the Plaintiffs claim that the McKittrick policy violates DOJ's responsibility under § 7 of the ESA to take no action which may adversely affect a threatened species without first consulting with the Fish and Wildlife Service (FWS). . . .

B.
APA REVIEWABILITY: THE MCKITTRICK POLICY IS AN
ABDICATION OF DOJ'S CRIMINAL ENFORCEMENT DUTIES
. . . Here, the nonenforcement decision is made by the Attorney General and the United States Attorneys, who have "broad discretion" to enforce the Nation's criminal laws which make the presumption against reviewability especially strong. . . .

Nevertheless, the Executive Branch's power to prosecute is not wholly "unfettered." "[P]rosecutorial discretion only encompasses the Executive Branch's power to decide whether to initiate charges for legal wrongdoing and to seek punishment, penalties, or sanctions. It does not include the power to disregard statutory obligations that apply to the Executive Branch." In other words, the Executive Branch may not re-write the statute. . . .

The Defendant argues that the Rule provides broad prosecutorial discretion because it does "not address which shootings are subject to criminal penalties as compared to civil or administrative penalties; each incident of take will be investigated and determinations regarding those investigations will be made on a case-by-case basis. Nothing in this rule predetermines the outcome of an investigation into the take of a Mexican wolf."

This discretion does not, however, negate the broad sweep of protections afforded ESA listed species. In *TVA v. Hill*, 437 U.S. 153, 180 (1978), the Supreme Court described the ESA as: "the most comprehensive legislation for the preservation of endangered species ever enacted by any nation." *Babbitt v. Sweet Home Chapt. of Comm. for a Great Oregon*, 515 U.S. 687, 698 (1995). "Whereas predecessor statutes enacted in 1966 and 1969 had not contained any sweeping prohibition against the taking of endangered species except on federal lands, . . . the 1973 Act applied to all land in the United States and to the Nation's territorial seas." *Id.* . . .

The McKittrick policy is to the contrary. . . .

Public welfare offenses, created by regulatory statutes, arose from the industrial revolution and in response to previously unimagined risks to people's health and welfare such as industrial accidents, high-speed automobiles, contaminated food and dangerous pharmaceutical drugs. . . .

In *International Minerals*, the Court construed a statute imposing criminal penalties on those who "knowingly violate[d]" Interstate Commerce Commission ("ICC") regulations, a short-cut reference for the regulations governing the transport of corrosive liquids. The Court stated that "where . . . dangerous or deleterious devices or products or obnoxious waste materials are involved, the probability of regulation is so great that anyone who is aware that he is in possession of them or dealing with them must be presumed to be aware of the regulation." Applying this presumption of awareness, the Court concluded that knowingly applies only to the specific acts or omissions which violate the Act because there is no exception to the rule that ignorance of the law is no excuse. . . .

Accordingly, a public welfare offense will, in all likelihood, impose liability upon at least some innocents—after all it is the purpose of such a regulatory statute, through its quasi-strict liability construct, to "heighten the duties of those in control of particular industries, trades, properties or activities that affect public health, safety or welfare." In such situations, the Supreme Court has reasoned that "as long as a defendant knows that he is dealing with a dangerous device of a character that places him "in responsible relation to a public danger, [*United States v.*] *Dotterweich*, [320 U.S. 277,] 281, he should be alerted to the probability of strict regulation, and we have assumed that in such cases Congress intended to place the burden on the defendant to ascertain at his peril whether [his conduct] comes within the inhibition of the statute. "Under such statutes we have not required that the defendant know the facts that make his conduct fit the definition of the offense."

[The court further discussed how the misdemeanor penalties under the Endangered Species Act are minimal and that shows that the knowledge requirement is more like the public welfare offense than requiring specific knowledge. The court then held that the McKittrick Policy is an abdication of the DOJ's prosecutorial responsibilities under the Endangered Species Act and declared it void.]

- However, on October 23, 2018, the Court of Appeals for the Ninth Circuit reversed the District of Arizona's *WildEarth Guardians* decision because the plaintiffs lacked standing to challenge the McKittrick Policy. *WildEarth Guardians v. U.S. Dep't of Justice*, Nos. 17-16677, -16678, -16679, 2018 WL 5278941 (9th Cir. Oct. 23, 2018). Therefore, as of this publication, the McKittrick Policy is still the policy of the Department of Justice throughout the United States.
- Based on your understanding of "knowing," is the McKittrick Policy a correct statement of the law or is it beyond what Congress intended when amending the Endangered Species Act to allow a misdemeanor for a "knowing" violation?
- Given that the Endangered Species Act provides only a misdemeanor for violating even the provisions implementing CITES' restrictions on the import and export of species listed within its appendices, the Lacey Act has become a valuable tool in enforcing the Endangered Species Act. The Endangered Species Act may serve as the underlying law violation for proving the Lacey Act's first prong so that if a defendant knowingly imports or exports a species that is prohibited by the Endangered Species Act (through CITES), then the Lacey Act's five-year felony applies. Thus, the Lacey Act has been used far more to enforce the Endangered Species Act than the Endangered Species Act has been.

C. THE MIGRATORY BIRD TREATY ACT

In 1916, the United States entered into a treaty with Great Britain to protect migratory birds in both the United States and Canada.[15] Both sovereigns sought to save migratory birds "from indiscriminate slaughter" and to ensure "the preservation of migratory birds as are either useful to man or are harmless."[16] To implement this treaty, Congress enacted the Migratory Bird Treaty Act (MBTA). 40 Stat. 755, Ch. 128 (1918). In the intervening years, Congress has amended the MBTA to include agreements between the United States and Mexico,[17] Japan,[18] and the then-known Soviet Union.[19] To keep its treaty commitments, Congress drafted the MBTA very broadly in terms of the number of birds covered and the prohibited conduct.

Instead of discussing which birds are covered under the MBTA, it is easier to discuss the few that are not covered. The United States Fish and Wildlife Service regulations implementing the MBTA define a "migratory bird" as:

> any bird, whatever its origin and whether or not raised in captivity, which belongs to a species listed in § 10.13, or which is a mutation or a hybrid of any such species, including any part, nest, or egg of any such bird, or any product, whether or not manufactured, which consists, or is composed in whole or part, of any such bird or any part, nest, or egg thereof.

50 C.F.R. § 10.12. The list of birds in 50 C.F.R. § 10.13 includes nearly every species that is found in North America.

In addition to the number of birds covered under the MBTA, Congress intended to regulate a great deal of conduct. For example, unless a person has a permit from the Secretary of the Interior,

> it shall be unlawful at *any time, by any means or in any manner*, to pursue, hunt, take, capture, kill, attempt to take, capture, or kill, possess, offer for sale, sell, offer to barter, barter, offer to purchase, purchase, deliver for shipment, ship, export, import, cause to be shipped, exported, or imported, deliver for transportation, transport or cause to be transported, carry or cause to be carried, or receive for shipment, transportation, carriage, or export, any migratory bird, any part, nest, or egg of any such bird, or any product, whether or not manufactured, which consists, or is

---

[15] Convention between the United States and Great Britain for the Protection of Migratory Birds, Aug. 16, 1916, 39 Stat. 1702.

[16] *Id.*

[17] Convention between the United States and Mexico for the Protection of Migratory Birds and Game Mammals, Feb. 7, 1936, 1937 U.N.T.S. 310, 50 Stat. 1311.

[18] Convention between the Government of the United States of America and the Government of Japan for the Protection of Migratory Birds and Birds in Danger of Extinction, and Their Environment, March 4, 1972, 25 U.S.T. 3329.

[19] Convention between the United States of America and the Union of the Soviet Socialist Republics Concerning the Conservation of Migratory Birds and Their Environment, Nov. 19, 1976, 29 U.S.T. 4647.

composed in whole or part, of any such bird or any part, nest, or egg thereof, included in the terms of the [treaties with Great Britain, Mexico, Japan, and the Soviet Union].

16 U.S.C. § 703 (emphasis added). Besides broadly prohibiting unpermitted take, Congress precluded the unpermitted foreign and interstate commerce of migratory birds, their parts, and their eggs. 16 U.S.C. § 705. Consequently, in terms of criminal enforcement, the MBTA focuses on two themes: (1) take; and (2) trafficking.

1. Prohibitions Against Take

Congress imposed a six-month misdemeanor for anyone who violates "any provision" of the MBTA. 16 U.S.C. § 707(a). Notice that Congress did not include the word "negligently," "knowingly," or "willfully." Instead, an unpermitted take of a covered migratory bird "at any time, by any means, or in any manner" is a strict liability offense.

United States v. Apollo Energies, Inc.
611 F.3d 679 (10th Cir. 2010)

TYMKOVICH, Circuit Judge.

"This would have remained a profoundly insignificant case to all except its immediate parties had it not been so tried . . . as to raise questions both fundamental and far-reaching in federal criminal law. . . ." And we might add, "No one may be required at peril of life, liberty or property to speculate as to the meaning of penal statutes. All are entitled to be informed as to what the State commands or forbids."

This case requires us to consider the scope of the Migratory Bird Treaty Act (MBTA or Act). The Act declares it a misdemeanor to "pursue, hunt, take, capture, [or] kill" birds protected by several international treaties. 16 U.S.C. § 703. The MBTA also specifies a maximum penalty of $15,000 and six months in prison for a misdemeanor violation, but does not require any particular mental state or mens rea to violate the statute. See 16 U.S.C. § 707(a). The question this case presents is whether the MBTA constitutionally can make it a crime to violate its provisions absent knowledge or the intent to do so.

Appellants are two Kansas oil drilling operators who were charged with violating the Act after dead migratory birds were discovered lodged in a piece of their oil drilling equipment called a heater-treater.

After a trial before a magistrate judge, both Apollo Energies and Dale Walker (doing business as Red Cedar Oil) were convicted of taking or possessing migratory birds, each misdemeanor violations. Apollo was fined $1,500 for one violation, and Walker was fined $250 for each of his two violations. The federal district court affirmed the convictions, concluding that violations of § 703 of the MBTA are strict liability offenses, which do not require that defendants knowingly or intentionally violate the law.

On appeal, Apollo and Walker renew their challenges to the MBTA, claiming (1) it is not a strict liability crime to take or possess a protected bird, or, (2) if it is a strict liability crime, the Act is unconstitutional as applied to their conduct. We conclude the district court correctly held that violations of the MBTA are strict liability crimes. But we hold that a strict liability interpretation of the MBTA for the conduct charged here satisfies due process only if defendants proximately caused the harm to protected birds. After carefully examining the trial record, we agree Apollo proximately caused the taking of protected birds, but with respect to one of his two convictions, Walker did not. Due process requires criminal defendants have adequate notice that their conduct is a violation of the Act.

Consequently, . . . we AFFIRM in part and REVERSE in part the district court's decision.

Apollo and Walker own many heater-treaters, a device commonly used in oil drilling operations. Heater-treaters are cylindrical equipment up to 20 feet high and more than three feet wide that separate oil from water when the mixture is pumped from the ground. The heater-treaters at issue in this case have vertical exhaust pipes that are approximately nine inches in diameter, and Walker's heater-treaters included movable louvers that can be opened to access heating equipment at the base. Birds can crawl into the exhaust pipes or through the louvers to form nests. Once inside the heater-treaters, escape can be difficult for some birds.

Acting on an anonymous tip, an agent with the U.S. Fish and Wildlife Service (Fish and Wildlife, or Service) inspected more than a dozen of Apollo's heater-treaters in December 2005. He found bird remains in about half of the heater-treaters he inspected. In February 2006, Fish and Wildlife officers expanded their investigation in the region (southeast Kansas), finding more than 300 dead birds in heater-treaters, 10 of which were identified as protected species under the MBTA.

As a result of the investigation, Fish and Wildlife embarked on a public education campaign to alert oil producers to the heater-treater problem. The Service sent letters to 36 of the oil companies involved in the February 2006 inspections, including Apollo. The record does not disclose, however, that Walker's company, Red Cedar, received the notice. Fish and Wildlife also created a poster describing the problem, which it distributed to oil equipment supply companies. Service representatives made presentations to the Kansas Independent Oil and Gas Association and at a Kansas Corporation Commission Oil and Gas meeting. Finally, a Kansas television station and the Associated Press news service each ran a story about heater-treaters' threat to protected birds. Fish and Wildlife chose not to recommend prosecution for MBTA violations related to heater-treaters through the end of 2006, while the education campaign was ongoing.

In April 2007, after Fish and Wildlife's grace period ended, agents searched heater-treaters belonging to Apollo and Walker. The search of Apollo's heater-treaters yielded the carcass of a Northern Flicker, an MBTA-protected species. Agents found four protected birds in Walker's heater-treaters, as well. When confronted with the dead birds, Walker is reported to have said "that's not good." A year later, in April 2008, the Service again conducted a search of Walker's heater-treaters. Although Walker had placed metal caps on the exhaust pipes— where birds previously had been found—a Fish and Wildlife agent retrieved a protected bird that he found lodged in a heater-treater's louvers.

Apollo was convicted of one violation of the MBTA based on the April 2007 bird death. Walker also was convicted of two violations based on the April 2007 and April 2008 deaths.

II. DISCUSSION

Appellants make one statutory and several due process arguments. Their statutory argument is that the MBTA does not create a strict liability crime to take or possess migratory birds, and, under that statutory construction, they lacked the necessary imputed mental state to commit an MBTA violation. Our precedent forecloses Appellants' statutory construction, and consequently we are obliged to address Appellants' broader arguments about the MBTA's constitutionality.

As to their constitutional due process claims, Appellants argue: (1) the MBTA is unconstitutionally vague because it provides inadequate notice of what conduct is criminal, (2) due process requires that they caused an MBTA violation to be guilty of a crime, and (3) the district court erred in applying the law to the facts in this case. . . .

Appellants first contend § 703 is not a strict liability offense, but contains a scienter requirement.

Section 703 makes it a crime to "take" protected birds:

> [I]t shall be *unlawful at any time, by any means or in any manner, to . . . take [or] . . . attempt to take . . . any migratory bird*, any part, nest, or egg of any such bird, or any product, whether or not manufactured, which consists, or is composed in whole or part, of any such bird or any part, nest, or egg thereof, included in the terms of [various treaties between the United States and Great Britain, Mexico, Japan, and the U.S.S.R.]. (Emphasis added).

16 U.S.C. § 703. Regulations implementing the statute explain that the term "take" means to "pursue, hunt, shoot, wound, kill, trap, capture, or collect." Under § 707(a), "any person, association, partnership, or corporation" is "guilty of a misdemeanor" if they "violate any provisions" of the Act. The statute does not supply a mens rea requirement.

Appellants' contention is foreclosed by our holding in *United States v. Corrow*, 119 F.3d 796 (10th Cir. 1997), which squarely addressed § 703's mens rea requirement. In *Corrow*, we considered and resolved the mens rea requirement of § 707(a), and concluded that "misdemeanor violations under § 703 are strict liability crimes." In that case, the defendant was charged with illegal possession of protected Golden Eagle and Great-Horned Owl feathers. We upheld the conviction, finding it persuasive that a plain reading of § 703's text—"it shall be unlawful" to possess protected birds—did not require any particular state of mind or scienter. We relied on the fact that "[l]ike other regulatory acts where the penalties are small and there is 'no grave harm to an offender's reputation,'" the Supreme Court has long recognized a different standard applies to those federal criminal statutes that are essentially regulatory. "*Simply stated, then, 'it is not necessary to prove that a defendant violated the Migratory Bird Treaty Act with specific intent or guilty knowledge.'*" *Id.* at 805 (quoting *United States v. Manning*, 787 F.2d 431, 435 n. 4 (8th Cir. 1986) (emphasis added)).

Our holding in *Corrow* fell in line with those of other circuits at the time of that case. At least seven other circuits either had held that MBTA misdemeanors are strict liability crimes or noted the MBTA's lack of mens rea in passing. *See, e.g., United States v. Pitrone*, 115 F.3d 1, 5 (1st Cir. 1997); *United States v. Hogan*, 89 F.3d 403, 404 (7th Cir. 1996); *United States v. Boynton*, 63 F.3d 337, 343 (4th

Cir. 1995); *United States v. Engler*, 806 F.2d 425, 431 (3d Cir. 1986); *United States v. Catlett*, 747 F.2d 1102, 1105 (6th Cir. 1984) (per curiam); *United States v. FMC Corp.*, 572 F.2d 902, 907–08 (2d Cir. 1978); *Rogers v. United States*, 367 F.2d 998, 1001 (8th Cir. 1966). *See also United States v. Morgan*, 311 F.3d 611, 614–16 (5th Cir. 2002) (citing *Corrow* and holding misdemeanor MBTA violations are strict liability crimes). *But see Newton County Wildlife Ass'n*, 113 F.3d 110, 115 (8th Cir. 1997) ("Strict liability may be appropriate when dealing with hunters and poachers. But it would stretch this 1918 statute far beyond the bounds of reason to construe it as an absolute criminal prohibition on conduct, such as timber harvesting, that indirectly results in the death of migratory birds."); *Mahler v. U.S. Forest Serv.*, 927 F. Supp. 1559, 1579 (S.D. Ind. 1996) (questioning the MBTA's application to bird deaths caused indirectly by logging).

Despite this applicable precedent, Appellants challenge the extension of *Corrow* to the conduct alleged here. They reason our holding in *Corrow* was limited to the MBTA violations at issue there—possessing and selling protected bird feathers. For support, they point to Fish and Wildlife's regulations that define "possession" as "detention and control," and "to take" as to "capture, or collect." 50 C.F.R. § 10.12. They say the linguistic differences imply an active state of mind to violate the Act, and the conduct here was passive—they merely failed to bird-proof the heater-treaters.

We see no express or implied limitation to our holding in *Corrow*. In fact, that decision broadly held "misdemeanor *violations* under § 703 are strict liability crimes." *Corrow*, 119 F.3d at 805 (emphasis added). Nothing in the structure or logic of the opinion lends itself to carving out an exception for different types of conduct, and therefore a scienter requirement for the takings here. Nor is there any reason to find that capturing or collecting birds implies a higher mens rea than detaining or controlling them. In short, the conduct alleged here has the same mental state requirement as the sale and possession of protected birds we considered in *Corrow*.

Appellants also point to Supreme Court case law on the books at the time we decided *Corrow* as fatally undermining its holding. They contend three years before *Corrow*, the Supreme Court in *Staples v. United States*, 511 U.S. 600 (1994), cast doubt on the presumption of strict liability when a statute omits a mens rea requirement. The Court in *Staples* held that strict liability crimes "generally are disfavored," and suggested some indicia of congressional intent, "express or implied," is necessary before courts can dispense with the traditional mens rea requirement.

While we did not cite to *Staples* in *Corrow*, our reasoning was that although the MBTA was silent as to mens rea, its "plain language"—an indicia of legislative intent—supported a strict liability interpretation. Congress, moreover, in 1986 added the word "knowingly" to create the felony offense of selling migratory birds, while leaving intact the language of the misdemeanor provision without an explicit mens rea requirement. This is further evidence the legislative scheme invokes a lesser mental state for misdemeanor violations. *See* S. Rep. No. 99-445, at 15 (1986), *reprinted in* 1986 U.S.C.C.A.N. 6113, 6128 ("Nothing in this amendment . . . is intended to alter the 'strict liability' standard for misdemeanor prosecutions under 16 U.S.C. 707(a), a standard which has been upheld in many Federal court decisions."). Finally, the Court in *Staples* took pains to reaffirm the basic proposition that "public welfare" or "regulatory" offenses can "impose a form of strict criminal liability." *Staples*, 511 U.S. at 606. . . .

In sum, *Corrow* squarely addressed the mens rea requirement for an MBTA violation, and we are bound by its holding. As a matter of statutory construction, the "take" provision of the Act does not contain a scienter requirement.

C. Due Process: Notice and Causation

Having concluded the MBTA applies a strict liability standard to the taking or killing of migratory birds, we must address Appellants' additional arguments that the Act is unconstitutional facially and as applied to the conduct in this case. Appellants' broader argument is that the MBTA violates their due process rights because of its scope and application to their conduct.

By way of background, although § 703 is a strict liability crime, a few historical elements are worth remembering. At common law, crime was a "compound concept" consisting of both an "evil-meaning mind" and an "evil-doing hand." . . .

Yet by the middle of the twentieth century, the Supreme Court was confronted with a new category of crimes for which no mens rea was required. In *Morissette v. United States*, for example, the Supreme Court gave a stamp of approval to regulatory crimes that lacked or had a minimal mens rea element. But the Court did not do so in unequivocal terms. The Court reasoned that while the strict liability crimes at that time technically did not require mens rea, the "accused, if he d[id] not will the violation, usually [wa]s in a position to prevent it with no more care than society might reasonably expect and no more exertion than it might reasonably exact from one who assumed his responsibilities." *Id.* at 256. Moreover, the "penalties commonly [we]re relatively small," and did not cause "grave damage to an offender's reputation." *Id.* . . .

A line of subsequent cases suggest several important limiting principles to strict liability crimes. Two due process limitations are especially relevant here.

First, due process requires citizens be given fair notice of what conduct is criminal. A criminal statute cannot be so vague that "ordinary people" are uncertain of its meaning. However, even when a statute is specific about which acts are criminal, our due process analysis is not complete. When, as here, predicate acts which result in criminal violations are commonly and ordinarily not criminal, we must ask the fair notice question once again. In the context of laws criminalizing the possession of dangerous items such as drugs or explosives, the Supreme Court has stated when items have characteristics such that a reasonable person would expect the items to be regulated, strict liability for violations of those regulations passes constitutional scrutiny. But when the items lack those special characteristics—that is, when persons would not reasonably foresee the items' regulation—strict liability becomes constitutionally suspect.

Second, criminalizing acts which the defendant does not cause is unconstitutional, as is criminalizing acts based on the defendant's status. Put differently, the concept of causation limits criminal sanctions to a defendant's conduct—whether the conduct includes affirmative actions or proscribed omissions. More pertinent to this case, "[b]y interpreting such public welfare offenses to require at least that the defendant know that he is dealing with some dangerous or deleterious substance" the Supreme Court "avoided construing criminal statutes to impose a rigorous form of strict liability." *Staples*, 511 U.S. at 607 n.3.

Apollo and Walker make several arguments based on these principles which fall into three general categories: (1) the statute provides inadequate notice of what conduct would violate the MBTA, (2) due process requires they caused an MBTA violation to be guilty of a crime, and (3) the district court erred in applying the preceding principles to them.

. . . The MBTA is not unconstitutionally vague. It criminalizes a range of conduct that will lead to the death or captivity of protected migratory birds, including to "pursue, hunt, take, capture, [and] kill. . . ." 16 U.S.C. § 703. The actions criminalized by the MBTA may be legion, but they are not vague.

Furthermore, the MBTA's language does not encourage arbitrary enforcement—at least as far as vagueness is concerned. The arbitrariness at which a vagueness challenge takes aim is the "standardless sweep [of a statute's language, which] allows policemen, prosecutors, and juries to pursue their personal predilections." In contrast, the MBTA's terms are capable of definition without turning to the subjective judgment of government officers. We thus reject Appellants' vagueness contention.

In a variation of their vagueness argument, Appellants also contend the statute does not provide fair notice of prohibited conduct because of the sheer breadth of the Act. They argue the Act applies to innocuous conduct several steps removed from bird deaths or takings. No reasonable person, they contend, would be on notice that those predicate acts are potentially criminal.

. . . Questions abound regarding what types of predicate acts—acts which lead to the MBTA's specifically prohibited acts—can constitute a crime. Conceptually, the constitutional challenge to the criminalization of these predicate acts can be placed under the rubric of notice or causation. The inquiries regarding whether a defendant was on notice that an innocuous predicate act would lead to a crime, and whether a defendant caused a crime in a legally meaningful sense, are analytically indistinct, and go to the heart of due process constraints on criminal statutes.

Recognizing these notice and causation concerns, the district court attempted to cabin the MBTA's reach by holding the defendants must "proximately cause" the MBTA violation to be found guilty, and that they did so here. In other words, the court found the government had found "'proximate causation' or 'legal causation' beyond a reasonable doubt" by "showing that trapped birds are a reasonably anticipated or foreseeable consequence of failing to cap the exhaust stack and cover access holes to the heater/treater."

. . . We agree with the district court's assessment of proximate cause. Central to all of the Supreme Court's cases on the due process constraints on criminal statutes is foreseeability—whether it is framed as a constitutional constraint on causation . . . and mental state . . . or whether it is framed as a presumption in statutory construction. . . . When the MBTA is stretched to criminalize predicate acts that could not have been reasonably foreseen to result in a proscribed effect on birds, the statute reaches its constitutional breaking point.

[W]e agree with the district court's legal conclusion and hold that the MBTA requires a defendant to proximately cause the statute's violation for the statute to pass constitutional muster.

Applying these principles to Appellants' claims, we reject the contention that the Act violates due process, with one important exception.

As to Apollo, the record shows it had notice of the heater-treater problem for nearly a year-and-a-half before the bird death resulting in its conviction. Indeed, Apollo admitted at trial that it failed to cover some of the heater-treaters' exhaust pipes as Fish and Wildlife had suggested after the December 2005 inspection.

In effect, Apollo knew its equipment was a bird trap that could kill.

In contrast, Walker was charged and convicted for dead birds found in both the April 2007 and April 2008 inspections. Walker contends the conviction arising from the April 2008 inspection should be reversed because on that occasion the bird was found in his heater-treater's louvers, not the exhaust pipe, for which he had no knowledge of a problem. Fish and Wildlife argues it warned Walker of the louver problem when, in its 2007 letter, it admonished Walker to secure all heater-treater cavities in which a protected bird might become trapped. Regardless, we find that once Walker was alerted to protected birds' proclivity to crawl into the heater-treaters' exhaust pipes, it was reasonably foreseeable protected birds could become trapped in other of the heater-treaters' cavities.

The conviction for the April 2007 bird death is a different matter. Walker's testimony—which the Fish and Wildlife agent does not dispute—is that prior to April 2007, he was not aware of problems with heater-treaters in the oil industry or in his specific operations. Fish and Wildlife did not send him a letter about the issue before the April 2007 inspection, and he was not a member of the trade association to which the Service advertised the oil field equipment problem. Nor was Walker aware of the one television report or newspaper article about heater-treaters. Given the state of this record, we agree no reasonable person would conclude that the exhaust pipes of a heater-treater would lead to the deaths of migratory birds.

. . . Therefore, the magistrate judge's finding as to the April 2007 bird death is reversed.

III. CONCLUSION

For the foregoing reasons, we AFFIRM in part, REVERSE in part, and REMAND for further proceedings consistent with this opinion.

- Assume that an electrical utility company erects a field of power-generating windmills in an effort to reduce reliance on coal-fired power plants. However, migratory birds keep getting killed in the spinning blades of the windmills. Consequently, the United States Fish and Wildlife Service (USFWS) shows up at the electrical utility, conducts an inspection, and finds over 100 migratory birds laying at the base of the windmills. The gruesome find clearly shows that these birds were chopped up by the whirling propellers of the windmills. The special agent for the USFWS tells the environmental compliance officer for the utility company that he is going to refer the company to the United States Attorney's Office for prosecution for violating the MBTA by taking over 100 migratory birds. Suppose that you represent the company. Does *Apollo Energies* help you in terms of arguing that your client's conduct cannot be prosecuted?

- Suppose you work for the United States Attorney's Office. How would you argue the decision in *Corrow* to justify a prosecution?
- Would it make a difference to you if the utility company had studies conducted prior to constructing the windmills that showed that the construction site was a major migration corridor for migratory birds and that moving the windmills a half mile to the west would greatly reduce bird mortalities without sacrificing wind power?
- Although the majority of courts have long held that an unpermitted take of a migratory bird is a strict liability offense, a recent opinion from the Solicitor at the Department of the Interior (i.e., the chief counsel) contends that take under the MBTA is not a strict liability offense. The Department of the Interior is in charge of investigating violations of the MBTA.

The Migratory Bird Treaty Act Does Not Prohibit Incidental Take
M-37050 (Dec. 22, 2017), Opinion by the Solicitor of the Department of Interior[20]

I. INTRODUCTION

This memorandum analyzes whether the Migratory Bird Treaty Act, 16 U.S.C. § 703 ("MBTA"), prohibits the accidental or "incidental" taking or killing of migratory birds. Unless permitted by regulation, the MBTA prohibits the "taking" and "killing" of migratory birds[.] "Incidental take" is take that results from an activity, but is not the purpose of that activity.

This issue was most recently addressed in Solicitor's Opinion M-37041— Incidental Take Prohibited Under the Migratory Bird Treaty Act, issued January 10, 2017 (hereinafter "Opinion M-37041"), which concluded that "the MBTA's broad prohibition on taking and killing migratory birds by any means and in any manner includes incidental taking and killing." Opinion M-37041 was suspended pending review on February 6, 2017. In light of further analysis of the text, history, and purpose of the MBTA, as well as relevant case law, this memorandum permanently withdraws and replaces Opinion M-37041.

Interpreting the MBTA to apply to incidental or accidental actions hangs the sword of Damocles over a host of otherwise lawful and productive actions, threatening up to six months in jail and a $15,000 penalty for each and every bird injured or killed. As Justice Marshall warned, "the value of a sword of Damocles is that it hangs—not that it drops." Indeed, the mere threat of prosecution inhibits otherwise lawful conduct. For the reasons explained below, this Memorandum finds that, consistent with the text, history, and purpose of the MBTA, the statute's prohibitions on pursuing, hunting, taking, capturing, killing, or attempting to do the same apply only to affirmative actions that have as their purpose the taking or killing of migratory birds, their nests, or their eggs.

---

[20] The Office of the Solicitor in the Department of the Interior is the equivalent of the office of general counsel in other federal agencies. Thus, the Solicitor for the Department of Interior is the equivalent of the agency's chief counsel.

In order to fulfill the United States' obligations under [the migratory bird treaty with Great Britain], Congress [passed] what came to be known as the "Migratory Bird Treaty Act." As originally passed, the MBTA provided:

> That unless and except as permitted by regulations made as hereinafter provided, it shall be unlawful to hunt, take, capture, kill, attempt to take, capture or kill, possess, offer for sale, sell, offer to purchase, purchase, deliver for shipment, ship, cause to be shipped, deliver for transportation, transport, cause to be transported, carry or cause to be carried by any means whatever, receive for shipment, transportation or carriage, or export, at any time or in any manner, any migratory bird, included in the terms of the convention between the United States and Great Britain for the protection of migratory birds concluded August sixteenth, nineteen hundred and sixteen, or any part, nest, or egg of any such bird.

Violation of MBTA was a misdemeanor criminal offense, punishable by a fine of no more than $500 and/or up to six months in jail. This time, relying in part on the federal treaty power, the legislation survived constitutional scrutiny. . . .

III. THE CURRENT STATE OF THE LAW
a. The Migratory Bird Treaty Act
Section 2 of the MBTA provides:

> Unless and except as permitted by regulations made as hereinafter provided, it shall be unlawful at any time, by any means or in any manner, to pursue, hunt, take, capture, kill, attempt to take, capture, or kill, possess, offer for sale, sell, offer to barter, barter, offer to purchase, purchase, deliver for shipment, ship, export, import, cause to be shipped, exported, or imported, deliver for transportation, transport or cause to be transported, carry or cause to be carried, or receive for shipment, transportation, carriage, or export, any migratory bird, any part, nest, or egg of any such bird, or any product, whether or not manufactured, which consists, or is composed in whole or part, of any such bird or any part, nest, or egg thereof. . . .

Violations of the MBTA are criminal offenses. . . . Courts have held that misdemeanor violations of the MBTA are strict-liability offenses. Accordingly, if an action falls within the scope of the MBTA's prohibitions, it is a criminal violation, regardless of whether the violator acted with intent. Felony violations, however, require knowledge. As one court noted, "[l]ooking first at the language of the MBTA itself, it is clear that Congress intended to make the unlawful killing of even one bird an offense." At times the Department of Justice has taken the position that the MBTA permits charges to be brought for each and every bird taken, notwithstanding whether multiple birds are killed via a single action or transaction.

b. Judicial Decisions Regarding Incidental Take

This Opinion is not written on a blank legal slate. Beginning in the 1970s, federal prosecutors began filing criminal charges under the MBTA against persons, including oil, gas, timber, mining, and chemical companies, whose activities "incidentally" resulted in the death of migratory birds. In response, courts have adopted different views on whether Section 2 of the MBTA prohibits incidental take, and, if so, to what extent. Courts of Appeals in the Second and Tenth Circuits, as well as district courts in at least the Ninth and District of Columbia Circuits, have held that the MBTA criminalizes some instances of incidental take, generally with some form of limiting construction. By contrast, Courts of Appeals in the Fifth, Eighth, and Ninth Circuits, as well as district courts in the Third and Seventh Circuits, have indicated that it does not.

Courts holding that the MBTA does not extend to incidental take generally trace their roots to the Ninth Circuit's ruling in *Seattle Audubon Society v. Evans*. The court in *Seattle Audubon* held that the MBTA did not criminalize the death of birds caused by habitat destruction. According to the court, the regulatory definition of "take" "describes the physical conduct of the sort engaged in by hunters and poachers, conduct which was undoubtedly a concern at the time of the statute's enactment in 1918." The court went on to compare "take" under the MBTA, and its applicable regulatory definition, with the broader statutory definition of "take" under the Endangered Species Act, which includes "harm":

> We are not free to give words a different meaning than that which Congress and the Agencies charged with implementing congressional directives have historically given them. . . . Habitat destruction causes "harm" to the [birds] under the [Endangered Species Act] but does not "take" them within the meaning of the MBTA.

The court further distinguished actions leading "indirectly" to the death of birds, such as habitat destruction, from actions that lead directly to the death of birds, such as exposing birds to a highly toxic pesticide, leaving open whether the law reaches the later conduct.

Building upon *Seattle Audubon*, the district court in *Mahler v. United States Forest Service* held that the cutting of trees by the U.S. Forest Service that could destroy migratory bird nesting areas did not violate the MBTA, ruling "[t]he MBTA was designed to forestall hunting of migratory birds and the sale of their parts" and "declin[ing] [the] invitation to extend the statute well beyond its language and the Congressional purpose behind its enactment." In response to plaintiff's motion to alter or amend judgment, the court reaffirmed that the MBTA did not reach the Forest Service's activity, holding "[p]roperly interpreted, the MBTA applies to activities that are intended to harm birds or to exploit harm to birds, such as hunting and trapping, and trafficking in bird and bird parts. The MBTA does not apply to other activities that result in unintended deaths of migratory birds."

The Eighth Circuit in *Newton County Wildlife Association v. United States Forest Service* likewise rejected a claim that the destruction of forests containing migratory birds violated the MBTA. Citing to *Seattle Audubon* and *Mahler*, among other cases, the *Newton County* court held:

> [I]t would stretch this 1918 statute far beyond the bounds of reason to construe it as an absolute criminal prohibition on conduct, such as timber harvesting, that indirectly results in the death of migratory birds. Thus, we agree with the Ninth Circuit that the ambiguous terms "take" and "kill" in 16 U.S.C. § 703 mean "physical conduct of the sort engaged in by hunters and poachers. . . ."

Following *Newton County* as "controlling precedent," the court in *United States v. Brigham Oil & Gas, L.P.* held that the MBTA did not impose criminal liability on an oil company for the deaths of several migratory birds after coming into contact with a "reserve pit." In doing so, the *Brigham Oil* court concluded "as a matter of law, that lawful commercial activity which may indirectly cause the death of migratory birds does not constitute a federal crime." In addition to relying on the *Newton County* decision, the court in *Brigham* examined the text of the MBTA, concluding that the text "refers to a purposeful attempt to possess wildlife through capture, not incidental or accidental taking through lawful commercial activity." The court also noted that "to extend the Migratory Bird Treaty Act to reach other activities that indirectly result in the deaths of covered birds would yield absurd results," potentially criminalizing "driving, construction, airplane flights, farming, electricity and wind turbines . . . and many other everyday lawful activities."

Most recently, the Fifth Circuit in *United States v. CITGO Petroleum Corporation* examined "the statute's text, its common law origin, a comparison with other statutes, and [a] rejection of the argument that strict liability can change the nature of the necessary illegal act" and "agree[d] with the Eighth and Ninth circuits that a 'taking' is limited to deliberate acts done directly and intentionally to migratory birds." The court further noted that "[t]he scope of liability under the government's preferred interpretation is hard to overstate," and "would enable the government to prosecute at will and even capriciously (but for the minimal protection of prosecutorial discretion) for harsh penalties." *CITGO* is the most recent decision on this topic and triggered the Department's further evaluation of the question.

IV. ANALYSIS OF INCIDENTAL TAKE UNDER THE MBTA. . . .
a. The Relevant Text of the MBTA Is Limited to Affirmative Actions that Have as Their Purpose the Taking or Killing of Migratory Birds . . .

The relevant portion of the MBTA reads "it shall be unlawful at any time, by any means or in any manner, to pursue, hunt, take, capture, kill, attempt to take, capture, or kill . . . any migratory bird, [or] any part, nest, or egg of any such bird." Pursuant to the canon of *noscitur a sociis* ("it is known by its associates"), when any words "are associated in a context suggesting that the words have something in common, they should be assigned a permissible meaning that makes them similar." Section 2 of the MBTA groups together five verbs—pursue, hunt, take, capture, and kill. Accordingly, the canon of *noscitur a sociis* counsels in favor of reading each verb to have a related meaning.

Of these five verbs, three—pursue, hunt, and capture—unambiguously require an affirmative and purposeful action. . . .

By contrast, the verbs "kill" and "take" may refer to active or passive conduct, depending on the context. When read together with the other active verbs in Section 2 of the MBTA, however, the proper meaning is evident. The operative verbs ("pursue, hunt, take, capture, kill") "are all affirmative acts . . . which are directed immediately and intentionally against a particular animal—not acts or omissions that indirectly and accidentally cause injury to a population of animals." This conclusion is also supported by the U.S. Fish and Wildlife Service's implementing regulations, which define "take" to mean "to pursue, hunt, shoot, wound, kill, trap, capture, or collect" or attempt to do the same. The component actions of "take" involve direct and purposeful actions to reduce animals to human control. As such, they "reinforce[] the dictionary definition, and confirm[] that 'take' does not refer to accidental activity or the unintended results of other conduct." . . .

A number of courts, as well as the prior M-Opinion, have focused on the MBTA's direction that a prohibited act can occur "at any time, by any means, in any manner" to support the conclusion that the statute prohibits any activity that results in the death of a bird, which would necessarily include incidental take. However, this language does not change the nature of those prohibited acts and simply clarifies that activities directed at migratory birds, such as hunting and poaching, are prohibited whenever and wherever they occur and whatever manner is applied, be it a shotgun, a bow, or some other creative approach to deliberately taking birds.

b. Interpreting Strict Liability as Dispositive Conflates Mens Rea and Actus Rea

In reaching a contrary conclusion, Opinion M-37041 assumed that because Section 703 is a strict-liability provision, meaning that no mens rea or criminal intent is required for a violation to have taken place, any act that takes or kills a bird must be covered as long as the act results in the death of a bird. . . .

The prior M-Opinion posited that amendments to the MBTA that imposed mental state requirements for certain specific offenses were only necessary if no mental state is otherwise required. Again, this mixes separate questions—the definition of the prohibited acts and the mens rea, if any. The conclusion that the taking and killing of migratory birds is a strict-liability crime does not answer the separate question of what acts are criminalized under the statute.

The Fifth Circuit explained in *CITGO*:

> [W]e disagree that because misdemeanor MBTA violations are strict liability crimes, a "take" includes acts (or omissions) that indirectly or accidentally kill migratory birds. These and like decisions confuse the mens rea and the actus rea requirements. Strict liability crimes dispense with the first requirement; the government need not prove the defendant had any criminal intent. But a defendant must still commit the act to be liable. Further, criminal law requires that the defendant commit the act voluntarily. WAYNE R. LAFAVE, CRIMINAL LAW § 5.2(e) (5th ed. 2010). "To some extent, then, all crimes of affirmative action require something in the way of a mental element—at least an intention

to make the bodily movement that constitutes that act which the crime requires." *Id.* Here, that act is "to take" which, even without a mens rea, is not something that is done unknowingly or involuntarily. Accordingly, requiring defendants, as an element of an MBTA misdemeanor crime, to take an affirmative action to cause migratory bird deaths is consistent with the imposition of strict liability.

There is no doubt that a hunter who shoots a migratory bird without a permit in the mistaken belief that it is not a migratory bird may be strictly liable for a "taking" under the MBTA because he engaged in an intentional and deliberate act toward the bird. A person whose car accidentally collided with the bird, however, has committed no act "taking" the bird for which he could be held strictly liable. Nor do the owners of electrical lines "take" migratory birds who run into them. These distinctions are inherent in the nature of the word "taking" and reveal the strict liability argument as a non-sequitur. . . .

Thus, there appears to be no explicit basis in the language or the development of the MBTA for concluding that it was intended to be applied to any and all human activity that causes even unintentional deaths of migratory birds.

The use of the words "affirmative" and "purposeful" serve to limit the range of actions prohibited under the MBTA to activities akin to hunting and trapping and exclude more attenuated conduct, such as lawful commercial activity that unintentionally and indirectly results in the death of migratory birds. . . .

d. The MBTA Should Be Interpreted Narrowly to Avoid Constitutional Doubt

The Supreme Court has recognized that "[a] fundamental principle in our legal system is that laws which regulate persons or entities must give fair notice of conduct that is forbidden or required." "No one may be required at peril of life, liberty or property to speculate as to the meaning of penal statutes." . . .

The "scope of liability" under an interpretation of the MBTA that extends criminal liability to all persons who inadvertently or accidentally kill or take migratory birds incidental to another activity is "hard to overstate" and "offers unlimited potential for criminal prosecutions." "The list of birds now protected as 'migratory birds' under the MBTA is a long one, including many of the most numerous and least endangered species one can imagine." Currently, over 1000 species of birds—"nearly every bird species in North America"—are protected by the MBTA. According to the U.S. Fish and Wildlife Service, the top "human-caused threats to birds" are:

- Cats, which kill an estimated 2.4 billion birds per year;
- Collisions with building glass, which kills an estimated 303.5 million birds per year;
- Collisions with vehicles, which kill an estimated 200 million birds per year;
- Poisons, which kill an estimated an estimated 72 million birds per year;
- Collisions with electrical lines, which kill an estimated 25 million birds per year;

- Collisions with communications towers, which kill an estimated 6.5 million birds per year;
- Electrocutions, which kill an estimated 5.4 million birds per year;
- Oil pits, which kill an estimated 750 thousand birds per year; and
- Collisions with wind turbines, which kill an estimated 174 thousand birds per year.

Interpreting the MBTA to apply strict criminal liability to any instance where a migratory bird is killed as a result of these "human-caused threats" would be a clear and understandable rule. It would also turn every American who owns a cat, drives a car, or owns a home—that is to say, the vast majority of Americans—into a potential criminal. Such an interpretation would lead to absurd results, which are to be avoided. . . .

V. CONCLUSION

The text, history, and purpose of the MBTA demonstrate that it is a law limited in relevant part to affirmative and purposeful actions, such as hunting and poaching, that reduce migratory birds and their nests and eggs, by killing or capturing, to human control. . . . Interpreting the MBTA to criminalize incidental takings raises serious due process concerns and is contrary to the fundamental principle that ambiguity in criminal statutes must be resolved in favor of defendants. Based upon the text, history, and purpose of the MBTA, and consistent with decisions in the Courts of Appeals for the Fifth, Eighth, and Ninth circuits, there is an alternative interpretation that avoids these concerns. Thus, based on the foregoing, we conclude that the MBTA's prohibition on pursuing, hunting, taking, capturing, killing, or attempting to do the same applies only to direct and affirmative purposeful actions that reduce migratory birds, their eggs, or their nests, by killing or capturing, to human control.

- Does the Solicitor's Opinion adequately deal with the fact that no mens rea is mentioned in 16 U.S.C. § 707(a)? Does it adequately deal with prohibition against take "any time, by any means, or in any manner"?
- Does the fact that the vast majority of the birds protected under the MBTA are not and have never been game birds undermine the argument that the MBTA was primarily an anti-hunting statute? Does the fact that the vast majority of migratory birds are killed by industry also cut against why strict liability taking is outside the protective purpose of the MBTA?
- By which rationale are you persuaded: that the MBTA's take provisions are strict liability that include acts not intended to take birds, or that they are strict liability for which a volitional act against birds must be proven?

2. Prohibitions Against Trafficking

In addition to the misdemeanor provision, the MBTA contains a two-year felony for take if done "knowingly" and "with intent to sell, barter, or offer to barter such bird" or if a person knowingly sells, offers to sell, barters, or offers to barter any migratory bird regardless of whether the person was responsible for the take. 16 U.S.C. § 707(b)(1). As with the other crimes discussed previously, the question of what the defendant must know regarding the take and the regulated status of the bird is always a question, which the Court of Appeals for the First Circuit answered in an opinion full of bird puns.

United States v. Pitrone
115 F.3d 1 (1st Cir. 1997)

SELYA, Circuit Judge.

This harlequinade requires us to examine a matter of first impression: the degree of scienter needed for a felony conviction under 16 U.S.C. § 707(b) (1994), a part of the Migratory Bird Treaty Act (MBTA). Detecting no reversible error in the district court's rejection of the defendant's proffered jury instruction or in any other respect, we affirm the judgment of conviction.

I. THE STATUTORY SCHEME

. . . This case pirouettes around a provision of the MBTA which criminalizes the taking and selling of migratory birds:

> Whoever, in violation of this subchapter, shall knowingly—
> (1) take by any manner whatsoever any migratory bird with intent
> to sell, offer to sell, barter or offer to barter such bird, or
> (2) sell, offer for sale, barter or offer to barter, any migratory bird
> shall be guilty of a felony and shall be [punished as provided].

16 U.S.C. § 707(b) (1994). Under this proviso, it is unlawful for a taxidermist to receive money or compensation in exchange for a migratory bird other than from a person who originally provided the bird and requested the taxidermy services. *See* 50 C.F.R. § 21.24(c)(1), (2) (1996). In other words, a taxidermist may receive, transport, possess, and mount migratory birds for another person, but he may not sell any migratory birds (mounted or not) which he has taken out of the wild.

II. BACKGROUND . . .

Defendant-appellant William P. Pitrone is a taxidermist by trade and a huntsman by choice. Pitrone frequented sportsmen's shows at which he offered for sale mounted game birds. In early 1993, a browser, Chris Giglio, spotted a protected migratory bird (a Common Eider) among the birds that Pitrone displayed for sale at a show held in Boston. When Giglio began questioning Pitrone about the Eider, Pitrone immediately inquired whether Giglio was "a warden" and, upon receiving an assurance that Giglio was not, freely discussed his operation and produced a business card. Giglio suspected that Pitrone was violating federal law and informed the Interior Department's Fish and Wildlife Service (FWS) of his suspicions.

At the behest of the FWS, Giglio contacted Pitrone by telephone and arranged to visit him at his home in Medford, Massachusetts. Once inside, Giglio observed that Pitrone maintained a large inventory of mounted waterfowl. Pitrone declared that all the mounts were for sale. When Giglio reported this information to the FWS, the agents smelled smoke. They outfitted Giglio with cash and a clandestine body recorder, and sent him back to Pitrone's residence in search of fire. During the ensuing conversation, Pitrone volunteered that he had recently been to Alaska to hunt Harlequin ducks (a protected species of migratory bird) and claimed to have bagged 42 of them. He also said that he sold standing mounts for $50 apiece, flying mounts for $60 apiece, and Harlequin mounts for $75 apiece.

On May 13, 1993, Giglio returned to Pitrone's abode, this time accompanied by an undercover FWS agent. During this meeting (which Giglio surreptitiously recorded), Pitrone crowed that he had sold the 42 Harlequin mounts for $75 each, and he described in colorful language the enthusiasm with which decoy carvers clamored to purchase them. When asked why Harlequins cost more than other mounts, Pitrone replied that the price differential reflected the additional cost he had incurred in travelling to Alaska to hunt them.

By the fall of 1995, the FWS had its ducks in a row and a federal grand jury returned an eight-count indictment. At trial, the prosecution relied, inter alia, on the testimony of Giglio, FWS agent Robert Garabedian, and four of Pitrone's customers. One customer, James Olenick, told Pitrone in advance of the Alaska hunting trip that he would be interested in purchasing a Harlequin duck if Pitrone bagged one. Olenick subsequently bought such a duck from Pitrone (a transaction that formed the basis for the count of conviction). After the FWS investigation surfaced, Pitrone contacted Olenick and suggested that, if approached, he should tell the FWS agents that the duck was merely a "leftover," implying that Pitrone gave it to him as a gift. James Boone, another customer, stated that he had purchased mounts from Pitrone and had provided him with a "wish list" of mounts he sought to purchase. A third customer, Donald Todd, testified that Pitrone contacted him after a sale of two mounts and requested that Todd, if questioned by the FWS, tell the agents that his payment to Pitrone had not been for merchandise received but for services rendered. A fourth customer, George Anzivino, said Pitrone bragged that he had sold all the Harlequin ducks he had shot in Alaska, that the hunt had cost him $2400, and that he had recouped the cost by selling the birds. Later, Pitrone admonished Anzivino not to mention their conversation to anyone.

The trial lasted for six days. In the end, the jury acquitted Pitrone on seven counts, but found him guilty on count 2 (the knowing sale of a Harlequin duck). Following the imposition of sentence, Pitrone sought refuge in this court.

III. ANALYSIS

On appeal, Pitrone grouses about two rulings. One complaint implicates the jury instructions. . . .

A. The Jury Instructions . . .

In this instance, Judge Gertner instructed the jurors that, in order to convict on count 2, they must find that Pitrone acted knowingly. This meant, the judge explained, that "he was conscious and aware of his actions, realized what he was doing and what was happening around him, and did not act because of ignorance, mistake, or accident." The government, she added, did not need "to prove that the defendant knew that his actions were unlawful," but he "must know within the meaning of the statute that he was selling a bird." Pitrone requested a more lenient instruction and objected to the instruction actually given on the ground that it did not require the government to prove that the defendant knew his actions contravened federal law.

On appeal, Pitrone widens the scope of his barrage. While he renews his claim that the government should have been required to prove beyond a reasonable doubt that he knew his conduct was unlawful (and, therefore, that the jury should have been so instructed), he goes on to raise a new and entirely different point: that the instruction afforded the jury was defective because it did not require the government to prove that he knew he was selling a migratory bird. We address the second claim first. . . .

For present purposes, we need look only to the last element of the test. In the district court, there was never any issue about whether a Harlequin duck was a migratory bird (it is) or whether Pitrone, a nimrod of note, knew as much (it strains credulity to suggest he did not). In this regard, the instructions that he proposed are telling; he beseeched the lower court to charge the jury "that the government must prove beyond a reasonable doubt: first, that Mr. Pitrone actually knew that he was selling the migratory birds, as opposed to giving away the birds and charging only for his mounting services." This proposed instruction assumes that Pitrone knew he was selling migratory birds, as demonstrated by the repeated use of the article "the." And, moreover, Pitrone has limned no plausible basis for believing that he lacked such knowledge. . . .

We turn next to the compass of the term "knowingly" as that word is used in MBTA § 707(b). The statute proscribes, inter alia, "knowingly" taking migratory birds with intent to sell them and "knowingly" selling such birds. Since the meaning of the word "knowingly" is neither precisely defined in the statute itself nor immediately obvious in the statutory context, we resort to the legislative history.

For most of its existence, the MBTA contained no scienter requirement whatever; its felony provision, like its misdemeanor provision, 16 U.S.C. § 707(a), imposed strict liability. But in 1985, the Sixth Circuit held that the felony provision—section 707(b)—ran afoul of the Due Process Clause on this account. The following year, Congress amended section 707(b) to meet the . . . court's objection by including an element of scienter, that is, by adding the modifier "knowingly." Congress clearly indicated that, by inserting this word, it sought only to require proof that "the defendant knew (1) that his actions constituted a taking, sale, barter, or offer to sell or barter, as the case may be, and (2) that the item so taken, sold, or bartered was a bird or portion thereof." At the same time, Congress warned that: "It is not intended that proof be required that the defendant knew the taking, sale, barter or offer was a violation of the subchapter, nor that he know the particular bird was listed in the various international treaties implemented by this Act."

Against this backdrop, Pitrone's assertion that the word "knowingly" modifies the phrase "in violation of this subchapter" and, thus, requires proof of specific intent in order to convict, is unconvincing. When it is necessary to go beyond the text in construing criminal statutes, meaning ordinarily should be derived by "draw[ing] upon context, including the statute's purpose and various background legal principles, to determine which states of mind accompany which particular elements of the offense." The appellant's interpretation of the MBTA flouts this precept: it not only involves a forced reading of the text but also flatly contradicts Congress's stated purpose. We are, therefore, disinclined to swallow it. . . .

Pitrone tries to make an end run around the lessons taught by the legislative history, citing a plethora of cases. . . . But this argument overlooks (or, at least, fails to acknowledge) that the element of willful intent and the element of scienter are birds of a very different feather: the cases which the appellant includes in this string citation stand for the proposition that knowledge of the unlawfulness of one's conduct is required when the statutorily prohibited behavior includes an element of willful intent.

Here, the proposition is beside the point. The applicable statute, section 707(b), requires the government to prove a knowing act, but it does not require proof of willfulness. That makes a world of difference. "Knowingly" has a meaning distinct from "willfully" in the lexicon of statutory construction. Thus, courts consistently have rejected arguments—as we do here—which posit that the term "knowingly," standing alone, requires the prosecution to show that the defendant knew his behavior was unlawful, instead interpreting "knowingly"—as we do here—to require no more than that "the defendant know he was engaging in the prohibited conduct." By contrast, "willfully"—a word which is conspicuously absent from section 707(b)—sometimes has been construed to require a showing that the defendant knew his behavior transgressed the law. We decline either to read into a statute a word that Congress purposely omitted, or, on our own initiative, to rewrite Congress's language by ascribing to one word a meaning traditionally reserved for a different word. . . .

Finally, the appellant hawks the importance of the Supreme Court's decision in *Liparota v. United States*, 471 U.S. 419 (1985). There, the Court held that, when prosecuting a person for violation of the statute governing food stamp fraud (which prohibits the "knowing" acquisition of food stamps in an unauthorized manner), the government must prove the defendant knew that his conduct was unauthorized. We think *Liparota* is distinguishable. First, unlike in this case, the legislative history of the provision before the *Liparota* Court shed no light on what Congress meant by the term "knowing violation." Second, the Food Stamp Act covers a variegated array of conduct undertaken by literally millions of people, many of whom are unencumbered by a working knowledge of the regulatory labyrinth. These facts, together with the sheer volume of food stamp transactions which occur, create a high probability of unauthorized, yet innocent, transfers. Thus, the *Liparota* Court sought to prevent the criminalization of a wide range of innocent behavior.

In sharp contrast, the felony provision of the MBTA prohibits conduct that occurs on a much smaller scale and which is much more likely to be committed by individuals familiar with existing protections for migratory birds (e.g., hunters, taxidermists, scientists, or artisans whose trades require knowledge of birds' habits and attributes). Consequently, applying the scienter requirement in the manner described in the legislative history of section 707(b) does not pose the same type of threat that prompted the *Liparota* Court to condition a conviction under the Food Stamp Act upon proof that the defendant knew his behavior was unauthorized by law. . . .

IV. CONCLUSION

We need go no further. From aught that appears, Pitrone was tried fairly and convicted lawfully in a proceeding untainted by reversible error. No more is exigible.

Affirmed.

- Is the sale of taxidermized birds a public welfare crime that is highly regulated enough to create a presumption that the public is aware of the regulation?

Case Study: Extra Money for College

Assume that a college student is selling trinkets through an online auction website to pay for education expenses. Further assume that one of the items the student sold was a taxidermized migratory bird that the student bought at a local garage sale. After the sale, a photo of the sold migratory bird mount remained on the student's seller profile on the auction website. A frequent customer of the auction website and an avid bird enthusiast sees the seller's profile and notices the bird mount that the student had recently sold. Disgusted with the student's action, the bird enthusiast reports the sale to the United States Fish and Wildlife Service. After investigation, a special agent for the United States Fish and Wildlife Service investigates and verifies that the student sold a migratory bird. The special agent talks to the student, who readily confesses to having sold the mount but claims that he had no idea that "those creepy taxidermized birds were protected or that the sale was illegal." Could the student be charged with a felony under the MBTA for selling a migratory bird? If so, should the student be charged?

D. THE BALD AND GOLDEN EAGLE PROTECTION ACT

In 1782, the Continental Congress adopted the bald eagle as the national symbol of the fledgling nation.[21] However, by 1939, the bald eagle was in jeopardy of extinction in the United States. According to the Acting Secretary of the Department of Agriculture, "if the destruction of the eagle and its eggs continues as in the past this bird will wholly disappear from much the larger part of its former range and eventually will become extinct."[22] Consequently, in 1940, Congress enacted the Bald Eagle Protection Act, ch. 278, 54 Stat. 250. The Act provided that

> whoever . . . without being permitted . . . shall willfully take, possess, sell, purchase, barter, offer to sell, purchase or barter, transport, export or import, at any time or in any manner, any bald eagle . . . alive or dead, or any part, nest or egg thereof, shall be fined not more than $500 or imprisoned not more than six months or both.

Ch. 278, 54 Stat. 250, 250-51. The Act exempted any bald eagle or its parts taken prior to 1940 but required the possessor to prove the pre-Act possession if charged

---

[21] Bald Eagle Protection Act, ch. 278, 54 Stat. 250 (recognizing that Continental Congress adopted bald eagle as national symbol in 1782).

[22] H.R. Rep. No. 2104, 76th Cong., 3d Sess. 1 (1940). For an excellent summary of the Bald and Golden Eagle Protection Act, 16 U.S.C. § 668, see Rebecca F. Wisch, *Detailed Discussion of the Bald and Golden Eagle Protection Act*, Animal Law Legal and Historical Center (July 7, 2018), https://www.animallaw.info/article/detailed-discussion-bald-and-golden-eagle-protection-act.

with a violation of the Act. Congress also defined "whoever" to include "associations, partnerships, and corporations." The Act also defined "take" as "pursue, shoot, shoot at, wound, kill, capture, trap, collect, or otherwise willfully molest or disturb." Based on this definition, the Act was construed to contain a "willful" mens rea.

In 1962, Congress amended the Bald Eagle Act to include golden eagles because their "population . . . has declined at such an alarming rate that it is now threatened with extinction." Pub. L. No. 87-884, 76 Stat. 1246. Also, Congress recognized that protecting the golden eagle "will afford greater protection for the bald eagle . . . because the bald eagle is often killed by persons mistaking it for the golden eagle." *Id.* Other than including "golden eagle" into the Act, the Act remained relatively unchanged in terms of its prohibitions, penalties, and definitions.

However, in 1972, Congress felt compelled to amend the Bald and Golden Eagle Protection Act (BGEPA) after learning from an August 3, 1971 article in the *Washington Post* that 500 bald and golden eagles had been killed from helicopters over ranches in Wyoming and Colorado. S. Rep. 92-1159, 4285, 4286 (1972). The pilot of one of the helicopters testified before Congress after he was granted immunity. *Id.* During his testimony, the pilot stated that ranchers paid $80 a day or from $10 to $25 per eagle, and that some hunters "were not paid and just shot the eagles for sport." *Id.* In fact, the pilot confessed that "[w]e had a regular haystack of these eagles when we first started bringing them in. . . . At least one time last November . . . more than 65 dead eagles were piled up . . . and that Wyoming game and fish wardens saw them there but did nothing." *Id.* at 4287. Congress also noted that only 35 convictions had occurred under the BGEPA and that sentencing was light because it averaged "only about $50 per incident." *Id.* at 4288. Accordingly, "[i]n order to prevent, or deter, the taking of eagles in the future, violations should be subjected to greater penalties . . . and the amount of knowledge required to be proved in order to obtain a conviction in this type of case should be reduced." *Id.*

To accomplish these objectives, Congress imposed a stronger penalty for violating the BGEPA. For a first violation, the defendant will be subject to a one-year misdemeanor and fined no more than $5,000. 16 U.S.C. § 668(a). However, Congress expressly provided that each dead eagle constitutes a separate charge, *id.*, and if the defendant is convicted of another violation of the BGEPA, even in the same case, then the penalty for that second violation is a felony with up to two years' imprisonment and up to a $10,000 fine. *Id.*; *United States v. Street*, 257 F.3d 869 (8th Cir. 2001) (holding that felony provision for a second violation applies to second BGEPA count in same indictment as misdemeanor count). In addition to increasing the misdemeanor penalty and adding a two-year felony, Congress removed the "willful" mens rea and replaced it with "knowingly, or in wanton disregard for the consequences." *Id.* Therefore, the BGEPA now provides:

> Whoever . . . shall knowingly or in wanton disregard for the consequences of his act take, possess, sell, purchase, barter, offer to sell, purchase or barter, transport, export or import, at any time or in any manner, any bald eagle . . . or any golden eagle, alive or dead, or any part, nest, or egg thereof of the foregoing eagles . . .

> shall be fined not more than $5,000 or imprisoned not more than
> one year or both: *Provided*, That in the case of a second or
> subsequent conviction for a violation of this section . . . shall be
> fined no more than $10,000 or imprisoned not more than two years
> or both. . . .

Id. Additionally, Congress amended the definition to take to include "poison." Consequently, "take" now includes "pursue, shoot, shot at, poison, wound, kill, capture, trap, collect, molest, or disturb." 16 U.S.C. § 668c.

United States v. Moon Lake Electric Association
45 F. Supp. 2d (D. Colo. 1999)

BABCOCK, District Judge.

On June 9, 1998, the United States of America ("the government") filed an Information charging defendant, Moon Lake Electric Association, Inc. ("Moon Lake"), with seven violations of the Bald and Golden Eagle Protection Act ("the BGEPA"), 16 U.S.C. § 668 (1997), and six violations of the Migratory Bird Treaty Act ("the MBTA"), 16 U.S.C. §§ 703 & 707(a) (1997) (collectively, "the Acts"). in connection with the deaths of 12 Golden Eagles, 4 Ferruginous Hawks, and 1 Great Horned Owl. Moon Lake moves for dismissal of the charges, arguing that the Acts do not apply to unintentional conduct that is not the sort of physical conduct normally exhibited by hunters and poachers. . . . The issues are fully briefed and the parties presented oral argument on November 13, 1998. For the reasons set forth below, I deny Moon Lake's motion.

I. BACKGROUND

I glean the following from the parties' briefs and oral arguments. Moon Lake is a "rural electrical distribution cooperative" that provides electricity to customers in northeastern Utah and northwestern Colorado. At issue in this case is Moon Lake's supply of electricity to an oil field near Rangely, Colorado. The electricity is conveyed by power lines strung across 3,096 power poles. The oil field is located near the White River in an area that is home to several species of protected birds, including Bald Eagles, Golden Eagles, Ferruginous Hawks, and Great Horned Owls. The oil field is mostly treeless, making Moon Lake's power poles preferred locations for perching, roosting, and hunting by birds of prey. The government alleges that Moon Lake has failed to install inexpensive equipment on 2,450 power poles, causing the death or injury of 38 birds of prey during the 29-month period commencing January 1996 and concluding June 1998.

As noted above, the Information charges Moon Lake with causing the deaths of 12 Golden Eagles, 4 Ferruginous Hawks, and 1 Great Horned Owl. Specifically, the Information alleges that Moon Lake did "take and kill" those 17 protected birds. . . .

III. WHETHER DEFENDANT'S ALLEGED CONDUCT CONSTITUTES A VIOLATION OF THE MBTA OR THE BGEPA

Moon Lake argues that the electrocutions, even if they occurred as alleged, do not constitute violations of the MBTA or the BGEPA because the electrocutions were unintentional and not caused by the sort of conduct normally exhibited by hunters and poachers. Moon Lake contends that, in proscribing the taking or killing of protected birds, Congress intended to target only poaching, hunting, trapping, and other "intentionally harmful" acts directed toward protected birds. In contending that its alleged conduct was unintentional, Moon Lake focuses on the mens rea, or mental state, required for conviction. By arguing that Congress intended to punish only conduct normally exhibited by hunters and poachers, Moon Lake directs my attention to the actus reus, or the physical act, required for conviction.

When courts interpret statutes, the initial inquiry focuses on the language of the statute itself. Courts do not, however, read specific statutory language in isolation: courts "'must look to the particular statutory language at issue, as well as the language and design of the statute as a whole.'" If congressional will "'has been expressed in reasonably plain terms, "that language must ordinarily be regarded as conclusive."'" Courts should assume Congress intended the words to be given their ordinary meaning, which may be discovered through the use of dictionaries. While contemporaneous dictionary definitions of words in a statute are relevant, the existence of alternative dictionary definitions may themselves indicate that the statute is ambiguous. Only if statutory language is ambiguous do courts resort to legislative history as an interpretive aid. . . .

The BGEPA states, in relevant part:

> Whoever, within the United States or any place subject to the jurisdiction thereof, without being permitted to do so as provided in this subchapter, shall knowingly, or with wanton disregard for the consequences of his act take, possess, sell, purchase, barter, offer to sell, purchase or barter, transport, export or import, at any time or in any manner, any bald eagle commonly known as the American eagle, or any golden eagle, alive or dead, or any part, nest, or egg thereof of the foregoing eagles, or whoever violates any permit or regulation issued pursuant to this subchapter, shall be fined not more than $5,000 or imprisoned not more than one year or both. . . .

16 U.S.C. § 668. "Take" under the BGEPA "includes also pursue, shoot, shoot at, poison, wound, kill, capture, trap, collect, or molest or disturb. . . ." 16 U.S.C. § 668c.

a. Whether the Acts Proscribe Only "Intentionally Harmful" Conduct

The plain language of the Acts belies Moon Lake's contention that the Acts regulate only "intentionally harmful" conduct. In *United States v. Corrow*, 119 F.3d 796 (10th Cir. 1997), the Tenth Circuit joined the majority of Circuit Courts of Appeal in holding that § 707(a) of the MBTA is strict liability crime. *Id.* at 805 (collecting cases). "Simply stated, then, 'it is not necessary to prove that a defendant violated the Migratory Bird Treaty Act with specific intent or guilty knowledge.'" *Id.* (quoting *United States v. Manning*, 787 F.2d 431, 435 n. 4 (8th Cir. 1986)); see also S. Rep. No. 445, at 16, *reprinted in* 1986 U.S.C.C.A.N. 6113, 6128 ("Nothing in this amendment is intended to alter the 'strict liability' standard for misdemeanor prosecutions under 16 U.S.C. § 707(a), a standard which has been upheld by many Federal court decisions."). Thus, whether Moon Lake intended to cause the deaths of 17 protected birds is irrelevant to its prosecution under § 707(a).

The BGEPA, in contrast to § 707(a) of the MBTA, is not a strict liability crime. The BGEPA applies only to those who act "knowingly, or with wanton disregard for the consequences" of their acts. 16 U.S.C. § 668c; see also S. Rep. No. 92-1159, at 5, reprinted in 1972 U.S.C.C.A.N. 4285, 4289 (the defendant "must be conscious from his knowledge of surrounding circumstances and conditions that conduct will naturally and probably result in injury" to a protected bird). Accordingly, I reject Moon Lake's contention that the MBTA and the BGEPA prohibit only intentionally harmful conduct. Whether Moon Lake took or killed protected birds knowingly, or with wanton disregard for the consequences of its acts, is a question of fact for the jury's determination. . . .

b. Whether the Acts Proscribe Only Physical Conduct Normally Associated with Hunting or Poaching

Moon Lake next argues that the Acts prohibit only physical conduct normally exhibited by hunters or poachers. After reviewing the plain language of the Acts, their respective legislative histories, and their designs as a whole, I disagree.

1. The MBTA

[The court undertakes a lengthy analysis as to why the MBTA is not limited only to intentional conduct to hunt migratory birds.]

2. The BGEPA

Congress modeled the BGEPA after the MBTA. Similar to the MBTA, the BGEPA proscribes taking, possessing, selling, purchasing, bartering, selling, purchasing, bartering, transporting, exporting, importing, pursuing, shooting, shooting at, poisoning, wounding, killing, capturing, trapping, collecting, molesting, and disturbing. 16 U.S.C. §§ 668(a) & 668c. Only taking, shooting, shooting at, capturing, and trapping constitute acts normally associated with hunting and poaching. By prohibiting "poisoning," "killing," "possessing," "molesting," and "disturbing" in addition to the acts normally associated with hunting, the BGEPA, like the MBTA, suggests that Congress intended to regulate conduct beyond the sort engaged in by hunters and poachers. And, as does the MBTA, the BGEPA proscribes taking or killing "at any time or in any manner." 16 U.S.C. § 668(a). I conclude, therefore, that the plain language of the Acts prohibits the alleged conduct of Moon Lake.

The BGEPA's legislative history, although sparse in comparison [to] that of the MBTA, is less equivocal. In 1940, Congress passed, with little debate, "An Act for the Protection of the Bald Eagle." . . .

The 1962 amendments to the act also authorize the Secretary of Interior to permit, when appropriate, the taking of eagles for various reasons, including "for the scientific or exhibition purposes of public museums, scientific societies, and zoological parks, or for the religious purposes of Indian tribes." Congress further amended the BGEPA in 1972, increasing its criminal penalties and reducing the mens rea required for conviction. Notably, during congressional hearings on the 1972 amendments, eagle electrocution was discussed before the Senate Committee on Commerce:

Sen. Spong: What progress is being made in protecting eagles from electrocution in the West?

Mr. Hansen: We are very gratified to report that substantial progress has been made within the past year to correct this situation. Electrocution on power transmission poles in the West has been a low grade but constant source of eagle deaths for many years. The problem in general has been well identified and is now well understood. A great many specific electrocution sites have been located and corrective modifications to the power transmission system have been developed.

Cooperation between land and resource management agencies, both Federal and States, and the various power administrations, has been excellent. We are getting on top of this situation very well.

Mr. Reed: There is a meeting, Mr. Chairman, of the power companies, the National Audubon Society, the National Wildlife Federation, the Colorado Department of Fish and Game, Rural Electrification Administration and the Bureau of Sport Fisheries and Wildlife in September, in Denver, Colo., to again go over some of the emergency work that is being implemented by the power companies to get their stringers further apart. As you know, the great problem is when the bird lands with his wings outspread and takes off with his wings outspread. He can make contact between two wires and that will electrocute him. And, of course, the power line is a place which a bird of prey enjoys sitting on because he has a great view of the countryside and can see his prey. So they are naturally attracted. If the stringers are placed further apart it avoids the problem of accidental electrocution.

  * * *

Sen. Spong: Please explain, with examples, what is gained by deleting "willfully" and substituting for it "knowingly or with negligent disregard for the consequences of his act."

Mr. Smith: Senator Spong, what we are addressing here is the difference between a person "willfully" committing an act and a person "knowingly" causing damage to a fish and wildlife resource. The current legislation under consideration indicates a person must knowingly cause damage to the resource. We feel that this type of language would certainly improve our authority for enforcement. The present language is "willful." We are suggesting the change to "knowingly." Our position would have been much stronger in recent Eagle cases had we had the language that is being proposed. For example, if an individual in placing a poison should kill an eagle we have to prove that this was a wilful action. With the change in language this will indicate to us that if the person using the poison knows that the poison has the capability to kill wildlife, and is using it with negligent disregard for the consequences of his act, it makes our enforcement position much stronger.

Sen. Spong: So it would be easier to gain conviction?

Mr. Smith: Correct, sir.

Sen. Spong: What effect would the change in language have on power companies as far as the electrocution is concerned?

Mr. Smith: I know of no effect that this would have on present operation of power companies, Senator. We will provide a legal opinion to you on the impact of this language change on future transmission line construction.

Bald Eagle Protection Act: Hearings on S.2547, H.R.12186, and H.R.14731 Before the Subcomm. on the Environment of the Senate Comm. on Commerce (hereinafter "Hearings"), 92nd Cong. 22-24, Serial No. 92-63 (June 29, 1972) (statements of Senator William B. Spong, Jr. (Virginia); Henry Hansen, Acting Chief, Division of Management and Enforcement; Nathaniel P. Reed, Assistant Secretary of the Interior for Fish and Wildlife and Parks; and Spencer H. Smith, Director, Bureau of Sport Fisheries and Wildlife) (Congress passed the 1972 BGEPA amendments without floor debate.) The following opinion letter was subsequently submitted for the record:

> . . . [S]ince power lines have a tendency to destroy eagles, such lines erected after the date of enactment should provide such safeguards as are available in order for the power companies to avoid the charge of acting with "negligent disregard for the consequences" of their acts. This obligation would be no more of a burden upon power companies than upon any other person or organization performing operations which had a tendency to destroy wildlife. In every case, reasonable precautions would have to be taken to prevent the killing of eagles.

(Ltr. from C. Brester Chapman, Jr., Associate Solicitor, U.S. Department of the Interior, to Spencer H. Smith of 7/20/92, reprinted in Hearings at 24.) Thus, even if I did not regard the plain language of the BGEPA as conclusive, its legislative history suggests that it proscribes conduct beyond the sort typically exhibited by hunters and poachers.

In summary, I reject Moon Lake's argument that the Acts prohibit only physical conduct normally exhibited by hunters or poachers. After reviewing the plain language of the Acts, their respective legislative histories, and the judicial opinions cited by the parties, I conclude that the Acts must be interpreted as the government suggests. I next address Moon Lake's contention that § 707(a) of the MBTA is unconstitutional as applied under the circumstances of this case. . . .

Accordingly, I ORDER that defendant's motion to dismiss is DENIED.

- Did Congress's reduction of the mens rea standard under the BGEPA to make conviction easier work too well? Congress stated that "wanton disregard for the consequences" means that the defendant "must be conscious from his knowledge of surrounding circumstances and conditions that conduct will naturally and probably result in injury" to a protected bird. S. Rep. No. 92-1159, at 5, reprinted in 1972 U.S.C.C.A.N. 4285, 4289. Assume that in an attempt to reduce reliance on fossil fuels and to help air quality, a power company erects giant, power-generating windmills in Wyoming where bald eagles are known to fly. Suppose that the windmills kill two dozen bald eagles in addition to other raptors that are protected under the MBTA. By erecting these windmills in an area known to be bald eagle habitat, has the power company violated the "wanton disregard for the consequences" standard? Should the United States prosecute companies that are seeking to produce renewable energy, such a wind power, for killing bald and golden eagles?

- Additionally, as to the "knowingly" mens rea, there is a conflict between the courts as to whether the prosecution must show that the defendant knew that the bird that he/she killed was, in fact, an eagle. *Compare United States v. Zak*, 486 F. Supp. 2d 208, 221-22 (D. Mass. 2007) (holding that United States had proven a BGEPA violation even though defendant said he thought the bird was "a big brown hawk"); *and United States v. Allard*, 397 F. Supp. 429, 432 (D. Mont. 1975) ("The effect of the word 'knowingly' is to require that the Government prove that the defendant knew that the feathers were golden eagle feathers, and I think it clear that a conviction would not be had were a person to sell golden eagle feathers thinking them to be turkey feathers.").

- Given the religious and cultural significance that bald and golden eagles have for many Native American tribes, Congress exempted the taking, possession, or transportation of bald and golden eagles and their parts for use in Native American ceremonies. 16 U.S.C. § 668a. However, the exemption applies only if the Secretary has issued a permit for the take or possession of a bald or golden eagle. 50 C.F.R. Ch. I, Part 22. Additionally, if a live take of a bald or golden eagle is not allowed, Congress requires Native Americans to apply for and obtain whole eagles or their parts from the National Eagle Repository in Commerce City, Colorado. The National Eagle Repository receives eagle carcasses, eagle parts, and eagle feathers that are collected from all over the United States. *United States v. Wilgus*, 638 F.3d 1274, 1278-79 (10th Cir. 2011) (explaining the National Eagle Repository system). Native Americans that belong to a federally recognized tribe who seek to obtain an entire eagle or any of its parts must fill out an application with the United States Fish and Wildlife Service and wait for their request to be filled by the National Eagle Repository. The Repository receives far more requests for entire eagle carcasses than it has on hand and, often, it is years behind in filling requests for eagle parts. *Id.* at 1279, 1282-84 (describing limitations on the Repository). Not surprisingly, the BGEPA has produced several, albeit unsuccessful, challenges to the statute based on the Religious Freedom Restoration Act and the Free Exercise Clause of the First Amendment to the United States Constitution. *Wilgus*, 638 F.3d at 1296; *United States v. Oliver*, 255 F.3d 588, 589 (8th Cir. 2001) (per curiam); *Gibson v. Babbitt*, 223 F.3d 1256, 1258-59 (11th Cir. 2000) (per curiam); *United States v. Hugs*, 109 F.3d 1375, 1378 (9th Cir. 1997) (per curiam); *Rupert v. U.S. Fish & Wildlife Serv.*, 957 F.2d 36 (1st Cir. 1992).

E. ANIMAL WELFARE ACT

Animal cruelty laws in the United States are older than the United States itself. For example, around the mid-1600s, the Massachusetts Bay Colony outlawed anyone from exercising "Tirrany or Crueltie towards any bruite Creature which are usuallie kept for man's use."[23] The policy bases for such a law reflect both the intrinsic value of animals as living creates in addition to what cruelty toward animals demonstrates about the humans who abuse them. Indeed, regardless of their "use" to humanity, animals have value simply because they exist. Additionally, many, like eighteenth-century German philosopher Immanuel Kant, have long observed that "[h]e who is cruel to animals becomes hard also in his dealings with men. We can judge the heart of a man by his treatment of animals." Behavioral science concurs with observations like Kant's by finding significant ties between animal cruelty and acts of violence toward humans.[24]

When the prospect of making a profit accompanies exhibitions of animal cruelty, then far too many are willing to participate in the abhorrent spectacle. As one court observed, "Professional dog fighting is both lucrative and well organized." *United States v. Berry*, No. 09-CR-30101-MJR, 2010 WL 1882057, at *3 (S.D. Ill. May 11, 2010). Senator John Kerry of Massachusetts noted that "[d]ogfighting is an interconnected, nationwide, lucrative commercial industry. In addition to high-stake gambling, dogfighters exchange tens if not hundreds of millions of dollars annually on the purchase and the sale of fighting dogs. . . ." *Dogfighting*, 153 Cong. Rec. S10409 (daily ed. July 31, 2007). Cockfighting generates even more revenue because in 2007, "the total value of the gamefowl industry to the economy of the United States [was] a staggering total of $2 billion to $6 billion annually" and producing fighting cocks is the majority use of the game fowl industry. *United States v. Gibert*, 677 F.3d 613, 625 (4th Cir. 2012) (citations and quotations omitted).

The amount of money at issue in these blood sports generates more animal cruelty than just the carnage of the fight itself. Consider Judge Reagan's observations in the Southern District of Illinois during sentencing for a dog fighting violation of the Animal Welfare Act.

United States v. Berry
No. 09-CR-30101-MJR, 2010 WL 1882057 (S.D. Ill. May 11, 2010)

REAGAN, District Judge.

The lives of fighting dogs are not to be envied. These dogs do not lead normal lives, but rather every aspect of the dog's life is carefully calculated to antagonize and thereby increase the aggression level of the dog. Many fighting dogs spend their entire lives without basic nutrition, shelter and healthy socialization with humans and other animals. Rather, fighting dogs spend the majority of their lives in filthy conditions, pinned in small cages or chained up with heavy chains across their neck. As the dog grows, owners will add weights to the chains in order to increase the dog's strength. Generally, the dogs are kept in close proximity to other fighting dogs in order to further antagonize and increase anxiety levels. The dogs are also beaten and goaded on a daily basis in order to raise the dog's tolerance

---

[23] Collections of the Massachusetts Historical Society 232 (Charles C. Little & James Brown eds.).

[24] Cheryl L. Currie, *Animal Cruelty by Children Exposed to Domestic Violence*, 30 Child Abuse & Neglect 425-35 (2006).

towards pain and increase the "fight" within the dog. At the professional level, fighting dogs receive better care in that they are at least fed on a daily basis and their exercise is monitored. However, these dogs are often injected with steroids, and various other legal and illegal drugs to increase the size, strength, and aggressiveness in the dog. If the dog fighters are hobbyists or even street dog fighters, the dogs may receive significantly less care. To increase aggression, these dogs may be starved, have lit cigarettes burned into their coats, or may be beaten with a variety of crude instruments including broken bottles, pipes, or even machetes.

Further adding to the suffering of these animals, some handlers purposefully disfigure their dogs in a crude attempt to give their dog an advantage in a fight. Handlers will cut off a dog's ears and tail, lest another dog latches onto them during a fight.

While tail docking, as it is referred to by the veterinarians, can be done without anesthesia, cropping a dog's ears is a very invasive procedure and requires anesthesia and extensive care for the dog to successfully recover. Both procedures are often done in the dogfighting world with dull, unsterilized objects, such as scissors or knives, without any anesthetic and without proper medical attention, leaving the dog disfigured and at risk for infection or other serious health problems. Dog fighters also employ teeth filing or teeth sharpening as another method to increase their dog's prowess in the ring. . . .

One of the more sadistic training methods utilized by handlers is referred to as the "Catmill or Jenny." Similar to a "carnival horse walker with several beams jetting out from a central rotating pole," the Jenny is used to increase the dog's stamina by attaching the dog to one part of the pole and attaching "bait" to another end of the pole, thus allowing the dog to run continuously for long periods of time. The bait can range anywhere from toys to actual animals, including rabbits, cats, or even small dogs, and in some instances, these "bait" animals are household pets that have been stolen from backyards. After the workout, the dog is usually rewarded with the bait animal and mauls it to death.

Early in the dog's training, it may be forced to participate in a "roll," which is a controlled fight where young dogs are taught to lunge at each other. As the dog's training progresses, the dog is paired against an older dog to ascertain the dog's demeanor and "gameness." Trainers will also steal larger dogs, such as German Shepherds, Doberman Pinchers, or Labs, from neighborhoods to stage "rolls" against their fighting dogs. Often times, these bait dogs are muzzled in an attempt to limit injuries to the fighting dogs, while the trainer encourages the fighting dog to attack. Other times, handlers utilize metal wiring to tie bait animals' legs together in order to prevent the bait from fleeing. During any of these rolls, the trainers attempt to determine the aggressiveness, strength, and willingness to fight present in the dogs. If the dog shows the requisite level of aggression, it is deemed ready to fight, but if the dog exhibits any signs of disinterest in fighting or fear, the dog will most likely be neglected, abandoned or killed.[25]

Given the barbarity of animal-fighting culture, in addition to the criminal enterprises that operate within it, Congress amended the Animal Welfare Act of

[25] Trainers kill underperforming dogs by hanging, electrocution, drowning, and fatal beatings. *United States v. Peace*, 3:07CR274, ECF No. 46 (E.D. Va. Aug. 24, 2007).

1966 in 1976, 2007, 2008, and in 2014 to include and then strengthen the penalties for animal fighting provisions. 7 U.S.C. § 2156. Section 2156 prohibits "any person" who knowingly: (1) sponsors or exhibits an animal in an animal fighting venture; (2) attends an animal fighting venture; (3) causes an individual who is under the age of 16 to attend an animal fighting venture; (4) sells, buys, possesses, trains, transports, delivers, or receives any animal for the purpose of having the animal participate in an animal fighting venture; (5) advertising an animal fighting venture; and (6) selling, buying, transporting, or delivering in interstate commerce a knife, a gaff, or any other sharp instrument designed to be attached to the leg of a bird in an animal fighting venture. 7 U.S.C. § 2156(a)-(e). Congress imposed five-year felonies upon all the foregoing acts except for attending an animal fighting venture and causing someone younger than 16 years old from attending. For those crimes, Congress imposed a one-year misdemeanor and a three-year felony respectively. 18 U.S.C. § 49. However, Congress also included a provision that exempts "fighting ventures involving live birds" from being a federal crime if the state in which the fighting venture occurs allows it under state law. 7 U.S.C. § 2156(a)(3). Congress did not include a similar exemption for dog fighting.

Congress defined the term "animal fighting venture" to mean "any event, in or affecting interstate or foreign commerce, that involves a fight conducted or to be conducted between at least 2 animals for purposes of sport, wagering, or entertainment, except that the term 'animal fighting venture' shall not be deemed to include any activity the primary purpose of which involves the use of one or more animals in hunting another animal." 7 U.S.C. § 2156(g)(1). Thus, in order to prove the element of an "animal fighting venture," the prosecution must show that the event affected interstate commerce. Notice how the Court of Appeals for the Fourth Circuit addressed this element in a cockfighting case out of South Carolina.

United States v. Gibert
677 F.3d 613 (4th Cir. 2012)

BARBARA MILANO KEENAN, Circuit Judge:
. . . Jeffrey Brian Gibert and certain other defendants (collectively, Gibert) were indicted for their roles in organizing, operating, and participating in "gamefowl derbies," otherwise known as "cockfighting." Gibert entered a conditional guilty plea to the charge of conspiring to violate 7 U.S.C. § 2156 (the animal fighting statute), which prohibits, among other things, "sponsor[ing] or exhibit[ing] an animal in an animal fighting venture." The term "animal fighting venture" is defined in the statute, in relevant part, as "any event, in or affecting interstate or foreign commerce, that involves a fight conducted or to be conducted between at least 2 animals for purposes of sport, wagering, or entertainment." 7 U.S.C. § 2156(g)(1).

In his plea agreement, Gibert reserved the right to challenge the constitutionality of the animal fighting statute. . . . Gibert contends that animal fighting is inherently an intrastate activity that has no substantial [e]ffect on interstate commerce and, thus, is a matter reserved for regulation by the states, rather than by the federal government. He also advances an argument regarding the scienter requirement of the animal fighting statute, contending that the government was required to prove that he had knowledge that the animal fighting venture "was in or affected interstate commerce." Upon our review of the parties' arguments, we hold that the animal fighting statute is a legitimate exercise of Congress' power under the Commerce Clause. We also hold that the statute does not require the government to prove the defendants' knowledge regarding the particular venture's nexus to interstate commerce. Accordingly, we affirm Gibert's convictions.

I.

In November 2009, a federal grand jury returned an indictment against Gibert, alleging one count of participating in a conspiracy to violate the Animal Welfare Act, and one count of participating in, and/or aiding and abetting, an unlawful animal fighting venture. The indictment alleged that Gibert and his co-defendants each entered one or more roosters in one or more "cockfighting derbies" held in Swansea, South Carolina in July 2008 and April 2009.

The indictment described a "cockfighting derby" as a series of fights between roosters, in which the owner of the rooster with the most victories in a series of fights wins a monetary "purse," which is comprised of the derby participants' entry fees minus the amount retained by the derby organizers. Before the fights, the roosters are equipped with a knife, gaff, or other sharp instrument that is affixed to the roosters' legs. As stated in the indictment, "[t]he fight is ended when one rooster is dead or refuses to continue to fight. If not killed during the fight, the losing rooster is typically killed after the fight." Spectators not otherwise involved in the fights pay an admission fee to attend the derbies, and gambling routinely occurs between the spectators and the owners of the roosters. Paraphernalia, such as gaffs, tie cords, cages, training equipment, medication, and veterinary supplies, some of which are manufactured in or transported from other states, are sold before or during the fights.

. . . Gibert entered a conditional guilty plea to Count I of the indictment alleging a conspiracy to violate the animal fighting statute. In his written plea agreement, Gibert stipulated that the government could satisfy its burden of proving the elements of 7 U.S.C. § 2156, including that he: "(A) [ ] knowingly sponsored or exhibited; (B) [a]n animal; (C) [i]n an event that was in or affecting interstate commerce and that involved a fight between at least two animals for the purpose of sport, wagering or entertainment; and (D) [w]hich event also violated State Law."[26] Pursuant to the plea agreement . . . Gibert reserved the right to challenge on appeal Congress' powers under the Commerce Clause to enact the animal fighting statute, as well as the district court's ruling that the government need not establish as an element of the offense Gibert's knowledge that the cockfighting derbies affected interstate commerce.

The district court accepted Gibert's plea and sentenced him to a three-year term of probation and a monetary fine. Gibert appeals his conviction. . . .

---

[26] The element of proving that the cockfighting operation violated state law applies here because of the exemption from federal prosecution for cockfighting that Congress provided in the Animal Welfare Act where state law allows cockfighting. 7 U.S.C. § 2156(a)(3).

II. . . .

Because congressional findings of fact are an important consideration in determining whether a federal statute may survive a challenge under the Commerce Clause, we begin our analysis by discussing the legislative history of the animal fighting statute. . . .

In enacting the animal fighting statute, Congress initially focused its concern on dogfighting. In the House Report discussing the Amendments, the House Committee on Agriculture (the Committee) observed the rise of dogfighting and its connection to interstate commerce:

> [Dogfighting], a minor problem prior to World War II, has unfortunately grown and prospered to the point that Regional Conventions are held which attract fighting dogs and 'dog fanciers' from numerous states. They frequently are advertised in [dogfighting] magazines of nationwide circulation. In addition [to] the 'sporting element' of these enterprises, there apparently has grown up also a sort of traveling circus in which vans will travel from state to state and set up for brief periods offering patrons the opportunity to witness and gamble upon a series of dog fights and to indulge at the same time many questionable and criminal activities.

Accordingly, the Committee made factual findings that "animals and activities which are regulated under this Act are either in interstate or foreign commerce or substantially affect such commerce or the free and unburdened flow thereof, and that regulation of animals and activities as provided in this Act is necessary to prevent and eliminate burden[s] upon such commerce, to effectively regulate such commerce, to protect the human values of this great Nation from the subversion of dehumanizing activities, and to carry out the objectives of the Act."

The animal fighting statute has been amended and expanded since its passage in 1976 to reflect the increasing national consensus against this activity. In strengthening the animal fighting prohibition, members of Congress have emphasized the nexus between animal fighting and interstate commerce. . . .

The current version of the animal fighting statute, under which Gibert was indicted and convicted, was amended in 2008. In its present form, the animal fighting statute provides in relevant part that "it shall be unlawful for any person to knowingly sponsor or exhibit an animal in an animal fighting venture." 7 U.S.C. § 2156(a)(1). The statute sets forth the following definition of an "animal fighting venture":

> [T]he term 'animal fighting venture' means any event, in or affecting interstate or foreign commerce, that involves a fight conducted or to be conducted between at least 2 animals for purposes of sport, wagering, or entertainment. . . .

7 U.S.C. § 2156(g)(1). Thus, as this definition plainly illustrates, a conviction for violating the animal fighting statute requires (a) that the activity be in or affect interstate or foreign commerce, and (b) be for purposes of sport, wagering, or entertainment. . . .

Thus, to convict a defendant of violating the animal fighting statute, the government must allege and prove that the individual participated in an animal fighting event that had a connection with or effect on interstate or foreign commerce. This express requirement in the animal fighting statute of a connection to, or effect on, interstate commerce thus satisfies the Supreme Court's concern . . . that the statute at issue have a nexus to interstate commerce as an element of the offense.

[T]here are ample congressional findings in the statute and its legislative history that support the judgment that animal fighting has a substantial effect on interstate commerce. As we have noted, the AWA's statement of policy declares that the animals regulated under the Act "are either in interstate or foreign commerce or substantially affect such commerce or the free flow thereof." Additionally, the House Committee Report pertaining to the original enactment of the animal fighting prohibition in 1976 discussed the growing rise of commercial animal fighting and its strong connection to interstate commerce. . . .

[T]he link between animal fighting ventures and its effect on interstate commerce is not attenuated. Rather, the link is direct, because animal fighting ventures are inherently commercial enterprises that often involve substantial interstate activity. Thus, in contrast to the statute at issue in *Lopez*, there is no need to "pile inference upon inference" in order to establish the link between animal fighting and interstate commerce. Cf. 514 U.S. at 567, 115 S. Ct. 1624.

In sum, . . . the animal fighting statute was a legitimate exercise of Congress' power under the Commerce Clause.

III.

We next consider Gibert's argument that the district court erred in its construction of the scienter element of the animal fighting statute. As stated above, the animal fighting statute provides, in relevant part, that "it shall be unlawful for any person to knowingly sponsor or exhibit an animal in an animal fighting venture." 7 U.S.C. § 2156(a)(1). An "animal fighting venture" is defined as "any event, in or affecting interstate or foreign commerce, that involves a fight conducted or to be conducted between at least 2 animals for purposes of sport, wagering, or entertainment. . . ." 7 U.S.C. § 2156(g)(1). . . .

We find no merit in Gibert's scienter argument, because Gibert's conviction for violating the animal fighting statute required proof of knowledge of the stated factual elements of the offense, but did not require proof of knowledge that the activity was "in or affected interstate commerce." *See, e.g., United States v. Langley*, 62 F.3d 602, 605–06 (4th Cir. 1995) (conviction under felon-in-possession statute, 18 U.S.C. § 922(g)(1), does not require knowledge of firearm's interstate nexus as an element of the offense); *United States v. Darby*, 37 F.3d 1059, 1067 (4th Cir. 1994) (conviction for transmitting threatening interstate communications, 18 U.S.C. § 875(c), does not require proof of knowledge that threatening telephone call was an interstate call); *United States v. Squires*, 581 F.2d 408, 410 (4th Cir. 1978) (conviction under National Stolen Property Act, 18 U.S.C. § 2314, does not require proof of knowledge of interstate nature of transportation of counterfeit securities).

As these decisions plainly illustrate, "criminal statutes based on the government's interest in regulating interstate commerce do not generally require that an offender have knowledge of the interstate nexus of his actions." Accordingly, we agree with the district court that the animal fighting statute does not require that the government establish a defendant's knowledge that the animal fighting venture was in or affecting interstate commerce. . . .

AFFIRMED.

- What must the prosecution do to prove that an animal fighting venture affected interstate commerce?
- What type of evidence would you want to use to meet this element?
- The *Gibert* court held that the prosecution need not prove that the defendant knew that the animal fighting venture affected interstate commerce. If proof of knowledge is not required, why is the effect on interstate commerce an element of the crime?
- The defendant in *Gibert* received a sentence of probation and a fine for his cockfighting enterprise. However, other courts have not been so lenient, especially where the prosecution establishes evidence of the cruelty of the operation. *United States v. Hargrove*, 701 F.3d 156, 164-65 (4th Cir. 2012) (affirming five-year sentence for defendant's horrific treatment of dogs in his fighting operation even though the United States Sentencing Guidelines recommended a sentence of zero to six months for defendant's actions).
- In addition to the Animal Welfare Act's prohibitions on dog and cockfighting, Congress has also enacted legislation to combat the production and distribution of "crush videos." A crush video:

  > (1) depicts actual conduct in which 1 or more living non-human mammals, birds, reptiles, or amphibians is intentionally crushed, burned, drowned, suffocated, impaled, or otherwise subjected to serious bodily injury; and
  > (2) is obscene.

  18 U.S.C. § 48(a). The Court of Appeals for the Fifth Circuit clinically but horrifically described a crush video for which a defendant had been indicted in the Southern District of Texas:

  > Generally, the videos portray [the defendant] binding animals (a kitten, a puppy, and a rooster), sticking the heels of her shoes into them, chopping off their limbs with a cleaver, removing their innards, ripping off their heads, and urinating on them. [The defendant] is scantily clad and talks to both the animals and the camera, making panting noises and using phrases such as "you like that?" and "now that's how you fu* * a pu*** real good."

  United States v. Richards, 755 F.3d 269, 272 (5th Cir. 2014). Congress imposed criminal sanctions for "any person" who "knowing create[s]" such a video if "the person intends or has reason to know that the animal crush video will" move in interstate commerce. 18 U.S.C. § 48(b)(1). Additionally, Congress prohibited any person from "knowingly" selling, marketing, advertising, exchanging, or distributing any crush video in foreign or interstate commerce. 18 U.S.C. § 48(b)(2). Criminal penalties include up to seven years in prison.

CHAPTER 9

CONVENTIONAL CRIMINAL STATUTES

Randy owns an e-waste recycling company called "E-Recy" in Miami, Florida. Businesses and government entities pay E-Recy to come and pick up old computers, cell phones, and other electronic equipment so that these items can be recycled instead of being thrown into the landfill and causing environmental harm. E-Recy's website and the brochures that it mails to prospective clients state that all of the e-waste that E-Recy receives is recycled domestically in an environmentally friendly manner according to the law. The website and brochures state that using E-Recy is a great way to help the environment. Many businesses like E-Recy's business model and prices, which, in turn, provides E-Recy plenty of e-waste to recycle as well as good profits. However, E-Recy is doing so well because, instead of domestically recycling e-waste, it loads most of it into shipping containers, marks them as "computer monitors for schools," and sends them overseas to China where criminal cartels pay for the e-waste so that the precious metals can be extracted using a crude, open burning process that pollutes the environment significantly. For the e-waste that is not sent overseas, Randy has his workers break it into small pieces so that it can be mixed into municipal waste and disposed of at the local landfill. Much of the e-waste that E-Recy handles is hazardous for toxicity. When the state hazardous waste regulators ask Randy what he does with his hazardous e-waste, he tells them that his workers use an elaborate process that recycles the e-waste without harming the environment. After visiting with the hazardous waste regulators, Randy tells his workers that no one can talk to the regulators upon the pain of being fired, and if the regulators force the workers to talk, then they had better not tell the truth or else they will not have a job.

From what you have already studied in this course, you have undoubtedly identified the potential RCRA violations in which Randy is engaged. However, RCRA, like many of the environmental crimes previously discussed, is complex and, therefore, creates challenges to proving a criminal violation beyond a reasonable doubt. Consequently, prosecutors often search for other charges that provide a sufficient penalty to address wrongdoing like Randy's but do not implicate the complexity of RCRA's provisions. These "other charges" may be brought just in case the RCRA charges fail or in lieu of RCRA to avoid its complexity all together. When in search of such a charge, prosecutors typically look to the following five conventional statutes, which contain a level of generality that make them applicable across all types of factual scenarios: (1) mail fraud, 18 U.S.C. § 1341; (2) wire fraud, 18 U.S.C. § 1343; (3) false statements, 18 U.S.C. § 1001; (4) obstruction of justice, 18 U.S.C. § 1519; and (5) smuggling, 18 U.S.C. § 554. Each statute is discussed below, but mail fraud and wire fraud will be discussed together because of their similarity. As you study each statute, consider whether Randy has violated any of them.

A. MAIL AND WIRE FRAUD

Congress has long been concerned with fraudulent schemes. In fact, the mail fraud statute was originally enacted in 1872 and proscribed "using the mails to initiate correspondence in furtherance of 'any scheme or artifice to defraud.'" *McNally v. United States*, 483 U.S. 350, 356 (1987). The sponsor of the mail fraud bill said that it was needed "to prevent the frauds which are mostly gotten up in the large cities . . . by thieves, forgers, and rapscallions generally, for the purpose of deceiving and fleecing the innocent people in the country." *Id.* (quoting Cong. Globe, 41st Cong., 3d Sess., 35 (1870) (remarks of Rep. Farnsworth)). Following amendments in 2008, the mail fraud statute now provides:

> Whoever, having devised or intending to devise any scheme or artifice to defraud, or for obtaining money or property by means of false or fraudulent pretenses, representations, or promises . . . places in any post office or authorized depository for mail matter, any matter or thing whatever to be sent or delivered by the Postal Service, or deposits or causes to be deposited any matter or thing whatever to be sent or delivered by any private or commercial interstate carrier, or takes or receives therefrom, any such matter or thing, or knowingly causes to be delivered by mail or such carrier according to the direction thereon, or at the place at which it is directed to be delivered by the person to whom it is addressed, any such matter or thing, shall be fined under this title or imprisoned not more than 20 years, or both.

18 U.S.C. § 1341. Other than the above-referenced statements for the mail fraud statute in the 1870s, its legislative history is scant, which is why the law surrounding it has largely been developed through the courts.[1]

As communications technologies became more modern and ubiquitous, many criminal enterprises started using interstate wire communications to defraud the citizenry. Consequently, in 1952, Congress enacted the wire fraud statute by patterning it after the mail fraud statute. 18 U.S.C. § 1343. S. Comm. on Interstate and Foreign Commerce, *Communications Act Amendments*, S. Rep. No. 85-44 at 14 (1951) (stating that wire fraud statute was "a parallel provision now in the law for fraud by mail"). Not surprisingly, the text of the wire fraud statutes provides:

---

[1] Donald V. Morano, *The Mail Fraud Statute: A Procrustean Bed*, 14 J. Marshall L. Rev. 45, 45-47 (1980).

> Whoever, having devised or intending to devise any scheme or artifice to defraud, or for obtaining money or property by means of false or fraudulent pretenses, representations, or promises, transmits or causes to be transmitted by means of wire, radio, or television communication in interstate or foreign commerce, any writings, signs, signals, pictures, or sounds for the purpose of executing such scheme or artifice, shall be fined under this title or imprisoned not more than 20 years, or both.

18 U.S.C. § 1343. Thus, instead of trying to create legislation to address every type of scheme to defraud that humanity is able to concoct, Congress simply required the prosecution to prove that the defendant had a scheme to defraud and that he/she used the mail or wire communications in furtherance of the scheme.

United States v. Sawyer
85 F.3d 713 (1st Cir. 1996)

STAHL, Circuit Judge.

Appellant F. William Sawyer appeals his convictions for mail and wire fraud, interstate travel to commit bribery, and conspiracy to commit those offenses. The district court imposed a $10,000 fine, and sentenced him to imprisonment for twelve months and one day. In this appeal, Sawyer claims that the district court erred in its jury instructions and in evidentiary rulings, and that the evidence was insufficient to establish his guilt beyond a reasonable doubt. For the reasons that follow, we vacate the convictions and remand for further proceedings.

I.

FACTS . . .

During the indictment period, 1986 to March 1993, the John Hancock Mutual Life Insurance Company ("Hancock") employed the defendant-appellant, F. William Sawyer, as a senior lobbyist within its Government Relations Department. As the largest life insurance company in Massachusetts, Hancock had a continuing and abiding interest in the state's insurance laws. Sawyer's job was to lobby the Massachusetts Legislature on Hancock's behalf. . . .

A principal focus of Sawyer's lobbying activities was the Legislature's Joint Insurance Committee ("Insurance Committee"), composed of state representatives and senators. . . .

During the indictment period, Sawyer focused his lobbying activities on the house members of the Insurance Committee, some of whom took action that directly or indirectly affected Hancock's interests. Representative Francis H. Woodward was the House Chair of the Insurance Committee from 1986 to 1990. Research analyst Smith identified Sawyer as the lobbyist he saw most often with Representative Woodward during Woodward's tenure as the Committee's House Chair. During this time, the Insurance Committee never rejected Woodward's recommendations on bills affecting the life insurance industry and Woodward "carried" most of the bills sought by the industry. Representative Frank Emilio, a member from 1986 to 1990, sponsored a September 1990 bill on behalf of Hancock. Representative John F. Cox sponsored bills that Hancock supported in November

1990 and December 1991. In addition, Representatives Walsh, Mara, and Driscoll sponsored legislation sought by the life insurance industry.

"Legislative Reports" issued by the Hancock Government Relations Department to senior Hancock officers, and signed by Sawyer, outlined specific lobbying efforts and proceedings in the Massachusetts Legislature pertinent to Hancock's interests. In July 1990, Sawyer wrote a memorandum to Hancock's Management Committee summarizing the successful efforts of Hancock lobbyists, including himself, in excluding Hancock from a bill that would have subjected it to a $100-million tax liability. In a September 1990 memorandum to the Management Committee, Sawyer referred to a 1990 bill, filed by Representative Emilio, that allowed Hancock to assess and report its real estate advantageously. A November 1990 letter from Ralph F. Scott, Hancock's Assistant Legislative Counsel, to Representative Cox indicated that Sawyer and Scott planned to work with Cox in obtaining favorable action on a specific bill that he had sponsored for Hancock.

During the indictment period, Sawyer paid for numerous meals, rounds of golf, and other entertainment for and with Massachusetts legislators, including many members of the Insurance Committee. Although Sawyer initially paid for most of these activities himself, they were treated as business expenses and reimbursed by Hancock (hereinafter "expenditures"). In accordance with Hancock's procedures, Sawyer would complete monthly expense vouchers, attaching receipts and a handwritten calendar that identified the recipients of the expenses. Sawyer's supervisor, Raeburn B. Hathaway, the head of Hancock's Government Relations Department, reviewed Sawyer's expense vouchers and approved them for reimbursement. Hathaway's secretary would then detach the detailed calendars from the vouchers, keeping the calendars within the Government Relations Department, and forward the voucher, alone, to the accounting department for payment.

Analysis of Sawyer's expense vouchers and calendars during the indictment period revealed that the top three recipients of his expenditures were: Representative Woodward, who received more than $8,000 worth of expenditures during his tenure as Insurance Committee House Chair; Robert Howarth, an Insurance Committee member from 1986 to 1992 (over $3,000); and Representative Emilio (over $2,500). After these three legislators left office, Sawyer, on behalf of Hancock, expended practically nothing on entertaining them (Woodward, $0; Howarth, $8.33; and Emilio, $85.65).

Specifically, Sawyer's expenditures included thousands of dollars for golf—in and out of state—with various Massachusetts legislators. . . . Sawyer also hosted dinners for legislators and their families. In September 1992, Sawyer provided Representative Mara and his wife tickets for a show in Hancock's private box at the Wang Center and ordered an accompanying dinner.

The apparent catalyst for this prosecution was a December 1992 trip to Puerto Rico where Sawyer, other lobbyists, and a group of legislators, including Representative Mara, travelled for a legislative conference. The group did not stay at the conference site, but instead went to a different resort where Sawyer paid for many of the legislators' meals, transportation, and golf. Hancock reimbursed Sawyer for some $4,000 of entertainment expenses from the Puerto Rican trip.

Both Sawyer and his supervisor, Hathaway, had reason to believe that these expenditures could or did violate certain state laws. In his office, Sawyer kept internal Hancock memoranda, newspaper articles, and opinions of the Massachusetts Ethics Commission, all explaining or reporting on Massachusetts ethics-in-lobbying. While some of the documents varied in their interpretations, they nonetheless advised on compliance with laws regarding gratuities, gifts, and lobbying expenditures.

In April 1993, a reporter from the Boston Globe newspaper queried Richard Bevilacqua, Hancock's Director of Employee and Customer Communications, about Sawyer's entertainment of legislators during the 1992 Puerto Rico trip and about Hancock's legislative agenda during that period. Bevilacqua, in turn, asked Sawyer about the trip, and Sawyer opined, "it's difficult to take anyone out to lunch or dinner these days without going over [the] amount [permitted by law]." This set of events prompted Hancock to begin an internal investigation into Sawyer's legislative expenditures. Bruce A. Skrine, vice president, corporate counsel and secretary for Hancock, asked Sawyer for his expense records. Contemporaneous with Sawyer's production of the records, Sawyer told Skrine that the expenses were "consistent with the way . . . things were done on Beacon Hill." Sawyer also told Skrine that his reason for making the expenditures was "to get to know" the legislators and to develop "a certain relationship so that you could turn to them"; he further indicated that he made these expenditures to "build and maintain relationships," gain "access to legislators," and get legislators to "return his calls as a result of [the expenditures]."

Sawyer caused the mailing of items related to the expenditures on legislators, including golf bills, reimbursement requests, and credit card bills. Sawyer also caused the making of interstate telephone calls to arrange for some of the entertainment.

Following a nine-day trial, the jury convicted Sawyer of fifteen counts of mail fraud, nine counts of wire fraud, eight counts of interstate travel to commit bribery, and one count of conspiracy. The jury acquitted Sawyer of two additional mail fraud counts.

II.

MAIL AND WIRE FRAUD COUNTS

The government charged that Sawyer and his unindicted co-conspirator—his Hancock supervisor, Hathaway—engaged in a scheme to deprive the Commonwealth of Massachusetts and its citizens of the right to the honest services of their state legislators, and used the mails and interstate telephone wires in furtherance of the scheme, in violation of 18 U.S.C. §§ 1341, and 1343.

Sawyer contends that his convictions impermissibly involve the federal government in setting standards of good government for local and state officials. He argues that this case is exemplary of the "dangers of standardless federal criminal enforcement and unbridled prosecutorial discretion long-recognized under the mail fraud statute." We have already considered and rejected these arguments, however. Congress may protect the integrity of the interstate mails and wires by forbidding their use in furtherance of schemes to defraud a state and its citizens, whether or not it can forbid the scheme itself.

Sawyer also contends that the government has failed to establish that he committed "honest services" mail and wire fraud ("honest services fraud") within the meaning of the statutes. To explain our resolution of this issue, we provide a brief overview of the law of honest services fraud. The ultimate issue is whether or not the "scheme" presented at trial actually targeted the Massachusetts' citizens' right to "honest services" within the meaning of the mail fraud statute.

To prove mail and wire fraud, the government must prove, beyond a reasonable doubt: (1) the defendant's knowing and willing participation in a scheme or artifice to defraud with the specific intent to defraud, and (2) the use of the mails or interstate wire communications in furtherance of the scheme.[2] Because the relevant language in both the mail and wire fraud statutes is the same, we analyze both offenses together for the purposes of this case and, for simplicity, we refer only to mail fraud.

Traditionally, the mail fraud statute reached schemes that deprived the fraud victim of property or some other item of economic value. Some courts later expanded the scope of the statutes to encompass schemes intended to defraud citizens of their intangible, non-property right to the honest services of their public officials. Those courts rationalized that a public official "acts as 'trustee for the citizens and the State . . . and thus owes the normal fiduciary duties of a trustee, e.g., honesty and loyalty' to them."

In 1987, the United States Supreme Court held, contrary to every circuit court that had decided the issue, that the mail fraud statute did not prohibit schemes to defraud citizens of their intangible, non-property right to honest and impartial government. *McNally v. United States*, 483 U.S. 350, 359 (1987). Congress quickly reacted to the *McNally* decision by enacting 18 U.S.C. § 1346, which provides that, for the purposes of, inter alia, the mail and wire fraud statutes, "the term 'scheme or artifice to defraud' includes a scheme or artifice to deprive another of the intangible right of honest services." We have recognized that § 1346 was intended to overturn *McNally* and reinstate the reasoning of pre-*McNally* case law holding that the mail fraud statute reached schemes to defraud individuals of the intangible right to honest services of government officials. . . .

A. Scheme to Defraud

Here, the government did not prosecute Sawyer on the theory that he, as a lobbyist, directly owed a duty of honest services to the Commonwealth or its citizens. Rather, the government sought to prove that Sawyer engaged in conduct intended to cause state legislators to violate their duty to the public. The government sought to establish this scheme by proving that Sawyer intentionally violated, or caused members of the legislature to violate, two Massachusetts statutes.

Briefly, these two Massachusetts statutes . . . are: (1) the "gift" statute, which prohibits—under threat of civil penalties—a "legislative agent" from offering or

---

[2] [Fn. 6] The use of the mails or wires to further the fraudulent scheme need only be "incidental." *United States v. Grandmaison*, 77 F.3d 555, 566 (1st Cir. 1996). Moreover, the "[d]efendant[ ] need not personally use the [mails or] wires as long as such use was a reasonably foreseeable part of the scheme in which [he] participated." *United States v. Boots*, 80 F.3d 580, 585 n. 8 (1st Cir. 1996).

giving to a public official (or an official's acceptance of) "gifts" aggregating $100 or more per year; and (2) the "gratuity" statute, which prohibits—under threat of civil and criminal penalties—anyone from giving to a legislator (or a legislator from soliciting or accepting) anything of "substantial value . . . for or because of any official act performed or to be performed" by that person. Through the violation of these laws, the government contended, Sawyer stole the honest services of the legislators. . . .

[T]he government alleges that the defendant violated federal laws, mail fraud and wire fraud, by intentionally violating or causing Massachusetts legislators to violate certain state laws. Accordingly, in order to prove the first element of the mail fraud and/or wire fraud, that the defendant devised a scheme to defraud, the government must prove beyond a reasonable doubt that the defendant intentionally violated or caused members of the Massachusetts Legislature to violate at least one of the following two state laws. . . .

The jury was permitted to find the first element of mail and wire fraud, the scheme to defraud, upon proof that either the gift statute or the gratuity statute was violated. The gift statute as charged, however, was a legally insufficient basis upon which to find the scheme to defraud. Although the gratuity statute was properly instructed in terms of honest services mail fraud, we cannot tell if the convictions were based on that statute or the insufficiently charged gift statute. When a jury has been presented with several bases for conviction, one of which is legally erroneous, and it is impossible to tell which ground the jury convicted upon, the conviction cannot stand. . . .

In view of the possibility that the government may choose to retry this case, we think it is useful to add a cautionary word. . . .

B. Intent to Deceive

Whether or not a new trial on the mail and wire fraud counts is allowable requires us to reach Sawyer's additional contention that the evidence was insufficient to establish his intent to deceive the public. To this end, Sawyer contends that because the government did not establish that he had a duty to disclose his illegal gifts and gratuities to the public, his intent to deceive the public had to be shown through affirmative acts of deception, which he claims are absent here.

To establish mail fraud—in cases involving honest services fraud and otherwise—the alleged scheme must involve deception in the deprivation of money, property, or the right to honest services. While a misrepresentation of fact is not required to establish mail fraud, a demonstrated intent to deceive is required.

When the conduct of a government official is involved, "the affirmative duty to disclose material information arises out of [the] official's fiduciary relationship to [the public]." Thus, an official's intentional violation of the duty to disclose provides the requisite "deceit."

Here, although the issue has not been clearly presented by the parties, it appears that the requisite intent to deceive could have been shown either through Sawyer's own acts of deception toward the public with respect to the gift/gratuity statute violations, or through his efforts to ensure that the legislators deceived the public with respect to the violations. The latter requires evidence only that Sawyer intended to cause the legislators intentionally to fail to disclose material information about the violations, although evidence that he intended the legislators to affirmatively misrepresent themselves in this regard would also suffice. At bottom, the evidence must be sufficient to establish Sawyer's intent that, in the end, the public be deceived with respect to his unlawful gifts and gratuities.

Therefore, we must determine if the admissible evidence, viewed in light most favorable to the jury's verdict, is sufficient for a rational jury to find that Sawyer intended that the public be deceived. . . . [T]he specific intent to deceive may be proven (and usually is) by indirect and circumstantial evidence.

At first blush, it may appear that bribery of a public official necessarily incorporates a finding that the offender intended to "trick" or "deceive" the public into thinking that the official was acting independently when, in fact, the official was actually motivated by the bribe. While we have little doubt that bribes are usually given in secrecy, bribery and gratuity statutes generally, as here, do not require a separate element of deception. Ostensibly, a person could offer an illegal bribe to a public official and not be concerned with its secrecy. Thus, the evidence presented must permit a finding that Sawyer not only gave the unlawful gifts or gratuities with the intent to deprive the public of honest services, but that he also intended to deceive the public about that conduct.

Here, the government presented evidence that Sawyer gave the unlawful gifts and gratuities during the seven years of the indictment period until the Boston Globe exposed the practice in May 1993. Much of his entertainment of lobbyists took place out-of-state—usually at industry and legislative conferences—where members of the Massachusetts citizenry generally would not observe the questionable activities. Unlike his acts of "non-public" entertainment, Sawyer ensured compliance with state ethical standards for a 1993 Boston Marathon brunch, potentially a high-profile event. In his office, Sawyer kept newspaper articles reporting legislators' activities with lobbyists, and in particular, the ethical ramifications of such relationships. In one article, Representative Mara (a recipient of Sawyer's unlawful gifts or gratuities) is quoted as saying, "Everyone picks up their own tabs at [legislative] conferences. . . . These conferences have become almost nonexistent." These articles were kept in notebooks with other materials regarding lobbying laws.

A jury rationally could infer that Sawyer was cognizant of his ethical obligations in lobbying, knew of the public awareness of lobbying activity, and repeatedly gave hidden unlawful gifts and gratuities until he was publicly exposed. While not overwhelming, the combined evidence is sufficient to permit a reasonable jury to find, beyond a reasonable doubt, that Sawyer intended to deceive the public about his unlawful expenditures on legislators.

For the foregoing reasons, Sawyer's mail and wire fraud convictions must be vacated and remanded for a possible new trial.

- As the court in *Sawyer* observed, "[t]he use of the mails or wires to further the fraudulent scheme need only be 'incidental,'" which means that mail fraud and wire fraud do not require the fraudulent materials to be sent through the mail or over interstate wires but only that the mail and interstate wires support the fraudulent operation. With the elements of mail and wire fraud in mind, consider whether Randy, in the example at the beginning of this chapter, committed mail and wire fraud. Recall that Randy used the mail and the internet to advertise that his e-waste recycling business did not send any e-waste overseas and that it was recycled in an environmentally friendly manner. However, Randy actually did send significant e-waste overseas, and, for the waste he did keep domestically, he did not recycle the waste at all but disposed of it in the landfill. Did Randy commit mail fraud and wire fraud?

- Keep in mind that the wire fraud statute provides that communications must move "in interstate commerce" instead of the more lenient standard that communications are "in or affecting interstate commerce." Thus, wire fraud "requires the additional element of a communication crossing state lines." *Cent. Cadillac, Inc. v. Bank Leumi Trust Co. of N.Y.*, 808 F. Supp. 213, 227 (S.D.N.Y. 1992). This requires investigation into where the servers are located and whether anyone out of state has viewed the materials, among other things. *United States v. Kieffer*, 681 F.3d 1143, 1153-54 (10th Cir. 2012).

- As to mens rea, recall that movement in interstate commerce is a jurisdictional element about which proof of the defendant's knowledge is not required.

- Although wire fraud requires the crossing of state lines, mail fraud does not. Instead, Congress criminalized merely placing something with either the United States Postal Service or a commercial mail-delivery enterprise in furtherance of a fraudulent scheme. *United States v. Photogrammetric Data Serv., Inc.*, 259 F.3d 229, 248 (4th Cir. 2001) *abrogated on other grounds by Crawford v. Washington*, 541 U.S. 36 (2004). Accordingly, interstate travel of a mailing is not a required element.

B. FALSE STATEMENTS

During the Civil War, Congress became concerned about all of the false claims that were being submitted for payment to the United States government. *United States v. Bramblett*, 348 U.S. 503, 504 (1955). Consequently, in 1863, Congress enacted a statute that imposed criminal penalties for those who "'make or cause to be made, or present or cause to be presented for payment . . . any claim . . . knowing such claim to be false, fictitious, or fraudulent.'" *Id.* (quoting Act of March 2, 1863, 12 Stat. 696). To assist in the prosecution of those seeking payment for false claims against the United States, Congress added, "any person [in the armed forces] who shall, for the purpose of obtaining, or aiding in obtaining, the approval or payment of such [false] claim" by false representations to the government would also be punished criminally. *Id.*

In 1934, Congress significantly amended its 1863 act at the behest of the Secretary of the Interior, who found his agency subject to land swindles based on false claims. *Id.* The 1934 amendments allowed prosecution for those who

> knowingly and willfully falsify or conceal or cover up by any trick, scheme, or device a material fact, or make or cause to be made any false or fraudulent statements or representations . . . knowing the same to contain any fraudulent or fictitious statement or entry,

in any matter within the jurisdiction of any department or agency of the United States. . . .

48 Stat. 996.

Since 1934, Congress has expanded this provision to include false statements to the judicial and legislative branches in addition to agencies of the executive branch. Now known as 18 U.S.C. § 1001(a), the prohibition on false statements provides a felony with up to five years' imprisonment for:

whoever in any matter within the jurisdiction of the executive, legislative, or judicial branch of the Government of the United States, knowingly and willfully—

(1) falsifies, conceals, or covers up by any trick, scheme, or device a material fact;

(2) makes any materially false, fictitious, or fraudulent statement or representation; or

(3) makes or uses any false writing or document knowing the same to contain any materially false, fictitious, or fraudulent statement or entry[.]

Congress exempted false statements from a party or his/her counsel during litigation from § 1001(a)'s reach. 18 U.S.C. § 1001(b). Additionally, Congress limited the false statements that are prosecutable under § 1001 within the jurisdiction of the legislative branch to claims for payment and property from Congress in addition to investigations that Congress conducts. 18 U.S.C. § 1001(c). Therefore, to prove a violation of § 1001(a), the prosecution must establish that (1) the defendant; (2) regarding a matter within the jurisdiction of the executive, legislative, or judicial branches; (3) knowingly and willfully made a false statement, representation, or omission (orally or in writing); (4) that is material.

As the case below illustrates, § 1001(a) provides a very useful alternative to prosecuting many dishonest act environmental crimes. As you may recall from the previous discussion concerning the Clean Water Act, Clean Air Act, and RCRA, false statements are prosecuted thereunder for documents that each statute requires to be filed or maintained. Section 1001(a) not only allows prosecution of false statements or omissions in documents that those environmental statutes require to be filed or maintained but also allows for prosecution for false statements whether given orally or in documents and other correspondence that the aforementioned environmental statutes do not require but may still have an impact on agency decisionmaking. Courts have found no impediment to charging a false statement under the substantive environmental statute in addition to § 1001. *United States v. Shaw*, 150 Fed. App'x 863, 873-74 (10th Cir. Oct. 13, 2005) (holding that § 1001 count for false statements relating to asbestos can be prosecuted under § 1001 even though Clean Air Act also contains false statement provision).

1. Matters Within the Jurisdiction of the United States Government

United States v. Wright
988 F.2d 1036 (10th Cir. 1993)

STEPHEN H. ANDERSON, Circuit Judge.

Appellant, Gerald Wright, entered a conditional guilty plea to a charge of violating 18 U.S.C. § 1001, which, inter alia, makes it a crime to make a false written report "in any matter within the jurisdiction of any department or agency of the United States." The false reports submitted by Mr. Wright contained water quality data required by regulations promulgated by the Environmental Protection Agency ("EPA") pursuant to the Safe Drinking Water Act, 42 U.S.C. § 300f-300k (the "Act"). The reports were filed with the Oklahoma State Department of Health, through the Sequoyah County Department of Health; and the EPA had granted primary enforcement authority over drinking water standards to the State of Oklahoma. Mr. Wright unsuccessfully moved to dismiss the indictment against him, on the ground that the reports he filed were not matters within the jurisdiction of the EPA and, therefore, the district court lacked jurisdiction. On appeal he reasserts his position. We hold that the reports were matters within the jurisdiction of the EPA. Accordingly, we affirm the district court's denial of the motion to dismiss, and the conviction.

BACKGROUND

During the period 1987-1989, Mr. Wright was the superintendent and manager of a water treatment plant and distribution system at Lake Tenkiller, near Vian, Oklahoma. As part of his managerial duties he prepared and filed with the Sequoyah County (Oklahoma) Health Department monthly operating reports containing data on the suspended particulate matter (turbidity) in the water at his plant. These reports were false in that they purported to show information on turbidity from water samples when, in fact, no samples were analyzed or taken.

The reports, sampling, analytical, and record keeping requirements resulting in the type of data in question are required by federal regulations promulgated by the EPA pursuant to its authority and responsibility under the Act. The regulations require, among other things, daily monitoring of turbidity and submission to the state of monthly reports of the daily values within 10 days of the end of the month.

The Act permits a state to apply to the Administrator of the EPA for primary enforcement responsibility over drinking water standards. On March 30, 1977, the Administrator approved Oklahoma's application for primary enforcement responsibility, and Oklahoma had that authority during the period in question. Within the State of Oklahoma, responsibility for enforcing drinking water standards has been given to the Department of Health, which provided the forms which Mr. Wright filled out and filed with the County Health Department. The County Health Department forwards filed forms to the State Health Department.

A federal grand jury indicted Mr. Wright on January 9, 1992, charging him with seven counts of violating 18 U.S.C. § 1001 by making false written statements in a matter within the jurisdiction of the EPA. After the district court denied his motion to dismiss the indictment on jurisdictional grounds, Mr. Wright entered into a plea agreement with the government pursuant to which he pled guilty to three counts of violating 18 U.S.C. § 1001, reserving his right to appeal the denial of his motion.

As part of the plea agreement, the parties stipulated that if Mr. Wright testified he would state that: (1) he at no time knew of the jurisdiction of the EPA or any other federal agency or department in connection with the requirement to file turbidity reports; (2) he did not have notice, at any time, that the turbidity reports would be reviewed by the EPA or by any other federal agency or department, or that the turbidity reports could serve as the basis of an enforcement action by the EPA or any other federal agency or department; and (3) that all of the monthly reports he prepared concerning water turbidity were submitted by him to the Sequoyah County Health Department, and not to the EPA or any other federal agency or department.

The parties also stipulated that if a named responsible official of the EPA testified he would state that the EPA: (1) conducts annual evaluations of the Oklahoma public water system program under the Act; (2) makes semiannual visits to the Oklahoma State Department of Health to review the state public water system; (3) conducts biannual audits of the state program, during which operational reports are randomly selected for review; and (4) makes annual grants to the Oklahoma Department of Health which have ranged from approximately $500,000 to $700,000 since 1987. In addition, it was stipulated that such annual financial grants are dependent, in part, on the outcome of EPA's evaluation of the state public water program. The district court and the parties have treated these recitations as established facts, as do we.

DISCUSSION . . .

The parties agree that "jurisdiction," as it is used in section 1001, is to be defined broadly. "The most natural, nontechnical reading of the statutory language is that it covers all matters confided to the authority of an agency or department." Thus, an agency has jurisdiction under section 1001 "when it has the power to exercise authority in a particular situation." A false statement falls within that jurisdiction when it concerns the "authorized functions of an agency or department," rather than "matters peripheral to the business of that body."

The false statement need not be made directly to the federal agency to be within its jurisdiction. In addition, federal agency jurisdiction is not affected by a defendant's awareness of that jurisdiction, or by his or her awareness that the false information would be submitted to or influence the action of a federal agency.

Mr. Wright asserts that a writing does not fall within the jurisdiction of an agency unless there is a "direct relationship" between the writing and an authorized function of the agency. He then contends that there was no direct relationship between the reports he submitted and a function of the EPA "[b]ecause the EPA had surrendered primary authority for enforcement of Safe Drinking Water Act standards to the State of Oklahoma," and because he filed the report with the state, not the EPA. We disagree.

Regardless of the standard employed, the false turbidity data filed by Mr. Wright fell within the jurisdiction of the EPA. A grant of primary authority is not a grant of exclusive authority. Congress passed the [Safe Drinking Water] Act "'to assure that water supply systems serving the public meet minimum national standards for the protection of public health.'" *Montgomery County v.*

Environmental Protection Agency, 662 F.2d 1040, 1041 (4th Cir. 1981) (quoting H.R. Rep. No. 93-1185, 93d Cong., 2d Sess. 1, reprinted in 1974 U.S.C.C.A.N. 6454). The Act requires the Administrator to promulgate maximum contaminant level goals and national primary drinking water regulations. 42 U.S.C. § 300g-1(b)(1). The regulations relating to the collection and reporting of turbidity data, described above, were promulgated pursuant to that charge and authority. The EPA retains the authority, in the discharge of its duties under the Act, to enforce its regulations; and, turbidity data clearly concern an authorized function of the EPA.

Furthermore, in this situation, the EPA is actively involved in assuring state compliance with national safe water standards. It audits, reviews, and evaluates the state of Oklahoma's program, including an inspection of the monthly reports of the type involved in this case. Such reports, therefore, directly implicate the ongoing function and mission of the agency. In addition, the Act expressly authorizes the EPA to take enforcement actions in states having primary enforcement authority. 42 U.S.C. § 300g-3(a), (b).

Finally, EPA's funding of the Oklahoma public water program is conditioned, in part, on the results of its annual evaluations of that program. This court is in accord with other circuits which have found that a state agency's use of federal funds, standing alone, is generally sufficient to establish jurisdiction under section 1001.

CONCLUSION
For the reasons stated, we agree with the district court's denial of Wright's motion to dismiss the indictment, and we AFFIRM the judgment of conviction.

- Under *Wright*, a defendant need not knowingly misrepresent a matter to a federal agency to have that matter be deemed one within the federal agency's jurisdiction. Lying to a local agency may be enough to support a federal criminal charge under § 1001 if that local agency is working in conjunction with another federal agency on the matter about which the misrepresentation was made.
- *Wright* also shows that the knowing and willful mens rea for § 1001 applies only to the misrepresentation and not to whom the misrepresentation is made. Accordingly, the prosecution does not need to establish that the defendant intended to lie to a federal entity; only that the lie was part of what the federal entity regulated.

2. Mens Rea for the Misrepresentation

United States v. Gonsalves
435 F.3d 64 (1st Cir. 2006)

BOUDIN, Chief Judge.
Wallace Gonsalves, Jr., an osteopathic doctor, conducted a solo medical practice in Cranston, Rhode Island. In 1971, he was certified as a "civil surgeon" with the former Immigration and Naturalization Service ("INS"), performing blood tests and administering immunizations to immigrants seeking permanent

residence in the United States. Gonsalves, like most doctors, kept drugs in his office premises, including vaccines needed for immunizations.

In June 2002, Catherine Cordy, Chief of the Board of Pharmacy of the Rhode Island Department of Health ("DOH"), received an anonymous complaint about Gonsalves' medical practice, later determined to have come from Kelly Walsh. Walsh, a former employee, reported that Gonsalves was engaged in workers' compensation fraud and was illegally selling drug samples to a local pharmacist. Cordy referred this complaint to the Attorney General and the DOH's Board of Medical Licensure, and Walsh was interviewed on July 8, 2002.

Walsh told investigators that Gonsalves had instructed employees to immunize immigrant patients with diluted vaccines and to administer to those patients only a half-dose of the already-diluted vaccines. She also reported that Gonsalves was falsely certifying to the INS that patients had been tested for various diseases when no such tests had been performed and requiring payments of $150-$300 in cash (which he did not record in his books) for the INS examination, even though the examinations were covered by the patients' insurance.

On August 16, 2002, the Rhode Island Attorney General's office executed a search warrant in Gonsalves' office for general patient and business records, the DOH executed an administrative subpoena for twelve specific patient records, and Cordy, relying on her statutory authority to inspect without a warrant locations where drugs are held, conducted an inspection for misbranded or adulterated drugs. Cordy seized various drugs as misbranded or adulterated—evaluations later confirmed in testing by the Food and Drug Administration.

In due course, Gonsalves was indicted in federal court for drug adulteration and tampering, making false statements to the government, 18 U.S.C. § 1001 (2000), and tax violations. At trial, the government's evidence permitted a jury to conclude that Gonsalves was criminally responsible for, among other things, the dilution and improper storage of vaccines, false certifications to the INS that patients had been tested for HIV and syphilis, falsely reporting that patients had been properly immunized, and the failure to report over $400,000 in income. The jury convicted Gonsalves on all submitted counts.

For these offenses, the district court sentenced Gonsalves to ten years in prison and fined him heavily. . . .

[Gonsalves challenges] the instruction for the false statement counts under 18 U.S.C. § 1001. The core of the district court's charge on scienter was that the government was required to show that the "defendant knowingly made a material false statement" to the INS and "that the defendant made the statement voluntarily and intentionally," that is, knowing "that it was false or demonstrat[ing] reckless disregard for the truth with a conscious purpose to avoid learning the truth."

Gonsalves says that a good faith instruction (which he requested) should have been given—a position not seriously developed and already rejected by the case law. Then, more to the point, he argues that the scienter requirement for the offense was not sufficiently explained and that an "intent to deceive" instruction should have been given. It is debatable how far the full objection was preserved, but it warrants comment because of some tension in our own case law.

Two of our older cases associate section 1001 with an "intent to deceive" requirement. Our more recent decisions impose no such requirement but do say that the false statement must be made knowingly and willfully. Normally, the more recent cases would control, but in this instance they govern also because the Supreme Court has itself rejected the claim that an "intent to deceive" is required. *See United States v. Yermian*, 468 U.S. 63, 73 (1984).

Willfulness—a term our cases do endorse—means nothing more in this context than that the defendant knew that his statement was false when he made it or—which amounts in law to the same thing—consciously disregarded or averted his eyes from its likely falsity. This is just what the district judge told the jury in this case, i.e., that the defendant made the statement knowing that it was false or demonstrating "reckless disregard for the truth with a conscious purpose to avoid learning the truth." . . .

Affirmed.

- Unlike willfulness in other contexts, willful under § 1001 does not require the prosecution to prove that the defendant intended to break the law. Instead, § 1001's knowing and willful requirement only imposes the requirement of proving that the defendant knew that the information he/she gave or failed to give was false at the time the information was given.

- However, even though the prosecution need not establish the defendant's intent to deceive, the government can prove such an intent to show that a literally true statement is a violation of § 1001. In *United States v. Stephenson*, 895 F.2d 867, 873-74 (2d Cir. 1990), the defendant told a government official that the vice-president of a company had offered the defendant a bribe. That statement was literally true. However, what the defendant failed to divulge was that he was a willing participant, and his failure to divulge this critical fact was a misrepresentation to the government by making it appear that the defendant was "an unwilling victim of a bribery scheme" by the company's vice-president. Thus, a literally true statement that omits critical details may be a violation of § 1001.

3. Materiality

United States v. Brittain
931 F.2d 1413 (10th Cir. 1991)

BALDOCK, Circuit Judge.

A jury convicted defendant-appellant, Raymond T. Brittain, of eighteen felony counts of falsely reporting a material fact to a government agency, 18 U.S.C. § 1001, and two misdemeanor counts of discharging pollutants into the waters of the United States in violation of [the Clean Water Act]. Defendant appeals, contending: (1) the government did not establish materiality as required by 18 U.S.C. § 1001. . . . We affirm.

I.

We first consider materiality under 18 U.S.C. § 1001. The Clean Water Act prohibits the discharge of pollutants from any point source into the navigable waters of the United States unless such discharge complies with a permit issued by the EPA pursuant to the National Pollutant Discharge Elimination System (NPDES) or by an EPA authorized state agency. NPDES permits impose limits on the point sources and amounts of discharged pollutants, and the EPA monitors compliance through monthly discharge monitoring reports from the permittee. See generally 33 U.S.C. § 1342 (NPDES system); 40 C.F.R. § 122 (1989) (NPDES regulations). Defendant, as public utilities director for the city of Enid, Oklahoma, had general supervisory authority over the operations of the Enid wastewater treatment plant and was responsible for filing the plant's discharge monitoring reports. Defendant directed the plant supervisor to falsify eighteen monthly discharge monitoring reports and the supporting laboratory records by recording 25 to 30 milligrams per liter of effluent for two specific pollutants regardless of the actual measurements at the point of discharge. Defendant's convictions under 18 U.S.C. § 1001 resulted from these falsifications.

. . . Defendant concedes sufficient evidence on all of the elements of § 1001 except materiality. Therefore, we limit our discussion to whether defendant's false statements were of a material fact, a separate and distinct element of the offense. . . .

A false statement is material if it "'has a natural tendency to influence, or [is] capable of influencing, the decision of the tribunal in making a determination required to be made.'" Defendant contends that the government did not establish materiality because it did not demonstrate that his false statements were capable of influencing government action. He relies on a plant laboratory technician's personal diary offered by the government. The diary reflected the true levels of pollutant discharge to be below the falsely reported levels and within the plant's NPDES permit limits. Defendant also urges us to consider the testimony of Sharon Parrish, an expert witness for the government. Ms. Parrish testified that an EPA enforcement action would result if the discharge monitoring reports reflected pollutant discharges outside the NPDES permit limits. According to defendant, the government did not establish materiality since its only evidence reflected the actual levels of pollutant as within permit limits and enforcement action would result only if the levels exceeded permit limits. As authority, he cites *United States v. Radetsky*, 535 F.2d 556 (10th Cir.).

Radetsky involved a Medicare fraud scheme whereby the defendant doctor attempted to obtain reimbursement from the government for medicinal drugs that he did not prescribe. We held, as matter of law, that the government could not establish materiality under 18 U.S.C. § 1001 because the doctor's false reports were of drugs that were noncompensable under Medicare regulations. The doctor's false reports therefore were incapable of influencing the government to reimburse. Defendant contends that the circumstances of his case parallel those of *Radetsky* because the government's evidence, the laboratory technician's diary, reflected no need for EPA enforcement because it recorded the true levels of pollutants to be within NPDES permit limits. The record, however, reveals that defendant's reliance on *Radetsky* is misplaced.

Contrary to defendant's position, the lab technician's diary was not the only evidence the government produced as to the true levels of effluent. The record contains expert testimony to the effect that it was impossible for the treatment plant to meet its NPDES permit limitations during the indictment period, May 1985, to September 1986. The government expert testified that he examined the plant in

November 1986, and found it in a state of disrepair. When asked his opinion of the operation of the plant during the indictment period, the witness responded: "Well, they hadn't taken care of the plant. They hadn't ordered new parts and installed them when they were needed. . . . The place was just kind of a mess." The expert testified in detail regarding the specific problems resulting from the plant's poor condition and why such problems rendered it impossible for the plant to meet its NPDES permit requirements during the indictment period. Furthermore, the laboratory technician's diary reflecting discharge levels within permit limits covered only two months of the indictment period. The expert testimony, on the other hand, considered the entire eighteen-month period. This expert testimony allowed the government to establish that defendant's false statements could have influenced an EPA enforcement decision. *See* 40 C.F.R. § 122.41(a) (1990) ("Any [NPDES] permit noncompliance constitutes a violation of the Clean Water Act and is grounds for enforcement action. . . .").

. . . The Ninth Circuit has noted that "[t]he NPDES program fundamentally relies on self-monitoring." *Sierra Club v. Union Oil Co.*, 813 F.2d 1480, 1491 (9th Cir. 1987), *vacated and remanded on other grounds*, 485 U.S. 931, 108 S. Ct. 1102, 99 L. Ed. 2d 264 (1988). The same court held that discharge monitoring reports showing exceedances were conclusive evidence of NPDES permit violations. *Id.* at 1492. Also, the legislative history of the Clean Water Act reveals that Congress sensed a need for accurate self-reporting:

> One purpose of these new requirements [self-reporting requirements] is to avoid the necessity of lengthy fact finding, investigations, and negotiations at the time of enforcement. Enforcement of violations of requirements under this Act should be based on relatively narrow fact situations requiring a minimum of discretionary decision making or delay.

S. Rep. No. 414, 92 Cong., 1st Sess. 64, reprinted in 1972 U.S.C.C.A.N. 3668, 3730.

Defendant's false statements served to undermine the integrity of the self-monitoring permit system. Our finding of materiality in this case, however, turns on the evidence that defendant's false statements had the tendency to influence or were capable of influencing an EPA enforcement action. . . .

AFFIRMED.

- What evidence did the court in *Brittain* look to for support that the defendant's misrepresentations were capable of influencing the EPA's decisions when the defendant's lies were given to a state agency with delegated authority to run the Clean Water Act program in Oklahoma?
- Notice that "material" does not mean that the misrepresentation actually influenced a government decision. "Material" simply means that the misrepresentation was "capable" of influencing a government decision. What EPA decisions were the defendant's lies capable of influencing?
- Given the fact that many environmental statutes rely on self-reporting to carry out the regulatory program, is there a place for having two different sources to prosecute false statements: § 1001 and the false statement statutes within the Clean Water Act, Clean Air Act, RCRA, and others?

- Once again, consider the hypothetical with Randy and E-Recy from the beginning of this chapter. Recall that Randy met with state hazardous waste regulators and told them that his workers use an elaborate process to recycle the e-waste that businesses pay E-Recy to collect. Would you charge Randy with a violation of § 1001? Would you want to know more information? If so, what would you want to know?

C. OBSTRUCTION OF JUSTICE

As the Tenth Circuit observed in *Brittain*, the administrative environmental regulatory regime relies heavily on self-reporting from the regulated entities. Because of the self-reporting nature of environmental regulation, the information necessary to prove compliance or non-compliance with environmental laws is kept within the entity that is being regulated. This means that, to a large extent, the regulatory body is at the mercy of the regulated entity for obtaining information necessary to establish non-compliance with environmental laws. Although society expects regulated entities to be transparent and honest with government regulators, the incentives for not getting caught for an environmental violation sometimes outweigh the values of honesty and transparency. Where regulated entities succumb to this temptation, prosecution for obstructing the regulatory agency in its efforts to determine compliance can be an effective deterrent to improving candor in self-reporting. To incentivize honesty with administrative agency proceedings, Congress enacted 18 U.S.C. § 1505, which provides, in relevant part:

> Whoever corruptly, or by threats or force, or by any threatening letter or communication influences, obstructs, or impedes or endeavors to influence, obstruct, or impede the due and proper administration of the law under which any pending proceeding is being had before any department or agency of the United States . . . [s]hall be fined under this title, imprisoned not more than 5 years or, if the offense involves international or domestic terrorism . . . imprisoned not more than 8 years, or both.

Courts have interpreted § 1505 to require "three essential elements." *United States v. Price*, 951 F.2d 1028, 1031 (9th Cir. 1991). First, the prosecution must prove that there is a proceeding pending "before a department or agency of the United States." *Id.* Second, the prosecution must establish that the defendant knew about the pending proceeding. *Id.* Finally, the prosecution must prove that the defendant intentionally endeavored corruptly or by force or intimidation to influence, obstruct, or impede the pending proceeding. *Id.* The following cases illustrate what a "proceeding" means in terms of § 1505 in addition to what the prosecution must show to prove that the defendant corruptly endeavored to obstruct a proceeding.

United States v. McDaniel
Case No. 2:12-CR-0028-RWS-JCF, 2013 WL 3993983 (N.D. Ga. Jan. 29, 2013)

J. CLAY FULLER, United States Magistrate Judge.

This case is before the Court on the motions to dismiss Count One of the Indictment filed by Defendants. . . . Because the Federal Bureau of Investigation ("FBI") lacks adjudicative and rulemaking powers, a criminal investigation conducted by the FBI is not a "proceeding" for purposes of 18 U.S.C. § 1505, and Count One of the Indictment fails to allege a violation of that statute. Therefore, it is RECOMMENDED that Defendants' motions to dismiss Count One of the Indictment be GRANTED.[3]

PROCEDURAL HISTORY

Count One of an Indictment filed September 4, 2012 charges Defendants King, Brown, and McDaniel with obstructing and impeding "the due and proper administration of the law under which a proceeding was pending before the Federal Bureau of Investigation, an agency of the United States," by influencing, obstructing, and impeding, and attempting to influence, obstruct, and impede, "an investigation being conducted by Special Agents of the Federal Bureau of Investigation in which D.B.S. was acting as a confidential informant," in violation of 18 U.S.C. § 1505 and 18 U.S.C. § 2 (aiding and abetting statute). . . .

DISCUSSION

All Defendants move to dismiss Count One of the Indictment on the ground that it fails to state a criminal offense under 18 U.S.C. § 1505. . . . Defendants argue that the Government's allegations in Count One are insufficient to satisfy the elements of Section 1505 because an FBI investigation is not a "proceeding" under that statute. The Government responds that "the Court should find that an FBI investigation is a proceeding under Section 1505 and deny defendants' motions." . . . Case law from other circuits, however, provides persuasive authority that an FBI criminal investigation is not a "proceeding" for purposes of 18 U.S.C. § 1505.

The definition of the word "proceeding" as used in § 1505 is a question of law to be determined by the court. Courts have noted that, for purposes of § 1505, the term "proceeding" is defined broadly, "'encompassing both the investigative and adjudicative functions of a department or agency.'" Even a broad definition has limits and in this instance, courts have generally found that only agencies that engage in rulemaking, adjudicative, or civil enforcement activities conduct "proceedings" for purposes of § 1505.

The few courts squarely addressing the issue have found that a purely federal law enforcement criminal investigation, including an FBI investigation, is not a proceeding under § 1505. In *United States v. Higgins*, 511 F. Supp. 453 (W.D. Ky. 1981), for example, the court granted the defendant's motion to dismiss a § 1505 charge, where the defendant was alleged to have obstructed an FBI investigation.

---

[3] Under 18 U.S.C. § 636(b)(1)(B), a district court judge may designate a magistrate judge to hear and determine any pretrial motion pending before the court and to make a report and recommendation with the district court as to the pending motion.

Id. at 454. The court acknowledged that in *Fruchtman*, the Sixth Circuit had stated that "proceeding" is a "term of broad scope, encompassing both the investigative and adjudicative functions of a department or agency." *Id.* at 455. The *Higgins* court concluded, however, that based on "careful examination of the case law and pertinent legislative history, the meaning of 'proceeding' in § 1505 must be limited to actions of an agency which related to some matter within the scope of the rulemaking or adjudicative power vested in the agency by law." *Id.* The court distinguished *Fruchtman*, which involved the Federal Trade Commission, "an agency which by law possesses both investigative and adjudicative functions." *Id.* The FBI, on the other hand, is a "criminal investigatory agency" with "no rulemaking or adjudicatory powers regarding the subject matter of this indictment." *Id.* Accordingly, the *Higgins* court found that an FBI investigation was not a "proceeding" within the meaning of § 1505. *Id.* at 456.

In explaining why it found that an FBI investigation is not a "proceeding" under § 1505, the court in *Higgins* found "very persuasive" the legislative history of 18 U.S.C. § 1510, a statute which prohibits obstruction of criminal investigations. *Higgins*, 511 F. Supp. at 455. That legislative history supports a finding that § 1505 does not proscribe attempts to obstruct a criminal investigation before a proceeding is initiated. *See id.* In *United States v. Kohler*, 544 F.2d 1326 (5th Cir. 1977), the court noted the same legislative history referenced by the court in *Higgins*, i.e., House Report No. 658 dated September 21, 1967, which explained the purpose of passing § 1510:

> Sections 1503 and 1505 of chapter 73, title 18, presently prohibit attempts to influence, intimidate, impede, or injure a witness or juror in a judicial proceeding, a proceeding before a Federal agency, or an inquiry or investigation by either House of the Congress or a congressional committee. *However, attempts to obstruct a criminal investigation or inquiry before a proceeding has been initiated are not within the proscription of those sections.* The proposed legislation would remedy that deficiency by providing penalties for attempting to obstruct the communication to a Federal penal law, thus extending to informants and potential witnesses the protections now afforded witnesses and jurors in judicial, administrative, and congressional proceedings.

Kohler, 544 F.2d at 1328 n. 3 (quoting 1967 U.S. Code Cong. & Admin. News p. 1760 (emphasis added)).

In addition, the *Higgins* court observed, "It is significant to the Court that in the eighty-two years this statute or its predecessor has been on the books, it has apparently never been applied to a criminal investigation by a federal law enforcement agency." *Higgins*, 511 F. Supp. at 455. "Indeed, each reported decision applying this statute has involved an agency with rulemaking or adjudicative authority in addition to investigative functions." *Id.* (listing cases). A review of the case law since the 1981 *Higgins* decision reveals that the Government's position that a criminal investigation by the FBI is a proceeding under § 1505 lacks more contemporary support, as well.

Even in cases where the courts found that agency investigations were "proceedings" under § 1505, the courts distinguished investigations conducted by agencies with adjudicative, rulemaking, or civil enforcement authority, such as the Internal Revenue Service ("IRS"), the Securities and Exchange Commission ("SEC"), or the Food and Drug Administration ("FDA"), from criminal investigations performed by law enforcement agencies without such authority, such as the FBI.

CONCLUSION

Given the weight of authority, the reasoning articulated in the above-discussed cases, the legislative history of §§ 1505 and 1510, and the absence of contrary authority, the undersigned finds that the FBI investigation referenced in Count One of the Indictment was not a "proceeding" under 18 U.S.C. § 1505. Therefore, it is RECOMMENDED that Defendants' motions to dismiss Count One of the Indictment be GRANTED, and that Count One be DISMISSED as to all Defendants.

- As the *McDaniel* court observed, many courts have held that only agencies with rulemaking, adjudicative, or civil enforcement authority can have "proceedings" for purposes of § 1505. However, the plain language of § 1505 provides that a "proceeding" can be "before any department of agency of the United States." 18 U.S.C. § 1505. The United States Supreme Court has interpreted the word "any" to have "an expansive meaning, that is, 'one or some indiscriminately of whatever kind.'" *United States v. Gonzales*, 520 U.S. 1, 5 (1997). Given the plain language of § 1505, have courts misread Congress's intent by limiting the word "proceeding" to only those agencies that are not exclusively for law enforcement?
- Section 1001 allows for the prosecution of false statements to law enforcement officers. What is the policy reason for allowing the prosecution of false statements to law enforcement under § 1001 but to not allow prosecution for obstruction of justice in a law enforcement investigation under § 1505?

United States v. El-Sherif
Case No. 17-20006-01-JAR, 2018 WL 358284 (D. Kan. 2018)

Defendant Ahmed El-Sherif was charged in a two-count Indictment with knowingly storing hazardous waste without a permit from March 2012 through October 2013, in violation of 42 U.S.C. § 6928(d)(2)(A), and obstruction of an agency proceeding, in violation of 18 U.S.C. § 1505. This case was tried to the Court beginning on February 1, 2018. This decision represents the Court's findings of fact and conclusions of law. As described more fully below, the Court finds Defendant guilty of Count 1 and not guilty of Count 2. . . .

FINDINGS OF FACT

The following facts are either stipulated by the parties, or found by the Court beyond a reasonable doubt based on the evidence admitted at trial.

Defendant Ahmed El-Sherif obtained a master of science degree in chemistry from Arkansas State University in 1983 and studied chemistry at Arizona State

University in pursuit of a doctoral degree, although he did not obtain a doctoral degree. Following his education, he worked in several laboratories in the field of radioactive synthesis. In 1996, Defendant incorporated Beta Chem, Inc. ("Beta Chem"), a small laboratory that focused on the synthesis of radioactive isotopes utilized in research and medical applications. Defendant was Beta Chem's owner, president, and sole shareholder. On July 15, 1998, Beta Chem was forfeited as a corporation, but Defendant continued to operate the laboratory as a sole proprietorship. In September 1998, Defendant entered into a lease agreement for Beta Chem to lease space at a 30-unit office/warehouse complex in Lenexa, Kansas. Beta Chem acquired commercially available chemicals and substances from wholesale vendors for use in its laboratory work. Defendant primarily stored these chemicals in their original containers. . . .

ABILITY TO PAY INQUIRY

In 2014, the EPA approached Defendant and his attorney, William Session, and asked whether Defendant would be performing the Superfund cleanup. Session responded that Defendant could not afford to pay for the cleanup. Based on Session's response, the EPA commenced a review of Defendant's ability to pay for the cleanup (known as an "ATP" analysis). The EPA conducts this review when a party that will potentially be responsible for paying for a cleanup asserts an inability to pay. The EPA sent ATP forms to Session to document Defendant's claimed inability to pay. Defendant submitted an ATP form to the EPA through Session on September 29, 2014. Defendant also executed an IRS Form 4506-T, or a "Request for Transcript of Tax Return," so that the EPA could obtain Beta Chem's income tax returns for 2010, 2011, 2012, and 2013.

On October 22, 2014, after the EPA submitted Defendant's Form 4506-T to the IRS, the IRS responded to the EPA that it could not provide the returns for Beta Chem for 2010, 2012, or 2013, and that the EPA needed to contact the taxpayer to determine why the IRS could not provide the requested information. On the same date, the IRS sent to Defendant a notice stating that "we can't provide tax information for tax year[s] 2010, 2012, or 2013 because you didn't file a return." The EPA asked Session for copies of Beta Chem's 2012 and 2013 corporate income tax returns on January 6, 2015. On January 12, 2015, the IRS received three tax returns for Beta Chem for tax years 2010, 2012, and 2013, which were dated March 15, 2011, March 10, 2013, and March 16, 2014, respectively. Also enclosed in the packet of returns was a letter from Defendant, dated November 7, 2014, stating that "[t]his responds to your notice that says I did not report tax documents for 2010, 2012, and 2013, copy enclosed. I previously filed these taxes using form 1120S." Also on January 12, 2015, the EPA received from Session copies of Beta Chem tax returns for 2010, 2012, and 2013, along with the cover letter from Defendant he wrote to the IRS that was dated November 7, 2014.

Several of the figures contained in these tax returns are irreconcilable with other evidence of Beta Chem's earnings and expenses presented at trial. For example, each of the returns state that Beta Chem incurred $6,900 of deductible rental expenses. Although this figure is compatible with the amount of rent Beta Chem owed each year, it is inconsistent with FBI Special Agent Shara McGowan's calculation of the rental payments Beta Chem made in each year based on Defendant's personal tax return figures: $4,025 in 2010, $4,025 in 2012, and $0 in

2013.99 The income reported on Beta Chem's returns for each year is also inconsistent with the income for Beta Chem that Defendant reported on his personal tax returns. The 2010 Beta Chem return reports net income of $0, while his personal return reports $10,000 for Beta Chem income. Beta Chem's 2012 return reports a net income of negative $18,404, but his personal return reports a loss of $10,426 for Beta Chem that year. Finally, the 2013 Beta Chem return reports a loss of $10,426, but Defendant's 2013 personal return states Beta Chem's income was $11,500.

Jacob Nicholls, an accountant at EPA Region 7, conducted the ATP analysis for Defendant. He reviewed, among other documents, Beta Chem's corporate tax returns for 2010, 2012, and 2013, and Defendant's personal returns for 2011 and 2012. Nicholls testified that he understood Defendant had filed the Beta Chem returns on the dates stated on the returns. But Nicholls also testified that as of November 2014, he knew the IRS did not have tax returns on file for Beta Chem for tax years 2010, 2012, and 2013. Nicholls also testified that he was aware of differences between Defendant's personal returns and Beta Chem's returns before he completed his ATP report. Nicholls did not contact Defendant or Session to gain additional information about these discrepancies.

In conducting the ATP analysis, Nicholls used a computer model, INDIPAY, that ran "an analysis and calculate[d] out potential future cash flows, along with additional debt capacity that a respondent might have in order to help pay . . . for the cleanup costs." To enable INDIPAY to calculate these figures, Nicholls plugged in numbers from Defendant's personal income tax returns because Defendant was the potentially responsible party. Nicholls did not use numbers from the Beta Chem corporate returns, and he never analyzed Beta Chem's ability to pay cleanup costs, because Beta Chem was not the potentially responsible party.

Nicholls submitted his ATP report to EPA attorney Nazar on February 18, 2015. He explained that the INDIPAY model predicted Defendant could fund $16,761 of the proposed CERCLA removal action amount of $520,700, but that "it is my opinion that Mr. Sherif cannot afford to pay any of the proposed ceiling for the CERCLA removal action of $520,700 without placing an excessive financial hardship on him and his family." Nicholls therefore recommended that the EPA not seek the $16,761 from Defendant.

CONCLUSIONS OF LAW
Defendant is charged with one count of knowingly storing hazardous wastes without a permit under RCRA, in violation of 42 U.S.C. § 6928(d)(2)(A), and one count of corruptly influencing, obstructing, and impeding an agency proceeding in violation of 18 U.S.C. § 1505. The Court addresses each count in turn. [The court found Defendant guilty of violating RCRA.]

COUNT 2: OBSTRUCTION OF AGENCY PROCEEDING CHARGE
Defendant is charged with obstructing an agency proceeding in violation of 18 U.S.C. § 1505. Section 1505 provides criminal penalties for "[w]hoever corruptly . . . influences, obstructs, or impedes or endeavors to influence, obstruct, or impede the due and proper administration of the law under which any pending proceeding is being had before any department or agency of the United States." Thus, a conviction on Count 2 requires proof beyond a reasonable doubt that (1)

on or about January 2015, a proceeding was pending before a department or agency of the United States; (2) Defendant knew that a proceeding was pending before a department or agency of the United States; and (3) Defendant corruptly endeavored to influence, obstruct, or impede the due and proper administration of the law in that proceeding.

The first two elements of this analysis are not in issue. The Government proved beyond a reasonable doubt that an agency proceeding was pending in January 2015 before an agency of the United States, and that Defendant knew of this proceeding. That is, Defendant knew of the ability to pay inquiry that the EPA was pursuing during this time. Thus, the remaining question is whether Defendant corruptly endeavored "to impede the due and proper administration of the law" during the ATP proceeding.

The term "corruptly" as used in section 1505 means "acting with an improper purpose, personally or by influencing another, including making a false or misleading statement, or withholding, concealing, altering, or destroying a document or other information." The Supreme Court has held that the term "endeavor" includes "any effort or essay to accomplish the evil purpose that the section was enacted to prevent." The obstruction need not be successful to constitute a § 1505 violation; "an endeavor suffices."

Although the obstruction need not be successful, the Supreme Court has adopted a "natural and probable effect" requirement in the context of 18 U.S.C. § 1503, an obstruction statute nearly identical to § 1505. Under this standard, the "endeavor must have the natural and probable effect of interfering with the due administration of justice." Several courts have applied the "natural and probable effect" requirement in the § 1505 context, and the Court will do the same because of the similarities between § 1503 and § 1505.

Defendant cites *United States v. Wood*, in which the Tenth Circuit applied the "natural and probable effect" standard in a case involving a charge of obstruction of justice under § 1503. The defendant in *Wood* made false statements to FBI agents about a car he had loaned to the chairman of the Navajo Nation of Indians during the course of an investigation the agents were conducting into political corruption involving the chairman. The government later learned that the statements were false, but did not further investigate the facts involved in the statements. In upholding the District Court's dismissal of the obstruction charge, the Tenth Circuit found that the FBI agents did not rely exclusively on the defendant's false statements and terminate their investigation, but instead continued to investigate the case and revealed the truth about the car. The court thus concluded that the false statements "did not have the natural and probable effect of impeding the due administration of justice in the sense required by 18 U.S.C. § 1503."

Defendant argues that as in *Wood*, any false statements in the tax returns here did not have the natural and probable effect of impeding the ATP proceeding because the EPA did not rely on the inaccurate information in Defendant's corporate tax returns in evaluating his ability to pay. The Court agrees. The evidence at trial tended to show that Defendant submitted post hoc corporate tax returns to the IRS in November 2014 after he was made aware that the IRS did not have tax returns on file for Beta Chem for tax years 2010, 2012, and 2013. Certain figures on these corporate tax returns are irreconcilable with those reflected on

Defendant's personal tax returns for the same years. The Government, however, did not present evidence suggesting that the figures on Defendant's personal tax returns are false or inaccurate.

Even assuming the figures on Defendant's corporate income tax returns are false, the Court finds that these figures did not have the natural and probable effect of obstructing the EPA's inquiry. Jacob Nicholls testified that he was aware the IRS did not have tax returns for Beta Chem on file in November 2014 for tax years 2010, 2012, and 2013, and he was also aware of the discrepancies between the corporate and personal tax returns when he was conducting the ATP analysis. Nicholls did not follow up with Defendant or his counsel to gain additional information about these discrepancies. Instead, he used the information contained on Defendant's personal returns, and ignored the figures on the corporate returns because he was not focused on Beta Chem's ability to pay. As in *Wood*, the EPA did not rely on the false statements in the corporate returns in conducting its inquiry.

Certainly, as Nicholls testified, false statements contained on the corporate tax returns would give the EPA reason to question the truth of figures contained on Defendant's personal tax returns. But the Government presented no evidence that the EPA further investigated the figures on Defendant's personal tax returns based on the discrepancies it knew existed between the corporate and personal returns, and there was no evidence that the information in Defendant's personal returns was inaccurate. The Court therefore finds that obstruction of the ATP proceeding was not a natural and probable effect of the inconsistent information contained in Beta Chem's corporate tax returns. Accordingly, the Court finds Defendant not guilty of the Count 2 obstruction charge.

CONCLUSION
Based on the above stated findings of fact and conclusions of law, the Court finds that Defendant is adjudged guilty of Count 1, in violation of 42 U.S.C. § 6928(d)(2)(A), and not guilty of Count 2. . . .

- Recall that 18 U.S.C. § 1001 requires that any intentional misrepresentation to government officials be "material," which means that the misrepresentation has the ability to influence a government decision. Conversely, to prove that the defendant endeavored to obstruct justice, the prosecution must prove that "the natural and probable effect" of the endeavor to obstruct has an adverse effect on the agency "proceeding." Does 18 U.S.C. § 1505's standard regarding endeavoring to obstruct impose a more difficult standard to prove than § 1001's materiality requirement?

- If § 1505's standard is more difficult to prove than § 1001's materiality requirement, what is the advantage to prosecuting a matter under § 1505? Does § 1505 cover crimes that § 1001 does not?

- The beginning of this chapter provided a hypothetical involving Randy and his company E-Recy. Recall that Randy had to respond to questions from state regulators about his e-recycling business. Randy told his workers that if any of them spoke with state hazardous waste regulators, they would be fired. Randy then told his workers that if they were compelled to speak with state hazardous waste regulators, they had better lie so that the company did not get in trouble. Did Randy obstruct justice under 18 U.S.C. § 1505? What additional evidence that is not provided in the hypothetical would you need to know before presenting charges to a grand jury?

D. SMUGGLING

Elbert Hubbard, an American writer from the nineteenth century, once quipped, "Forbid a man to think for himself or to act for himself and you may add the joy of piracy and the zest of smuggling to his life." Consistent with Hubbard's view, smugglers seem to have attained a folkloric status in some circles. For example, Han Solo of *Star Wars* is a well-known and beloved smuggler as is Captain Jack Sparrow from *Pirates of the Caribbean*. Additionally, there are many television shows in the United States and in many other nations around the world in which the hero is a smuggler while law enforcement is the villain.[4] Although Hubbard and Hollywood have associated smuggling with personal freedom, not everyone sees smuggling's allure. For example, the English theologian Robert Hardy once said:

> Of all the occupations, I look upon Smuggling to be the most pernicious. It introduces habits of *Art*, and *Slyness*, and *Deception* and *Concealment*; it leads to the way of *Lying*, and *Cheating*, and *Pilfering*, and *Fraud*; it breaks up the course of honest and useful labour; it excites a fondness of spiritous liquors and makes men sots and drunkards; it lays the foundation of bad health, of painful and fatal diseases, and of premature death.[5]

Regardless of society's views regarding smuggling as an occupation and of those who engage in it, all can agree that smuggling deprives the government of the ability to tax smuggled goods and that some of those smuggled goods are contraband for which society is willing to pay great sums of money to possess contrary to other laws that the government has promulgated.

Although far too long to recite here, the history of smuggling laws in the United States reflects the need to protect the government's ability to collect taxes on goods entering the United States in addition to ensuring that imports and exports do not thwart other laws. Congress codified these dual aims when it enacted 18 U.S.C. § 545. To show it was serious, violating either of § 545's criminal provisions carries a maximum penalty of 20 years of imprisonment. Accordingly, § 545 contains two crimes: (1) defrauding the United States; and (2) importing merchandise contrary to law. The elements of each are discussed below.[6]

---

[4] For example, see *Señor de los Cielos* ("Lord of the Heavens") from Telemundo, which features a powerful drug lord named Aurelio Casillas.

[5] Robert Hardy, *Serious Cautions and Advice to All Concerned in Smuggling: Setting forth the mischiefs attendant upon that traffic; together with some exhortations to patience and contentment under the difficulties and trials of life* (London, 1818) quoted in Alan L. Karras, *Smuggling: Contraband and Corruption in World History* (Rowman & Littlefield Publishers, 2009).

[6] Similar provisions for exports are found in 18 U.S.C. § 546.

1. Intent to Defraud the United States

The earliest smuggling laws came into existence to protect the government's abilities to tax merchandise coming into the country. This is the primary purpose of the crime capsulated in the first paragraph of 18 U.S.C. § 545, which provides:

> Whoever knowingly and willfully, with intent to defraud the United States, smuggles, or clandestinely introduces or attempts to smuggle or clandestinely introduce into the United States any merchandise which should have been invoiced, or makes out or passes, or attempts to pass, through the customhouse any false, forged, or fraudulent invoice, or other document or paper;

Thus, to prove the crime in § 545's first paragraph, the prosecution must show that the defendant: (1) brought or attempted to bring merchandise into the United States; (2) knew that the merchandise should have been declared or reported to customs authorities; and (3) acted knowingly and willfully with intent to defraud the United States. If attempt to defraud the United States is charged, then the prosecution must also prove that the defendant took a substantial step toward committing the crime that was reasonably calculated to result in the crime's commission. Because the defendant needs to know that failure to declare the merchandise is illegal, the definition of "willful" that has been previously and repeatedly discussed applies in § 545's first paragraph. However, the requirement to prove "intent to defraud the United States" has been the subject of a split between the federal circuit courts of appeals.

United States v. Menon
24 F.3d 550 (3d Cir. 1994)

BECKER, Circuit Judge.

Thekkedajh Menon appeals from a judgment in a criminal case in which he was convicted by a jury of violating 18 U.S.C. §§ 2 and 545 by knowingly and willfully, with intent to defraud the United States, making out and passing through the customhouse false and fraudulent invoices and other documents in order to conceal the identity of the exporters of certain products, and of violating those same sections by reimporting shrimp that had previously been rejected as contaminated by the Food and Drug Administration ("FDA").

Menon's first contention on appeal, a contention he failed to raise in the district court and hence one that we review for plain error, is that to obtain a conviction for passing false invoices under § 545, the government must prove that he intended to deprive the United States of revenue, not just that he intended to evade federal regulations. Menon's second argument is that the evidence was insufficient to show that he reimported previously rejected shrimp, a point which ultimately turns on whether a search of Menon's office, which exceeded the scope of a search warrant, was nonetheless valid under the "plain view" doctrine even though the agent who happened upon the documents at issue did not appreciate their significance until she brought them to a more knowledgeable agent.

Agreeing with Menon's construction of the first paragraph of § 545 and holding that the district court's construction constituted plain error, we reverse his convictions for passing false invoices through the customhouse. The meaning of "defraud" varies from statute to statute, and here the evidence supports Menon's interpretation of "defraud." When Congress codified the criminal code, it changed the language of § 545 (then § 159 of title 19 (U.S.C. 1940 ed.)) from "defraud the revenues of the United States" to "defraud the United States" but it did not mean to change the substance of the statute; it meant to continue the previous requirement of an intent to defraud the revenues of the United States. Thus, we continue to give the statute its former meaning, and finding plain error on the basis that the district court's misinterpretation went to the existence vel non of criminal responsibility, we reverse Menon's convictions for passing false invoices. . . .

I. FACTS AND PROCEDURAL HISTORY

The FDA is responsible for ensuring the safety of seafood entering the United States. In performing this function, the agency analyzes data to see if it establishes a pattern demonstrating that seafood which importers have bought from particular exporters is likely to be unsafe. Foreign exporters which have a history of shipping contaminated goods are placed on a block list; shipments from these exporters are automatically detained, and the importer must obtain a private laboratory report demonstrating that the seafood is free of contamination before the FDA will release it. Other exporters are placed in an intermediate category, which means the FDA is more likely to sample their products before admitting them into the country than it is to sample those of other exporters.

Menon was President and two thirds owner of Flag Imports, Inc. ("Flag"), a business that purchased seafood both overseas and domestically for resale to distributors. On numerous occasions, Menon directed his employees to list falsely on invoices a different exporter of seafood than the one from which Flag had actually purchased the seafood. By listing exporters with no history of contamination rather than the actual exporters, who were either on the block list or subject to an increased risk of surveillance sampling by the FDA, Menon intended to deceive the FDA so that Flag's imports entered the United States more readily.

Nonetheless, the FDA discovered that one of Flag's shipments, a March 22, 1991 shipment of 1200 cases of shrimp, contained salmonella. It thereupon issued a Notice of Refusal of Admission for this shipment, and ordered that the cases be either exported or destroyed within 90 days. On May 25, 1991, Flag shipped the shrimp to Jabeco Transport ("Jabeco") in Rotterdam, Holland. The ultimate fate of that shrimp is a question of much moment in this case; the government contends that Menon illegally reimported it into the United States whereas Menon claims that there is insufficient evidence to prove reimportation beyond a reasonable doubt.

On January 19, 1993, a federal grand jury returned a 142-count indictment against Menon. Counts 1 through 110 charged that, in violation of 18 U.S.C. §§ 2 and 545, Menon did knowingly and willfully, with intent to defraud the United States, make out and pass through the customhouse, false and fraudulent invoices and other documents in order to conceal that the exporter of these products had been block-listed by the FDA. Counts 111 through 139 charged Menon with similar conduct with respect to seafood obtained from exporters in the intermediate category. Count 140 charged Menon with reimportation of shrimp that had previously been rejected as contaminated by the FDA, also in violation of 18 U.S.C. §§ 2 and 545. Finally, Counts 141 and 142 charged that, in violation of 16 U.S.C. § 3372(d) and 18 U.S.C. § 2, Menon knowingly made and used false invoices and decoy packaging to conceal that shipments identified as shrimp from Bangladesh were largely composed of frog legs subject to automatic detention and special permit requirements.

During the course of the jury trial, the government voluntarily dismissed counts 16 and 33 of the indictment. At the close of the evidence, the district court granted a judgment of acquittal on Counts 141 and 142 (the frog legs counts). On March 10, 1993, the jury found Menon guilty of all of the remaining counts. Menon filed a motion for a judgment of acquittal on Count 140 alleging that the government had presented insufficient evidence of his guilt. Menon also moved for a new trial, asserting that 1) the district court had improperly barred him from presenting evidence that no one had ever reported being sick as a result of Flag seafood; 2) Count 140, alleging reimportation of contaminated shrimp "contrary to law," was deficient for failing to specify the law to which the reimportation was contrary; and 3) evidence seized during a search of Flag's property should have been suppressed. The district court denied these motions.

The district court held a sentencing hearing after which it imposed concurrent sentences of 20 months on each of Counts 1 through 15, 17 through 32, and 34 through 140. The court also imposed concurrent terms of two years supervised release on each count of conviction, a total special assessment of $6,900, and a fine of $50,000. . . .

On appeal, Menon presses two additional arguments. First, he asserts that his convictions for making out false invoices should be reversed because he did not intend to defeat the customs laws nor to defraud the United States government of money. . . . After considering the many difficult issues, we hold that paragraph 1 of § 545 does require an intent to deprive the United States of revenue and that Menon's convictions on counts 1-15, 17-32, and 34-139 should therefore be reversed. . . .

II. THE MEANING OF 18 U.S.C. § 545

The jury convicted Menon of 137 counts of violating the first paragraph of 18 U.S.C. § 545. As we have noted, this paragraph makes it illegal to "knowingly and willfully, with intent to defraud the United States . . . make[ ] out or pass[ ], or attempt to pass through the customhouse any false, forged, or fraudulent invoice." The jury concluded that Menon, in his position as President of Flag, violated this provision by writing invoices that misrepresented the name of the seafood exporter from which Flag had bought the seafood it was importing. Menon contends that the district court misread § 545, because "an intent to defraud the United States" by passing false invoices "through the customhouse" requires 1) an intent to defeat the customs laws and 2) an intent to deprive the United States of revenue.

Menon's argument that § 545 requires an intent to deprive the United States of revenue would place a new gloss on a 45-year-old statutory provision that has been interpreted to the contrary by two courts of appeals, *see United States v. Borello,*

766 F.2d 46, 51 (2d Cir. 1985); *United States v. McKee*, 220 F.2d 266, 269 (2d Cir. 1955); *United States v. Kurfess*, 426 F.2d 1017, 1019 (7th Cir. 1970). . . .

In a very similar case, in which the plaintiff argued that the district court had improperly instructed the jury that the mail fraud statute did not require an intent to deprive another of money or property, we indicated that if the district court had given such an improper instruction, it would have constituted plain error. As in that case, we think that, assuming Menon's interpretation of the statute is correct, the district court's failure to instruct the jury that § 545 requires an intent to deprive the government of money or property constituted manifest injustice and thus constituted plain error. And, despite the contrary decisions of two courts of appeals, we hold that Menon's interpretation of § 545 is correct.

While the meaning of "defraud the United States" generally extends beyond defrauding the government of revenue, the history of § 545 demonstrates that Congress did not intend such a broad reading here. We first note that until recently, the Supreme Court generally interpreted "defraud" to extend to actions preventing the government from carrying out its lawful functions even when the government did not lose any revenue. This interpretation took root in *Hammerschmidt v. United States* which analyzed the statutory predecessor of 18 U.S.C. § 37, a statute making it illegal to "conspire to . . . defraud the United States in any manner or for any purpose." In *Hammerschmidt*, the Supreme Court concluded that

> [t]o conspire to defraud the United States means primarily to cheat the Government out of property or money, but it also means to interfere with or obstruct one of its lawful governmental functions by deceit, craft or trickery, or at least by means that are dishonest. It is not necessary that the Government shall be subjected to property or pecuniary loss by the fraud, but only that its legitimate official action and purpose shall be defeated by misrepresentation, chicane, or the overreaching of those charged with carrying out the governmental intention.

Id. at 188.

Recently, however, the Supreme Court has significantly narrowed the category of statutes in which the meaning of "defraud" extends beyond a deprivation of property rights. In *McNally v. United States*, 483 U.S. 350, 359 (1987), the Court interpreted the mail fraud statute, which made it illegal "to defraud" or to "obtain[ ] money by means of false or fraudulent pretenses," to require a finding that the defendant intended to deprive others of property or money. 18 U.S.C. § 1341. In so doing, the Court rejected "a long line of court of appeals decisions that had interpreted the statute as proscribing schemes by government officials to defraud citizens of their intangible rights to honest and impartial government." In justifying its decision, the Court quoted *Hammerschmidt* for the proposition that, "the words to defraud 'commonly refer to wronging one in his property rights by dishonest methods or schemes.'" *McNally*, 483 U.S. at 359. The Court concluded that this common understanding combined with the rule of lenity meant that the mail fraud statute required an intent to deprive someone of money or property.

The Court distinguished the actual ruling of *Hammerschmidt* on the basis that the mail fraud statute aimed to prevent fraud against any member of the public, while the statute discussed in *Hammerschmidt* aimed to protect the United States against fraud. A statute that has for its "'object the protection and welfare of the government alone'" aims to prevent fraud in a broader sense than deprivation of property rights, but a statute aiming to prevent fraud against members of the public is likely using fraud in its usual, narrower sense. *Id.* at 358.

Another case distinguishing *Hammerschmidt* is *United States v. Cohn*, 270 U.S. 339, 343 (1926). There the Supreme Court was faced with interpreting the meaning of Section 35 of the Penal Code, 40 Stat. 1015 (1918), which provided that actions "for the purpose of obtaining or aiding to obtain the payment or approval of any claim upon or against the United States . . . for the purpose and with the intent of cheating and swindling or defrauding the Government of the United States . . . shall be punishable." The Court construed Section 35 as requiring the defendant to cheat the government out of property or money. The Court distinguished *Hammerschmidt* on the grounds that the term defraud within Section 35 "is used in connection with the words 'cheating or swindling,' indicating that it is to be construed in the manner in which those words are ordinarily used, as relating to the fraudulent causing of pecuniary or property loss." *Id.* at 346–47.

The message we derive from this potpourri of Supreme Court cases is twofold. First, the meaning of "defraud" must be interpreted in the context of the particular statute that uses the term. In each case in which the Court has evaluated the meaning of "defraud," it has determined the intent of Congress based on the purpose of the particular statute and on the surrounding statutory language. Second, an intent to defraud generally requires an intent to deprive someone of property or money but does not generally require such an intent in the context of statutes making it illegal to defraud "the United States." It seems appropriate therefore to construe § 545 as prohibiting acts that prevent the United States from carrying out its statutory duties unless there is countervailing evidence on the meaning of the statute.

Here, strong countervailing evidence exists. Menon points out that § 1593 of title 19 (U.S.C. 1940 ed.), the predecessor statute to 18 U.S.C. § 545, required that the defendant intended "to defraud *the revenues* of the United States" (emphasis added). Although Congress left out the language "the revenues" when it recodified the Federal Criminal Code in 1948, Menon contends that Congress made it clear that it did not intend to make any substantive change in the statute by making this deletion. Thus, he concludes that the concept "defraud the revenues" is still a part of the statute.

As support for his view that Congress intended no substantive change, Menon cites the House Report which states that, "[r]evision [of the Criminal Code], as distinguished from codification, mean[s] the substitution of plain language for awkward terms, reconciliation of conflicting laws, omission of superseded sections, and consolidation of similar provisions." H.R. Rep. No. 304, 80th Cong., 1st Sess. (1947). The House Report does not indicate that substantive changes were included as part of the revision. The House Report concludes that, "[t]he reviser's notes are keyed to sections of this bill and explain in detail every change made in text," and W.W. Barron, chief reviser of the code, testified to the House Committee on Revision of the Laws that "[e]very substantive change, no matter how minor, is fully explained [in the reviser's notes]." Because the reviser's notes for § 545 say only that "[c]hanges were made in phraseology," H.R. Rep. No. 304, 80th Cong., 1st Sess. at A46, and do not specify that any substantive changes were intended,

Menon concludes that the current statute, like its predecessor, requires that the defendant have intended to deprive the United States of revenues to which it was entitled.

We agree. Although we might ordinarily discount legislative history, we are unwilling to do so where that history consists of committee reports and statements by the chief reviser and where the statutory change we are interpreting occurred in the context of codification of the entire criminal code. In that context, Congress was unlikely to have been able to carefully consider every change made to prior statutes. We think it was reasonable for Congress to rely on representations made to it by the chief reviser, among others, that all substantive changes were explicitly set forth in the revisers' notes and for Congress to indicate that it intended no other substantive changes. Absent a compelling need, we should not read as substantive a change initiated by the revisers and probably not considered by Congress.

At a minimum, we think that the legislative history makes the meaning of "defraud the United States" in § 545 ambiguous given that, as we have seen, the meaning of defraud varies from statute to statute. As the Court did in *McNally*, we rely on the rule of lenity to hold that because the meaning of defraud is ambiguous in the context of § 545, that section requires an intent to cause a deprivation of property or money. As Menon points out, and the government does not deny, the government made no showing that he had such an intent. Thus, we must reverse his conviction on Counts 1-15, 17-31, and 33-139. . . .

V. CONCLUSION

For the foregoing reasons, we will reverse Menon's convictions on Counts 1 through 15, 17 through 32, and 34 through 139. . . .

United States v. Ahmad
213 F.3d 805 (4th Cir. 2000)

DIANA GRIBBON MOTZ, Circuit Judge:

In this in rem civil action the government appeals an order denying forfeiture of the defendant funds. The government contends that some of the funds were used to structure financial transactions in violation of 31 U.S.C. § 5324 (1994), and that the remainder constitutes a substitute for property involved in customs fraud in violation of 18 U.S.C. § 545 (1994). The district court ruled that neither statute provided a basis for forfeiture of the defendant funds and that, in any event, the forfeiture would be a constitutionally excessive fine. We reverse.

I.

This civil action follows certain related criminal proceedings, which derived from a complex operation involving transfers of currency to individuals in Pakistan and the importation of surgical equipment from Pakistani manufacturers. We set forth the details of this operation in *United States v. Ismail*, 97 F.3d 50, 52–54 (4th Cir. 1996). We restate only the most relevant facts here.

Shakeel Ahmad operated a money exchange business that primarily served Pakistanis living in the United States who wanted to transfer funds back to their families in Pakistan. Ahmad deposited the funds into checking accounts held at

First Virginia Bank. Following a conversation with a bank officer on September 25, 1989, Ahmad structured all of his cash deposits in amounts less than $10,000 in order to avoid the filing of currency transaction reports. From January 1, 1990 to October 25, 1993, Ahmad deposited $5.6 million in cash, cashier's checks, and wire transfers into his First Virginia Bank accounts.

In order to obtain a better exchange rate under Pakistani trade regulations, Ahmad used the funds he received from his Pakistani clients to supply bridge loans to various Pakistani companies. The companies would repay the bridge loans by distributing rupees to the family members of Ahmad's clients. This method also allowed Ahmad to "bundle" numerous transfers into one transaction and thereby avoid multiple transaction fees. Ahmad's business dealings included many different companies, but he was charged with making false statements to the United States Customs Service only in relation to his association with Falcon Instruments.

Falcon Instruments imported surgical equipment manufactured in Pakistan for resale in the United States. During the relevant time period, the surgical instruments were non-dutiable goods. When a Pakistani manufacturer would ship the products, it would list on the invoice a significantly inflated purchase price. Upon receipt of the shipment, Falcon would request a "discount," which was generally the difference between the inflated invoice price and the price at which the manufacturer would make a small profit. Ahmad would then deposit an amount equal to the discount into Falcon's account—an account also maintained at First Virginia Bank. Falcon, in turn, would send the Pakistani manufacturer the full amount of the inflated invoice price, as required by Pakistani law, and the manufacturer would then grant the "discount" and distribute the difference between the inflated price and the "discounted" price to the family members of Ahmad's clients. Through this arrangement with Falcon, Ahmad transferred approximately $1.3 million to families in Pakistan. Falcon, for its part, caused Customs agents to list the inflated invoice price as the "transaction value" of the imported goods on Customs forms.

The government's investigation into all of these dealings ultimately resulted in the seizure and forfeiture of $186,587.42 pursuant to the criminal forfeiture statute, 18 U.S.C. § 982. . . .

Ahmad filed a motion for return of the seized funds; days later, on November 11, 1996, the government filed this action for civil forfeiture of these funds. Ahmad intervened in the action to file a claim for the property. On January 21, 1998, after the United States and Ahmad stipulated as to all relevant facts, the district court entered judgment in favor of Ahmad finding no statutory basis for the forfeiture and concluding that, in any event, the forfeiture would constitute an excessive fine. On appeal, the government contends that [among other things] . . . the remaining $101,587.42 of the defendant currency is forfeitable as a substitute for property involved in customs fraud violations. . . .

The government argues that the remaining portion of the defendant currency, $101,587.42, is forfeitable under 18 U.S.C. § 545 as substitute assets for the value of the imported surgical equipment introduced into the United States through the use of fraudulent invoices. Section 545 provides that merchandise introduced into the United States by smuggling, clandestine activity, or fraudulent invoicing, or "the value" of such merchandise "recovered from" a person engaging in such activity "shall be forfeited to the United States." 18 U.S.C. § 545. In order to effect the forfeiture, the government must demonstrate probable cause that a violation of § 545 has occurred. An unrebutted probable cause showing will suffice to justify the forfeiture.

To satisfy its burden of demonstrating probable cause that a § 545 violation occurred, the government relies on the asserted collateral estoppel effect of Ahmad's criminal convictions, which we have affirmed, for conspiracy to defraud the United States under 18 U.S.C. § 371 and customs fraud under 18 U.S.C. § 542 (which is violated when a person "introduces . . . into the commerce of the United States any imported merchandise by means of any fraudulent or false . . . statement").

Ahmad fails to offer any evidence to rebut this probable cause showing. Instead, he maintains that § 545 must be interpreted so as to require the government to prove an intent to defraud the United States of "revenues," which he admits is not a requirement of § 542. The district court relied on this interpretation to hold that the government failed to demonstrate probable cause that § 545 had been violated. The court reasoned that because the surgical equipment was not subject to duty, the customs forms overstating the value of the equipment did not deprive the government of revenues but only of accurate information.

The first paragraph of § 545 provides in relevant part that anyone who "knowingly and willfully, with intent to defraud the United States . . . makes out or passes . . . through the customhouse any false, forged, or fraudulent invoice, or other document or paper" violates federal law. 18 U.S.C. § 545. Thus, the first paragraph of the statute plainly does not require that the United States be deprived of "revenues" in order for a violation of the statute to occur.

The predecessor statutes to this portion of § 545, the Tariff Acts of 1842 and 1930, did require an intent to defraud the "revenues of the United States." In 1948, those predecessor statutes were recodified in § 545 and the words "the revenues of" deleted. Until 1994, our sister circuits had uniformly given effect to the plain language of the recodified statute and held a violation of § 545 need not be based on an intent to defraud the United States of "revenues." *See, e.g., United States v. Borello*, 766 F.2d 46, 51–52 (2d Cir. 1985); *United States v. Kurfess*, 426 F.2d 1017, 1019 (7th Cir. 1970); *United States v. Boggus*, 411 F.2d 110, 113 (9th Cir. 1969).

In holding to the contrary, the district court relied on the Third Circuit's more recent decision in *United States v. Menon*, 24 F.3d 550 (3d Cir. 1994). The *Menon* court ruled that "the meaning of 'defraud' must be interpreted in the context of the particular statute that uses the term. . . . [A]n intent to defraud generally requires an intent to deprive someone of property or money but does not generally require such an intent in the context of statutes making it illegal to defraud 'the United States' . . . unless there is countervailing evidence on the meaning of the statute." The Third Circuit identified as "countervailing evidence" the legislative history of the 1948 revision of the United States Code, specifically, the House Report, which explains that Congress did not intend any substantive changes unless explicitly discussed in the Reviser's Notes. Because the Reviser's Note to § 545 states only that "[c]hanges were made in phraseology" and fails to discuss the impact of deleting the words "the revenues of," the *Menon* court held that Congress did not intend to work a substantive change in the statute by interpreting "to defraud the United States" more broadly.

In other words, the Third Circuit in *Menon* relied on a negative inference, based on the Reviser's Note, to construe § 545 contrary to the statute's plain language. This seems to us a perilous course, at odds with the Supreme Court's repeated admonition that statutory construction begins with examining the language of the statute, and that when the language is clear, the judicial inquiry "in all but the most extraordinary circumstance, is finished."

The Supreme Court's recent decision in *United States v. Wells*, 519 U.S. 482, 497 (1997), heightens our unease with the *Menon* rationale. There the Court specifically refused to extend similar interpretive deference to the Reviser's Notes. The statute at issue in *Wells*, 18 U.S.C. § 1014 (1994), makes it a crime to knowingly make false statements to a federally insured bank. Notwithstanding language in some of § 1014's statutory predecessors establishing a falsehood's materiality as an element of the offense and the Reviser's Note that the consolidation of many prior provisions into one statute "was without change of substance," 519 U.S. at 496, the *Wells* Court refused to hold that materiality was an element of § 1014 given the lack of any such requirement in the statutory language.

The Court explained that the Reviser's Note did "nothing to muddy the ostensibly unambiguous provision of the statute as enacted by Congress . . . [and] the revisers' assumption that the consolidation [of various provisions] made no substantive change was simply wrong. . . . Those who write revisers' notes have proven fallible before." *Id.* at 497; *see also United States v. Robinson*, 147 F.3d 851, 853 (9th Cir. 1998) (rejecting the *Menon* rationale and holding instead that § 545 "protects governmental interests extending beyond mere property rights," and thus, "the intent to defraud element . . . should be construed as meaning intent to avoid and defeat the United States customs laws, . . . rather than the narrower construction 'intent to deprive the United States of revenue'"); *United States v. Nathan*, 188 F.3d 190, 204 (3d Cir. 1999) (citing *Robinson*, rather than its own decision in *Menon*, and noting that a number of courts have applied a broad construction to the intent to defraud element of § 545).

In sum, the plain language of § 545 does not require the government to prove that it suffered a loss of revenue any more than § 542 does. Ahmad has failed to articulate any compelling reason why we should not follow the statutory language. Therefore, Ahmad's conviction for conspiracy to violate § 542 satisfies the government's burden of demonstrating probable cause that a violation of § 545 has occurred. Accordingly, § 545 entitles the government to civil forfeiture of the $101,587.42 recovered from Ahmad as a portion of "the value" of the surgical equipment introduced into this country in violation of that statute, but only if this forfeiture does not constitute an excessive fine prohibited by the Eighth Amendment. . . .

IV.

For these reasons, the judgment of the district court is REVERSED.

- Which interpretation of "defraud the United States" is more compelling, that of the *Menon* court or the *Ahmad* court?

- What change in meaning occurred as a result of the word "revenues" being excised from the phrase "defraud the revenues of the United States"? Was it really a minor cleanup of superfluous statutory language, or a change that expanded the scope of the reach of 18 U.S.C. § 545's first paragraph?
- Currently, the Second, Fourth, Seventh, and Ninth Circuits hold that "defraud the United States" does not require the prosecution to prove that the undeclared goods were subject to duty. Only the Third Circuit holds otherwise. Eight circuits have yet to opine on the subject; however, the Pattern Criminal Jury Instructions for the Fifth and Tenth Circuits seem to follow the majority of circuits and reject *Menon*'s holding. Pattern Crim. Jury Instr. 5th Cir. 2.24A ("It is not necessary, however, to prove that any tax or duty was owed on the merchandise"); Pattern Crim. Jury Instr. 10th Cir. 2.29 (2018) (same).

2. Importing Merchandise Contrary to Law

In addition to protecting the United States' taxing abilities, Congress imposed criminal penalties on those who import merchandise intending to thwart other civil and criminal laws. This provision is known as the "second paragraph" of § 545, which provides:

> Whoever fraudulently or knowingly imports or brings into the United States, any merchandise contrary to law, or receives, conceals, buys, sells, or in any manner facilitates the transportation, concealment, or sale of such merchandise after importation, knowing the same to have been imported or brought into the United States contrary to law—

To prove this crime under 18 U.S.C. § 545, the prosecution must establish that (1) the defendant fraudulently or knowingly (2) imported or brought into the United States (3) any merchandise (4) contrary to law. *United States v. Patel*, 762 F.2d 784, 790 (9th Cir. 1985). This provision is similar to but broader than the Lacey Act's trafficking provisions. Recall that a Lacey Act trafficking violation requires the prosecution to prove that the defendant knowingly imported fish, wildlife, or plants into the United States where the defendant knew (for the felony) or reasonably should have known (for the misdemeanor) that the fish, wildlife, or plants were taken, possessed, transported, or sold in violation of foreign, state, tribal, or federal *wildlife* law (whether civil or criminal). However, the Lacey Act will not apply if the wildlife is smuggled into the United States where the defendant knows that he/she possesses it contrary to some non-wildlife law. Consequently, smuggling merchandise, which includes wildlife, into the United States contrary to *any* law fills the gap that the Lacey Act leaves. Additionally, § 545 provides another mechanism to enforce the provisions of CITES. Consider the following case.

United States v. Lawson
618 F. Supp. 2d 1251 (E.D. Wash. 2009)

FRED VAN SICKLE, Senior District Judge.

THIS MATTER came before the Court on April 27, 2009, based upon the defendants' motions for judgment of acquittal [which defendants filed after a jury convicted them but before the court imposed sentence].

BACKGROUND

Gypsy Lawson and Fran Ogren flew to Thailand during 2007. While there, they searched for a monkey to take back to the United States. Ultimately, they purchased a Rhesus Macaque. When it came [time] to return to the United States, they sedated the monkey. Once the monkey was sedated, Ms. Lawson hid it under her clothing[,] creating the appearance that she was pregnant. Ms. Lawson and Ms. Ogren did not seek permission from Thai officials to take the monkey out of Thailand, nor did they disclose the monkey's presence to American officials when they arrived in Los Angeles. Ms. Lawson and Ms. Ogren knew that they were violating the law, and that they could be punished if they were caught. As it turned out, neither Thai nor American officials detected the monkey while the women were traveling. It was not until after they had returned to the Eastern District of Washington that American officials learned of the monkey's existence, and then only because they received a tip from a concerned citizen. On July 22, 2008, the government filed a Superseding Indictment. Count One charged Ms. Lawson and Ms. Ogren with conspiracy. Count Two charged them with violating 18 U.S.C. § 545. A jury found both women guilty of both crimes. They filed a timely motion for judgment of acquittal. Fed. R. Crim. P. 29(c).

A. Alternative Methods of Committing a Single Crime

Section 545 of Title 18 is divided into paragraphs. The first two paragraphs create separate crimes. The defendants were convicted of violating the second paragraph, which makes it unlawful to:

> fraudulently or knowingly import[ ] or bring[ ] into the United States, any merchandise contrary to law, or receive[ ], conceal[ ], buy[ ], sell[ ], or in any manner facilitate[ ] the transportation, concealment, or sale of such merchandise after importation, knowing the same to have been imported or brought into the United States contrary to law[.]

18 U.S.C. § 545. The defendants argue that the second paragraph of § 545 creates at least two crimes. In their opinion, one crime consists of importing merchandise into the United States contrary to law; the other crime consists of receiving, concealing, buying, selling, or in any manner facilitating the transportation, concealment, or sale of such merchandise after importation. The government disagrees with the defendants' interpretation of the second paragraph of § 545. According to the government, the second paragraph describes alternative means by which a person may commit a single crime.

Neither the Ninth Circuit nor any other circuit court of appeals has addressed the parties' competing interpretations of the second paragraph of § 545. However, the Ninth Circuit has provided guidance. In *United States v. Arreola*, 467 F.3d 1153, 1157 (9th Cir. 2006), the circuit court explained that it employs the analytical framework established in *United States v. UCO Oil Co.*, 546 F.2d 833 (9th Cir. 1976), when asked to determine whether a statute creates separate offenses or simply describes alternative means of committing the same crime. "Under *UCO Oil*, we consider . . . (1) [the] 'language of the statute itself,' (2) 'the legislative history and statutory context,' (3) the type of conduct proscribed, and (4) the 'appropriateness of multiple punishment for the conduct charged in the indictment.'"

It is appropriate to begin with the language of the statute. Congress could have divided the second paragraph of § 545 into separate paragraphs. This would have strongly suggested that Congress intended to create more than one crime. Instead, Congress left the second paragraph as a single unit. The fact that Congress did so indicates an intent to create a single crime. Granted, the second paragraph of § 545 is composed of several clauses. As the defendants observe, it is unlawful either to "fraudulently or knowingly import[ ] or bring[ ] into the United States, any merchandise contrary to law, *OR* receive[ ], conceal[ ], buy[ ], sell[ ], or in any manner facilitate[ ] the transportation, concealment, or sale of such merchandise after importation[.]" 18 U.S.C. § 545 (capitalization and emphasis added). The fact [that] the preceding clauses are divided by a disjunctive "or" is relevant, but not especially helpful to the defendants. Ordinarily, the fact [that] a statute uses a disjunctive "or" means the statute is specifying two or more ways in which a single crime can be committed. This reading of the second paragraph of § 545 is reinforced by considering the penalty provision. Punishment does not vary depending upon whether a person imports merchandise contrary to law or whether he facilitates the transportation of unlawfully imported merchandise. In either event, the punishment is the same. Uniformity of penalty suggests that Congress intended to create a single crime. Indeed, that is the most sensible interpretation of the second paragraph of § 545. The various clauses of that paragraph are simply alternative means by which a person may commit a single crime.

B. Merchandise

The term "merchandise" is not defined by § 545. As a result, the Ninth Circuit uses the definition set forth in 19 U.S.C. § 1401(c). Under § 1401(c), "[t]he word 'merchandise' means goods, wares, and chattels of every description, and includes merchandise the importation of which is prohibited [.]" The Rhesus monkey was the defendants' chattel. Black's Law Dictionary 229 (7th ed. 1999). Thus, the monkey constituted merchandise within the meaning of § 545.

C. Contrary to Law

The government presented overwhelming evidence that the defendants left Thailand with a monkey and brought the monkey into the United States with them. Witnesses variously described the defendants' monkey as a "Rhesus monkey" and a "Rhesus Macaque." It was clear that the witnesses were referring to the defendants' monkey. After considering all of the evidence, the jury found that the defendants imported, concealed, and transported a Rhesus Macaque, i.e., a monkey. It is common knowledge that a monkey is a primate. For example, anyone who has toured a reputable zoo can attest to that fact. Consequently, it was unnecessary for the government to offer expert testimony in order to establish that a monkey is a primate. *Cf. United States v. Miller*, 981 F.2d 439, 443 (9th Cir. 1992) ("The common knowledge of even schoolchildren that saguaro is cactus made expert testimony on its botanical character unnecessary.").

All primates are included in either Appendix I or Appendix II of the Convention on International Trade in Endangered Species of Wild Fauna and Flora ("CITES" or "Convention"), 27 U.S.T. 1087, T.I.A.S. No. 8249. Both Thailand and the United States signed the Convention. The United States implemented its CITES obligations through the Endangered Species Act, 16 U.S.C. § 1531 et seq. ("ESA"). Under the ESA, "[i]t is unlawful for any person subject to the jurisdiction of the United States to engage in any trade in any specimens contrary to the provisions of the Convention[.]" 16 U.S.C. § 1538(c)(1). Congress authorized the Secretary of the Interior to promulgate regulations in order to enforce the ESA. 16 U.S.C. § 1540(f). In response, the Secretary promulgated Part 23 of Title 50 of the Code of Federal Regulations. 50 C.F.R. § 23.1(a) ("[t]he regulations in [Part 23] implement the Convention on International Trade in Endangered Species of Wild Fauna and Flora").

The jury convicted the defendants of violating the second paragraph of 18 U.S.C. § 545. In order to convict them, the jury had to find that they imported merchandise contrary to law. Administrative regulations do not necessarily constitute "law" for purposes of 18 U.S.C. § 545. "The term ['law'] includes a regulation only if there is a statute (a 'law') that specifies that violation of that regulation is a crime." Here, there is such a statute. Section 1538(c)(1) of Title 16 makes it unlawful "to engage in any trade in any specimens contrary to the provisions of the Convention[.]" The United States' obligations under the Convention are embodied in the regulations contained in Part 23. 50 C.F.R. 23.1(a). Since § 1538(c)(1) makes it unlawful to engage in trade that is "contrary to the provisions of the Convention," and since the relevant provisions of the Convention are embodied in Part 23, a person who violates the regulations set forth in Part 23 violates the law. This interpretation is consistent with the Secretary's understanding of the consequences of violating the regulations that are contained in Part 23:

> Except as provided in § 23.92, it is unlawful for any person subject to the jurisdiction of the United States to conduct any of the following activities unless they meet the requirements of this part: (a) Import, export, re-export, or engage in international trade with any specimen of a species listed in Appendix I, II, or III of CITES.

50 C.F.R. § 23.13.

Even if the Part 23 regulations are not "law" for purposes of 18 U.S.C. § 545, the government nonetheless presented evidence which is sufficient to prove that the defendants imported a primate contrary to law. Article IV of the Convention imposes restrictions upon the trade in Appendix II species, of which the Rhesus Macaque is one. Not only were the defendants required to obtain an export permit from Thailand, but also they were required to obtain an import permit from the United States. CITES, Art. IV, ¶¶ 2, 4. The defendants did not attempt to obtain either permit. Consequently, when they removed a Rhesus Macaque from Thailand and brought it into the United States, they violated 16 U.S.C. § 1538(c)(1) by engaging in trade that is contrary to the provisions of the Convention. In other words, they acted contrary to law within the meaning of the second paragraph of 18 U.S.C. § 545.

D. Genus and Taxon

The Superseding Indictment alleged, in part, that the "Rhesus Macaque (*macaca mulatta*)" is subject to "Appendix II permit requirements." Given that allegation, the defendants argue it was incumbent upon the government to prove both the Genus (*Macaca*) and Taxon (*Macaca mulatta*) of the Rhesus monkey. The defendants are incorrect. The government is not required to prove all of the facts that are alleged in an indictment simply because the indictment alleges them. To the contrary, the government is obligated to present "only enough facts to prove the essential elements of the crime [charged in the indictment]." *Id.* As explained above, there is more than one method by which a person may violate the second paragraph of § 545. However, each method requires proof that merchandise was imported into the United States contrary to law. Here, the merchandise was a primate. In order to prove that the primate was unlawfully imported, the government had to prove it is covered by CITES. Were only some primates covered by CITES, it might be necessary for the government to offer evidence concerning a particular primate's Genus and Taxon in order to prove that it is covered. However, all primates are covered by either Appendix I or Appendix II of the Convention. There are no exceptions. Thus, it was unnecessary for the government to identify a particular primate by Genus and Taxon. The Superseding Indictment's reference to a *Macaca mulatta* is mere surplusage. As such, it need not be proved. . . .

I. Unduly Harsh Punishment

The defendants argue that Congress did not intend persons who engage in conduct like theirs to be prosecuted under 18 U.S.C. § 545. According to the defendants, Congress has enacted more specific statutes—e.g., the Lacey Act, 16 U.S.C. § 3371, et seq.—to address the type of conduct that they engaged in. The defendants argue that the government could have, and should have, prosecuted them under the Lacey Act. Had the government done so, say the defendants, they would be facing punishment that is commensurate with the seriousness of their acts. Instead, in their opinion, they face unduly harsh punishment. The defendants urge the Court to protect them from felony convictions by granting judgment of acquittal under either the rule of lenity or, perhaps, the Due Process Clause of the Fifth Amendment. The Court declines to do so. "When, as here, conduct violates more than one criminal statute the government may generally elect which statute it wishes to charge. . . . This is so even though one statute imposes felony penalties and the other merely imposes misdemeanor penalties." Given this principle, the defendants are not entitled to judicial review of the government's decision to charge them with felonies under 18 U.S.C. § 545 rather than charging them with misdemeanors under some more specific statute. Nor are the defendants entitled to relief under the rule of lenity. As the government points out, "the rule of lenity applies only when the statutory language contains grievous ambiguity or uncertainty and when, after seizing everything from which aid can be derived, [a court] can make no more than a guess as to what Congress intended." The second paragraph of § 545 is not so ambiguous that the Court must guess at its meaning. To the contrary, its reasonably clear. As a result, the rule of lenity is inapplicable.

IT IS HEREBY ORDERED:
1. Fran Ogren's motion for judgment of acquittal is denied.
2. Gypsy Lawson's motion for judgment of acquittal is denied.
IT IS SO ORDERED. The District Court Executive is hereby directed to enter this order and furnish copies to counsel.

- Why did the prosecution rely on 18 U.S.C. § 545 instead of the Lacey Act?

- Despite alleging that their punishment was too harsh, the defendants in *Lawson* had not yet been sentenced when they filed their motions for acquittal. Do you think that the difference in penalties between the Lacey Act (5-year maximum) and § 545 (20-year maximum) really makes a difference in how the defendants in *Lawson* were sentenced? The answer is "apparently not" because the defendants in *Lawson* were sentenced to 60 days in jail, three years of supervised release, and $4,500 in restitution for the medical tests needed to be performed on the monkey. *United States v. Lawson*, 2:08CR26, ECF Nos. 314, 316.

- In addition to addressing illegally imported wildlife, § 545 prosecutions have proven useful as to the Clean Air Act's prohibitions on certain types of engines and products containing CFCs. *United States v. LeBlanc*, 1:97CR34 (D. Me. 1998), ECF No. 58 (defendant sentenced to 15 months' imprisonment and a $28,000 fine for smuggling CFC-12, which is precluded from importation under the Clean Air Act).

- The mens rea for this crime is "fraudulently" or "knowingly." What is the difference between the two words? Unlike many instances of the word "knowing" that have been discussed previously, "fraudulently" and "knowingly" here require the prosecution to prove that the defendant knew that his/her conduct was unlawful even though the government need not prove that the defendant specifically knew which law he/she was violating. *See, e.g., Babb v. United States*, 252 F.2d 702, 708 (5th Cir. 1958).

- Congress relied on the second paragraph of § 545 to punish those who "fraudulently or knowingly export[] or send[] from the United States, or attempt[] to export or send from the United States" any merchandise or object contrary to any law or regulation of the United States. 18 U.S.C. § 554(a). Thus, if a person intentionally exports something that the person knows is contrary to federal law, then that person faces a maximum of ten years in prison.

- Once again, consider the hypothetical at the beginning of this chapter involving Randy and E-Recy. Recall that Randy exported much of the e-waste he collected from businesses to China in shipping containers marked "Computer Monitors for Schools." If the e-waste inside the shipping containers is hazardous, have Randy and E-Recy violated 18 U.S.C. § 554(b) by fraudulently or knowingly exporting merchandise contrary to RCRA and its regulations? Recall that RCRA does not allow for the export of hazardous waste without permission from both the EPA and the receiving nation.

Table of Cases

Principal cases appear in **Bold**

Table of Statutes

INDEX

Federal Insecticide, Fungicide,
and Rodenticide Act
(FIFRA) Felony, 276
History, 274-75
Labeling, 275-76
Mens rea, 276-77
Misdemeanor
  Class A, 277
  Class C, 277
  Commercial applicator, 277
  Private applicator, 277
Registration, 275
  General use, 275
  Restricted use, 275
FIFRA. *See* Federal Insecticide,
  Fungicide, and Rodenticide
  Act

G

Grand Jury, 34
  Indictment Authority, 36
  Investigatory Powers, 36
  Nature and composition, 35

I

Investigative Discretion, 17-18

K

Knowingly. *See* Mens rea
Knowingly and willfully. *See*
  Mens rea

L

Lacey Act, 288
  Labeling offenses, 303
    mens rea, 303
  Trafficking Offenses
  Mens rea

knowledge of underlying
  illegal activity, 289
Trafficking offenses, 289
Mens rea
    felony, 289
    misdemeanor, 289
Love Canal, 1

M

Mail fraud. *See* Wire Fraud
Mens rea, 49-98
  Criminal negligence, 92
  Knowing, 56
    Collective Knowledge, 87
    Jurisdictional facts, 66
    Knowledge of the facts, 57
    Knowledge of the law, 69
    Willful blindness, 82
    Strict liability, 97
    Willful, 50
Mental state. *See* Mens rea
Migratory Bird Treaty Act
  (MBTA), 97, 311
  Strict liability, 312-25
  Trafficking
    Felony, 325-30

N

Negligence
  See Mens rea, Criminal
    negligence
NESHAP. *See* Clean Air
  Act:National Emissions
  Standards for Hazardous Air
  Pollutants
NPDES. *See* Clean Water Act